ACCLAIM FOR Morton N. Cohen's

# *Lewis Carroll*

A BIOGRAPHY

"Surely the most authoritative life of Dodgson we will have. . . . Cohen patiently dismantles [the] myth in his meticulous biography." —*Wall Street Journal*

"A wonderful study worthy of its subject—an honest but elegant tribute to an extraordinary man. . . . Cohen stands apart. His percipient affection for Lewis Carroll is contagious." —*Washington Times*

"Superbly researched and altogether engrossing." —*Washington Post Book World*

"[Cohen is] the world's premier Carroll scholar . . . no one has ever known so much about Carroll . . . he takes on the subjects most likely to make us sweat and squirm, handling them with a plain-speaking dignity, an ease in his own judgments and an unmistakable decency that do more than even his scholarly credentials to cement his authority." —*Boston Globe*

"Cohen is a thorough and . . . perceptive biographer . . . the ultimate expert." —*The New York Review of Books*

"Deeply moving . . . a convincingly full portrayal of [Carroll's] large heart and busy mind . . . [told] with matchless knowledge and profound empathy." —*Chicago Tribune*

"It is hard to believe there will ever be a better book on the subject than this one." —*The Spectator* (London)

# Morton N. Cohen

## *Lewis Carroll*

Morton N. Cohen, Professor Emeritus of the City University of New York, was born in Calgary, Canada, and grew up on the North Shore of Boston. He holds a B.A. from Tufts University and received his M.A. and Ph.D. from Columbia University. He has taught English at West Virginia University, Rutgers University, Syracuse University, and the City College and the Graduate Center of the City University of New York. He has written children's books, travel articles, fiction, and biographical works on Rider Haggard, Rudyard Kipling, and other Victorian subjects. He edited the two-volume edition of *The Letters of Lewis Carroll* (1979) and has written or edited six other books on Lewis Carroll.

ALSO BY MORTON N. COHEN

*Rider Haggard: His Life and Works*

*Rudyard Kipling to Rider Haggard*

*The Letters of Lewis Carroll*

*The Selected Letters of Lewis Carroll*

*Lewis Carroll and Alice: 1832–1932*

*Lewis Carroll, Photographer of Children: Four Nude Studies*

*Lewis Carroll and the Kitchins*

*Lewis Carroll and the House of Macmillan*

*Lewis Carroll: Interviews and Recollections*

LEWIS CARROLL

*Charles Lutwidge Dodgson*

# Lewis Carroll

A BIOGRAPHY

by

Morton N. Cohen

VINTAGE BOOKS
A DIVISION OF RANDOM HOUSE, INC.
NEW YORK

The Library of Congress has cataloged the Knopf edition as follows:
Cohen, Morton Norton, [date]
Lewis Carroll : a biography / by Morton N. Cohen. — 1st ed.
p. cm.
ISBN 0-679-42298-6
1. Carroll, Lewis, 1832–1898—Biography. 2. Authors, English—19th
century—Biography. 3. Mathematics teachers—Great Britain—Biogra-
phy. 4. Oxford (England)—Biography.
I. Title.
PR4612.C588 1995
828'.809—dc20
[B]  95-2663
CIP
Vintage ISBN: 0-679-74562-9

*Book design by Peter A. Andersen*

Random House Web address: http://www.randomhouse.com/

Printed in the United States of America
10 9 8 7 6 5 4 3 2 1

# Contents

# Illustrations

# Preface

In the last twenty-five years or so, many papers relating to the life and works of Lewis Carroll (Charles Lutwidge Dodgson) have become available for the first time for perusal and use. *The Diaries of Lewis Carroll* that Roger Lancelyn Green edited in two volumes in 1953 contain about 65 percent of the surviving text, based on an edited typescript prepared by Carroll's niece Menella Dodgson. In 1969 the Dodgson heirs sensibly sold the surviving volumes to the British Library, where they are now housed with a two-hundred-page index which Mr. R. E. Thompson, sometime indexer for *The Times*, prepared at my request, and they are now accessible to all. The passages omitted from Green's edition are neither inflammatory nor riveting, but they are revealing and help us form a more nearly complete image of their author.

Other materials have also enriched our knowledge of Carroll. In 1974 a proof copy of the "Wasp in a Wig" chapter omitted from *Through the Looking-Glass* (John Tenniel, the famous *Punch* cartoonist, had insisted that he could not produce an appropriate drawing) was sold at a Sotheby sale. In 1977 W. W. Bartley's edition of *Lewis Carroll's Symbolic Logic* appeared, containing the previously unknown "Part II, Advanced Logic." In 1979 *The Letters of Lewis Carroll* (two volumes) appeared, and in 1987 *Lewis Carroll and the House of Macmillan*, the three volumes together containing both full and partial texts of more than two thousand Carroll letters. To these we can add some recent smaller collections of letters: *Some Oxford Scandals: Seven "Letters to the Editor"* (1978); *Lewis Carroll and the Kitchins* (1980); and *Letters to Skeffington Dodgson from His Father* (1990). In 1989 *Lewis Carroll: Interviews and Recollections* was published, containing some 125 reminiscences, mostly written by people who knew Carroll. In 1993 Edward Wakeling's edition of *The Oxford Pamphlets . . . of Charles Lutwidge Dodgson* and in 1994 Francine F. Abeles's edition of *The Mathematical Pamphlets . . .* appeared as the first two in a projected series of six volumes to assemble Carroll's printed pamphlets, leaflets, and circulars. This new material has made a world of differ-

ence to those who have sought to see Lewis Carroll more clearly and accurately than we were able to before. It has also, however, raised new questions
and presented literary historians with new puzzles, not least of all the one
that arose on the discovery that someone—not Carroll himself—had used
a razor to cut out certain pages of the surviving Carroll diary.

Much is still missing besides the excised pages: four volumes of the full
diary; the various letter registers that Carroll kept during his mature life—
the one for his personal use, as his nephew Stuart Dodgson Collingwood
tells us, comprising an astronomical 98,721 letters sent and received; many of
the photographs that he took and sent or gave to so many different recipients; and bundles of letters still probably housed in shoe boxes in attics or
trunks in basements or hiding in private collections.

But the material that has become available in the last quarter century
along with the files of as-yet-unpublished Carroll letters that will fill at least
three further volumes are inestimably valuable to a biographer: they have
provided light that illuminates dark corners; they afford a close look at the
development of Carroll's myriad interests; they document and define, as
nothing has before, the man's religious faith; and they allow a closer, more
assured examination of his mind and his emotional life.

Carroll's diaries and letters are, to be sure, the two principal biographical
sources extant, and I have used them unsparingly. In order to limit super-
scripts in the text and an inordinate number of endnotes, I have put the date
of the diary entry or letter into the text along with the quotation; a reader
who wishes to see it whole or how it appears in context may simply turn to
the published *Diaries* or the *Letters* of Lewis Carroll, as the case requires.
Both are arranged chronologically with dated running heads, and finding
the source is easy. When an unpublished entry from the diary or an unpublished letter appears here, an endnote identifies the source. Actually the surviving diaries are now being edited in their entirety for publication by
Edward Wakeling and two of the nine volumes have already appeared. Letters to and from Carroll's publisher appear, also chronologically, in *Lewis
Carroll and the House of Macmillan*.

Carroll's works are another indispensable wellspring, and again I have not
given detailed publishing information for those I cite because anyone wishing more information about any work by Carroll can easily find it in the
most recent revision of *The Lewis Carroll Handbook* (1979). Editions of the
*Alice* books, *The Hunting of the Snark*, and anthologies of Carroll's prose and
poetry abound.

While this life of Carroll generally adopts customary biographical conventions, following the grave advice of the King in *Alice's Adventures in Wonderland*— to begin at the beginning, and, when you get to the end, to stop—several chapters, in treating specific themes in Carroll's life, either break chronology or employ a chronology of their own. In order to see how the man's religious faith developed, one must assemble the relevant material in isolation; one must also deal separately with Carroll's special relationship with Dean Liddell, his wife, and of course Alice; and his most particular interest in and pursuit of child friends is best examined on its own, as is what we know of his emotional life.

One of my overwhelming concerns throughout was to listen to voices—to Carroll's voice and to the voices of the people who knew him. Those voices are as close as we can get to him. We have a sound recording of Tennyson's voice, and Tennyson died six years before Carroll—but, sadly, we have no recording of Carroll's voice. What one would give to have it, or a film of him standing before a group of pupils at the Oxford High School for Girls, urging them to scale the ethereal heights of logic. Still, we have the words on paper, and we must content ourselves with them. Fortunately Carroll's "paper voice" is articulate, voluble, and more and more readily available. So too are the voices of his family and friends.

Then again, it is not enough to record the facts, to examine the words on paper. I have tried, therefore, to paint a total picture, and, to complete it, I have sought fresh connections, innuendos, intimations, in the hope of breaking through Victorian reticence and detecting the motives that lived behind the conventional social mask. The picture that emerges differs from earlier portraits, but, after carefully examining the facts and weighing them for some thirty years, I hope that I have assembled a portrait of the man entire.

Some readers will object to my using Lewis Carroll's given name, Charles, throughout the work. I have done so simply because it seems most appropriate in a book dealing with the intimacy of his life. I hope that the following pages will provide others, too, with a close and companionable acquaintanceship with this remarkable man.

M.N.C.

# Acknowledgments

Throughout my work on Lewis Carroll, I have enjoyed the singular pleasure and privilege of my friendship with Philip Dodgson Jaques, Lewis Carroll's great-nephew, and I wish to thank him most particularly, as executor of the Charles L. Dodgson Estate, for permission to quote freely from his great-uncle's diaries, letters, and manuscripts.

Other persons have helped me in various ways, and I wish to acknowledge their kindness. They are Anne Clark Amor, Peter Atkinson, Malvina Balogh, Carol Martin Brent, Keith Batey, Mavis Batey, Lionel Casson, Mark Curthoys, Lloyd deMause, David Elkind, Martin Gardner, H. R. Harcourt Williams, Ellis Hillman, Rosella Howe, Jon A. Lindseth, Myra Livingston, and George Max Saiger.

For permission to quote from copyright material, I am grateful to A. K. S. Lambton and Robert, the sixth Marquis of Salisbury.

I want to thank the private collectors, the curators, and the institutions that have supplied copies of manuscripts and illustrations: the Berg Collection (New York Public Library), the British Library, the Dodgson Family Collection in the Guildford Muniments Room, the Houghton Library (Harvard University), the Huntington Library (San Marino, California), F. Manier, the National Portrait Gallery (London), Jennifer Macrory (Rugby School), Marvin Taylor (the Fales Library of New York University), Graham Ovenden, the Pierpont Morgan Library, M. A. T. Rogers, the Rosenbach Foundation (Philadelphia), Alexander D. Wainwright (the Parrish Collection, Princeton University), the Humanities Research Center, University of Texas (Austin), and H. J. R. Wing and the Governing Body, Christ Church, Oxford.

I owe a special debt to the friends and associates who have read part or all of this book before it went to press. They are Francine Abeles, James Algie, Sandor Burstein, Selwyn Goodacre, Peter Heath, Cecil Lang, J. F. A. Mason, Iain McLean, Richard N. Swift, and Edward Wakeling.

# Introduction

How ever in the world did Lewis Carroll, a fastidious, reserved, and deeply religious Victorian mathematics don, manage to create the stories that have become the most popular children's classics in the English language?

Readers and critics have been asking that question since 1866, when *Alice's Adventures in Wonderland* first took them down the rabbit hole into a curious world of highly opinionated characters like the Caterpillar, the Cheshire Cat, the Hatter, an ugly duchess, and a queen with a penchant for chopping off heads. But the paradox persists, even as the popularity of the *Alice* books grows, attracting generation after generation of children of all ages and from all lands, who wander wide-eyed through Wonderland and who step into the world behind the looking-glass.

The paradox is linked to the name Lewis Carroll, which is really all air, for the author of those magical books was in fact the Reverend Charles Lutwidge Dodgson, who spent his entire mature life at one of Oxford's most fashionable colleges, Christ Church, first as an undergraduate and then as a lecturer. And just as he invented a fanciful name for himself, he also invented incomparable adventures, particularly when he had an audience of young female friends before him who wanted him to tell them a story. Just how Lewis Carroll, a bachelor living a cloistered life within college walls, could capture the interest of children and engage their young emotions is part of the paradox. He evidently possessed a special gift for understanding children that continually endeared him to them. For him, on the other hand, female children embodied the essence of romance: he admired their natural beauty; he valued their spontaneous utterances; he treasured their untrammeled innocence; and he devoted his time, energy, and imagination to amusing and edifying them. He loved to make them laugh, he invented games to play with them, he encouraged them, plied them with gifts, photographed them—he simply worshiped them.

The paradox remains, however, for he never married and never had children of his own. Instead he lived his life pursuing child friendships. In his own terms, he succeeded when, in his prime, he could count in his circle dozens of young female friends. He reached an apogee in his relationship with the three daughters of his college dean, the Liddell sisters, and most particularly with his favorite child friend of all time, the middle sister, Alice.

But Carroll's girl friends grew up, most of them found husbands near their own age, and all too often he was left behind. As the years passed and his hair turned silver, the numbers of his friends diminished, and he had to sustain himself with memories of past glories.

He was an extraordinarily gifted man and, in spite of a deaf right ear and an incurable stammer, lived a busy and productive life. But it was not an ordinary life, nor are the products of his labors merely plentiful or sufficient. They are, in fact, overpoweringly numerous and often brilliant.

Had he never written his children's books, he would still enjoy a permanent place in posterity in more than one discipline. His bibliography contains over three hundred separately published items. He was one of the earliest art photographers and has been acknowledged to be the finest photographer of children of the nineteenth century. He was also an inventive and prodigious letter writer; in fact, a letter register he began to keep halfway through his life indicates that in his last thirty-five years he sent and received 98,721 letters. Although early critics failed to grasp the significance of his work in mathematics and logic, recent writers have come to grips with these esoteric studies and have shown that he broke new ground in numerous branches of this specialty and that his work was occasionally ahead of its time. While not in a class with his predecessors Augustus DeMorgan and George Boole, nor producing authoritative compendiums as did his contemporaries John Venn and John Neville Keynes, his work is unique, meaningful, and influential. Reevaluations of his labors on social choice, or voting theory, and his proposed rules for fairer methods of eliminating players in lawn tennis have also heightened his reputation among specialists, and current assessments claim that his proposals for improving voting methods are highly innovative and more nearly just than those used today.

But even these attainments do not tell the whole story. He argued in favor of the benefits of vaccination. In the face of religious opposition to the stage as a source of entertainment, he supported the theater as wholesome, uplifting, and educational; and he was instrumental in helping to found a school that would eventually become the Royal Academy of Dramatic Art. Though politically conservative, he opposed sham and greed wherever he saw it; he worried about the poor and the sick and did all he could to assuage hardships wherever he encountered them.

Undeniably he is best remembered for his lighter works, his whimsy, his nonsense. *The Hunting of the Snark*, the longest nonsense poem in English, has attracted fans through the years, and Snark clubs have grown up in England and the United States. Carroll's other poetry, both humorous and serious, is less popular but deserves a fresh look and reappraisal. The volumes of games and puzzles that he invented are being reissued and continue to attract droves of young people.

The man responsible for all these creations has provoked curiosity at all times, and literary historians and psychologists have tried to discern what made him tick. But their efforts have resulted largely in contradictory assessments. No consensus has emerged. Lewis Carroll remains an enigma, a complex human being who has so far defied comprehension. The man himself is a puzzle, on the surface a tall, straight figure dressed in black, formal, precise, exacting, and proper in every detail of behavior. But his severe exterior concealed a soaring imagination, a fountain of wit, a wide-ranging and far-reaching appreciation of the human condition, and the knowledge of how to touch others, how to move them, and how to make them laugh.

Beneath the bubbles and the froth lived yet another force, however, a brooding guilt, and Lewis Carroll's letters and diaries which have become available in recent years enable us to see deeper into this troubled well than ever before. He was a good practicing Christian, but he nonetheless saw himself as a repeated sinner. Stern Victorian that he was, he could never give voice or employ pen and ink to record the nature of his sins, but the painful appeals to God for forgiveness that he confided to his diary reveal a man in spiritual pain for transgressions that surely go beyond ordinary failings like idleness or indolence. Lewis Carroll's strong and virile imagination must also have bred sexual fantasies. His dreams probably reached out beyond what he considered acceptable terrain and ventured into dangerous precincts. A severe disciplinarian, he never transgressed propriety or violated innocence. He was a master at regulating his life, and superhuman, in today's terms, in controlling his impulses during waking hours. But the nights brought troubled thoughts for which he saw himself a miscreant.

Much of his serious poetry and his writings on religious subjects trace his efforts to find a sinner's road to salvation. And his constant labors, his books and essays, are his offerings to a higher force, his struggles to earn forgiveness. He drove himself relentlessly, especially in his later years, to write purposeful, serious works which he hoped would have lasting value. So determined was he in pursuing this task that he grew almost asocial, ate and slept too little, and virtually wrote himself into the grave before his sixty-sixth birthday. Ironically, although the products of his later years—the *Sylvie and Bruno* books and his writings on symbolic logic—take their honored place on library shelves, these results of his feverish efforts are not the ones that come to mind when we first think of Lewis Carroll.

The name Lewis Carroll is for most of us synonymous with the tales of those two magical journeys, *Alice's Adventures in Wonderland* and *Through the Looking-Glass*. For today, a century and a quarter after they first appeared, they are more popular than ever. Neither book has ever gone out of print. Along with the Bible and Shakespeare's works, they are the most widely quoted books in the Western world. Millions of copies of the *Alice* books have been printed, and they have been translated into virtually every language spoken and read on earth. (Some thirty different translations into French alone have appeared.) They have been adapted for the stage, made into films, and remade several times for television. They have provoked a mountain of parodies, retellings, poems, musical compositions, ballets, and monuments. Everywhere one goes, one sees Alice-inspired theme parks, exhibitions, and artifacts, and the *Alice* industry has produced countless pieces of children's pottery, soap and soap dishes, wallpaper, glass and ivory figures, postcards, games, chess sets, umbrella handles, tea towels, teapots, stained-glass hangings, decorative wall plates, posters, all manner of clothing (especially, in recent times, T-shirts), and "collectibles" that enliven any jumble sale or flea market.

But these trivia aside, the most important fact is that Carroll revolutionized writing for children: children's books after Carroll were less serious, more entertaining, and sounded less like sermons and more like the voices of friends than earlier prototypes. It follows naturally that the influence of the *Alice* books upon children as they grow up and upon the minds and hearts of mature people has been considerable. It is difficult to think of a great writer of the last century who has not written about Carroll and his books; the list includes W. H. Auden, Max Beerbohm, Kenneth Burke, G. K. Chesterton, John Ciardi, Robert Graves, Walter de la Mare, William Empson, Robert Graves, James Joyce, Harry Levin, Vladimir Nabokov, Joyce Carol Oates, J. B. Priestley, V. S. Pritchett, Saki, Allen Tate, Edmund Wilson, Virginia Woolf, and Alexander Woollcott. Leonard Bernstein brought up his children on the *Alices*, and the books have inspired Deems Taylor, David del Tredici, and other composers.

Distinguished writers make sense in what they say of Carroll and the *Alice* books. But we have also been bombarded by a horde of wild surmises, mostly from the psychological detectives determined to unlock deep motives in the man and to discover hidden meanings in the books. These analysts sometimes seem to be engaged in a contest to win a prize for the most outlandish reading of the texts. One such writer has proved to his satisfaction that *Alice* was written not by Lewis Carroll at all, but by Queen Victoria. Another sees *Alice's Adventures in Wonderland* as an allegory of the Oxford Movement, a third as an allegory of Darwinian evolution. Still another tells us that *Alice* represents Carroll's own birth trauma in the isolated Cheshire parsonage where he first saw the light of day, and some Freudians suggest that the book is about a woman in labor, that falling down the rabbit hole is an expression of Carroll's wish for coitus, that the heroine is variously a father, a mother, a fetus, or that Alice is a phallus (a theory that, at least, provides us with a rhyme). We can see her as a transvestite Christ if we choose or, if we follow the tortured reasoning of a more modern writer, we can consider Carroll himself as the first "acidhead." One eminent critic tells us that the story is about toilet training and bowel movements, and a recent paper even suggests that Alice is a symbol of the fallen woman (after all, she does fall down the rabbit hole). Unfortunately these eccentric readings, while they may amuse, do not really bring us any closer to understanding Carroll or his work.

The task of the biographer is to look behind the writings and into the artist to try, by closely studying the evidence, to bring him clearly and truthfully to life. With the help of newfound Carroll letters, with full access to the nine surviving volumes of his diaries, and with the connections that link this new material, the man and his subtle mixture of mind and feeling emerge more clearly than ever before, as does a sharper and deeper picture of the genius we know as Lewis Carroll.

LEWIS CARROLL

*Charles's birthplace, Daresbury Parsonage. Although the parsonage itself was destroyed by fire in 1884, the site is now a shrine cared for by the Lewis Carroll Birthplace Trust.*

# CHAPTER ONE

# *Beginnings*

*Through him the gale of life blew high.*

A. E. HOUSMAN

The man who came to be known the world over as Lewis Carroll breathed his first breath on January 27, 1832, during the reign of William IV, in the parsonage of Daresbury in Cheshire. He would be christened Charles Lutwidge Dodgson, and his father, Curate of the parish, paid to have his first son's birth announced in *The Times* of London:[1]

---

### BIRTHS.

On Saturday, the 28th inst., in Spring-gardens, Mrs. Joseph Freeman, of a daughter.

On the 29th inst., in Baker-street, the lady of Robert Cuninghame Taylor, of a daughter.

On the 25th inst., the lady of the Rev. E. H. Orme, M.A., of a daughter.

On the 21st inst., Mrs. W. B. Bell, of Frederick-street, Mecklenburg-square, of a son.

On the 27th inst., at the Parsonage, Daresbury, Cheshire, the lady of the Rev. Charles Dodgson, of a son.

On the 29th inst., at Highfield-house, Winchmore-hill, the lady of Peter Pope Firth, Esq., of a son.

On the 29th inst., the lady of Alexander Dobie, Esq., Palsgrave-place, of a son.

The Daresbury parsonage must have rung with joy at the news: parents, two sisters (aged three and one), grandparents, servants, neighbors, and members of the congregation would all have shared in the celebrations.

Another Charles Dodgson (1722?–95), Bishop of Elphin, was the grandfather of both Charles's parents. The Dodgsons descended from north country people going back beyond the eighteenth century. In 1827 Charles Dodgson, Lewis Carroll's father, married his first cousin Frances Jane Lutwidge. The newborn son was the third of what eventually became a family of eleven children, and if these bloodlines deserve credit for the creative genius we know to be Lewis Carroll's, so perhaps must they bear the blame for the stammer endemic in Charles's speech and in the speech of most of his brothers and sisters.

The older north country Dodgsons were county families, gentry and nobility. But immediate antecedents were mostly men of the cloth, an army captain, a lawyer. While privileged, they were neither exceptionally gifted nor depraved: no geniuses, no knaves.

The Dodgsons we meet here typify the slice of Victorian society often described as upper middle class, falling between those who worked with their hands and those who did not work at all. Lacking aristocratic bearings, inherited wealth, land, or other property, they could aspire to rise in the world only by developing their minds—which they did. Money was generally a constant concern, but it never crowded out their religious fervor, devotion to social good, pursuit of learning, and dedication to improving the human condition.

The living at Daresbury that the newborn boy's father held was entirely obscure, a small subsidiary of a larger parish. The Reverend Mr. Charles Dodgson received the curacy from his college, Christ Church, Oxford, in 1827, six years after taking a double first in classics and mathematics. Daresbury, seven miles from Warrington and twenty-one from Liverpool, a hamlet of 599 acres and 143 people, pleasantly situated and commanding fine prospects of the surrounding country, was virtually lost in the farming landscape. The parsonage, situated on a glebe farm a mile and a half from the small village, stood in rustic isolation, where "even the passing of a cart was a matter of great interest."[2]

Daresbury sowed deep seeds in young Charles's mind during his eleven years there, and his scribblings, sketches, and early efforts at verse hearken back to these days. Memories of Daresbury also color the mature works. One of the early pieces, "Lays of Sorrow, No. 1," is a tale of a dead chick in the henhouse and a youth's "bursting heart" on discovering it; in another, "Faces in the Fire," he reminisces about

> An island-farm—broad seas of corn
> Stirred by the wandering breath of morn—
> The happy spot where I was born.

S. D. Collingwood, Charles's nephew-biographer, who heard about life in the Daresbury parsonage at first hand, recorded that "in this quiet home the boy invented the strangest diversions for himself; he . . . numbered certain snails and toads among his intimate friends. He tried also to encourage civilised warfare among earthworms. . . ." He "seemed at this time to have . . . lived in that charming 'Wonderland' which he afterwards described so vividly; but for all that he was a thorough boy, and loved to climb the trees and to scramble about in the marl-pits."[3] In *Alice's Adventures in Wonderland* and *Through the Looking-Glass,* the White Rabbit, the animals in the Caucus-Race, the Caterpillar, the garden of flowers, and much more owe their origin to the barnyard, the fields, and the gardens of Daresbury. Here too Charles encountered a literary form, the acrostic, that he would make his own and use throughout his life. He read this one as it appears on the old tower addressed to the church bell ringers; it is based on the name of their village:

> Dare not to come into this sacred place
> All you good Ringers, but in awfull Grace.
> Ring not with Hatt, nor Spurs nor Insolence.
> Each one that does, for every such offence
> Shall forfeit Hatt or Spurs or Twelve Pence.
> But who disturbs a Peal, the same Offender
> Unto the Box his sixpence shall down Tender.
> Rules such no doubt in every Church are used
> You and your Bells that may not be abused.[4]

The elder Dodgson and his family were living through the memorable events of the age of reform. He at least would have read with interest in *The Times* of the reform bills, the abolition of slavery in the colonies, the Factory Act forbidding the employment of children under nine years old, the New Poor Law establishing workhouses, the Chartist agitation for wider suffrage and parliamentary reform, the opium war in China, the death of William IV, the accession of Victoria and her marriage to Prince Albert. But these events must have appeared remote to the family. Collingwood, in fact, characterizes Charles's eleven years at Daresbury as "years of complete seclusion from the world."[5]

At Daresbury the father tended his flock, giving special attention to the poor; he initiated Sunday school and held service in a barge chapel of his own devising for those who worked on the canal running through the parish. He was reputed to exhibit wit and humor "in moments of relaxation," but in the main, he "was a man of deep piety and of a somewhat reserved and grave disposition."[6] To augment his meager income, he took in paying pupils. In addition to all his other work, he somehow managed to produce a monograph on religion at least once a year.

Life in the Dodgson household was busy and followed a strict regimen. Hours were allocated for games, but lighter activities did not encroach upon the severe Christian responsibilities or on time needed for lessons, reading, memorizing. Religious rituals dominated the Daresbury parsonage. The family assembled for prayers morning and evening; Bible reading was a staple; on Sunday they attended two church services and the children went to Sunday school. Both work and play were

*Silhouette of Charles as a boy*

forbidden on Sunday, replaced by reading religious tomes, and the family ate cold meals to insure that the servants did not have to work on the Lord's day. Even though Mr. Dodgson augmented his income by tutoring, he was pinched financially and sent reports back to Christ Church of "anxieties incidental to my situation."[7]

For her part, the cleric's lady kept busy helping her husband with parish work and bearing, rearing, and shaping her ever-increasing family: ten of her children were born in Daresbury. Complying with custom, she educated her daughters at home. Mrs. Dodgson was in her own way as remarkable as her husband, remaining cheerful and loving, taking on all her duties and burdens without complaint. One observer remembered her as "one of the sweetest and gentlest women that ever lived, whom to know was to love. The earnestness of her simple faith and love shone forth in all she did and said. . . . It has been said by her children that they never in all their lives remember to have heard an impatient or harsh word from her lips."[8] Charles's great-aunt Mary Smedley later recalled that when she and Charles's mother were walking together one day, Mrs. Dodgson "spoke . . . of her rare and exceeding happiness . . . that she was very happy at Daresbury but that . . . such a life as she led [after Daresbury] at Croft . . . [was] the perfection of earthly happiness . . . that sometimes when remembering this it was almost startling to find how exactly her wishes had been fulfilled and that for seven . . . years she had been living precisely the life that she had most delighted to dwell upon in fancy,—and then she spoke most touchingly and beautifully of the responsibility incurred by a lot of so much happiness— and that it really at times was 'alarming' to look round her and feel that she had not a wish unfulfilled. . . ."[9]

Charles was her special pet; the few surviving letters she wrote to her sister Lucy show her sensitive to Charles's uncommon nature. She kept a three-part record of Charles's early reading: "Religious Reading: Private," "Religious Reading with Mama," and "Daily Reading: Useful—Private." Among the tomes he tackled at age seven was *The Pilgrim's Progress*. For his part, he sensed her angelic qualities and worshiped her above all others. Many years later, when his sister Mary gave birth to her first child, Charles wrote her: "May you be to him what your own dear mother was to *her* eldest son. I can hardly utter for your boy a better wish than that."[10]

"Charlie," as well as the other sons, received their earliest lessons from their father. Charles progressed rapidly in his studies. When he was eight or so, Charles's mother, writing to him from Hull, where she was visiting her parents, congratulated him on "getting on so well with your Latin, and . . . [making] so few mistakes in your Exercises."[11] All children are curious, but not many so precocious as Charles: "One day, when . . . [he] was a very small boy," Collingwood wrote, "he . . . showed . . . [his father] a book of logarithms, with the request, 'Please explain.' Mr. Dodgson told him that he was much too young to understand . . . such a difficult subject. The child listened . . . and appeared to think it irrelevant, for he still insisted, '*But*, please, explain!' "[12] The father was evidently successful in tutoring Charles and Charles diligent in his application, taking easily to his study of Latin, mathematics, the classics, and English literature. The father imbued the son with his own religious principles, and the son, in these early days, accepted the parental teachings, especially in matters of Christian doctrine, and sought to mirror his accomplished sire.

A silhouette of Charles made at this time, when he was eight, reveals the profile of an ordinary boy, well proportioned, erect, with no hint of his com-

plex character. For he was exceptionally gifted, sensitive, eager, but handi-
capped from an early age, not only by his stammer but also by deafness in
his right ear, which his mother ascribed to "Infantile fever."[13]

For sixteen years, Mr. Dodgson struggled in obscurity at Daresbury. But
then, in 1843, when Charles was eleven, on the urging of Mr. Dodgson's old
friend Charles Longley, Bishop of Ripon, and other notables, the Prime
Minister, Robert Peel, awarded the elder Dodgson the living of Croft-on-
Tees in the North Riding of Yorkshire, four miles south of Darlington,
twenty-five miles north of the cathedral town of Ripon. Daresbury would
live in Charles's memory, but the parsonage does not survive, having burned
to the ground in 1884. Lewis Carroll is, however, honored by a plaque at the
site of the old parsonage, and the church where Charles was baptized and
first heard his father preach contains a stained-glass window depicting characters from the *Alice* books.

On the family's departure from Daresbury, the churchwarden summarized, in tribute, Mr. Dodgson's achievements in that outlying parish. He
recalled that when the Dodgsons first came to Daresbury,

> no Sunday-school existed, no week-day Lectures were given—no effi-
> cient visitations to the sick and poorer classes took place and the Sun-
> day congregations in our Church were lamentably small.
>
> It is, Sir, to your persevering energies . . . that we are indebted
> for . . . the establishment . . . of a Sunday School. . . . To your unwea-
> ried exertions, we owe . . . no less than three Lectures in each week. . . .
> By your open-handed charities . . . the sick, the poor, and the afflicted,
> have been constantly relieved, instructed and comforted.
> . . . Your labours . . . have been shared by the excellent and amiable
> Ladies of your family. We have gratefully observed their warm interest
> in the Parish . . . and we have witnessed their assiduous attention to
> the wants and comforts of the Poor. . . .[14]

The prospect the Dodgsons beheld when they arrived at Croft was immensely superior to Daresbury's. The rectory, a large, three-storied Georgian
edifice across the road from an ancient heavy stone Gothic church, stands to
this day, boxlike, solid, and dignified. The size alone must have given great
satisfaction. Paintings and later photographs show a surround of spacious
gardens, flowers, bushes, and trees in bloom. Photographs of the assembled
Dodgsons, taken perhaps by Skeffington Lutwidge, the mother's brother, or

by Lewis Carroll himself, depict an expanse of lawn ideal for croquet. Charles later memorialized the Dodgsons' home in the *Rectory Umbrella:*

> Fair stands the ancient Rectory,
>     The Rectory of Croft,
> The sun shines bright upon it,
>     The breezes whisper soft.
> From all the house and garden
>     Its inhabitants come forth,
> And muster in the road without,
> And pace in twos and threes about,
>     The children of the North.

Acacia trees in the front garden bloom there still, and the cluster of old chimneys catches the eye. Inside the front hall hang framed pictures of the Dodgson era, one a photograph of Charles in his student days and the verse he composed about the Old Rectory. Although the interior is much altered, the warren of hallways, stairs, and rooms, and not least the dark, mysterious basement, evoke the busy life the Dodgsons led here for a quarter of a century, from 1843 to 1868.

Just as the new Croft home was a vast improvement for the Dodgsons, so was the village of Croft itself, with its town hall and a posting inn for coaches plying the London-Edinburgh route. "This place is much noted for its sulphureous spa waters," reads an early nineteenth-century directory, "which resemble both in smell and medicinal properties the Harrogate sulphur spa."[15] The town was also a center for horse racing and for hunting. Compared to Daresbury, Croft appeared a veritable metropolis to the Dodgsons.

The father plunged into his parish with his accustomed zeal, soon replaced a decrepit chancel roof on the church, made necessary repairs to the rectory, and built a proper school where a barnlike structure sufficed earlier.[16] He induced members of his family to join him in teaching. He now had an

*Charles's exaggerated version of Croft Rectory and how its inhabitants poured forth to watch a knight mount a steed*

*Charles's father, Archdeacon Charles Dodgson*

income of more than a thousand pounds a year and could provide adequately for his family and help support worthy charitable programs.

The home was dominated by an Evangelical orderliness and rule of denial. Family prayers were again conducted both morning and evening. Sundays were sacrosanct; everyone read the Bible and prescribed religious tomes. The mother gave birth to her eleventh child, a son, and busied herself caring for her family and the parish poor. The father ruled imperiously.

Charles was remembered as "thin, tallish . . . always very serious, as though in deep study, but particularly pleasant when spoken to and in subsequent conversation." He was often seen "sitting or lying full length on the lawn under the noble acacia tree in the rectory garden, writing."[17]

"[The Dodgsons] . . . were very nice, kind people, very generous," one recollection reads. "They gave away all they had. They kept cows and anyone was welcome to a can of milk. I remember that the Misses Dodgson, Lewis Carroll's sisters, wore very long, full skirts like umbrellas, but their dresses were very plain. Miss Elizabeth was my teacher in Sunday school,

*Charles's seven sisters in the garden at Croft Rectory*

and I remember that she often gave us apples from the tree in the rectory garden."[18]

The earliest passenger railway line in England ran from nearby Darlington to Stockton in the east, and its magic soon bewitched Charles. He constructed a miniature replica in the rectory garden, "a rude train [made] out of a wheelbarrow, a barrel and a small truck" that conveyed his "passengers" from one "station" to another. All "passengers" had to buy tickets in advance, and each station had a refreshment room. Charles devised a timetable and rules governing the operation. "Station master can put anyone who behaves badly to prison," and passengers "may not get in or out of the train when moving. . . ."[19] Charles also wrote a three-act comic opera called *Guida di Bragia*, burlesquing *Bradshaw's Railway Guide.* He began to draw and kept a notebook for sketches and pictures "afterwards painted by his brothers and sisters."[20]

The inhabitants of the rectory were the subjects of a rhyming spoof that Charles wrote some years later, "Lays of Sorrow, No. 2." It depicts a crowd emerging from the rectory to witness "a gallant feat of horsemanship" that turns out to be no more than a "knight" (Charles's younger brother Skeffington) mounting and riding a "steed," which Charles's drawing reveals to be a donkey. The beast proves unmanageable; another brother, Wilfred, comes to the rescue: he blocks the steed's path while the "knight" dismounts and then clears a path for the beast to gallop away. The piece ends with a glimpse of the rectory interior, where "often in the evening . . . the fire is blazing bright . . . books bestrew the table. . . . And moths obscure the light . . . crying children go to bed . . . [a] struggling, kicking load. . . ."

In Croft Rectory, the boy grew into a youth, and his native talents emerged. Even before he was thrust in with others of his age and station at school, he proved supple in matters mechanical, creative in art, and a responsible leader and instructor of the other Dodgson children. With a carpenter's help, he built a marionette theater, composed plays, and learned to manipulate the marionettes for the presentations. Wearing a brown wig and a long white robe, he became an Aladdin, a nimble magician performing tricks to amaze and delight an admiring throng. He created charades and acted them out. He built for his elder sister Elizabeth a miniature toolbox and inscribed it "E.L.D. from C.L.D."

Drawings, verses, and short stories sprang forth, and while none is stamped with Mozartian genius, all are more than ordinary. Charles's early compositions in prose and poetry and his artwork show that his handwriting was already remarkably adult, strong, confident; his vocabulary and allusions prove him well ahead of his years; and if his drawings are crude, they do not lack force or humor. So mature does he appear so early that one wonders whether he moved from childhood directly into adulthood, somehow skipping boyhood.

Like so many other Victorian families, the Dodgsons initiated a series of domestic magazines, scrapbooks for everything of interest—newspaper cuttings, pressed leaves and flowers no doubt, perhaps family memorabilia, and certainly any creative efforts by the rectory clan. Eight of these magazines came into being, but only four survive. The eldest son was the driving force behind them all and made the only significant contributions to them.

The earliest booklet is a slender thing called *Useful and Instructive Poetry*. It consists of sixteen items on the right-hand pages and crude illustrations on the left. It is entirely the work of thirteen-year-old Charles, who tells us in the last of the magazines, *Mischmasch*, that it appeared "about the year 1845, the idea of the first poem being suggested by a piece in the *Etonian*. . . ."

Fifteen of the pieces are in verse, the sixteenth an adaptation of some dialogue from Shakespeare's *Henry IV, Part 2*. Of the fifteen, the piece entitled "Melodies" contains four limericks in a style that would become associated with Edward Lear. These limericks may well have preceded Lear's, or were at least contemporaneous with Lear's first book of nonsense in 1846. The last in the group is perhaps the best:

> His sister named Lucy O'Finner
> Grew constantly thinner and thinner,
>> The reason was plain,
>> She slept out in the rain,
> And was never allowed any dinner.

Charles wrote these verses for his younger brother Wilfred and sister Louisa, and most of them end with moral tags, giving the mock impression that the older brother was instructing the younger two in proper behavior. One of the moral tags is "Don't dream," another "Never stew your sister."

The booklet shows a sophisticated wit for a thirteen-year-old and an impressive range of literary allusion and influence: the humorist poet W. M. Praed, Shakespeare, Blake, the Romantic poets, Izaak Walton, Tennyson. We see the influence of his religious upbringing and recognize the seeds of a later harvest—"The Mouse's Tail," the cook and her stew, some of the words that Humpty Dumpty will utter, intimations of "Phantasmagoria" and *The Hunting of the Snark*. Young Charles clearly took pleasure in playing with words, even in coining a few, and delighted in parody and humor.

True, the metrics, the rhymes, even the grammar leave something to be desired, and if Charles's drawings are incondite, they at least show early signs of his interest in art. The self-confidence throughout suggests an exceptional young man in the making. Perhaps most remarkable is the tone, how he treats cherished subjects without offending. The verses bear serious titles ("Punctuality," "Charity," "Rules and Regulations"), but what he does with these virtuous subjects often surprises. In one after another, he dispatches conventional and ponderous Victorian concerns with a fresh and light stroke, with banter, irreverently but endearingly spoofing solemn rubrics. The neatest composition is the first poem, "My Fairy":

> I have a fairy by my side
> Which says I must not sleep,
> When once in pain I loudly cried
> It said "you must not weep."

> If, full of mirth, I smile and grin
> It says "You must not laugh";
> When once I wished to drink some gin
> It said "You must not quaff."
>
> When once a meal I wished to taste
> It said "You must not bite";
> When to the wars I went in haste
> It said "You must not fight."
>
> "What *may* I do?" at length I cried,
> Tired of the painful task.
> The fairy quietly replied,
> And said "You must not ask."
>
> *Moral:* "You mustn't."

Here, then, Charles's brand of humor, his singular vein of genius, emerges: at thirteen, he already knows how to use it to excellent effect. These juvenile outpourings contain more than meets the eye. Behind the parodies of life at Croft lurk both a keen observer and a critic, a commentator on domestic and social conventions, a judge of family relationships, and, above all, an independent spirit. And beneath the banter run a dark strain of complaint, a smarting resentment, even gratuitous violence, all of which appear more forcefully later.

By the time Charles composed *Useful and Instructive Poetry*, he was no longer being tutored by his father but, in fact, was a resident at Richmond School, ten miles from home. Richmond is an old, solidly built market town of gray stone and cobbled roads sited picturesquely on the sloping ground above the "foaming Swale," with the remains of a monastery, abbey, and castle, and walking access to Yorkshire's magnificent Swaledale. At Richmond, Charles boarded with the headmaster, James Tate, his wife, six children, and a handful of other pupils, in a large edifice, Swale House.

Within a week of his arrival he wrote home. His new life in a society dominated by masters and boys must have jolted him, but he did not complain. Dated August 5, 1844, his letter went not to his parents but to his two elder sisters, Frances and Elizabeth. He reports that "the boys have played two tricks on me," but he is able to add that they "play me no tricks now.

The only *fault* (tell mama) that there has been, was coming in one day to dinner *just* after grace." On Sunday he attends church service morning and evening, and in the afternoon the headmaster reads to the boys a discourse on the Fifth Commandment ("Honour thy father and mother . . ."). At his father's request, he reports on the sermon's text, but adds that at the morning service he could hear neither text nor sermon. He concludes the letter by noting that "the chief games are foot-ball, wrestling, leap frog, and fighting." Charles's inability to hear the sermon may have had something to do with acoustics, but more likely was the result of his deafness.

In spite of the difference between Croft Rectory and Swale House, the two had much in common: a multiplicity of children, a schoolish atmosphere, an emphasis on Christian ritual and behavior. Nor did the subjects that Charles studied in the large schoolroom differ much from those he had learned under his father's wing: Latin, Greek, religion, mathematics, English literature, and French. The instruction was conducted primarily by the headmaster, assisted by his brother and a French master. Perhaps the most evident difference between the two scenes was the absence of sisters.

Charles did well during his sixteen months at Richmond, won prizes, and apparently "loved his 'kind old schoolmaster,' as he affectionately called . . . [Tate]." The headmaster, for his part, reported to the Dodgsons that their son possessed "a very uncommon share of genius," that "he is capable of acquirements and knowledge far beyond his years, while his reason is so clear and so jealous of error, that he will not rest satisfied without the most exact solution of whatever appears to him obscure. He has passed an excellent examination just now in mathematics, exhibiting at times an illustration of that love of precise argument, which seems to him natural."[21]

Tate may have fed Charles's hunger for mathematical answers and helped him enter the lists of higher mathematics. Quite possibly, Charles left Richmond "with a rudimentary interest in the conceptual gaps in traditional algebra," according to the historian Helena M. Pycior. She believes "that a critical perspective on traditional algebra . . . prevailed at the school during . . . [Charles's] school years." Furthermore, "if poorly defined algebraic concepts were criticized by any Richmond students . . . [Charles] would surely have been among the critics."[22]

Altogether Richmond was a success. Charles proved resourceful, held his own among the 120 boys, and emerged intellectually superior to most of them. Here, "in later school days," Collingwood tells us, Charles became "famous as a champion of the weak and small, while every bully had good reason to fear him. . . . Long after he left school his name was remembered as that of a boy who knew well how to use his fists in defence of a righteous cause."[23]

Charles returned to Croft at the end of 1845 to contemplate the next step in his education. He was home for the Christmas holidays and perhaps during this time away from books he assembled his verses and drawings for *Useful and Instructive Poetry*.

On January 27, 1846, Charles's fourteenth birthday, he again left home, this time to enter Rugby. Why Rugby, when Charles's father and Uncle Hassard Dodgson had both been King's Scholars at Westminster and when Westminster offered the high road to Christ Church, taken by the two elder Dodgsons? One reason must have been Westminster's steady decline, which began even before the elder Dodgsons went to school there, and reached its nadir at the time that Charles was ready to enter a public school. In the area around Westminster School, in what Dickens would label "Hell's Kitchen," crime flourished, factories and other buildings multiplied, adding to London's noxious air. Within the school, masters and prefects fought unresolved battles. The decline was so pronounced that student enrollment sank from three hundred in 1821 to ninety in the year Charles entered Rugby.[24]

Rugby offered geographical advantages. It was some eighty-five miles closer to Croft than London, and the smaller town did not conjure up the dangerous stews or the unhealthy atmosphere of the capital. Perhaps most important was that Rugby School was enjoying its reputation as England's best public school, the result of the fourteen-year rule, from 1828 to 1842, of the exuberant Dr. Thomas Arnold.

When Arnold came to Rugby in 1828, it too had the reputation of being a nursery for vice, but he was determined to turn it into a training ground for Christian gentlemen. In his view, the school's chapel was at least as important as its classrooms: Christian faith, if blended well with classical learning, would produce a superior breed, a new brand of Englishman. Arnold introduced a hierarchy, from masters to preceptors to fags. For him, the manner of teaching was more important than the matter, and he carefully selected masters for their ability to teach, not only their subjects but moral righteousness as well, and to set a moral example in how they themselves lived. He sought to instill in each member of the school a missionary zeal and to elicit from the community a genuine love of God and devotion to duty, a moral earnestness. He served as Rugby's chaplain as well as headmaster and with dramatic sermons sowed conscience in his boys' minds. Arnold saw the rows of boys arrayed before him as vessels of sin from which he had to exorcise the devil. He cajoled his charges, making each feel that the great doctor was addressing him personally. Life on earth, Arnold thundered, was no fool's paradise, but a battlefield where everyone must fight and where the stakes were enormous.

The boys listened, mesmerized—they quaked. They heard the learned doctor rant against evil behavior, and they learned that in their idol's scale of values, moral behavior stood above gentlemanly conduct and gentlemanly conduct above intellectual achievement. Arnold also taught spiritual introspection: sinners must look for help within themselves even as they must set high standards for all their thoughts and actions. If a boy cultivated a strong will, a strong mind would follow. Truthfulness was one of Arnold's special virtues, and, as we know from *Tom Brown's Schooldays*—Thomas Hughes had been a Rugby student five years before Charles—the wrath of both heaven and headmaster descended upon a boy caught lying. Arnold had an enormous influence upon his lads, many became eminent Victorians, and Rugby became the model for all good schools in Britain and beyond.

Charles never actually heard Dr. Arnold. He arrived at Rugby more than three years after Arnold preached his last sermon. His headmaster, Archibald Campbell Tait, later Archbishop of Canterbury, succeeded Arnold. Tait lacked Arnold's theatricality, but he preached good sermons, continued his predecessor's policy of making the chapel central to life, and saw the pulpit as a vital source of the boys' education. He was also, like Arnold, courageous. Arnold had openly preached and written about his Broad Church liberalism, attacking the rigid theology of the Tractarians; Tait lashed out against restrictive thought and practice. His censure of John Henry Newman's *Tract XC* caused Newman to discontinue his *Tracts for the Times*. When, in 1844, W. G. Ward's *Ideal of a Christian Church* appeared, calling for stricter religious tests in the universities, Tait denounced the proposal. "There is no need," he wrote, "of our narrowing the limits of the Church of England because some among us wish to make it too wide."[25]

Charles heard Tait preach, but the legend of the great Dr. Arnold still rang through the halls and in the ears of Charles's generation. If, when Charles arrived at Rugby in 1846, he went into the school chapel to explore its aisles and recesses, he likely stopped in reverence before the communion table in the chancel, beneath which lay the late headmaster's body. One of the prizes he earned here was Arnold's *Introductory Lectures on Modern History,* and when Arnold's collected sermons were published while Charles was at Rugby, he surely took note. Charles's later writings sometimes echo Arnold's sermons, particularly in the image of life as a battleground where one must take up arms against the devil.

When Charles left Croft for Richmond, he left childhood and domesticity behind, but he could and did come to terms with change. Going from Richmond to Rugby was another matter altogether. Rugby's reputation must have inspired respect in the lad from the provincial north, and the town itself, already a major railway junction, must have appeared a bustling municipality. The school, with its ancient buildings, would have had its own impact, as Charles moved along its paths and through its chambers, his eye caught by arched doorways, Gothic halls, crenellated towers, machicolated parapets, a clock tower, turrets and turret staircases, quadrangles, courtyards, cloisters, manicured playing fields, a close, bays, and mullioned windows.

More trials awaited Charles here than at Richmond. The challenges came from Rugby's social structure and from cracks in the disciplinary stone wall that Arnold had sought to construct. Boys will be boys, and despite Arnold's and Tait's preaching and prodding, some of the five hundred pupils still preferred a rough-and-ready lifestyle and the excesses of fagging and bullying.

The curriculum was unremarkable. Arnold had liberalized it somewhat, but the classics and classical languages still reigned supreme. Mathematics, French, and Scripture filled out the schedule. The one new element was history, but science had not yet earned a place for itself.

Charles took his studies in stride, not particularly troubled by the long hours required. On Mondays, Wednesdays, and Fridays, he had two classes in the morning, from 7 to 8 and from 9:15 to 11, and two more in the afternoon, from 2:15 to 5; on Tuesdays and Thursdays, the same morning classes, but a third from 11 a.m. to 1 p.m., and no afternoon classes; on Saturday, morning classes as usual, but no class after 11. These make about twenty classes a week, each between one and two hours long. Of the twenty, sixteen were in classics, Scripture, and history; two in mathematics, two in French.

In spite of Arnold's obsession with boys' inherent wickedness and Tait's efforts to continue Arnold's policies, fagging, bullying, and even worse elements persisted. Initiating ceremonies were sometimes brutal. Thomas Hughes describes "lamb-singing" in chapter 6 of *Tom Brown's Schooldays,* and at the end of the century W. H. D. Rouse, classicist and Rugby master, reported:

The most remarkable of . . . [Rugby] customs which still survive is the "lamb-singing." . . . New boys are conducted to one of the small dormitories. The head of the house and the captain of the . . . [Rugby football team] sit on a bed, as a bench of judges; the other boys crowd inside . . . or without. Then on another bed each new boy is made to stand up in turn, a fag on either side lighting his face with a . . . [candle] set in a tin candlestick. The lamb must now sing a song. If it pass muster, good; if not, the judges start "Rule Britannia," which is taken up by all present, and the unsuccessful songster formerly had to drink a concoction of tooth-powder, salt, mustard, and other ingredients, mixed with water.

Charles had a good singing voice, but one shudders to think of the consequences if he had stammered during his lamb-singing.[26]

Fagging was, in fact, one of the sanctioned elements in the Arnold-Tait hierarchy, where older boys governed the houses and imposed discipline on the younger ones. Ruled by the elite sixth form, undisciplined youths were supposed to be transformed into responsible, religious, dutiful men.

Two types of fagging existed: school fagging and house fagging. If a member of the sixth wanted a fag for any outdoor activity, like umpiring cricket, he merely picked one of the three hundred or so boys in the lower forms. House fagging was more arduous and humiliating, ranging from scullery work to running errands. On call virtually all the time he was not in class, the fag could not call his life his own.

If a fag did not perform his duties or was found wanting, he was punished. "For minor offenses," Rouse wrote, "there was a 'study-licking' of three strokes; for others, a more serious chastisement administered before the Sixth, or 'hall licking.' "[27] One of Charles's contemporaries recalls that the "most common punishments [impositions] consisted of writing out many hundred lines of Virgil or Homer by a particular time, and the severity of the punishment chiefly lay in the time allowed to do it. If not brought up on time it was doubled, and some boys were generally a few hundreds in arrear, which were occasionally wiped off by a flogging. . . ."[28]

The boys lived in dens; some pillaged others' dens and certainly they played tricks upon one another. A boy "might come in to find everything in the place turned wrong way up: the table tied to the ceiling, each chair hung up on the walls upside down, the sofa on the top of the door, pens and pencils glued to the roof, every picture face downwards on the floor, the books on their heads, and the geraniums standing on their flowers. Even the ink-stand would be turned over, but so cunningly that the ink remained in it."

"There was a great deal too much drinking of strong liquors," Rouse wrote. Neither Arnold nor Tait was able to rid the school of drunkenness. The boys were served beer with their meals—water was unsafe—and from beer to stronger libations is not a long leap.

James Warner, a boy who entered Rugby the year Charles left, wrote home: "I have got on quite well with bullying, except their coming into my study pulling all my books about and preventing my learning by asking me to repeat the most horrid words, by pretending to know such things as boys ought not to know. . . . Stealing here is not uncommon and they alter the 8th commandment to 'Thou shalt steal nothing except. . . .' . . . Swearing and vile language are but too frequent although prayers are said in private by some."[29]

Of Charles's years at Rugby we have slender record. He did well in his studies and won prizes. His mathematics master, R. B. Mayor, wrote to Charles's father in 1848: "I have not had a more promising boy at his age since I came to Rugby." At the close of 1849, when Charles was about to leave, Tait also sent words of praise to Croft about "the very high opinion I entertain of him. . . . His mathematical knowledge is great for his age, and I doubt not he will do himself credit in classics. . . . His examination for the Divinity prize was one of the most creditable exhibitions I have ever seen. . . . During the whole time of his being in my house, his conduct has been excellent."[30]

Two letters Charles wrote home from Rugby survive. Sensitive but staunchly self-reliant, he was not one to complain: whatever unpleasantness he encountered remained at Rugby; nothing disagreeable traveled to Croft. He writes to his older sister Elizabeth about his prizes, a visit to a nearby Roman camp, the books he is reading, and others he wants to buy. He asks about the family magazines, and reports buying a new hat and gloves. A series of questions in the letter dated May 24, 1849, constitutes a humorous barrage that conceals the feelings of a homesick lad but also gives a glimpse of the busy life at Croft Rectory:

> Will you answer my questions about the clocks, when you next write? How do you get on with the poetry book with Willy and Louy? Shall I send or bring you any more numbers of it? And have you seen *The Vast Army?* There is a 3d part of *Laneton Parsonage* come out, have

you seen it? How do you like the *Diversions of Hollycott?* Will my room
be ready for me when I come home? . . . Have you been many walks
with Aunt and Cousin Smedley? And how long are they going to stay
with you? Are my two pictures of cricketing framed yet? When is Papa
going to the Ordination? And when to the Durham examination? Has
Fanny yet finished Alison's *Europe?* . . . Are the mats finished? Is
Skeffington's ship finished? Have you left off fires yet? Have you begun
the evening walks in the garden? Does Skeffington ride Henderson's
donkey much now? Has Fanny found any new flowers? Have you got
any new babies to nurse? Mary any new pictures to paint? . . . Will you
tell me whose and when the birthdays in next month are? Will you
condense all these questions into one or answer each separately? Lastly,
Do you believe that I subscribe myself your

Affectionate Brother, sincerely or no? Is this letter long enough?

Charles's health was good, but during his school years he suffered both
whooping cough and mumps. He got over the first in good form, and his
mother wrote to her sister that he was back in the rectory garden entertaining his brothers and sisters: "At the *Railroad* games, which the darlings *all
delight* in, he *tries and proves* his strength in the most persevering way."[31]
The mumps came later, but these illnesses were not exceptional. An old
Rugbeian of the time writes about "the annual visitation of epidemics, that
took this opportunity of looking up those who had escaped before, and seeing that the great mump-and-measle tax . . . was duly paid."[32]

Charles's nephew reproduced a paragraph from a missing diary which
Charles wrote in 1855, making clear that Charles was unhappy, even miserable, at Rugby: "During my stay I made I suppose some progress in learning of various kinds, but none of it was done *con amore,* and I spent an
incalculable time in writing out impositions—this last I consider one of the
chief faults of Rugby School. I made some friends there . . . but I cannot say
that I look back upon my life at a Public School with any sensations of pleasure, or that any earthly considerations would induce me to go through my
three years again."[33]

Nor did Charles escape bullying. In one of his school books, where he
wrote his name, his Rugby house, and the date (November 13, 1846), another
hand added "is a muff."[34] He was not athletic, and in sports, as in lamb-
singing, he must have come in for a good amount of hazing.

We get another insight into these difficult days from Charles's diary, where he records a visit to another public school, Radley (March 18, 1857):

> I was particularly struck by the healthy happy look of the boys and their
> gentlemanly appearance. The dormitory is the most unique feature of
> the whole: in two large rooms, by a very trifling expense in wood-work,
> every boy has a snug little bedroom secured to himself, where he is free
> from interruption and annoyance. This to little boys must be a very
> great addition to their happiness, as being a kind of counterbalance to
> any bullying they may suffer during the day. From my own experience
> of school life at Rugby I can say that if I could have been thus secure
> from annoyance at night, the hardships of the daily life would have
> been comparative trifles to bear.

Charles was at Rugby for almost four years, until 1849, when he returned
to Croft to spend almost a year preparing for Oxford. That time at home,
free of the rowdy school atmosphere, relieved of rigid schedules, must have
been joyous. Even though he was preparing for Oxford, he had leisure, he
had the opportunity to be with his brothers and sisters, and he could soak
up the love and attention of his doting mother. He could also return to the
family magazine project and let his imagination soar. Two of the surviving
family magazines date from this time. *The Rectory Magazine* (1848) describes
itself as "Being a Compendium of the best tales, poems, essays, pictures,
etc., that the united talents of the Rectory inhabitants can produce, Edited
and printed by C.L.D., Fifth Edition, carefully revised, & improved, 1850."
It contains 128 pages, all in Charles's hand script, with a table of contents
and an index. Most of the compositions are by Charles, but other family
members contributed too. It begins with a dedication: "To the Inhabitants
of the Rectory, Croft, and especially to the younger members of that house,
this Magazine, their own united labour and produce, is respectfully Dedicated by The Editor." In reminiscing about the volume in the introduction
to *Mischmasch*, Charles wrote: "This was the first started for general contribution, and at first the contributions poured in one continuous stream, while
the issuing of each number was attended by the most violent excitement
through the whole house; most of the family contributed one or more articles to it. About the year 1848 the numbers were bound into a volume. . . ."
*The Rectory Magazine* is an accumulation of fanciful jottings, a ragbag of
verse, stories, essays, drawings, mock book reviews, and faked letters. The
contributions that come from the other family members are less luminous
than Charles's but are not to be dismissed: they contain some wit, like

Charles's, and some talent. Charles's contributions, however, add a touch of real distinction. While *Useful and Instructive Poetry* demonstrates a highly gifted family satirist at work, the whole is monochromatic. Here, in *The Rectory Magazine,* Charles plays with many bows; the result is a blend of instruments that produces a much more mature and engaging piece of music. The strains and devices of the earlier efforts reappear here: puns, plays on words, word coinage, and social parody. New are portmanteau words and a fresh prose narrative. Once more Charles's extensive reading is on display: he quotes or alludes to or shows the influence of Coleridge, Cowper, Crabbe, Dickens, Goldsmith, Gray, Ossian, Scott, Shakespeare, Tennyson, Thomson, and Wordsworth.

How young was Charles, one wonders, when he took his first railway journey? He was fascinated by the railway but also aware of the engine's grotesque qualities, which inspired one of his poems here:

Terrors
. . . Is not that an angry snake?
Lo! he twists his writhing tale!
Hear the hisses he doth make!
See his yellow coat of mail.

Distant howls still louder grown,
Angry mutterings sounding near,
All proclaim with solemn tone,
Something dreadful coming here!

Lo! it comes, a vision grim!
Puffing forth black coils of smoke!
While amid these terrors dim
I listened, thus the monster spoke,

"Clear the line there! clear the rails!
'Stop the engine! hold there! Steady!
'Stoker! hand me up those pails!
'Euston station! tickets ready! . . .' "*

Charles signed the poem "B.B.," one of six pseudonyms he used in the magazine. In the verse "Screams," he shows his familiarity with the slang of

---

* The punctuation is Charles's.

the day, but for less worldly readers, he supplies a glossary ("peeler": police-
man; "shiners": money). He adds an amusing essay on the discovery of ink
and how it changed the world of letters. His best work is in his prose narratives. "Crundle Castle" is a tale with strong Dickensian overtones that draws
characters who would reappear more fully developed in the *Sylvie and Bruno*
books. The most elaborate tale, and the best, is "Sidney Hamilton," about a
prodigal son and a stern father. It ends in reconciliation, with the father reduced to complaining that toast is being wasted at breakfast.

In an essay entitled "Rust," Charles warns that "there is no fate which we
dread more for our magazine than that it should become rusty. We would
have its wheels run smoothly on, the axletrees well oiled by a copious and
constant stream of contributions," but "we opened our Editor's box this
morning, expecting of course to find it overflowing with contributions, and
found it—our pen shudders and our ink blushes as we write—empty!"

The single contribution made by Aunt Lucy Lutwidge gives us another
window through which to see into the domestic life of the rectory. It is a
mock advertisement for

> a Maid of all work, in a large but quiet family, where cows, pigs, and
> poultry are kept. . . . She will be required to have breakfast on the table
> at 9, Luncheon at 12, Dinner at 3 (when she will wait at table), Tea at
> 6, and Supper at 9. Baking done at home as also the washing, and in
> winter brewing. No perquisites allowed or going out without leave. All
> leisure time to be spent in gardening. A cheerfulness of disposition and
> a willingness to oblige indispensable. Wages £3. 3s. 0d. a year, with or
> without tea and sugar accordingly as she gives satisfaction.

Charles is the sole author of the next family magazine, *The Rectory Umbrella,* apparently begun in 1850 and completed during vacations back at
Croft from Oxford. Later, in the preface to *Mischmasch,* he reports that it
originated "in 1849 or 1850," that it was "wholly unsupported, and it took us
a year or more to fill the volume by our own unaided efforts."

Charles had grown and his talents had matured. At eighteen, he showed
a polish not evident earlier. The works are more complex, longer, sustained.
He begins with an allegorical drawing showing a smiling, bearded poet sitting beneath an umbrella on which appear Charles's categories of the various branches of literature: jokes, riddles, fun poetry, tales. From the sky
above, a band of devilish creatures, all male, throw rocks down upon the umbrella; the rocks are labeled: woe, crossness, alloverishness, ennui, spite, and

gloom. And flying on the wind, toward the bohemian poet, seven
angelic females bring good
humor, taste, liveliness,
knowledge, mirth, con-
tent, and cheerfulness.

Some readers have
been troubled by the
poet's garment, think-
ing it is a dress. But it
is not. He wears a
tabard or tunic, but
Charles's skill in draw-
ing the recumbent fig-
ure is inadequate; he
draws him better, stand-
ing, on the last page. That
the garment is only knee-
length is the clincher: no
woman either in medieval times
or during the nineteenth century
would wear a dress ending above the
knees. A good many other sketches
skip and scamper here and there, illustrating both prose and poetry.

*Charles's Aunt Lucy Lutwidge, who
cared for the family after his mother died*

Again we get glimpses of life at the rectory and its precincts. In the first
"Lays of Sorrow," we have mayhem in the rectory henhouse; in the second,
Skeffington and his effort to ride the steed. "Moans from the Miserable, or
The Wretch's Wail" is a complaint by the rectory rabbits against too much
petting and affection from the children. Charles exhibits, in one piece in his
series of "Zoological Papers," mock concern over a number of technological
and scientific subjects. He includes an ornithological piece on "The Lory,"
a "species of parrot." Here he comes close again to the Lear connection; in
any case, the bird will later reappear in *Alice*. We also get an amusing zoological paper on "Fishs."

He is clever at mimicking old ballads and has a good ear for regional dialects. In two essays entitled "Difficulties," we come on Charles's early concern with time. In one, he dwells on time zones, a subject that interested

*Top, Charles's allegory of the poet being attacked by demons*
*Bottom, the poet as victor, the demons having been dispatched by angels*

him all his life and on which he later both lectured and wrote, posing the problem "Where Does the Day Begin?" Greenwich mean time, time zones, and the date line were not seriously discussed until the 1870s, and the confusion over the time of day and the day of the week in various localities around the world troubled Charles's orderly mind. When, in February 1857, he saw the subject written about in the *Illustrated London News,* he wrote a letter to the paper summarizing the complexity of the problem of fixing time relatively, and ending with the plea for "a rational solution. . . ." Three years later, still vexed by the issue, he lectured on it at the Ashmolean Society, and he evidently "cast a gloom" over parties on his social rounds by going on about this complex question.[35] The other essay is about "two clocks: one doesn't *go at all,* and the other loses a minute a day." He asks "Which is the best . . . ?" and has a ready answer: the clock that loses a minute a day is right only once in two years, but the broken clock is right twice a day.

Charles's longest and most interesting composition is an eight-part serial called "The Walking-Stick of Destiny," a medieval tale, with footnotes and drawings, populated by two barons, a magician, a poet, innumerable servants, and a villain who, with the aid of a magic walking-stick and a magical toad, is reduced to a heap of mashed potatoes.

At the end of this considerable anthology, we have "The Poet's Farewell," where Charles descants on the succession of the Dodgson family magazines. The final drawing of the volume shows the poet of the frontispiece standing erect, the umbrella closed at his feet, the devilish rock-throwers fleeing in the distance, the angelic muses hovering over the recumbent umbrella.

While *The Rectory Umbrella* does not possess the charm, the freshness, or the disarming naïveté of the earlier magazines, it is a much more sophisticated effort than the earlier booklets, vividly showing a developing genius. Greater things were to come, for Charles now prepared to leave his home, his school, and his provincial life behind and enter a much larger, more challenging arena, where he would be his own master and try his mettle as he had not done before.[36]

*The Great Hall, Christ Church, the largest of its kind in Oxford*

# CHAPTER TWO

# Cap and Gown

*. . . that sweet City with her dreaming spires,*
*She needs not June for beauty's heightening.*

MATTHEW ARNOLD

Rugby seasoned Charles and made him more confident, and the year at home provided an agreeable reprieve from public school schedules and routines, from the rough-and-tumble of dormitory life. He could now contemplate his future coolly and calmly, a future that his father had already designed for him. He does not question his father's decisions; he will gratefully follow in his father's footsteps. He is, in fact, traveling a course open to only a small minority of British youngsters.

Almost a full year before Charles left Rugby, his father, looking ahead, wrote to his old friend Canon E. B. Pusey of Christ Church, Oxford, to ask him whether he would nominate young Charles to a studentship (the equivalent of a fellowship at other colleges) at the cathedral college "should [Charles] fairly reach the standard of merit by which these appointments were regulated." Pusey, who bore a strong aversion to favoritism, replied that he would be pleased if circumstances permitted him to nominate Charles.[1] Charles's Rugby record and his early command of the classics and mathematics assured his admission to Christ Church, and on May 23, 1850, he journeyed to Oxford to present himself to Osborne Gordon, Censor of Christ Church, for matriculation—that is, enrollment on the *matricula,* or roll, of the university. By custom, Gordon presented Charles to the Vice-

Chancellor of the university, before whom he swore on his knees to comply with the statutes of the university and signed the Thirty-nine Articles, the official creed of the Church of England. He was now a member of Oxford University.

We do not know whether matriculation provided Charles with his first view of Oxford and its walled-in entities of names and reputations that echo round the world. Perhaps he saw it as a fellow Oxonian first did, from Magdalen Bridge, when one could look "straight across the Christ Church cricket-ground to the meadows beyond Cherwell . . . [for] an uninterrupted view of every tower in the city from Magdalen to the Cathedral . . . a fairyland of spires and pinnacles, rising from a foreground of trees and verdure . . . 'the noblest of cities.' "[2]

One can only imagine the irrepressible delight that must have arisen within him as he approached his college. What exactly did he feel as he gazed up at Cardinal Wolsey's miter on the corner turrets and beheld that powerful yet graceful Wren magnificence, Tom Tower, reaching heavenward at the entrance over the gate? Or as he walked through to the grandest quadrangle in Oxford, Tom Quad, and made his way to the cathedral, lofty of structure, rich in ornament? It would have been natural for him to enter and give thanks for his gifts and good fortune. Then, passing through yet another archway to another quadrangle, he would have stood before the neoclassical library, where strong and sturdy pillars without mark the way to precious tomes within.

Crossing Tom Quad again, Charles would have come to the entrance to the Great Hall. If the sun were shining, he would have been momentarily blinded as he entered the shaded passage to find the broad, arched staircase, worn down by the tread of student-scholars from century to century. Looking up, he would have seen a ceiling of some of the most delicate tracery in the world. The Hall itself—the largest of its kind in Oxford—which, in Matthew Arnold's words, cast a "line of festal light"[3] for miles, is a revelation. It is, in John Ruskin's words, "about as big as the nave of Canterbury Cathedral, with its extremity lost in mist, its roof in darkness."[4] It must have made a bewildering assault on Charles's senses, with its height, length, graceful lines, light and shadow, tints and textures, at once striking, awesome, massive yet elegant. He would have admired the stained-glass windows, walked down the aisles of old, polished wood tables and benches, passed the tiers of portraits of the rich, noble, wise, and powerful, of great men and world movers who had preceded him, feeling their eyes staring down upon him.

*Christ Church Cathedral*

There, ahead of him, would have been Cardinal Wolsey and King Henry VIII, founders of the college; Elizabeth I, who stayed here; Charles I, who took refuge at Christ Church during the Civil War; John Locke, whom the younger Dean Fell expelled for being a Whig; John Wesley; and a host of other dignitaries. He would have stood in the very place where Parliament assembled during the divisive events of 1644. Looking farther, Charles would have seen any number of eminent divines, viceroys, ministers, leaders from all walks of life, gracing the wainscot. Where else could one encounter such a blend of the magisterial and the monastic? Where but in the finest museums could one behold such a collection of artwork by the great masters, among them Romney, Kneller, Holbein, Lely, Gainsborough, and Reynolds?

His sensations as he walked up and down the staircases, through the chambers, across the paths that lead from building to building, are unknown. But he must have been pleased that he would be making his home among these ancient monuments for years to come. In the stillness, the grandeur and solemnity must have moved him. Is that undergraduate there, his gown fluttering in the wind, a preview of what he himself would soon look like? Is that wizened don, stooped and shuffling, to be one of his tutors? He might well have been agitated, shaken, awed, baffled, stunned, overwhelmed by this powerful setting.

As he traveled back to Croft, he must have regained his calm, and we can conjecture the scene there when he recounted his visit, the father pleased with the son, the mother loving and proud, the brothers and sisters wide-eyed and gripped by the adventure.

Charles still had eight months to prepare himself before taking up residence at Oxford. He was, as usual, busy at Croft. His sisters and brothers were always delighted when he was home because he was a source of constant invention, entertainment, and amusement, adding jollity to what could otherwise be glum days. He felt responsible, too, for helping his parents with the young ones, assisting with their instruction and refinement. Certainly he took a keen interest in the parish and did what he could to help with the care of the poor and needy. He also had to prepare for Oxford, and, probably with the help of his father, set himself a stern schedule of reading and studying. With all that, however, he still had time for some frivolities, for writing, for sketching, for fun and games. And then, early in the new year, on January 24, 1851, three days before his nineteenth birthday, he returned to Oxford, a full-fledged member of Christ Church.

But two days after he arrived to begin his studies, he had to travel back to Croft because his mother had suddenly died, of "inflammation of the brain," a diagnosis covering a broad spectrum of Victorian medical ignorance. The shock was surely enormous, the loss inconsolable.

In the midst of his grief, Dodgson *père* faced a domestic crisis. The two youngest children were seven and four. The eldest two girls, twenty-two and twenty, were thought neither old, experienced, nor competent enough to take over so large a household. Another solution had to be found. At first, a cousin, the poet Menella Bute Smedley, came to help, to be replaced soon by the dead mother's younger unmarried sister, Lucy Lutwidge, a sometime contributor to the family magazines and a frequent visitor. This gentle woman lived with and cared for the family for the remainder of her long life.

Back at Oxford, Charles resumed his daily routine. He submitted dutifully to the university's dress code. The cap and gown were the formal exteriors, to be worn throughout the early part of the day. Noblemen sported a gold tassel, commoners like Charles a black one.

The city of Oxford, the university, and Christ Church itself were all much smaller and different in 1851 from what they are today. Although the railway had already reached the town's perimeter, Oxford remained essentially provincial, a country town with unpaved roads, horse-drawn carriages, and coaches still arriving from major cities. The horse was the main means of transport, and many dons owned horses and rode. The suburban sprawl had not yet begun; fields, meadows, and hedgerows met the eye on all sides in an era that nestled between the Industrial Revolution and the age of high technology and science, a time rooted in traditional ways and laborious inconvenience.

Although gas came into use in 1819, candlelight remained the dominant means of lighting Oxford homes and college rooms. Water was pumped directly from the reservoir without being filtered, carrying with it all sorts of aquatic specimens. Oxford firefighters had only primitive equipment, mainly hand pumps. No system of drainage had yet come into being and all varieties of filth were disgorged into Oxford streams and rivers. Cesspools intruded on wells; typhoid and tuberculosis lurked everywhere; sensible people shunned unboiled water; the city suffered outbreaks of cholera in 1832, 1849, and 1854.

For much of the winter, Oxford was flooded because of the weirs that millers had built to dam water to work their mills. (The Great Western railway line was actually washed away by a flood in 1852.) While those waters provided sporting people with the opportunity to sail in mild weather and skate in frosts, a fishy smell pervaded the atmosphere in the spring and early summer, when the floods subsided. Oxford was almost a thousand years old, and it looked it. Many buildings were decrepit, their fronts black and crumbling. The era of restoration and preservation had not yet dawned.

Although it was possible to be a serious and purposeful student at Oxford, the prevailing tone was frivolous, self-indulgent, decorative, even flamboyant. Most young men came because it was the right course for their social class. Thomas Hughes describes Tom Brown's arrival and those he encountered:

> Three out of the four were gentlemen-commoners, with allowances of £500 a year at least each; and, as they treated their allowances as pocket-money, and were all in their first year, ready money was plenty and credit good, and they might have had potted hippopotamus for breakfast if they had chosen to order it. . . .[5]

Men with intellectual interests and ambitions were in the minority. Noblemen's sons came to fritter away their time; country gentlemen's heirs, who had grown up riding, shooting, and hunting, came to Oxford unwilling to give up their habits or horses and continued to ride to hounds. They kept dogs too, and Oxford's colleges were as much the provinces of dogs and horses as of men. One master estimated that at University College the dog population averaged five to a set of rooms. The dogs' owners often pitted them against rats and used them as retrievers in pigeon shooting.[6]

Matthew Arnold, reporting on a visit to Oxford in October 1854, wrote: "I am much struck with the apathy . . . of the people here . . . compared with the students of Paris or Germany or even of London."[7] And G. M. Young, looking back on the scene, depicted the "exasperated fascination" that Oxford dons exercised upon the outside world: "They were clerical; they were idle; they were dissipated; they reflected those odious class distinctions by which merit is oppressed and insolence fostered; their studies were narrow, their teaching ineffective."[8]

The *Oxford Spectator*, that irreverent record of undergraduate days and ways, described the more figged-out student frequently encountered about college quads as one who had

> furnished himself with a curiously devised coat in velvet, and a pair of breeches of a wondrously close cut . . . [a] hat with curiously curved brim, the very spacious satin scarf, and the sealskin waistcoat. [This] slim and graceful youth [is] highly perfumed; his voice is soft and his manners attractive, if perhaps a trifle artificial . . . his lair, a spot strewn with every elegance of luxury and art; with albums full of fair faces or amusing "sketches," with graceful trifles from foreign lands, and little notes from all the ladies in Oxford. [He] acts in private theatricals, and sleeps till midday . . . [and commands] ornaments of language which flourish in Oxford under the name of slang.[9]

When Charles entered Christ Church, it wore two faces, not exactly tragic and comedic, but dissimilar enough to reflect a split in the student body. On the one hand, the House, as insiders call Christ Church (because it embodies the Cathedral House of Christ), was (and is) known as a rich man's college, with royal and aristocratic connections, a surfeit of money, and a minimum of intellectual aspiration. It was ruled by Dean Thomas Gaisford, a scholar who preferred poring over classical texts to dealing with college affairs. As a result, the college languished. Gaisford spoke earnestly, judged generously, and built nothing, although he lent his name to a prize for Greek verse and prose. He alone was not to blame for the stagnation, for he inherited the tone of apathy and self-indulgent indolence from far back, and both were difficult to change.

The reminiscences of Christ Church men do little to redeem the college. One reads of dinner parties lasting through the night and into the morning; large breakfast parties followed chapel, larger "spreads" flourished. Although morning chapel was compulsory, "behaviour . . . [in church] was generally irreverent, and sometimes disgraceful." Often, when a student earned an imposition for missing chapel, "this exercise was . . . performed by a deputy."[10] Breaking off door knockers and bell handles was a favorite pastime, and when Mercury, the pool at the center of Tom Quad, was drained, a bed of these and other misappropriated objects was revealed.[11] The deanery doors were, on occasion, painted red and the deanery garden mutilated.

One graduate recalls that "towards the close of Dean Gaisford's reign," some students redressed what they considered the "wrongs" they "had undergone in being put under processes of instruction . . . [and] burnt the tables and benches."[12] On another occasion "a violent explosion," devised and executed by some students, "shook the college to its foundations," leaving an enormous ravine in the center of the quadrangle. Charles records in his diary (October 5, 1867) that "the usual town and gown disturbances . . . intensified into a 'bread riot' which . . . was considered by the Home Secretary (Gathorne-Hardy) formidable enough to justify his sending down a company of the guards."

As late as 1894, after a particularly bibulous celebration, some five hundred panes of glass were broken in the college. The previous December, Charles witnessed what happened when the Dean refused to allow students to attend the Duke of Marlborough's ball at Blenheim Palace and they then went on a rampage, painted the walls of Tom Quad "with gross abuse of the Dean and the Senior Censor," and cut the bell rope of Tom. Much earlier, when Balliol suffered a student uprising, a friend remarked to Benjamin Jowett that it reminded him of prisoners breaking out of jail. "Worse than that," Jowett replied, "[it] reminds me of Christ Church."[13]

In Charles's early days at Oxford, he experienced two college rows. On May 29, 1856, while preparing, at the Dean's invitation, his paper on the life of Richard Hakluyt, the eminent sixteenth-century geographer and a Christ Church graduate, for an oration at an upcoming end-of-term Gaudy,* he observed that at "about ½ past 1 in the morning, the men began to explode fireworks in Chaplain's Quad, and 3 of them came out and threw bottles into LLoyd's windows. . . . We saw the last fireworks come, but the offenders

* A formal college dinner for old members.

had beat a retreat."[14] Two nights later, after Charles delivered his oration, he records that during dinner in Hall "the noise was tremendous and Gordon turned several men out. . . ."

The other face of Christ Church was one of intellectual distinction. Not only had Charles's father and his friend E. B. Pusey emerged from Christ Church, but many more men of achievement graced the roster. In the first half of the century, the crumbling walls embraced some of the most eminent churchmen in the land, some of the world's great classical scholars, and, for a time, the Professor of Poetry. "In those days," recalls one chronicler, "Christ Church nearly monopolised the class list, and was the focus and centre of the intellectual life of the University."[15]

Martin Tupper recalls that in about 1830 a visitor might, by pushing open the door of the lecture room next to the Hall staircase, encounter a group of future world-shakers, among them "two head masters to be; three bishops; three Regius professors; three viceroys, Canning, Dalhousie and Elgin; Gladstone, Newcastle, and Cornewall Lewis. [Robert] Lowe [Viscount Sherbrook] sometimes looked in, and Sidney Herbert [Baron Herbert of Lea] regularly came across from Oriel." The group worked at translating Aristotle's *Rhetoric* "in turn at the feet of . . . [Thomas] Briscoe [later Chancellor of Bangor Cathedral]."[16]

The collection of great names from before the nineteenth century also bespeaks intellectual splendor: Philip Sidney, Locke, Richard Hakluyt, George Peele, the Wesleys, "Monk" Lewis, and Henry Hallam. When a friend of Samuel Johnson announced that he planned to enter Pembroke College in 1730, Johnson overcame his loyalty to his own college and urged his friend to enter Christ Church instead, where he would find the ablest tutor in all of Oxford, a Mr. Bateman.[17] The nineteenth century added Wellington, Peel, Gladstone, Liddell, A. P. Stanley, Ruskin, Salisbury, Rosebery, and Liddon.

As Charles arrived, he, Oxford, and Christ Church all stood at a major crossroad. All three would undergo dramatic change and emerge much altered. "At Christ Church, when a man came up," recalls a graduate, "he was put into any room that happened to be empty, until he had an opportunity of changing . . . by-and-by."[18] Charles was apparently unable to get a room allocated to commoners at Christ Church, but fortunate in not having to seek lodgings in town because he was offered "a couple of rooms" in the Christ Church residence of his father's friend, Senior Student Jacob Ley.[19]

Charles did not join any of the "sets" or clubs that were the rage; he preferred to stand apart and follow his own program of studies and recreation. On February 16, 1857, he allowed his name to go forward for membership in the Oxford Union, but he added: "It might be worth while *now* to be a member—I have avoided it hitherto, as it would have been too great a temptation to wasting time." He did not exactly devote himself to Wordsworth's "plain living and high thinking," but he was purposeful and ambitious. A birthday letter he sent his sister Mary six weeks after moving in with Ley shows how he differed from the general run of undergraduate. Compulsory chapel was at eight, and many students straggled into the cathedral, partially dressed, still half asleep. But not Charles. He tells his sister that he is in the habit of being called at six-fifteen "and generally managing to be down soon after 7." He strove for punctuality in all he did, attending lectures in the mornings, chapel a second time later in the day, and dinner at five. We get a picture of dinner in Hall, Charles in his place, from a contemporary who recalls

the batches of half-a-dozen undergraduates who dined together at the different tables in the hall, and the disgraceful way the dinner at that time was served. . . . Though the spoons and forks were silver—some of them very old, the gift of former members of The House—the plates and dishes were pewter. The joint was pushed from one to another, each man hacking off his own portion, and rising from the table without waiting for one another, without even waiting for the ancient Latin grace. . . . We all . . . sat in the same hall and some of us even at the same table with Dodgson without discovering . . . the wit, the peculiar humour, that was in him. We looked upon him as a rising mathematician, nothing more. He seldom spoke, and the slight impediment in his speech was not conducive to conversation.[20]

Charles worked hard, and while he was often silent, he was neither unsociable nor entirely a bookworm. In that same letter to his sister Mary, he writes: "I have got a new acquaintance of the name of Colley, who has been here once or twice to tea, and we have been out walking together."

Within the year Charles moved from Ley's into his own rooms, on staircase 4 in Peckwater Quadrangle, in view of the library. Here, for the first time, he was completely independent. He already knew the head porter, and soon met the scout on his staircase. As Tom Brown knew, "the scout was an institution! Fancy me waited upon and valeted by a stout party in black, of quiet, gentlemanly manners, like the benevolent father in a comedy. He takes the deepest interest in my possessions and proceedings, and is evidently used to good society, to judge by the amount of crockery and glass, wines, liquors, and grocery, which he thinks indispensable for my due establishment."[21] In June, in a birthday letter home, Charles reports in mock medieval English that "Onne Moone his daye nexte we goe yn forre Responsions,* and I amme uppe toe mine eyes yn worke." Responsions, the first real Oxford test of his abilities, safely behind him in July, he rewarded himself with a visit to London, and then sent a glowing account back home of the Great Exhibition that had opened in the Crystal Palace: "I am afraid it will be impossible to give you any idea of all I have seen," he wrote his sister Elizabeth (July 5), and went on to describe some of the exhibits that particularly impressed him.

> I think the first impression produced on you when you get inside is of bewilderment. It looks like a sort of fairyland. As far as you can look in any direction, you see nothing but pillars hung about with shawls, carpets, etc., with long avenues of statues, fountains, canopies, etc., etc., etc. The first thing to be seen on entering is the Crystal Fountain, a most elegant one about 30 feet high at a rough guess, composed entirely of glass and pouring down jets of water from basin to basin. . . . The centre of the nave mostly consists of a long line of colossal statues, some most magnificent. A pair of statues of a dog and child struck me as being exceedingly good. In one the child is being attacked by a serpent, and the dog standing over to defend it. The child is crying with fear, and making I think an exceedingly ugly face. In the other the dog has conquered: the body of the serpent is lying at one side, and the head, *most thoroughly* bitten off, at the other. . . . The child is leaning over and playing with the dog, which is *really* smiling with pleasure and satisfaction.

Back at Christ Church in the autumn, he plunged into work again and did well. In November he won the Boulter Scholarship, worth twenty pounds a year. But he found time for occasional literary spoofery too. "The Christ Church Commoner," which he wrote out on the mourning letter paper he used after his mother's death, purports to be a "fragment of an unpublished novel by G.P.R. James" and is a tongue-in-cheek description of a

---

* Responsions, or "Smalls," was an early examination for the B.A., involving written papers on Latin, Greek, and arithmetic (with an option for algebra or Euclidean geometry) and an oral examination (*viva voce*).

Christ Church undergraduate sitting for the "Little Go," or Moderations, the first of two public examinations for the bachelor's degree. It surely dates from about the time that Charles himself took the examination.

## THE CHRIST-CHURCH COMMONER
### A Tale
### Chap: I.
*"Respond! Respond! oh Muse!"*

GOLDSMITH

It was a glowing summer morning: the Orient sun had long risen, and gilded with his dazzling beam the topmost fane of Tom, the great tower of Christ Church. Out of the Eastern gate, known by the name of Canterbury, is walking a young man, solitary, downcast. His years are scarcely enough for a clergyman, and yet he wears a white neck-cloth and bands. . . . Let us follow him: he approaches a vast range of buildings, ugly and un-architectural: they are called "the schools." . . . Let us follow him in. A long table, covered with books, and surrounded with chairs; two gloomy-browed examiners, and twelve pale-faced youths complete the picture. Seats, like those in a circus, slant up at the end of the room: these are crowded with spectators.

### Chap: II.
*"Veni, vidi, vici"*

CAESAR

The youth is sitting at the table: before him lies a small edition of Sophocles. Sternly does the examiner remark "Go on at the four hundred and fiftieth line." . . . In a low, musical tone, he commences. Some mistakes he makes, small and few: he is given two passages to translate—They are done: they are handed in: they are looked over. What is the examiner saying—"you may go." All is over.

A more significant manuscript survives, "*Formosa facies muta commendatio est,*" a quotation attributed to Publilius Syrus that translates as "A beautiful face is a silent recommendation." Above the title is the signature "C. L. Dodgson"; at the close of the four hundred words is the legend "Read out in Hall, November 22, 1851." John Ruskin, who preceded Charles at Christ Church by fourteen years, describes the frame into which this early unpublished essay by Charles fits: "It was an institution of the college that every week the undergraduates should write an essay on a philosophical subject, explicatory of some brief Latin text of Horace, Juvenal, or other accredited and pithy writer; and, I suppose, as a sort of guarantee to the men that what they wrote was really looked at, the essay pronounced the best was read aloud in hall on Saturday afternoon, with enforced attendance of the other undergraduates. . . ."22

Charles's essay, published here in the Appendix, discusses beauty and pleasure and suggests that at nineteen, he is not only stirring with thoughts and feelings but also analyzing them and trying to understand his own nature. He notes that the ability to see and be moved by beauty is among the highest possible pleasures, the most ennobling and enduring. Love and admiration for what we perceive as beautiful arise naturally, even though we may know nothing of the character of the person who possesses the beauty. Charles resents this trap that nature sets for us. Falling in love with a beautiful person is unjust to both the person being loved and the person who loves, he asserts, because neither has done anything either to acquire beauty or to enable him or her to enjoy it. Surely all this aesthetic theorizing was provoked by emotional stirrings he has recognized within himself and must deal with seriously.

Two other moral essays, also published for the first time in the Appendix, date from early undergraduate days. One, headed by a Latin tag from Ovid, translates as "Nothing aids which may not also injure us." Charles read this one out in Hall six months after the earlier one. Again his fascination with language is evident; once more he couches the essay in the philosophical mode. The burden of the essay is a text that he heard often preached from the pulpit, in his father's church and certainly again in Rugby Chapel: the struggle between good and evil and the need for arming oneself against the devil. He believes that man has the will to choose good over evil and that doing good is the source of the greatest happiness on earth. Acquiring riches or striving to do so is not good unless one uses those riches to good ends.

These manuscripts are probably among the earliest expressions of Charles's fear of some forces he felt operating within him and of his intention to control them, to follow the righteous road, to serve God in every deed. This struggle is a keynote to his character, and in understanding it, as articulated here in an objective, detached confession, we recognize what would become one of the overpowering themes of his life: the determination to devote so much of his energy to doing good for others, his generosity to his family, friends, and strangers. Here too is an early clue to understanding his anguish when, in his own merciless judgment, he fails to live up to the lofty goals he sets for himself.

*Charles's Uncle Skeffington Lutwidge, who introduced Charles to photography*

The third essay bears no date, but the handwriting is of this same period, and the Latin tag, from Tacitus, reads in translation: "To despise fame is to despise merit." Charles here may be reflecting on the many poets who have discoursed on the subject of fame, from Chaucer to Milton to Shelley. But here again the underlying theme is good versus evil. Fame is essentially an ideal pursuit, but it can easily be perverted. What our fellow creatures think of us is a measure of our success, but moderation is important, and we must guard against excess. Desiring fame, however, is much nobler than desiring money, power, or pleasure for its own sake, and can actually deter one from baser pursuits. It can bring out our finer qualities, our inner strengths and courage, and help us perform deeds worthy of emulation. Those among us who can idolize fame and avoid its excesses are the noblest of our breed and make the highest contribution to civilization.

Charles absorbed the postulates embedded in these essays from his parents at home and from his teachers and spiritual advisers at Richmond and Rugby. Early on he accepted the simple doctrine of life as a battleground between good and evil. What is particularly interesting is that he saw it so clearly, accepted it unconditionally, and could express it so eloquently so early, implicitly recognizing the danger of giving his emotions full rein.

On June 24, 1852, he wrote a long letter to his sister Elizabeth, while staying with his favorite uncle, Skeffington Lutwidge, a barrister and Commissioner in Lunacy. Lutwidge provided Charles with London hospitality, shared with his nephew his interest in microscopes, telescopes, and gadgets generally. Before long Skeffington introduced Charles to photography. In the letter, Charles reports that his uncle "has as usual got a great number of new oddities, including a lathe, telescope stand, crest stamp, a beautiful little pocket instrument for measuring distances on a map, refrigerator, etc., etc. We had an observation of the moon and Jupiter last night, and afterwards live animalcula in his large microscope. . . ." He continues: "Before I left Oxford, I had a conversation with Mr. Gordon and one with Mr. [Robert] Faussett [Mathematical Lecturer at Christ Church] on the work of the Long Vacation: I believe 25 hours' *hard* work a day *may* get through all I have to do, but I am not certain." In the meantime, however, he enjoyed London.

His twenty-five-hour day of hard work reaped rewards. On December 9 he reports the good news to Elizabeth:

> You shall have the announcement of the last piece of good fortune this wonderful term has had in store for me, that is, *a 1st class in Mathematics*. Whether I shall add to this any honours at collections I cannot at present say, but I should think it very unlikely, as I have only today to get up the work in The Acts of the Apostles, 2 Greek Plays, and the Satires of Horace and I feel myself almost totally unable to read at all: I am beginning to suffer from the reaction of reading for Moderations . . . I am getting quite tired of being congratulated on various subjects: there seems to be no end of it. If I had shot the Dean, I could hardly have had more said about it.

In spite of his apprehension, when he sits for Moderations he adds second-class honors in classics to his achievements.

Impressed by Charles's performance, Dr. Pusey wrote on December 2, 1852, to Charles's father. "I have great pleasure in telling you that I have been enabled to recommend your son for a Studentship. . . . One of the Censors brought me to-day five names; but in their minds it was plain that they thought your son on the whole the most eligible. . . . It has been very satisfactory to hear of your son's uniform steady and good conduct."[23]

It was not wholly exceptional for the best undergraduates to be appointed to studentships at Christ Church even before they earned their B.A. degrees, but the honor was conferred on few. The appointment crowned Charles's achievements with glory and security. He might, if he chose, now remain a Student the rest of his life, with lodgings, an honored place in the academic community of the finest college in the oldest university in the land, and a secure income. Although his emoluments came to thirty pounds a year, he soon augmented that by lecture fees; and as a result of the 1858 Ordinance, he earned as Senior Student two hundred pounds per annum.[24]

The appointment came with restrictions. He must proceed to holy orders and must not marry, for if he did, he would automatically lose the studentship, as his father had done. But he was not required to teach if he chose not to, nor was he expected necessarily to publish or to achieve any other distinction. If he wished, he might recline in his easy chair, his feet up by the fire, drink his claret, and smoke a pipe for the rest of his life. Indolence was not, however, the style that Charles yearned for. He took quite the opposite course.

Congratulations on his appointment poured in, but perhaps he valued his father's letter most. "My dearest Charles," it begins.

> The feelings and thankfulness with which I have read your letter just received . . . are, I assure you, beyond *my expression;* and your affectionate heart will derive no small addition of joy from thinking of the joy which you have occasioned to me, and to all the circle of your home. I say "*you* have occasioned," because, grateful as I am to my old friend Dr. Pusey for what he has done, I cannot desire stronger evidence than his own words of the fact that you have *won,* and well won, this honour for *yourself,* and that it is bestowed as a matter of *justice* to *you,* and not of *kindness* to *me. . . .*"[25]

Charles was now well set on a career and continued to improve his accommodation. Having lived for three terms in Peckwater, he moved in the spring of 1852 to the Cloister staircase, where, for five terms, he shared rooms with his friend G. G. Woodhouse, later Perpetual Curate of Upper Gornal, Staffordshire. Charles addressed his one-hundred-line mock epic "The Ligniad" to Woodhouse, perhaps in gratitude: he was the "*very* first who spoke to me—across the dinner table in Hall" in Charles's earliest college days.[26] In time, however, Charles sought rooms of his own. He had his eye on Tom Quad, but did not quite get there yet. At the end of Michaelmas term 1853, he moved next door, where he had two rooms to himself, and where he remained for eight years.

In 1853 he was still an undergraduate working for his B.A. and did well in mathematics. But Collingwood tells us that "philosophy and history were not very congenial subjects to him." Indeed in these subjects he did no better than a third class.[27] The results at least confirmed his strengths and his weaknesses, and he could plan accordingly. Perhaps because he made such a poor showing in philosophy and history, he compiled an ambitious list of what he called "general reading." On March 12, 1855, he devised a plan for "looking over all the Library regularly, to acquaint myself generally with its contents, and to note such books as seem worth studying. . . ." On the following day he asked: "Has any writer ever given us a *system* of Classical Reading? What a grand thing a system of general reading would be. . . ." He then assembled a formidable list of readings in classics, divinity, history, languages, mathematics, novels, miscellaneous studies, divinity reading for ordination, and "other subjects."

On May 3, 1854, as his undergraduate days came to an end, Charles read a declamation in Hall—not, it appears, the usual weekly essay, but something rather more special, perhaps connected in some way with his classical studies. It was a disquisition on Aristotle's *Nicomachean Ethics*, and the declamation itself was liberally peppered with both Latin and Greek.[28] It is a courageous essay, in fact, which analyzes a passage in the *Ethics* about the relative value in life of seeking the good (practical rules for living) on the one hand and the truth (wisdom) on the other and concludes that Aristotle is not a true philosopher because he errs in allowing the practical considerations of life (the search for the good) to outweigh the theoretical (the search for truth or wisdom). Charles had naturally steeped himself in Plato and Aristotle and later dedicated *Symbolic Logic, Part I* to "the memory of Aristotle." But while he praised Aristotle here and there in his utterances, he was also a staunch critic of Aristotle as logician. Later, in *Symbolic Logic, Part I*, he writes of Aristotle's logical method as "an almost useless machine, for practical purposes, many of the conclusions being incomplete, and many quite legitimate forms being ignored."[29]

His studies and examinations took up most of his energies, but he found time to relax a bit in the spring of 1853. Not much of a sportsman, he nevertheless keenly observed the boat races. "The Ligniad," moreover, which dates from this period, shows a keen knowledge of cricket. He spent the long vacation of 1854 at Whitby as a member of a reading party in mathematics coached by Professor Bartholomew Price, Sedleian Professor of Natural Philosophy (the Bat in *Alice*). One member of the group recalled that, at times when they were not deep in their studies, Charles . . . would "sit on a rock on the beach, telling stories to a circle of eager young listeners of both sexes."[30] Charles also took time to compose and publish in the *Whitby Gazette* a poem, "The Lady of the Ladle," and a short story, "Wilhelm von Schmitz," and signed himself with the pseudonym "B.B."

"The Lady of the Ladle" is a thirty-line set of rhyming couplets about a "very heavy swell" who "drinks his fill" at the "Royal on the Hill" and then sways about the town gawked at by the loungers. The piece incorporates a number of Whitby landmarks that readers would recognize. The four chapters of "Wilhelm von Schmitz" are also set in Whitby and tell a tale in mock prolixity of a young English poet who applies too much grease to his hair and not enough soap to his hands and, in order to be accepted in society, adopts a foreign name, the title of the story. He comes to Whitby in search of his long-lost love, Sukie, a barmaid. After some extraordinary adventures, he finds her, a generous friend arranges for them to run a vacant public house, and they live happily ever after. Charles pasted a copy of "The Lady of the Ladle" and copied chapters 3 and 4 of "Wilhelm Von Schmitz" into *Mischmasch*.

Writing to his sister Mary from Whitby on August 23, 1854, he reports on an expedition the mathematics reading party took to Goathland, where they examined the machinery that drew the trains up the steep cliff; he also tells of a foolhardy climb he and another student attempted up the sheer cliff: at one moment during the adventure, he writes, "both my feet had lost hold at once, and if the root I was hanging to had broken, I must have come down, and probably carried him with me."

Back at Oxford in the autumn, he was preparing for "Greats," the final examinations for the bachelor's degree. "For the last three weeks before the examination," Collingwood wrote, "he worked thirteen hours a day, spending the whole night before the *viva voce* over his books."[31] The result was gratifying. He made first-class honors in the Final Mathematical School. On December 13 he wrote to Mary:

> Enclosed you will find a list, which I expect you to rejoice over considerably: it will take me more than a day to believe it, I expect—I feel at present very like a child with a new toy, but I daresay I shall be tired of it soon, and wish to be Pope of Rome next. . . . I have just given my Scout a bottle of wine to drink to my First. We shall be made Bachelors on Monday. . . . I hope that Papa did not conclude it was a 2nd by not hearing on Wednesday morning. . . . All this is very satisfactory. I must also add (this is a very boastful letter) that I ought to get the Senior Scholarship next term. . . . One thing more I will add, to crown all, and that is—I find I . . . stand next . . . for the [Mathematical] Lectureship. And now I think that is enough news for one post.

Five days later Charles received his Bachelor of Arts.

Charles was back with his family, all staying at Ripon, for much of the

Christmas vacation. He tried to do some studying, but mostly failed because of the festivities and social whirl. "Got my likeness photographed by Booth," he wrote in his diary on January 10, 1855, just before his twenty-third birthday. "After three failures he produced a tolerably good likeness, which half the family pronounced the best possible, and the other half the worst possible." It is perhaps the photograph opposite, showing a pensive, attractive young man with an amplitude of hair, a waistcoat, and a bow tie.

When he returned to Oxford later that month, he was no longer a youth but a man among men, a professional embarking upon his career with a pocketful of impressive credentials and a future full of promise and challenge. He had moved up considerably in the world and could now claim a well-earned place among the dons. Oxford dons are not known for geniality or for their interest in chitchat. They are generally reputed to be aloof, singular, and eccentric. One of their number has written vividly about the life of a don: "It fosters solitariness and independence and self-sufficiency. You live in a comfortable, self-contained flat. You are probably doing the work which you have always wanted to do and most enjoy doing, and . . . you may have to work very hard indeed. It is no small temptation to be engrossed in your own activities, to shut out all other interests, and to end up by being indifferent to anything except that which comes directly to you in a way of business, or to any person except those who, like your pupils, are dependent on you."[32]

"These Dons," writes another, "live by themselves and for themselves, until they are become perhaps the most refinedly selfish men on the face of the globe. . . . As they cannot be said to possess any feelings whatever, their whole existence is intellectual. . . . Society is not to them a pleasure—but a mere relaxation from work. Consequently their hatreds and jealousies are of the most complicated and fierce nature—their friendships and likings variable and unsatisfactory."[33]

Praise for a tutor here, a don there, appears, but virtually no all-embracing compliments for the society. Still, young Charles could not but think himself fortunate in joining this academic enclave. Among his new duties was taking his turn at "pricking," ticking off the names of men who turn up for chapel. He also patrolled the town at night in search of wayward Christ Church men.

Probably during his third year at Oxford, he started to keep his diary, which he then added to faithfully until the end of his life. Fortunately the larger part of it survives, nine of thirteen volumes, the other four having ei-

*Charles as a young man*

ther been misplaced, thrown out in error, lost in moving house, or perhaps even intentionally destroyed when some keeper of the flame came upon some entries that he or she found unpleasant or unflattering. The surviving volumes provide us with a remarkable record and allow us to observe Charles closely. The first volume, covering his early days as undergraduate, is missing, but volume 2 begins on New Year's Day 1855, just after Charles has secured his B.A., while he is still home in Yorkshire, getting ready to take up his new life.

On January 1, 1855, Charles wrote the first entry in this volume at The Residence, Ripon, where, since 1852, his father, Canon of Ripon Cathedral, was required to spend at least three months a year: "Tried a little Mathematics unsuccessfully. Sketched a design for illumination in the title page of Mary's book of Sacred Poetry. Handbells in the evening, a tedious performance."

The next entry (January 4) reveals mental exploration: "Might not complicated mathematical figures (in solid geometry, etc.) be well represented on paper by first modelling the figure, and then taking a photograph from the model?" And he adds alongside: "The next time I am in town, it would be worthwhile to try and buy a small printing press, for printing mathematical tables, etc." Clearly he is thinking of the life that lies ahead as teacher and as mathematician.

On January 19 he returned to Oxford for the new term and on the twenty-first read the first lesson in afternoon chapel. On the following day he called on Mr. Price "and arranged to coach with him this term till the Scholarship comes off." On the twenty-third Osborne Gordon asked him to take a pupil preparing for Little Go. On the twenty-seventh Charles records "23rd birthday" and notes that his father has sent him a photograph of himself; his sisters, (Walter Farquhar) Hook's *Church Dictionary* (1842); and his Aunt Lucy, a sofa cover. On the thirtieth his life as a tutor begins properly: "Had my first interview with Burton, my first pupil. He seems to take in Algebra very readily." The diary allows us to infer the elation Charles felt over this first session, the first time the tables were turned and he was doing the coaching rather than receiving it. His excitement erupts in a letter to his younger sister and brother Henrietta and Edwin the following day. It is a brilliant spoof of the occasion and tingles with the thrill of his new life:

My one pupil has begun his work with me, and I will give you a description how the lecture is conducted. It is the most important point, you know, that the tutor should be *dignified*, and at a distance from the pupil, and that the pupil should be as much as possible *degraded*—otherwise you know, they are not humble enough. So I sit at the further end of the room; outside the door (*which is shut*) sits the scout; outside the outer door (*also shut*) sits the sub-scout; half-way down the stairs sits the sub-sub-scout; and down in the yard sits the *pupil.*

The questions are shouted from one to the other, and the answers come back in the same way. . . . The lecture goes on, something like this.
*Tutor.* "What is twice three?"
*Scout.* "What's a rice tree?"
*Sub-scout.* "When is ice free?"
*Sub-sub-scout.* "What's a nice fee?"
*Pupil* (timidly). "Half a guinea!"
*Sub-sub-scout.* "Can't forge any!"
*Sub-scout.* "Ho for Jinny!"
*Scout.* "Don't be a ninny!"

*Tutor* (looks offended, but tries another question). "Divide a hundred by twelve!"

*Scout.* "Provide wonderful bells!"

*Sub-scout.* "Go ride under it yourself."

*Sub-sub-scout.* "Deride the dunder-headed elf!"

*Pupil* (surprised). "Who do you mean?"

*Sub-sub-scout.* "Doings between!"

*Sub-scout.* "Blue is the screen!"

*Scout.* "Soup-tureen!"

And so the lecture proceeds.

Becoming a tutor was only the beginning of Charles's professional life; more appointments and honors followed. But through it all, ties with the family at Croft remained strong. While at home for the summer of 1855, he inaugurated what was to be the last of the family magazines. Although it is more a scrapbook than a unified anthology (perhaps because Charles was away from home so much), it offers some mature pieces. Like *The Rectory Umbrella*, it contains contributions from other members of the family and, for the first time, clippings of some of Charles's published works. The preface provides information about the previous magazines and tells something of this one: "The name is German, and means in English 'midge-madge,' which we need not inform the intelligent reader is equivalent to 'hodge-podge': our intention is to admit articles of every kind, prose, verse, and pictures, provided they reach a sufficiently high standard of merit." Some of the pieces would be published in the *Comic Times* in 1855 and a review of a photographic exhibition in the *Illustrated Times* in 1860.

An early poem in *Mischmasch* is "The Two Brothers," which begins: "There were two brothers at Twyford School," perhaps alluding to some discussion at the rectory of an appropriate school for Charles's two younger brothers, Skeffington and Wilfred. It is the tale of two loutish lads who, instead of studying their Greek and Latin, go fishing in the River Tees. The older and stronger brother impales the younger and weaker upon his rod for bait.

Another poem, "Lays of Mystery, Imagination, and Humour, No. 1, The Palace of Humbug," rejected by the *Comic Times*, the *Train*, and *Punch*, eventually found a place in the *Oxford Critic* (May 29, 1857). It appropriates Alfred Bunn's famous line "I dreamt that I dwelt in marble halls" and much of Tennyson's rich tapestry from "The Palace of Art" to outline a vision of fuzzy morbidity that makes neither sense nor engaging nonsense.

It is followed by a faked parchment containing four lines of verse entitled "Stanza of Anglo-Saxon Poetry," for which Charles provides a "modern" rendering. The poem will become the first four lines of "Jabberwocky." Charles follows the transcription with a scholarly explication of the words, defining nonsense word after nonsense word ("Bryllyg," he reports, is "derived from the verb to Bryl or Broil" and means "the time of broiling dinner, i.e. the close of the afternoon").

"Lays of Mystery, Imagination, and Humour, No. 2" is "The Three Voices," a witty parody of Tennyson's "The Two Voices," the longest poetic effort in the volume and the most successful. It adumbrates attitudes that characters in *Alice* later express.

"Wrote a sort of imitation of Sydney Dobell's poem 'Tommy's Dead,' for the amusement of the party," Charles noted in his diary on the last day of 1857 at Croft. It is number three of the "Lays of Mystery," etc., in *Mischmasch*. Charles documents his debt to Dobell, but where the monologue in Dobell is uttered by a father grieving for his son, Charles tells us in a note at the end that his speaker is grieving after the death of a cat.

"Lays of Mystery . . . , No. 4," entitled "Melancholetta"—"a name I invented in a dream," Charles noted (April 6, 1857)—would appear in 1862 in *College Rhymes*. As it appears in *Mischmasch,* it has nineteen six-line rhymed verses and tells the tale of the poet's eponymous sister, who sighs and weeps and moans without respite. The poet can do nothing to wrest her from her melancholy. The final poem in the volume appears as "Lays of Mystery . . . , No. 5" with the title "Bloggs' Woe" and would appear also in *College Rhymes,* in 1863, as "Size and Tears," the plaint of a fat man who suffers abuse because of his obesity.

The volume contains a number of other pieces that would also appear in print in coming years: "Ode to Damon (from Chloë, Who Understood His Meaning)," "The Willow Tree," "Faces in the Fire," and "Lines" (which later became "A Valentine"). It also contains the review he wrote of the Photographic Exhibition and signed "The Lounger"; a poem by his sister Louisa and one by his brother Wilfred; two drawings rejected by the *Comic Times* and other sketches; a verse riddle entitled "A Monument—Men All Agree—"; and a full-page sketch of a maze.

On February 14, 1855, Charles was appointed Sub-Librarian at Christ Church: "This will add £35 to my income," he noted, but conceded that it will not be "much towards independence." Three days after he received his new appointment, he told his diary that Robert Faussett had gone off as a commissioned officer to the Crimea. "Report says the Dean does not mean to appoint a successor," Charles wrote, "an anomalous state for Christ Church—otherwise it would come to me, there being no one else to take it. I fancy his real motive is his objection to appoint a B.A."

Charles meanwhile settled into a routine. By the end of February he had taken on another pupil to coach, and on the last day of the month he invited the B.A.'s in Hall to his rooms for wine. Two evenings later he gave "a large wine, that is to all I know at Christ Church, about 40 in number." He was busily reading mathematics and working out problems, attending to his library duties, spending a morning "over a Latin Theme to be read out in Hall," taking walks with friends, reading Shakespeare and a society novel, skating ("got a severe fall, cutting open my forehead . . ."), rowing on the river, attending a public lecture on the Crimean War.

His hope to become Mathematical Lecturer persisted. "Faussett has returned and will stay, I believe, till the end of this term," he wrote (March 4), "so that the Dean's final decision about the lectureship may not be known till the beginning of next [term]."

On March 5 he acquired a third pupil; teaching now took up fifteen hours a week, "which does not leave me much time for scholarship." Then, on March 22, he sat for the mathematical scholarship: "I only succeeded in doing 5 questions in the morning," he writes, "and 4 in the afternoon." On the next day: "I did only 2 questions in the morning, and accordingly gave up, and did not go in for the afternoon one." On the twenty-fourth he learned that the scholarship had gone to another member of the Whitby reading party: "It is tantalising to think how easily . . . I might have got it, if I had only worked properly during this term, which I fear I must consider as wasted. However, I have now got a year before me, and with this past term as a lesson . . . I mean to have read by next time, Integral Calculus, Optics (and theory of light), Astronomy, and higher Dynamics. I record this resolution to shame myself with, in case March 1856 finds me still unprepared, knowing how many similar failures there have been in my life already."

He sat for yet another scholarship, but that too did not come to him. "This completes the lesson read me by this wasted term," he wrote (March 28). ". . . I do not think the work of this term worth recording," and he packs to leave for the Easter vacation.

Was he being too hard on himself? With pupils to coach, library duties to perform, and the need to sort out his priorities during this first term in professional harness, some slippage was inevitable. His return to Croft could not have been as jubilant as the previous Christmas homecoming, but he no doubt received a warm welcome—a consoling kiss perhaps from his aunt and some understanding words from his father to assuage the anguish over his failures. In the midst of the family circle, with their love and encouragement, care and ministrations, he might attack his difficulties calmly and forge reasonable plans for the future.

While at home, he continued to read and to work on mathematical problems and he started to learn Italian. On April 20 he was back in Oxford, resolutely facing the new term. He received a five-pound fee for coaching one of his pupils during the previous term: "This is the first *earned* money I ever received," he wrote, "—the first that I can fairly call *mine*." He agreed, with G. W. Kitchin, Mathematical Examiner, to coach a group of fourteen pupils. "[It] will give me no official position," he wrote (April 25), "as it is merely a private arrangement between ourselves: it is decidedly favourable to my getting the lectureship hereafter, though it by no means secures it. We calculated roughly that I shall get £50 by it." He devised a scheme to meet with his students individually and in small groups.

He still found time to row on the river with his friend Henry Parry Liddon, to walk with Professor Price, to attend a lecture on the Creed given by the Lady Margaret Professor of Divinity, and another on Tennyson, and to take in an exhibition of paintings.

He continued with his charges through the spring, when, on May 10, he struck another poignant note in the diary: "This morning, in a Trigonometry lecture with . . . [two of his pupils], I tried to teach them a proof I once did of the formula opposite, but failed entirely—a lesson not to attempt anything beyond book-work in lecture, without having gone over it beforehand." Any teacher, remembering early days with pupils, would sympathize. In any case, on May 12, he "began arranging a scheme for teaching systematically the first part of Algebraic Geometry: a thing which hitherto no one seems to have attempted. I find it exceedingly difficult to do it in anything like a satisfactory way."

On May 14 he received good news: "The Dean and Canons have been pleased to give me one of the 'Bostock' Scholarships, said to be worth £20 a year. This very nearly raises my income this year to independence. Courage!" At the end of May he reported achievements: "During the last month I have again written out in an improved form the *Fifth Book of Euclid Proved Algebraically* and have made considerable progress in my treatise in Algebraic Geometry. . . ."

*Charles's photograph of his Putney relatives: Uncle Hassard Hume Dodgson, Aunt Caroline, and their children*

Gradually, 1855 became a year of dramatic change, both for Christ Church and for Charles. On June 2 Dean Gaisford died, and five days later Charles and the world learned that Henry George Liddell, nephew of Baron Ravensworth, headmaster of Westminster School, co-compiler of the famous *Greek-English Lexicon*, and Chaplain to Prince Albert, who had preached to the Court at Windsor, would succeed. Term ended and on the nineteenth Charles traveled up to London for a few days before heading north. He indulged himself, went twice to the Royal Academy, to the Botanic Gardens, to the opera twice for *Norma* and *The Barber of Seville*, to Lord's for cricket, to another lecture on the Crimean War, to the theater to *Henry VIII* with Charles Kean and Ellen Tree, to his relatives in Putney, and to dine with his Uncle Skeffington. After eight days he took the overnight train home.

The report he could make to the family this time must have been easier and should have elicited gratifying comments. He settled into life at Croft quickly, undertook a considerable program of study, and, for the first time, taught in his father's school. Looking ahead to the likelihood that he would be made Mathematical Lecturer at Christ Church and be required to give public lectures, he took this opportunity to see how he would fare before rows of faces in a classroom, apprehensive as he must have been over his stammer and deafness. On July 5 he wrote: "I went to the Boys' School in the morning to hear my Father teach, as I want to begin trying myself soon," and three days later: "I took the first and second class of the Boys' School in the morning. . . . I liked my first attempt at teaching very much." On July 16 he recorded: "All this week I took the first class of boys." He read Latin with a neighbor on Wednesday evenings and Saturday mornings and summed up his teaching schedule as about nine hours a week. He read English history, a historical novel by James Grant, Coventry Patmore's *Angel in the House*, and Ruskin's *Stones of Venice*. On August 5 he began to analyze Coleridge's *Aids to Reflection*, and on the fourteenth, when Tennyson's *Maud* arrived, he spent much of the day reading it. Within the week he was off on a visit to his favorite cousins, the Wilcoxes, at Whitburn. Although a rumor that Charles would be Mathematical Lecturer reached the north, the appointment was not confirmed. Still, Charles's father wrote his son a long letter "on the subject of my new appointment and prospects in life." Collingwood prints part of it:

I will just sketch for you a supposed case, applicable to your own circumstances, of a young man of twenty-three, making up his mind to work for ten years, and living to do it, on an Income enabling him to save £150 a year—supposing him to appropriate it thus:

|  | £ | s. | d. |
|---|---|---|---|
| Invested at 4 per cent. | 100 | 0 | 0 |
| Life Insurance of £1,500 | 29 | 15 | 0 |
| Books, besides those bought in ordinary course | 20 | 5 | 0 |
|  | £150 | 0 | 0 |

Suppose him at the end of the ten years to get a Living enabling him to settle, what will be the result of his saving:

1. A nest egg of £1,220 ready money, for furnishing and other expenses.

2. A sum of £1,500 secured at his death on payment of a *very much* smaller annual Premium than if he had then begun to insure it.

3. A useful Library, worth more than £200, besides the books bought out of his current Income during the period. . . .[34]

Exactly when Charles learned of his appointment is not clear, but when he returned to Oxford in October 1855, he bore the new title. The year's last quarter goes uncharted because another volume of the diary is missing. When the autumn term ended, Charles went back to Croft for Christmas in triumph. Collingwood, who had the missing volume of Charles's diary at hand, reports that Charles wrote at the close of this remarkable year: "I am sitting alone in my bedroom this last night of the old year, waiting for midnight. It has been the most eventful year of my life: I began it a poor bachelor student, with no definite plans or expectations; I end it a master and tutor in Christ Church, with an income of more than £300 a year, and the course of mathematical tuition marked out by God's providence for at least some years to come. Great mercies, great failings, time lost, talents misapplied—such has been the past year."[35]

Having achieved financial independence and academic security, Charles could now, just before turning twenty-four, look forward to being an Oxford don and to living a dignified life as a lecturer, scholar, and member of a high social order. True, as a mathematician without clerical credentials, he would not be a full-fledged member of the ecclesiastical establishment, not part of the inner circle—the Chapter of Canons, the Professors of Divinity, Hebrew, and the like. But his title of Lecturer, while it put him on a low rung of the ladder in this august society, did launch him properly on his career.

Back home, his father and his brothers and sisters were certainly impressed with his achievement, and proud. He knew that when he returned to Oxford, his duties would multiply, but he was prepared. He had spread his wings in classrooms at Croft, he had gained self-confidence as a teacher and enjoyed conducting classes. Gone were the dismal failures in philosophy and history, in the mathematical scholarship competitions. He now rejected the notion of sitting for the scholarships again and used his time to advance his career, prepare his lectures, write his mathematical treatises, and let his imagination roam.[36]

*Charles, probably taken by his friend Reginald Southey*

# CHAPTER THREE

# The Don, the Dean, and His Daughter

*Alas! The slippery nature of tender youth.*

CLAUDIAN

In assuming the deanery of Christ Church, Henry George Liddell acquired a post of great influence and responsibility. Not only does the Dean run the college and oversee its vast wealth and property, but, as Dean of Christ Church Cathedral, he is also the most important ecclesiastical figure in Oxford, playing a major role in appointing canons and in consecrating the Bishop of Oxford. In Liddell's case, he found Christ Church mired in old ways, his predecessor, Thomas Gaisford, having staunchly opposed all change, as he labored quietly in the academic groves of ancient Greece and Rome.

Studentships at Christ Church, when the new dean took up his duties, were still given for life (they later became renewable seven-year appointments). Undergraduates numbered about 180, and the faculty comprised six classical tutors and one mathematician, who was solely responsible for all the instruction in mathematics.

The college maintained discipline by "gating"—confining pupils to its precincts—and by "impositions"—requiring undergraduates to copy passages from the classics, often Homer. Attendance at chapel was compulsory. Dinner in Hall was at six during the week, at five on Sundays. Candles lit the Hall, as they did other rooms. Mercury, the pool in the center of Tom Quad, provided the water that the scouts carried to their staircases.[1]

Servitors, like Thomas Hughes's Hardy in *Tom Brown at Oxford*, still existed, but they no longer performed menial duties. Undergraduate noblemen dined apart at High Table; Students and undergraduate commoners sat below in the body of the Hall. Seating was fixed by class and position; all sat on benches, only the Dean had a chair.

When Charles became Mathematical Lecturer in 1855, his routine did not alter significantly because he was not called upon to begin formal lecturing that term. Nevertheless, his life was busy. Andrew Lang recalls that the "hardest worked of men is a conscientious college tutor. . . . They deliver I know not how many sets of lectures a-year. . . . The knowledge and the industry of these gentlemen is a perpetual marvel."[2]

Charles's new life confirms Lang's description. But he was young, eager, able—and new inducements appeared. Early in the autumn term of 1855, he was made Master of the House. As "M.A. of House," he had no additional duties and few new privileges, but the honor made him eligible to participate in more ceremonies, including the Christ Church festive banquets, the Gaudies. It underscored his elevated standing in the college and provided a useful stopgap until 1857, when he could claim his own M.A.

Charles was well aware of Liddell's reputation: as a schoolboy at Rugby, he had written home (October 9, 1848) asking permission to purchase Liddell and Scott's "Larger *Greek-English Lexicon.*" The man himself—exceptionally tall, handsome, self-assured, twenty-one years Charles's senior—must have awed the younger man. Liddell reminded one don of Leonardo da Vinci;[3] for Ruskin, he was "one of the rarest types of nobly-presenced Englishmen."[4] He made an Olympian impression at Oxford as he glided across the quadrangles and through the arched edifices of his domain, and quickly became a natural candidate for all important appointments.

Liddell's thirty-six-year reign at Christ Church is amply recorded, particularly his determination to change everything from eating arrangements in Hall to liberalizing the curriculum and refashioning the shape and fabric of the college. He even got involved in civic enterprise, particularly in the problem of drainage. The story goes that when a visiting German professor sought a glimpse of the great author of the *Lexicon,* he was led out to Christ Church Meadow, where, inquiring of a workman, he was told, " 'Oh, yes . . . he has just gone down the drain.' An adjacent man-hole was then approached, and in answer to a call, a loud voice was heard from below, and soon the majestic head emerged from the lower depths."[5]

Liddell had a remarkable wife. Born Lorina Hannah, youngest daughter of the Lowestoft Reeves, landed gentry, she married Liddell on July 23, 1846. He was already a man of considerable reputation, having published the famous *Lexicon* (1843) and served as Chaplain to the Prince Consort. Liddell, as headmaster of Westminster School, was an astonishingly good catch, and the wedding, held in Lowestoft, created a great stir.[6] Thackeray, a fellow schoolmate of Liddell, wrote to a friend about the match: "Dear brave old Liddell! . . . He is full of learning and honour and simplicity, and has taken a 3d rate provincial lady (rather first rate in the beauty line though I think) for a wife. They are like the couples in the old comedies."[7]

At Westminster School, the couple met the right people and did all the right things. Mrs. Liddell took a maternal interest in the boys and grew popular. The London chapter endured for nine years, and by the time Christ Church summoned them to Oxford, Mrs. Liddell had given birth to two sons (one, named Arthur, after the Queen's third son, died in 1853 of scarlet fever) and three daughters.

When Charles's diary resumes at the start of 1856, he and the Dean were already on a professional footing. On January 21, back in Oxford after a busy, sociable vacation in the north and four days swanning about London, Charles called on the Dean and got his consent "to arrange public lectures as I find best." Later that day he sent a notice round in Hall, "the first I have issued as Mathematical Lecturer," asking the students concerned "to attend in the lecture room at 10 tomorrow." But of the sixty men sent for, only twenty-three appeared: "I have sent for the rest to my rooms." He drew up a reading list to go with his lectures and on the following day sent out his second notice in Hall, but, alas, it produced no better results. He again sent for the men individually and called on the Dean "to consult him on various questions connected with the lecture." The two agreed on how Charles would monitor his pupils' preparedness, attendance, and progress: "The idle are to be at once reported to the Dean."

Charles consulted his mentor Bartholomew Price for advice on "the order in which men should read their subjects for Moderations," and Price provided him with an appropriate list. He gave a lecture in trigonometry on Saturday the twenty-sixth, "the first this term," and two days later his first two lectures in the lecture room: "9 men at the Euclid, 11 at the Algebra lecture (there ought to be 12 at each)."

So it went: new duties took their place alongside old, and once Charles hit his stride, he ceased to record details. With lectures to prepare and tutorials to give, he led a busy life. But he was, by nature, orderly, and order helped him survive. "I am thinking of beginning a sort of day-book for entering *everything* in, another private one, and gradually form special books," he wrote (January 22). On February 5 he devised a "system of readings" for himself, in the classics and English history. "Thoroughness must be the rule of all this reading," he added.

Undaunted by his work schedule, he wrote (January 22) asking his Uncle Skeffington "to get me a photographic apparatus, as I want some other occupation here than mere reading and writing." Nor was he yet content: on January 29, 1856, he arranged to teach classes in the local school, St. Aldate's, opposite Tom Gate, three times a week, where he tried for the first time (February 5) introducing a number of sums for the students to work out as part of a story, a technique he developed and used in later years.

A week later disillusionment set in: "The school class noisy and inattentive—the novelty of the thing is wearing off. . . ." The classes continued "noisy and troublesome," and by the end of the month he gave up and stopped teaching there.

He concealed his difficulties from his Croft audience. His father, writing to Charles's brother Skeffington, in Keswick cramming for the Oxford matriculation examination, reported that Charles "gives a good account of himself and his doings at Christ Church. He seems to be making good friends with the Dean and to be succeeding in his Lectures."[8]

On February 25 Charles went to the river to watch the boat races and there met "Mrs. Liddell, her sister, and two eldest children [Harry and Lorina]." This may have been his first encounter with the family.

On March 6, 1856, he made "friends with little Harry Liddell. . . . He is certainly the handsomest boy I ever saw." Two days later he joined "about half the college" at the deanery for a musical party: "I took the opportunity," he wrote, "of making friends with little Lorina . . . the second of the family."

Not until the following term, after Charles returned from the Easter vacation, did he encounter Alice, Lorina's younger sister, just under four years old. The meeting occurred on Friday, April 25, 1856, when Charles, having ordered his camera during the vacation, went with his friend-in-photography, Reginald Southey, "to the Deanery, to try to take a photograph of the Cathedral"; but "both attempts proved failures." He added: "The three little girls were in the garden most of the time, and we became excellent friends: we tried to group them in the foreground of the picture, but they were not patient sitters." He concludes: "I mark this day with a white stone."[9]

*The deanery garden, Christ Church, where Charles played croquet with the Liddell sisters, and the cathedral in the background*

Charles and Southey returned to the deanery on three successive days the next week, taking photographs (mostly failures) of some of the children. From then on, Charles's path led frequently to the deanery. On May 6 the Dean asked him to give the oration at the upcoming Gaudy. Four days later Charles and Southey tried photography again: "As it was so good a day for it," Charles writes, "I went over to the Library, and called to Harry Liddell from the window, and got him to come over to Southey's room. We had great difficulty in getting him to sit still long enough. . . . [Southey] succeeded at last, by placing him in a bright light, in getting a fair profile."

On May 13 Charles went over to the deanery to show the Dean his son's likeness. The Dean, himself a photography enthusiast, asked Charles to stay to lunch. "Invitation to dine at the Deanery on Saturday next," Charles notes. On the appointed Saturday, May 17, dinner was followed by another large musical party, "fair as far as music went, but too much crowded for enjoyment. . . ."

A crush at the deanery was now not unusual. Mrs. Liddell, keenly aware of her family's standing, enjoyed mixing in society and staging large functions. With the deanery and all of Christ Church available, she turned what might have remained a dull, silent enclave into a lively, bustling social center.

Charles's photography gave him instant access to the inner circle. On June 3 he spent the morning at the deanery "photographing the children," and later in the day he and his Putney cousin Frank Dodgson, a Junior Scholar at Christ Church, took Harry Liddell rowing. Harry was stroke "and he steered back." Two days later the same three, accompanied by Lorina, went rowing, Lorina "much to my surprise having got permission from the Dean to come," Charles wrote. "We went down to the island, and made a kind of picnic there, taking biscuits with us, and buying gingerbeer and lemonade. . . . Considering the wild spirits of the children, we got home without accident, having attracted by our remarkable crew a good deal of attention from almost everyone we met." Charles exults: "Mark this day, annalist, not only with a white stone, but as altogether *dies mirabilis.*" Two days after the river picnic, Charles called at the deanery to bid adieu to the Liddells, and that evening he left Oxford for the long vacation.

He spent most of the summer of 1856 in pleasant diversions, traveling with his photography equipment to London, Croft, and even on a walking-coaching excursion through the Lake District. He visited relations in Whitburn and Alvaston and spent a week at Whitby. He wrote some verses, studied Italian and botany, and photographed family and friends. On October 10 he returned to Oxford with his brothers Wilfred and Skeffington, now about to enter Christ Church.

Twelve days later he encountered Harry and Ina Liddell in Christ Church Meadow "and took them up to see my book of photographs." On November 1, after the Gaudy in Hall, "we adjourned . . . to the Deanery for dessert, and health-drinking. I arranged with the Dean to go over some fine day soon, and have one more try at the view of the Cathedral and the children's portraits."

Mrs. Liddell was eager to have her carefully turned-out children photographed to secure their images for posterity. On Monday, November 3, Charles met Miss Prickett, the governess, walking with Ina, and settled that he would come over on Wednesday morning, if fine, to take more photographs. "I also asked her," he adds, "to try to secure some of the Aclands coming over to be taken: there are 5 or 6 of them, and Southey says they are a beautiful family."

Charles's photographs of Lorina, Alice, and
Edith Liddell. He must have taken dozens of
photographs of the Liddell children. "Being
photographed," Alice wrote, "was . . . a joy to
us and not a penance."
Alice as "Beggar Child" (above left)
The young Alice (above)
Alice's younger sister,
Edith (below)

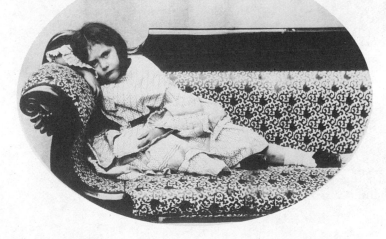

*Alice's older sister, Lorina*

*Young Alice in profile*

*Lorina with ukulele*

*Alice feigning sleep (above)*
*Alice wreathed (below)*
*Alice in a verdant setting (right)*

*The three Liddell sisters: "Open your mouth, and shut your eyes"*

*Alice and Lorina: "the Chinese group"*

Henry Wentworth Acland, Fellow of All Souls and soon Regius Professor of Medicine, and his family were friends of the Liddells, and Acland was their physician. It was a natural leap for Charles to approach the Aclands through the Liddells, but in so doing he committed, in the Liddells' view, an inexcusable social gaffe. Was he appropriating the deanery for his photographic studio and inviting whomever he wished to sit for him? The Liddells lowered the boom. On the appointed Wednesday: "The morning was fair, and I took my camera over to the Deanery—just in time to see the whole party . . . set off with the carriage and ponies—a disappointment for me, as it is the last vacant morning I shall have in the term."

Either oblivious of the rebuff or determined to ignore it, Charles marked time, and, evidently, the Liddells relented. On the following Monday (November 10), a sunny day, he went to the deanery "to take portraits at 2, but the light failed, and I only got one of Harry. I spent an hour or so afterwards with the children and governess, up in the schoolroom, making them paper boats, etc."

Two days later he reported "becoming embarrassed by the duties of the lectureship": he was so occupied tutoring pupils that he had little time to prepare adequately. He reprimanded himself for not having done better during the long vacation and resolved to do more in the future: "Something must be done, and done *at once,* or I shall break down altogether." A fortnight later (November 26), he elaborated: "I am weary of lecturing, and discouraged. . . . It is thankless, uphill work, goading unwilling men to learning they have no taste for, to the inevitable neglect of others who really want to get on." He did not suggest, however, that his attention to photography or to the Liddells had anything to do with his difficulties.

Two days later still, on November 14, 1856, he was back at the deanery "in the morning taking pictures, and . . . again in the afternoon at Harry's request to take him and Ina." Mrs. Liddell bristled; she said "they were not to be taken till all can be taken in a group," and Charles began to suspect that something was wrong. "This may be meant as a hint that I have intruded on the premises long enough: I am quite of the same opinion myself, and, partly for this reason, partly because I cannot afford to waste any more time on portraits at such a bad season of the year, I have resolved not to go again for the present, nor at all without invitation, except just to pack up the things and bring them back."

But tempers cooled and Mrs. Liddell, again assuaged, invited Charles to the deanery to photograph her father-in-law. A week later Charles attended another musical party and on December 3 went to pack up his equipment. He showed Mrs. Liddell two portraits of the children which he had had colored.

Term over, Charles called before leaving Oxford: "The Dean and Mrs. Liddell are going abroad for 4 months," he notes, "for his health." The Dean had bronchitis. "The children are to remain in Oxford: LLoyd has undertaken to teach Harry his Latin and Greek. I offered to teach him sums, etc., but Mrs. Liddell seemed to think it would take up too much of my time."

Free of lectures, Charles headed for London for five days of theater, music, and visits with relations. He returned to Oxford on December 17 to help a pupil prepare for Honour Moderations. While back he presented Harry with a mechanical tortoise as a Christmas present. On the twenty-fourth, having stayed up all night packing, he made the twelve-hour journey to Croft.

Thirty minutes before year's end, exhausted after a long day of entertaining more than eighty children with a magic lantern, he sat down with his diary to review 1856 and

to take counsel with myself for the future. I must with sorrow confess, that my bad habits are almost unchanged. I am afraid that lately I have been even more irregular than ever, and more averse to exertion: though the labour of last term has been nearly as heavy as at any period in my life, it has been forced on me by my position, rather than taken up voluntarily. As to the future, I may lay down as absolute necessities: *Divinity Reading,* and *Mathematical Reading.* I trust to do something this Vacation, but most of the Long Vacation must be devoted to work, and I think my best plan will be to take lodgings wherever Price has his reading party and so get occasional help from him.

On other subjects I think there is no use in making resolutions. (I hope to make good progress in Photography in the Easter Vacation: it is my one recreation, and I think should be done well.) . . . Midnight is past: bless the New Year, oh heavenly Father. . . .

Charles's resolve was productive. On returning to Oxford for Hilary term, he recorded (January 23, 1857) having done a fair amount of work during the vacation, especially in algebraic geometry.

With the Dean and Mrs. Liddell by now in Madeira, Charles's path to the deanery was unobstructed. The day after he returned, he sent some Christmas cake to the children, and five days later, disregarding Mrs. Liddell's wishes, he arranged "with Miss Prickett for Harry Liddell to come to me 3 days a week . . . to learn sums." A week later (February 5), Charles, taking a walk, "fell in with Ina Liddell and the governess, and returned with them to the Deanery, where I spent about an hour with the young party in the schoolroom. Miss Prickett showed me a letter the other day," he adds, "from Mrs. Reeve (Mrs. Liddell's mother), in which she expressed great alarm at Harry's learning 'mathematics' with me! She fears the effect of over-work on the brain. As far as I can judge, there is nothing to fear at present on that score, and I sent a message to that effect." Harry appeared for his customary lesson two days later with news that the Dean's health had improved. Charles then took him to two picture galleries. On the following Sunday (February 8), Charles, in surplice, read the second lesson in the afternoon cathedral service. "Harry ran up to me afterwards," he reports, "to tell me 'You've got your white gown on, and you *read in the church!*' "

Throughout 1857 Charles worked at mathematical manuscripts, but he found time to volunteer to bring Common Room record books up to date, and to attend public concerts, exhibitions, and a succession of dinner parties.

During the winter, while the Liddell parents were away, he met the children and their governess frequently in various combinations. Then suddenly, on February 23, the children were whisked off to their grandmother in Lowestoft to escape a scarlet fever outbreak. Hoping perhaps that the children would return soon, Charles decided on March 31 "on staying up this Vacation," and indeed the next day encountered "the two youngest Liddells. They tell me that they came back yesterday."

Charles resumed tutoring Harry, walked with the children, and visited the deanery. One evening he read them the whole of one of his favorite comic dramas, J. M. Morton's *Away with Melancholy*, probably taking all the parts himself, mimicking the characters, raising his voice for the female parts, gesticulating, acting. He took Harry rowing again, and on May 17 found "to my great surprise that my notice of . . . [the children] is construed by some men into attentions to the governess, Miss Prickett." To shield Miss Prickett from further embarrassment, he planned not to take "any public notice of the children in future unless an occasion should arise when such an interpretation is impossible."

Attracting Miss Prickett was the furthest thing from Charles's mind, but she may not have found his attentions unwelcome. Why, when the Dean and Mrs. Liddell had made clear their disapproval of Charles's attentions to the children, had Miss Prickett been so amenable, allowing Charles to come so often to the deanery, to take Harry on as pupil, and shown him letters from the parents and from the grandmother? Perhaps she hoped that with repeated exposure, she might win her way into Charles's heart. In any case, Charles's resolve not to notice her and her charges in public evaporated soon enough, and he continued meeting them all. On one occasion (June 2), he spent an entire morning with Ina and Alice: "To try the lens, I took a picture of myself, for which Ina took off the cap, and of course considered it all her doing!"

The Dean and Mrs. Liddell returned the following day, and Charles kept his distance. But, almost three weeks later, on the twenty-second, he joined them all at a musical event at New College, and three days after that called "to show Mrs. Liddell the photographs she had asked about," getting leave to return on the morrow to photograph the Dean.

Four days later, camera in hand, he spent the whole day at the deanery. It turned out to be one of the "pleasantest" times he had ever spent there, with all four children, taking photographs, swinging in the garden, and playing backgammon. Naturally, he marked the day with a white stone. On the thirtieth he left for the long summer vacation: "So ends my five months stay at Oxford, during which I have learned almost nothing, taught not much more, and forgotten a great deal."

Charles's resolve to join Price's reading party vanished, and his summer activities consisted largely of visits, photography, and novel-reading. He even neglected his diary for a week or more at a time, but did record (August 13) that Mrs. Liddell had written, thanking him for some photographs he had sent her and (September 3) acknowledging an album of photographs.

While at Croft, he managed some work. But soon he packed up his gear and set off on a journey to Berwick, Edinburgh, Hawthornden, Roslin, Glasgow, and ultimately to the Lakes. He returned to Croft for twelve days at the beginning of October and traveled back to Oxford on the sixteenth.

At the deanery three days later, he learned that the parents intended to leave again for Madeira, this time taking the girls with them. On November 2, using Ina, "whom I met coming in from the Meadow," as messenger, he sent his photograph album for Mrs. Liddell's perusal. On the eighteenth he bade the Liddells goodbye: "It took a long time to get to the end of the adieus of the dear, loving little children; and I spent more than an hour there instead of a quarter, as I had intended."

Back in Oxford after the vacation, with the Liddells away, Charles went about his work routinely. On February 24 he began a system of reading Scripture before chapel. He invented "another cipher, far better than the last,"[10] read novels and poetry, and worked on physiology and anatomy. At the close of the Easter vacation, he journeyed from Croft to London with his twelve-year-old brother, Edwin, shepherding him to the theater, art galleries, the Zoological Gardens, and Madame Tussaud's. They visited relatives and the Photographic Society Exhibition, where, for once in his lifetime, Charles had four of his own photographs on show.

Although Charles worked hard at his profession, he did not altogether neglect the larger world, as most Oxford academics were inclined to do. True, we find no mention of the war with China in 1857–58, and only a single reference (January 7, 1858) to the Indian Mutiny in his diary. The Crimean War did catch his notice, however. A year after the outbreak, he noted (February 17, 1855) that R. G. Faussett, Mathematical Lecturer at Christ Church, departed for the Crimea, leaving his position vacant. Less than a month later (March 16), Charles attended a "good" lecture in Oxford on the defenses of Sebastopol; and in London (June 22), he attended another, "very good" lecture, on "the model of Sebastopol." On September 11 he reacts jubilantly to the "glorious intelligence . . . of the *Fall of Sebastopol.* The whole town is in the hands of the allies," he added. After the Russians capitulated, Charles accompanied his family (March 26, 1856) "to see the Crimean photographs [by Roger Fenton]" on view in Ripon, and on the last day of March, elated, he writes: "*News of the signing of Peace* came by telegraph. The cathedral bells were ringing most of the day, and flags flying all over the town. Thus March does for once 'go out like a lamb,' " he adds, "leaving us once more in peace, '*qua sit perpetua!*' " He was, almost immediately, moved to write a poem in praise of Florence Nightingale, and it appeared in the May number of the *Train.*

As busy as he was at Oxford, Charles did not slight his creative promptings. Beginning back in 1854, he managed to get some of his literary efforts into print. Two poems appeared in the *Oxonian Advertiser* under pseudonyms, but no one has yet identified them with certainty. That summer, as we have seen, he published a poem and a short story in the *Whitby Gazette.* Then, a distant cousin maneuvered some of Charles's early efforts into the *Comic Times,* a competitor of *Punch.* The August 18, 1855, number contained "The Dear Gazelle," a parody of lines from Thomas Moore's *Lalla Rookh,* headed by a prose preface, which Charles confessed *Punch* had already rejected. The ballad, meant to be sung, laments the transiency of life. It is more meaningful than its thin film of nonsensical jollity would indicate, for beneath the surface runs a disquieting despair.

Three more pieces appeared in the *Comic Times* before the paper's demise in November 1855, all in keeping with the magazine's humorous stance: "She's All My Fancy Painted Him" took its impetus from the first line of "Alice Gray," a song by William Mee. (In time it became, in more polished form, the White Rabbit's "evidence" in the trial scene of *Alice.*) This too is non-sense, a miscellany of shifting pronouns. But here again, as in "The Dear Gazelle," Charles strikes chords of loss and sadness. "Hints for Etiquette, or Dining Out Made Easy," a prose parody of a guide to social conduct, is a forced bit of wit mocking conventional rules of society: "To use a fork with your soup, intimating at the same time to your hostess that you are reserving the spoon for the beef-steaks, is a practice wholly exploded." "Photography Extraordinary" also appeared, a spoof suggesting that the new art of photography could capture weak and formless thoughts, which, by appropriate treatment, could be elevated to a higher, more potent plane. Charles wonders whether the technique could "be applied to the speeches of Parliament."

When the *Comic Times* dissolved, its staff reorganized and formed a new humor paper, a monthly this time, called the *Train.* Contributors went un-paid, but even that stratagem did not keep the paper solvent: it lasted only from 1856 to 1858. Eight of Charles's pieces appeared there, seven in verse, one in prose. A poem entitled "Solitude," written in 1853, is a straightfor-ward Romantic exercise by a twenty-one-year-old posing as a wealthy an-cient yearning to recapture his youth and the feelings he felt then. Its sad undercurrent has something in common with "The Dear Gazelle." Edmund Yates, editor, in turn, of the *Comic Times* and the *Train,* required a signature for the poem, and Charles manufactured one based on a Latinized reversal of his first two names, Charles Lutwidge, making "Solitude" the first piece to bear the signature Lewis Carroll.

Among other verse contributions to the *Train* are "Ye Carpette Knyghte," a mock medieval poem built on puns; "The Path of Roses," a long senti-mental poem in blank verse celebrating the end of the Crimean War and hailing Florence Nightingale as a model of what a woman can contribute in wartime; "Upon a Lonely Moor," a nonsense parody of Wordsworth's "Res-olution and Independence" (it later becomes the White Knight's ballad in *Looking-Glass*); "The Three Voices," the humorous parody of Tennyson's "The Two Voices" embodying a bravura display of Platonic metaphysics; "The Sailor's Wife," another sentimental dream poem about an imagined shipwreck; and, perhaps most amusing of all, "Hiawatha's Photographing," a long verse parody of Longfellow's American Indian ballad that captures the absurdities inherent in the vogue among the nouveaux riches to get every member of the family photographed in flattering poses.

The single prose piece, "Novelty and Romancement," is a delightful if overdrawn tale about a hero named Stubbs, who, in search of "romancement," believes he has finally found it when he sees it advertised, but, alas, the sign really touts "Roman Cement." Another verse, "The Palace of Humbug," a fuzzy nightmare, rejected by *Punch,* the *Comic Times,* and the *Train,* ultimately finds a home in the *Oxford Critic.*

The diary record breaks off on April 17, 1858, and the next two volumes, covering four crucial years, to May 1862, are missing. Only Charles's publications, surviving letters, and the few diary excerpts that his nephew S. D. Collingwood quotes from the diary that was later lost allow us some insights into his life and thoughts during that time.

No further publications appear during the eight and a half blackout months of 1858, but one literary effort, "Stanzas for Music," although not published until a decade later, and then under a different title, bears the date 1859 in *Mischmasch.* It is another lovelorn poem, this time spoken by a jilted maid viewing with tearful eyes from beneath a distant willow tree, where she once was wooed, her beloved's wedding to another.

In 1860 Charles published two pieces on photography. "A Photographer's Day Out," in the obscure *South Shields Amateur Magazine,* is a humorous story of an amateur photographer in pursuit of his beloved, camera in hand. The other, a review of that year's Photographic Exhibition, appeared in the *Illustrated Times.*

Onward and upward Charles moved. After the photography pieces, a poem of his surfaced in Dickens's weekly periodical *All the Year Round.* "Faces in the Fire" reverberates with melancholy and wistful nostalgia. Again an old man, reminiscing by the fire at dusk, bemoans his lost childhood and the unrequited love of a "gentle maid." The refrain is what might have been; in the end, the old man sits lonely facing the oncoming night.

During 1860 and 1861 he made four contributions to *College Rhymes,* an Oxford-Cambridge literary journal first published in 1859, and one poem in July 1862 in *Temple Bar.* "A Sea Dirge," a splendid diatribe against the spurious virtues of the seaside, metrically patterned on Edgar Allan Poe's "Annabel Lee," is a prime example of Charles's ability to dress himself in attitudes totally foreign to his nature, for he was devoted to the seaside. In

"The Dream of Fame" (later the title poem of Charles's posthumous book of verse, *Three Sunsets and Other Poems*), an old man returns to the scene of his youth and tells a tale of unfulfilled love. In "Ode to Damon," a forceful Chloë, by tolerating Damon's foibles, imposes domestic bliss upon their marriage. "Those Horrid Hurdy-Gurdies!" is a short monody complaining about annoyances of everyday life, including hurdy-gurdies. "After Three Days," the poem that appeared in *Temple Bar,* is Charles's tribute to William Holman Hunt's painting *The Finding of Christ in the Temple,* which he judged "about the most wonderful picture I ever saw."

Two poems bear dates near the end of the blackout period, one serious, one humorous. The serious one (dated February 17, 1862) appeared in *College Rhymes* in March. Charles must have been reading about Jonathan Swift, and his attention was caught by an item found among the Dean's effects after his death, labeled "Only a woman's hair," a phrase that Charles adopted as his title.

The humorous poem, "Disillusionised" (dated March 15, 1862, reprinted as "My Fancy"), also appeared in *College Rhymes* that summer. Here again Charles parodies William Mee's "Alice Gray" in a tongue-in-cheek complaint of a swain's disappointment in wooing the object of his desire: first believing that she has years "perhaps a score," he discovers that she has "At least a dozen more." He concludes:

> She has the bear's ethereal grace,
>     The bland hyena's laugh,
> The footstep of the elephant,
>     The neck of the giraffe;
> I love her still, believe me,
>     Though my heart its passion hides;
> She's all my fancy painted her,
>     But oh! *how much besides!*

Charles labored away at his profession, not just in tutorials and lectures but in writing. He published, at his own expense, aids to students of mathematics and logic and, later, works that explore new dimensions of those disciplines. His concern with logical problems appeared early—even, as we know, in the family magazines. His interest in games persisted, and in January 1858, at the close of the Christmas vacation, he completed the rules for a card game, *Court Circular,* which he later improved and saw through two printings.

Charles's first book appeared in 1860: *A Syllabus of Plane Algebraical Geometry, Systematically Arranged, with Formal Definitions, Postulates, and Axioms,* a 154-page attempt to translate some of Euclid into algebraical terms and to claim for analytical geometry a greater role in developing reason and logical thinking than was generally conceded.

Also in 1860 he published an eight-page pamphlet, *Notes on the First Two Books of Euclid, Designed for Candidates for Responsions,* and in 1861 *The Formulae of Plane Trigonometry, Printed with Symbols (Instead of Words) to Express the "Goniometrical Ratios"* (nineteen pages) and *Notes on the First Part of Algebra* (sixteen pages). These works reflect Charles's tutoring and lecturing and his desire to help his students grasp the subjects and prepare for examinations more easily and effectively.

That, in sum, is Charles's publication record up to May 1862, when his diary resumes, he having passed his thirtieth year the previous January. And what does one make of it? The mathematical works speak for themselves: they are professional and, if not altogether elegant, genuine attempts to change mathematical practices and to help students. His literary treasury is not large: his witty verse succeeds, but the serious pieces, while personally revealing, often mystify. They reflect Charles's inner self, but no single authorial voice emerges; if anything, we have a jangle of themes. Charles dons disguises easily, perhaps deliberately to throw the reader off course. Possibly, however, he had not yet found his true literary self and was experimenting. Yet some of these pieces, though derivative, are mature. Perhaps he was not so much shaping his literary stance as finding a way to secrete an emotional struggle beneath a polished veneer or even devising a manner of expression to conceal him from himself.

These early literary efforts display a true wit, an ability to toy engagingly with language, to entertain. Their strength lies in their inventive humor. The serious poems are sentimental, traditional, glum. One wonders why Charles chose such morose subjects, why tragedy is so strong an element, why gloom and doom predominate while he, in fact, has met with overwhelming professional and personal success. Why the recurring themes of dashed hopes, disappointment in love, despair echoing despair? Something is gnawing away at him, and whatever it is will not lie quiet; it demands a hearing.

These persistent themes cannot be accidental. And yet we have no clue whatsoever that any object of desire had even entered his life, let alone rejected him. He had not yet fallen in love or been thwarted in it; we do not see even a flirtation. Alice Liddell had still not become his ideal child friend;

she remains just one of the three points in the triangle of Liddell sisters.

But wait: a connection is possible between the poseur seeing himself re-peatedly as the old man reminiscing about an unfulfilled or lost love and the melancholy accompaniment reverberating in these early verses. Conceiv-ably, by now Charles has confronted his inner self, his nature, and his at-traction to prepubescent females. He is different from other men and astute enough to realize that the difference will create difficulties, cause him pain, leave his unconventional yearnings unsatisfied. He sees, perhaps, that be-cause he is bent upon a course outside the stream of social acceptability, he will have to live as an outsider.

In 1859 Charles undertook therapy for his stammer from James Hunt, fore-most speech correctionist, who lived near Hastings, where Charles was able to stay with his maternal aunts. Also undergoing therapy there was the poet-novelist-cleric George MacDonald, whom Charles met, and with whom he developed a firm friendship.

Letters that Charles wrote home in April 1860 provide further glimpses into his activities. He reports attending a concert and an illustrated lecture on the Arctic, meeting his thirteen-year-old brother Edwin at Rugby (prob-ably to be on hand for the lad's first day at the school), and approving Dr. Hunt's therapy.

Then, from the Eagle in Rugby on April 19, he described his London out-ing, where he had gone to Joseph Cundall and Company, who developed and stored his photographs (he got them done a hundred at a time and re-tailed them himself). He gate-crashed a private showing of Holman Hunt's *The Finding of Christ in the Temple* and talked with the artist. Later Hunt would give Charles an introduction to Mrs. Millais, the former Effie Gray, John Ruskin's bride, now married to the painter John Everett Millais, and he became a frequent caller at the Millais', photographing the parents and their children.

During 1860 Charles had printed a list of 159 photographs he had taken successfully. It fell into three categories: eighty-seven portraits of eighty-four persons, relatives, Christ Church colleagues, and friends. The list in-cludes himself, his father, two of his three brothers, Kitchin, Liddon, Longley, Friedrich Max Müller, and Price. A second group contains nine-teen photographs of thirty-nine persons, including Thomas Woolner, Bishop Wilberforce, groups of Christ Church choristers, and Twyford School boys. A miscellaneous group includes fifty-three photographs of forty-four places, sculptures, skeletons, and the like, including Croft Rectory, Daresbury Parsonage, and sculptures by Alexander Munro. Although he had photographed the Dean, his children, and almost certainly Mrs. Liddell, they do not enter the list. Nor do the Tennysons or the female members of his own family.

In November Charles gave a lecture entitled "Where Does the Day Begin?" at the Ashmolean Society and on December 12 attended a very special party at the deanery. The Prince of Wales had entered Christ Church as an undergraduate in October 1859, and on December 12, 1860, his mother came on a visit to Oxford, no doubt to see for herself how Edward was getting on. The Dean and Mrs. Liddell were honored to have the Queen stay at the deanery, and they entertained the royal party.

She arrived in Christ Church about twelve [Charles writes in his diary], and came in Hall with the Dean. . . . I had never seen her so near before [Charles writes home on the eighteenth], nor on her feet, and was shocked to find how short, not to say dumpy, and (with all loyalty be it spoken), how *plain* she is. She is *exactly* like the little full-length photograph published of her. I have got the whole set of the Royal Family, and will bring them with me.

You will be sorry to hear that I have failed, finally and completely, in getting H.R.H. to sit for his photograph. . . . I did not fail for want of asking and . . . if ever impudence and importunity deserved to succeed, *I* did.

He gives a long and detailed account of how he pursued the Prince, through the Prince's "Governor." He does at least get to talk to H.R.H. at the deanery party:

The Prince . . . shook hands very graciously, and I began with a sort of apology for having been so importunate about the photograph. He said something about the weather being against it. . . . Edith Liddell coming by at the moment, I remarked on the beautiful *tableau* which the children might make: he assented, and also said, in answer to my question, that he had seen and admired my photographs of them. I then said I hoped, as I had missed the photograph, he would at least give me his autograph in my album, which he promised to do. Thinking I had better bring the talk to an end, I concluded by saying that, if he would like copies of any of my photographs, I should feel honoured by his accepting them, he thanked me for this, and I then drew back, as he did not seem inclined to pursue the conversation.

In his letter home, Charles reports writing to the Prince's governor for permission to bring his photograph album round for the Prince to see. On Saturday morning at ten, Charles accordingly presented himself:

The Prince came in directly . . . and seemed very friendly and more at his ease than he was at the Deanery. . . . When the box was opened, he looked through the second album, the "cherry" group, the Chinese group, and the large one of the two Haringtons.*

He said he had no time to finish looking through them then, and proposed they should be left, but on my saying (an awful breach of court etiquette, no doubt), that I was expecting some friends that morning to see them . . . he fixed on Tuesday (today) to have them sent over again. He consented to give the autograph then, but would not use my gold pen, as I wanted, saying that he wrote best with quill, and went to fetch a good one, with which he signed, adding the place and date at my suggestion. There ends my interview with Royalty. I have sent over my box this morning, and General [Robert] Bruce [governor to the Prince] is to send me a list of those of which he would like to have copies. We must do them if possible in the Easter Vacation: I expect there will be no lack of volunteers to print for the Prince—of course none but *first-raters* must be sent.

On February 20, 1861, he grasped "an hour without a lecture" to answer a letter from his sister Mary. She apparently asked about his mathematical books, and he provides a list of seven mathematical works completed or in progress.[11]

Charles continues: "Not much going on here but the usual botheration of lectures. . . . I need not say I have given . . . [my small friends the Liddells] a copy of *College Rhymes*—they say the 'Sea Dirge' is 'not true'—rather a sweeping condemnation."

A great deal of Charles's energies at this point was going into professional writing and there was much more he intended to do. He was aware of the standard texts and the work already done in the fields he was tilling

---

* The first two photographs are of the Liddell sisters in different poses, the third of the two daughters of the Principal of Brasenose College, Richard Harington.

and sought to be in touch with others working in similar areas, among them Robert Potts, a distinguished mathematician at Cambridge and an agitator for educational reform. Potts had published an edition of Euclid's *Elements* in 1845; his schools edition of *Elements* became a standard text and was much reprinted. Charles sent Potts a copy of his *Notes on the First Two Books of Euclid,* suggesting perhaps a collaboration on a text suitable for Oxford and Cambridge. Charles's letter is missing, but Potts's reply (March 20, 1861) makes clear that he believed that Charles's *Notes* gave students too much help.

The earliest letter that has come to light from Charles to a child friend is dated March 30, 1861. It went from Christ Church to the ten-year-old Kathleen Tidy of Littlethorpe in Yorkshire, daughter of a Major Thomas Tidy. Charles had photographed Kathleen sitting on the limb of a tree, and he sent her a letter bearing a characteristically Carrollian sharp edge to its humor. He wishes her "many happy returns of your 72d birthday" and sends a promised penknife with instructions for using it as a weapon against her brothers.

During this same year Charles became involved in a controversy concerning Benjamin Jowett, the Professor of Greek, earning an annual stipend, fixed in the sixteenth century, of forty pounds, and never raised since. A movement to increase Jowett's stipend was afoot, and Charles made his first speech in Congregation* on the subject.[12] Jowett, a champion of the liberal cause in religion, education, and politics, had been dubbed a heretic by the Oxford establishment for his *Epistles of Paul* (1855) and his "Interpretation of Scripture" in *Essays and Reviews* (1860). Charles opposed Jowett's cause and two days later printed and circulated a broadside on university politics entitled *Endowment of the Greek Professorship.* Appearing anonymously, but known even then to have been by Charles, it proposed that "the Professor of Latin be substituted for the Regius Professor of Greek." Charles published other jabs at Jowett, both in prose and verse, but when Charles and Jowett met at the Tennysons' on the Isle of Wight in April 1862, *odium theologicum* was kept at bay: "I walked down here [to his hotel from the Tennysons'] with . . . Mr. Jowett," Charles wrote to his sister Mary (April 19); and much later, in 1883, when Charles decided to contribute new

---

* Congregation is the legislative assembly of all resident M.A.'s, both academic and administrative; Convocation is the university assembly of all registered M.A.'s.

backs to the gallery seats at St. Mary's, Oxford, he met amiably with Jowett, then Vice-Chancellor, three times.

Charles had for several years been preparing for ordination. At the beginning of the long vacation, 1859, he sought an interview with Samuel Wilberforce, Bishop of Oxford, probably to clear up what he saw as some puzzles or obstacles. By August 5, 1861, he had resolved his difficulties and desired to offer himself at the Bishop's examination in September. On December 22, 1861, Wilberforce ordained Charles a deacon in the Church of England.

Charles's involvement in these religious ceremonies did not interfere with his holiday celebrations, however, and he selected as a Christmas present for Lorina, Alice, and Edith Liddell a copy of Catherine Sinclair's *Holiday House.* He wrote on the front inner cover in his careful script an acrostic poem made on the three sisters' names with built-in echoes of the title of the book, and on the flyleaf: "L. A. and E. Liddell a Christmas gift from C. L. Dodgson."

Choosing *Holiday House* was meaningful. When it first appeared in 1839, it broke with the tradition of children's books for the "better classes." Sinclair's preface records how Sir Walter Scott provoked her to write the book by predicting ominously that "in the rising generation there would be no poets, wits or orators, because all the play of the imagination is now carefully discouraged, and books written for young persons are generally a mere dry record of facts, unenlivened by any appeal to the heart, or any excitement to the fancy." A child's library would contain books "as dry as a road-book; but nothing on the habits or ways of think-

Little maidens, when you look
On this little story-book,
Reading with attentive eye
Its enticing history,
Never think that hours of play
Are your only **HOLIDAY**,
And that in a **HOUSE** of joy
Lessons serve but to annoy:
If in any **HOUSE** you find
Children of a gentle mind,
Each the others pleasing ever—
Each the others vexing never—
Daily work and pastime daily
In their order taking gaily —
Then be very sure that they
Have a *Life* of **HOLIDAY**.

*An acrostic verse, in Charles's hand, that appears on the front inner cover of a copy of Catherine Sinclair's* Holiday House; *on the flyleaf Charles wrote: "L. A. and E. Liddell / a Christmas gift / from C. L. Dodgson."*

ing, natural and suitable to the taste of children; therefore, while such works are delightful to the parents and teachers who select them, the younger community are fed with strong meat instead of milk, and the reading which might be a relaxation from study becomes a study in itself."

Sinclair endeavored "to paint that species of noisy, frolicsome, mischievous children . . . now almost extinct, wishing to preserve a sort of fabulous remembrance of days long past, when young people were like wild horses on the prairies, rather than like well-broken hacks on the road; and when, amid many faults and many eccentricities there was still some individuality of character and feeling allowed to remain."[13]

Sinclair tells a tale of hearty, healthy, lively Harry and Laura (names not all that different from Harry and Lorina), full of energy, plans, and questions. They are overseen by a prickly governess—not Miss Prickett, but Mrs. Crabtree—and they have a great friend in their Uncle David (Dodgson?), a font of hilariously funny stories.

*Holiday House* was an immediate success. Parents, weary of the didactic gloom suffusing other books, bought it, and it was reprinted time and again through the Victorian age, making it "one of the most important books in the history of children's literature . . . ,"[14] "the first real story of happy child life, and the first real bit of nonsense literature."[15]

Between 1858 and 1862 Charles moved to new rooms in Tom Quad, staircase 7, room 3. He involved himself in college and university politics; set his course toward ordination; developed his interest in photography; and labored mightily at his lecturing and at producing mathematical works. He was full of resolve, ambition, energy. He succeeded magnificently, except in his teaching. He tested some men going in for the Moderations and found "hardly one" fit for the examination, a depressing experience.

Why, given his distress, had Charles chosen to lecture in mathematics? Surely he knew that the subject would not appeal to all or even many undergraduates, that they would not warm to a required subject as they might to one they chose to study. He had solid reasons, however, for his choice. First and foremost, he, like his father, was exceptionally gifted at mathematics. Taking a first in mathematics proved his ability. Charles's early agreeable experiences in the classrooms at Croft and his sheer enjoyment in mathematics propelled him further.

Charles's trouble lay in the system that brought unprepared undergraduates to Oxford. They should have come up with enough mathematics and

Euclid to pass Responsions, but they did not, and it was too much to ask a youth, fully shaped but without the proper preparation, to swot it all up in no time at all.

Charles became aware of the problem early. He vented his concern in the letter to Robert Potts in 1861, and in replying, Potts held out some hope "that the disgraceful ignorance of Elementary Mathematics with which many students come into residence both at Oxford and Cambridge, will shortly be removed. Eton and Public Schools are now requiring an adequate knowledge of these subjects as a condition for moving up in the higher forms. The Oxford and Cambridge Local Examinations also . . . are exerting a most wholesome influence both on scholars and schoolmasters."[16]

Potts's promise of a rosier mathematical future did not, however, materialize, and Charles was doomed to Sisyphean labors, helping individual unprepared students. He certainly did not give up and tried every means to draw the unprepared and untrained into his world of intellectual excitement. He continued inventing stories by which to teach mathematics, he added humor to his equations and syllogisms. But he met with no great success. Teaching mathematics to the unteachable proved, in the end, impossible.

Charles pressed on. In the midst of a rising tide of university reform, a movement began to lower requirements. On April 11, 1864, the first effort at dilution failed. The advocates of change were not vanquished, however, and, early the following year, resurfaced. Charles, furious at efforts to cheapen degrees, composed *Examination Statute* on the eve of Congregation, a satirical squib in rhyming couplets of twenty-six lines, each beginning with a letter in the alphabet representing the name of a well-known member of the university who would be voting. He supplied a line for every letter in the alphabet, but printed only the first letter of the name followed by a dot for each omitted letter. Here are a few of the lines with names supplied:

> A is for [Acland], who'd physic the masses,
> B is for [Brodie], who swears by the gases.
> I am the Author, a rhymer erratic—
> J is for [Jowett], who lectures in Attic:
> K is for [Kitchin], than attic much warmer,
> L is for [Liddell], relentless reformer!
> U's University, factiously splitting—
> V's the Vice-Chancellor, ceaselessly sitting.
> Y are the Young men, whom nobody thought about—
> Z is the Zeal that this victory brought about.

This second time, however, the proposals passed, and on February 25, after Convocation, the university's legislative assembly, also adopted the new statute, 281 to 243, Charles, as a protest, wrote and printed *The New Examination Statute,* sent it off to be published in the *Morning Post* (March 4), and resigned as Mathematics Examiner. He considered the lowering of standards degrading and believed the new dispensation harmed both mathematics and classics, "*essential* part[s] of an Oxford education."

Charles remained vigilant and on numerous occasions sought to bring rationality to play in the circus of student examinations. Later, in 1877, for instance, he again printed a copy for circulation of a letter he had written to the Vice-Chancellor. This one, *Responsions, Hilary Term, 1877,* dealt with devastating discrepancies in the examination results as revealed by precise statistics he had collected between 1875 and 1877. He continued to keep score and in 1882 wrote a letter to the *Guardian* on "Oxford Responsions" and published another broadside, *An Analysis of the Responsions-Lists,* this time defending the examination's fairness.

If Oxford was to give examinations, Charles wanted them rigorous, but on the whole he opposed the examination system and was even depressed by it. In 1890, when he wrote *Sylvie and Bruno Concluded,* he found an outlet for his frustration. Mein Herr reminisces (chapter 12):

"Our favourite teacher got more obscure every year. . . . Well, his pupils couldn't make head or tail of . . . [moral philosophy], but they got it all by heart; and, when Examination-time came, they wrote it down; and the examiners said 'Beautiful! What depth!'

"But what good was it to the young men *afterwards?*" [the listener asks.]

"Why, don't you see?" replied Mein Herr. "*They* became teachers in their turn, and *they* said all these things over again; and *their* pupils wrote it all down and the Examiners accepted it and nobody had the ghost of an idea what it all meant!"

A fair amount of froth has surfaced from those who knew Charles as a colleague and others who sat before him in tutorials and in lectures. Canon Henry Scott Holland "always thought that Dodgson . . . ought to have lived in the Middle Ages in the palmy days of Scholasticism. His peculiar gifts of mind would . . . have enabled him to rout all other schoolmen, and to produce subtleties and dialectical terms which would have beaten and confounded the whole of Europe." Holland imagines Charles "lecturing . . . to eleven thousand enthusiastic students. They would have flocked to him

from all the Universities—Paris, Padua, Bologna, etc., to hear him turn the
theories of other great men inside out and upside down."[17]

Thomas Banks Strong, who later succeeded Charles as Curator of
Common Room and became Dean of the college and Bishop of Oxford,
recalled that

> efforts which . . . [Charles] made to enliven the proceedings did not al-
> ways succeed. There was a rule-of-three question which he told me he
> occasionally set—in hopes of ascertaining whether his pupils had
> thought at all of the relevance of arithmetic to things. If it takes 10 men
> so many days to build a wall, how long would it take 300,000 men? The
> answer would come, giving a very short space of time. When Dodgson
> would comment: "You don't seem to have observed that that wall
> would go up like a flash of lightning, and that most of those men could
> not have got within a mile of it." [And the Bishop adds:] A baffling
> comment such as this upon a successful calculation cannot have en-
> couraged confidence.[18]

A don of later vintage wrote during the centenary of Charles's birth: "I
asked one of . . . [his former pupils] if Carroll's lectures were bad. He said
they were dull as ditchwater. I asked another if he was a poor tutor. He said
that he and others once signed a round robin to the head of the college, asking to be transferred to other hands. Dodgson himself probably realized his
deficiencies here [the don writes], for though his tutorial duties were slight
he gave them up before he was fifty."[19]

Sir Herbert Maxwell, seventh Baronet of Monreith, an undergraduate at
Christ Church in the 1860s, reminisced about the "lean, dark-haired person . . . [and] the singularly dry and perfunctory manner in which he im-
parted instruction to us, never betraying the slightest personal interest in
matters that were of deep concern to us."[20]

John Henry Pearson, an Oxford clergyman, recalled Charles as "my
mathematical tutor and certainly his methods of explaining the elements of
Euclid gave me the impression of being extremely lucid, so that the least intelligent of us could grasp at any rate 'the Pons Asinorum.' I remember he
gave me a copy of a game he had invented, something after the manner of
chess."[21]

An undergraduate who signed himself "The Last of the Servitors" writes:
"As one connected with the House first in the same year as Mr. Dodgson
took his degree, 1854, I should like to . . . bear witness to the innate kindness

of his disposition. On entering the House as an undergraduate in 1864 I received from him a note, asking me to call upon him. I went to his rooms in Tom . . . and he said, 'Mr. ——— if you are intending to read mathematics, I shall be glad to give you any help you need.' "[22]

A former pupil of Charles's confessed: "I always hated mathematics at school, but when I went up to Oxford I learnt from Mr. Dodgson to look upon my mathematics as the most delightful of all my studies. His lectures were never dry."[23]

Although Charles received mixed reviews as a college lecturer, he was a resounding success as an extracurricular lecturer in mathematics and logic and as a private instructor to members of his family and to individuals or small groups of child friends.

The discrepancy is not difficult to grasp. It does not hinge, as some claim, on any dislike of boys as opposed to girls, which is false, because he worked doggedly to help even his unskilled male students to prepare for examinations. His niece Violet Dodgson saw the case clearly: "The fact was that the 'unwilling men' found him a very uninspiring lecturer."[24]

Charles reaped satisfaction from the students who succeeded, but the burden of the others took its toll. When his illustrator Harry Furniss became a popular comic lecturer, Charles wrote to him (March 29, 1888): "I congratulate you on the success you have had as a Lecturer, a role which I tried for 26 years, without ever attaining such world-wide celebrity as you have done!"

When the diary blackout ends, Charles, now thirty, was nearing the end of another year's work. The initial entry in the new volume announces a new poem, "Stolen Waters."

From May 1862 Charles's life was orderly and calm, governed by an unruffled diurnal placidity. Now entirely free of lectures on Tuesday, Thursday, and Saturday and the anxieties that once accompanied them, he was totally in control of his work. He led an active social life, made his rounds cheerfully, called on friends, went to dinner parties. Photography still had an important place in his schedule, as he arranged sittings for various portraits and groupings. More and more, he trained his lens on children.

He gave dinner parties in his rooms, and he entertained two sisters and an aunt on a visit. On Sunday (June 15), he went to three church services. And something new: accepting an invitation from his friend W. H. Ranken, Vicar of Sandford-on-Thames, he preached at Sunday evening service, resolving to do more of the same in the future. Later, he assisted for the first time at Communion (August 17), and took his first funeral service (October 5) and first baptism (February 18, 1863).

Charles's relationship with the Liddells was equally relaxed, with only an occasional moody objection from Mrs. Liddell. He visited the deanery frequently and took the children on long walks and on river expeditions. The young ones visited his rooms so often that they virtually dominate his diary. The friendship with them was now deeply rooted, and if it is obvious that Charles was now very much attached to them, it is equally clear that they were enormously fond of him, often proffering their own invitations, seeking him out, wanting his company and companionship. Alice Liddell's reminiscences of this period resonate with Proustian detail:

> We used to go to his rooms . . . escorted by our nurse. When we got there, we used to sit on the big sofa on each side of him, while he told us stories, illustrating them by pencil or ink drawings as he went along. When we were thoroughly happy and amused at his stories, he used to pose us, and expose the plates before the right mood had passed. He seemed to have an endless store of these fantastical tales, which he made up as he told them, drawing busily on a large sheet of paper all the time. They were not always entirely new. Sometimes they were new versions of old stories: sometimes they started on the old basis, but grew into new tales owing to the frequent interruptions which opened up fresh and undreamed of possibilities. In this way the stories, slowly enunciated in his quiet voice with its curious stutter, were perfected. . . . Being photographed was . . . a joy to us and not a penance as it is to most children. We looked forward to the happy hours in the mathematical tutor's rooms.
>
> . . . He used sometimes to come to the Deanery on the afternoons when we had a half-holiday. . . . On the other hand, when we went on the river for the afternoon with Mr. Dodgson, which happened at most four or five times every summer term, he always brought out with him a large basket full of cakes, and a kettle, which we used to boil under a haycock, if we could find one. On rarer occasions we went out for the whole day with him, and then we took a larger basket with luncheon— cold chicken and salad and all sorts of good things. One of our favourite whole-day excursions was to row down to Nuneham and picnic in the woods there, in one of the huts specially provided by Mr.

*Nuneham Park, where Charles and the Liddell sisters enjoyed picnics. "Sometimes," wrote Alice, "we spent the afternoon wandering in the more material fairyland of the Nuneham woods until it was time to row back to Oxford in the long summer evening."*

Harcourt for picnickers. . . . To us the hut might have been a Fairy King's palace, and the picnic a banquet in our honour. Sometimes we were told stories after luncheon that transported us into Fairyland. . . . On these occasions we did not get home until about seven o'clock.[25]

Nuneham was one of the Liddells' cherished destinations for a day's outing. With a landscaped park and deep woods, it provided the freedom and mystery to please young appetites and imaginations; it also stimulated Charles's storytelling. The estate was owned by William Vernon Harcourt, distinguished scientist and Canon of York, a Christ Church graduate himself and uncle of Charles's friend and colleague A. G. Vernon Harcourt, who sometimes accompanied Charles and the Liddells on their jaunts. Nuneham is five miles downstream, an ideal distance and in the right direction for the children to row. Alice provides the details: "After we had chosen our boat with great care, we three children were stowed away in the stern, and Mr.

Dodgson took the stroke oar. . . . He succeeded in teaching us in the course of these excursions, and it proved an unending joy to us. When we had learned enough to manage the oars, we were allowed to take our turn at them, while the two men [Charles and Harcourt] watched and instructed us. I can remember what hard work it was rowing upstream from Nuneham, but this was nothing if we thought we were learning and getting on. It was a proud day when we could 'feather our oars' properly."[26]

The first stanza of the prefatory poem in *Alice* captures the sight of the children rowing:

> All in the golden afternoon
>    Full leisurely we glide;
> For both our oars, with little skill,
>    By little arms are plied,
> While little hands make vain pretence
>    Our wanderings to guide.

And in the "Wool and Water" chapter of *Looking-Glass,* Alice rows the Sheep and is offended at the Sheep's instructions to "feather."

Charles chronicled the day-to-day encounters with the Liddell children during what must have been glorious spring and summer days of 1862. The rowing parties became routine, but on June 17 he recorded a river journey that included his sisters Frances and Elizabeth and his Aunt Lucy Lutwidge, and it turned out anything but ordinary:

> Expedition to Nuneham. Duckworth . . . and Ina, Alice, and Edith came with us. We set out about 12½ and got to Nuneham about 2: dined there, then walked in the park, and set off for home about 4½. About a mile above Nuneham heavy rain came on, and after bearing it a short time I settled that we had better leave the boat and walk: 3 miles of this drenched us all pretty well. I went on first with the children, as they could walk much faster than Elizabeth, and took them to the only house I knew in Sandford. . . . I left them . . . to get their clothes dried, and went off to find a vehicle, but none was to be had there. . . . Duckworth and I walked on to Iffley, whence we sent them a fly. We all had tea in my rooms about 8½, after which I took the children home, and we adjourned to Bayne's rooms for music and singing, "Adelaida," etc.

Robinson Duckworth, Fellow of Trinity College, was an early friend of Charles who later became Chaplain to the Queen and Canon of Westmin-

*Robinson Duckworth, the "Duck" in* Alice, *was present on the rowing party when Charles first told the Liddell sisters the story. Duckworth had a good singing voice and could help to entertain the children. It was he who suggested that Lewis Carroll ask John Tenniel to illustrate* Alice's Adventures in Wonderland.

ster. He was a man of great charm with a good singing voice. The rain that day probably inspired the pool of tears in *Alice.*

The river expeditions were special to all of them. Ina had already been on fourteen by 1862. Another favorite destination for a river picnic was upstream, at Godstow, and on July 4, the day after rain had forced the party to postpone a journey, Charles, Duckworth, and the three Liddell sisters set off for Godstow for one of their picnics, this one destined to make literary history. Here is Charles's diary entry:

> Duckworth and I made an expedition *up* the river to Godstow with the 3 Liddells: we had tea on the bank there, and did not reach Christ Church again till ½ past 8, when we took them on to my rooms to see my collection of micro-photographs,* and restored them to the Deanery, just before 9. [On February 10, 1863, Charles adds a note on the blank page opposite:] On which occasion I told them the fairy-tale of *Alice's Adventures Under Ground,* which I undertook to write out for Alice, and which is now finished. . . .

A quarter of a century later Charles reminisced about that day:

> Many a day had we rowed together on that quiet stream—the three little maidens and I—and many a fairy tale had been extemporised for their benefit—whether it were at times when the writer was "i' the

---

* Ingenious miniature versions of photographs he had taken and sometimes had set in tiny ivory telescope viewers which, when held up to the eye, reveal the photograph.

vein," and fancies unsought came crowding thick upon him, or at times when the jaded Muse was goaded into action, and plodded meekly on, more because she had to say something than that she had something to say—yet none of these many tales got written down: they lived and died, like summer midges, each in its own golden afternoon until there came a day when, as it chanced, one of my little listeners petitioned that the tale might be written out for her. That was many a year ago, but I distinctly remember, now as I write, how, in a desperate attempt to strike out some new line of fairy-lore, I had sent my heroine straight down a rabbit-hole, to begin with, without the least idea what was to happen afterwards. . . . In writing it out, I added many fresh ideas, which seemed to grow of themselves upon the original stock; and many more added themselves when, years afterwards, I wrote it all over again for publication. . . .

Full many a year has slipped away, since that "golden afternoon[27]" that gave thee birth, but I can call it up almost as clearly as if it were yesterday—the cloudless blue above, the watery mirror below, the boat drifting idly on its way, the tinkle of the drops that fell from the oars, as they waved so sleepily to and fro, and (the one bright gleam of life in all the slumberous scene) the three eager faces, hungry for news of fairy-land, and who would not be said "nay" to: from whose lips "Tell us a story, please," had all the stern immutability of Fate![28]

Alice herself added to the record of that exceptional adventure. Collingwood, when writing the life of his uncle, must have asked her to share her memory of the occasion and then published an excerpt from her reply:

Most of Mr. Dodgson's stories were told to us on river expeditions to Nuneham or Godstow. . . . My eldest sister . . . was "Prima," I was "Secunda," and "Tertia" was my sister Edith [Charles refers thus to the trio in the prefatory poem in *Alice*]. I believe the beginning of Alice was told one summer afternoon when the sun was so burning that we had landed in the meadows down [*sic*] the river, deserting the boat to take refuge in the only bit of shade to be found, which was under a new-made hayrick. Here from all three came the old petition of "Tell us a story," and so began the ever-delightful tale. Sometimes to tease us— and perhaps being really tired—Mr. Dodgson would stop suddenly and say, "And that's all till next time." "Ah, but it is next time," would be the exclamation from all three; and after some persuasion the story would start afresh. Another day, perhaps the story would begin in the boat, and Mr. Dodgson, in the middle of telling a thrilling adventure, would pretend to go fast asleep, to our great dismay.[29]

Thirty-four years after she sent this reminiscence to Collingwood, she again cast her mind back to that day:

> Nearly all of *Alice's Adventures Under Ground* was told on that blazing summer afternoon with the heat haze shimmering over the meadows where the party landed to shelter for a while in the shadow cast by the haycocks near Godstow. . . . I have such a distinct recollection of the expedition, and also, on the next day I started to pester him to write down the story for me, which I had never done before. It was due to my . . . importunity that, after saying he would think about it, he eventually gave the hesitating promise which started him writing it down at all.[30]

Robinson Duckworth also described that day for Collingwood:

> I rowed *stroke* and he rowed *bow* . . . , when the three Miss Liddells were our passengers, and the story was actually composed and spoken *over my shoulder* for the benefit of Alice Liddell, who was acting as "cox" of our gig. I remember turning round and saying, "Dodgson, is this an extempore romance of yours?" And he replied, "Yes, I'm inventing as we go along." I also well remember how, when we had conducted the three children back to the Deanery, Alice said, as she bade us goodnight, "Oh, Mr. Dodgson, I wish you would write out Alice's adventures for me." He said he would try, and he afterwards told me that he sat up nearly the whole night, committing to a MS. book his recollections of the drolleries with which he had enlivened the afternoon. He added illustrations of his own and presented the volume, which used often to be seen on the drawing-room table at the Deanery.[31]

More river picnics followed, more visits to the deanery, and, on August 6, another journey to Godstow when Charles "had to go on with my interminable fairy-tale of 'Alice's Adventures.' "

In early July Charles became editor of *College Rhymes* and remained so until the end of March 1863. During those nine months the review became more Oxonian than Cantabridgian and favored Christ Church contributions. He published some of his own work in the journal and cast his editorial net wide in an unsuccessful effort to attract literary giants like Keble, Charles Kingsley, Thackeray, and Tennyson.

Charles finished lecturing for the term, marked his papers, and turned in the results. On August 8 the Liddells went off to their holiday house in Wales, and Charles caught "a last sight of my young friends" in the two flies that sped them away. He lingered on in Oxford, traveled to Worcester, to London, and then finally, on September 9, to Croft.

When he returned a month later, the Liddells were already back in residence. Six days after he arrived, on October 17, out walking in the afternoon, he fell in "with Mrs. Liddell and the children, driving." Eleven days later he called on Mrs. Liddell to ask her permission for a local artist he had engaged to color his photographs of the children to call at the deanery "so as to get good likenesses." But Mrs. Liddell "simply evaded the question." Charles adds parenthetically: "I have been out of her good graces ever since Lord Newry's business."

Charles Francis Needham, Viscount Newry and Morne, a nineteen-year-old Christ Church undergraduate and purportedly a favorite of Mrs. Liddell, as eligible noblemen tended to be, was planning a Christ Church ball that would end after the college curfew. Charles discussed the problem with Newry, without resolution: "The two parties cannot agree on the rules and I am afraid much ill-feeling will result," he wrote (May 25). Mrs. Liddell saw Charles as one of the dons who refused to lift the curfew for the ball, and some ill feeling did ensue, though not between Charles and the Viscount. On June 25, when Charles took the Liddell party out on the river again, Lord Newry accompanied them, and on December 17, 1865, Newry called on Charles to see his photographs and confide in him about a play he had written.

Mrs. Liddell's displeasure, however, kept Charles away from the deanery. But by the twenty-first Mrs. Liddell's *froideur* had melted, as Charles jubilantly notes: "Was surprised by a message from Mrs. Liddell, asking whether the children should come over to me, or if I would go to them. No other alternative being offered, I chose the latter, and found that Alice and Edith had originated the idea. . . . I had a very pleasant 2 hours with them (Ina being in bed with a cold, and Mrs. Liddell did not appear)."

Charles's visits to the deanery resumed and continued in the New Year; after the Christmas vacation, he was there frequently and took the children with Miss Prickett to the University Museum and to the University Press to show them the printing equipment and the art collection belonging to

Thomas Combe, director of the Clarendon Press and Printer to Oxford University.

In early March Alice asked Charles to escort her on March 10 to see the Oxford illuminations. For days now, all of Oxford had been busily preparing a grand celebration for March 10, the wedding day of the Prince of Wales to Alexandra, Princess of Denmark. Oxford, and especially Christ Church, planned a grand display of visual delights and activities to demonstrate their pride at the royal connection and their loyalty and devotion. The city drew upon its ample resources and those of the surrounding towns and villages, and the various colleges competed with one another for variety and originality in decorations and festivities.

Charles's brother Edwin arrived on the day before the event and was on hand to assist. The day began bright and sunny. The town and colleges were all dressed up in their finery: flags, bunting, plumes, and feathers everywhere. A royal gun salute started the ceremonies, and all day long bands played, parades passed, and balloons were released. One of the high moments was a Christ Church enterprise: the three Liddell daughters each planted a memorial tree along the Cherwell and "delivered a short speech." Charles and Edwin escorted the Liddells to see an ox roasted whole near Worcester College, "which was *not* an exciting spectacle," Charles adds, and in the afternoon they attended the eight-oared Torpids race,* "for which we went on to the barge, and of course met the Liddells again."

Charles and Edwin dined in Hall, and as evening came on, the Oxford night sky yielded to the illuminations, bonfires, and fireworks. They made their way to the deanery to claim Alice, ready, eager, and waiting. Hand in hand they went, buffeted by the crowds, making the rounds of the principal streets for two hours. "The mob was dense," Charles tells us, "but well conducted, the fireworks abundant, and some of the illuminations very beautiful." Christ Church displayed three large stars, illuminated by twelve hundred gas jets, and a replica of Cardinal Wolsey's miter. Special lamps lighted the quadrangles, and on one side a transparency of the Prince of Wales's emblem and the initials of the bride and groom glowed. Most impressive was "a large, beautiful, revolving crown in variegated lamps, high up on the top of the Canterbury gate entrance to Christ Church."[32]

Charles made amusing comments as they went along, devised answers to every question, explanations for every gaseous display, and he shared in

---

* Hilary term boat race at Oxford.

every exclamation of his young charge. Emotions ran high, he sensible of the privilege of having this remarkable eleven-year-old, his favorite young friend, beside him, she excited by the celebration, content to be cared for by this adoring gentleman, her favorite adult friend. "It was delightful to see the thorough abandonment with which Alice enjoyed the whole thing," Charles writes, adding: "The Wedding-day of the Prince of Wales I mark with a white stone." Alice in later years remembered the evening as one of the great adventures of her young life, how she "clung tightly to the hand of the strong man on either side."[33]

So memorable was the occasion for Charles, the illuminated images so graven upon his mind, that he later transformed the excursion with Alice into art. At the very outset of *Looking-Glass,* Alice, sitting in the huge Victorian armchair winding up the tangled worsted into a ball, addresses the kitten sitting on her lap: "Do you know what to-morrow is, Kitty? . . . You'd have guessed if you'd been up in the window with me. . . . I was watching the boys getting in sticks for the bonfire—and it wants plenty of sticks, Kitty! . . . We'll go and see the bonfire to-morrow." And then Alice, who is forever playing "Let's pretend," recalls that only yesterday she had said to her sister: "Let's pretend we're kings and queens"; now Alice wants Kitty to pretend she's the Red Queen, and before we know it, Alice is telling Kitty all about Looking-Glass House and we are off on another great adventure.

The royal wedding set the stage for the tale; the chess figures that dominate the story are Alice's own memory pieces of that exciting celebration. The story is in fact royalty- and nobility-ridden, with two queens, a king, a white knight, royal messengers and soldiers, and even a lion and a unicorn who step out of the royal crest and become opponents in a futile battle for the crown, to which the King clings determinedly. If Charles was parodying the Whigs and the Tories, his joke was not lost on his young friend, and she recognized the dusty town with the old bridge and marketplace as Oxford, not London, and she could also identify his characters. The Red Queen, for instance, is surely an exaggerated "Pricks," the Liddell governess: she admonishes Alice on how to behave in the presence of royalty, and Charles himself, in his essay " 'Alice' on the Stage," describes the Red Queen as "the concentrated essence of all governesses." The story is laced with barely disguised incidents that Charles and the Liddell children shared and caricatures of persons they knew.

The celebration over, life returned to something like normal. But Charles's elation did not subside entirely. Three days after the festive day, he

*Broad Walk, Christ Church, taken by Charles. He strolled many times with the Liddell daughters through Christ Church Meadow and down the Broad Walk, an avenue of noble elms.*

encountered Alice, Edith, and Miss Prickett in the Broad Walk and spent "a very pleasant two hours' walking with them round the meadow." He also began "a poem . . . in which I mean to embody something about Alice (if I can at all please myself by any description of her) and which I mean to call 'Life's Pleasance' "—Pleasance being Alice's second name. "I gave up the name 'Alice,' " he adds, "as I want to print it in *College Rhymes* and have had a poem sent in with that name." But "Life's 'Pleasance' " did not appear in *College Rhymes* at all; instead he saved it to use as the dedicatory verse in *Looking-Glass*.

Charles often went to the Broad Walk to meet the Liddells. They frequently walked together; he raced with Ina "on the bridge over the reservoir," and on the twenty-fifth accompanied Alice, Edith, and Miss Prickett to the railway station "to see them off [to Cheltenham] and to get a few minutes more of the society of my little favourites." Later in the day he wrote Alice a long letter, enclosing for her and Ina "micro-photographs" of themselves.

On April 3 Charles received an invitation to lunch on the following Saturday at Hetton Lawn, where the children were staying. After lunch and an exuberant walk, the youngsters, back in their element of fun and games, probably urged Charles to remain. He did and the invitation to lunch ended up becoming a four-day visit.

Charles left to spend eight days visiting relations at Tenby, but on April

15 he returned to Cheltenham and, as before, put up at the Belle Vue. He wrote ahead proposing an expedition into the country, but when he found no reply waiting at the hotel, he assumed the children had already returned to Oxford and went over to Gloucester to attend the cathedral service. It turned out that the answer to Charles's note was sent to Tenby and missed him there. But all was not lost, for the 2:40 train brought the children and Miss Prickett to Gloucester, and Charles and the Liddells completed "a very merry journey . . . together" back to Oxford.

Later the train journey was transmuted into *Looking-Glass,* and another important element for the tale emerged from the visit to Charlton Kings: an enormous looking-glass sitting above the drawing-room fireplace at Hetton Lawn may have inspired the idea of climbing up to the mantelpiece and going through to the other side.

Back at Oxford, the usual pattern of river trips and long walks resumed. On the twenty-fifth he called to see Alice, laid up with a sprained leg. He remained with her and young Rhoda Liddell, a fourth sister born in 1858, for about an hour. "Alice was in an unusually disagreeable mood by no means improved by being an invalid," he notes, a sentence in his diary which a later family custodian sought unsuccessfully to obliterate.

"There is no variety in my life to record just now," he writes (April 29, 1863), "*except* meetings with the Liddells, the record of which has become almost continuous. I walked with them in the meadow this morning."

When Mrs. Liddell gave birth to another son and the baby grew gravely ill and died, Charles did what he could to help: to divert the children, he took them and Miss Prickett on another river journey to favored Nuneham. "A very pleasant day, to be marked with a white stone."

Even before this river journey, Charles, the Liddells, indeed much of Oxford, were preparing for a return visit by the Prince and Princess of Wales, fixed to coincide with the degree-awarding Encaenia. They would, of course, stay at the deanery, and excitement broke through the sadness clinging to the place.

Charles was marking end-of-term papers, but on the thirteenth he went over to the deanery in the afternoon to see the royal chamber, splendidly furnished. He also noticed a magnificent album (for *cartes de visite*), hired from a local stationer, and offered to fill it with his photographs. The offer accepted, he had "an hour or two of work in transferring the pictures. While I was there," he adds, "a note came from Ina (at the Bazaar in St. John's gardens) begging me to come and help them. Accordingly I went about 3 and worked till 7 putting up cards, arranging, etc."

The bazaar was arranged to honor the royal visit, and the proceeds went toward building a new Radcliffe Infirmary. All major Oxford families mounted stalls, and the Liddells' was as grand as it ought to have been. Mrs. Liddell gathered together items to be sold, the children helped arrange the offerings.

The great day dawned, and once more Oxford was festooned with bunting, flowers, and many decorations, while bands and tintinnabulating bells filled the air. Defying heavy clouds and rain, city and university dignitaries welcomed the royal couple in a ceremony on Magdalen Bridge. The procession then moved down High Street to St. Aldate's and Tom Gate. At 12:45 the gates swung open and the royal carriage entered Tom Quad. The band played the national anthem, the onlookers cheered, the royal couple left the carriage on the East Terrace to see the Volunteers present arms. Under an awning and on a red carpet stood Dean and Mrs. Liddell, the Canons of Christ Church, and the Liddell children. The Princess took the

*The visit of the Prince and Princess of Wales to Christ Church, June 16, 1863. Charles watched the ceremony welcoming the royal couple through his telescope. He could also see Alice and her sisters on the dais.*

Dean's arm and the royal pair were led under umbrellas through the rain to their quarters.

Charles observed the "lovely day" from Bayne's rooms, where he had brought his telescope and "for the accommodation of which . . . [T. Vere Bayne, Charles's childhood friend and student at Christ Church] broke out a pane of one window. . . . We managed to see them wonderfully well. . . ." After lunch Charles went to the bazaar and made himself useful to the Liddells.

> After I had helped in their stall a short time the Royal party arrived. There were very few admitted with them and the place was comparatively clear: I crept under the counter and joined the children outside, and the Prince (I don't know whether he knew me) bowed and made a remark about a picture. The children are selling some white kittens . . . and as Alice did not dare offer hers to the Princess, I volunteered to plead for her, and asked the Prince if the Princess would not like a kitten—on which she turned round and said to me, "Oh, but I've bought one of those kittens already" (which I record as the only remark *she* is likely ever to make to me). Ina's had been the favoured one. For some while I went about with the children, trying to get their kittens sold, when suddenly the Bazaar opened, and the place filled with a dense mob. Rhoda was missing, and I set out to hunt her up, with Edith . . . and after some time spied her out in a stall: I begged them to hand her over to me, and, carrying her, and pushing Edith, I fought my way down the whole Bazaar, through a tremendous crush, back to their stall. I remained there all the afternoon, sometimes behind the counter.

The banquet honoring the Prince and Princess took place that evening in Hall, "gorgeously done," according to Charles, "with a large collection of grandees and many ladies, music (much too loud) during dinner, and singing by the Orpheus Club after the healths. . . . A day to be remembered as unique and most interesting."

The following day the Prince received an honorary doctorate of civil law, but Charles skipped the ceremony; instead he went again to the bazaar, this time finding it nearly empty. He could not cover all the festive events but attended "a very successful" collation at All Souls and observed the departure of the royal party on the eighteenth in a procession to the railway station with cheering crowds lining the way.

These extraordinary happenings—the celebration of the royal wedding in early March and the royal visit in mid-June—intertwined as they were for Charles with the Liddell children, afforded him pleasures verging on ecstasy. When he came to invent the two books that would make him famous and live for posterity, he worked these memories ingeniously into his tales. The river expeditions, the walks, the croquet games, the long deanery visits, and most particularly the two royal occasions—all presented Charles with the raw material for the *Alice* books. He had provided and witnessed the stimuli that excited the children; he wanted to reawaken that excitement with his stories. Although Charles had already invented the tale of *Alice* and was writing it out in its earliest draft, the story would grow to twice its size before he finished it. As for *Looking-Glass,* many of the events that inspired the tale were just then occurring in 1863; they would germinate for years before Charles produced his sequel.

Charles continued working with his camera after the royal visit and on the twenty-third photographed the royal bedstead at the deanery, the deanery itself, and the cathedral. For the latter, "Ina and Alice sat in the window of the Royal chamber and have come out very well in the picture." In the evening Charles "went with the three children and Miss Prickett to Sanger's Circus, returning in the carriage." On the following day Charles fell in with the Liddells at the Great Volunteer Review in Port Meadow and saw them "safe off." On the twenty-fifth of June, at about ten in the morning,

> Alice and Edith came over to my rooms to fetch me over to arrange about an expedition to Nuneham. It ended in our going down at 3, a party of ten, the Dean and Mrs. Liddell and the Dean's father, the 3 children and Rhoda, Harcourt, Lord Newry and myself: we took a 4-oar, and the last 3 rowed all the way, the others taking it in turns to man the stroke-oar. We had tea under the trees at Nuneham, after which the rest drove home in the carriage . . . while Ina, Alice, Edith, and I (*mirabile dictu!*) walked down to [the] . . . station, and so home by railway: a pleasant expedition with a very pleasant conclusion.

Charles's pleasure in this railway journey home must have been thrilling indeed: perhaps for the first and only time, he had the children alone to himself, without either a parent or Miss Prickett present. Days good for photography continued, and on the twenty-seventh, Saturday, he wrote to Mrs. Liddell urging her to send the children over to have their pictures taken.

\* \* \*

For June 27, 28, and 29, no record appears in the diary. Charles often skipped a short period, but this omission is unique. He accounted for those days, but the page on which he wrote was later cut out. In fact, by her own admission many years later, Charles's niece Menella Dodgson owned to having cut some pages from the diary, and this page was evidently one of them. It contained information that offended her sensibilities, and she took a razor to it.

That the page recorded a crisis in Charles's relations with the deanery is certain. Something occurred during those three days that caused a break in the relationship, something that exiled Charles and cut him off from the children. No more visits follow, no outings, no photography, no croquet games, no more walks together. And for more than five months afterward, not a single mention of a Liddell appears in Charles's diary. The next reference to them (December 2) is not of a happy reunion. On that day Charles attended a Christ Church theatrical and noticed Mrs. Liddell and the children: "But I held aloof from them," he wrote, "as I have done all this term."

What could have happened to cut the cord? One thing is clear: it was something that Charles himself confronted and recorded straightway, but something that his prim niece could not bear to let stand.

No conclusive evidence exists about the rupture. Given the frequent, almost daily, visits that Charles and the children shared for so long before it, Mrs. Liddell obviously overcame her early objections. Perhaps the parents decided that the advantages of the connection outweighed any possible difficulty. The children were so fond of their Mr. Dodgson, reaped such joy and comfort from their meetings with him, it would have been cruel to deny them his friendship. But the parents may have detected or imagined a new and serious danger on the occasions marked by the missing page. They must have discussed whatever it was that troubled them and decided rationally on a break with Charles out of a deep desire to protect their young.

We can dismiss the notion that Mrs. Liddell's displeasure over the "Lord Newry affair" was involved: that is totally unrealistic, for Charles's relations with the aristocrat were amiable throughout. Equally unrealistic is the idea that the Dean and Charles fell out over academic politics. Although the Dean was wedded to change and Charles opposed, no acrimony arose between them this early. Indeed as late as December 2, 1896, Charles referred to the Dean as "my dear friend."

Some speculate that Charles, aged thirty-one, "proposed marriage" to Alice, aged eleven. Oxford gossip had it so. Margaret Woods, daughter of Charles's friend George Granville Bradley, sometime Master of Marlborough, wrote: "When the Alice of his tale had grown into a lovely girl, he asked, in old-world fashion, her father's permission to pay his addresses to her."[34] Mrs. Woods was, however, reporting gossip, without any real evidence. But Lord Salisbury wrote Lady John Manners (August 25, 1878): "They say that Dodgson has half gone out of his mind in consequence of having been refused by the real Alice (Liddell). It looks like it."[35] Now, Lord Salisbury was an archenemy of gossip and speculations about people's private lives. For him to be so forthright argues that he had something more than gossip to go on, but what revived his conjecture more than a decade after Charles's break with the Liddells remains a mystery.

The fact that Alice is Charles's "ideal child friend,"[36] that she sparked his creative energy, that he devoted so much of his time to her and fashioned his two remarkable fantasies with her as heroine is proof enough of a deep attachment, certain affection, even a kind of love. That he might desire a holy union with her is understandable. An entry in the diaries concerning Charles's brother Wilfred, long withheld from view, supports this notion.

At age twenty-seven, Wilfred fell in love with fourteen-year-old Alice Jane Donkin. On October 7, 1865, over two years after the events recorded on the missing diary page, Charles wrote Wilfred "a long letter on the subject of Alice Donkin, as things are not on a satisfactory footing at present," and urged on him the wisdom of keeping away from Barmby Moor [where the Donkins lived] for a couple of years."

A year later (October 17, 1866), Charles reported dining twice with his mentor-uncle Skeffington Lutwidge, "and on each occasion we had a good deal of conversation about Wilfred, and about A.L. It is a very anxious subject." The two brothers, both in their prime, were attached to two teenage youngsters named Alice. In the end, Wilfred may have taken his elder brother's advice: he did not marry Alice Donkin for another six years, when he was better situated financially and Alice more mature.

But Charles made no such alliance with "A.L.," not necessarily, however, for want of trying. The question remains: did Charles propose marriage to Alice and cause the rift?

He would certainly not have proposed to Alice directly or even asked her parents for her hand then and there. That simply was not done. However insensitive he was or appeared to be in some matters, he was well trained and responsive to Victorian conventions. Besides, he was extraordinarily intelligent, rational, and reasonable. The most he would have undertaken would have been to suggest that perhaps, in the future, if her affection for him did not diminish, he would be happy to propose an alliance.

As for the twenty-year difference in their ages, May-September marriages were common in Victorian Britain. It took men longer to establish themselves financially and professionally than it does today, and upper-class parents desperately wanted their daughters to marry men of wealth as well as position. If Charles and Wilfred required examples of marriages of older men and young brides, they could have found them easily. In 1848 Ruskin, aged twenty-nine, married Effie Gray, ten years his junior. True, ten years is not twenty. But the age of legal capacity to marry in Britain at the time was twelve for females. The 1861 census shows that in Bolton 175 women married at the age of fifteen or under, in Burnley 179.[37] By her own confession, Henrietta Mary Ada Ward (later a painter of the royal family) fell in love with the artist Edward Matthew Ward when she was ten or eleven and married him at sixteen.[38] The future archbishop E. W. Benson, aged twenty-four, approached the parents of Mary Sidgwick, aged twelve, about marrying her, and they did marry when she was eighteen.[39]

But Charles needed to look no further than the deanery to find an example of a successful marriage between an older man and a younger woman, for when the Dean courted Lorina Reeve, she was nineteen, he thirty-four, and, by his own confession, his hair was already "falling off and going grey."[40] The age gap between Charles and Alice was five years wider, but that in itself would not have troubled Victorian parents.

We must remember that marital bliss and regal pomp were much in the air in 1863. Talk of the royal couple and their visit must have lingered in the deanery for some time. Marriage for her superior daughters was certainly on Mrs. Liddell's mind. And marriage would have been on the girls' minds as well, especially with Lorina now fourteen. Mrs. Liddell was most particular about the candidates for her daughters' hands, and perhaps in the midst of all this thought and talk of royal marriage, the girls suddenly began to talk openly about themselves and marriage. "Whom would you like to marry?" would have been a likely question one might have asked another, even in their parents' presence. And Alice might have impetuously piped up: "I'm going to marry Mr. Dodgson." And if Charles were present, perhaps taking it as a teasing remark, or not, he might have picked up the thread and replied: "Well said, and why not!"

Ah, teasing. That might have had much to do with the case. Young females can bat their eyes, shake their heads, toss their locks about, feign innocence, and make outrageous suggestions—all with the intent to shock and call attention to themselves. And the three clever Liddell sisters were probably expert in these arts.

Charles too would have been capable of asking the question, seemingly in jest, when they were discussing the royals: "And do you want to marry a Prince when you grow up?" And the answer might have been, "No, I want to marry you." And if Charles seemed to welcome the idea, he may well have set off alarms in the parents' minds. There would have been no explosion, no immediate crisis, no finger pointing to the deanery door. The Dean would have seen Charles privately and told him, in the most gentlemanly way, that, for the present at least, he must avoid the children.

A letter that Alice's son Caryl wrote in 1951 to Menella Dodgson, Charles's niece, confronts what he calls the "coolness" that evolved between Charles and the Liddells. He writes that his grandmother was wont to keep a "strict eye" on her daughters' male friends and "shooed" many of them away. He insists, however, that Mrs. Liddell did not "hate" Charles.[41] But perhaps Alice herself gives something away when, toward the end of her life, she recalls, through her amanuensis-son Caryl, that "nobody then expected that this shy . . . tutor . . . would in years to come be known all over the civilized world."[42] Mrs. Liddell expected nothing of him and clearly did not always welcome Charles's close and constant attentions to her daughters.

In a letter that Ina wrote Alice in old age (May 2, 1930), she asks her whether she remembers when Mr. Dodgson ceased coming to the deanery. Florence Becker Lennon, writing her book on Charles,[43] had asked her that. "I said his manner became too affectionate to you as you grew older and that mother spoke to him about it, and that offended him so he ceased coming to visit us again—as one had to find some reason for all intercourse ceasing. . . . Mr. D. used to take you on his knee. . . . I did *not* say that!"[44]

Caryl Hargreaves may not have known all the facts, and Ina, by her own admission, was withholding some. With the critical page missing from the diary, we cannot know what happened at that crucial time. Certainly Charles somehow offended and was exiled.

A confession that Charles made, in an aside, may bear on the case. Long after Alice married and the infrequent exchanges between him and the deanery had assumed a formal cordiality, he wrote Mrs. Liddell (November 19, 1891) to thank her for arranging that the Duchess of Albany and her children should call on him, and he asked if he might have a visit from the two youngest Liddell daughters, Rhoda and Violet, adding: "If I were 20 years younger, I should not, I think, be bold enough to give such invitations: but, but, I am close on 60 years old now: and all romantic sentiment has quite died out of my life: so I have become quite hardened as to having lady-visitors of *any* age!" The remark may not refer to his relationship with Alice, but if "romantic sentiment" had not played a role in the break that occurred in the 1860s between Charles and the Liddells, one may argue, he need hardly have mentioned it. It must have been small consolation for him to entertain the two younger Liddells, now fully grown young ladies, when they came, but he surely realized at that age that only small consolations were left to him.

# CHAPTER FOUR

# The Child

*Columbus only discovered America; I have discovered the child.*

VICTOR HUGO

Wherever we look in Charles's works, his diaries, his letters, we find involvement with the child, an overwhelming fascination with what he himself calls "child nature." "Any one that has ever loved one true child," he writes in the preface to *Alice's Adventures Under Ground*, "will have known the awe that falls on one in the presence of a spirit fresh from God's hands, on whom no shadow of sin . . . has yet fallen."

Some see Charles's devotion to the child as an obsession, a manifestation of some inadequacy, a maladjustment, even a perversion. Others who have sought to understand his intense attraction by using what they term "analysis" have often promulgated warped fantasies of their own. Until we have better tools for exploring a dead author's impulses and motives, we are on sounder ground by looking for the roots of Charles's attachment to the child in the domestic, social, and cultural forces that shaped him.

Growing up at Daresbury and Croft, Charles was surrounded by children. As the eldest brother, he had responsibilities which he willingly assumed and fulfilled. He not only created theatricals, games, a garden railway, charades, and family magazines to edify and amuse his brothers and sisters, but also monitored their behavior, their manners, their moral fiber. In fact, as a surrogate parent, he helped rear them.

When the Dodgsons came to Croft and Charles's father, dismayed by the lack of a proper school there, immediately set about building one, to "train up the Children in Christian Knowledge,"[1] the young and impressionable Charles very likely lent a hand. Some fifty to sixty children came to the school and swarmed about the Dodgson enclave. Charles was thirteen when the school opened, and he entered the classroom as a teacher in July 1855, when he was twenty-three.

Almost all his juvenilia were designed for his brothers and sisters. Ever in the company of children as he grew, he became accustomed not only to their presence but also to their childish ways. He noticed how their minds and hearts were moved naturally, spontaneously. In time, perhaps through a combination of biological, spiritual, and psychological forces, this interest developed into a need, an essential component of his own happiness. Given this domestic background, Charles as a young adult at Oxford paid particular notice to his colleagues' children and to the children of all the families he encountered there, on visits to London and elsewhere.

Charles's upbringing at Croft and the larger social setting in which his family lived and moved were surely factors in his attachment to children, but other forces exerted their influence too. He was a serious reader, and some of the books he read helped shape his personality, his character, his faith. Next to the Bible and Shakespeare, Charles was devoted to the writings of Blake, Wordsworth, Coleridge, Dickens, and Tennyson—all Romantics and all variously commentators on the nature of the child and the child's place in the universe. Indeed, except for Tennyson, they all dwell extensively on the whys and wherefores of the child or childhood. Their works, the literature that Charles grew up with, proved a bond with other hearts and minds, nurtured and acclaimed his particular brand of love, and gave him the courage to recognize his inner needs and to cultivate unusual friendships; their works helped him justify himself to himself.

The child was a central subject of literature long before Blake. In the seventeenth century, the works of Traherne, Vaughan, Prior, and Vanbrugh took the child as subject. The early eighteenth century saw an increase of interest in childhood, in the works of Thomson, Gray, Cowper, and Scott. But these early outpourings centered mostly on the poet's own self and expressed nostalgia for a lost childhood. They did not address the phenomenon of childhood itself, or, as it later becomes, the nature and mystery of the untutored child.

Rousseau was the first to train his lens outward to explore the idea of the child, to capture the delicate texture of childhood. He exploded the belief that the child is an adult in miniature, that childhood is a condition to be passed through as quickly as possible. He rejected outright the Calvinist principle of original sin and replaced it with the notion of inborn divinity. The child, for Rousseau, was a primitive in the grandest sense, unblemished and noble, uncorrupted and pure. He argued against rooting out and destroying the devil in the child, against training the child away from his natural state, and sought to instill respect for these virginal beings as such and yearned to encourage their natural growth; he wanted children to develop with a minimum of interference. His novel *Emile,* published in translation in England in 1763, proved an instant success and became one of the strongest forces in the movement away from eighteenth-century Reason to nineteenth-century Feeling.

Blake later wed the primitive nobility that Rousseau saw in the child to the angelic simplicity inspired by Christ's injunction that those who seek the kingdom of heaven must "become as little children." Blake went even further, enveloping this ideal being in a cloud of mystic beauty. He did not indulge in personal nostalgia; like Rousseau, he addressed the condition of childhood and found in it a vision that moved him to reverence. In the child he saw flashes of divinity, the messenger come from above who brings with him or her intimations of paradise. For Blake, the child was both deceptively simple and intricately complex.

Charles's view of childhood is Blakean; he too revered the mystic combination of the primitive and the pure, the noble, and the divine. These innocents possessed a charm he could not resist. He yearned for their favor and friendship; they, more than any other force, fired his imagination, and he found, like Blake, that they saw into the heart of complex truths more clearly and perceptively than weary adults. Charles would have agreed with Blake when he wrote: "I am happy to find a Great Majority of Fellow Mortals who can Elucidate My Visions, and Particularly they have been Elucidated by Children, who have taken a greater delight in contemplating my Pictures than I even hoped. Neither Youth nor Childhood is Folly or Incapacity."[2]

W. M. Rossetti's description of Blake suits Charles perfectly: "gentle and affectionate, loving to be with little children, and to talk about them."[3] Peter Coveney also wrote about Blake in words that apply to Charles: "For Blake children were no occasional interest, no vehicle for a mere personal nostalgia. They were for him a symbol of innocence, without which, as a religious artist, he could not have worked."[4]

Charles may have read Rousseau. He certainly uses the Romantic com-

monplace "children of nature" derived from Rousseau.⁵ He definitely read
Blake, probably from his school days on, perhaps even earlier. He owned
Blake's works and Alexander Gilchrist's magisterial life of Blake. At Oxford,
in 1863, he commissioned Thomas Combe to print for him on large paper
some of Blake's *Songs of Innocence.* He presumably had a quantity of copies
struck, perhaps to give to child friends. Whatever his intent, his admiration
for the poems is clear. Many years later (November 11, 1896), he asks a young
friend, Dorothy Joy Poole, if she can identify some lines of modern poetry
and quotes Blake's "Infant Joy":

> What shall I call thee?
>   "I happy am—
> Joy is my name."
> Sweet Joy befall thee!

One need only look into Charles's work to see that Blake colored his creative strain. His poem "Stolen Waters" ends with a sinner finding salvation
when he hears "a clear voice" celebrating infant joy:

> "A rosy child,
> Sitting and singing, in a garden fair,
>     The joy of hearing, seeing,
>     The simple joy of being—
> Or twining rosebuds in the golden hair
>     That ripples free and wild. . . ."

The message the sinner hears is:

> "Be as a child—
> So shalt thou sing for very joy of breath—
>     So shalt thou wait thy dying,
>     In holy transport lying—
> So pass rejoicing through the gate of death,
>     In garment undefiled."

Some of Charles's words and ideas are Blake's: the divinely linked angel-
child, the marriage of song and joy, song and innocence. Charles cloaked the
verse in Victorian sentiment, but, sentiment aside, he inherited from his literary models the idea that a child can teach an adult repentance and the way
to salvation.

Blake's words and images occur repeatedly in Charles's work. The world of nature, abounding with beasts and flowers, is there, and into this natural setting the untrammeled child descends from heaven to the accompanying chorus of birds, in the brilliant radiance of the sun, watched over by angels. The child, whose intuitions, dreams, and visions suggest eternal truths, is often the center of the verse, whether found in a cradle, at its mother's breast, running free, awake or asleep.

Blake's "Night" is a reverent rendering of the setting sun and the mysterious moment when angels descend to watch over God's creatures. The speaker bids farewell to the green fields

> Where flocks have ta'en delight.
> Where lambs have nibbled, silent move
> The feet of angels bright. . . .

Charles's "Acrostic" to Agnes Hull finds the speaker at his "lonely hearth," where among shadows "ghostlike"

> Now here, now there, a childish sprite,
> Earthborn and yet as angel bright,
> Seems near me. . . .

And in Charles's "A Song of Love," the speaker asks:

> . . . whose is the skill . . .
> That flecks the green meadow with sunshine and shadow,
> Till the little lambs leap with delight?

Then, in Charles's "The Valley of the Shadow of Death," his line "My guardian-angel seemed to stand" could very well be a remembrance of Blake's "O'er my angel-guarded bed" in his poem "A Dream." At the close of Charles's poem, he seeks to confirm Blake's notion of guardian angels:

> . . . if there be—O if there be
> A truth in what they say,
> That angel-forms we cannot see
> Go with us on our way. . . .

Charles insists that Love is the secret of life, a notion not far from Blake's view that

> . . . we are put on earth a little space
> That we may learn to bear the beams of love.

The first line in Charles's verse to Rachel Daniel echoes the opening lines of Blake's "The Tiger":

> What hand may wreathe thy natal crown
>> O tiny tender Spirit-blossom,
> That out of Heaven hast fluttered down
>> Into this Earth's cold bosom?

The verse does not ponder the mysterious origin of the fierce tiger, but it strikes again the theme of welcoming a child, a "pure and perfect Maiden," to this "sin-begrimed and sorrow-laden" earth. When, toward the end of the poem, Charles asks

> What human loves and human woes
> Would dim the radiance of thy glory. . . .

we hear Blake's oft-repeated theme as well as his description of the charity children in St. Paul's Cathedral in "Holy Thursday":

> Seated in companies they sit, with radiance all their own.

In the same poem, Charles adds:

> Only the Lark such music knows
> As fits thy stainless story

—recalling the skylark that sings in the first stanza of Blake's "Schoolboy."

In "Beatrice," inspired by a new acquaintance, five-year-old Beatrice Ellison, Charles again worships heaven-sent innocence and the miracle of that innocence in taming the wildest of beasts:

> In her eyes is the living light
>> Of a wanderer to earth
> From a far celestial height:
>> Summers five are all the span—
>> Summers five since Time began
> To veil in mists of human night
>> A shining angel-birth.
>
> Does an angel look from her eyes?
>> Will she suddenly spring away,
> And soar to her home in the skies?

. . . . . . .

> For I think, if a grim wild beast
>   Were to come from his charnel-cave,
> From his jungle-home in the East—
>   Stealthily creeping with bated breath,
>   Stealthily creeping with eyes of death—
> He would all forget his dream of the feast,
>   And crouch at her feet a slave.

For both Blake and Charles, the child is the measure of all good, and the child's intrinsic qualities show how mankind has moved away from eternal values. For both, the child points up the man-made evils in the world and beckons the worn and tarnished sinner to repent and worship at the shrine of child innocence.

Blake's visions and dreams also adumbrate some of Charles's. In Charles's "Stolen Waters," the speaker hears a "clear voice," evidently divine, that brings salvation. The verse is dreamlike, as in so many of Charles's serious poems, and Charles's belief that love "makes the world go round" carries with it the contrapuntal notion that life is but a dream.

Charles's *An Easter Greeting to Every Child Who Loves "Alice,"* a printed letter to what he hoped would be a large audience of children, adapts Blakean ideas to Victorian sensibilities. He addresses his child readers directly: "Do you think . . . [God] cares to see only kneeling figures, and to hear only tones of prayer—and that He does not also love to see the lambs leaping in the sunlight, and to hear the merry voices of the children, as they roll among the hay? Surely their innocent laughter is as sweet in His ears as the grandest anthem that ever rolled up from the 'dim religious light' of some solemn cathedral?" Earlier in the *Easter Greeting,* Charles pictures the child waking to a summer morning "with the twitter of birds in the air," which could be an echo of Blake's "The Schoolboy," who confesses:

> I love to rise on a summer morn,
>   When birds are singing on every tree. . . .

The *Easter Greeting* seeks to dispel the child's fear of death and suggests that the child think of death as "that great morning when the 'Sun of Righteousness shall arise with healing in his wings,' " when the child will see "a brighter dawn than this—when lovelier sights will meet your eyes than any waving trees or rippling waters—when angel-hands shall undraw your cur-

tains, and sweeter tones than ever loving Mother breathed shall wake you to
a new and glorious day—and when all the sadness, and the sin, that darkened life on this little earth, shall be forgotten like the dreams of a night that
is past!"[6]

We have here a living mother and a happy child. Elsewhere in Charles's
poetry, he paints a child clutching at a mother's breast. The image is possibly a metaphor for his own attachment to his mother mingled with Victorian sentiment, but its literary ancestor may very well be Blake's "Infant
Sorrow," where the newborn child, having leapt into "the dangerous world,"
thinks it best to "sulk upon my mother's breast."

Dripping as Charles's words and phrases do with Victorian treacle, comparing them with Blake's evocative simplicities is almost irreverent; but the
quality of the verse is beside the point. Charles learns from, agrees with, admires, and echoes Blake; and we understand Charles better by recognizing
as much. Like Blake, he refused to moralize childhood, he revered it in all
its manifestations.

Beyond the question of literary influence, Blake's work probably affected
the tenor of Charles's faith. Some of Blake's anticlerical poetry doubtless
strengthened Charles's discontent with conventional High Church Angli-
canism. In Blake's "The Chimney Sweeper," for instance, the child's stern
Calvinist parents deplore his natural happiness, dress him "in the clothes of
death," teach him "to sing the notes of woe." They themselves go off to
church to pray,

> . . . to praise God and his priest and king,
> Who make up a heaven of our misery.

In Blake's "The Little Vagabond," the child cries out: "Dear mother, dear
mother, the Church is cold," and says that he fares better in the "healthy, and
pleasant, and warm" alehouse, adding the unorthodox notion that if the
Church would give its parishioners some ale and build a pleasant fire, all
would gladly go to church and listen to the parsons, who "with wind like a
blown bladder swell," and God would have no further quarrel with the
Devil. In "A Little Boy Lost," Blake condemns the priest who sends the
child to burn at the stake for uttering simple, instinctive truths.

Charles also rebukes the Church and its ministers for being too rigid, too
dogmatic, and certainly too parochial. Both Blake and Dodgson reach beyond Anglican and Catholic dogmas to embrace all humanity. "It will not
matter in the *least*," Charles wrote (July 7, 1885) to the mother of two child

friends, ". . . what form of religion a man has professed. . . . Many who have never even *heard* of Christ, will in . . . [the last day] find themselves saved by His blood." In "The Divine Image," Blake teaches humanitarianism:

> And all must love the human form,
> In heathen, Turk, or Jew.
> Where Mercy, Love, and Pity dwell,
> There God is dwelling too.

Charles's occasional comments on social issues also have something in common with Blake's. His poem "The Deserted Parks" (1867), modeled on Goldsmith's "The Deserted Village," deplores the effect that turning the Oxford University Parks into cricket grounds would have upon the poor, the young, and especially the children:

> How often have I paused on every charm,
> The rustic couple walking arm in arm—
> The groups of trees, with seats beneath the shade
> For prattling babes and whisp'ring lovers made—
> The never-failing brawl, the busy mill
> Where tiny urchins vied in fistic skill—
>
> . . . . . . .
>
> These round thy walks their cheerful influence shed;
> These were thy charms—but all these charms are fled.
>
> . . . . . . .
>
> And trembling, shrinking from the fatal blow,
> Far, far away thy hapless children go.

Much earlier (January 7, 1856), when Charles read Charles Kingsley's *Alton Locke,* he observed that "it tells the tale well of the privations and miseries of the poor, but I wish he would propose some more definite remedy, and especially that he would tell us what he wishes to substitute for the iniquitous 'sweating' system in tailoring and other trades. . . . If the book were but a little more definite, it might stir up many fellow-workers in the same good field of social improvement. Oh that God, in His good providence, may make me hereafter such a worker!"

When Charles went twice (January 6 and 11, 1883) to the Royal Academy exhibit of D. G. Rossetti's paintings, he described *Found* as "one of the most marvellous things I have seen done in painting." It is one of those sentimental Victorian story pictures, "of a man," as Charles puts it, "finding, in the streets of London, a girl he had loved years before in the days of her innocence. She is huddled up against the wall, dressed in gaudy colors . . . trying to turn away her agonized face, while he, holding her wrists, is looking down with an expression of pain and pity, condemnation and love. . . ." The girl is a "fallen" creature, and Charles must have realized that Rossetti's mistress had posed for it. It is not a particularly good work of art, not representative really of Rossetti's style, and remained unfinished at his death. What attracted Charles to the painting? Was his social conscience pricked by the scene? Was he angry at the way the world corrupts innocence? Or did the painting evoke in him a missionary call? Perhaps all three; in any case, his response was not far from Blake's when the earlier poet saw social deprivation. Charles lacked an imaginative, innovative vision on social issues, but he was concerned about the oppressed and the less fortunate.

The world Charles entered as an adult was full of confused and battling forces, torn and driven in conflicting and bewildering directions, defined by rational sciences that clashed with intuitive faith. Confronting greed and chaos, Charles chose not so much to join in the struggle to sort matters out as to retreat to the past, to the inspirational words of visionaries like Blake. He clung to the simple affections of childhood, refusing to trade them in for the duplicities of Victorian adulthood, while he struggled against what, in his poem "Solitude," he terms the "slow result of Life's decay." Blake suited Charles superbly and gave him the strength and courage to pronounce the child the highest form of life on earth and to render friendship with children his principal purpose and mainstay, to let the child spark his creative powers, to see the child as the main audience for his tales.

It comes as no surprise that Wordsworth, "the poet of childhood" who "depicts the moods and activities of children more extensively" than any earlier writer,[7] would be another favorite. Charles knew and quoted from his work. As early as March 13, 1855, when Charles resolved to read "whole poets," he placed Coleridge and Wordsworth on his list. In May 1881 he suggested that his publisher, Alexander Macmillan, include Wordsworth in the Globe Series of authors. "You never made a more judicious present than when you gave me your Golden Treasury Wordsworth," Charles wrote Macmillan (August 22, 1886). Charles's library contained a good many earlier volumes of Wordsworth's poetry, he gave anthologies of Wordsworth's poems as gifts to child friends, and he knowledgeably recommended Matthew Arnold's selection of Wordsworth's poems (1879) as best. Even if

Wordsworth believed Blake to be an "insane genius" and Blake considered Wordsworth to be a "pagan,"[8] Wordsworth sometimes echoes Blake. In addition to that famous pronouncement "The Child is father of the Man," Wordsworth confides, in book 2 of *The Prelude*, how he treasures the memory of childhood enchantment. Occasionally his thoughts are similar to Blake's, as, for instance, in book 5:

> Our childhood sits,
> Our simple childhood, sits upon a throne
> That hath more power than all the elements.
> I guess not what this tells of Being past,
> Nor what it augurs of the life to come;
> But so it is, and, in that dubious hour,
> That twilight when we first begin to see
> This dawning earth, to recognise, expect,
> And in the long probation that ensues,
> The time of trial, ere we learn to live
> In reconcilement with our stinted powers. . . .

and in book 12:

> Oh! mystery of man, from what a depth
> Proceed thy honours. I am lost, but see
> In simple childhood something of the base
> On which thy greatness stands.

Wordsworth looks inward and writes about himself, but from his own life he generalizes about all life. He too idealizes childhood, sees it as ennobling, venerates and deifies it even, and he seeks to capture the subtle sensations one experiences as one passes through the stages from childhood to maturity. He insists that we all possess an essential divinity because he recalls the intimations of immortality of his own childhood, and when he dwells on the quality of childhood, Charles would find him speaking for his own feelings. Picture Charles reading these lines from Wordsworth's famous "Ode: Intimations of Immortality from Recollections of Early Childhood," that moving celebration of the child:

> Our birth is but a sleep and a forgetting:
> The Soul that rises with us, our life's Star,
> Hath had elsewhere its setting,

And cometh from afar:
Not in entire forgetfulness,
And not in utter nakedness,
But trailing clouds of glory do we come
From God, who is our home:
Heaven lies about us in our infancy!
Shades of the prison-house begin to close
Upon the growing Boy. . . .

Wordsworth's child feels most at home in a natural setting. The child communes easily with birds and beasts and finds an easy relationship with flower, bush, and tree. Society draws the child, as he or she grows, away from nature, dulls the child's perceptions and instincts, and imposes a restricting rationality upon him or her. Even to the grown adult, nature is still a source of consolation and comfort, as Wordsworth assures us in "Lines Composed a Few Miles above Tintern Abbey":

. . . well pleased to recognise
In nature and the language of the sense
The anchor of my purest thoughts, the nurse,
The guide, the guardian of my heart, and soul
Of all my moral being.

In "Solitude," Charles, aged twenty-one, also celebrates the magical qualities of nature. Has he been reading Wordsworth, one wonders, in whose poetry the words *solitude* and *solitary* appear more than two hundred times, or Coleridge's long poem "Fears in Solitude"? In any case, the poem overflows with echoes of Blake, Wordsworth, Coleridge, and, in its feigned weariness, Tennyson's disillusioned hero of "Locksley Hall." The message is simple: the speaker flees society to commune with nature, where he can wax nostalgic for his lost childhood.

In both Blake and Wordsworth, the child is a mystical creature, flesh and blood limned with divine spirit, visible but intimating the invisible, possessed of an energy that cannot rationally emerge from such tiny, immature vessels, born with intuitive good sense, even with wisdom.

Charles's child also enjoys this immortal energy, this sacred, intuitive force that is related to energy in nature. In his *Easter Greeting*, Charles sees his child reader as feeling "life in every limb" and by intuition "eager to rush out into the fresh morning air." Thirteen years later, in his public letter

"Stage Children," Charles, quoting from Wordsworth's "We Are Seven," characterizes the child's life on the stage as "natural and rewarding."

Like Wordsworth, Coleridge looks inward for meaning, and, like Blake and Wordsworth, sees the child as possessing the clear, unobstructed intuitive spark. The child is supernatural. Observing the child leads to understanding. The intuition of childhood should be sheltered, encouraged, revered—and retained as long as possible into maturity.

Charles's attitude toward the child is closer to Coleridge's than to Wordsworth's. Like Coleridge, he recognizes the pure, unblemished, intuitive force in the child and seeks not only to enjoy it but also to preserve it. He clings to that magical quality he sees in the child and wants to retain what he can of it in himself. Where Wordsworth finds that the prison-house of adulthood must inevitably replace the spontaneity of childhood, Charles believes it possible to arrest, or at least delay, the change. Charles strives to retain in adulthood a measure of the visionary gleam.

Coleridge objects to Wordsworth's extreme idealization of the child, but his idea of the "child of nature" runs parallel to Wordsworth's, particularly as Wordsworth describes the phenomenon in the fifth book of *The Prelude*. The fact that their natural child is male would not present any obstacle to someone with Charles's dexterous mind. Coleridge also subscribes to a mystical tie between the "child" and the natural world, as opposed to the man-made world. The child is at home in his natural habitat. Here is how he depicts the foundling in "The Foster-Mother's Tale":

> A pretty boy, but most unteachable—
> And never learnt a prayer, nor told a bead,
> But knew the names of birds, and mock'd their notes,
> And whistled, as he were a bird himself. . . .

When Charles, in his early twenties, first picked up Coleridge's *Aids to Reflection*, he must have noticed this passage in chapter 15: "In the state of perfection, perhaps, all other faculties may be swallowed up in Love, or superseded by immediate vision; but it is on the wings of the CHERUBIM, *i.e.* . . . the *intellectual* powers and energies, that we must first be borne up to the 'pure empyrean.' It must be seraphs, and not the hearts of imperfect mortals, that can burn unfuelled and self-fed." Charles employs the word *seraph* in his poem "Beatrice" and *seraph-choir* in his birthday poem to Rachel Daniel.

Charles knew Coleridge's poetry as well as his prose and quoted it. When, for instance, he made friends with a bright and pretty child, about five years old, he described her (August 2, 1877), quoting "Christabel," as realizing "Coleridge's 'little child, a limber-elf, etc.' She seems to be on springs, and was dancing incessantly. . . ." Much later, Charles concludes his preface to *Sylvie and Bruno* with a quotation from "The Rime of the Ancient Mariner," and he quoted from the same poem in a sermon he preached at St. Leonards-on-Sea in 1897.[9]

Blake, Wordsworth, and Coleridge etch the lyrical landscape of pure and innocent childhood that becomes almost doctrine for many Victorian writers. Their poetry rings with such sonority and captures so many basic emotional elements that their utterances about the world's natural beauty and the divine qualities of the child soon ripple through the writings of their contemporaries. The Romantic surge of feeling sweeps into all literature, not just the poetry but even into sermons; it floods the new fiction and inundates the works of its prime practitioner, Charles Dickens, where we find the most extensive and elegiac treatment of the new philosophy of childhood.

Dickens's attitude toward the child is actually more complex than the poets'. While he too sings paeans to the child's inborn purity and divinity, he goes further and portrays the child as the victim of a depraved social order. He castigates society, and in particular unfeeling parents as tools of that society, for dehumanizing children. Oliver Twist is innocent—and victimized. In an altogether different social setting, David Copperfield too is innocent—and victimized. Similarly Paul Dombey and a host of other Dickens children. Some, like Little Nell and Smike, although they possess a moral purity and exemplify unblemished and natural goodness, are so brutalized that death is their only escape. But whether the innocent survives, triumphs, or is crushed, Dickens indicts the adult world for its insensitivity, ignorance, malice, and abuse of the child.

Charles knew and admired Dickens's novels, and he quoted from them repeatedly. He gave his friend Bayne an inscribed copy of *The Old Curiosity Shop;* he gave each of his brothers a set of Dickens when the sales of *Alice* began bringing a return. He published his poem "Faces in the Fire" in Dickens's *All the Year Round* in January 1860, and his copy of a first edition of *Pickwick Papers* bears his inscription: "Bought with the proceeds of a Poem, 'Faces in the Fire,' contributed to *All the Year Round*."[10] Later he may even have corresponded with Dickens, for on January 5, 1870, Alexander Macmillan, probably replying to Charles's request, sends him Dickens's address. Charles, impressed and deeply moved by Dickens's treatment of the child, particularly in *Dombey and Son*, seems to follow in his creative path, for in both *Alice* books and later in the two *Sylvie and Bruno* books, the innocent child is victimized by a brutal adult society. True, Charles is concerned not with stray waifs (but then Dickens is not either, at least not in the cases of David Copperfield and Paul Dombey), only with upper-class children, but they too can be persecuted by elders. Nor is Charles grinding the Dickens ax: where Dickens damns Malthusian and Benthamite dogma, Charles strikes at manners and the conventions of his class that, even in the best of Victorian homes, fostered thoughtless attitudes toward and neglect of children.

Charles attended carefully to Dickens's gift of humorous exaggeration and stinging irony, marking how the novelist used those techniques to undercut the society he deplored. Dickens's sentimentality, his effort to soften hard hearts and make them bleed for the child, to cause tears to flow, also suited Charles. In *Hard Times*, Dickens advocates freedom for the child's imagination to roam, for the child to dream, to build castles in the air; like Rousseau, he opposes regimentation, rigid rules of training, which inhibit the child. He puts it directly when he champions "the dreams of childhood—its airy fables; its graceful, beautiful, humane, impossible adornments of the world beyond: so good to be believed in once, so good to be remembered when outgrown. . . ."[11]

Tennyson's influence on Charles's thinking and work is enormous, even if one does not think of the Poet Laureate as a champion of the child. Children do enter Tennyson's poetry, and the child is the center of domestic harmony and unity. In "Eleänore," a juvenile verse, Tennyson captures the bliss of childhood, and Charles in his later *Easter Greeting* almost re-creates the scene. Here is Tennyson's description of the child:

> Or the yellow-banded bees,
> Through half-open lattices
> Coming in the scented breeze,
>     Fed thee, a child, lying alone,
>         With whitest honey in fairy gardens culled—
>     A glorious child, dreaming alone,
>     In silk-soft folds, upon yielding down,
> With the hum of swarming bees
>     Into dreamful slumber lulled.

In "The Two Voices," the protagonist, who has been on the verge of suicide, recommits himself to a Christian life on the dawn of Sunday and takes strength and comfort, on his way to church, as he "walked between his wife and child,/With measured footfall firm and mild." Appealing to Christ, the speaker of "Supposed Confessions of a Second-Rate Sensitive Mind," another morose poem of Tennyson's youth, sees that "Children all seem full of Thee!" In "Locksley Hall," when the hero indulges in a fantasy of the unhappiness that has supposedly befallen Amy, his lost love, a positive note intrudes:

> Nay, but Nature brings thee solace; for a tender voice will cry.
> 'Tis a purer life than thine; a lip to drain thy trouble dry.
>
> Baby lips will laugh me down: my latest rival brings thee rest.
> Baby fingers, waxen touches, press me from the mother's breast.
>
> O, the child too clothes the father with a dearness not his due.
> Half is thine and half is his: it will be worthy of the two.

Some Wordsworthian notions enter here, but Tennyson does not follow either Blake or Wordsworth: he does not idolize the child, nor does he urge upon us the notion that the child is closer to eternity than the tarnished adult. And yet Charles took much from Tennyson, not least of all his brooding sentiment, and, like Tennyson, tended to dwell upon loss and to portray abandoned, dejected, and rejected protagonists.

Although Tennyson helped Charles shape the form and emotion of his serious verse, Charles primarily enlisted Blake and Wordsworth in praising the divinity in the child and the beauty and innocence of childhood. While Charles could parody Wordsworth and Tennyson in his work and appropriate Coleridge's "Ancient Mariner" themes and meters, Blake's work remained sacrosanct. It influenced him, echoes of it entered his work, but he did not tamper with it: it was riven with divinity, it touched too closely all that he cherished, it confirmed what he saw and believed about the shape of heaven and earth.

Perhaps the most important fact that underlies all the attitudes of these artists whom Charles valued so is their rejection of the Calvinist, Wesleyan insistence on original sin, the belief that the child is born intrinsically evil, and that evil must be exorcised by applying strict measures. The household in which Charles grew up did not resemble the eighteenth-century Evangelical tomb of a home, but many elements of that demanding faith still prevailed at Croft Rectory. At the end of his life, for instance, Charles still believed that a stray thought, a lighthearted indulgence, a careless pleasure could instantly damn an unrepentant soul.

In Charles's case, a strange amalgam emerged from his attachment to the innocent child, his own childhood memories of the abuses he observed and probably suffered when he was young at the hands of unfeeling and unsympathetic adults, and the courage and inspiration he found in the works of his favorite authors. His own genius was, of course, the magic element that turned that amalgam into the art that he himself created.[12]

*Charles's own design for the title page of* Alice's Adventures Under Ground, *his Christmas gift to Alice Liddell*

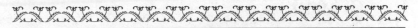

CHAPTER FIVE

# *The* Alice *Books*

*"Who are you?" said the Caterpillar.*

LEWIS CARROLL

I t had to happen. Charles's stern self-discipline, his determination to
control thought and action, his deep commitment to the child, his
friendship with the Liddell sisters, his suppressed emotional life, and
his fount of endless energy joined forces to produce a creative burst. The result was Alice's adventures, first underground, where Charles's emotional
promptings lived concealed, and later, after more careful deliberation, in
Wonderland.

It happened on that "golden afternoon" in the summer of 1862. The circumstances were ideal: Charles was in his element, with the three Liddell
sisters, ranging in age from eight to thirteen, and Duckworth, with his
singing voice, together gliding languidly over the shimmering water. There
they were, alone on the watery sanctuary, secluded in the world of the boat,
self-contained, close to one another, far away from family, governess, society, duty, unified by their banter, their joviality, their unaffected laughter.
"Tell us a story," the little priestesses demanded. And out it poured, the story
of Alice down the rabbit hole.

The tale is light as air, and it almost evaporated. It would have done, too,
but for the persistence of ten-year-old Alice. In later years she recalled that
the tale Charles told "must have been better than usual" because "on the next
day I started to pester him to write down the story for me which I had never

# Chapter I

Alice was beginning to get very tired of sitting by her sister on the bank, and of having nothing to do: once or twice she had peeped into the book her sister was reading, but it had no pictures or conversations in it, and where is the use of a book, thought Alice, without pictures or conversations? So she was considering in her own mind, (as well as she could, for the hot day made her feel very sleepy and stupid,) whether the pleasure of making a daisy-chain was worth the trouble of getting up and picking the daisies, when a white rabbit with pink eyes ran close by her.

There was nothing very remarkable in that, nor did Alice think it so very much out of the way to hear the rabbit say to itself "dear, dear! I shall be too late!" (when she thought it over afterwards, it occurred to her that she ought to have wondered at this, but at the time it all seemed quite natural); but when the rabbit actually took a watch out of its waistcoat-pocket, looked at it, and then hurried on, Alice started to her feet, for

quite dull and stupid for things to go on in the common way.

So she set to work, and very soon finished off the cake.

\*   \*   \*   \*   \*   \*

"Curiouser and curiouser!" cried Alice, (she was so surprised that she quite forgot how to speak good English) "now I'm opening out like the largest telescope that ever was! Goodbye, feet!" (for when she looked down at her feet, they seemed almost out of sight, they were getting so far off) "oh, my poor little feet, I wonder who will put on your shoes and stockings for you now, dears? I'm sure I can't! I shall be a great deal too far off to bother myself about you: you must manage the best way you can — but I must be kind to them," thought Alice, "or perhaps they won't walk the way I want to go! Let me see: I'll give them a new pair of boots every Christmas."

And she went on planning to herself how she would manage it.

"The Queen of Hearts she made some tarts
    All on a summer day:
The Knave of Hearts he stole those tarts,
    And took them quite away!"

"Now for the evidence," said the King, "and then the sentence."

"No!" said the Queen, "first the sentence, and then the evidence!"

"Nonsense!" cried Alice, so loudly that everybody jumped, "the idea of having the sentence first!"

"Hold your tongue!" said the Queen.

"I won't!" said Alice, "you're nothing but a pack of cards! Who cares for you?"

At this the whole pack rose up into the air, and came flying down upon her: she gave a little scream of fright, and tried to beat them off, and found herself lying on the bank, with her head in the lap of her sister, who was gently brushing away some leaves that had fluttered down from the trees on to her face.

We lived beneath the mat
    Warm and snug and fat
        But one woe, & that
            Was the cat!
                To our joys
                    a clog, In
                our eyes a
            fog, On our
        hearts a log
    Was the dog!
        When the
        Cat's away,
        Then
        the mice
        will
        play,
        But, alas!
            one day, (So they say)
                Came the dog and
                cat, Hunting
                    for a
                        rat,
                    Crushed
                    the mice
                all flat,
            Each
            one
        as
        he
        sat
    Underneath the mat, Warm, & snug, & fat. Think of that!

than she expected; before she had drunk half the bottle, she found her head pressing against the ceiling, and she stooped to save her neck from being broken, and hastily put down the bottle, saying to herself "that's quite enough— I hope I sha'n't grow any more— I wish I hadn't drunk so much!"

Alas! it was too late: she went on growing, and growing, and very soon had to kneel down: in another minute there was not room even for this, and she tried the effect of lying down, with one elbow against the door, and the other arm curled round her head. Still she went on growing, and as a last resource she put one arm out of the window, and one foot up the chimney, and said to herself "now I can do no more— what will become of me?"

36

"Everybody says "come on!" here," thought Alice, as she walked slowly after the Gryphon; "I never was ordered about so before in all my life— never!"

They had not gone far before they saw the Mock Turtle in the distance, sitting sad and lonely on a little ledge of rock, and, as they came nearer, Alice could hear it sighing as if its heart would break. She pitied it deeply: what is its sorrow?" she asked the Gryphon, and the Gryphon answered, very nearly in the same words as before," it's all its fancy, that: it hasn't got no sorrow, you know: come on!"

So they went up to the Mock Turtle, who looked at them with large eyes full of tears, but said nothing.

"This here young lady" said the Gryphon,

79

*Pages from* Alice's Adventures Under Ground, *the original version of the* Alice *story, in Charles's handwriting and with his own illustrations*

done before." She "kept going on, going on" at him until he promised to oblige her.[1] For one reason or another, however, it took him two and a half years to deliver the completed manuscript, illustrated with his own drawings.

In the meantime, encouragement to publish the story came from Mr. and Mrs. George MacDonald, friends whose taste and judgment he trusted. As the MacDonalds read the draft, they probably recognized elements of George MacDonald's *Phantastes,* his 1858 fairy tale, which Charles knew well. In any event, they read the *Alice* story to their household of children. One of them, Greville, remembered "that first reading well, and also . . . that I wished there were 60,000 volumes of it."[2] Mrs. MacDonald wrote announcing the verdict: "They wish me to publish," Charles proclaimed (May 9, 1863) to his diary.

He presented the green leather booklet containing the neatly hand-scripted text to Alice in 1864 as a Christmas gift, a year and a half after the break with the Liddells. The booklet found its way into the hands of visitors to the deanery. Henry Kingsley, novelist brother of Charles Kingsley, chanced upon it and insisted that Mrs. Liddell urge its author to publish it. Charles got the message, but by then he was already well along the publication road. He tells us later, in the preface to *Alice's Adventures Under Ground,* that "there was no idea of publication in my mind when I wrote this little book: *that* was wholly an afterthought, pressed on me by the 'perhaps too partial friends' who always have to bear the blame when a writer rushes into print."

Later, when composing the preface to the first facsimile edition, Charles described the early version as merely "the germ that was to grow into the published volume"; in fact, he decided that before publishing, he would have to flesh out the original with more chapters, incidents, and characters.

He needed a proper publisher. Although Oxford presses had been printing his esoteric pamphlets, he had no experience with high-powered London publishers. He now found one through a friend. On October 19, 1863, he went by invitation to visit Thomas Combe. Charles had visited him and his wife before and had already photographed the strikingly handsome Combe. But on this particular evening he went expressly "to meet the publisher [Alexander] Macmillan," Combe's guest, the younger of the Macmillan brothers who in the mid-1840s founded the now well-established publishing house.

Because Macmillan had published Charles Kingsley's *The Water-Babies* five months earlier, Charles may have hoped to interest him in his chil-

*John Tenniel, famous* Punch *political cartoonist, who illustrated the first published edition of*
Alice's Adventures in Wonderland. *He forced
Charles to delete a chapter in* Through the
Looking-Glass *because when he came to
illustrate it, he decided that "a* wasp *in a* wig *is
altogether beyond the appliances of art."*

dren's tale, or the subject of the *Alice*
story may have come up casually in
conversation. Whatever the case,
Macmillan liked Charles's story and
agreed to publish it.

The next step for Charles was to
find an illustrator. Duckworth mentioned John Tenniel, already a fa-
mous artist, whose drawings appeared regularly in *Punch*. His style suited
Charles perfectly, and he decided to see if the artist would collaborate. Two
months after the meeting with Macmillan (December 20, 1863), he wrote
his acquaintance Tom Taylor, the popular playwright, asking him if he knew
Tenniel well enough "to say whether he could undertake such a thing as
drawing a dozen wood-cuts to illustrate a child's book" and if so whether
Taylor would be willing to put him in touch with Tenniel. "The reasons for
which I ask," Charles wrote Taylor, ". . . are that I have written such a tale
for a young friend, and illustrated it in pen and ink. It has been read and
liked by so many children, and I have been so often asked to publish it, that
I have decided on so doing. . . . If [Mr. Tenniel] . . . should be willing to undertake [the illustrations] . . . , I would send him the book to look over, not
that he should at all follow my pictures, but simply to give him an idea of
the sort of thing I want."

A month later (January 25, 1864), Charles called on Tenniel in London,
carrying Taylor's letter of introduction. He "was very friendly," Charles
wrote, "and seemed to think favourably of undertaking the pictures." Tenniel first saw the early text and then the expanded tale, more than twice the
length of the original. Charles had worked hard on the story. The Mouse's
tale was much altered, the Mad Tea-Party appeared for the first time, and
the trial scene at the end of the story, occupying two pages in the early version, grew to two chapters of twenty-six pages.

90

of her own little sister. So the boat wound slowly along, beneath the bright summer-day, with its merry crew and its music of voices and laughter, till it passed round one of the many turnings of the stream, and she saw it no more.

Then she thought, (in a dream within the dream, as it were,) how this same little Alice would, in the after-time, be herself a grown woman: and how she would keep, through her riper years, the simple and loving heart of her childhood: and how she would gather around her other little children, and make their eyes bright and eager with many a wonderful tale, perhaps even with these very adventures of the little Alice of long-ago: and how she would feel with all their simple sorrows, and find a pleasure in all their simple joys, remembering her own child-life, and the happy summer-days. days.

*"The Hidden Alice": Charles first drew a picture of Alice at the end of the manuscript of* Alice's Adventures Under Ground; *then, dissatisfied with the result, he pasted over it a trimmed photograph he had taken of his ideal child friend.*

Charles also changed the title. He called the booklet he had given Alice *Alice's Adventures Under Ground.* But he was apparently unhappy with that title and, after casting about for a new one, settled on *Alice's Adventures in Wonderland.*

Throughout the summer and autumn of 1864, Charles discussed, in person and by letter, various production details with Macmillan and Tenniel. A stream of letters flowed back and forth between Charles and Macmillan through the autumn. The exchanges between Charles and Tenniel are not well documented because Tenniel probably destroyed Charles's letters, and only a few brief notes from Tenniel survive. But we know enough to correct the myth that paints Tenniel as a long-suffering illustrator victimized by the iron whim of a merciless, exacting fledgling. The myth probably originated with Harry Furniss, another *Punch* caricaturist who, three years after Charles's death, published a two-volume memoir in which he pilloried

Charles. He claimed that after *Alice,* "Tenniel had point-blank refused to il-lustrate another story," that Charles "was . . . 'impossible.'" He described Charles as "a wit, a gentleman, a bore and an egotist—and, like Hans An-dersen, a spoilt child. . . . Tenniel and other artists declared I would not work with Carroll for seven weeks!"[3]

But most of the letters that Charles wrote to Furniss when they collabo-rated later on the *Sylvie and Bruno* books, and the few from Furniss that sur-vive, reveal Charles patient and considerate on almost every point and Furniss ever-hasty and often provocative. In the end, Furniss lasted longer than seven weeks with Charles, but much of the credit for the successful col-laboration is owing to Charles, not to Furniss. True, Charles was a perfec-tionist and deluged his illustrators with suggestions, but he almost always gave way to the artist's taste when a disagreement arose. He suffered untold rebuffs from both Tenniel and Furniss but bore them in silence.

The most telling example of Charles's willingness to reconcile himself to the demands of an illustrator occurred just after *Alice's Adventures in Won-derland* appeared. The Clarendon Press printed two thousand copies of what has come to be known as the first edition. On June 27, 1865, Charles noted that the press had sent its first copies to Macmillan, and on July 15 he went to London to inscribe "20 or more copies of *Alice* to go as presents to vari-ous friends." Four days later, on July 19, came the shock: "Heard from Ten-niel, who is dissatisfied with the printing of the pictures." Charles himself expressed no displeasure either with Tenniel's drawings or with the printing. The next day he called on Macmillan and showed him Tenniel's letter: "I suppose we shall have to do it all again," he recorded. Less than a fortnight after that (August 2), Charles wrote: "Finally decided on the re-print of *Alice,* and that the first 2000 shall be sold as waste paper. Wrote about it to Macmillan, Combe and Tenniel."

Charles immediately tried to recall the copies already dispatched to friends, promising replacements from the new printing. He engaged a dif-ferent printer, Richard Clay of London, and the first copy of the new im-pression arrived at Christ Church on November 9. Charles heard from Tenniel, "approving the new impression." Because his arrangements with Macmillan called for him to pay all costs—printing, engraving, even adver-tising—and for the publisher, Macmillan, to receive a fixed commission on sales, Charles bore the entire loss. It cost him six hundred pounds to reprint the book, as he calculated it, "6*s.* a copy of the 2000. If I make £500 by sale," he added, "this will be a loss of £100, and the loss of the first 2000 will probably be £100, leaving me £200 out of pocket." For a thirty-three-year-old Oxford lecturer with a modest income, these figures make the head reel. But Charles, who himself refused to compromise on the quality of his books, respected Tenniel's objection and was determined to satisfy him. "If a second 2000 could be sold," he wrote in his diary, "it would cost £300, and bring in £500, thus squaring accounts: any other further sale would be a gain. But that I can hardly hope for," he concluded, unaware that he had on his hands one of the most lucrative children's books ever to come to market.

Some commentators have too hastily concluded that Charles, dissatisfied with the printing, scrapped the first edition, but it was entirely Tenniel's doing. Tenniel himself boasted to the brothers Dalziel, his engravers: "I protested so strongly against the disgraceful printing that . . . [Dodgson] *cancelled the edition.*"[4]

Both Charles and Tenniel would be stunned to learn that a single copy of that "inferior" first edition today commands a king's ransom when it comes up for sale. Collectors would trade whole segments of their libraries for a single copy of the "first" *Alice;* bibliographers dream of uncovering an unrecorded copy; and literary chroniclers are at a loss to explain how, even in the heyday of Victorian publishing, such extravagant decisions could have been made over a single children's book.

Charles sent copies of the new impression to his friends. Christina Rossetti wrote to offer "a thousand and one thanks . . . for the funny pretty book you have so very kindly sent me. My Mother and Sister as well as myself made ourselves quite at home yesterday in Wonderland: and . . . I confess it would give me sincere pleasure to fall in with that conversational rabbit, that endearing puppy, that very sparkling dormouse. Of the hatter's acquaintance I am not ambitious, and the March hare may fairly remain an open question. The woodcuts are charming."[5] Her brother Dante Gabriel Rossetti also wrote: "I saw *Alice in Wonderland* at my sister's, and was glad to find myself still childish enough to enjoy looking through it very much. The wonderful ballad of Father William and Alice's perverted snatches of school poetry are among the funniest things I have seen for a long while."[6] Henry Kingsley wrote: "Many thanks for your charming little book. . . . I received it in bed in the morning, and in spite of threats and persuasions, in bed I stayed until I had read every word of it. I could pay you no higher compliment . . . than confessing that I could not stop reading . . . till I had finished it. The fancy of the whole thing is delicious. . . . Your versification is a gift I envy you very much."[7]

*Alice's Adventures in Wonderland* was widely reviewed and earned almost unconditional praise. Charles's diary lists nineteen notices. The *Reader* (November 18, 1865) termed it "a glorious artistic treasure . . . a book to put on one's shelf as an antidote to a fit of the blues." The *Press* (November 25) liked its "simple and attractive style," judged it "amusingly written," and concluded that "a child, when once the tale has been commenced, will long to hear the whole of this wondrous narrative." The *Publisher's Circular* (December 8) selected it as "the most original and most charming" of the two hundred books for children sent them that year; the *Bookseller* (December 12) was "delighted. . . . A more original fairy tale . . . it has not lately been our good fortune to read"; and the *Guardian* (December 13) judged the "nonsense so graceful and so full of humour that one can hardly help reading it through." The *Athenaeum* (December 16) was a clear exception: "We fancy that any child might be more puzzled than enchanted by this stiff, overwrought story."[8]

The tale pleased the reading public. Sales started steady, then spiraled upward. The audience of admirers widened, translations into other languages followed, edition after edition was called for, through Charles's lifetime.

Reading the reviews and noting the agreeable sales reports, Charles bethought himself, considered his future as an author of children's books, and decided that he could do more with Alice. Nine months after the second impression of *Alice* appeared (August 24, 1866), he wrote to Macmillan: "It will probably be some time before I again indulge in paper and print. I have, however, a floating idea of writing a sort of sequel to *Alice,* and if it ever comes to anything, I intend to consult you at the very outset, so as to have the thing properly managed from the beginning." By the end of the year Charles had "added a few pages to the second volume of *Alice*"; and on February 6, 1867, he was "hoping before long to complete another book about 'Alice.' . . . You would not, I presume," he wrote Macmillan, "object to publish the book, if it should ever reach completion." The next mention occurs when Charles wrote a friend (December 15, 1867) that "Alice's visit to Looking-Glass House is getting on pretty well." Liddon apparently suggested the title *Through the Looking-Glass and What Alice Found There.*[9]

A major obstacle still loomed ahead, however: once again Charles needed an illustrator. Tenniel was an obvious choice—or was he, after the debacle of the first printing? Charles knew that it would be difficult to find a suitable replacement, someone as good and as famous. He made the approach. The answer, however, was a resounding no: Tenniel was too busy. Charles withdrew. He tried to find another artist—Richard Doyle, Sir Joseph Noël Paton, even W. S. Gilbert, whose *Bab Ballads* were then appearing with his own illustrations in *Fun*. For various reasons, however, none of these came to the rescue. In fact, two and a half years passed before Charles finally persuaded Tenniel to illustrate the book, and even then the artist consented to draw the pictures only "at such time as he can find."

Charles sent the first chapter of his looking-glass story to Macmillan on January 12, 1869, but two more years passed before he finished it. And even then further delays occurred. "*Through the Looking-Glass* . . . lingers on, though the text is ready," he noted in August 1871, adding, "I have only received twenty-seven pictures." Four days later he wrote to Tenniel "accepting the melancholy . . . fact that we cannot get . . . *Looking-Glass* out by Michaelmas."

When Tenniel supplied the drawing of the Jabberwock for a frontispiece, Charles grew concerned that the monster would frighten his young readers and sent copies of the drawing to thirty mothers asking their opinion. They confirmed his fears, and he substituted the drawing of the White Knight at the front of the book and tucked the Jabberwock away deep in the text.

Tenniel finally finished, and through the spring and summer of 1871 Charles kept up a flow of letters to Macmillan about reprinting *Alice* for Christmas and getting *Looking-Glass* out at the same time. When Charles suggested delaying *Looking-Glass* yet again, concerned lest haste mar the book's quality, Macmillan protested (November 6): "Your proposal is worse than the cruellest ogre ever conceived in darkest and most malignant moods. . . . Why, half the children will be laid up with pure vexation and anguish of spirit. Plum pudding of the delicatest, toys the most elaborate will have no charms. Darkness will come over all hearths, gloom will hover over the brightest boards. Don't think of it for a moment. The book must come out for Christmas or I don't know what will be the consequence. . . . Don't for any sake keep it back." Later that month the book went to press. Although the title page bears the publication date 1872, *Looking-Glass* appeared as a Christmas book for 1871.

It was an immediate success. On November 30, before Charles saw his first copy, he was amazed that Macmillan already had orders for seventy-five hundred *Looking-Glass*es: "They printed 9000," he noted, "and are at once going to print 6000 more!" Six days later he received the first copy, and three days after that three bound in morocco (for Alice, Ellen Terry's younger sister Florence, and Tennyson) and a hundred in cloth. Then, with the help of Parker's, the Oxford stationer, he packed them off to friends.

Having had his fingers burned by the original printing of *Alice,* he was ever watchful with the printing of *Looking-Glass.* He wrote to Macmillan (December 17, 1871):

> Whatever the *commercial* consequences, we must have no more artistic 'fiascos'—and I . . . write *at once* about it by your alarming words . . . "We are going on with another 6000 *as fast as possible.*" My decision is, we must have *no more hurry.* . . . You will think me a lunatic for thus wishing to send away money from the doors; and . . . that I shall thus lose thousands of would-be purchasers, who will . . . go and buy other Christmas books. I wish I could put into words how entirely such arguments go for nothing with me. . . . The only thing I *do* care for is, that all the copies that *are* sold shall be artistically first-rate.

Macmillan tried to assuage Charles's fears by reporting that the printer "thinks he can fulfil your requirements and let us have copies so as to be on sale by January 23." On January 27, 1872, a mere seven weeks after publication, Charles wrote: "My birthday was signalized by hearing from . . . Macmillan that they have now sold 15,000 *Looking-Glass*es and have orders for 500 more."

While sales soared, Charles received thanks from friends favored with inscribed copies. Henry Kingsley wrote: "I can say . . . that your new book is the finest thing we have had since *Martin Chuzzlewit.* . . . In comparing the new *Alice* with the old, 'this is a more excellent song than the other.' It is perfectly splendid."[10]

Critical reaction was favorable, with some dissent. The *Athenaeum* (December 16) now was enthusiastic about both *Alice* and *Looking-Glass:* "It is with no mere book that we have to deal here. . . . It would be difficult to over-estimate the value of the store of hearty and healthy fun laid up for whole generations of young people by Mr. Lewis Carroll and Mr. John Tenniel in the two books. . . ." The *Globe* (December 15) pronounced that "to write good nonsense is as difficult as to write good sense, but it must be more difficult, as there are very few who deal in the commodity so successfully as Mr. Carroll." The *Examiner* (December 16) found the sequel "hardly as good" as the original but "quite good enough to delight every sensible reader of any age." It praised the "wit and humour that all children can appreciate, and grown folks ought as thoroughly to enjoy."

The *Illustrated London News* (December 16) heaped praise upon both book and author. It judged the story "quite as rich in humorous whims and fancy, quite as laughable in its queer incidents, as lovable for its pleasant

*Charles compiled this list of reviews of* Alice's Adventures in Wonderland *in his diary.*

spirit and graceful manner as the wondrous tale of Alice's former adventures underground." Other rapturous reviews appeared in *Aunt Judy's Christmas Volume* for 1872, the *Saturday Review* (December 30), the *Spectator* (December 30), and elsewhere.

The two books continued to sell. A year after it first appeared, Charles rejoiced to a friend that "*Looking-Glass* is having such a tremendous sale. . . . We have sold about 25000!" By 1898, the year Charles died, Macmillan had printed over 150,000 *Wonderland*s and more than 100,000 *Looking-Glass*es.[11]

Although, as the novelist Charlotte Yonge observed, "it takes some cultivation to enjoy these wonderfully droll compositions,"[12] neither *Alice* book has ever gone out of print; both are, in fact, firm bulwarks of society, both in the English-speaking world and everywhere else. Next to the Bible and Shakespeare, they are the books most widely and most frequently translated and quoted. Over seventy-five editions and versions of the *Alice* books were available in 1993, including play texts, parodies, read-along cassettes, teachers' guides, audio-language studies, coloring books, "New Method" readers, abridgments, learn to-read story books, single-syllable texts, coloring books, pop-up books, musical renderings, casebooks, and a deluxe edition selling for £175. They have been translated into over seventy languages, including Swahili and Yiddish; and they exist in Braille.

Not only the books but Charles's life and Alice Liddell's have come under close scrutiny and been the subjects of stage plays, films, television dramas, and ballets. Lewis Carroll societies flourish in Britain and the United States, and one has been founded in Japan. Britain's Dodo Club has more than a hundred members. Two Lewis Carroll foundations have been incorporated to advance Carroll studies, and in Daresbury, Cheshire, the Lewis Carroll Birthplace Centre has been established, an attraction not only for tourists and Carrollians but for scholars as well.

Critics have pondered the books' magic and tried to explain it. What are they all about, they ask, and why so universally successful? What is the key to their enchantment, why are they so entertaining and yet so enigmatic? What charm enables them to transcend language as well as national and temporal differences and win their way into the hearts of young and old everywhere and always?

Commenting on *Alice,* Charles himself wrote: "The 'Why?' of this book cannot, and need not, be put into words. Those for whom a child's mind is a sealed book, and who see no divinity in a child's smile, would read such words in vain. . . . No deed . . . I suppose . . . is really unselfish. Yet if one can put forth all one's powers in a task where nothing of reward is hoped for but a little child's whispered thanks and the airy touch of a little child's pure lips, one seems to come somewhere near to this."[13]

Charming as that comment is, it does not help us grasp the meaning of the books. We must go beyond Charles's reflections. The critiques, commentaries, exegeses, and analyses that have appeared during the past hundred years and more—some profound and interesting, some absurd—offer many bewildering theories. Recalling a few simple facts, however, helps.

To begin with, Charles wrote both books with Alice Liddell and, to a lesser degree, her sisters and Robinson Duckworth in mind. All the occupants of the boat who first heard the tale of Alice are characters in the first book. The Dodo is Charles, the Duck is Duckworth, the Lory is Lorina, the Eaglet Edith. But they play hardly more than walk-on parts. The book is about Alice, the middle sister; it is she, and she alone, who stands at center stage throughout.

The actors in both *Alice* books are transplants from real life, as are the episodes, and those who sat in the gliding boat recognized them as Charles related them, just as they would later experience flashes of memory upon reading *Looking-Glass*. The landmarks, the language, the puns, the puffery—it was all rooted in the circumscribed enclave of their Victorian lives. Oxford provided the landscape, its architecture, its history, its select society, its conventions. In *Under Ground* and in the additions that Charles later made to the tale and in the sequel, his listeners (and readers) would have instantly picked up on the references, to the Sheep Shop on St. Aldate's, the treacle well at Binsey, the lilies of the Botanic Gardens, the deer in Magdalen Grove, the lion and the unicorn from the royal crests, the leopards from Cardinal Wolsey's coat of arms that graces the fabric of Christ Church and are known as "Ch Ch cats." Charles parodied familiar verses and songs, some of which they sang together as they rowed up or down river: "Twinkle, twinkle, little bat"; "Salmon come up" in "The Lobster-Quadrille"; "Turtle Soup"; "How doth the little crocodile"; and more. They would readily penetrate the thin disguises of John Ruskin as the conger eel, Bartholomew Price as the Bat, Humpty Dumpty as some egghead don pontificating, the Caterpillar as another conducting a *viva*. The Mad Tea-Party as a parody of Alice's birthday party would have elicited howls of laughter. A good many of the references are lost to us, so localized they were.[14]

*Looking-Glass,* too, grew directly out of shared experiences with the Liddell sisters. The royal celebrations in March and June 1863 supplied the book's characters and its essential theme, Alice's trials on the road to majesty. The looking-glass would have reawakened memories of the visit to Hetton Lawn. The opening scene of Alice with the kitten in her lap would have taken them back to the bazaar in St. John's gardens, when Charles helped Alice and her sisters sell their little kittens. And then, like Princess Alexandra at the bazaar, the White Queen has her own imperial kitten. The Red Queen lecturing Alice echoes either Mrs. Liddell's or Miss Prickett's injunctions to the girls: "Look up, speak nicely, and don't twiddle your fingers all the time"; "Curtsey while you're thinking what to say"; "Open your mouth a *little* wider when you speak, and always say 'your Majesty' "; and "Speak in French when you can't think of the English for a thing—turn out your toes when you walk—and remember who you are!" On those outings from Hetton Lawn into the country, they would have noticed the patchwork design of the fields, and one of the girls or Charles might have suggested their similarity to a chessboard. The "high wind" that blew their way as they walked across Leckhampton Hill later whistles in Alice's ears as she runs with the Red Queen through the chessboard country. The railway carriage scene reconstructs the "very merry" railway journey the girls and Charles had from Gloucester back to Oxford. The banquet at the end of the story is a replica of the one for the Prince and Princess of Wales in Hall in June 1863.

Underlying the characters, however distorted and exaggerated, is the cast-iron foundation of Victorian society, its shibboleths, class hierarchy, manners, conventions, proprieties, taboos, and, perhaps most of all, its foibles and follies. The Victorian idea—or, in Charles's terms, the misconception—of the child is at the heart of both stories, as are the child's observations of the adult world and the adult world's insensitive, abusive treatment of the child. We also have a running commentary on the human condition and especially a catalogue of human weaknesses—sliding away from rectitude, succumbing to frailties, escaping responsibilities, imagining infirmities.

Although the heroine is still young and learning, she is old enough both to reflect her training and to criticize it. She mirrors her society by showing that her sensitivity has already been blunted and that she has learned to mimic the haughty stance, the rude rebuke common in her social milieu. Her indelicate treatment of the Mouse and the birds in the early chapters of *Wonderland* are a mere prelude to the insolence and arrogance she herself encounters and criticizes. Almost everyone she meets mistreats her: the rabbit mistakes her for his housemaid and shouts orders at her, the caterpillar cross-examines her, the Duchess berates her, the Hatter criticizes the length of her locks, the March Hare lectures her on her use of language, the Gryphon chides her and tells her to hold her tongue, the Queen of Hearts shouts "Off with her head!"

Bad behavior is one thing, but violence is something else, and it too occurs in these books, some of it initiated by our heroine. Alice's fall down the rabbit hole is in itself not violent, but it certainly carries with it the fear of a violent crash. When Alice is jammed into the Rabbit's house, she kicks Bill the Lizard up the chimney like a skyrocket. Later she comes upon the scene of utter havoc in the Duchess's kitchen, where the Cook throws fire irons, saucepans, and plates at the Duchess and her baby and the Duchess in turn orders the Cook to decapitate Alice. While singing a lullaby urging punishment for sneezing, the Duchess tosses her baby "violently up and down" and then hurls it at Alice. A pigeon flies into Alice's face and beats her. The

Queen's croquet ground witnesses cruel incidents too. The company plays croquet with live flamingos for mallets and live hedgehogs for balls, the Duchess is in prison for boxing the Queen's ears, and the Queen's command to chop off various heads becomes a refrain. In *Looking-Glass,* there's the Jabberwock with jaws that bite and claws that catch, the oysters are all eaten, the Lion and the Unicorn engage in battle, and the red chess pieces are threatening.

The books reflect England's rigid social scale more than they criticize it. Charles has a good ear and captures the speech and manners of several social grades. His listeners were undoubtedly amused by his imitation of the Cockney, the parvenu, the social climber, the huffy academic. In fact, most slices of the social pie are represented, from the royals and the aristocratic Duchess to the pretentious Rabbit with his waistcoat, gloves, and watch, hobnobbing with the aristocracy, to the carpenter and the Gryphon, who favors double negatives.

The characters behave according to their stations, but a good many Victorian bromides transcend class, and Charles deals them out mercilessly. "I'm older than you, and must know better," says the Lory to Alice. When Alice asks exactly how old the Lory is, she vainly refuses to tell. Group games are the target in the Caucus-Race, with its solemn prize-giving ceremony. When the Mouse goes off in a huff after reciting its tale, the old Crab admonishes her daughter: "Ah, my dear! Let this be a lesson to you never to lose *your* temper!" Then the Caterpillar orders Alice to "keep your temper." Similar rebuffs and platitudes occur throughout.

What, then, does it all add up to besides art? The answer surely is a double-layered metaphor. The more obvious one, not much disguised, is the child's plight in Victorian upper-class society, which the Liddell sisters would easily recognize. But that same metaphor goes far beyond Charles's original purpose: it reaches beyond Victorian Oxford into the wide world. For Charles, intentionally or not, got at the universal essence of childhood and captured the disappointments, fears, and bewilderment that all children encounter in the course of daily living. He wove fear, condescension, rejection, and violence into the tales, and the children who read them feel their hearts beat faster and their skin tingle, not so much with excitement as with an uncanny recognition of themselves, of the hurdles they have confronted and had to overcome. Repelled by Alice's encounters, they are also drawn to them because they recognize them as their own. These painful and damaging experiences are the price children pay in all societies in all times when passing through the dark corridors of their young lives, and Charles miraculously captures their truth.

The second metaphor lives in Charles's own life. He could not have written about Alice's adventures had he not himself experienced the indignities that Alice suffers and the fears she feels. The *Alice* books become, in this metaphor, a record of Charles's childhood, the shocks dealt him by parents, teachers, all his elders. Bad manners and violence were commonplace in Victorian days, but their emphasis and frequency in these books, while capturing the ethos of the age, also tell us that Charles must have stored up an amount of hostility as he grew up, at home, at school, and at Oxford. At home and at school, he very likely smarted under innumerable commands from above, unreasoning and unreasonable, and as a sensitive observer, he saw and deplored society's artificial and meaningless minuets. The spare-the-rod philosophy was still dominant; whippings and beatings at school were customary. The bullying he witnessed, the knockabout games on the sporting fields, surely weighed on him. Accumulated resentment seeks outlets, and Charles took this opportunity to get even with the past.

If the Red Queen is a parody of Miss Prickett, she is also an exaggeration of someone in or near the Dodgson household in Daresbury or Croft. The metaphor holds true through both books. The Caucus-Race is a parody of games at Richmond and Rugby. The conversation between the Mock Turtle and the Gryphon, in its absurd, lethargic silliness, captures the essence of a conversation between intimate adults, perhaps between two dim-witted parsons or between two fossilized Oxford dons. And Alice's exchanges with both the Caterpillar and Humpty Dumpty parody academic pomposities.

In the end, however, the books are not mainly about fear and bewilderment. Once readers have associated with Alice and wandered with her through Wonderland, they are together on a survival course. They are thrown back upon their own inner resources, determining whether their resources are strong enough to get them through. Does Alice have the wit necessary to master the maze of childhood and emerge a tried and tested teenager? Charles's answer is affirmative. He endows his heroine, and by extension all children, with the means of dealing with a hostile, unpredictable environment. At the close of both books, we have a catharsis, an affirmation of life after Wonderland and life on this side of the looking-glass. Although unconventional, the endings are happy, as fairy-tale endings should be. In both cases, Alice should meet a strong male rescuer, a Prince Charming, and they should fall in love and live happily ever after. But she does not. She succeeds, but not through the formula of grand romance. Instead of honeyed happiness, she gains confidence, a way of dealing with the world; instead of love, she finds advancement, recognition, acceptance. It is a reasonably happy ending for Charles himself, for he is at the heart of the tales.

The *Alice* books affect all children of all places at all times in a similar way. They tell the child that someone does understand; they offer encouragement, a feeling that the author is sharing their miseries and is holding out a hand, a hope for their survival as they pass from childhood into adulthood.

But this discussion sounds too serious, really, because Charles's most successful device is laughter. Anyone who abhors a pun does not appreciate its usefulness as a tool to exercise the mind, to urge the growing child to wed sense to sound. Charles Dodgson, like Charles Lamb, knew the worth of the pun even as he valued many other forms of humor, not only as educational tools but as elements that offer relief from the ordinary, the arduous, the boring. When, in reading the *Alice* books, the child sees and gets the pun or some other joke all on his or her own, the child suddenly senses an awakening pride in his or her ability and, at least for a moment, laughter replaces a troubled emotion.

Many of the critiques of the *Alice* books seem to have been written by people who seldom laugh. If so, they cannot come to grips with these books, where the jests, the shattered shams, the punctured pretenses, and the peals of laughter are essential elements to understanding and enjoying. What child, young or old, can resist the Mock Turtle's account of his schooldays, where they learn the different branches of Arithmetic: Ambition, Distraction, Uglification, and Derision? Or his description of the subjects he and others studied when young: "Reeling and Writhing, of course, to begin with. . . . Mystery, ancient and modern, with Seaography: then Drawling— the Drawling-master . . . taught us Drawling, Stretching, and Fainting in Coils." And the Classical master taught them Laughing and Grief. Those seabed lessons, everyone knows, took ten hours the first day and nine the next, and so on: how could they be called lessons if they did not lessen from day to day?

Such entertaining stuff is a balm for whatever ails us. Education at the bottom of the sea is as funny today as it was in 1866, and it will continue to amuse for centuries to come because it appeals to something basic—our sense of the ridiculous, our yearning for relief from seriousness, our preference for fun.

Charles's juvenilia record how the Dodgson children took refuge in puns and parodies, concocting absurdities to escape their elders' impositions. The *Alice* books provide an avenue of escape from the child's burdens.

*Calendar of events connected with composing and publishing* Alice's Adventures in Wonderland, *also entered in Charles's diary*

Finally, one must ask again why these books have become such widely read classics while other children's books that were, in their time, equally popular—books by such famous authors as Catherine Sinclair, Mrs. Margaret Gatty, Charles Kingsley, George MacDonald, and Christina Rossetti—are no longer read and have largely perished.

Children's books had existed for centuries before Charles came along. He did not invent the genre. But he did something significant. He broke with tradition. Many of the earlier children's books written for the upper classes had lofty purposes: they had to teach and preach. Primers taught children religious principles alongside multiplication tables. Children recited rhymed couplets as aids to memorizing the alphabet—*A:* "In Adam's fall we sinned all"; *F:* "The idle Fool is whipped at school." Children learned their catechism, learned to pray, learned to fear sin—and their books were meant to aid and abet the process. They were often frightened by warnings and threats, their waking hours burdened with homilies. Much of the children's literature of Charles's day, the books he himself read as a boy, were purposeful and dour. They instilled discipline and compliance.

The prose of children's books before *Alice* was also formularized. Most earlier writers (contemporaries and later writers too) wrote down and condescended to children. They rarely gave the young credit for much intelligence, let alone sensitivity or imagination. The sentiment was heavy, often couched in purple prose. The language tended to be monosyllabic and dull. The Puritan tradition forbade anything lighthearted. Growing up was a serious affair, and the devil had his pitchfork ready, waiting to lead the child into evil ways.

The *Alice* books fly in the face of that tradition, destroy it, and give the Victorian child something lighter and brighter. Above all, these books have no moral. About a year after *Wonderland* appeared, when Charles sent a more conventional children's book to a young friend, he wrote (January 5, 1867): "The book is intended for you to look at the outside, and then put it away in the bookcase: the *inside* is not meant to be read. The book has got a moral—so I need hardly say it is *not* by Lewis Carroll." He was fed up with all the moral baggage that burdened children, that perhaps he himself had struggled with when a boy, and he was not purveying any more. Not only not purveying it—he went further and parodied the entire practice of adult moralizing. In chapter 9 of *Wonderland:* Alice "was a little startled when she heard . . . [the Duchess's] voice close to her ear. 'You're thinking about something, my dear, and that makes you forget to talk. I can't tell you just now what the moral of that is, but I shall remember it in a bit.' 'Perhaps it hasn't one,' Alice ventured to remark. 'Tut, tut, child!' said the Duchess. 'Everything's got a moral, if only you can find it.' "

Charles's prose is also unconventional. He uses big, polysyllabic words, sophisticated concepts, notions that a child cannot possibly be expected to grasp. But he embeds these words in a string of adventures that a child can follow easily. If the child is engrossed in the story, he or she is provoked to ask questions about the difficult words and concepts. If an adult is reading the story to the child, the child might interrupt and ask, even as early as the first chapter of *Alice,* "What's that word mean, Mummy, what's *antipathies?*" The parent might suggest that the child look up the word in a dictionary, hinting at a good learning habit. Or in the case of *antipathies,* the intelligent reader might introduce the child to double meanings and the concept of similar-sounding words.

What do the *Alice* books mean? everyone asks. To understand what they mean, we have to realize that Wonderland and the world behind the looking-glass are mysterious places where characters do not live by conventional rules and that meaning does not play a conventional role. Even the laws of nature, the law of gravity for instance, do not work as they should. But, for Charles, meaning is only one quality that words possess, and why, he implies, is meaning so important? To put it another way, is the meaning of a word really the most important thing about it? After all, words make sounds, and perhaps the sound of a word, like music without words, has a role to play, perhaps an even more important role than meaning. That is the point: the sound of words, like music, makes us feel. Sound and feeling, in these books, are as important as, perhaps even more important than, sense and meaning. The sounds help us associate with Alice and her adventures. The reader feels along with Alice throughout her wanderings, and those feelings are the most important part of the journey. The sound of words and the feelings they provoke emerge as a new phenomenon in children's books, thanks to Lewis Carroll. It is not surprising that James Joyce knew the *Alice* books well.

Charles's language suits the mood and contributes a good deal to the piece. He is a genius at double meanings, at playing games with words, and he challenges every child who picks up the book to play the game with him. And when the child catches Charles's second meaning (" 'We called him Tortoise because he taught us' "), the child experiences a sense of satisfaction unparalleled elsewhere. The child has played the game right and can share a private joke with the author.

By banishing seriousness, Charles turns the tables on the old, menacing books proffered to children. Although the characters in the *Alice* books take themselves seriously, no child reader is meant to do so. The language the characters use, the games they play, the lives they lead—all evoke mirth and laughter, at least from the child's point of view. The Rabbit, the Duchess, the Queen of Hearts, the Hatter, and the White Knight are all figures of fun.

Perhaps the most important difference between the *Alice* books and more conventional children's stories of mid-Victorian Britain is a difference in the author's attitude toward his audience. For a middle- and upper-class child, growing up in Victorian times may have been something less than a happy experience. It was an age of the nanny and the governess; children were shunted off to the nursery, brought out to spend an hour with their mothers in the late afternoon, and then whisked off again. When they reached school age, they were packed off to preparatory and then public schools, where they learned to fear schoolmasters and mistresses and, even more, one another. School was too often the arena of the bully: violence was rampant. To survive at the English boarding school, one had to be strong and resourceful enough to outwit one's classmates.

By a magical combination of memory and intuition, Charles keenly appreciated what it was like to be a child in a grown-up society, what it meant to be scolded, rejected, ordered about. The *Alice* books are antidotes to the child's degradation. Like Dickens, Charles knew that when harsh reality becomes unbearable, the child seeks escape through fantasy. Charles also knew how to make the adult reader sympathize with the child Alice, the victim of the unpredictable, undependable world of adults into which she has accidentally fallen. Charles champions the child in the child's confrontation with the adult world, and in that, too, his book differs from most others. He treats children, both in his book and in real life, as equals. He has a way of seeing into their minds and hearts, and he knows how to train their minds painlessly and move their hearts constructively. As an adult, he devotes more of his time, money, and energy to doing things for children than to anything else.

The theme of survival echoes all through Charles's work, just as it is a major concern in his life. If the *Alice* books are symbols of his own struggle to survive, they are also formulae for every child's survival: they offer encouragement to push on, messages of hope in the wilderness of adult society. Time and again Charles articulates that message, through his works and in his personal relationships. Ethel Rowell, a child friend, recorded her debt to him for teaching her logic and for compelling her "to that arduous business of thinking." And she added: "He gave me a sense of my own personal dignity. He was so punctilious, so courteous, so considerate, so scrupulous not to embarrass or offend, that he made me feel I counted."[15]

Charles's devotion to children and their plight are at the heart of the *Alice* books. They are his way of embracing and comforting the child. He first tells the tale in order to entertain three real children, then he publishes it to make the world of children a bit happier. In a letter to the father of one of his child friends, he wrote (January 31, 1877): "The pleasantest thought I have, connected with *Alice*, is that she has given real and innocent pleasure to children."

The element of respect and the absence of condescension are crucial, and

Charles's acceptance of the child as an equal makes all the difference, for it is these components that render the books timeless. Despite the Victorian furniture built into the tales, they do today for young people what they did for Ethel Rowell and other Victorian children. A seventeen-year-old student of mine confirmed this notion, writing in a paper on nineteenth-century fantasy: "Lewis Carroll gives equal time to the child's point of view. He makes fun of the adult world and understands all the hurt feelings that most children suffer while they are caught in the condition of growing up but are still small. I find myself constantly identifying with Alice as I move through this bewildering world of ours. The *Alice* books help the child develop self-awareness and assure her that she is not the only one feeling what she feels. Maybe they even show adults how to be more aware of the child and the needs of children. They really made it easier for me to grow up."

Charles does not play jokes on children—he shares jokes with them and, in doing so, gives them the self-confidence they need, the extra boost to make them take another step forward in the often precarious process of leaving childhood and entering adulthood. Along the road he makes them laugh without requiring them to pay for their laughter.

Even today the formula works: Charles helps children see themselves anew and to like what they see. That is why the *Alice* books have been translated into practically every language that children speak and why Charles commands an audience in every new generation.

But how did he come to understand the child and the predicament of childhood? Well, we have come full circle. If we look back to the family hearth at Croft, we see a highly sensitive eldest son growing up in surroundings that make enormous demands upon him. The heroine of the two books is modeled on Alice Liddell, but she and her adventures would not have materialized had the boy Charles Dodgson not earlier lived through those trials and adventures.

*Agnes and Amy Hughes, daughters of the artist Arthur Hughes, feigning sleep. Charles took the Hughes sisters to a pantomime and wrote them amusing letters suggesting how they might fairly divide the kisses he sent them and how best to press cats between leaves of blotting paper.*

# CHAPTER SIX

# The Pursuit of Innocents

*Surely it is thus that cherubs and seraphs sing,*
*and charm the saints of heaven.*

CHARLES READE

All his life Charles Dodgson conducted an ardent search for beauty—in drawings and paintings, on the stage, in the elegance of mathematical proofs, in the mysteries of the Bible and the works of God, in nature, in literature, and in the minds and hearts of children.

We know that, even as a boy, he nurtured artistic ambitions: the family magazines he composed and edited are populated by early efforts of his to sketch and to paint. His letters, even those from school, contain drawings and literary flourishes. Then, later, he himself drew the illustrations for *Alice's Adventures Under Ground.* Later still, his letters to artists illustrating his books are weighted with sketches he hoped would help them fulfill his intentions in their finished drawings.

As the lad matured, the visual arts claimed his serious notice. When he left Yorkshire and childhood behind and came to Oxford, he moved from marionettes and domestic charades to the real theater, from puppets and amateur thespians to professional actors and actresses. A similar transition occurred with drawing and painting, as his attraction to artists and their work intensified. He visited galleries and museums regularly, occasionally bought pictures, and cultivated friendships with artists. He took instruction in drawing and tried to shape his talent, but could never achieve the professional quality he yearned for. Soon he realized the truth of John Ruskin's verdict that he would never command artistic authority and polish. He reconciled himself to sketching as a hobby and used it for practical purposes, as a diversion, and to entertain his young visitors.

He had an eye for the beauty around him and a good intuitive sense of composition. With his limited ability to draw, however, he saw photography as a door opening onto an aesthetic world where he might succeed better than he had with drawing and sketching. Photography appealed also because he was at heart a gadgeteer, an amateur inventor, a devotee of technological progress.

He was by no means alone in his newfound interest. Photography became a popular pastime in the 1850s. The "glass house," where photographs were taken, was almost as common on the Victorian landscape as the television aerial in ours. Taking and looking at photographs was the kind of diversion that television viewing would become a hundred years later.

It was not, by any means, an era of easy, instant photography. To take a photograph in the 1850s, when Charles began, he needed a darkroom at hand before and after he took his picture. He first had to prepare his sitter for the "take"; then, when all was ready, he had to dart off to his darkroom to prepare the "plate" (film did not come into use until the 1880s), by pouring collodion, a gummy solution of guncotton in ether that dries rapidly, onto a 10-by-8-inch oblong glass plate which he had rubbed and polished like a conscientious waiter with a wineglass. In pouring the collodion, he had to make sure that he coated the glass evenly and completely and that no foreign specks or liquid touched it. Then, working quickly and carefully, he had to sensitize the plate by dipping it into a silver nitrate solution, again making sure that the liquid spread evenly over the surface. That done, he could take the picture, providing, of course, that no accident occurred on the way from the darkroom to the camera and back. If the wet plate brushed against his cuff or smeared against a curtain, it was ruined; if Charles bumped up against anything, or if, in moving to and from the camera, he stirred up a cloud of dust and particles settled on the wet plate, he had to begin again. It was all delicate and further complicated by the need to hurry: the collodion plate had to remain wet throughout the various stages; "wet collodion" was no misnomer.

As soon as Charles exposed the plate (by lifting a cap from the front of his camera by hand and replacing it after a prescribed number of seconds), he had to rush, plate in hand, back to the darkroom to develop it on the spot, and after developing it in one carefully prepared solution, he had to "fix" it in another. If all went smoothly, if the sitter remained stone-still for, say, the forty-five seconds required, if the daylight was strong enough, if the temperature had not changed significantly, if the chemicals were pure, potent, and properly applied, if dust particles had not settled on the plate, then perhaps Charles had a negative that pleased him. But successful or not, he was a marked man—he emerged from his darkroom with black stains on both his hands and probably his clothing. The chemicals splashed when he used them, and he had to use his hands on the wet plates. The stains, coupled with the fact that they occurred in a darkroom, earned for photography the sobriquet "the black art."

But even now Charles was not finished. He had yet to varnish the negative, by first holding the glass plate before a hot fire until it was evenly heated, then pouring varnish over it, allowing it to drain and dry. Only after he had a firm negative fixed and varnished could he make a positive print. Victorian photograph albums are often testimonials not so much to the marvels of photography as to photographic failures. That Charles achieved so many clear, unblemished photographs in perfect focus says much for his technical ability and efficiency.

In Charles's day a photographer's equipment was extensive and cumbersome. If he wanted to take photographs in the open country, he had to bring with him a darkroom tent, a large box camera, numerous lenses, a tripod, bottles containing chemicals, a quantity of glass plates, numerous trays and dishes, scales and weights, glass graduates, funnels, a pail or two, and even water for rinsing when no fresh source was available. So unwieldy were his crates and boxes, he had to hire a porter to help transport them, and he certainly needed a carriage or horse-drawn van to take him to his destination.

Although Charles only infrequently photographed landscapes, he did move his equipment about; he packed and carted it to Croft, Guildford, Whitby, to the Lakes, and to London, where he shunted it from one friend's home to another. When Charles Longley, a friend of the family, became Archbishop of Canterbury, Charles used Lambeth Palace, with its rich architectural backdrops, as a photographic venue. He packed and unpacked his equipment himself, sent it by rail, and moved it around London and Oxford in hired vehicles. We do not know whether Charles ever used a perambulator or wheelbarrow, as other photographers did, but he might well have done.

Actually both Charles and photography passed through their formative years at about the same time. As we have seen, Charles was twenty-three when, home in Yorkshire from Oxford for the Christmas vacation, he sat for a commercial photographer in nearby Ripon. On September 10, 1855, his Uncle Skeffington Lutwidge, visiting Croft, took "several photographs, the church, bridge, etc.," and two days later Charles accompanied him to Richmond, "photographing."

Charles's interest in photography grew serious the following year, when he was twenty-four. His chum Reginald Southey, a fellow Student at Christ Church, already absorbed in photography, aided and abetted him. Southey's enthusiasm reinforced Charles's experience with his uncle. Just before he turned twenty-four, on January 16, Charles visited the Photographic Exhibition in London and commented about the pictures in detail in his diary. Two days later he and Southey called on Hugh Welch Diamond, Secretary of the Photographic Society, and Charles came away with some of Diamond's own photographs, including one of Uncle Skeffington.

The die was cast. On March 18, 1856, at the beginning of the Easter vacation, Charles, in London, bought a "camera and lens, etc.," for "about £15." On May 1 Charles's camera arrived, and a week later a shipment of fresh chemicals. "I am now ready to begin the art," he noted on May 13. The rest is history. A man of compulsive orderliness, he arranged his photographs in albums, with appropriate indexes, numbered his negatives, and kept a photography register. He tried his hand at landscapes, architecture, a human skeleton, a fish skeleton, at drawings and sculptures. But mostly people, first his family and his Oxford colleagues and associates.

He sought out worthwhile subjects, especially handsome, striking, and beautiful sitters. He arranged them and the background carefully. He had a knack for making people enjoy sitting still for the required eternity, relaxed, not fidgety. Especially with children, he used his ebullience, charm, volubility, and his treasure trove of anecdotes to divert the sitter's attention from the mechanics of picture-taking. He also examined other artists' arrangements and techniques. When he went to the Exhibition of the British Artists in London on April 22, 1857, he noted: "I took hasty sketches on the margin of the Catalogue of several of the pictures, chiefly for the arrangement of hands, to help in grouping for photographs." He collected good examples of other photographers' work, particularly those of Oscar Gustav Rejlander, for whose lens he also sat. He developed a keen eye for proportion and balance. When a friend sent him a photograph of his daughter, he returned it asking for a cropped copy, "that I may have her *without her feet!* The artist has managed his lens badly, and has magnified them: no English child ever had such huge feet! I have so often photographed, and drawn, children's feet (generally in their natural beauty . . .) that I speak from experience."

His observations and practice led to a storehouse of knowledge and a clear notion of right and wrong. "In taking portraits," he wrote in his review of the 1860 Photographic Exhibition, "a well-arranged light is of paramount importance . . . as without it all softness of feature is hopeless." When taking groups, one must give "to the different figures one object of attention. . . . In single portraits the chief difficulty . . . is the natural placing of the hands; within the narrow limits allowed by the focussing power of the lens there are not many attitudes into which they naturally fall, while, if the artist attempts the arrangement himself he generally produces the effect of the proverbial bashful young man in society who finds for the first time that his hands are an encumbrance, and cannot remember what he is in the habit of doing with them in private life."[1]

His devotion to natural realism clashed with Julia Margaret Cameron's notions. When he visited the Photographic Exhibition on June 23, 1864, he "did *not* admire Mrs. Cameron's large heads taken out of focus" and wrote his sister Louisa (August 3, 1864) that some of them were "nearly hideous." Mrs. Cameron apparently did not admire Charles's work either: in a letter to Henry Taylor, she wrote: "Your photograph by Dodgson I heard described as looking like 'a sea monster fed upon milk.' . . . The Tennysons abhor that photograph."[2] All the same, Charles and the Camerons managed genial personal relations. At Mrs. Cameron's request, Charles brought his photographs for her to see, and by July 28, 1864, came to think some of hers "very beautiful."

Because Charles could achieve with a camera the success and fulfillment that eluded him with a sketchbook, the newfangled art form became much more than a personal indulgence—it was a passport to the rarefied world of art, enabling him to sign photographs that he gave away as "from the Artist." The possibilities were boundless. When Charles visited relatives in the Lake District, a cousin showed "some interesting drawings of mining machinery in America, and some ground plans and elevations which he took in the Holy Land. These inspired me," Charles wrote (August 27, 1856), "with two new ideas, both of which I hope to carry out: to collect ground plans of English Abbeys and other ruins, and to make a Long Vacation tour to the Holy Land: the latter would be far more enjoyable if I could only manage to carry my Photography with me."

How it all changed his life! Word of his skill spread, and Oxford society, and later select London circles, offered themselves up to his lens. Theologians, grammarians, philosophers came, the crème de la crème of Church and University. The road led from photographing fellow dons and clerics to photographing their children, and before long, proud mothers were leading their little darlings through Tom Quad and up the stairs to Charles's rooms. Charles was ecstatic. Photography provided instant access to his heart's delight, to the acquaintance, converse, and, in many cases, prolonged and affectionate friendships with beautiful, pure, unaffected, natural female children.

Appreciating the companionship of children, particularly the female of the species, was not new with Charles. We see from the earliest surviving diary volume and his letters his early penchant for the young. His involvement manifested itself at Croft, even before he entered his father's schoolhouse as a teacher. On July 3, 1855, Charles and two sisters drove over to Melsonby to call on some friends, who had as visitors Mrs. Richard Harington, widow of the Principal of Brasenose College, Oxford. "I made great friends with Mrs. Harington's nice little children, Bob and Beatrice, 4 and 3 years old," Charles wrote. His friendship with the Haringtons matured and endured.

A week after the initial meeting with the Haringtons, Charles took a class in his father's girls' school for the first time "and liked it very much." On August 17 he noted that the two youngest Aireys, Augusta and Georgina, daughters of a "theatrical family" visiting Croft, "are very pleasant and conversable." On the twenty-first, on a visit to Tynemouth, he called on a Mrs. Crawshay "with three nice little children; I took a great fancy to Florence, the eldest a child of very sweet manners—she has a very striking, though not a pretty, face, and may possibly turn out a beautiful brunette."

While Charles was staying with his cousins at Whitburn, a chance meeting occurred that adumbrated the later Liddell connection. On a walk he took (August 27, 1855), he encountered "little Frederica[3] Liddell. . . . Each time I see her," he added, "confirms me in the impression that she is one of the most lovely children I ever saw, gentle and innocent looking, not an inanimate doll-beauty." Two days later "I went on the cliff . . . and as little Frederica Liddell happened to be sitting on a stile near, I put her into . . . [a] sketch also."

Frederica was a cousin of the three Liddell girls who later become so significant a part of Charles's life, and she enters the diaries once more when Charles joined his cousins and the Liddells on the beach, "which gave me

CHARLES'S PHOTOGRAPHS OF CHILD FRIENDS
*Above, three Ellis sisters. Connyngham Ellis, father of these sisters and Vicar of Cranbourne, Berkshire, was one of Charles's friends-in-photography. Charles visited the family from time to time and became a favorite of at least five Ellis sisters.*
*Below, "Xie" Kitchin: "Where dreamful fancies dwell!"*

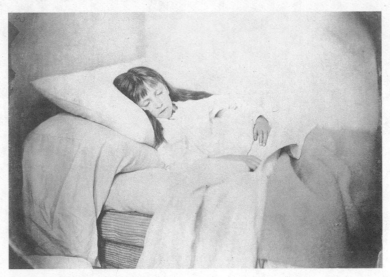

*Grace Denman*

*Effie Millais*

*Alice Constance Westmacott*

*Irene MacDonald*

*Beatrice Henley*

*"Coates," the daughter of an employee at Croft Rectory*

*Alice Jane Donkin*

the opportunity, of making acquaintance with the elder of them, one of the nicest children I have ever seen, as well as the prettiest: dear, sweet, pretty Frederica!" Then, after an evening of charades, presumably with Frederica present, in which Charles himself took "an old man part," he added: "Mark this day, oh Annalist, with a white stone."

The pattern was established. A week later, on a visit to the Tates at Richmond, he made "acquaintance with the eldest of the little Cochranes, a plain queer little child, Constance"; and ten days after (September 21), he fell "in with my favourite little Liddells, coming over to the house," and spent "about an hour with the little party, storytelling, etc." He added: "The youngest Liddell, Gertrude, is even prettier than my favourite Freddie: indeed she has quite the most lovely face I ever saw in a child." Again he marked this day with a white stone.

At the outset of the long summer vacation of 1856, he went from Oxford to London and stayed with his relations at Putney, where, at a party, he met the four children of T. W. C. Murdoch, later Special Commissioner to Canada. A week after the party, on the nineteenth, the Murdochs came over to be photographed and stayed for the evening. Charles composed a verse addressed to the youngest Murdoch, Alice, then four years old, addressing her as

> O child! O new-born denizen
> Of life's great city!

and wrote it in his album alongside his photograph of her.[4]

Back at Croft at the end of June, he rode over to Dinsdale to dine with a friend and encountered a family named Brown. "Spent most of the evening with the children," he wrote. He also took his camera over to Whitby and photographed the family of Lieutenant Bainbridge, whom he knew from previous visits to Whitby. He dined with the Bainbridges to celebrate Florence's birthday and read aloud J. M. Morton's play *Away with Melancholy*.

Home for Christmas 1856, he helped with festivities in his father's school and gave two magic lantern performances. At the first, he had "the largest audience I ever had, about 80 children, and a large miscellaneous party besides. . . . I introduced 13 songs . . . 6 for myself and 7 for the children." After the second, he advised himself "to give rather more time to views, to make the comedy more palpable, for example, in imitation of animals, voices, etc."

During Hilary term, while walking (March 7, 1857) with a friend through Christ Church Meadow, he met "with . . . the Norrises [James Norris was

President of Corpus Christi College and a distant relative], which gave me the opportunity I have long been wishing for, of being acquainted with them. . . . They seem to be very nice children, and the eldest is certainly pretty (I must find an opportunity of taking their photographs)." And on the following day he "met in the Broad Walk the eldest of the Norris party (Lydia), with the governess, and made further acquaintance with my newly-discovered little cousin. Unless the parents now make some advances . . . , this acquaintanceship with the children may prove awkward," he adds. Some agreeable arrangement must have been achieved, for Charles lent his photograph album to them, Mrs. Norris asked him to call, and the friendship prospered.

Attending a Choral Society concert (May 29, 1857), he noticed "a family party . . . next to me, one of whom . . . was a little girl with the most perfect little French face I ever saw, like one of the French beauties one sees painted on enamel, the effect being carried out by a head of flaxen hair dressed 'à l'Impératrice.' "

Back in Yorkshire for the summer, Charles photographed children a good deal. On August 18 Mrs. C. R. Weld, Tennyson's sister-in-law, brought her daughter Agnes Grace to sit for Charles. The Tennyson connection intrigued Charles: "I was much interested in talking about him with one who knew him so well. She told me . . . that he wishes much to learn photographing. . . . The children [Hallam and Lionel] are noticed even by strangers for their remarkable beauty. . . . He has addressed one sonnet to the little Agnes Grace: she hardly merits one by actual beauty, though her face is very striking and attractive, and will certainly make a beautiful photograph. I think of sending a print of her, through Mrs. Weld, for Tennyson's acceptance."

In late summer he set off on a journey to Scotland, then swung back toward the Lakes again on his way home. On September 18 he walked toward Coniston, intending at first only to "*see*" Tent Lodge, where the Tennysons were staying. On arriving, he "at last" made up his mind "to take the liberty of calling." The poet was not at home, but Charles sent in his card all the same, "adding . . . 'artist of "Agnes Grace". . . .' " Mrs. Tennyson received him, and he spent almost an hour with her and her sons, "the most beautiful boys of their age I ever saw." Mrs. Tennyson agreed to let Hallam and Lionel sit for Charles's camera and "even seemed to think it was not hopeless that Tennyson himself might sit, though I said I would not request it, as he must have refused so many that it is unfair to expect it. She also

*Alfred Tennyson, taken by Charles. Although Charles disliked being lionized, he himself felt no scruples about lionizing the great. When the Tennysons were visiting friends in the Lake District, Charles appeared uninvited, camera at the ready, and managed to photograph the family.*

promised that I should have an autograph of the poet's. Both the children proposed coming with me when I left—how far seemed immaterial to them." Another white stone ends the diary entry.

Three days later Charles reappeared on the Tennysons' threshold, ready to photograph. "After I had waited some little time [in the drawing room] . . . a strange shaggy-looking man entered: his hair, moustache and beard looked wild and neglected; these very much hid the character of his face. . . . He was dressed in a loosely fitting morning coat, common grey flannel trousers, and a carelessly tied black silk neckerchief. His hair is black: I think the eyes too; they are keen and restless—nose aquiline—forehead high and broad; both face and head are fine and manly. His manner was kind and friendly from the first: there is a dry lurking humour in his style of talking."

Charles dined with the Tennysons and showed them his photographs: "A most delightful evening. I left at what I believed to be a little after nine, but which to my horror I found to be after eleven. . . . *Dies mirabilis!*" On the twenty-eighth Charles photographed everyone in sight—all the Tennysons, their hosts, and a visitor—and on the following day repeated the exercise.

Two years later, during the Easter vacation of 1859, when Charles was on the Isle of Wight, he called again on the Tennysons at Farringford. He reported to his cousin William Wilcox (May 11, 1859) that he had come upon the Poet Laureate mowing his lawn. Tennyson was welcoming, showed Charles around the house, where his own photographs of the Tennysons hung upon the wall. Charles paid several visits to Farringford, engaged Tennyson in conversation, and got Hallam, the elder son, to autograph the photograph that Charles had taken of him up north.

\* \* \*

When the diary recommences after the critical four-year gap, the same concerns and activities dominate, and his letters of the period also reflect those interests. Friendships with children and photography intertwined freely. Photography often provided the entrée to acquaintanceships, even as it advanced, enhanced, and cemented earlier connections. Charles devoted a great deal of time and energy first to finding appropriate child sitters, then to cultivating their friendship while photographing them and amassing his pictorial oeuvres. Photographing children individually, with their parents, sometimes in pairs, and in groups became a main occupation.

At Croft in the autumn of 1862, he took "several good photographs . . . including Dr. Dukes' children: Mary, Ernest, Gertrude and Caroline." On October 8 he was at Barmby Moor, the home of Wilfred's intended, Alice Donkin: "Took pictures of some of the children, and the house"; and on the morrow: "Photographing most of the day: took a composition picture, 'the elopement,' Alice Donkin having climbed out of her bedroom window to pose a staged escape with a rope and ladder and one of 'the little brides-maids,' Alice and Polly seen through a picture frame."

He was forced to abandon photography in late autumn for lack of proper light, but remained on the *qui vive*. He was by now a minor photographic celebrity with access to many homes and the children they sheltered. In fact, even before he was able to return to photography in 1863, toward the end of March, we find a list of 108 names in the diary, "Photographed or to be photographed." It comprises the names of female children arranged alphabetically: 5 Alices, 5 Beatrices, 6 Constances, 6 Ediths, 5 Florences, 12 Marys. After each of the eighteen appears a date, indicating their birthdays and ages, a considerable treasure to the compiler.

Later, beginning in 1871, Charles prepared more lists of "new friends." Opposite the entry at the end of a Whitby holiday (August 26, 1871), Charles added "a list of the friends made during my 3 weeks' stay here," comprising five families, with the names, occupations, and addresses of the parents, their children's names, ages, and, here and there, birth dates. On August 27, 1872, he wrote of the "several very pleasant friends" made during a similar holiday at Bognor.

"My child-friends during this seaside visit have been far more numerous than in any former year," Charles wrote (September 27, 1877) after his summer sojourn at Eastbourne, and added a list opposite of thirty-four names, all female. A year later (September 30, 1878), he notes that his new child friends have been few that year, and he lists three. But fortune smiled more brightly in 1879, when he made two lists (September 15 and 28), enumerating twenty-two. And similar lists appear each year from 1880 to 1886. Then, at the beginning of October 1887, he writes: "No new child-friends at *Eastbourne* this summer. My new friends have been . . ."—and he lists four in Oxford and nine in London.

Seven more names appear in early October 1888. "My new child-friends this summer include Princess Alice and Lady Marjorie Manners, whom I met at Hatfield," he writes in mid-September 1889. More lists appeared in the early 1890s, though none for 1893. But in late October 1894 he writes: "My new girl-friends, this summer, have been . . ."—and he lists sixteen. New friendships occur thereafter, but he compiles no further lists.

Charles kept an enormous store of delights for his young friends in his Christ Church rooms, but nothing caught their imaginations more than photography, with all its built-in sorcery. Even before he moved into his large set of rooms, he envisaged (June 21, 1868) the "bare possibility of my erecting a photographing room on the top, accessible from the rooms, which would be indeed a luxury. . . ." It seems inconceivable that the college authorities would risk marring the classic lines of Tom Quad with such a structure. But even the Canons and dons of the House succumbed to the blandishments of the new art. They allowed Charles to erect his glass house, above his chambers. He could then escort his sitters upward into the light and place them before his camera even in inclement weather. The structure was finished and ready to use by October 1871. Charles fitted it out, arranged for proper heating, and on March 16, 1872, took his first photograph there.

Photography continued to open wider and broader possibilities for friendships. As with the Tennysons, it helped him again and again to gain entrée into the circles of the high, the mighty, the famous, the noble, the rich. His overtures were usually straightforward, designed to ease him into their good graces. First he offered to show his photograph albums, containing not only photographs of the Liddells and the Tennysons but also many more fascinating images. Although he never managed to get the Queen or the Prince of Wales, he bagged some lesser royals and a large array of notables. Many of the photographs are inscribed by the sitters and accompanied by some verse or other quotation which Charles added in his neat script beneath the photograph, explaining the story the photograph is meant to tell. Imagine the running commentary that flowed from his lips and the appreciative sighs from his viewers as he turned the pages for them, revealing the Queen's youngest son, Prince Leopold; Frederick, Crown Prince of Denmark; John

Ruskin; the Rossetti family; the Millais clan; Charlotte Yonge and her mother; the Henry Taylors; the dramatist Tom Taylor; the artist Arthur Hughes; George MacDonald and his family; the sculptor Alexander Munro; Holman Hunt; Henry Parry Liddon; Archbishop Longley and family (at Lambeth Palace); F. D. Maurice; Bishop Wilberforce; Sir Michael Hicks Beach (Chief Secretary for Ireland); the sculptor Thomas Woolner; the poet Aubrey de Vere; the Bishop of Lincoln, John Jackson; Robert Bickersteth, Bishop of Ripon, and his family; Friedrich Max Müller, the orientalist, and his family; Gathorne-Hardy, Home Secretary; C. C. Clerke, Archdeacon of Oxford; Thomas Combe; C. W. Corfe, Christ Church organist; C. W. Faraday, Professor of Chemistry; Sir Frederick Ouseley, Professor of Music; Bartholomew Price; a smattering of canons; and, somewhat farther afield, J. Baker, Chaplain of Winchester College; H. D. Erskine, Dean of Ripon; George Kitchin, then headmaster of Winchester College; a number of Kitchin's masters and groups of his boys; masters of Radley and Rugby; A. P. Saunders, Dean of Peterborough; and many more.

If the season was right and the acquaintanceship ripe enough, the next adventure was to photograph the young sitters. Charles strove to capture his subjects as they appeared in real life, almost as though taken unawares. His familiarity with the theater led him to value stage props, and he used them: a book, a lens, a croquet mallet, a table, a bicycle, a mirror, a doll, a basket, a column, a trellis, a flower. He disliked elaborate and artificial surroundings and leaned toward the clean and the simple. He shunned ornate backdrops and used a blanket, a cloth, or a plain curtain, a flight of stairs, a classical pillar, a Gothic arch.

He developed special techniques for photographing children. "He could not bear dressed-up children, but liked them to be as natural as possible," one observer recalled. "He never let them pose for their photographs and it did not matter a bit if their hair was untidy; in fact, it pleased him better."[5] "You don't seem to know how to *fix* a restless child, for photography," he wrote his artist friend Gertrude Thomson (October 2, 1893). "*I* wedge her into the *corner* of a room, if standing; or into the angle of a sofa, if lying down."

Out in the open, Charles placed one young charmer on a flight of stone steps, near a brick wall, and had her lean her head on her braced arm, her dress falling in folds down to her high-buttoned shoes. He arranged a trio of lasses in an almost perfect semicircle. He gave a child in a cape a stuffed bird to hold; he had another clasp her huge hat in one hand to let her hair

*Above, "The Dream": the Barry children, whom
Charles caught in a double exposure that was meant
to capture the mystery of dreamland. The Barry family
were early friends in Yorkshire; the father, John Barry,
was Rector of Smeaton. Charles photographed the
children a number of times.*
*Right, "Reflections": Charles's sister Margaret beside a
looking-glass. Margaret was the ninth of the eleven Dodgson
children.*

flow freely over her shoulders, one of her arms propped on a classical column, her eyes turned away toward a distant object. He put his sitters into a
variety of different seats and settees, stood them before leafy or brick backgrounds, posed them in a corner holding a doll, sat them on stairs grasping
a mallet or before an ornate archway, an arm upraised and a hand held up
against the wainscot. One, wearing a frilly dress, holds a plant in her lap; another sits in profile, the fingers of her hand curled around the back of the
chair she graces. He took a group cleverly arranged before an open window;
a child caught pensive as she contemplates writing with a pencil into a notebook; one climbing a garden ladder; another holding a large book open in
her lap. Two he posed with a seesaw, one by a high-backed chair playing a
violin, one in a plaid skirt sits on a lower limb of a tree.

   He created story photography: a child portrayed in a nightdress, mouth set grim, hair disheveled, a brush and mirror in her hands—with the title "It Won't Come Smooth"; the Cherry Group: the three Liddell sisters, one holding a cherry out for another to reach with her lips. Others depict characters from literature or lore: the Beggar Maid, Little Red Riding Hood, a group arranged in tableau vivant entitled "St. George and the Dragon," a youngster as Viola in *Twelfth Night,* an actress dressed in chain mail as a heroine in Scott's *The Lady of the Lake.* Once he asked a bride of two weeks to dress up again in her wedding gown and prevailed on her three young sisters to don their bridesmaids' dresses so that he could record the marriage. The bride was Mary Augusta Arnold, after her betrothal Mrs. Humphry Ward.

Charles bought up theatrical costumes and borrowed others from the Ashmolean to dress his sitters in dramatic finery. Some appear in the typical dress of nations around the world—Greece, Turkey, Denmark—and from time to time a young female poses as a "Chinaman." He tried trick photography. He placed his sister Margaret before a mirror and got two images of her head in a photograph called "Reflections." He double-exposed a group of the Barry children to make the son appear as a ghost and called the result "The Dream."

The adventures shared in taking photographs, of deciding on the pose, arranging the clothes, or choosing the costume, the artifacts, the props, draping the clothing, adjusting the limbs, seeking the right facial expression—it was all an elaborate game the children and he played together and enjoyed. Charles, for his part, joked with and teased his young friends as he performed his elaborate ritual; the children were thrilled with every minute of the game, delighted with all the attention showered upon them.

And there was more. When Charles had to dash off to his darkroom, the young, curious minds wanted to know what happened *in there.* He obliged, even allowing them to accompany him into his sanctum sanctorum, to observe his magic. Alice Liddell recalled her induction into the mysteries:

> Much more exciting than being photographed was being allowed to go into the dark room, and watch him develop the large glass plates. What could be more thrilling than to see the negative gradually take shape, as he gently rocked it to and fro in the acid bath? Besides, the dark room was so mysterious, and we felt that any adventures might happen then! There were all the joys of preparation, anticipation, and realization, besides the feeling that we were assisting at some secret rite usually reserved for grown-ups! Then there was the additional excite-

ment, after the plates were developed, of seeing what we looked like in a photograph.[6]

Not every young child friend "endured the torture" of being photographed, as Isabel Standen put it,[7] although Ethel Arnold did, and could "never catch a whiff of the potent odour of collodion nowadays without instantly being transported on the magic wings of memory to Lewis Carroll's dark-room, where, shrunk to childhood's proportions, I see myself watching, open-mouthed, the mysterious process of coating the plate, or, standing on a box drawn out from under the sink to assist my small dimensions, watching the still more mysterious process of development."

While Charles used all manner of dress for his sitters—ragged garments, party frocks, fancy costumes—he also took them with no dress at all. Not right away, to be sure. In a sense he worked his way slowly toward the nude child model. First he took a number, besides Alice Liddell, costumed as beggar children, with bare feet; he also took photographs of children in bed, lying in their nightdresses, propped up on settees. Then, on July 8, 1866, he succeeded in taking "a good many" successful photographs of little Ella, daughter of Sir Monier Monier-Williams, Professor of Sanskrit, "of whom I did several pictures with no other dress than a cloth tied round her, savage fashion."

Eleven years after he acquired his camera, when he was thirty-five, he had his child models dispose of garments altogether. On May 21, 1867, he recorded this simple fact: "Mrs. Latham [an Oxford neighbor] brought Beatrice, and I took a photograph of the two, and several of Beatrice alone, *sans habillement*." In the next thirteen years Charles took other nude photographs of female children, sometimes during sustained sittings, some, but not all, in his studio. On October 9, 1869, in Guildford, he brought "cameras, sofa, etc., into the Haydons' garden" and took a number of photographs, "Tommy, Ethel (2 of the latter undraped)."

Although he took a good many nude photographs, only four have come to light.[8] Other nude photographs of children, all pale and loitering, are occasionally attributed to Charles's camera, but they are clearly not his work, mainly because they are photographic failures, and he diligently destroyed failures. Before he died, moreover, he destroyed most of the negatives and prints of his nude studies. Those that remained he asked his executors to destroy, and they apparently complied with his wish.

Charles was extremely careful about giving away pictures of nude children

Four nude photographs taken by Charles (and professionally colored, with drapery and backgrounds supplied by the artists): Beatrice Hatch seated before white cliffs (left); Evelyn Hatch as a gypsy sitting by a brook (below); Evelyn Hatch lying on the ground (opposite top); and Annie and Frances Henderson as castaways (opposite bottom). Charles began to photograph children *sans habillement*, as he put it, in 1867, when he was thirty-five. "Their innocent unconsciousness is very beautiful," he wrote to the mother of the Henderson girls, "and gives one a feeling of reverence, as at the presence of something sacred."

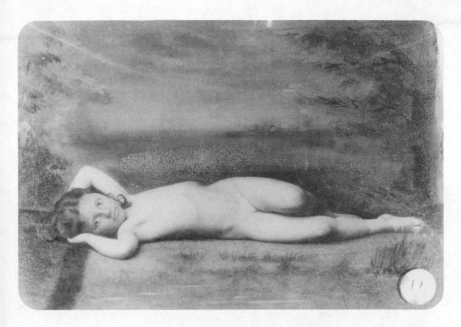

and even about letting them be seen. On June 21, 1881, he addressed Mrs. Henderson: "I write to ask if you would like to have any more copies of the full-front photographs of the children. I have 2 or 3 prints of each, but I intend to destroy all but one of each. That is all I want for myself, and (though I consider them perfectly innocent in themselves) there is really *no* friend to whom I should wish to give photographs which so entirely defy conventional rules. Miss Thomson is the only friend who has even *seen* them, and even to *her* I should not think of giving copies. . . . The negatives are already destroyed."

And to Beatrice Hatch he wrote (March 4, 1895): "I have, as you know, 5 coloured photos . . . of you and Evelyn. . . . I want to leave written instructions, for my Executors, as to what to do with these pictures. It shall be exactly what you and your sisters would like best. Please consult them, and let me know." Of those that survive, two must be of these five, one of the Henderson girls and the fourth a watercolor tracing of a photograph of Beatrice Hatch, all embellished by a colorist. Despite the color and painted backdrops and, in one instance, a painted loincloth, they are valuable examples of Charles's photographic art.

How did he manage it? His letters and diaries trace the way he approached parents, first to get their permission to photograph the children and then, if all went well, to photograph them unclothed. The Hendersons are a case in point. He first approached the father, P. A. W. Henderson, Fellow of Wadham College (June 18, 1877): "I have been told so often, and so forcibly, that I *ought* (as an amateur-photographer whose special line is 'children'), to apply for leave to take your 2 little girls (whom I don't even know by sight yet), that I write to say I expect to be here till the end of the month, and shall be much pleased if you, or Mrs. Henderson, could at any time look in with them—*not* [to] be photographed then and there (I never succeed with strangers), but to make acquaintance with the place and the artist, and to see how they relished the idea of coming, another day, to be photographed."

A year and a half passed, and then, on November 1, 1878, "Henderson brought his 2 little girls, Annie and Frances. . . ." On December 2 Charles called on Mrs. Henderson "to take her my photos of the 2 little girls." Winter set in and Charles put his camera by. In mid-July of the following summer (1879), he wrote to Mrs. Henderson:

I hope my mention of my admiration of children's feet did not make you think I meant to propose taking *Annie* with bare feet. I shall propose no such thing, as I don't think she knows me well enough, and is also too nervous a child, to like it. So I hope she has heard nothing of it, as it might make her afraid to come. . . . With children who know me well, and who regard dress as a matter of indifference, I am very glad (when mothers permit) to take them in any amount of undress which is presentable, or even in none (which is more presentable than many forms of undress) but I don't think your Annie is at all a child of that sort. If you ever meet with any such "children of Nature," I shall be glad to hear of them.

Within the week (July 18), "Mrs. Henderson brought Annie and Frances. . . . [I] was agreeably surprised to find they were ready for any amount of undress, and seemed delighted at being allowed to run about naked. It was a great privilege to have such a model as Annie to take: a *very* pretty face, and a good figure. . . ."

Charles's delicate concern for the children's nervousness was, in this instance, misplaced. According to Mrs. Diana Bannister, Annie's daughter, "My mother was the eldest of three girls [a third would be born in 1880] all of whom adored Lewis Carroll. . . . Annie and Frances had gone to visit him with their father and spent the afternoon 'dressing up.' They heard him say how much he would like to photograph them in the nude. They promptly hid under the table, which had a cloth nearly reaching to the ground, and emerged with nothing on, much to the amusement of their host."[9]

The Henderson parents admired Charles's art and were completely easy about having the children photographed nude, delivering them to him and allowing them to stay without supervision. Two days after the July 18, 1879, sittings, Charles wrote Mrs. Henderson to ask whether Gertrude Thomson, who was coming to Oxford as his guest, might be present at a nude sitting. "I'm sure she would thoroughly enjoy helping to arrange the children for a few photographs." He insisted that the children themselves must be willing to come, and if the idea of Miss Thomson's presence did not put them off, he suggested that Mrs. Henderson deposit them at Christ Church at about eleven-thirty. He would give them their midday "dinner." Charles saw the advantage of Miss Thomson's doing some sketches "out of which . . . she might make *a* really pretty drawing. . . . I don't think she *could* have a better subject than Annie."

Readers who question Charles's motives in requesting to have the children left on their own must consider another paragraph in his July 20 letter to the mother: "I have only mentioned the *children,* as you talked of sending them alone: but if you are not too busy to come yourself, it would make the thing all the pleasanter. Even if too busy in the morning, couldn't you come to luncheon at 1½? That will make a nice party, 2 ladies and 2 gentlemen . . . as I am asking Mr. Bayne to luncheon." Charles added a postscript: "It is very pleasant to me to think that the children are so absolutely at their ease with me, and . . . I take it as a great compliment and privilege that you are willing to trust me with them so entirely. I have never seen anything more beautiful in childhood than their *perfect* simplicity."

On the following day (July 21, 1879), Miss Thomson and Charles "brought Frances down with us (Annie had a cold and could not come) and took a photo of her, lying on the sofa in her favourite dress of 'nothing.'" True to plan, Bayne—and Mr. and Mrs. Henderson—joined the party for lunch. Four days later, on the twenty-fifth, Charles fetched "Mrs. Henderson, Annie, and Frances, in a cab, and did some more photos of them in the same dress as before." On the twenty-ninth he "brought over Annie . . . alone (Frances having a cold) and did some photos of her—two excellent ones of her lying on a blanket, naked as usual."

On January 5, 1880, Charles wrote Mrs. Henderson to ask "whether you would have any objection to my giving to Miss E. G. Thomson . . . any of my photos of the children," adding that he would not give her, or "any one, any of the full front views."

In the late seventies, when Charles was photographing the Mayhew girls, daughters of another Oxford don, a sudden break in the friendship occurred. Margaret, one of the daughters, later explained: "My mother raised no objection to my younger sister, aged about six or seven, being photographed in the nude, or in very scanty clothing . . . but when permission was asked to photograph her elder sister, who was probably then about eleven, in a similar state, my mother's strict sense of Victorian propriety was shocked, and she refused the request. Mr. Dodgson was offended, and the friendship ceased forthwith."[10]

In the spring of 1880, he resumed work with the Henderson children. On May 22 "Annie and Frances . . . were brought at 11. . . . I did a photo of the two as Princes, and one of Annie naked (a back view, standing)." A week later "Annie and Frances . . . were brought at 11 . . . and I did 4 pictures of them, mostly in their favourite state of 'nothing to wear.'" Two days later (May 31, 1880), Charles wrote their mother:

I do hope you did not think I had taken a step not warranted by the circumstances, in allowing the children to live for 3 hours in their favourite costume, up in the studio. But I felt so confident that, when you told Annie they must not be taken naked because it was too cold, it was your *only* reason, that I thought that objection cleared away by the fact that the studio was . . . nearer 80° than 70°.

Their innocent unconsciousness is very beautiful, and gives one a feeling of reverence, as at the presence of something sacred: and, if you had only those two girls, I should see no objection (in spite of "Mrs. Grundy"*) in their repeating the performance, if they wished, next year, or even for 2 or 3 years to come. But, for the sake of their little brother, I quite think you may find it desirable to bring such habits to an end after this summer. A boy's head soon imbibes precocious ideas, which might be a cause of unhappiness in future years. . . . So I shall be quite prepared to find, next year, that they have learned to prefer *dressed* pictures. I am not so selfish as to wish for pictures, however valuable as works of art, the taking of which involved any risk for others.

Mrs. Henderson did not think Charles's behavior unwarranted, and cordiality reigned, and another photographic session followed (June 18), the last recorded instance of the Henderson children sitting for Charles's camera. In fact, Charles took his very last photograph less than a month later, in July 1880. A current of whispers ran through Oxford about Charles's nude photography, and he was aware of it. He was not one to fear wagging tongues, because he knew that he had not compromised his standards of moral rectitude, but he would have been concerned had the whispers reached the ears of his child friends. He nowhere suggests that his ingenuity was at an end or even flagging, or that he had tired of the art.

Other forces were weighing heavily upon him. For one thing, he felt keenly time's winged chariot at his heels and began referring to himself as an "elderly gentleman," an "old fogey," as "old and grey" and " 'elderly' if not 'old.' "[11] And he had yet to write a number of books, some already begun, others on the drawing board, serious works on logic, works on religious and moral subjects dealing with the meaning of life and death and bearing messages of comfort for young and old. It is no accident that within a year after he stopped photographing and six months before his fiftieth birthday, he gave up something even more central to his life—his mathematical lectureship, saying clearly (July 14, 1881) that in doing so he was looking forward to

---

* Thomas Morton's character in his play *Speed the Plough* (1798) became a symbol of rigid Victorian propriety.

"the additional time I shall have for book-writing." From this time forward, his diaries and letters echo his fears that he might not have enough time left to finish his books.

Another circumstance helps explain Charles's break with his "one amusement," photography: the rapid change taking place in photographic equipment and technique. The year he stopped taking photographs, 1880, heralded the advent of the dry plate process. Charles became acquainted with it, examined the results, and rejected them as artistically inferior. To stay with the old method would have been too time-consuming, to change to the new would have compromised his art. Instead he gave it up entirely.

The decision to abandon photography was, however, neither instantaneous nor deliberate. It seems to have evolved naturally. Eight days after he took his last photograph, he left for his summer at Eastbourne. Photography was out of the question while he was there: Eastbourne time was for writing. On his return to Oxford in the autumn, the pressures of academic life made him forgo photography until good weather and bright sunshine returned. He clearly intended to take more photographs. Twelve days after the last session with the Henderson girls, for instance, he wrote to their mother: "I have now made about all the pictures I can think of, of these 2 children: so I don't expect to ask for them again till next year—and then, if Annie retains her present simplicity, and if you see no objection to her coming again, she will probably be a finer subject than she is now, even."

A year later, not having taken any photographs in the interim, he wrote again to Mrs. Henderson (June 21, 1881); hoping that one of the nude photographs on her drawing-room table would "serve as a sort of 'decoy duck' and reveal to you (and through you to me) other parents who possess well-made children who have a taste for being taken without the encumbrances of dress." Mrs. Henderson must have replied that although Annie and Frances were no longer of an age suitable for Charles's camera, her youngest daughter would be available. Charles replied on the thirtieth: "Many thanks for the promise of another model in the future—4 or 5 years hence will be time enough. I shall trust it to you to bring her a year before she reaches the outside limit of age, within which she is available."

Mrs. Henderson made good her promise, but by that time Charles had abandoned photography. Instead, on July 2, 1885, he celebrated "a new experience in Art. Little Lilian Henderson (aged 5½) was brought down by Annie and Frances, for me to try some sketches of her, naked, up in my studio. She has a charming little figure, and was a very patient sitter. I made 4 studies of her. The only previous occasion when I have had a naked child to draw from was a hasty attempt (which quite failed) at Beatrice Hatch (I think), which would have been in 1872. To draw the figure from *life* seems to give one quite new powers." He confided his jubilation to Gertrude Thomson a fortnight later: "It is 3 or 4 years now since I have photographed—I have been too busy. . . . There was never time, in photographic days, to try *drawing*. . . . [Lilian] *is* such a sweet little figure! If only you, or some other person who *can* draw, had been here! *Then* there would have been some result worth showing. I could have had her here again and again, but did not like to tax the patience of so young a sitter any more. Next year they say she may come again: and then I shall venture on a rather long sitting. . . . The results were, I think, about 10 times as good as I ever draw out of my own head: but what good is it to multiply zero by 10? The mathematical result is zero!"

Charles continued to draw nudities. It was a less demanding indulgence, and it diverted him from his more intellectual enterprises. From time to time during the 1880s and 1890s, he visited artists' studios in London to draw from life, and he frequently encouraged Gertrude Thomson to arrange drawing sessions with a model for both of them. He even prodded her into hiring the latest model camera for photographing nudes: "*All* 'dry-plate' photography is inferior," he wrote her (July 28, 1893), "in artistic effect, to the now-abandoned 'wet-plate': but, as a means of making *memoranda* of attitudes, etc., it is invaluable. Every figure-artist ought to practice it. If *I* had a dry-plate camera, and time to work it, and could secure a child of a really *good* figure . . . I would put her into every pretty attitude I could think of, and could get, in a single morning, 50 or 100 such memoranda. Do try this, with the next pretty child you get as a model, and let me have some of the photos."

Less than two months before his death, on November 20, 1897, Charles went to Miss Thomson's studio in London, where she had a camera and a model for taking "photographic memoranda" to help her in drawing the nudities required for a book that he was preparing to publish. "A delightful day," he wrote in his diary. ". . . Had about an hour and a quarter" with Miss Thomson "and her little model . . . a very nice and pretty child, aged 13. We tried one hasty sketch of her lying down."

Glancing back upon the quarter century in which Charles practiced the black art, one is struck again by how he developed on parallel tracks his two strong interests, his photography and his friendship with children. In the years that preceded the fashionable art-for-art's-sake movement of the

1890s, Charles evolved an art form celebrating the child. Two incontrovertible facts emerge: Charles Dodgson produced some of the most remarkable photographs of the nineteenth century, earning for himself the garland as the finest photographer of children of the age; and with the help of photography he came to terms with his true self. He was interested in young females before he took up the camera, and even after he gave it up, but with his camera at the ready and his sitters before him, true beauty as he saw it registered in his eye and was transferred onto his glass plate. The pleasure he reaped from this process helped him develop as a man and shine as an artist. His photographs stand apart from other Victorian amateurs. Where so many efforts are blurred, off-center, or recording wooden or stiff figures, Charles's work is pliant and liquid. He gets sharp, three-dimensional results. The person sitting, the furniture, the drapery all catch the eye, one leading to the next, ultimately providing a satisfying result, an object of art.

Child friendships became a necessity early, and he devised means for both obtaining them and keeping them alive. He sought them out singly and in groups, while walking in parks and along the beach, on railway journeys, in homes, in theater dressing rooms, in classrooms. He discovered them by word of mouth, by letter, by begging introductions. Where friendships succeeded, he clung to them tenaciously, doing all he could to foster them. He confided to the mother of a child friend (November 7, 1896): "The friendship of children has always been a great element in my enjoyment of life, and is very *restful* as a contrast to the society of books, or of men." Isa Bowman recalled that when she asked him whether children never bored him, he replied: "They are three-fourths of my life," adding that he could not understand how anyone could be bored by children.[12]

Charles traveled much by rail, and these journeys often provided new child friends. Never shy in railway carriages, he sought out and engaged fellow travelers in conversation and games, particularly families with children. He met the three Drury sisters on a railway journey, and we have an account of the meeting: "He took off his grey and black cotton gloves, opened his bag and found inside it three puzzles. He had made them himself . . . and he gave one to each of them to find out. When they were tired of this game he produced three little pairs of scissors and papers so that they could cut out patterns. There were many other surprises in that wonderful bag. No journey could ever have passed more quickly. The little girls were disconsolate when the train slowed down and they reached their destination."[13] The copy of *Alice* that Charles subsequently sent the Drury sisters bears a verse inscription recalling the railway journey:

Minnie, Ella, and Emmie Drury
To three puzzled little girls from the Author

Three little maidens weary of the rail,
Three pairs of little ears listening to a tale,
Three little hands held out in readiness
For three little puzzles very hard to guess.
Three pairs of little eyes open wonder-wide
At three little scissors lying side by side.
Three little mouths that thanked an unknown Friend
For one little book he undertook to send.
Though whether they'll remember a friend, or book, or day
In three little weeks is very hard to say.

He did not always succeed. "I met him at Reading station," the novelist Margaret L. Woods wrote, "where I was changing for Oxford. He was seated in a first-class carriage, and found that I was alone, and travelling third-class. This horrified him. . . . [He] left his first-class carriage and joined me there. Seating himself at the farthest end to myself, he put arithmetical puzzles to me during the rest of my journey. My education had been neglected, and . . . [I was not] interested in arithmetic. . . . Consequently I could not solve one of those conundrums, and he doubtless concluded me to be a stupid girl, for he took no further notice of me."[14] Ellen Terry's son, Edward Gordon Craig, was another with whom he had no success: "I can see him now," he writes, "on one side of the heavy mahogany table—dressed in black, with a face which made no impression on me at all. I on the other side of the . . . table, and he describing in detail an event in which I had not the slightest interest—'How five sheep were taken across a river in one boat, two each time—first two, second two—that leaves one yet two must go over'—ah—he did this with matches and a matchbox—I was not amused—so I have forgotten how these sheep did their trick."[15] Although the Queen's granddaughter, Princess Alice (Countess of Athlone), welcomed his attentions when a child, she later complained that "he was always making grown-up jokes to us" and "we thought him awfully silly."[16]

Children whom he attracted he treated as treasured friends and lavished every indulgence upon them. He encouraged their confidences, rooted out

their likes and dislikes, esteemed their childish vanities, elicited their uncer-
tain, childish utterances, propped up their self-confidence, assuaged their
fears and misgivings, provoked them to peals of laughter, and whisked them
off to all sorts of adventures they had never even imagined. He fetched them
and brought them to his gated, guarded castle in Tom Quad, produced
fairy-tale pictures and stories, staged tea parties overflowing with fancy
cakes, sticky buns, and sweets. He emptied full cupboards of mechanical
toys, music boxes, and any number of devices, gadgets, and games bought
up or invented for their amusement. He took them on tours of Christ
Church, up narrow staircases, inside Tom Tower to the huge bell, which
they could strike with a hammer. He led them into the college kitchen and
accompanied them hand in hand on walks and on picnics.

They went rowing together; he would "borrow" them for a day's outing in
London and take them to the theater to introduce them to the world of actors and acting; he escorted them to art galleries, museums, to the homes of
friends to be well fed. He created games, both indoor and out, for them;
played these and others with them; taught them mathematics and logic;
bought them any number of objects, from pens to clothing. He escorted
them on visits to Oxford; took them to stay with his sisters at Guildford; had
them to stay with him in his lodgings by the sea, paying for their journeys
down and back; read to them; sang to them. He explained his religious faith
to them in frank and simple terms; proffered moral tutelage when they
seemed to want it. He showered them with gifts; gave them books, inscribed
copies of his own, sometimes with acrostic verses he had composed for them
written out neatly on the half-title page. He prayed for them; he cherished
locks of their hair; he paid for their art lessons, French lessons; he took them
to the doctor, to the dentist.

He kept careful records of their full names and birthdays, and he marked
their changing height on the back of a door. He held them on his knees,
hugged, cuddled, and kissed them. He sent them streams of letters, many
bearing squiggles, drawings, jokes, japeries. He created puzzles, puns, and
pranks; he teased, feigned, fantasized. He devised new kinds of letters—
rebus letters; circular pinwheel letters; looking-glass letters that must be
held up to the mirror to be read; back-to-front letters to be read from the
end to the beginning; letters with riddles, hoaxes, and acrostics; fairy letters
in tiny writing that require a magnifying glass to read, written on letter
paper the size of a postage stamp; letters in verse; verse letters written in
prose (to see if the recipient would detect the hidden meters and rhymes);

The 🔴🔴🔴🔴

My 🦌 Ina,

    Though 👁 don't give birthday presents, still 👁

April ... write a birthday ✉.

June ... came 2 your 🚪 2 wish U many happy returns of the day, 🛢 the 🐱 met me, 🖐 took me for a 🐀, 🖐 hunted me 👉 and 👈 till 🐾 could hardly ⌂ However somehow 👁 got into the 🏠, 🖐 there a 🐭 met me, 🖐 took me for a 🐱, and pelted me

I       113

Charles's rebus letter to Georgina Watson, the daughter of the Postmaster of Merton College. He also photographed "Ina" and her two sisters.

Ch. Ch.
Feb. 3. [1874]

My dear B,
        You were so gracious the other day that I have nearly got over my fear of you. The slight tremulousness, which you may observe in my writing, pro-duced by the thought that it is *you* I am writing to, will soon pass off. Next time I borrow you, I shall venture on having you alone: I like my

*Charles wrote a tremulous letter to Beatrice Earle, daughter of John Earle, Professor of Anglo-Saxon. He entertained the Earle children in his rooms at Christ Church and taught them his game "Mischmasch." Beatrice later married George Buckle, editor of* The Times.

7, Lushington Road.
Sep. 25./94

My dear Winifred,

I suppose you are going to
the school whether you like it or not
whether etc. & a few of the
elder girls, like to try
to learn "Symbolic Logic", &
if so whether the whether etc. of
a ? full town, ?

? I think I write, you
teach you think ? that
? If ? ? whether the ?
to you advise whether I "say"
better, you know, the ? or
if all later: it will make
you understand it all if the
letter.

Your affectionately,
C. L. Dodgson.

*Charles's looking-glass letter to Winifred Schuster. He became acquainted with the Schusters late in life, during a summer holiday at Eastbourne. He taught the children ("first-rate pupils") logic and took Winifred on an excursion to Brighton.*

long was that, see you,
then But. "Dodgson
Uncle for pretty, thing
some make I'll now",
it began you when,
yourself to said you
that, me telling her
without, know I course
of and : ago years many
great a it made had
you said she. Me told
Isa what from was it?
For meant was it who
out made I how know

you do! Lasted has it
well how and. Grandfather
my for made had you
Antimacassar pretty
that me give to you of
nice so was it, Nelly
dear my.

*A letter that must be read back to front, from Charles to Nellie Bowman. Nellie was Isa Bowman's younger sister. Both Isa and Nellie went on to become professional actresses. Nellie was the more successful one, appearing in* Peter Pan *(1906-10) and as late as 1946 in* Arsenic and Old Lace.

letters with visual effects, with a beetle or a spider crawling across the page. He poured the essence of himself into these letters and unwittingly earned a place in the history of epistolary art.

Some of these friendships were more intense than others; some lasted decades, others a brief while, a good many ended abruptly at one point or another, usually with Charles arbitrarily rejected. When a friendship was in bloom, the child often enjoyed it enormously. Upper-class Victorian parents did not pay much attention to their children and relegated them to the care, and often to the neglect, of nannies and governesses, sometimes dour creatures, uneducated, unsympathetic, and unimaginative. What a difference when the children came to know Mr. Dodgson: "My friendship with him was probably the most valuable experience in a long life, and . . . it influenced my outlook more than anything that has happened since—and wholly for the good," wrote Enid (Stevens) Shawyer.[17] Isa Bowman tells us: "He was so good and sweet, so tender and kind. . . . To have been with him for long as a child, to have known so intimately the man who above all others has understood childhood, is indeed a memory on which to look back with thanksgiving. . . ."[18] Beatrice Hatch agreed that "he was the most gentle, affectionate, and sympathetic of companions" and remembered the "well-known bright smile whenever we met; the long calls, when one felt oneself a child again . . . and life one vast holiday; the familiar . . . handwriting in the frequent and amusing notes; above all, the true affection."[19]

For Charles, his child friends were more than a source of pleasure—they were his mainstay, as essential as the air he breathed. They provided the impetus for his actions, regulated and punctuated his daily rounds, defined the purpose of his labors, fired his energies, and sparked his imagination. Understandably, he was constantly on the lookout for new friends and for means of advancing old ones.

But young girls grow up, they embark on careers, go off to foreign parts, become engaged, get married—and they would abandon him. After 1880, when he stopped photographing, the well often dried up. He made repeated efforts to acquire new friends, but he was not always successful. On April 8, 1897, he confided to Enid Stevens about unsuccessful efforts at getting young ladies to come to dine with him singly at Christ Church: "I'm afraid it's 'no go,' " he wrote. ". . . It's a very good thing that *some* girls are more get-at-able! What a nuisance it would be if your mother were to say 'I can only lend Enid in sets of *three!*" He met with failures, but he also succeeded: a new friend, acquired the very month he complained to Enid, was Dorothy

Rivington, the daughter of a former pupil. Dorothy came to dine, and more dinner parties followed.

His tenacity is ever evident, but so are a number of other personal traits, and some temper his excesses. He always sought, for instance, to protect the children's well-being and went to great lengths to assure himself (and their parents) that the children themselves desired the connection and benefited from it. He was aware that his entanglements with them were extraordinary, and he took precautions to see that he compromised neither the child nor his own stern conscience. He was aware of the tittle-tattle and confronted it. He wrote mothers long letters pointing out the benefits of his friendship, larding his letters with layers of assurance, making clear his innocent intent. In the early years, when still an eligible bachelor, he was especially cautious to abide by all the proprieties, but as he grew older and reached the age when Victorians believed men harmless as companions, no longer possible suitors, he flew in the face of censure, often with wit and whimsy, particularly when dismissing his favorite paper tiger, Mrs. Grundy. Living, by his own confession, as a lonely man, he remained determined to alleviate his solitary state in his own way.

Early and late he was at pains to have the parents approve his efforts. "I hope you will not have thought I took too great a liberty in making friends with your very friendly little daughter," he wrote to C. H. M. Mileham (August 12, 1884), four days after encountering the ten-year-old May on the Eastbourne beach. "I am fond of children, and their society is a great refreshment, sometimes, to an old bachelor. Also I hope I shall have your kind permission to continue the friendship so suddenly begun." Permission was forthcoming and the friendship lasted.

A cousin of May's recalled Charles's initial meeting with her. While "on one of our low-tide explorations," he wrote, ". . . [May] slipped and fell full-length in a few inches of water. Refusing to see the funny side . . . and regarding with dismay her sodden garments, she set up a piercing howl. . . . From the distant crowded parade emerged a black-coated figure of clerical aspect, striding in haste over shingle and sand-flat. Gathering up in his arms the wet mess of my amphibious cousin, he bore her with soothing words to . . . [our] lodgings."[20]

"I have a request to make of you," Charles, aged sixty-four, wrote (November 7, 1896) Mrs. R. L. Poole, the mother of one of his logic pupils, aged thirteen, at the Oxford High School, ". . . that I may be allowed to try the experiment of making friends with Joy. . . . If you give your sanction, I will ask to be allowed to fetch her, some evening, to dine with me." Mrs. Poole consented and a week later Charles had the child to dinner: "I think we both much enjoyed the evening."

Another time he wrote (May 26, 1879), anticipating a mother's objection to his photographing her daughter in scanty dress or none, "that people will be sure to hear that such pictures have been done, and that they will *talk*. As to their *hearing* of it, I say 'of course. All the world are welcome to hear it, and I would not on any account suggest to the children not to mention it— which would at once introduce an objectionable element'—but as to people talking about [it]"—and he cites an old Scottish motto which simply means "Let them talk."

He grew bolder, but ever with a clear conscience. On April 14, 1884, he confided to one of his young friends that he dreams of "careering about . . . [with her] in hopes of meeting Mrs. Grundy and giving that worthy lady something definite to talk about. Just now she—Mrs. G.—is no doubt busy talking about me and another young friend of mine—a mere child, only 4 or 5 and 20—whom I have brought down [to Guildford] from town to visit my sisters."

In 1885 he experimented with child guests at his seaside lodgings—without any sisters present. His first visitor was Phoebe Carlo, an eleven-year-old actress, whom he befriended after seeing her on the London stage. "I went up to town [from Eastbourne] and fetched Phoebe down here," he reports in a letter (July 29?, 1885), ". . . and we spent *most* of Saturday upon the beach—Phoebe wading and digging, and 'as happy as a bird upon the wing' . . . four days of sea-air, and a new kind of happiness, did her good, I think. I am rather lonely now she is gone. . . . It was very touching to see . . . the far-away look in her eyes, when we talked of God and of heaven—as if her angel, who beholds His face continually, were whispering to her."

Eager though he was, he did not make friends with every child he ran into—he was particular. "I do *not* (as is popularly supposed of me) take a fancy to *all* children, and instantly: I fear I take *dis*likes to *some* . . .," he wrote one mother (February 12, 1887). When a child friend shows up with some unpleasant cousins, he avoids them: "Her cousins are a rough lot. . . . One *must* draw the line somewhere!" To Mrs. Stevens he wrote (February 28, 1891): "It's such a lottery, the finding of any *lovable* ones," and went on to explain his attachment to her daughter Enid: "Please don't think it's only her *beauty* that has attracted me: a face may be very beautiful, and yet very unattractive (for instance if the owner is self-conscious)." "I *do* sympathise so heartily with you in what you say about feeling shy with children when you have to entertain them!" he wrote to Edith Blakemore (March 31, 1890). "Sometimes they are a real *terror* to me. . . . I'm *not* omnivorous!—like a pig. I pick and choose."

Even when he liked a child but found her self-conscious or otherwise not at ease with him, he refused a second immediate meeting. "I don't think I *did* succeed, as you think, in setting Lottie 'at her ease,' " he wrote to Mrs. Rix (June 7, 1885). "I feel no doubt that, if she had *quite* felt that, she would have talked more, and not merely *replied*. . . . I shouldn't dare, at present, to ask her over here for a day. She would feel constrained, and the hours would drag. . . ."

"Will you kindly name a day, or days, when I could fetch my pet Enid for walk and tea?" he wrote Mrs. Stevens (October 20, 1882). "Also the same for Winifred (*different* days, please, as I will *not* have them together!); but, with *her*, I should prefer 'dinner and evening': it would be much more leisurely and comfortable. Would this be possible? And would it be *de rigueur* that there should be a 3rd to dinner? 'Tête-à-tête' is so much the nicest!" Twelve days later Mrs. Stevens and Winifred came to tea and Winifred remained for dinner and the evening—"the first Oxford resident who has so far defied 'Mrs. Grundy.' "

In the mid-1890s, when he was giving logic lectures to girls at school and college, he repeatedly sought permission to have one pupil at a time for a tête-à-tête dinner. On March 9, 1894, he had Evelyn Hatch, then at St. Hugh's Hall, having obtained permission from Charlotte Moberly, the principal. "At Lady Margaret Hall they are stricter," Charles noted. Edith Olivier, also at St. Hugh's, recalled that Charles's position in Oxford "was such that in his case alone our rigid rule of chaperonage was waived. If our authorities were sticklers for chaperons he was equally a stickler for none. 'I like tête-à-tête dinner,' he said. 'And if you don't come alone, you shan't come at all.' Miss Moberly gave in, saying with her gay smile: 'Once more, we must make a virtue of necessity.' "[21]

Holding hands with his young friends and sitting the very young ones upon his knees were part of the ritual of friendship. Audrey Fuller recalled that when she was twelve and Charles took her for her birthday to the Garrick to see J. M. Barrie's play *The Professor's Love Story*, he "sat all the time with my hand in his; we had about the third row of the stalls and I loved it."[22] Winifred Holiday, the daughter of the illustrator of *The Hunting of the Snark*, remembered: "When he stayed with us he used to steal on the sly into my little room after supper, and tell me strange impromptu stories as I sat on his knee in my nightie."[23] Isa Bowman recorded that Charles held her

*Charles's drawing of Gertrude Chataway in fisherman's jersey and cap. He met the Chataway family on a late-summer vacation on the Isle of Wight in 1875 and saw a good deal of them. On October 2 he "got Gertrude . . . to come across in her wading attire . . . and made a drawing of her." Gertrude later wrote that at age eight and a half, she was "absolutely entranced with the lodger next door."*

hand while walking and while giving her a lesson in geography. Once, standing on a cliff with her at sunset, he was so moved by the beauty of the scene that tears came to his eyes, and when they turned to leave he held her hand more tightly than usual.[24]

When Phoebe Carlo came to visit Charles at Oxford (June 26, 1885), they "had a little dinner together at 7.30, after which my tired little friend had a good nap on my knee, from which I had to wake her to come off by the 9.5 train to town." When he took Irene Burch, aged seven, to see *Cinderella* at the Lyceum (February 16, 1894), "they let me bring her without a ticket, to sit on my *knee:* and about once in every half-hour she turned round to give me a kiss."

Charles sent and received kisses by post: to Amy and Agnes Hughes, the daughters of the artist Arthur Hughes, at the outset of 1870; and he exchanged kisses with Gertrude Chataway, in an amusing letter (December 9, 1875):

This really will *not* do, you know, sending one more kiss every time by post: the parcel gets so heavy that it is quite expensive. When the postman brought in the last letter, he looked quite grave. "Two pounds to pay, sir!" he said. "*Extra weight,* sir!" . . . "Oh, if you please, Mr. Postman!" I said, going down gracefully on one knee (I wish you could see me go down on one knee to a Postman—it's a very pretty sight). "Do excuse me just this once! It's only from a little girl!"

. . . I promised him we would send each other *very* few more letters. "Only two thousand four hundred and seventy, or so," I said. "Oh!" he said. "A little number like *that* doesn't signify. What I meant is, you mustn't send *many.*" So you see we must keep count now, and when we get to two thousand four hundred and seventy, we mustn't write any more, unless the postman gives us leave.

In the summer of 1884 Charles, on the beach at Eastbourne, met the ten-year-old daughter of an architect, and a friendship began. On December 30 of that year he wrote to "My dearest May": "Thank you very much indeed for your two letters: and extra thanks and kisses for the lock of hair. I have kissed it several times—for want of having you to kiss, you know, even hair is better than nothing." "I don't mean to forget such friends as you and your lovable daughter," he wrote to Mrs. H. A. Feilden (February 12, 1887). "Doesn't *that* show what an old man I am, when I can say to a mother 'I love your daughter,' and *not* get the reply 'what are your intentions, and what is your income?' And I will even be bold enough to add that I *regret* the break (of some years) in my meetings with Helen, which caused us to change from kissing to hand-shaking! Others of my child-friends have kept up the old habit continuously, though married years ago!"

The Bowman sisters, child actresses, were an important addition to Charles's life in the 1880s, Isa, the eldest, becoming his favorite. On April 14, 1890, he sent her this letter, in response to one from her, just before she was to embark on a theatrical tour of the United States:

*A letter from Charles to Isa Bowman about kissing. Isa Bowman had a small part in the original West End production of* Alice *and played Alice in the first revival of the dream play. In later years, she became one of Charles's favorite child friends.*

The Stevens girls also played a major role in the autumn of Charles's life. On February 28, 1891, he wrote their mother:

> I have lost a considerable fraction (say .25) of my heart to your little daughter: and I *hope* that you will allow me further opportunities of trying whether or no we can become real *friends*. She would be about my only child-friend in Oxford. The former ones have grown up: and I've taken no trouble to find others. . . . You may have noticed as one of the Facts of Life, that, if one doesn't blow one's own trumpet, it has a way of not getting blown: so let me humbly mention that I would *very* much like a kiss from *another* daughter of yours, besides Enid (as to whom I took it for granted that *any* child under 12 is 'kissable'): only, as I had promised I would wait for *her* to indicate if she would like to be on those terms, and as she didn't, I of course forbore, being *more* than content to treat her as she likes best.

Charles sent one of the Moberly Bell children, Hilda, aged fourteen, another mock-serious letter (October 5, 1893): "It *is* sweet, of you children, to sign your letters to me, after only *once* seeing me, as you do! When I get letters signed 'your loving,' I always kiss the signature. You see I'm a sentimental old fogey!"

To A. H. G. Greenidge, Fellow of St. John's College, Oxford, and the fiancé of Edith Lucy, who had been a child friend, Charles wrote (May 24, 1895): "I would like you to know, from myself, how *entirely* I approve of Edith's wise suggestion that she and I had better now drop the 'kissing' which used to mark our greetings. It is a real pleasure to me to feel that, in carrying out her suggestion, I am doing what will I hope be satisfactory to one she loves so well."

When Charles was giving logic lectures at the Oxford High School for Girls in the mid-1890s, he perceived a keen logic student in Ethel Rowell, a head girl, and undertook to give her (and her sisters) private lessons. Permitted to take Ethel on an outing to London, he wrote to her mother (June 25, 1895): "The being entrusted with the care of Ethel for a day is such a great advance on mere acquaintanceship, that I venture to ask if I may regard myself as on 'kissing' terms with her, as I am with many a girl-friend a great deal older than *she* is. Considering that—she being 17 and I 63—I am quite old enough to be her *grandfather,* I hope you won't think it a very out-of-the-way suggestion. Nevertheless, if I find you think it wiser that we should only shake hands, I shall not be *in the least* hurt. Of course I shall, unless I hear to the contrary, continue to shake hands only."

After having Edith Olivier over from St. Hugh's Hall for dinner, Charles wrote (December 7, 1896) to Evelyn Hatch, by then teaching in Putney: "Yes: Miss Edith Olivier is a very nice girl, and *I,* at any rate, enjoyed the evening I had with her: though I can't say she was a *perfect* substitute for the other 'E.' It's *one* thing, you know, to have a guest with whom one is on 'Miss' terms, and quite *another* to have one with whom one is on 'Kiss' terms!"

Sometimes Charles seems to blind himself to selected realities. To Edith Miller, aged twenty-seven, he wrote (November 23, 1897): "I own to being a *little* puzzled at your feeling free to go up to town, for a day, with me as your sole escort, while you do *not* feel free to come to my room for an evening. Are you sure that your mother draws a line between these two things? The distinction is unintelligible to *me*. . . . I *hope* it won't occur to her to forbid *kissing!* That will be the *next* privilege cut off, I fear."

From time to time he ran into heavy weather. "I promised a *Snark* to quite a new little friend, Lily Alice Godfrey, from New York: aged eight; but talked like a girl of fifteen or sixteen," he wrote (September 3, 1880), "and declined to be kissed on wishing goodbye, on the ground that she 'never kissed gentlemen.' It is rather painful to see the lovely simplicity of child-hood so soon rubbed off: but I fear it is true that there are no children in America."

He encountered difficulty with Mrs. Owen. On February 5, 1880, Charles "brought in 'Atty' Owen and her brother in my rooms" to wait for their fa-ther, S. J. Owen, Tutor and Reader in Law and Modern History at Christ Church. "She does not look 14 yet," he wrote in his diary, "and when, hav-ing kissed her at parting, I learned (from Owen) that she is 17, I was aston-ished, but I don't think either of us was much displeased at the mistake having been made!" Charles wrote a mock apology to Mrs. Owen, assuring her that the incident had been " 'as distressing to her daughter as it was to myself!' but adding that I would kiss her no more." But Mrs. Owen took of-fense. Charles confided in Mrs. Kitchin (July 25, 1880): "I met Mr. S. Owen a few days ago, and he looked like a thundercloud. I fear I am permanently in their black books now: not only by having given fresh offence—appar-ently—by asking leave to photo Atty (*was* that such a very offensive thing to do?) but also by the photos I have done of *other* people's children. Ladies tell me 'people' condemn those photographs in strong language; when I enquire more particularly, I find that 'people' means 'Mrs. Sidney Owen'! It is sad."[25]

Word of Charles's unusual friendships traveled all the way up to Sunder-land, where his sister Mary lived, and it must have taken considerable courage for her to write to her older brother about the gossip. Her letter appears not to survive, but Charles's reply (September 21, 1893) does:

> I *do* like getting such letters as yours. I think all you say about my girl-guests is most kind and sisterly, and almost entirely proper for you to write to your brother. But I don't think it at all advisable to enter into controversy about it. There is no reasonable probability that it would modify the views either of you or me. I will say a few words to explain my views: but I have no wish whatever to have "the last word": so please say anything you like afterwards.
>
> You and your husband have, I think, been very fortunate to know so little, by experience, in your own case or in that of your friends, of the wicked recklessness with which people repeat things to the disadvantage of others, without a thought as to whether they have grounds for asserting what they say. I have met with a good deal of utter misrepresentation of that kind. And another result of my experience is the conviction that the opinion of "people" in general is absolutely worthless as a test of right and wrong. The only two tests I now apply to such a question as the having some particular girl-friend as a guest are, first my own *conscience*, to settle whether I feel it to be entirely innocent and right, in the sight of God; secondly, the *parents* of my friend, to settle whether I have their *full* approval for what I do. You need not be shocked at my being spoken against. *Any*body who is spoken about at all, is *sure* to be spoken against by *somebody:* and any action, however innocent in itself, is liable, and not at all unlikely, to be blamed by *somebody*. If you limit your actions in life to things that *nobody* can possibly find fault with, you will not do much!

Charles was, in the main, right: none of his child friends seemed to have suffered any scars from his attentions, and he certainly boosted their morale, flattered their vanities, helped them achieve the courage of their convictions, and, in sum, did for them what their elders had neither the time nor the inclination to do. Many of them would concur with Isa Bowman when she wrote: "Now that he is dead . . . I can still be glad that he has kissed me and that we were friends."[26]

Ultimately, the futility of his position bore in upon him. In late summer 1897 Miss Thomson tried to entice him to join her in sketching some nudities she had seen running about at the seashore. In his reply, he demurred, suggesting that it would be hopeless . . . to try to make friends with any of the little nudities. . . . A *lady* might do it: but what would they think of a *gentleman* daring to address them! And then what an embarrassing thing it would be to *begin* an acquaintance with a naked little girl! What *could* one say to start the conversation? Perhaps a poetic quotation would be best. "And ye shall walk in silk attire." But would *that* do? . . . Or one *might* begin with Keats' charming lines, "Oh where are you going, with your love-locks flowing, And what have you got in your basket?" . . . Or a quota-tion from Cowper (slightly altered) might do. *His* lines are "The tear, that is wiped with a little address, May be followed perhaps by a smile." But *I* should have to quote it as "The tear, that is wiped by so little a dress"![27]

Humor aside, some essential questions remain. Charles's emotional tar-gets clearly differed from most men's; the difference affected, even shaped, his behavior. But to what extent did he dwell upon the difference or believe that it impeded his progress in relationships? How did he accommodate the sometimes harsh and cruel response he suffered at the hands of others? And what was it, after all, that shaped his emotional equipment and made it what it was?

None of these questions is easy to answer. Charles recognized earlier than one might suppose that his inner springs differed from most men's, that his heart beat to a different drum, that in order to be true to himself he would be compelled to lead a life that not only was outside the norm but would come under particular scrutiny and raise suspicions, one not generally con-doned and subject to severe reprimand, sneers, lampoons, and ridicule. Be that as it may, he determined to follow his own star in spite of raised eye-brows and possible social censure. "Let them talk" was his answer; his own conscience would be his only judge.

So much we are sure of. But why he was what he was and how he came to be so are almost unanswerable questions. Some muster metaphors and symbols from Charles's writings to propound their theories, others use all manner of psychologizing and psychoanalyzing to try to pry into his inner self, still others reject hard and established facts and impose upon Charles's life a character they themselves invent.

We find among these efforts some interesting observations. "For some reason, we know not what, his childhood was sharply severed," wrote Vir-ginia Woolf. "It lodged in him whole and entire. He could not disperse it.

And therefore as he grew older this impediment in the center of his being, this hard block of pure childhood, starved the mature man of nourishment."[28] Bert Coote, the actor who was one of Charles's male child friends, speculated along a similar vein: "May be he had the brain of a clever and abnormal man with the heart of a normal child."[29]

These writers presume that Charles suffered an arrested development, that in some respect he remained a child all his life. Others have seen a split personality, a bifurcation, a dual persona, but that view is easily disposed of. Charles did try to isolate C. L. Dodgson from Lewis Carroll. He returned unopened letters that arrived at Christ Church addressed to Lewis Carroll; he sought, unsuccessfully, to have Bodley's Librarian delete from the catalogue cross-references to his two names; he wrote third-person letters objecting to correspondents making the connection. He appealed plaintively to the editor of a forthcoming *Dictionary of Anonymous and Pseudonymous Literature* to "erase the paragraph" in which he was mentioned, adding that if she had ever reaped any pleasure from reading his works, "do not, I entreat you, repay it by the cruelty of breaking through a disguise which it is my most earnest wish to maintain," and here he succeeded.[30]

But none of these efforts arose out of a deep-seated duality; they aimed only at retaining a semblance of privacy. "A good deal of play has been made of the difference between the personalities of C. L. Dodgson and Lewis Carroll," wrote Winifred Holiday. "To us I feel sure there was no such distinction. It was just as much 'Mr. Dodgson' who had written the *Alice*s as it was Mr. Dodgson who always took photographs of everyone and had to have a cellar all to himself for a dark room whenever he came to stay; who was my parents's loved friend as well as my adored one . . . always the same gentle-voiced, quietly happy, and whimsical soul, his faint stammer and slight touch of Oxford dryness of manner only serving to enhance his charm. . . . May it not have been," Miss Holiday asks, "because there is always something of the child in the artist?"[31]

"I use the name of 'Lewis Carroll' in order to avoid all *personal* publicity," Charles told one correspondent (October 31, 1883), echoing many similar assertions he made in person and in letters. On the other hand, he himself broke his rule of disavowal often, usually with children whose friendships had ripened to the point where he wished to confide in them, to share a great secret with them, but sometimes even earlier, when he was in pursuit and he rightly assumed that the fame of the author of the *Alice* books would help to break the ice with the parents of likely candidates.

He certainly did not live a double life, no Mr. Hyde lurked behind a Dr. Jekyll here. He knew what he wanted and how to achieve it. Consistency had naught to do with it. He did his best to appear ordinary to his young friends: if they saw him as a famous man, a literary monument, they would grow shy and tongue-tied, and a natural friendship might never develop. His reasons for keeping his two identities separate and under control were rational and reasonable.

Nor was his emotional life stunted; he did not suffer from arrested development. His responses were not those of a schoolboy. Schoolboys do not spend their energies or their time cultivating the friendship of young females or pursuing their companionship; they are more interested in sweets, sports, and their fellow schoolboys.

He was, in fact, a highly charged, fully grown male, with strong, mature emotional responses. True, what we today see as Victorian sentimentality found a home in his breast and utterance in his work, but so it did in polite society throughout three-fourths of the nineteenth century. If Dickens did not invent it, he certainly gave it his imprimatur, and it soon became the addiction of the age. But there was nothing childish about sentimentality; it lived comfortably if cloyingly in the world of polished, adult society.

Too bad, we might say, that Charles did not rise above it. But sometimes he did, for he could also strike subtle tones of emotional clarity, both in his life and in his works, that range up and down a large scale. The *Alice* books and the *Snark,* and more too, show him capable of substantial emotional feeling and expression, of a level of irony and sarcasm that does not live cheek by jowl with sentimentality.

Although usually silent on emotional matters, Charles thought carefully and philosophically about life and its meaning; and his words on the subject are illuminating. As early as September 1855, when he was twenty-three, he muses in his diary about the nature of pain and pleasure. He writes about music, but the passage is equally applicable to the child-friendship question: "There is, I verily believe, a sensation of pain in the *realisation* of our highest pleasures, knowing that now they must soon be over; we had rather prolong anticipation by postponing them. In truth we are not intended to rest content in any pleasure on earth, however intense: the yearning has been wisely given us, which points to an eternity of happiness, as the only perfect happiness possible."

In the same month, he read Tennyson's *Maud,* published that year, a second time. *Maud* is the tragic story of a young man whose love for the six-

teen-year-old Maud is thwarted. Charles singles out the first verse in section 8 as "true, passionate poetry":

> I have led her home, my love, my only friend.
> There is none like her, none.
> And never yet so warmly ran my blood
> And sweetly, on and on
> Calming itself to the long-wished-for end,
> Full to the banks, close on the promised good.

The young man is desperately in love, with all the natural inclinations and
good intentions in the world. But Charles knew that those natural inclinations, those good intentions, that passionate love would never be fulfilled.
He identifies with the lover and the hopelessness of his case and sympa-
thizes with the isolation, the exile, the lover must endure. For Charles, it was
not merely good poetry, it was passionate poetry, poetry he felt personally
and deeply, just as he increasingly felt the emotional pull toward child
friends, all the while sensing that he would never gratify his emotions. Underlying the parallel with the lover in Tennyson's poem is the implicit
tragedy that Charles faces.

The emotions that Charles shares with the forlorn lover of *Maud* are full-
blooded and ripe, not the emotions of a schoolboy or of an emotionally arrested adult. His fatalistic observations about the condition of life on earth
compose a mature philosophical construct that takes full account of the particular brand of suffering that he will have to endure all his life. But his suffering is a metaphor for all suffering and leads logically to the consolation he
finds in religious faith, one which he believes is available to everyone. The
quality of his emotions and the subtlety of his argument refute the suggestion
that he was not a full-grown man, either emotionally or intellectually.

But why did Charles's emotions focus on children and not on adults? The
answer may be somewhere in the volumes of studies that tell us that some
children undergo permanent shifts in personality and emotional orientation
because of early childhood experiences, particularly restrictive, fear-
inducing, punitive experiences. And we know that, however gentle and loving Charles's mother was, and however considerate and concerned his father
was, life at home in Daresbury and at Croft was governed by an iron set of
rules and regulations.

The large size of the Dodgson family, the frequency of new births in the
rectory, the comings and goings of midwives and physicians, must have made

an impression. As the children grew, their close proximity to one another, the wrestlings, the touchings, would have insured an early sexual awareness. Complying stringently with Victorian restraint, emotions cowered, never revealing themselves. While bodily functions and sexual implications were ever present, the subject of sex was never addressed directly. And the father, that pillar of righteousness and accomplishment, set the standard of sanctity and propriety and sought to mold his eldest son into another pillar of righteousness and accomplishment, a mirror image of himself. All the rules and principles of right conduct and proper thought must have come from this fountainhead of learning. The yeas and the nays descended on Charles, and his brothers and sisters, as virtually the word of the Lord.

But what if the young man, gifted and sensitive, had stirrings that the older man knew nothing of, could not even imagine? What if the son, eager, ambitious, industrious, bright, resourceful, intellectually hungry, saw beyond the horizons that the father defined? And what if, at some point in his apprenticeship, Charles's very nature revolted against the prescribed schedule, the predetermined rules, the enforced agenda, even against the very nature, the personality, the overpowering strength of the older man? What if, somewhere within the younger man, a resentment began to stir, leading his thoughts and his emotions in a direction his father would not approve? What if, without even articulating it, he gradually began to feel an inner urge to heed a call that he embark on a journey that would lead away from his father's hearth into an exceptional country, an exotic land with far fewer inhabitants than the one his father dwelt in? Perhaps Virginia Woolf was right in inferring that Charles's childhood was severed. Perhaps some single incident caused the rupture, or, more likely, perhaps the young man withdrew, slowly and silently, from the stern and rigid fortress and sought the more natural world that he described in his poem "Solitude," substituting an inner voice for external authority.

The young man followed a different road from the one charted for him and arrived in a land where he could live at ease with himself, where he could find untarnished beauty and innocence. Here, he found companionship without censure, affection without rebuke. Here, stern strictures and social restraints were banished, he could share simple innocent pleasures, speak his heart, encourage honest expression from his companions. He could please easily, he could laugh, he could sing his song of love.

The record of his departure from his father's hearth is seen nowhere better than in the *Alice* books. These corroborate the difficulties that Charles encountered as he grew at Daresbury and Croft, and they document his rejection of much of what he was tutored to think and believe. True, the books trace the adventures of a young female. But that is an easy disguise. Charles began to tell a story to the Liddell girls, and decided that one of them, his favorite, would be the heroine. But then, when he had to go on with the tale—to invent the incidents, and ultimately to revise and expand the text, to create more, and to polish the whole—he not only drew upon his own childhood memories but poured his soul into them, enshrining the agonies and bewilderments he himself had endured as a youth. The metaphors in the books are the external signals of his internal emotional life. The physical model for Alice wandering through Wonderland is Alice Liddell; the spiritual and psychological Alice is Charles himself. Alice's attitudes, her fears, her aggressions, her strengths, her weaknesses, her sharp retorts, her ineptitudes, her confusions, her insensitivities—and, in the end, her determination to survive—they all belong to Charles.

*Charles sometimes had one of his child friends take a photograph of him by lifting the cap from the lens and counting the seconds needed for the exposure. This could have been one such photograph.*

## CHAPTER SEVEN

# The Fire Within

*Fire that's closest kept burns most of all.*
WILLIAM SHAKESPEARE

Reticent Victorian, inbred Oxonian, upright cleric, rational mathematician—conservative, formal, controlled—Charles Dodgson presents a formidable figure, a prototype of his time and class, a sharp portrait of an age graven into a single human being. The rules he lived by never bent in the wind: conventions were the very motors of his life. Rooted in the rituals of his time, he never addressed an equal, a colleague, an associate, or even a friend by a given name. Only members of his family and children were called "Mary," "Wilfred," "Alice," "Edwin." Others were "Bayne," "Southey," "Kitchin," "Liddon," "MacDonald," "Miss Terry," "Miss Thomson," "Mrs. Henderson," "Mrs. Burch," and so on.

All personal exchanges in conversation and in writing were equally restrained. Ritual was all: it kept everyone in place, allowed for no confidences, no breach of the social charade. What was left unsaid was at least as meaningful, if not more so, as the words uttered. Emotions lived and burned within, tightly sealed, undeclared. How, then, are we to understand the inner man that was Charles Dodgson? Seek as we may, we find no outpouring of inner thought or feeling in confidence to a friend. Even his diaries, replete with prayers, protestations, and self-chastisements, offer little introspection.

Nonetheless, some unintended outcroppings of Charles's inner life here and there help us make some fresh connections that more than hint at the real man behind the mask.

"Nearly all of the following seventy-two problems," Charles writes in his introduction to *Curiosa Mathematica, Part II, Pillow-Problems Thought Out During Sleepless Nights* in 1893, "are veritable 'Pillow-Problems,' having been solved, in the head, while lying awake at night." The book is for the general reader, who might, in working the problems, glean "as much advantage and comfort as I have done" when "haunted by some worrying subject of thought, which no effort of will is able to banish. Again and again I have said to myself, on lying down at night, after a day embittered by some vexatious matter, 'I will *not* think of it any more! . . . It can do no good whatever to go through it again. I *will* think of something else!' And in another ten minutes I have found myself, once more, in the very thick of the miserable business, and torturing myself, to no purpose, with all the old troubles."

One cannot banish the dreaded subject by resolve, but "it *is* possible . . . to carry out the resolution 'I *will* think of so-and-so.' Once fasten the attention upon a subject so chosen, and you will find that the worrying subject, which you desire to banish, is *practically* annulled."

The formula applies not only to ordinary, commonplace worries but to "mental troubles, much worse than mere worry. . . ." These more serious sources of worry include "skeptical thoughts, which seem for the moment to uproot the firmest faith; . . . blasphemous thoughts, which dart unbidden into the most reverent souls; . . . unholy thoughts, which torture, with their hateful presence, the fancy that would fain be pure."

These are strong words, and in the preface to the second edition, Charles changed the words "sleepless nights" in the title to "wakeful hours," and explains that he altered it

to allay the anxiety of kind friends, who have written to me to express their sympathy in my broken-down state of health, believing that I am a sufferer from chronic "insomnia," and that it is as a remedy for that exhausting malady that I have recommended mathematical calculation. . . . The title was not, I fear, wisely chosen; and it certainly *was* liable to suggest a meaning I did not intend to convey, viz. that my "nights" are very often *wholly* "sleepless." This is by no means the case: I have never suffered from "insomnia": and the over-wakeful hours, that I have had to spend at night, have often been simply the result of the over-sleepy hours I have spent during the preceding evening! Nor is it as a remedy for *wakefulness* that I have suggested mathematical calculation; but as a remedy for the *harassing thoughts* that are apt to invade a wholly-unoccupied mind. I hope the new title will express my meaning more lucidly.

The explanation is illuminating but throws no further light upon the nature of Charles's harassing thoughts.

Even earlier, in 1889, in the preface to *Sylvie and Bruno,* Charles confided his plan to publish two anthologies, one containing passages from the Bible, the other passages from secular works, all fit to be memorized, an occupation that not only fills vacant hours but also helps "to keep at bay many anxious thoughts, unholy thoughts." He takes as his inspiration a passage from the liberal churchman Frederick William Robertson's *Expository Lectures on St. Paul's Epistles to the Corinthians* (1859): "If a man finds himself haunted by evil desires and unholy images . . . let him commit to memory passages of Scripture, or passages from the best writers in verse or prose. Let him store his mind with these, as safeguards to repeat when he lies awake in some restless night, or when despairing imaginations, or gloomy, suicidal thoughts, beset him. Let these be to him the sword, turning everywhere to keep the way of the Garden of Life from the intrusion of profaner footsteps."

The theme of avoiding temptation, in fact, became a refrain in Charles's life, reverberating through his mature years. "Absence of temptation is no doubt sometimes a blessing," he wrote Edith Miller (April 9, 1893), "and it is one I often thank God for. But one has to remember that it is only a short breathing-space. The temptation is sure to come again: and the very freedom from it brings its own special danger—of laying down the weapons of defence, and ceasing to 'watch and pray': and then comes the sudden surprise, finding us all unprepared, and ready to yield again. I speak of my own experience, the result of many many failures in my own life: and I *am* truly thankful when God grants me the happiness of helping others . . . in the battle we all have to fight."

On September 10, 1893, when he preached to a congregation of two hundred at the Ocklynge Mission-Room in Eastbourne, he "took as text Luke II:4: 'Lead us not into temptation,' which I have preached on 4 [actually five] times already." The following Sunday he preached there again: "I took the same line as before, viz., the *uses* of temptation: on the text, James I:2, which I have already preached on 3 times."

"Sin is the one unendurable agony of life," Charles wrote Mary Brown

(December 26, 1889). "One's own sins crush one to the dust more than all possible sorrows that could come from without."

W. H. Hewett, Vicar of Christ Church, Eastbourne, who engaged Charles to preach, recalled that "he gave several addresses at our Children's Services. . . . The subject he took was an original allegory, entitled 'Victor and Arnion,'" a story which, apparently, Charles never recorded and has gone lost. "Its purpose," the chronicler continues, "being to illustrate the temptations to which children are exposed, and to teach them how they may be avoided and conquered. The addresses were delivered with deep feeling, at times the speaker was scarcely able to control his emotions."[1]

Nor did these concerns with temptation and sin obsess only the elderly Charles, a man preparing to confront his Maker. They arose more than a quarter of a century before, when Charles was in his twenties and thirties. At the end of 1856 and 1857 he chastised himself for unfulfilled resolves, bad habits, inconsistency. But on the last day of 1863, approaching his thirty-first birthday, he went far beyond his earlier reprobations: "Here, at the close of another year, how much of neglect, carelessness, and sin have I to remember! Oh God . . . take me, vile and worthless as I am. . . . Help me to be Thy servant. . . ." Two months later, on March 6, 1864, he wrote: "Oh God . . . help me to live to Thee. Help me . . . to remember the coming hour of death. For myself I am utterly weak, and vile, and selfish. . . . Oh deliver me from the chains of sin." *Sin, vile,* and *worthless* were new weapons in Charles's battery of self-recrimination, harsh and devastating. Three years later, on February 6, 1867, he struck out again for a better life:

Self-discipline must be my chief work for a long while to come. Ere I can hope to be of use to others, I must learn to bring my rebellious will into subjection to the will of God. . . . Oh merciful Father, I come before Thee a sinner: be merciful. . . . Strengthen my weakness; raise me from the dust; lead me in Thy way! Oh grant me the great blessing that I may look back on this night as the beginning of better things—that so when Thou shalt call me, I may welcome the call, knowing that though I have long wearied Thy patience and love by my sins, yet that the precious blood of Jesus has washed away those sins, and that Thou has graciously forgiven me "all that is past."

On April 14, after Charles and Liddon hatched a scheme for collaborating on a commentary on the Epistles, Charles laments: "Yet how unfit am I to aid in any such work for God! To have entered into Holy Orders seems almost a desecration, with my undisciplined and worldly affections. Help me, dear Lord, to put away self, and to give my will wholly to Thee. Purify me from sin and make me Thine. . . ."

Charles's diary brings us closer to his spiritual self than any other surviving record. It is unlikely that the missing first volume, which chronicled his life before 1855, contained any of these *crises d'esprit.* More probably he lived contented in those early years, with a clear conscience, for, through the first nine months of the earliest diary that we do have, starting in January 1855, we find no self-rebukes or appeals to heaven. The earliest of these self-examinations occurs at the outset of 1856, when Charles was approaching his twenty-fourth birthday. But even then he does not allude to unholy thoughts, but merely complains about his youthful indolence. He asks himself: "Am *I* a deep philosopher, or a genius? I think neither. What talents I have, I desire to devote to His service, and may he purify me, and take away my pride and selfishness. Oh that *I* might hear 'Well done, good and faithful servant'!" Later he complains about "getting into habits of unpunctuality" and sees that he "must try to make a fresh start. . . . I record this resolution," he adds, "as a test for the future." Toward the end of the year he is in something of a panic: "I am becoming embarrassed by the duties of the Lectureship, and must take a quick review of my position, to see what can be done." He goes on to list the individual pupils' problems that require him to prepare separate lectures and deplores the lack of time for reading divinity and other subjects. "I am daily becoming more and more unfit for the lectureship," he writes and bemoans how little he has accomplished during the long summer vacation. He resolves that "next Long *must* be devoted to work."

On the last day of December we find another resolve: "I do trust most sincerely to amend myself in those respects in which the past year has exhibited the most grievous shortcomings, and I trust and pray that the most merciful God may aid me in this and all other good undertakings."

Early in 1857 Charles and his brother Wilfred argued about college duties, Wilfred believing that each man should decide for himself which rules to obey and which not. Charles insisted that one must submit unconditionally to the rules. Neither brother could sway the other, and Charles was depressed at his inability to convince Wilfred. It "suggests to me grave doubts as to the work of the ministry which I am looking forward to: if I find it so hard to prove a plain duty to one individual, and that one unpractised in argument, how can I ever be ready to face the countless sophisms and ingenious arguments against religion which a clergyman must meet with!"

Later in the year, at Croft, Charles reports good news: "I am now settled into a tolerably regular habit of 3 or 4 hours work every morning, Divinity and Mathematics alternately. One good result, at least, springs out of my former habits of indolence, and that is, a continual spurring motive to work, as a kind of self-retribution for so much lost time." At year's end, again at Croft, he sits down to his diary: "Five minutes more, and the Old Year comes to an end, leaving how many promises unfulfilled! As a last deed for it, I have begun on the opposite page a scheme . . . by which I hope in future to save a great deal of waste time. Especially the six days . . . unavoidably consumed every year in travelling to and from Oxford." He lists "things to be learned by heart"; resolves to read for ordination and to settle "the subject finally and definitely in my mind"; to make himself "a competent Mathematical Lecturer"; and to effect "constant improvement of habits of activity, punctuality, etc." The detailed scheme that appears on the facing page records his intention to make a list "of things to be learned by heart and kept up at such times as Railway-travelling, etc.," including poetry, elements of mathematical subjects, formulae proofs, formulae, chronology by memoria technica, and geometry problems.

The diary volume that ends the four-year blackout contains a steady flow of self-criticism, importunities, fresh resolves, pleas and prayers, largely adhering to the traditional pattern of Christian self-examination and resolution of other diarists. As the flow increases, however, a gnawing, deep-seated guilt emerges, accompanied by spiritual weariness and gloom: they are the cries of a man keenly dissatisfied with himself.

Charles appeals to God to help him lead a more earnest life, "a more thoughtful and Christian life," and to "live more recollectively, more consciously in His presence." In rapid succession he sends up prayer after prayer for change, better habits, and a holier life.

He complains that he has "little time for any religious duties" and longs for leisure. He is indeed busy, traveling here and there, taking photographs, and dealing with family matters at Croft. When he is away from Oxford, the exhortations vanish. But they reappear when he returns to Oxford and resolves again to put his life into good order.

He thinks about getting Sunday duty, but cannot decide where to offer his service. "Meanwhile I need both prayer and watchfulness to grow in grace myself. Oh God help me for Christ's sake." He deplores the lack of time for "Bible reading, etc., lately" and adds: "Oh God help me to lead a holier life." The appeals and resolves continue to the end of 1862.

The litany goes on: six entreaties (one written at 2 a.m.) appear during the first three months of 1863, and on April 1 he adds "Amen." Other appeals follow in May and June: "Tonight on my knees I pray to God to give me a new heart, that here, at this milestone on my way, I may begin a new life." Thirteen similar outpourings appear between late June and mid-December. On December 28 he writes: "God grant that with this dying year may die in me all the old evil life, and that a new life may begin," and he adds "Amen. Amen" on December 30.

The chants resound through 1864. In midyear he expresses the "earnest hope that from this may date, by God's blessing, the commencement of a new and better life. The spirit is willing but the flesh is weak." More entries follow and then, on December 16: "Would that I could leave my old bad habits behind. Help me, Oh God. . . ."

On the last day of 1864 we have another passionate confession: "I desire to record my intense gratitude to God, for his abundant mercy, in having spared me suffering and sorrow, and given me many and great pleasures—and my shame and sorrow for the sin, the coldness and hardness of heart by which I have provoked Him—and a prayer, from my heart, that He will grant me grace to put away the old sins of the dead year, and with this on-coming year to begin a holier and better life, that so, in His mercy, I may be spared to 'recover my strength, before I go hence, and be no more seen.' "

The stream courses on through 1865 and 1866. In mid-1866 he regrets that "too long, too long, I have lived away from God. Gracious Lord, send Thy Holy Spirit to dwell in this cold love for Thee, to strengthen this failing faith, to lead back from the wilderness this thy wandering sheep, to make real my repentance, my resolution to amend my struggles against the temptation of the devil, and the inclinations of my own sinful heart." Similar cries appear in July.[2]

These guilt-ridden apostrophes are the cries of a man with an uneasy conscience, not the utterances of a soul at peace, at one with God. They are not routine or mechanical, resonating as they do with pain and suffering. To understand Charles Dodgson, we must strive to apprehend what lies behind this inner torment, the struggle to live closer to God. What transgressions, what sins does he seek to expiate?

The frequency of these obtestations, as well as their intensity and timing, gives us clues. The following chart lists chronologically the number of entries containing personal evaluations, self-chastisements, fresh resolutions to mend, and appeals to God for mercy, forgiveness, and the strength to carry out his resolve to live a holier life:

| | |
|---|---|
| 1855 (9 months) | 0 |
| 1856 | 4 |
| 1857 | 4 |
| 1858 (3½ months) | 0 |
| Four years of missing diaries | |
| 1862 (8 months) | 14 |
| 1863 | 24 |
| 1864 | 16 |
| 1865 | 14 |
| 1866 | 17 |
| 1867 | 12 |
| 1868 | 9 |
| 1869 | 8 |
| 1870 | 5 |
| 1871 | 11 |
| 1872 | 5 |
| 1873 | 3 |
| 1874 | 1 |
| 1875 | 1 |
| 1876 | 2 |
| 1877 | 1 |
| 1878 | 0 |
| 1879 | 1 |
| 1880 | 0 |
| 1881 | 3 |
| 1882 | 1 |
| 1883 | 2 |
| 1884 | 2 |
| 1885 | 0 |
| 1886 | 2 |
| 1887 | 0 |
| 1888 | 1 |
| 1889 | 0 |
| 1890 | 0 |
| 1891 | 1 |
| 1892 | 3 |
| 1893 | 0 |
| 1894 | 0 |

|      |   |
|------|---|
| 1895 | 0 |
| 1896 | 0 |
| 1897 | 1 |

In addition to these soul-searching, soul-searing entries, Charles uses another device for easing his conscience. Frequently he returns to one of these extended entries in his diary and adds a second, sometimes a third, date, and a varying number of "Amen"s. These addenda do not enter this count, although they bear upon the case; the numbers refer only to the full prose pleas. The largest clusters occur from 1862 (the diary covers only eight months of the year) to the end of 1867, with entries in each of these years numbering between twelve and twenty-four. The numbers then decline from twelve in 1867 to five in 1870, but surge to eleven in 1871. From then onward, we get only an occasional appeal.

A few correlations are evident. The early sixties were Charles's busiest years, full of tension and pressure. He strove to shape his lectures, to devise systems for working efficiently and productively. These were, moreover, the early years of his photography. He was perfecting this craft, busily taking sittings and performing for himself all the steps, from ordering and mixing chemicals, preparing plates, taking photographs, developing, printing, varnishing, and recording his work. They were also the years in which he shaped his social life, when he became a habitual London visitor, attending the theater and taking in art exhibitions, calling on and staying with friends (sometimes laden with his photographic equipment), hunting for apt sitters, seeking out child actors, enlarging his circles of acquaintances.

In 1860 and 1861 he was preparing himself for holy orders. Troubled lest his attachment to the theater prove an obstacle to entering the ministry, he consulted both Wilberforce and Liddon on the possible conflict. They assured him that as a deacon, if not as a priest, he might abstain from direct ministerial duty. On the strength of their opinions he proceeded, and then became a deacon on December 22, 1861. But Charles's qualms lived on. Within the year (October 21 and 22, 1862), he appealed to Dean Liddell, who, after some dithering, assured him that he need not take priest's orders.

Charles wrote various mathematical treatises in the early sixties. Although mainly aids for students, some show an unusual flair. His *Formulae of Plane Trigonometry* (1861), for instance, coins symbols for conventional terms; his keen ability to organize material comes to the fore in his sixteen-page pamphlet intended to help students prepare for Responsions, *The*

*Enunciations of the Propositions and Corollaries, together with Questions on the Definitions, Postulates, Axioms, etc., in Euclid, Books I and II* (1863), and in the twenty-seven-page *Guide to the Mathematical Student in Reading, Reviewing, and Working Examples, Part I, Pure Mathematics* (1864).

He carried on his literary efforts as well. In 1860 he published a humorous tale called "A Photographer's Day Out" and reviewed a photographic exhibition for the *Illustrated Times;* he published poems in *All the Year Round* and *Temple Bar;* and he edited and probably supervised his sisters' *Index to "In Memoriam."* He contributed more than a dozen items, mostly verse, to *College Rhymes,* the Oxford-Cambridge literary magazine that flourished from 1860 to 1873 (he himself edited it from July 1862 to March 1863). The crowning achievement of the early sixties is the first *Alice* story. And that brings us to the crux of the matter. Full as these years were of activities professional, photographic, and social, and overburdened as Charles was with doubts about his abilities and remorse over his indolence and his "selfishness"—they were years dominated by his emotional involvement with the Liddell children.

Charles's first recorded meeting with Dean Liddell took place on January 21, 1856. Relations were amicable as both men settled into their new jobs. In early 1856 the Dean lived at Christ Church without his family, overseeing renovations at the deanery. His wife, son, and three daughters did not arrive until the house was fully habitable and appropriately resplendent, boasting a new grand staircase (later christened the Lexicon Staircase because the royalties that Liddell received on his major opus paid for it). The children appeared during the last week of February, and Charles encountered Harry and Ina almost immediately, on the twenty-fifth, at the boat races. But the acquaintance must already have been established, for Charles would not otherwise have taken the liberty of joining them there. From that point on, his meetings with the Liddells, in various combinations, were frequent and legion; in fact, the friendship with the Liddell children became an obsession.

In the early years no apparent connection appears between the dates and frequency of the visits with the Liddell children and the guilt-ridden diary entries. During 1856 and 1857, although Charles's meetings with the children are frequent and often prolonged, the few entries of self-reproach in his diary relate more to his work, his preparation for the ministry, his inefficiency, and his falling short of his own goals. No link between these entries and his friendship with the Liddells emerges.

These two years trace the budding of the friendship, to be sure, when

Charles was paying court, as it were, at the deanery, seeking to become a favored friend. At the outset, the children were extremely young: Harry, the eldest, not yet nine; Edith a baby; the middle two, Lorina and Alice, six and three. Charles's efforts at forging a friendship naturally centered more on the two elder children, Harry and Ina. They appear by name often in his diary; the younger two do not. The first mention of Alice by name does not occur until May 5, 1857 (when she is five), and she appears by name only twice more by that year's end.

Now comes the four-year blackout period, during which Charles's friendship with the children flowered and their mutual affection bloomed. For these years we have only three fleeting glimpses into Charles's relationship with the deanery. On December 18, 1860, he is present at the Liddells' reception for the Queen when she visits Oxford to see the Prince of Wales. We have an incomplete letter that Charles sent home to Yorkshire recounting the event, but the Liddell children do not appear there by name. In another letter home (February 20, 1861), Charles reports: "My small friends the Liddells are all in the measles just now. . . . Alice had been pronounced as commencing and looked *awfully* melancholy—it was almost impossible to make her smile." Finally, for Christmas that year Charles gives the three girls a copy of Catherine Sinclair's *Holiday House* inscribed with an acrostic verse of his creation, their names construed by reading the first letter of each line downward.

That is all we have between 1858 and 1862. But when the record resumes, on May 9, 1862, the friendship is flourishing. Older now, the children are more interesting, can go on outings and wander over to Charles's rooms. Charles is *persona grata,* and relationships seem relaxed. On May 17, for instance, he goes to the deanery in the evening; and nine days later he rows on the river with Ina, Alice, and Edith, after which they all play croquet in the deanery garden. These meetings lead up to the memorable river expedition of July 4, when Charles creates his tale of Wonderland.

But what about those self-rebukes during this time of exultant companionship with the Liddells? They are there, and in unprecedented numbers. Over a period of eight months in 1862, twenty-nine entries involve the Liddells; and we have fourteen guilt-ridden adjurations, some of them painful to read, even today. The very first time that year that Charles alludes to the Liddells, he concludes that day's entry with an appeal to God to help him to live a better and more earnest life. The July 4 river expedition is actually scheduled for the previous day, but is rained out. Instead Charles has lunch at the deanery and stays on to hear the Liddell girls sing; afterward they play croquet.

On the glorious Fourth, the river picnic takes place. On the following day he chances to meet the Liddells on the Oxford railway station platform, and they travel up to London together. On the seventh, in London, Charles meets the Liddells at an art gallery at noon, presumably by appointment, and on the tenth, back in Oxford, he enters another plea for help in leading a new life. On the fourteenth he wishes he "could get away, and begin, perhaps, a system of better habits and a holier life." On the sixteenth he calls on the Dean about college business and sees "also Mrs. Liddell and the children." On the twenty-second he writes: "God help me to lead a new and better life"; and on the twenty-fourth he puts off going to Streatley, "where I was to have preached next Sunday . . . till I can rule myself better, preaching is but a solemn mockery—'thou that teachest another, teachest thou not thyself?' God grant this may be the last such entry I may have to make! that so I may not, when I have preached to others, be myself a castaway."

Early August sees frequent meetings with the Liddells. On the first Charles visits the children at the deanery and hears the three girls sing "Beautiful Star," which he later parodies as "Turtle Soup" in *Alice*. On the second they go on another river expedition and return to the deanery for croquet and dinner. On the third Charles joins the children for dinner. On the fifth he is again at the deanery, playing a game of "Ways and Means." On the sixth they go on the river again to Godstow, where they have tea. "On the way," Charles writes, ". . . I had to go on with my interminable fairy-tale of 'Alice's Adventures.' We got back soon after 8, and had supper in my rooms, the children coming over for a short while. A very enjoyable expedition," Ina's "14th time."

On August 8 the Liddells leave Oxford for their summer holiday. Charles too leaves Oxford, and while he and the Liddells are apart, his lamentations and prayers disappear. He returns to Oxford on October 11, and six days later, on the seventeenth, while out walking, falls in "with Mrs. Liddell and the children." That very day, the appeals to heaven resume. The contrapuntal chronicle continues for the remainder of 1862, and he ends the year with his usual assessment and fresh resolve.

The meetings with the Liddell children continue unabated through the first half of 1863, his friendship with them intense and in full flower, with Alice by now his clear favorite. He completes writing out the *Alice* story by February 10 and on February 17 observes: "It seems I am destined to meet the Liddells perpetually just now. I walked in the Broad with them in the morning, and in the afternoon . . . I went to the Christ Church Athletic Sports, and fell in with them and kept with them most of the afternoon."

On March 6 he receives a letter in French from Alice, and three days later the note asking him to escort her round to see the illuminations the following evening. They celebrate the Prince of Wales's wedding to Princess Alexandra all day and into the night of March 10. Charles, as Alice's chosen escort, is in his element; he records many of the details and at the end marks the day with a white stone. From March to June the Liddells command much of Charles's attention, time, and energy. On the last day of March he makes another appeal: "Now at the close of this month and of the 1st Quarter of the year, on my knees I beseech Almighty God to help me put away my old sins, and lead a new life." On the following day he adds "Amen." In early April he joins the children at their grandmother's near Cheltenham. On May 4 he gives Alice a book as a birthday present. On May 19 he utters another plea. In June he takes the children on a river picnic to Nuneham; they return by rail, and Charles has tea with them at the deanery: "A very pleasant day," he writes, "to be marked with a white stone." Three days later, however: "Not all days are to be marked with white stones: Collections are over, and Vacation (in a way) begun; and tonight on my knees I pray to God to give me a new heart, that here, at this milestone on my way, I may begin a new life. Help me, oh God. . . ."

The following days bring more delights, while Oxford and most particularly Christ Church prepare for the visit of the Prince and Princess. On June 15 Charles gets to see the chamber made ready for the royals, spends an hour or two at the deanery filling an album with samples of his photographs on the chance that the visitors will look at them, and then is summoned to help the children set up their stall at the bazaar. After the Prince and Princess arrive, Charles, as we have seen, is at the bazaar with the children. Then, on the twenty-third, he photographs the royal bedstead and, from afar, Ina and Alice sitting in the window of the royal chamber. That evening he accompanies the three girls and Miss Prickett to the circus. On the twenty-fourth, the day of a Volunteer Review, he falls in again with the Liddells, and on the twenty-fifth Alice and Edith come over to him "to fetch me over to arrange about an expedition to Nuneham," which turns out to be the large party of ten. After the row to Nuneham, he and the three girls return to Oxford by train: "a pleasant expedition with a *very* pleasant conclusion." On the twenty-seventh he writes to Mrs. Liddell urging her to send the children over to be photographed. There the break occurs, the crucial page cut from the record by a later hand—and the Liddells vanish from the diary for five months. Even when they reenter on December 5, Charles merely sees them from a distance and keeps apart.

What of the breast-beating imputations, which in fact continue and intensify after Charles no longer sees the Liddell children? During the second half of the year, when he is not in touch with them, we find thirteen recantations and prayers. Ironically, during this period, when he must have been missing the children keenly, he sets in train the publication of *Alice*.

The break with the Liddells in June 1863 is nowhere explained, and equally enigmatic is the resumption of the relationship at the end of the year. Some overture must have come from the deanery, for twelve days after Charles noticed Mrs. Liddell and the three children at the Christ Church theatricals but remained apart, he wrote the mother and offered to go over to the deanery. But she "put off [the visit] till Saturday." On the nineteenth, the appointed Saturday, "went over to the Deanery [at 5], where I staid till 8, making a sort of dinner at their tea. The nominal object of my going was to play croquet, but it never came to that, music, talk, etc., occupying the whole of the very pleasant evening. The Dean was away: Mrs. Liddell was with us part of the time. It is nearly 6 months since I have seen anything of them, to speak of. I mark this day with a white stone."

But if June 25, the date of the river expedition to Nuneham and the return journey by train, is the last time "to speak of," surely there is another date that follows hard on its heels that is not to be spoken of, the date of the diary entry accounting for the break with the Liddells.

In any case, ties were reestablished by December 19. But on January 29, 1864, Charles and the Dean clashed on college business. Charles read in *The Times* that Christ Church would award six scholarships in February, one to go to the candidate showing the greatest proficiency in mathematics. He wrote the Dean forthwith to point out that the Electors of the college had the right to choose those whom they believed most fit in all respects, not merely in a given discipline. The Dean replied that he thought "my objection 'hyper-critical and unnecessary,' but that he would on future occasions modify the notice." Not satisfied, on the following day Charles wrote again, thanking the Dean "for his concession"; "it did not affect my objection to the *present* notice," he added; "this, however, he declined to alter, and so I wrote once more, saying that I must decline to act this time as assessor, but should be happy to do so again when the notice has been altered to meet my views. This brought our rather disagreeable correspondence to an end."

The two men managed, however, to keep college and personal matters separate. Charles, in London on January 25 on one of his sprees, bought a small musical box worked by a handle as a birthday present for Edith, and presumably gave it to her. But he recorded no visits with the Liddells from January to May. Then, on May 6, out for a walk, Charles encountered Ina, Alice, Edith, and Miss Prickett and together they "inspected the new 'grand-stand' intended for spectators of boat-races." On May 12 he wrote that during the past few days he had "applied in vain for leave to take the children on the river, i.e., Alice, Edith, and Rhoda: but Mrs. Liddell will not let *any* come in future: rather superfluous caution." And he added: "Help me, oh God, for Christ's sake, to live more to Thee. Amen."

Not a single mention of the Liddells appears for the next six months, while Charles was drawing the pictures in the manuscript booklet for Alice. On September 13, 1864, while still at Croft for the long vacation, he rejoiced in finishing the pictures. On his way back to Oxford for the new term, he made his usual detour to London and called on Macmillan and Tenniel to talk about the *Alice* book. His diary entry for that day is accompanied by one of his conventional prayers. On November 26 he sent the manuscript booklet to Alice. Significantly, he did not feel able to deliver the gift in person, nor have we any indication that it was ever acknowledged.

On February 2, 1865, the Dean issued a notice on appointing Junior Students. Charles found the notice consistent with the proviso that the Electors do the judging, and he wrote "to tell him I should be happy to serve as assessor, if it were wished." The Dodgson-Liddell estrangement nevertheless continued. Then, on March 16, while out walking, Charles met Ina and Miss Prickett and had a short talk with them: "It is long since we interchanged a word," he wrote, "but we met as if it had been yesterday."

Silence closed in. On April 1 Charles talked with the Dean, "who thinks something should be done to help men in Arithmetic. I undertook to give a lecture in it next term." On April 6 Charles, again in London, went to an exhibition to see W. B. Richmond's "very pretty picture" of the three Liddell girls, "Ina looking a little too severe and melancholy, much as I am sure she would have looked, sitting to a stranger. Alice very lovely, but not *quite* natural. Edith's is the best likeness of the three." Eight days later, on Good Friday: "Grant me grace this day for ever to put away the sins of my former life, to hate them more and more, to love Thee more and more. . . ." And on the following day he adds: "Amen." On May 11 he met "Alice and Miss Prickett in the quadrangle. Alice seems changed a good deal, and hardly for the better—probably going through the usual awkward stage of transition."

Through the spring, silence persisted. Charles was working on the publication of *Alice*, checking proofs, approving the binding. He also continued to repine. On June 2 he utters a plea to cultivate more holiness and to live nearer to God; other pleas appear on June 6 and 27. On July 4, the anniversary of the memorable river excursion that produced the *Alice* tale, in London, he went to the Royal Academy. There he chanced on the Dean, Ina, Alice, and Edith, but records only the fact. He saw a painting of Mrs. Liddell by Mrs. C. J. Newton (daughter of Joseph Severn) but judged it "most disagreeable." At the end of June *Wonderland* rolled off the presses, and Charles ordered Macmillan to send Alice a copy on July 4.

Only one contact with the Liddells is recorded during the rest of the year in which *Alice* was twice printed, and that was with the Dean, at the end of October, when Charles called on him to report that his mathematical workload was too heavy for one: "I have now about 70 men to look after," he wrote in his diary, justifying his suggestion that he should have an assistant. "The Dean said he would call a meeting to consider the subject."

On November 9 Charles received the new impression of *Alice*, and on December 14 he sent a copy to Alice. Again we have no indication that the Liddells responded to these events.

Another year passed without change, without any gestures from or to the deanery. But the self-inflicted tortures and the resolves to mend continue. On June 5, the particularly poignant cry already cited (see page 203) appears, an agonizing outburst followed by more invocations, four in July. On the first day of the month, after taking Communion, Charles yearns "for the grace to partake of that holy mystery more faithfully, more penitently, with more real resolve of amendment of life! . . . There is yet half a year before me in 1866. Grant me grace, dear Lord, that it may be spent better than the half gone by! Forgive me the miserable past." Then another painful confession on July 10: "My heart is very heavy. I resolve to pray, but seem to beat the air. Oh, God, who hast given me the will to pray, give me also Thy Holy Spirit to cleanse and sanctify me. . . . Oh how blessed would be my future life, if from this night of heaviness and sorrow for sin I could begin anew, striving more and more to return unto the Lord, that he may have mercy, and abundantly pardon my sin!"

On November 30 a curious entry appears: "For the evening, I had 2 invitations, to the Deanery, and to Price's, and took the latter." He recounts a succession of visits he made during the day before going to dinner at the Prices', evidence of his agreeable involvement in Oxford society, perhaps to console himself for the lost friendships. To buck up his *amour propre,* he demonstrates that he can refuse an invitation to the deanery.

On December 5 he suddenly took the road to the deanery once more and the dark clouds lifted: "Went to the Deanery at 4½ to a meeting of tutors." He stayed for dinner, "one of the pleasantest evenings I have had there for a very long time. . . . I had a good deal of talk with Mrs. Liddell and (*mirabile dictu!*) a long chat with Mrs. Reeve. Mrs. Liddell . . . showed me some very pretty new photographs of the children." Then Charles made one of his classic appeals to "leave behind, with the fast ending year, my old self." Three similar prayers appear in December. He deplores "wasted time and opportunities." Looking back at his "follies and . . . sins," he grows sadder every time: "Pardon, oh merciful Father, the sins of the past year . . . ," he writes, "and help me in the year now beginning to serve Thee more faithfully. Oh take me home again, as a sheep that has long wandered from Thy fold, and keep me Thine!"

Charles's conscience remained troubled in 1867, and on February 6 he unburdened himself again in his diary with an anguished plea: "God be merciful to me a sinner."

Visits with the Liddell children do not recur. On April 4, 1867, Charles had "a little talk" with the Dean and Mrs. Liddell at the University Museum, and on May 18 he visited Mrs. Liddell and had "a long chat with her, walking about the Deanery garden, a thing I have not done for years." And that is the last time any of the Liddells enter the diary until over three years later. Charles's self-recriminations continue, however, through 1867, 1868, and 1869.

The friendship with the idyllic trio was over—a wrench at the time of the break and a constant ache for years. How difficult it must have been for him to come to terms with so final and frustrating a reality. His work keeps him occupied. He takes his one journey out of Britain, to the Continent with Liddon. His photography and his friendships with other children, some especially gratifying, others less so, enable him to look to the future. By the time any sort of converse is reestablished with the Liddells, the three darlings are grown and entirely out of his reach.

On June 25, 1870, Charles recorded the events attendant upon Commemoration and added: "This morning an almost . . . wonderful thing occurred. Mrs. Liddell brought Ina and Alice to be photographed (that last occasion was [Charles, intending to look back for it, leaves the date blank]),[3] first visiting my rooms, and then the studio." The photographs he took of the two survive. Both young women, in their early twenties now, sit individually in one of Charles's leather armchairs; they look formal and grave. Gone the sparkle, gone the joy. Games have ceased, the laughter subsided, warmth cooled. Charles is left alone with his memories.

The ache of loss remained. On May 4, 1871, he wrote: "On . . . Alice's birthday, I sit down to record the events of the day, partly as a specimen of my life now, and partly because they include *one* new experience," a visit to a carpenter dying of tuberculosis. Charles read aloud to him from the Bible. "I *hope* that my visit may have been of some comfort to him, though I feel terribly unfit to comfort any one in such a time." His thoughts must bend to the past, to the birthday parties he attended at the deanery, to the Mad Tea-Party.

Charles and the Liddells strove for a semblance of propriety, even conviviality. On May 13 Charles went over to the deanery in the afternoon, "where they had croquet, and music in the Library." In the evening Alice came to dinner in Charles's rooms, with Charles's brother Wilfred and three sisters. On November 16 Charles encountered Edith, almost as a stranger, at a colleague's dinner party, but he finds her, "when the ice was once broken," a pleasant neighbor. *Looking-Glass* was published, and the first thing Charles did when he received his copies (December 8) was send three over to the Deanery, "the one for Alice being in morocco."

The success of *Wonderland* had led its author to write the sequel. But Charles was also spurred on by the need to keep his friendship with the Liddell daughters, and most particularly with Alice. He not unreasonably hoped to recapture some of the old glory, to placate the Liddell parents and to fan the dying embers of his friendship with the girls.

*Looking-Glass* is another reverie, like *Wonderland,* but the book is distinct from its predecessor. Similarities exist in the dramatis personae, in the play of words, the nonsense, and the verse. But the tone and texture are different, and even though both tales are episodic excursions into alien lands, the two landscapes differ sharply. Most of all, the underlying meaning, the imagery, and the message of each are unique.

*Wonderland* is the tale of a quest, a trial, and a test. It is a series of episodes that pits a young person against a bewildering cast of adult characters who behave incomprehensibly, according to arcane conventions. It illustrates how a young, inexperienced person can deal with this inexplicably chaotic world and survive as part of it. When Alice wakes, she returns to the reassuring comfort and companionship of her sister and, by extension, to the welcoming arms of her family. Though more experienced now, she is still young, but she is ready.

*Looking-Glass* is something else. Here we have a real chess game, with chess pieces representing the obstacles the young person encounters and must overcome. The game of life is more advanced, more adult, and the heroine must progress according to strict rules. The most important difference is that Charles's protagonist is the real Alice Liddell (the story opens in the deanery and Alice's companion is the real deanery cat) rather than the heroine of *Wonderland,* who is really Charles himself in disguise. Her progress after passing through the looking-glass does not really resemble what a child must learn to develop the character that will enable her to succeed in society, as it does in the earlier book. The journey here has a double purpose. Alice is climbing the social ladder and ultimately reaches the top, a queen, a figure of independence and power; and as she moves from square to square, she sheds her childishness and becomes adult. She endures the ritual of initiation, but her survival is not threatened.

Charles plays several roles in this book. He is, first, the Red Knight, his armor crimson (the color he preferred for his books' bindings), galloping down upon Alice, brandishing a great club. He tries to take her prisoner, but instead falls off his horse. Alice, for her part, fears for his safety more than she fears him. Then Charles tries again to come close to his heroine, this time with the gentler manner of the White Knight (Charles's presentation copies for Alice Liddell were bound in white). But first the two knights must engage in battle over her, an exercise that emphasizes their ineptitude as they keep falling off their horses and onto their heads. Then, all at once, the Red Knight gallops off, leaving the field and Alice to the White Knight. The White Knight is the only major character in the *Alice* books who treats her kindly, but she rejects him: "I don't want to be anybody's prisoner," she says. "I want to be a Queen."

The White Knight, his mind full of useless inventions, is a bumbler, a bad horseman. He sings Alice a melancholy song, and the author tells us that Alice will always remember the scene of the Knight crooning his lament. The song, about an old man sitting on a gate, is nonsense, but only on the surface: it serves as the White Knight's swan song to Alice, just before she leaves him at the edge of the wood to go in search of queenhood. The parody of Wordsworth, varnished with outrageous exaggeration, depicts an old man, an uncanny anticipation of how the aging Mr. Dodgson might look and behave:

And now, if e'er by chance I put
   My fingers into glue,
Or madly squeeze a right-hand foot
   Into a left-hand shoe,
Or if I drop upon my toe
   A very heavy weight,
I weep, for it reminds me so
Of that old man I used to know—
Whose look was mild, whose speech was slow,
Whose hair was whiter than the snow,
Whose face was very like a crow,
With eyes, like cinders, all aglow,
Who seemed distracted with his woe,
Who rocked his body to and fro,
And muttered mumblingly and low,
As if his mouth were full of dough,
Who snorted like a buffalo—
That summer evening, long ago,
   A-sitting on a gate.

Alice and the White Knight then part: " 'You've only a few yards to go,' he said, 'down the hill and over that little brook, and then you'll be a Queen—But you'll stay and see me off first?' he added as Alice turned with an eager look in the direction to which he pointed. 'I sha'n't be long. You'll wait and wave your handkerchief when I get to that turn in the road? I think it'll encourage me, you see.' " Alice complies and thanks him for the song. They shake hands, the Knight rides into the forest, Alice waves her handkerchief as he reaches the turn and disappears.

Charles also wrote a "Wasp in a Wig" episode, which he suppressed at Tenniel's insistence ("the '*wasp*' chapter doesn't interest me in the least," Tenniel wrote, ". . . a *wasp* in a *wig* is altogether beyond the appliances of art"[4]). The meeting with the Wasp echoes Alice's encounter with the White Knight. It too dwells on the subject of age and aging, the Wasp also serving as a mouthpiece for Charles's thoughts and feelings, disguised here, not by armor, but by a wig. "There's somebody very unhappy there," Alice observes as she hears the Wasp's moans. She looks about to find "something" like a very old man. "I don't *think* I can be of any use to him," she thinks, but he is so pitiful that she interrupts her journey to ask him what ails him. She listens "rather unwillingly" to his complaints about his old bones and offers to help him to a secluded spot, out of the wind, and to read to him out of a newspaper. As she reads, however, he interrupts her with irrelevancies. He is a vain old wasp, as his extended tale of how he came by his yellow wig proves. He makes some unflattering comments about Alice's appearance, and he stretches out one of his claws toward her hair, thinking it too is a wig. But Alice "kept out of reach." She finds his personal remarks unpleasant, and as the Wasp goes on talking and seems to have recovered his spirits, she moves off.

" 'Good-bye, and thank-ye,' said the Wasp, and Alice tripped down the hill again, quite pleased that she had gone back and given a few minutes to making the poor old creature comfortable." She leaps over the brook with relief: "Oh, how glad I am to get here!" She becomes a queen and enters her new life.

Like the two knights, the Wasp is depicted in exaggerated strokes, Charles's device both for concealing matter with manner and for injecting humor. The humor does not altogether succeed, but the theme is the same: an old man concerned with his infirmities, who, like the White Knight, is rejected. Neither succeeds completely as a figure of fun, but each reveals a kernel of truth about their creator.

Alice's encounter with all three of these pitiful characters is a transparent exaggeration of what had happened in real life to Charles and his favorite child friend. He sees into her heart, knows that she wants to be kind to these old, bumbling, complaining, overdrawn representations of himself, but that in reality she is all too ready to bid them adieu and get on with her own life. Charles conceals himself behind the armor and the wig, and while his humor distracts attention from himself, his knights and wasp have earnest missions. They bare their souls and tell us of the sad realities of life: they are old, she is young; they are bumblers, she is keen; they are resigned to their fate, she is ambitious; they are on their way out, she is entering a new life. They depart—she arrives.

The man who emerges as the aggregate of these three characters, with their painful admissions, is affecting and piteous. Loss and rejection have replaced friendship and conviviality, and Charles's only consolation now lies in nostalgia. *Looking-Glass* is bracketed by two carefully crafted poems that attempt to recapture some of the old sunshine. But both fail. The clouds have moved in, the emotion is at best recollected. That is why "the shadow of a sigh" trembles through the pages. A deep sadness hangs over these *évocations romantiques,* a sadness that Charles cannot disguise. Charles speaks out plainly in the poem:

Child of the pure unclouded brow
And dreaming eyes of wonder!
Though time be fleet, and I and thou
Are half a life asunder,
Thy loving smile will surely hail
The love-gift of a fairy-tale.

I have not seen thy sunny face,
Nor heard thy silver laughter;
No thought of me shall find a place
In thy young life's hereafter—
Enough that now thou wilt not fail
To listen to my fairy-tale.

. . . . . . . .

And though the shadow of a sigh
May tremble through the story,
For "happy summer days" gone by,
And vanish'd summer glory—
It shall not touch with breath of bale
The pleasance of our fairy-tale.

The verse that is the envoi at the end is similarly personal:

Long has paled the sunny sky:
Echoes fade and memories die:
Autumn frosts have slain July.

Still she haunts me, phantomwise,
Alice moving under skies
Never seen by waking eyes.

The final banquet in *Looking-Glass* is the last glimpse of the glorious days gone by, but again Alice shatters the scene, just as she shattered the trial scene in the earlier book. Nothing remains of the adventure behind the looking-glass. The dream vanishes and she awakes, a woman. But Charles's dream is also destroyed, and he must accept the new Alice.

How did the deanery take the new book? What manner of thanks did the Liddells render Charles? What emotions ran through the young trio when they read their own inscribed copies? We simply do not know. All we know is that the past exists only in memory, in fairy tales. There was no present, no meeting in 1872, and only two in 1873: on February 6 Charles went to the deanery to present Alice with a copy of the Italian version of *Wonderland;* and on April 24, calling on the Dean on college business, he met Mrs. Liddell, "who took me into the drawing room to see photos, where Alice showed me the large ones Mrs. Cameron had done of them."

On February 7, 1874, Charles tersely records: "Wedding-day of my old friend Ina Liddell." On March 7 he dines at the deanery but mentions no Liddell by name. Nor do any Liddells enter the diary in 1875. On June 26, 1876, Charles records the death, of peritonitis following measles, of "my old friend Edith Liddell," and her funeral (June 30). On December 11 Mrs. Liddell came over to Charles's rooms "to see the photographs (about which I had written) which I had taken, in 1858, 1859, and 1860, of Edith; and accepted several of them. In the evening she sent me 2 recent cartes of her." Nothing more, not even a note recording Alice's marriage to Reginald Hargreaves in 1880; years will pass before these old friends enter Charles's diary again.

His self-rebukes, his protests about his sinful life, his importunities for God to help him improve, decline as the thread that connects his life to the deanery unwinds: as the mentions of the Liddell children vanish, his complaints and resolves subside. The conjunction of these two currents, flowing side by side, must signify something. Charles's self-indictments often appear at crucial moments of the calendar, when a term begins, when a term ends, at the beginning of a new year, at its close, when he is about to leave Oxford for one of his other habitations or vice versa. Could they be connected exclusively with his work, his lecturing, his writing, his responsibilities as a member of Christ Church and his self-image as a cleric? The facts argue for more: the coincidence of his complaints with his meetings with the Liddell daughters cannot be overlooked.

What, then, lies behind and beneath those guilty appeals, those protests against past sins? Why should he characterize himself as vile and worthless, weak and selfish; why is he caught in the chains of sin; why does he confess to a rebellious will; what makes him yearn for a new life? What does he mean when he writes of mental troubles, skeptical or unholy thoughts "which torture the fancy that would fain be pure," blasphemous thoughts "which dart unbidden into the most reverent souls"? What temptations besiege him, to which, by his own admission, he succumbs?

We have no proven answers, for Charles, true Victorian, could not speak his whole heart, could not articulate anything that touched upon the forbidden province of sexual need or desire. We can, however, speculate; Charles himself provides clues.

He was not guilty of heresy, nor was he troubled by fine spiritual points. Unlike Carlyle, Mill, and Newman, he experienced no shattering spiritual crisis. His faith was secure, he could define it, and he lived with and by its dicta. He was not guilty of hidden crimes against individuals or society; he was guilty only in his own eyes—not so much of deeds as of thoughts. His "indolence" troubled him, but it did not cause those searing outcries. The protests and appeals, so deeply felt, came from a force within him that he finds difficult, even impossible, to harness—certainly emotional, very likely sexual.

He was highly strung and strongly emotional, and the imagination that produced those glorious adventures in Wonderland, behind the looking-glass, and in search of the Snark demanded its own life. So powerful a fancy could easily join forces with his fragile sensibility to cause him sleepless hours, to convey dangerous temptations, and perhaps, in his own scale of values, unholy thoughts and wilful, sinful desires. It is not the Baker who engages the Snark "every night after dark / In a dreamy delirious fight"—it is Charles.

In spite of some recent assertions that the Victorians knew about sex and enjoyed it,[5] Charles and his contemporaries did not, in fact, understand human sexuality, and what they thought about it they certainly concealed and ignored. Perhaps the most remarkable bit of Victorian sexual ignorance appears in a letter from Ellen Terry to G. B. Shaw: "I'll never forget my first kiss. . . . Mr. Watts kissed me in the studio one day . . . and I was in heaven. . . . I told no one for a fortnight, but when I was alone with Mother one day . . . I told her I *must* be married to him *now* because I was going to have a baby!!!! . . . Oh, I tell you I thought I knew everything then, but I was nearly 16 years old then—and I was *sure* that kiss meant giving me a baby."[6]

Most Victorians were taught to fear sex. The reemergence of the Evangelical restraint in the wake of Georgian excess led to stern social censors, like the fictional Mrs. Grundy, and to watchdog legislation, like the obscenity law of 1857. Even those intrepid souls who sought to learn more about sex by reading what passed for scientific tracts encountered more myth and misunderstanding than scientific knowledge. Healthy children, according to the dogma of the day, did not have sexual thoughts. Women had no natural sexual desires and merely submitted to the brutish needs of their husbands. For the married man, a duty and desire to procreate led to sexual experiments and often ended in tragedy. Birth control devices were rare, scorned, and dangerous. Women often died early from excessive child-bearing, and large families became burdens that fathers could not support nor mothers properly care for. For the unmarried, masturbation not only violated religious principle but was medically condemned as a form of deviance that led to blindness, madness, and early death. Sexual dreams were reprehensible, the result of moral wickedness. Sexual fantasies, even when unbidden, and nocturnal emissions were excrescences of a sinful, debauched, evil inner force. Many strove to live a pure life but found that their natural promptings collided with the strictures of the time. Chastity, the supreme virtue, was not enough; a clear conscience required not only abstinence, certainly for a bachelor, but an absence of desire, a mind free of sexual fantasies, however involuntary. What we today see as natural human impulses violated both religious faith and social morality.[7]

It is naïve to insist that Charles's troubled conscience stemmed solely from professional shortcomings or indolence. His letters and diaries are laced with inferences that allow us, with today's awareness, to deduce a fire raging beneath the surface. His literary effusions raise the same questions.

In the poetry he wrote and published during the years he was enjoying the Liddell connection and penning his personal recriminations, we find several splendidly humorous pieces which must have gratified him and his audience. But these verses are overshadowed by the serious poems that both show us Charles's limitations as a true poet and tell us much about him. One of the earliest, he called "Stanzas for Music" and later changed to "The Willow Tree." He did not publish it until 1869, but it appeared in 1859 in his own hand in *Mischmasch*, the family magazine, when he was twenty-seven. It tells the tale of a jilted female lover standing beneath a willow tree watching as in the distance her beloved weds another woman. Although the protagonist is female and the lines reek of Victorian sentimentality, the subject of rejection is apt. But she is resolved not to interfere with her lover's happiness: "I will hide myself away, / And nurse a lonely grief," she proclaims.

Another poem that he also copied into *Mischmasch* at about the same time (January 1860) is "Faces in the Fire," a tale of an older man sitting at dusk by the fire, recalling the love of his youth, but acknowledging that now

> . . . she is strange and far away
> That might have been mine own to-day—

That might have been mine own, my dear,
Through many and many a happy year—
That might have sat beside me here.

Ay, changeless through the changing scene,
The ghostly whisper rings between,
The dark refrain of "might have been."

The race is o'er I might have run:
The deeds are past I might have done;
And sere the wreath I might have won.

Sunk is the last faint flickering blaze:
The vision of departed days
Is vanished even as I gaze.

The pictures, with their ruddy light,
Are changed to dust and ashes white,
And I am left alone with night.

In the autumn of 1861 Charles published "The Dream of Fame," a long poem influenced by Tennyson's *Maud*. The young hero is smitten at first glance by a young woman, but for reasons not explained, the affair does not endure, and the "two lovers" meet "to bid farewell." The man departs. Many years later he returns, "a wanderer from a distant shore," to seek the landmarks of yore. "But those he sought were there no more." He remains, nursing "the ashes of a vain despair," hoping to catch a glimpse of the face he knew and loved. He is so absorbed in his anguish that he loses touch with reality. She, in fact, appears, but he dies without realizing that she stands and weeps over him.

Charles printed a prefatory note to a poem entitled "Only a Woman's Hair" (dated February 17, 1862). It reads: " 'After the death of Dean Swift there was found among his papers a small packet containing a single lock of hair and inscribed with the above words.' " The word *only* offends Charles. He speculates about the owner of the hair: was it a child's hair fringing a queenlike face, hair from a Gypsy's sunny brow, from an old woman, or from a supplicant kneeling and bathing Christ's feet? He ends with a sharp admonition:

The eyes that loved it once no longer wake:
  So lay it by with reverent care—

Touching it tenderly for sorrow's sake—
It is a woman's hair.

It would be wrong to look for absolute parallels between the characters, incidents, or emotional quotients in these verses and those in Charles's life. The poems could conceivably be postgraduate exercises in capturing the Gothic mood, the world-weary stance, the tainted hearts that Charles has observed in his reading, particularly in the poetry of the Romantics.

Why dwell on the pangs of unrequited love, untried love, and the hurt caused when a lock of a woman's hair found among the effects of a dead poet is brushed aside? Why choose these melancholy subjects? Do they give us some clues about his own emotional history and condition?

One major theme runs through them all: love. The subtext is that love does not come easily. No happy unions take place. Unsatisfactory love affairs and frustrated emotional states attract Charles. In the case of the lock of hair found in Swift's effects, Swift's love affair with Stella echoes Charles's own frustrations, and he responds feelingly. Other similarities appear when we look at the Swift-Dodgson histories. Swift often wrote letters to Stella in baby language. Charles knew, too, about Swift's relationship with Stella (and with the later Vanessa), which ended tragically.

The dull and doleful verses are not literally autobiographical, but they bring us close to Charles's inner fears. Given his unconventional inclinations, he fears the worst, and he strives to prepare himself for it, even as he seeks the means for preventing his life from ending in tragedy. By articulating the danger, by knowing how terrible the alternative, he can, he hopes, restrain his impulses and avoid disaster. He will suppress, he will control—these tragedies will not befall him because he will travel the narrow road. And yet, the rejected lovers are poignantly cast, their sad emotional condition consistently portrayed. Does Charles already feel the pang of rejection? And does he know that his life inevitably will be marked by repeated rejection?

These derivative poems of the later 1850s and early 1860s are unremarkable. They are traditional in structure, meter, rhyme, and imagery. The sun rises, the sun sets, Time, Nature, and Age play their roles, the language (locks, limbs, tresses, sobs) is strictly Victorian, formal. The verses are never innovative.

But beginning in 1862 we find a change. On May 9, the day which inaugurates the next surviving diary after the four-year loss, Charles records at the outset that he has finished and sent to the editor of *College Rhymes* his poem "Stolen Waters." It appears in the summer number. An allegory, it is more elaborate than the earlier serious ones and contains mysterious elements. Not for the first time, Charles here dons the cape of a fictitious figure, a youth who, in his journey into manhood, encounters a beautiful and bewitching maid. She smiles at him. "I followed her, I know not why." They consummate their love, and at that moment she turns into an old, withered hag. Realizing that he has sinned and forfeited his chastity, he flees his seductress, bearing with him a "cold, cold heart of stone." He is thought mad, he yearns to die. But suddenly he experiences an epiphany: he hears a child-angel singing about the purity of childhood, reminding him that, by striving to recapture his own childhood innocence, he may yet enter the kingdom of God. The singing voice is like the summer rain, and the youth matches it with his own repentant tears. Cleansed, his "human heart returned again." The youth has learned a lot by the experience: that he should not have sinned, but having done so, he can still be saved; that with remorse, a garland still awaits his brow, one that must be won with tears, with pain— with death.

Charles wrote "Stolen Waters" in the first person: it was his first public confrontation with sex, seduction. The imagery includes ripe fruit, a red sunset. The temptress has a glowing cheek, a gleaming eye, a lily brow. The knight drinks the juice of the forbidden fruit, the pair take their "pleasure."

The confessional mode descends from Coleridge's "Ancient Mariner," the narrative parallels Matthew Arnold's "The Strayed Reveller," and the imagery borrows from Tennyson's "The Lotos-Eaters." The whole is framed in Victorian melodrama and follows the well-worn course of innocence tempted, innocence seduced, innocence sinning, sinner repentant, and sinner redeemed. The poem's singular message is that if one sins, one is not necessarily doomed for eternity, a message that Charles preached for the rest of his life.

The earlier serious poems create fictional types who tell cautionary tales; "Stolen Waters" is the closest Charles comes to revealing his inner self, his biting fears. But it is probably not the report of anything he has experienced; at most, his Circe is the lithe creature of his dreams. Indeed there's the rub—his dreams. Without the benefit of later "scientific" work on dream interpretation, Charles, steeped in classical literature, knew that the ancient Greeks taught that dreams, sexual as well as otherwise, had to be regarded seriously; they bore real meaning for the dreamer. The fears that Charles makes implicit in these early poems sharpen and reappear in his later works, and the sins of his fancy, his dreams, haunt him relentlessly.

That is where Charles commits his sins, in his nocturnal waking hours and in his dreams. Perhaps for *dreams* we should read *fantasies*. Underscoring his faith and his philosophy was his belief that life is but a dream. But what were the dreams within that dream? Were they an escape from the larger dream into fantasy, where, like the unchaste knight, he took his imaginary pleasure? Were they infractions of his faith that led to self-contempt and the desperate prayers for change and renewal?

Charles wrote "Stolen Waters" when his attention to the deanery children was focused most intensely, when his friendship with them was firm and running smoothly and gratifyingly, when he had reason to hope that the affection the children bore him would ripen even further. It was early May 1862, the onset of the picnic season, the season for photography, less than two months before the magic moment in the boat when he would invent his children's classic. His hopes ran high, but his torments, recorded as some of them are in the diary throughout these months, plagued him. Hardly three and a half months had passed since he was ordained Deacon—and he writes, for the first time, of a knight allowing himself to be seduced by a false Eve, of copulating with her, and of having to suffer expulsion from Eden. The man is in trouble.

For the next three years, from 1862 to 1865, Charles busied himself, in one way or another, with telling, then writing out, and ultimately expanding and publishing the *Alice* tale. First he produced *Under Ground* and presented it to Alice at Christmastime 1864, then he published the expanded story in mid-1865. The imagery in *Alice* is not overtly sexual, as in "Stolen Waters." Where in "Stolen Waters" Charles writes of blatant, expressed sexuality, the *Alice* images record a suppressed sexuality. They appear so frequently and have been extracted by so many analysts that it will serve our purpose well enough to note just a few: the rabbit hole at the start; the emphasis on eating and drinking; Alice's changing size; Alice outgrowing the size of the Rabbit's house, almost causing it to burst at the seams; the explosive ejection of Bill the Lizard through the chimney of the house; the Pigeon referring to Alice as a kind of serpent; physical beatings, shakings, and sneezings; the numerous threats of decapitation.

If we accept the notion that the tale is an autobiographical allegory, that Alice is Charles in disguise, then surely these images reflect the intense relationship with the Liddell children on the one hand and Charles's troubled conscience on the other. If true, *Wonderland* emerges as an allegory of Charles's, not Alice's, journey, a journey beset by many pitfalls, a journey in search of one's identity (" 'Who are *you?*' " . . . " 'I—I hardly know . . .' "), a search for the right road, the one that will lead him to understand his impulses, to identify his sexuality and give it appropriate expression.

"The Valley of the Shadow of Death," a poem that Charles wrote in April 1868, is another rueful monologue with suicidal and sexual intimations. Charles wrote it at a time when no Liddell children entered his life, but when his lamentations and prayers continued. Here again, an old man looks back upon his life. From his deathbed he confides to his son about the "evil spells that held me thrall, / And thrust my life from fall to fall"; but he gives no details. He continues with generalities:

> The spells that bound me with a chain,
>   Sin's stern behests to do,
> Till Pleasure's self, invoked in vain,
>   A heavy burden grew—

Then, in the midst of his despair, wandering aimlessly like the knight in "Stolen Waters" after he has sinned, he comes upon a pair of innocent children reading aloud from the Bible, and all at once he sees the way to salvation: his tears cleanse his sinful soul, music descends from afar, and a voice beckons him to rest. He is transformed and lives in peace waiting for Death and reunion with his dead wife. The poem is another mawkish confession by a colorless and garrulous old man who would appear to have nothing in common with Charles Dodgson. But Charles creates him, a sinner who, by observing childish ways, finds a road back from the abyss of sin to redemption.

Abandoned by the Liddells, Charles's focus turned elsewhere, to other children, both for aesthetic and emotional satisfaction. He was still young, in his mid-thirties, his energy and impulses strong, and he needed friendship and affection. His diary and letters chronicle his numerous successes in achieving agreeable relationships. For the most part, he convinced himself, the children's parents, and even onlookers that his intentions were innocent and honorable, and, on the conscious level, they certainly were. For this stern self-disciplinarian never permitted himself to cross into the forbidden territory where he sent his knight of "Stolen Waters" and the ancient of "The Valley of the Shadow of Death." As tight-lipped as he was, however, the images that surface in his letters, diaries, and works reveal his sexual nature.

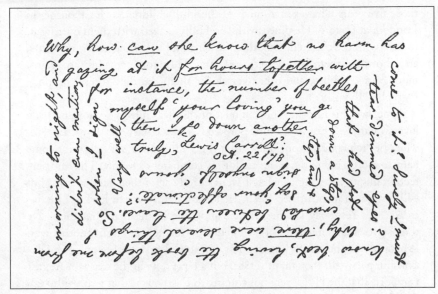

*Charles's spiral letter to Agnes Hull, who was another special child friend to whom he sent some of his most inventive letters. "At last I've succeeded in forgetting you!" he wrote teasingly in 1877. "It's been a very hard job, but I took 6 'lessons in forgetting,' at half-a-crown a lesson. After three lessons, I forgot my own name, and I forgot to go for the next lesson. . . . 'But I hope,' the Professor said, 'you won't forget to pay for the sessions!'"*

One example is a playful letter he wrote Gertrude Chataway (April 19, 1878): "When a little girl is hoping to take a plum off a dish, and finds that she can't have that one, because it's bad or unripe, what does she do? Is she sorry or disappointed? Not a bit! She just takes another instead, and grins from one little ear to the other as she puts it to her lips! This is a little fable to do you good; the little girl means *you*—the bad plum means *me*—the other plum means some other friend—and all that about the little girl putting plums to her lips means—well, it means—but you know you can't expect *every bit* of a fable to mean something!"[8]

Charles created some of his most amusing letters and other drolleries for Agnes Hull, one of his special child friends, who with her sisters offered him winning friendships from the summer of 1877, when he first met them at Eastbourne, to the summer of 1882, when the relationships ended. During those five years Charles saw much of the Hull children, at Eastbourne, in London, at Oxford. He dined with the Hulls, stayed with them overnight, walked with the children, took them rowing and to various entertainments, and showered them with letters and gifts. He wrote acrostics, anagrams, monograms, riddles, and other verses for them; he drew them, he photographed them.

Agnes was his favorite, and the relationship was filled with joy and little lovers' quarrels. Then a sour note entered Charles's diary on August 22, 1882, when he "reluctantly" concluded "that the 4 Hulls, tho' very pleasant company to me, do not in the least care for my company, or for me. They are perfectly obliging, so long as what I want exactly suits their inclinations, but will not go an inch further. Such friends are hardly worth having," he decided. ". . . Yesterday I joined Agnes and Evie in the road, but they gave themselves airs so much that I declined to go further, and went another way. It happened to be exactly 5 years, that day, since I first met them." The relationship persisted, though, into 1883, but a terse note in the diary on August 13 reports that the Hulls were not coming to Eastbourne that year. Although the Hulls returned in subsequent summers, Charles recorded no further visits with the children.

If the children's love was fleeting, perhaps Charles's love was too intense, too demanding. They were, after all, children; and Charles behaved like a lover scorned. In fact, Agnes Hull told her son that she broke off the friendship with Charles when she felt that one of his kisses was sexual.[9] Of course, just when a kiss ceases to be a sign of affection and becomes something more is subject to individual interpretation, but Charles's petulance and his overweening attachment to his "darling Aggie" could well have caused the Hulls some embarrassment.

We cannot know to what extent sexual urges lay behind Charles's preference for drawing and photographing children in the nude. He contended that the preference was entirely aesthetic. But given his emotional attachment to children as well as his aesthetic appreciation of their forms, his assertion that his interest was strictly artistic is naïve. He probably felt more than he dared acknowledge, even to himself. Certainly he always sought to have another adult present when nude prepubescents modeled for him. His artist friend Gertrude Thomson was sometimes on hand for the sessions, and he appealed to mothers to come with their sitter daughters to "arrange the dress," by which he meant to undress and then re-dress the child. Was he being cautious, one wonders, because he knew that reports would get about of his nude art, or was he insuring himself against any slipups? Perhaps neither; perhaps one ought to take him at his word, but the record he left behind does not altogether support his contention.

He brought his preference for purity-nudity into the illustrations of his later works. On May 7, 1878, he wrote to A. B. Frost, then illustrating his poems for *Rhyme? and Reason?*, that for the poem "Love among the Roses," he wished to have "a design on wood. . . . It should represent Cupid sleeping, fairies watching, and lots of roses. As this is for publication," he added, "I should like a draped Cupid—a tunic will do very well—but the critics would be down on me directly, if he were not enough dressed. His *face* should be, if possible, a portrait of little Sallie Sinclair." In the same letter, Charles requests another drawing, "a study from life (but *not* a Cupid) that I may keep it as a specimen of your power in drawing a beautiful figure. As it is *not* for publication, you need not put an atom of drapery on it, and I can quite trust you, even if you made it a full-front view, to have a simple classical figure. I had rather not have an adult figure (which always looks to me rather in need of drapery): a girl of about 12 is *my* ideal of beauty of form."

He wrote to Harry Furniss (November 29, 1886), instructing him on how he should draw Sylvie for *Sylvie and Bruno:* "I am charmed with your idea of dressing her in *white:* it exactly fits my own idea of her: I want her to be a sort of embodiment of Purity. So I think that, in Society, she should be *wholly* in white—white frock ('clinging,' certainly: I *hate* the crinoline fashion): white stockings (or wouldn't socks be prettier? When children have, what is not always the case, well-shaped calves to their legs, stockings seem a pity). . . . Also I *think* we might venture on making her *fairy*-dress transparent."

When he engaged Gertrude Thomson to provide the illustrations of nude female fairies that would ultimately appear in *Three Sunsets and Other Poems*, he wrote her (February 27, 1893) complaining that in one of her sketches a fairy looked like a boy. "If you would add to the hair, and slightly refine the wrist and ankles, it would make a beautiful girl. I had much rather have *all* the fairies *girls*. . . . For I confess I do *not* admire naked *boys* in pictures. They always seem . . . to need *clothes:* whereas one hardly sees why the lovely forms of girls should *ever* be covered up!"

Charles apparently convinced many of his friends that his attachment to the nude female child form was free of any eroticism. Later generations look beneath the surface. The price Charles paid for his delusions was the spiritual agony he endured in private and from which he sought relief by recantation and fresh resolves.

No one would doubt that Charles yearned for loving, reciprocal friendships. He believed that the ideal relationship evolved into a sanctified marriage, and he thought about marriage early. When he was thirteen, he wrote "A Fable" for *Useful and Instructive Poetry* in which a son owl pleads with his father owl for an inheritance because "he would married be." When Charles was twenty-five, he discussed with his father the appropriate time for taking out life insurance and concluded (July 31, 1857) that "if at any future period I contemplate marriage (of which I see no present likelihood), it will be quite time enough to begin paying the premium then." Later, in an undated essay, "Marriage Service," he wrote: "Plain facts are: God has implanted sexual desires, and has laid down conditions under which they are innocent, and blessed by Him—other conditions, under which they are sinful and accursed. It seems that God forbids us to arouse or encourage these desires except for the object, for which He gave them, marriage." Surely he believed that his own sexual promptings were natural and that to fulfill them in the marriage bed would be a holy act. But he never succeeded in making that fulfillment possible. Although he strove, perhaps more than once, to forge a permanent alliance with one with whom he felt himself in love, his love not being returned in kind, or the age gap intervening, he invariably failed. Psychoanalysts have suggested that an only or favored child's emotional makeup differs from other children's, that the only or favored child experiences difficulty in finding a spouse and often develops an atypical sexual orientation. If the theory is valid, it could explain much about Charles Dodgson.[10]

Charles's sexual promptings are evident. Because they could not be ritually fulfilled, he repeatedly felt frustrated, and saw himself as an inconsolable sinner. He became inhibited, irritable when his child friends did not respond to his advances. Lacking a marriage sanctioned by Church and God, he consoled himself with visits from child friends that lasted the time that "honeymoons" customarily last.[11] But the sexual force did not retreat; it was there and victimized him with nocturnal incursions. Even at the end of his life, he could not banish the horror of his transgressions: "Most truly," he wrote to William Mallalieu, the father of a child-actress friend (July 17, 1892), "I feel my own sinfulness more strongly than I could easily say in words: but I think, the more one feels one's sin, and the *wonderful* goodness of God who will forgive so much, the more one longs to help others to escape the shame and misery one has brought on one's-self."

For posterity, however, there were compensations. If Charles Dodgson's suppressed and diverted sexual energies caused him unspeakable torments, and they did, they were in all probability the source of those exceptional flashes of genius that gave the world his remarkable creative works.

*Charles's study at Christ Church, Oxford. "Those rooms of his!" wrote Isa Bowman. "I do not think there was ever such a fairyland for children."*

# CHAPTER EIGHT

# Years of Triumph

*With this for motto, "Rather use than fame."*
ALFRED TENNYSON

The early and mid 1860s witnessed Charles's deepest disappointment and spiritual anguish, and he was cast into even deeper despair in 1868 by his father's death. And yet, paradoxically, these same ten years constitute his golden age. At the close of 1857, approaching his twenty-fifth birthday, he was still struggling to perfect his professional techniques. As the year ebbed, he asked himself: "What do I propose as the work of the New Year?" and one of his answers was: "Making myself a competent Mathematical Lecturer for Christ Church." When the diary resumes in May 1862, he was more confident about his work, dealing with students efficiently, and arranging his lectures to permit time for his other interests. From the Isle of Wight he acknowledges to a sister (August 3, 1864) his "faculty of making friends . . . on the shortest notice."

He also seized an opportunity to move to better quarters. While living in staircase 7 of Tom Quad, directly below the expansive rooms Lord Bute occupied, Charles worked on the different versions of *Alice's Adventures.* When his lordship vacated his sumptuous suite, in June 1868, Charles, now a senior member of his college with some money to spare because of the returns on *Alice,* applied for and got the choice set of rooms, and moved in on October 30.

Charles did not move again, content with his comfortable "house," as he called his ten rooms, "perhaps the largest College set in Oxford,"[1] including two bedrooms, a dressing room, a dining room, a darkroom for his photography, and a scullery. His large sitting room, still architecturally intact, served as a wonderland for his child visitors, with its view up and down St. Aldate's, sun streaming in through leaded glass, and two magical towers, turret rooms well suited for imagining fairy kingdoms of knights and ladies and castles with secret passages and battlements.[2]

Gradually he installed a "ventilating globe chandelier," five asbestos fires to replace coal fires, and bookcases along the walls; he also engaged the renowned William De Morgan to design tiles depicting exotic animals for his fireplace.

Ethel Arnold, granddaughter of Dr. Arnold of Rugby, Matthew Arnold's niece, and Mrs. Humphry Ward's sister, wrote a year later: "What an El Dorado of delights those rooms were. . . . The large sitting-room was lined with well-filled bookshelves, under which ran a row of cupboards all round the four walls. Oh, those cupboards! What wondrous treasures they contained. . . . Mechanical bears, dancing-dolls, toys and puzzles of every description came from them in endless profusion! Even after I was grown up I never paid a visit to his rooms without finding my eyes stealing to those cupboards, experiencing over again the thrill of delicious anticipation as the doors of one of them swung open." Beatrice Hatch remembered

the climb up the winding, wooden staircase in the corner of Tom Quad; the unlocking of the great oak door with "the Rev. C. L. Dodgson" painted in white letters over it; yet another small door to be opened, and there we are in the large familiar room, with its huge windows overlooking St. Aldate's. . . . But let us go on to [Mr. Dodgson's] . . . "dinner parties. . . ." You are seated in a corner of the red sofa in front of the large fireplace, over which hang some painted portraits of his child-friends. . . . When dinner is announced you are led into another room much smaller than the first, and you may be quite sure you will never get the same *menu* that you had last time; for, besides other registers, lists and catalogues of letters, books, etc., Mr. Dodgson keeps a list of the dishes supplied every time he has guests at his table, and is careful always to look this up when he invites you, that you may not have the same thing twice. Two courses, and only two, is another of his rules—meat and pudding—and no one could wish for more. After dinner . . . there are games of his own invention, "Mischmasch," "Lanrick," and so on; also his own Memoria Technica to be explained and possibly learnt. And so the evening slips away, and it is time to be escorted home again.[3]

Reminiscing another time, Miss Hatch recalled that after dinner

you may play a game . . . or you may see pictures, lovely drawings of fairies, whom your host tells you "you can't be sure don't really exist." Or you may have music, if you wish it, and Mr. Dodgson will himself perform. You look round (supposing you are a stranger) for the piano. There is none. But a large square box is brought forward, and this contains an organette. Another box holds the tunes, circular perforated cards, all carefully catalogued by their owner. One of the greatest favourites is "Santa Lucia," and this will open the concert. The handle is affixed through a hole in the side of the box, and the green baize lining of the latter helps to modulate the sound. The picture of the author of *Alice,* keenly enjoying every note, as he solemnly turns the handle, and raises or closes the lid of the box to vary the sound, is more worthy of your delight than the music itself. Never was there a more delightful host for a "dinner-party," or one who took such pains for your entertainment, fresh and interesting to the last.[4]

Many more child friends waxed lyrical over visits to those rooms.[5]

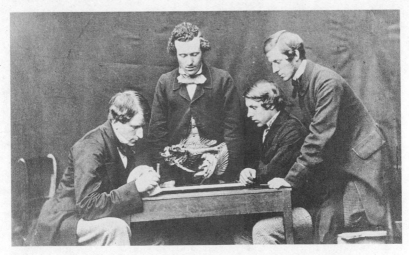

*Oxford dons examining a fish skeleton, photographed by Charles*

By now Charles was already a master photographic craftsman. As we have seen, the art of photography suited him and he triumphed with it. Taking a picture at the right moment was especially important, and Charles's personality had a great deal to do with creating it. He made his subjects forget self, so as to expunge stiffness and self-consciousness, to achieve for the crucial moment an easy, relaxed figure and expression. The technique came naturally to him, and he improved on it as he went along.

His photographs became masterpieces of composition, and when he turned from photographing adults to photographing children, he met new challenges and reached even greater heights, for child photographic portraiture was still in its infancy, and he showed the way to capture innocence and youthful bloom. Not even Mrs. Cameron's photographs of children challenged Charles's superior art. His studies of children reached the apex of the genre in the earliest days of photography and retain their authority today.

Photography provided him with a magic wand: it broke down social barriers and gave him access to many celebrities. On February 22, 1858, Charles met the sculptor Alexander Munro in Oxford. Munro soon proved a welcome host in London and swept Charles into his luminous circle of friends. He gave Charles carte blanche to his studio, and Charles photographed both sculptor and his work. Through Munro he met the dramatist Tom Taylor, who also made his home available for photography. On October 3, 1863, in fact, Charles arrived with all his equipment at the Taylor home in Wandsworth at eight-thirty in the morning, even "before they had assembled for breakfast," and succeeded "in getting some good portraits." He became acquainted with other artists, Arthur Hughes among them, who also sat for his camera. "Celebrities seem to come like misfortunes," Charles writes (October 1, 1863) after a dinner party at Munro's, " 'it never rains but it pours.' " Later Tom Taylor leads Charles to both Tenniel and the Terry family.

Charles set his cap at capturing the Terrys for his camera early, but it was not easy. On September 29, 1863, he wrote: "All my photographic victims seem to be available, but the Terrys, who are acting in Bristol." His journey toward the Terry hearth turned out to be painfully long. Not until August 20, 1864, did he manage, Tom Taylor's introduction in hand, to present himself at the Terry home in Stanhope Street:

*Mr.* Terry was away [Charles's diary reads], but luckily *Mrs.* Terry was at home, and I sent in the note to her, and she soon came out, and asked me into the little sitting-room: the only children with her were Marion (whom I saw in [Tom Taylor's play] *A Lesson from Life*) and the baby. I thought her particularly pleasant and ladylike. I stayed only a short time, but promised to come later with my photographs. . . . I took them over about 4½ and stayed till nearly 6, showing them to her, Polly [that is, Marion], Charlie, and Tom. . . . I gave Mrs. Terry my large photograph of Tom Taylor, and she gave me photographs of Polly, Florence, Charlie, Tom, and Kate as Ophelia. Before leaving I arranged as far as it can be done now, to try photographs of the whole party, including Mrs. Watts [Ellen Terry], in October, and so concluded a . . . very pleasant visit. . . . I mark this Saturday with a white stone.

Charles returned to the Terrys the following day: "I got Polly's autograph on her photograph, and offered to take her and Charlie on to Hampstead Heath with me, but Mrs. Terry did not like to let them go, in Mr. Terry's absence." When Charles was in London again in mid-October, the sunlight was too weak for photography. He called on the Terrys anyway on two successive days and enjoyed his visits.

Again in London on October 28, he called and remained "an hour or so with them, and told the children the old story of 'The [Three] Pixies' [he often told this story, but his rendition is not recorded]. On December 20, once more in London, Charles called again and met Kate for the first time: "She did me the honours of the house with ease and grace, and I thought her very ladylike and natural in manner—not an atom of shyness: that however one would expect." On his return the following day, he finally met Ellen, "the one I have always most wished to meet of the family. . . . I was very much pleased with what I saw of Mrs. Watts—lively and pleasant, almost childish in her fun, but perfectly ladylike. . . . However, both sisters are charming, and I think it a piece of rare good fortune to have made two such acquaintances in two days. I mark this day also with a white stone."

Charles's next visit to the Terrys was in the spring, on April 7, 1865, when he lunched with them and heard Ellen and Florence sing. Still hoping to photograph the family, he wrote to Mr. Terry to arrange a sitting during the summer vacation, and at the end of June Terry replied that they would be glad to see him but requesting "notice of your approach."[6] On July 10 Charles reported: "Heard from Miss [Kate] Terry, asking when I come to town, as Polly and Flo are leaving soon." He packed his equipment, went to London on the twelfth, and a four-day photography session ensued. On the twenty-

*The actress Ellen Terry.
Charles's "kindness to children
was wonderful," she wrote.
"He really loved them and put
himself out for them. . . .
Nothing could have been more
touching than his ceaseless
industry on their behalf."*

*Ellen Terry's younger sisters, Marion and Florence*

*Florence Terry. She gave up the stage in
1882 to marry a lawyer and raise a family.*

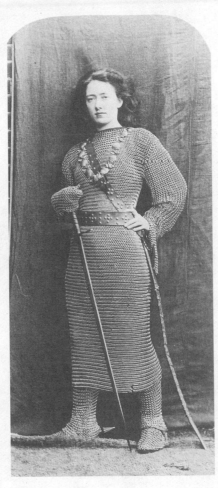

*Ellen Terry*

*The actress Kate Terry in mail. When Charles first met her, he "thought her very ladylike and natural in manner—not an atom of shyness."*

*Kate Terry*

*Dante Gabriel Rossetti, by Charles. Rossetti, according to Charles, was "most hospitable in his offers of the use of house and garden for picture-taking." He wrote to Charles in 1866: "I saw* Alice in Wonderland *at my sister's, and was glad to find myself still childish enough to enjoy looking through it very much."*

third, still in London, he showed them some of the results of the sittings.

When Charles was staying with the Munros in early October 1863, Munro took him to call on Dante Gabriel Rossetti, who turned out to be "most hospitable in his offers of the use of house and garden for picture-taking." That same day, Rossetti wrote to his mother: "The photographer (revd. W. [*sic*] Dodgson) is coming here on Wednesday to do the lot of us. . . . Will you stay dinner that day and I will ask the Munros . . . who are the means of bringing Mr. D."[7] On October 6 Charles took his camera over to the Rossetti house in Cheyne Walk. While he was unpacking, "Miss [Christina] Rossetti arrived and Mr. Rossetti introduced me to her. She seemed a little shy at first, and I had very little time for conversation with her, but I much liked the little I saw of her. She sat for two pictures, Mr. Rossetti for one. . . . I afterwards looked through a huge volume of drawings, some of which I am to photograph—a great treat, as I had never seen such exquisite drawing before. I dined with Mr. Rossetti, and spent some of the evening there. . . . A memorable day." Charles returned to Rossetti's house the following day and photographed the entire family. He spent the eighth photographing Rossetti drawings, and the ninth, one of Rossetti's models. Through the Rossettis, he met Swinburne and other dignitaries, including a cousin of the Rossettis, Teodorico Pietrocola-Rossetti, who later translated the first Italian *Alice.*

London attractions curtailed some of Charles's visits to Croft, but he did not neglect his family. When his father died in 1868 and he had to assume the management of the clan, he went house-hunting and found a spacious residence in Guildford, "The Chestnuts," for them, and from then onward spent much of his vacation time with them there, often stopping in London on his way to and fro.

Charles continued to write and publish. The volume and variety of his work during these years is extraordinary, his creative powers impressive. He evidently followed every impulse, his imagination provoked and nourished by what he saw and heard, by contemporary events and evocations. In 1862, while home at Croft, with the help of some sisters, he composed "Miss Jones," what he called a "Medley-song," "the tunes running into each other." He published verses in established papers and reviews, in *All the Year Round*, *Temple Bar*, and *Punch*. Some of his *College Rhymes* pieces are worth noting. "Poeta Fit, Non Nascitur" comprises eighteen six-line stanzas that add up to a lesson that an old poetaster gives to a lad asking how one becomes a poet. Charles produces clichés topped with banalities throughout in an amusing display of threadbare devices. The old man has the formula pat:

*"The Chestnuts," the Dodgson family home in Guildford. Charles procured it for his sisters and brothers in 1868 when their father died and they had to leave the Yorkshire rectory.*

"First fix upon the limit
  To which it shall extend:
Then fill it up with 'Padding'
  (Beg some of any friend):
Your great SENSATION-STANZA
  You place towards the end."

On November 15, 1862, Charles finished "'The Lang Coortin' which I began a week or two ago." It is a longish ballad (thirty-seven four-line rhymed stanzas) in Scots dialect about a suitor who waits for thirty years before proposing to the apple of his eye. The poem "Beatrice," which Charles completed on December 4, 1862, is another matter altogether. It is a serious celebration of innocence and harkens back to "Stolen Waters" and "The Valley of the Shadow of Death." It consists of nine seven-line rhymed stanzas. On March 5, 1863, he composed "The Majesty of Justice: An Oxford Idyll," nine eight-line stanzas satirizing the Jowett controversy.

He tried his hand at playwriting too. On January 25, 1866, he spent "2 or 3 hours in writing out, to send to Tom Taylor, a sketch of a domestic drama." Taylor took "a very favourable view" of the outline and promised to show it to Ellen Terry. Charles worked on the play, which he called "Morning Clouds," and sent a more nearly complete text to Taylor, but when he visited Taylor (April 5), he learned that "their opinion seems to be that it is impracticable—even my favourite ending. The public taste demands more sensation." Although Charles tried at least once more to get the play produced, nothing came of it.[8] Taylor and Terry's refusal to produce the play, one suspects, saved Charles considerable embarrassment at the hands of the critics.

In 1869 Charles published his first collection of verse, *Phantasmagoria and Other Poems,* containing over two dozen poems in all and covering over two hundred printed pages.

The world has crowned Charles Dodgson and Edward Lear monarchs of nonsense verse but turned its back on Charles the serious poet. Shackled as he was to the emotional tenor of his time, he was, as a serious poet, admittedly crippled. Sentimentality was his undoing; unlike the great Victorian poets, he cannot transcend it. Still, he was truly at home with nonsense verse, explored new poetical territory, and created a fresh landscape of the mind. But a third category of his verse, splendidly evident in *Phantasmagoria and Other Poems,* lies neglected—his straightforward humorous verse, and especially his provocatively amusing narrative pieces.

When the book appeared, most people had not even dreamed of electric lights. Homes were dark and shadowy, people feared the dark. Candles and oil lamps cast ominous shadows that swayed and danced on ceiling and wall. Corners of rooms, the inside of cupboards, even bureau drawers were recesses filled with mystery. We can understand why Charles was attracted to the occult, especially living as he did in a cloistered setting, in old buildings with winding staircases and long, gloomy corridors.

The initial poem, "Phantasmagoria," is a long, deftly wrought narrative, inspired by Victorian darkness and the ghosts that inhabit it. When it appeared, it proved Charles a master of witty verse fiction, sustained by entertaining language, meter, rhyme, and sound. He forges a tight story with numerous original twists. Charles provides a down-to-earth if appropriately eerie account of how his nocturnal creatures live and work. He reveals their *raison d'être*, delves into their thoughts, their feelings, their likes, their fears. In all, he produces a rounded 150 stanzas of five rhyming lines, the whole divided into seven cantos.

But leave it to Charles to find a new angle, to spring a surprise or two. "Phantasmagoria" is not about people afraid of ghosts—quite the opposite: it is about ghosts themselves and the troubles they encounter in trying to do their proper jobs of haunting people's homes. At one point, in fact, we get a monologue, an *apologia* of the terribly overburdened, put-upon little ghost who dilates on the onerous conditions under which he lives and works, often out of doors, cold, windblown, rain-soaked, sitting atop castle gates with no protection against the storm.

The poem is a dialogue between a middle-class gentleman and a ghost assigned to haunt his dwelling. The denouement surprises both. Toward the end, the ghost casually addresses the host as Tibbs. The host is puzzled and tells the visitor that his name is not Tibbs; it is Tibbets. "Why, then YOU'RE NOT THE PARTY!" exclaims the sad figure, realizing that, all this time, he has been haunting the wrong house. He explodes in anger at the host for not setting him right in the first place, but the host is his match and insists that he should have asked his name when they first met. The ghost succumbs to social propriety and agrees that the mistake was his.

The tale is too orderly and rational to have much in common with *Alice*, although they have elements in common—puns for instance, as in the ghost who is an Inn-Spectre. But the narrative style, the incidents, the characters are quite different. Perhaps we can, however, detect a reverse relationship. Alice, the innocent child, travels through a world of irrational, undependable, rude, and brutal adults, trying to make some sense of the grown-up society she encounters; in "Phantasmagoria," a small thing tries to disrupt a world that at least appears orderly. Here the "child" is petulant, rude, insensitive, and unmannerly and belongs to a hostile society. The *Alice* books and the ghost society in "Phantasmagoria" both strike at the foibles of human nature and question society's mores. But those undercurrents only attest to Charles's keen awareness of the ways of the world. The purpose of the long poem, which it achieves magnificently, is to amuse, to make us snicker and laugh.

The volume contains other bravura pieces. "A Sea Dirge" is a mock complaint about the seaside and all its ugliness and discomfort: miles of ugly salt water howling like a dog, tens of thousands of nursery maids leading children with wooden spades, stinging fleas in lodgings, coffee with dregs of sand or tea that hints of salt, fish in your eggs, no grass or trees, dampness everywhere. Charles also includes "The Lang Coortin'."

We also get Charles the parodist of Wordsworth, Swinburne ("Atalanta in Camden Town"), and Tennyson ("The Three Voices"), but while Tennyson's philosophical poem, "The Two Voices," is a debate about life and death, Charles's parody is a one-sided argument by a shrewish female berating her docile male companion.

A parody of Longfellow, "Hiawatha's Photographing," is a most amusing piece about the Victorian craze for photography. Charles published it in the *Train* as early as 1857, appropriating Longfellow's thumping meters to capture the fever of the time. Hiawatha, the photographer, sets up his tripod, affixes his rosewood camera, then instructs his sitters to stay motionless ("Mystic, awful was the process"). The entire family parades before the camera, one after another. The photographer produces a perfect likeness of the family group, but human nature being what it is, not one of the sitters is pleased with the results and together they heap abuse upon the photographer.

> "Really anyone would take us
> (Anyone that did not know us)
> For the most unpleasant people!"

Credit Charles with a facility for writing light verse that is amusing, for managing to ridicule the art form so dear to him in the very years when he is slaving to perfect his technique.

The humorous verse here reveals a refinement in Charles as a craftsman of wit. His juvenilia show an early facility with humor. Then with *Alice's Adventures* he took a major step forward in the play of language for humor's sake, in integrating his skill with mathematics and logic into the work to create absurdly laughable situations. In *Alice* we get Charles's first successful experiment with nonsense, a form that relies for its effect on something other than meaning. In the humorous verse in *Phantasmagoria,* the tales are all rational, they make sense; but Charles's technique and skill as a narrative artist leap forward as he produces entertaining, integrated pieces, easy, relaxed dialogue, in a colorful demotic idiom. This sharpened technique both in narrative and in poetic facility serves him well here and in the future.

The reviews of the volume were almost all laudatory: "This little book of poems, 'Grave and Gay,' . . . possesses considerable attractions for all who care to read stories in rhyme," wrote the *Pall Mall Gazette* (March 16). "The versification is, as a rule, harmonious and graceful. . . . 'Phantasmagoria' . . . reminds one in many places of 'Alice's Adventures.' . . ." The *Literary Churchman* notice (March 29) is brief: "Those who have not made acquaintance with these poems already have a pleasure to come. The comical is *so* comical, the grave so really beautiful. . . ." The *Guardian* (April 21) found "abundant proofs of ability . . . [and] real and playful wit, from which the writer passes, without the appearance of painful effort, to verse of graver mood."

Charles's mathematical wizardry manifested itself early, even in Daresbury, in the games and puzzles he invented. In 1863 he produced *Croquet Castles,* a complicated version of ordinary croquet (revised and published in *Aunt Judy's Magazine* in 1867), developed while playing croquet with the Liddell girls in the deanery garden. "Sitting up at night" on April 22, 1868, he "invented . . . *The Telegraph-Cipher,*" and on another occasion, probably that same year, *The Alphabet-Cipher,* almost a mirror image of *The Telegraph-Cipher,* both intended to challenge and amuse the developing minds of young friends.[9]

Photography was much on his mind, and after "Hiawatha's Photographing" comes "The Ladye's History" (1858) as a segment in "The Legend of 'Scotland.'" Charles wrote it for the Longleys, the children of the Bishop of Durham, old family friends, when they asked for a story about the ghost of Auckland Castle, where they then lived. In mock Old English, Charles tells the tale "writ down" in 1325 about a lady ghost called Gaunless (she wears a wrapper instead of a gown) who appears in a dream to Matthew Dixon, Chaffer, determined to tell her history. She wants to have her portrait painted, but painters of the day charge too much. Then "a certyn Artist, hight Lorenzo," appears, "having wyth hym a marveillous machine called by men a Chimera (that ys, a fabulous and wholly incredible thing)." She engages Lorenzo to take a full-length portrait of her, but in his takes, either the head is missing or the feet: not one gets her entire. Exasperated, the Ladye imprisons the photographer in her cellar; he wastes away into a ghost, and when she discovers him in a crack in the prison ceiling, she decides also to waste away into a ghost. Then, they both being shades, Lorenzo would be able to take her full likeness. But, alas, he never succeeds, and thereafter she simply haunts the castle.

In 1860 Charles wrote and published a romp called "A Photographer's Day Out" about an amorous young man in pursuit of his Amelia, whom he yearns to please. After overcoming numerous obstacles, he manages to take a picture of a cottage which Amelia has requested. But in doing so he trespasses on some farmer's land, and two brutes beat him up. In the fray the glass negative is shattered, and the swain-photographer ends up pictureless, shaken, sore, stiff, and bruised.

Inspiration never slackened during these crucial years. Charles grasped at every notion, at any hour. At 2 a.m. one morning (June 24, 1867), for instance, he was "sitting up writing, and listening to the music of the ball in the Corn Exchange. I have spent some hours today," he notes, "on a paper . . . for *Aunt Judy's Magazine,* to be called 'Bruno's Revenge.' " When Margaret Gatty, the editor, received it, she was delighted: "I need hardly tell you," she wrote Charles, "that the story is *delicious.* It is beautiful and fantastic and child-like, and I cannot sufficiently thank you. . . . Some of the touches are so exquisite, one would have thought nothing short of intercourse with fairies could have put them into your head. . . . Make this one of a series. You may have great mathematical abilities, but so have hundreds of others. This talent is peculiarly your own, and as an Englishman you are almost unique in possessing it. . . ."[10] It is a charming tale essentially about, not a girl this time, but a boy, and how he learns the rules for consorting with fairies. Bruno is naturally naughty, but his sister, Sylvie, and Bruno's keen desire to please her, transform him into a kindly, well-mannered lad. The narrative line is strong, even compelling. Although readers of *Aunt Judy's* clamored for "several more" Bruno stories, Charles did not comply. In time, however, the tale became the nucleus for Charles's longest work of fiction, *Sylvie and Bruno* and *Sylvie and Bruno Concluded.*

Charles was hardly a man of the world. One searches, almost in vain, for comments on events in central Europe or a mention of the American Civil

War. But he was very much on the *qui vive* in British politics. In London in July 1866, staying at a hotel near Trafalgar Square, he observed the mobs agitating for reform, and the following April, in London again, he managed to get into the House of Commons for the second reading of the Reform Bill drafted to extend voter suffrage and heard "several short speeches by Disraeli." A year later he was again at the House when it debated Gladstone's proposal to disestablish the Irish Church, and he heard a two-and-a-half-hour speech by Disraeli and an hour-and-a-half speech by Gladstone on the subject. He recorded in his diary entry for April 3, 1868, that he did not stay to learn the result. Three weeks later, however, Charles was back again at the House, hoping to hear Gladstone again on disestablishment, but, alas, Gladstone did not speak.

Increasingly, Charles took an interest in college and university affairs, in matters concerning the town of Oxford and its vicinity, and even in general public issues. Academia lent itself to easy parody, and Charles took advantage of his facile talent to mock conventions and ceremonials. In 1860 he printed *Dr. Acland's Tunny,* a line-by-line parody in Latin of an overblown inscription accompanying a stuffed fish that Dr. Acland had presented to the museum of the Anatomy School. In November 1861 he published his first squib, *Endowment of the Greek Professorship,* on the proposal to raise Benjamin Jowett's stipend; in 1862, the "Sequel to 'The Shepherd of Salisbury Plain' "; and in February 1864, *Examination Statute.*[11]

A year later, on February 15, 1865, he was struck by the idea of writing some mock American news reports based on dispatches about the Civil War embodying some proceedings at Christ Church, and two days later he sent off the manuscript, *American Telegrams,* to be printed. The "proceedings" concern the ongoing efforts by Christ Church Students to wrest from the Canons some of their decision-making powers. Charles's spoof contains numerous subtle allusions to persons and issues then relevant, now unknown, but clearly President L, who plays a major role, is Dean Liddell, and the Confederate Commissioners are the disgruntled Students. Annotations on a copy of the printed text in Christ Church Library identify some of the actors and issues involved.[12]

Esoteric though it is today, *American Telegrams* shows Charles ready and eager to reform education and administration at Christ Church and to join the movement that completely altered the oligarchic government of Oxbridge. Agitation began in the early part of the century to abolish the religious tests, which excluded all non-Anglicans, almost half the population of Britain, from its universities. Gladstone, not one of Charles's heroes, held the banner of reform; and Jowett, though not agreeing with Gladstone's program, also vociferously supported the idea. The first serious moves to abolish the tests and alter university government and education resulted from the recommendations of the University Commissions of 1850–52 that were incorporated in the Parliamentary Acts of 1854 and 1856. The acts did away with medieval constitutional regulations, required fellowships to be awarded on merit, opened the universities not only to non-Anglicans but to the middle class generally, and provided a wider, more liberal curriculum that more easily accommodated the needs of passmen (candidates not seeking degrees with honors) who wanted a good general education. The individual colleges were directed to modify their internal statutes to comply with the general reforms.

The reforms in 1854 and 1856 modified much, but at Christ Church left the Dean and the Canons in complete control. Disappointment among the teaching staff was rife, agitation to give the dons a voice in running their House mounted. The Dean and the Canons took note, and a succession of ordinances and amendments were promulgated, but not until 1857 were Students allowed to participate in the discussions.

During 1856 and 1857, when the Commissioners invited Christ Church Student-masters to meet and to lay propositions before them, Charles played a vigorous part in the deliberations, proposing and amending clauses and writing directly to the Commissioners with his own proposals for change. "He emerges . . . as a man of much practical sense in college affairs," write E. G. W. Bill and J. F. A. Mason.[13]

Even in the 1860s the Students still aimed at being raised to the position of Fellows with a statutory voice in governance. Support was growing for a direct petition to Parliament for a bill to alter the Constitution of Christ Church. On February 11, 1865, Charles attended a meeting of the Students. He gives no details of the meeting, but Arthur Hassall recorded some: "A memorable meeting . . . at which eighteen senior masters were present. . . . [Mr.] Bigg proposed that the position of the Students should be raised, and that proposal was carried by thirteen to four. Mr. Prout, supported by Mr. Dodgson, then carried . . . a proposal 'that the carrying out of the above proposition involves the admission of the Students into the Corporation of The House, with a due share of the administration of the revenues and in the government of the same, and also the possession of such other rights and privileges as commonly attach to the Fellows of other Colleges.' "[14] The Dean and the Canons appointed a committee, all but one of the four members to be of their own good selves, to look into the Students' grievances.

Five more meetings of the Students immediately followed, and Charles's *American Telegrams* spiced the proceedings. At least half of it, Bill and Mason point out,

> concerns the Students' agitation against the Dean and Chapter. The "Confederate 'platform'" of four points is Dodgson's version of the Students' proposals for the amendment of the constitution and domestic economy of Christ Church. The "General Grant" whose "almost dictatorial power" was to be "largely curtailed, if not altogether abolished," was the conveniently named Butler of Christ Church, Henry Grant, who was also the "General Butler" whose "enormities" were to meet with their "due reward." The demand "that the Treasury shall be placed under the control of Confederates [i.e., Students] and Federals [i.e., Canons] alike" speaks for itself. The Secretary of the Treasury who "would be a blot in any conceivable system of government" was the Under-Treasurer, Blott.[15]

Between February 1865 and March 1867 the Students held over two dozen meetings, Charles again in keen attendance. On February 18, 1865, Charles seconded a resolution to be sent to the Dean iterating the earlier demands. A delegation of Students met with the Dean and chapter delegates and put forth their demands, but the men in power were "not prepared to take steps towards promoting constitutional changes of the kind desired."[16] The Students decided to appeal to higher authority. The Canons, concerned lest the Students go over their heads, proposed arbitrating their differences, but the parties could not agree on the issues to arbitrate.

At a meeting on January 18, 1866, Charles expressed what proved to be the unanimous feeling of the Students: "He thought it better to agree with the . . . [Dean and the Canons] upon men who would draw up the scheme for arbitration than to have each party submit a Memorial to the Crown." Five distinguished Referees (including the close friend of the Dodgson family Archbishop Longley) were appointed to hear evidence. On June 25, Charles noted, he "sent some suggestions about Christ Church to the Archbishop, to show to the other Referees if he thinks fit." The upshot was that the Referees' seventeen recommendations and the award based on them satisfied all the Students' demands. According to one of the Referees, "It is intended that the new Governing Body shall be a little Republic, with the amplest powers, subject only to the double vote, and the casting vote, of the Dean, and the reserved right of the ecclesiastical Corporation."[17]

The Canons, not least of all Pusey, objected fiercely. In ensuing discussions and meetings with the Dean and the Canons, some Students, including Charles, were for making some accommodation in order to reach "a harmonious conclusion." Concessions were made in both directions, Parliament passed the Christ Church Ordinances (Oxford) Bill, and it received the Royal Assent on August 12, 1867. The Students had successfully curbed the Dean and the Canons, and a new era began at Christ Church, one in which they achieved higher status, more money, and a forceful voice in running the House and dealing with its revenues. What is more, they acquitted themselves with dignity and distinction. Charles played an important role in helping to bring the new order into being.[18]

The controversy over Jowett's salary continued to rage, and on March 3 Charles began a "sham mathematical paper on Jowett's case, taking $\pi$ to symbolise his payment," and had it printed on March 14. *The New Method of Evaluation as Applied to* $\pi$ is a clever jape devising five methods for calculating a just figure for Jowett's salary. In the second method, "The Method of Indifferences," Pusey and Liddon appear as EBP and HPL (in working out the formula, the "locus of HPL will be found almost entirely to coincide with . . . the locus of EBP"). Charles's conclusion is that it is "hopeless to obtain any real value for $\pi$ by this method." In spite of Charles's spoof and other conservative voices, however, Jowett's stipend was raised in 1865 from the absurd forty pounds that Henry VIII fixed as appropriate in the sixteenth century to five hundred pounds.

Doubtless pleased with the reaction to his *New Method* jape, Charles went on to concoct a more elaborate paper in the same vein: *The Dynamics of a Parti-cle*, a pamphlet of twenty-eight pages. The third chapter is a reprint of *The New Method of Evaluation as Applied to* $\pi$; the first two use Euclidian parodies to characterize the contest between Gladstone, who had been M.P. for the university for eighteen years and was to stand for reelection in July 1865, opposed by Sir William Heathcote and Gathorne Gathorne-Hardy (later the Earl of Cranbrook). Early in *Dynamics,* Charles pricks several political balloons with some definitions:

> PLAIN SUPERFICIALITY is the character of a speech, in which any two points being taken, the speaker is found to lie wholly with regard to those two points.
>
> PLAIN ANGER is the inclination of two voters to one another, who meet together, but whose views are not in the same direction.

Charles defines "RIGHT ANGER" and "OBTUSE ANGER" in a similar vein. Although Dean Liddell led a stream of Gladstone supporters to the polls, Hardy won. Clever and entertaining as Charles's puff is, it could hardly have influenced the voting one way or another. But it was something of a novelty, attracted attention, and went through three editions. Humor had not yet entered significantly into Charles's mathematical works, but he used it effectively here.

Charles detested Gladstone's liberalism and, about this time, vented his animosity in a series of anagrams:

> *William Ewart Gladstone*
> I, wise Mr. G. want to lead all.
> A wild man will go at trees.
> Wild agitator! Means well.
> Wilt tear down all images?[19]

When the Hebdomadal Council election of October 20, 1866, gave the Conservatives a clear majority, the Liberal Goldwin Smith, Professor of Modern History, wrote a letter to the Senior Proctor proposing that nonacademics be removed from Congregation and that the council itself be eliminated. Charles reacted with an eight-page verse parody, entitled *The Elections to the Hebdomadal Council,* addressed to the Senior Proctor:

> My scheme is this: remove the votes of all
> The residents that are not Liberal—
> Leave the young Tutors uncontrolled and free,
> And Oxford then shall see—what it shall see.
>
> . . . . . . .
>
> Sweep everything beginning with a "Con"
> Into oblivion! Convocation first,
> Conservatism next, and, last and worst,
> "*Concilium Hebdomadale*" must,
> Consumed and conquered, be consigned to dust!

Charles veers from politics to "The Science of Betting" in a letter to the *Pall Mall Gazette* (November 19, 1866). It describes a formula for winning a bet, which he devised in May 1857 and then published in *Bell's Life in London and Sporting Chronicle.* What provoked him to resuscitate it, he noted (November 15), was "an announcement in last night's *Pall Mall* that a certain firm 'the Messrs. H. & I. Smith' were offering £500 for a secret of the kind."

Charles's rule is this: "Write all the possible events in a column, placing opposite to each the odds offered against it: this will give two columns of figures. For the third column add together the odds in each case, and find the least common multiple of all the numbers in this column. For the fifth and sixth columns multiply the original odds by the several numbers in the fourth column. These odds are to be given, or taken according as the sum total of the sixth column is greater or less than the least common multiple. The last two columns give the *relative amounts* to be invested in each bet. . . ." Needless to say, Charles won no prize. Very likely, by the time an ordinary mortal made the required calculation, the race, game, or whatever would have ended.

Charles sent another letter to the *Pall Mall Gazette,* and it appeared on January 27, 1867. In "The Organisation of Charities," he disapproves of the chaos that charity-giving and charity-getting involves and suggests creating a National Philanthropical Society, "a central point *to* which, and again *from* which, the streams of benevolence should flow; one where contributions could be received . . . from all quarters, and for all charitable purposes, and handed over again, *without deductions,* to the objects designated. . . ." If such an organization existed, he believes, many more charitable gifts would be forthcoming.

In April 1867 some persons advocated turning part of the University Parks into a cricket ground, and Charles works out (May 22) "an idea . . . of adapting some of 'The Deserted Village,' and by one in the morning I had completed about a hundred lines, which I sent to . . . be set up in type." "The Deserted Parks," a poem of fifty-two couplets in Goldsmithian iambic pentameter, is a biting indictment of the proposal, which, according to Charles, would curtail the enjoyment of the parks by old and young, by town and gown alike. He cannot resist taking another swipe at Jowett; and yet his censure is mixed with praise:

> In peaceful converse with his brother Don,
> Here oft the calm Professor wandered on;
> Strange words he used—men drank with wondering ears
> The languages called "dead," the tongues of other years.
>
> . . . . . . . .
>
> A man he was to undergraduates dear,
> And passing rich with forty pounds a year.
> And so, I ween, he would have been till now,

Had not his friends ('twere long to tell you how)
Prevailed on him, Jack-Horner-like, to try
Some method to evaluate his pie,
And win from those dark depths, with skilful thumb,
Five times a hundredweight of luscious plum—
Yet for no thirst of wealth, no love of praise,
In learned labour he consumed his days!

Charles printed a hundred copies of the poem and distributed them. Whether his campaign had any effect, we do not know, but the proposal was withdrawn in early June. It raised its head again, however, on June 6, 1879, and Charles sent round more copies of the poem.

In January 1868 R. B. Clifton, Professor of Experimental Philosophy and Fellow of Merton, dispatched a letter entitled *The Offer of the Clarendon Trustees* to the Senior Proctor setting out the requirements of the Department of Natural Science. On February 6 Charles devised another parody bearing the same title, pointing out that a great opportunity now existed for providing space in the new museum for mathematical calculations. He calls for a "very large room for calculating Greatest Common Measures"; a "piece of open ground for keeping Roots and practising their extraction"; a "room for reducing Fractions to their Lowest Terms"; a "large room, which might be darkened, and fitted up with a magic lantern, for the purpose of exhibiting Circulating Decimals in the act of circulation"; a "narrow strip of ground, railed off and carefully leveled, for investigating the properties of Asymptotes, and testing practically whether Parallel Lines meet or not: for this purpose it should reach . . . 'ever so far' "; and as "Photography is now very much employed in recording human expressions, and might possibly be adopted to Algebraical Expressions, a small photographic room . . . both for general use and for representing the various phenomena of Gravity, Disturbance of Equilibrium, Resolution, etc., which affect the features during severe mathematical operations."

Righteous indignation lay behind many of Charles's public utterances, but his effusions were provoked also by a devotion to a set of humane values and a desire to castigate bad behavior. One is struck by the breadth and variety of subjects that concerned him.

He was far from a dilettante, however, as another stack of his publications during this decade shows. His mathematical writings are numerous, serious, disciplined, and impressive. In 1860 he published two: *A Syllabus of Plane Al-gebraical Geometry, Systematically Arranged, with Formal Definitions, Postu-lates, and Axioms* and *Notes on the First Two Books of Euclid, Designed for Candidates for Responsions.* The first contains 154 pages, the second a mere 8. *A Syllabus of Plane Algebraical Geometry* originated in 1855, the early days of Charles's lecturing.

He was keenly aware of the defects in available texts on the subject, and he dutifully persisted, keeping in mind that every undergraduate studying mathematics had to cover the first six books of Euclid. As a mathematical lecturer, he was expected to prepare students for examinations which he himself helped set. He labored at his task diligently and produced a work that would "occupy with regard to Algebraic Geometry, the same posi-tion . . . occupied by that of Euclid with regard to Pure Geometry." *Notes on the First Two Books of Euclid* continued Charles's effort to help his students prepare for examinations. It supplies definitions, an approach to proving theorems generally, and notes on several propositions.

The standard text of Euclid's *Elements* at this time was by Robert Sim-son, Professor of Mathematics at Glasgow in the eighteenth century. Charles sought to simplify later texts based on Simson's, to correct what he saw as gaps, inconsistencies, and inaccuracies in them. With students in mind, he wished also to clarify, to add definitions, and to develop clearer ap-proaches to proving theorems.

In 1861 Charles published two more mathematical works. In *The Formu-lae of Plane Trigonometry, Printed with Symbols (Instead of Words) to Express the "Goniometrical Ratios,"* a nineteen-page pamphlet, he invented new sym-bols to represent trigonometrical functions (sines, cosines, secants, cose-cants, and versed sines) to replace the more "cumbrous expressions" customarily used. The symbols help define the trigonometrical ratios and consequently make the material more accessible. In *Notes on the First Part of Algebra,* a sixteen-page pamphlet, he supplied a more elementary crutch to help his students prepare for examinations.

His efforts to clarify mathematical concepts and terms knew no bounds. On July 11, 1862, he sent off a first batch of proof sheets of what would be-come his *General List of [Mathematical] Subjects, and Cycle for Working Ex-amples,* along with printed letters entitled *Circular to Mathematical Friends* and seventy-five stamped covers addressed to himself for replies. The *Cir-cular,* dated 1862, asks friends to comment upon the "accompanying tables" devised to illustrate the entire subject matter of pure mathematics and to supply "a guide for working examples in the whole subject." Charles apparently received a good many replies. On February 6, 1863, he worked "hours . . . at the Cycle," and on the tenth sent it off to the press for printing after "many hours of work." The result confirms Charles's gift of ordering masses of information into intelligible categories.

On October 19, 1863, Charles sent to the University Press the manuscript of "a small [sixteen-page] book of enunciation, etc., for Euclid I, II" that aims at improving and clarifying earlier efforts by others on the same subject; it appeared anonymously as *The Enunciations of the Propositions and Corollaries, together with Questions on the Definitions, Postulates, Axioms, etc., in Euclid, Books I and II.*

In late 1864 he tried to improve upon his *General List of [Mathematical] Subjects* of 1862–63 by cutting up "two copies of my *Syllabus*" and filing "the whole, with some additional manuscript, to serve as scaffolding for the book." The result is a twenty-seven-page *Guide to the Mathematical Student in Reading, Reviewing and Working Examples,* dividing pure mathematics into twenty-six divisions and some five hundred subdivisions, providing students with an eight-page cycle of over sixteen hundred numbers defining the order in which they should study the topics. The list begins with rather elementary arithmetic and works its way up the ladder to calculus. Euclid and algebraic geometry are very much in evidence.

During the years Charles was writing *Alice* and preparing it for publication, he worked also at his mathematical projects, although few appeared in print. By January 25, 1866, however, he was printing again and noted that his mathematical publication that term was a card entitled *Symbols and Abbreviations for Euclid.*

That same year, 1866, brought forth one of Charles's important mathematical works, one that makes a claim for him as a significant mathematical theorist, *Condensation of Determinants, Being a New and Brief Method for Computing Their Arithmetical Values.* Charles was at work on "an elementary pamphlet on Determinants" as early as October 28, 1865. By February 27, 1866, he had discovered "a process for evaluating Arithmetical Determinants, by a sort of condensation: and proved it up to $4^2$ terms." Charles brought his discovery to the attention of the right people, through Bartholomew Price. "Heard from Mr. [William] Spottiswoode [Fellow and later President of the Royal Society]," Charles notes (March 25), "(to whom Price had sent my question as to the shortest way of computing Determinants arithmetically), saying that he knows of no short way, and that he will be very glad to hear from me."

That Spottiswoode, one of the most distinguished mathematicians of his day, would take Charles's work seriously is a great tribute. On March 29, 1866, Charles sent Spottiswoode "an account of my method of computing Determinants arithmetically by 'condensation,' and for applying the process to solving simultaneous Equations." On May 12 he finished "writing out my paper . . . which Price has undertaken to forward to the Royal Society for me"; on the seventeenth the paper was read before the Royal Society and then published in their proceedings,[20] matters in which Spottiswoode no doubt had a hand. On the following November 30, dining at the Prices', Charles met Spottiswoode and his wife "and was much pleased with them."

Charles Dodgson the mathematician was now ready to "go public." On February 11, 1867, he wrote to Alexander Macmillan:

I have got a little book, near completion, which I want you to publish for me—*not* one, I am afraid, that can be brought out as "by the author of *Alice's Adventures*." . . . It will be ready to bring out in another month or so. . . . The selling price we can settle hereafter: no price would repay me, I fancy, as I have made so many alterations. The reason I mention it now is, that you may be able to begin advertising it whenever you think fit. . . . That the book is much wanted there can be no doubt: that *my* book will meet the want, may well be doubted—but I am encouraged by the favourable opinion of Mr. Spottiswoode, who is I believe *the* authority on the new subject of Determinants and who has seen most of the book.

But Charles went on revising the text: "This little book . . . has given me more trouble than anything I have ever written: it is such entirely new ground to explore." Finally, copies of *An Elementary Treatise on Determinants with Their Application to Simultaneous Linear Equations and Algebraical Geometry* arrived "and look very well indeed in their brown binding," Charles wrote Macmillan (December 10, 1867).

Charles appended his Royal Society paper at the end of the 155-page book. The contents defy easy paraphrase. Some readers will know that a determinant is an "algebraic expression associated with a square array of numbers" and that "determinants simplify the solution of simultaneous linear equations."[21] Charles rejects the standard Leibniz notations on the subject; he coins a new symbol and a few words to accommodate his approach. His condensation method is important in two ways: it dramatically simplifies the computation of a determinant and provides a highly unusual way of viewing a determinant as a function. *An Elementary Treatise on Determinants* broke new ground, marked Charles's entry into the world of professional mathematics outside Oxford, which at the time lagged far behind Cambridge in mathematical distinction, and won him a place in mathematical histories.[22]

A notice in the *Pall Mall Gazette* (January 11, 1868) judged that "Mr. Dodgson's original monograph on determinants deserves the attention of mathematicians. . . . It serves to show . . . [his] ability . . . and it creates a hope that we may have from him the benefit of further investigation in the algebraical wonderland of his choice." (Charles must have cringed at the allusion to *Alice*.) The *Educational Times* reviewed it (June 1) along with other studies on determinants, concluding that, while it is "tedious . . . to read," it "forms a valuable addition to the Treatises we possess on modern Algebra." Humbled, Charles wrote Macmillan (June 4): "Thanks, first, for the *Educational Times'* notice of my *Determinants:* it is a more healthy one to read than if it were all praise—at the same time I cannot avoid a dim suspicion that the writer is not a mathematician and that he has not read much of the book. Nearly all he says is taken from the preface: then he talks of 'Proposition-Theorems,' an illogical phrase never used by me or any one else, but which he charges me with parading!"

That the treatise continues to be valuable more than a hundred years after Charles produced it is clear from recent literature.[23] Edward Wakeling sees the book as "an important step forward, not recognised at the time. Dodgson's method," he writes, "is 'computerisable'; it does not require the usual intermediary decisions to be made in the calculation; the procedure is robust."[24] Francine Abeles judges Charles's work on determinants "important. . . . Compared to the standard method of his time . . . Dodgson's method is a model of computational simplicity," she observes, pointing out, furthermore, that he "deeply understood the notion of the rank of a linear system. It is possible that Dodgson produced the first proof in print of . . . [a] fundamental theorem on rank. . . ."[25] Eugene Seneta writes of "Dodgson's startling contribution to linear algebra and to the theory of determinants."[26]

Abeles also sees a connection between Charles's work on determinants and the *Alice* books in their inversions and mirror imaging. "Determinants," she writes, "are rich in opportunities to exploit these notions. Complemental minors, adjugate blocks, row and column transformations permitted the full use of his creative imagination." Martin Gardner furthermore points out that "even in serious moments Carroll's mind, like that of the White

Knight, seemed to function best when he was seeing things upside down."
Edward Wakeling writes: "The method of condensation is like Alice
shrinking as a result of drinking from the bottle marked 'drink me.' A large
array of numbers gradually shrinks in size until a single number remains:
the determinant."[27]

The book was hardly a best-seller. About a month after publication,
Macmillan reported that they had sold thirty-three copies. But it remained
in stock and sold slowly but regularly, both in Britain and America, until
1880, when the last copy was accounted for. For Charles, *Determinants* was
nonetheless an important milestone, for it well and truly established his reputation as a gladiator among gladiators; and in the ensuing years he carved
out more and more ground for himself in the public arena.

In turning to determinants, Charles by no means abandoned his students.
In fact, he thought of *Determinants* as a text for the more advanced ones.
And even as he was writing and revising, he continued his efforts to make
Euclid more accessible. On January 16, 1868, he records: "I have written almost all of the pamphlet on *Euclid V* by Algebra, with notes." He strove in
*The Fifth Book of Euclid Treated Algebraically So Far As It Relates to Commen-
surable Magnitudes, with Notes* to provide a succinct explanation of Euclid V
with "hints on proving propositions" to help students prepare for examinations. His aim, Abeles writes, was to devise "a comprehensive treatment of
proportion for measurable quantities. . . . Because he intended the work for
pass-men, he omitted the more difficult material on nonmeasurable quantities. . . . Dodgson's contribution is in the methodical approach he uses to
develop the numerical part of ratio and proportion, and by removing the
more abstract concepts . . . [he makes] Euclid V (and Euclid VI) accessible
to ordinary undergraduates."[28]

On May 21, 1868, Charles took to the University Press "the MS for *Formulae in Algebra for [the Use of Candidates for] Responsions,*" another four-page
aid for students, which appeared as *Algebraical Formulae for Responsions.*

All these mathematical works are dead serious, without a flicker of
whimsy or humor. In time, in books meant for younger readers, in his continuing work in Euclid, and in logic, Charles would employ wit to good advantage and draw upon his storehouse of irony, paradox, and outright fun to
leaven the loaf.

These broadsides, books of verse, mathematical works, and pamphlets appear all the more remarkable because Charles worked on them while creat-

ing his masterpiece, the crowning glory of his inventive imagination, *Alice's Adventures in Wonderland.* He conceived it on July 4, 1862, when his mind was teeming with all manner of ideas, mathematical, social, political, literary. And he gave much of his energy to it during the next two years, scripting the early text into that leather-bound green notebook, leaving spaces for his own illustrations.

No wonder it took him more than two years to complete it. But despite negotiations with Macmillan, the University Press, and Tenniel, despite rewriting the text to double its length and waiting, waiting for Tenniel to supply the illustrations, despite Tenniel's rejection of the first edition and the cost of printing another edition, he forged ahead on all fronts: teaching, writing, thinking, puzzling out, inventing, creating into the long, still hours of the night, and, in season, photographing by day. Finally, the 1866 *Alice*, approved by Tenniel, was launched. In 1869 he held the first German *Alice* in his hands, then the first French. The agonized cries for help, we know, occurred frequently during this time, but pleasures were also sweet: they made it all worthwhile.

*Through the Looking-Glass* belongs to the 1860s as well. As early as August 24, 1866, Charles wrote to Macmillan about his "floating idea of . . . a sort of sequel to Alice," and most or all of the text was actually set in type by the end of 1869.

One marvels at how he did so much and still indulged in an active social life, for, during the 1860s, Charles was a virtual gadabout. Although rooted in Oxford during term time, he spent most of the holidays away, at Croft and in London. His hunger for the theater and art needed constant nourishment; his circles of friends multiplied as his reputation, first as an art photographer and then as the author of *Alice*, grew. Having undertaken to seek help for his stammer, he made regular visits to his speech therapist, Dr. Hunt.

Victorians were drawn to the sea in droves. They eagerly fled the soot and stench of the cities, and current medical advice offered few palliatives as effective as sea air, deemed far superior to country air, mountain air, and valley air. They did not seem to mind dressing up in hideous bathing costumes to take to the waves, splashing about with clenched teeth and Evangelical fortitude, braving the icy waters that ring the English coast even in summer. In spite of his spoof about the drawbacks of seaside holidays, Charles fell into the sea-adoring pattern. We have no evidence that he ever shed his heavy garments for a bathing costume (oh, for such a photograph of him!), but from childhood he participated in the seaside ritual, first with his family at Whitby, then at Freshwater and Sandown on the Isle of Wight, and from 1877 at Eastbourne.

As we know, Charles made his second assault on the Poet Laureate on the Isle of Wight, and when Charles went back to Freshwater at Easter 1862, he again called on the Tennysons. "I have seen hardly anything more of Mr. Tennyson," he wrote to his sister Mary (April 19), "and daytime does not seem propitious to getting much conversation out of him. Did I mention in my Thursday letter [missing] my lunching there on Wednesday? . . . After luncheon (the poet only turned up for a minute at the end)," Charles taught the Tennyson boys "Elephant Hunters" and played other games with them. On Thursday he encountered the two lads on the beach. "*After* luncheon" on that day, "(not having been invited to that meal) I went to the Tennysons, and got Hallam and Lionel to sign their names in my album. Also I made a bargain with the eight-year-old Lionel, that he was to give me some MS of his verses, and I was to send him some of mine." The letter then quotes some childish verses about the Battle of Waterloo from Lionel's pen accompanied by an effort on the "Death of the Prince Consort," a fit tribute to Albert, who had died on the previous December 14. Earlier in 1862, Tennyson's publisher, Edward Moxon and Company, published, with Tennyson's consent, *An Index to "In Memoriam,"* suggested and edited by Charles but largely compiled by one or more of his sisters. But all too soon, the relationship with the Tennysons soured, when Charles wrote to Tennyson asking his permission to retain a pirated edition of his poems. If anything infuriated Tennyson, it was the pirating of his work, and Charles should have known better than to make so indelicate a request.

Two years later, during the summer of 1864, Charles returned to Freshwater and called at Farringford the day after he arrived, and on August 13 he somehow managed, probably through the intervention of Mr. C. R. Weld, Mrs. Tennyson's brother-in-law, who was staying at Farringford and whom Charles knew from Croft days, to begin photographing at Farringford: "A long time was spent in getting out things and darkening a room." He took pictures not of the Tennysons but of their house, friends, guests, and servants. Although Charles's reception was not so warm at Farringford as he would have liked, he nevertheless made valuable connections through the Tennysons, whose neighbors and friends included Mrs. Cameron, a remarkably talented eccentric, and her family; and (Sir) Henry Taylor, the poet-dramatist, and his charming wife and children. Charles later sent Tennyson an inscribed copy of *Alice.*

Then, in 1870, Charles again pricked the poet's patience. In 1866 Tennyson wrote "The Window," a "German fashion" song cycle, for Arthur Sullivan. He had it privately printed in 1867, and it appeared in 1870 set to Sullivan's music. On March 3 Charles wrote to his idol telling him that a transcription of the unpublished poem had fallen into his hands, and he asked permission first to read it, then to keep it, and even to be allowed to give away copies to friends. If this were not enough to curdle the poet's blood, Charles's insensitively reminded the poet that some time ago, when he came into possession of an unpublished early poem, written in the Laureate's teens, entitled "The Lover's Tale" (which Charles carelessly misnamed "Lover's Life") he had, at Tennyson's request, destroyed the copy.

Mrs. Tennyson replied with a rebuke: a gentleman should understand that when an author chose to withhold any work from public view, he must have a good reason for doing so. Being accused of ungentlemanly conduct was more than Charles could bear, and he replied forthwith, pointing out that he had always sought to behave according to Tennyson's wishes and asking Tennyson to explain exactly how he had violated even the strictest code of propriety. More heated letters followed, and even though Charles sent Tennyson *Looking-Glass* as a "peace offering" and the poet acknowledged it, the breach was never healed.

Charles stopped taking holidays on the Isle of Wight after 1864. His photography, the attraction of the theater and art galleries, and his desire to see friends drew him to London for part of his summer vacations, his family ties continued to beckon him to Croft and after 1868 to Guildford, and his efforts to prepare himself for ordination also conspired to keep him from the seaside. He did have a week or ten days at Whitby in September 1865, 1866, and 1868; although he returned to the Isle of Wight for brief excursions in 1873 and 1876, apparently no further meeting with the Tennysons took place.

The inventive powers that drove Charles in so many directions and enabled him to reach such exceptional heights were evident in his letter writing as well. Writing letters was a ritual for him; he thought carefully about them and executed them with the greatest care and ingenuity. He often composed letters lying awake during the night, and for those sleepless hours he invented a device, the Nyctograph, that enabled him to take notes under the covers in the dark. Picture him, then, in the morning, fully dressed, standing before his upright desk, selecting the appropriate sheet of letter paper from the various sizes he kept in good supply, dipping his pen into purple ink, and writing out letters composed in the dark. The wit that we observed in earlier years achieved new dimensions in the 1860s as Charles created a dazzling array of letters.

Considering the enormous quantity that he penned, one would expect some to show signs of haste, of being scribbled off and occasionally appearing illegible. But there is none of that: each and every one, short or long, important or trivial, is clearly executed and totally legible—a remarkable achievement for one of the most assiduous letter writers of all time.

We get a hint of the mountains of letters he wrote from a "Register of Letters Received and Sent" that he kept for the last thirty-seven years of his life. The last entry, according to Charles's nephew S. D. Collingwood, who possessed it before it was lost, numbered 98,721. When we add to that total the merest estimate of letters that he must have received and sent in the earlier unrecorded twenty-nine years of his life, we end with an astronomical number, certainly well over 100,000.

Although letter writing gave him a great deal of pleasure, it could also be a burden. "One third of my life seems to go in receiving letters," he writes to a friend (May 8, 1879), "and the other two-thirds in answering them." "I'm generally 70 or 80 in arrears, and sometimes *one* letter will take me an afternoon," he complained to another (April 25, 1890). And to a third he wrote (February 14, 1887): "Life seems to go in letter-writing, and I'm beginning to think that the proper definition of 'Man' is 'an animal that writes letters.' "

He nevertheless devoted himself to the occupation, both out of a sense of duty and because he knew that his letters brought pleasure and comfort to others, primarily to child friends, and helped him advance and cement those child friendships. Many missives were designed to dispel fears, console grief, ease conscience, assuage pain—and, most of all, make his recipients laugh. If, as some critics suggest, letter writing obsessed him, he was at least sufficiently objective about it to laugh at his "obsession": "I hardly know which is me and which is the inkstand . . . ," he wrote a young correspondent (October 26, 1881). "The confusion in one's *mind* doesn't so much matter—but when it comes to putting bread-and-butter, and orange marmalade, into the *inkstand;* then dipping pens into *oneself,* and filling *oneself* up with ink, you know, it's horrid!"

Of course, he wrote mounds of serious letters, but those that emerged from his creative well provoked the laughter. The lightness of touch, the whimsy were unfailing, even as his invention was unique. He packed into tiny envelopes huge amounts of delight for his many friends. For them, the postman's knock must have been one of the world's happiest sounds. Many of these self-contained microcosms of Wonderland prove him to be, in both senses of the word, a man of letters. One of them went to ten-year-old Annie Rogers in 1867 after he forgot to keep an appointment he had with her:

My dear Annie,

This is indeed dreadful. You have no idea of the grief I am in while I write. I am obliged to use an umbrella to keep the tears from running down on to the paper. Did you come yesterday to be photographed? and were you *very* angry? why wasn't I there? Well the fact was this—I went out for a walk with Bibkins, my dear friend Bibkins—we went many miles from Oxford—fifty—a hundred say. As we were crossing a field full of sheep, a thought crossed my mind, and I said solemnly, "Dobkins, what o'clock is it?" "Three," said Fipkins, surprised at my manner. Tears ran down my cheeks. "It is the HOUR," I said. "Tell me, tell me, Hopkins, what day is it?" "Why, Monday, of course," said Lupkins. "Then it is the DAY!" I groaned. I wept. I screamed. The sheep crowded round me, and rubbed their affectionate noses against mine. "Mopkins!" I said, "you are my oldest friend. Do not deceive me, Nupkins! What year is this?" "Well, I *think* it's 1867," said Pipkins. "Then it's the YEAR! I screamed, so loud that Tapkins fainted. It was all over: I was brought home, in a cart, attended by the faithful Wopkins, in several pieces.

When I have recovered a little from the shock, and have been to the seaside for a few months, I will call and arrange another day for photographing. I am too weak to write this myself, so Zupkins is writing it for me.

Your miserable friend,
Lewis Carroll

Charles invented games for his correspondents to play; created stories to tell them later; prodded their ingenuity by inventing ciphers with complicated instructions; composed double acrostic verses to tax their ability to puzzle out the message or name hidden in the lines; deluged them with books, both his own and others, many beautifully inscribed; invented puzzles for them to solve. Not the most complex of his inventions, surely, but one of the most engaging, enumerates the names of the three Liddell sisters inscribed in the copy of *Holiday House* he gave them as a Christmas present in 1861 (see page 80).

* * *

A new experience lay in store for Charles in 1867, one shared with his friend, colleague, and mentor on religious matters, Henry Parry Liddon. Liddon's reputation as a brilliant preacher spread wide, and before long, while retaining his Christ Church studentship, he became Canon and Chancellor of St. Paul's Cathedral in London. Charles and Liddon met frequently in Oxford and in London, they took long walks together, they dined together, Charles heard Liddon preach. On July 4, 1867, Liddon "proposed to Dodgson that we should go together to Russia" and Charles was "much taken with the idea."[29] On the tenth Liddon was in Oxford discussing details with Charles, and on the eleventh Charles and he "decided on Moscow! Ambitious for one who has never yet left England."

They left on the twelfth, met at Dover, and spent the night there before sailing for Calais. "The pen refused to describe the suffering of some of the passengers during our smooth trip of 90 minutes," Charles recalls; "my own sensations—it was not for *that* I paid my money."[30] From Calais they traveled by rail to Brussels, where dinner was, according to Charles, "*très simple* . . . consisting of only 7 courses." On Sunday morning they went to church "just in time for the High Mass" and then observed the religious procession through the Grande Place. Charles went into considerable detail about the "Fête du Miracle du St. Sacrament" and regretted that the congregation did not participate more in the service. The parade he judged the "most splendid ceremonial I have ever seen" but also "theatrical and unreal." At the end of the day he and Liddon established a "common fund."

On to Cologne they traveled on the Monday, and Liddon had "difficulty in saving the train at Verviers, owing to Dodgson's delay about the tickets." At Cologne they spent an hour in the cathedral, "the most beautiful of all churches I have ever seen, or can imagine," Charles wrote. "If one could imagine the spirit of devotion embodied in any material form, it would be in such a building." Liddon reported Charles "overcome" by the cathedral's beauty. "I found him leaning against the rails of the Choir and sobbing like a child. When the verger came to show us over the chapels behind the Choir, he got out of the way: he said that he could not bear the harsh voice of the man in the presence of so much beauty."

Then overnight to Berlin, where they spent five days. They visited the usual Berlin sights, numerous churches and art galleries, and they attended a service at St. Peter's, impressed by both the orderliness of the service and the devotion of the congregation. Friday evening Charles insisted on finding the New Jewish Synagogue, and after breakfast he led them back there.

"The music was equal to some of the very best I have heard in Christian Churches," Liddon reports. For Charles, "the whole scene was perfectly novel . . . and most interesting. . . . We followed the example of the congregation in keeping our hats on." They spent an afternoon in Potsdam and returned to Berlin, where in the evening Liddon recorded "a long argument with Dodgson . . . about the obligation of the daily Service, an obligation which he fiercely contested."

*The renowned preacher Henry Parry Liddon, by his friend Charles Dodgson. Charles traveled with Liddon to Russia on the one journey that he took out of Great Britain.*

From Berlin they traveled to Danzig, which Charles described as a "fantastic and most interesting old town." They spent three hours together in the cathedral and another at the top of the tower, 328 feet above the street. Then to Königsberg, where Liddon came down with a stomachache and diarrhea, and after midnight Charles sent for a doctor, who applied blotting paper soaked in spirits of mustard and gave Liddon morphia powder and chamomile tea. While Liddon recuperated, Charles went to the theater, "which was fairly good in every way, and very good in singing and some of the acting," but he grasped little of the German dialogue.

The railway journey to St. Petersburg took twenty-eight and a half hours. "Unfortunately, the seats of the carriage we were in only allowed room for four to lie down, and as there were 2 ladies and another gentleman besides ourselves, I slept on the floor," Charles reports, "with a carpet-bag and coat for a pillow, and though not in great luxury, was quite comfortable enough to sleep soundly all night." During the journey Charles played three games of chess with the man in their compartment, who won them all.

They arrived at St. Petersburg on Saturday evening, July 27, with time "for a short stroll after dinner," Charles reports, "but it was full of wonder and novelty. The enormous width of the streets (the secondary ones seem to be broader than anything in London), the little droshkies that went running about, seemingly quite indifferent as to running over everybody . . . the enormous illuminated signboards over the shops, and the gigantic churches, with their domes painted blue and covered with gold stars—and the bewildering jabber of the natives—all contributed to the wonders. . . ."

On Sunday morning they went to St. Isaac's Cathedral. Charles found the service, "being in Slavonic . . . beyond all hope of comprehension. . . . The only share the congregation had . . . was to bow and cross themselves, and sometimes to kneel down and touch the ground with their foreheads. . . . The dresses of the officiating ministers were most splendid, and the processions and incense reminded me of the Roman Catholic Church at Brussels, but the more one sees of these gorgeous services, with their many appeals to the senses, the more, I think, one learns to love the plain, simple (but to my mind far more real) service of the English church." Charles must have voiced his opinion about the pomp and mechanical quality of the ceremonies, and Liddon wrote: "After church a long argument with Dodgson."

On Monday morning Charles bought a map and dictionary. Feeling adequately equipped and having been told, no doubt, that he must bargain over the price of services, he takes on a droshky driver:

> Myself. Gostonitia Klee—(Klees Hôtel).
> Driver. (utters a sentence rapidly of which we can only catch the words) Tri groshen—(Three groshen—30 kopecks?).
> M. Doatzat kopecki? (20 kopecks?).
> D. (indignantly) Tritzat! (30).
> M. (resolutely) Doatzat.
> D. (coaxingly) Doatzat piat? (25?).
> M. (with the air of one who has said his say, and wishes to be rid of the thing) Doatzat. (Here I take Liddon's arm, and we walk off together, entirely disregarding the shouts of the driver. When we have gone a few yards, we hear the droshky lumbering after us: he draws up alongside, and hails us).
> M. (gravely) Doatzat?
> D. (with a delighted grin) Da! Da! Doatzat! (and in we get).

Charles added: "This sort of thing is amusing for once in a way, but if it were a necessary process in hiring cabs in London, it would become a little tedious in time."

On Tuesday and Wednesday the two visitors went sightseeing, to the Cathedral of Saints Peter and Paul, where the Russian czars are entombed, and to the Hermitage. Charles comments particularly on the Murillos, the

Titians, and the "exquisite" Raphael of the Holy Family. On Thursday they went to Peterhof, twenty miles from the city, covering some of the distance by steamer across the Gulf of Finland, to visit the magnificent palace that the Nazis would destroy in World War II and which was later rebuilt. Charles was struck by the extensive gardens.

On August 2 they left for Moscow. They had a sleeping compartment, but Charles stayed up until about 1 a.m. and was "most of the time the sole occupant of the outside platform at the end of the carriage: it had a handrail and a roof, and afforded a splendid view of the country as we flew through it—its disadvantages being that the vibration and noise were much worse than inside." They reached Moscow in midmorning and gave "5 or 6 hours to a stroll through this wonderful city, a city of white and green roofs, of conical towers that rise one out of another like a fore-shortened telescope; of bulging gilded domes, in which you see as in a looking-glass, distorted pictures of the city; of churches which look, outside, like bunches of varie-gated cactus . . . and which, inside, are hung all round with Eikons and lamps, and lined with illuminated pictures up to the very roof. . . ."

They visited numerous churches and on Sunday searched out the English church for evening service. On Monday they went to the Kremlin and were dazzled by the rich thrones, crowns, and jewels in the Treasury; in the evening Roger George Penny, the English chaplain, took them to see a Russian wedding, for Charles "a *most* interesting ceremony," which he de-scribed in detail. After the ceremony, the priest introduced himself and gave Liddon and Charles the "kiss of peace."

On Tuesday, after sightseeing in Moscow, they set off for the World's Fair at Nijni Novgorod, which annually brought together some twenty thousand merchants and one hundred thousand visitors from the four corners of the earth. The journey entailed eighteen hours of discomfort, without sleeping carriages, and with the added adventure of having to get out of the train and cross a river on a footbridge in the pouring rain because the railway bridge had been washed away. They finally arrived at 1 p.m. on August 7 and spent most of the afternoon wandering through the fair "buying Eikons, etc.," Charles reports. "It was a wonderful place," he wrote to his sister Louisa on the seventh, swarming with "Greeks, Jews, Armenians, Persians, China-men, etc., besides the native Russians."

They were, Charles reports, "constantly meeting strange beings, with un-wholesome complexions and unheard-of costumes," the Persians the most picturesque. At sunset they came upon a Tartar mosque and stayed for the

service. In the evening Charles went to the theater and approved of the acting quality. They spent the night at a "villainous" hotel, whence Charles
wrote to his sister in pencil, no ink being available. They endured "beds consisting of boards covered with a mattress about an inch thick, a pillow, one
sheet and a quilt." Both were impressed by the music at the service at the
Nijni cathedral. At three in the afternoon they left Nijni for the homeward
journey to Moscow, again overnight, and for Charles, "if possible a more un-
comfortable one than the former." They reached Moscow "tired but delighted" with all they had seen.

On Friday the ninth they went to the Semonof Monastery, and on Saturday Liddon tried to connect with the Governor-General of Moscow and
Prince Vladimir Tcherchasky, a champion of the Orthodox Church, but
both were away. The rest of the day he and Charles spent at the Petrovski
Palace and at the Semonof Monastery for vespers. On Sunday Liddon complained that "Dodgson did not get up until 9:30." Nevertheless, they attended morning service at the English church, where Liddon preached.
Then they called on Bishop Leonide, the Suffragan of Moscow, to whom
Liddon had an introduction from Prince Nikolai Orloff, Russia's representative in Belgium, who was involved in negotiations between East and West
on Christian unity. Later in the day they visited the Strasnoi Nunnery,
where Charles was moved by the "effect of the women's voices, unaccompa-
nied . . . singularly beautiful."

"A most interesting day" was how Charles characterized Monday, August
12. They were up at five-thirty and off with Bishop Leonide and Mr. Penny
to the Troitska Monastery, where the Bishop took them into a side room of
the cathedral to witness the elaborate ceremony of the service. Then they
went to the Archbishop's palace and came face to face with the most influential figure in the Russian Church, Vasilii Drosdov Philaret, Metropolitan
of Moscow, who, though lacking a knowledge of English, was known to be
deeply interested in Western Christianity. The meeting lasted an hour and
a half and was devoted entirely to a conversation between Liddon and the
Russian churchman. Charles was merely a bystander through these high-
level negotiations, but he found the visit interesting and summarized it as
"one of the most memorable days of our tour."

Tuesday, August 13, was a holy day involving an elaborate service in the
cathedral and a grand procession to and from the river. Charles described
the huge crowds and the procession in detail, and Liddon estimated that five
bishops and eighty to a hundred clergy in splendid vestments participated.

He reported a "great argument with Dodgson on the character of Russian religion—he thought it too external, etc." Liddon was bothered on the following day as well: "Our whole morning was lost," he writes. "Dodgson did not get up until 9:30 . . ."; and later in the day he had "a warm argument with Dodgson about Prayers for the Departed. . . ."

On the fourteenth they went to the Strastny Monastery to visit its five churches and cemetery; and on the fifteenth to the Church of the Holy Sepulchre (or New Jerusalem) at Voskresensk, a replica of the one in Jerusalem, enduring a long and arduous journey, both by rail and carriage, in which, Charles reported, "we jolted along over 14 miles of quite the worst road I have ever seen. . . . Even with three horses, it took us nearly 3 hours to do the distance." En route, they stopped at a peasant's cottage to apply for bread and milk and Charles made two sketches of the cottage, "but in this was lost ¾ of an hour," an irritated Liddon complains.

They were shown through the monastery and the hermitage, but had to hire beds at the local inn in order to depart at four in the morning for the return journey. Charles recounted how they settled the bill with a deranged landlord: "He wrote . . . [the bill] in pencil on a scrap of rough paper, shouting out the different items as he wrote them down, and then handed it over to me to be added up. This I did, putting in an additional item . . . 'for service,' and on receiving the money he rose, bowed to the Icon in the corner of the room, crossing himself as he did so, then seized Liddon by the hand, kissed him on both cheeks, and then kissed his hand: I had to submit to the same affectionate farewell."

The day after they returned to Moscow, Saturday the seventeenth, was the jubilee honoring the fiftieth anniversary of Philaret's episcopate, and the pair went off from Moscow to Troitska to witness the celebration. On Sunday they visited the Cathedral of the Assumption. Liddon praised the sumptuous service, but Charles left in the middle "to go to the English Church." In the evening they walked through the Kremlin again and, as Charles records, "got our last impression of that most beautiful range of buildings, in perhaps, the most beautiful aspect of which it is capable—a flood of cold, clear moonlight, bringing out the pure white of the walls and towers, and the glittering points of light on the gilded domes, in a way that sunlight could never do—for it could not set them, as we saw them, in the midst of darkness."

They left Moscow on Monday afternoon for the overnight journey back to St. Petersburg. On the journey, according to Charles, "there was only one other gentleman in the carriage, so that, with an open window we might have managed: but as our friend . . . had a cold and so objected to this—and as the third bed, which naturally fell to the lot of the youngest, the writer, was situated immovably crosswise, with the head under one bed, and the foot under the other—I preferred air and fatigue, on the platform at the end of the carriage, to rest and suffocation within. From 5 to 6 a.m. I came in and had a nap, but that was all."

On Wednesday Count Poutiatine took them back to the Hermitage, where they saw paintings they had missed on their first visit and were shown into areas the public did not see. He took them also through the Winter Palace and the suite of rooms the Prince of Wales occupied when he had come to Russia the previous year to attend the wedding of his sister-in-law to Tsarevitch Alexander.

On Thursday, August 22, they crossed to Cronstadt and had "a most interesting day" inspecting the arsenal, the magnetic and astronomical observatories, the steam factory, the merchant harbor, and the main harbor. In the evening Charles reported that

Liddon had surrendered his over-coat early in the day [at Mr. Mc-Swinney's, the English chaplain], and when going, we found it must be recovered from the waiting-maid, who only talked Russian, and as I

*Success in retrieving Liddon's coat: Charles's*
*drawing in* The Russian Journal

had left the dictionary behind . . . we were in some difficulty. Liddon began by exhibiting his coat, with much gesticulation, including the taking it half off. To our delight, she appeared to understand at once—left the room, and returned in a minute with—a large clothes brush. On this Liddon tried a further and more energetic demonstration—he took off his coat, and laid it at her feet, pointed downwards (to intimate that in the lower regions was the object of his desire) smiling with an expression of joy and gratitude with which he would receive it, and put the coat on again. Once more a gleam of intelligence lighted up the plain but expressive features of the young person: she was absent much longer this time, and then she brought, to our dismay, a large cushion and a pillow, and began to prepare the sofa for the nap that she now saw clearly was the thing the dumb gentleman wanted. A happy thought occurred to me, and I hastily drew a sketch representing Liddon, with one coat on, receiving a second and larger one from the hands of a benignant Russian peasant. The language of hieroglyphics succeeded where all other means had failed, and we returned to Petersburg with the humiliating knowledge that our standard of civilisation was now reduced to the level of ancient Nineveh.

Charles draws a sketch in his journal to illustrate the delivery of the coat.

On Friday Charles wrote: "In our wanderings, I noticed a beautiful photograph of a child, and bought a copy, small size, at the same time ordering a full length to be printed. . . . Afterwards I called to ask for the name of the original, and found they had already printed the full length but were in great doubt what to do, as they had asked the father of the child about it, and found he disapproved of the sale. Of course there was nothing to do but return the carte I had bought: at the same time I left a written statement that I had done so, expressing a hope that I might still be allowed to purchase it."

On Saturday evening Charles and Liddon went to the Alexander Nevski Monastery and witnessed, Charles noted, "one of the most beautiful services I have heard in a Greek church. The singing was quite delicious. . . . One piece in particular, which was repeated many times in the course of the service . . . was so lovely a piece of melody that I would gladly have listened to it many times more."

Before the two left St. Petersburg on Monday the twenty-sixth, Liddon went alone on a round of calls and to the Roman Catholic church and the Kazan Cathedral. While Charles packed, the photographer called "to bring the pictures, as the father . . . had given them leave to sell them to me." They began their journey to Warsaw in the early afternoon. "A good view [from the train] of Jupiter through Dodgson's telescope," Liddon records.

Warsaw disappointed them. They visited numerous churches, "chiefly Roman Catholic," Charles adds, "which contained the usual evidence of wealth and bad taste. . . . The town, as a whole, is one of the noisiest and dirtiest I have yet visited." From Warsaw they traveled to Breslau, where, on their way to visit a church, they came upon a playground for the girls' school, "a very tempting field for a photographic camera," Charles mused, and added: "After the Russian children, whose type of face is ugly as a rule, and plain as an exception, it is quite a relief to get back among the Germans and their large eyes and delicate features."

On Saturday the thirty-first they set off for Dresden; on Sunday Charles writes: "Liddon attended the Roman Catholic Church, and I joined him there for a few minutes to hear the music." Liddon reports: "Some discussion with Dodgson in the evening. He thought the Roman Catholic church like a Concert-room—and went out. Dislikes the name Catholic because it connected us with Rome."

On Monday they went to the art gallery; in the evening Charles went to the theater, a disappointing experience, and then lost his way home in the dark. On Tuesday they traveled to Leipzig, arriving in time to take a walk through the old town in the evening. They noted that Napoleon had stayed in their hotel and that Luther and Eck had held their great disputation in the castle. They then traveled on to Giessen and Ems, through the Lahn valley. Charles comments on the scenery in a Ruskinian vein. On Friday, September 6, they went up the Rhine by steamer to Bingen and from Bingen on to Paris.

In Paris they stayed at the Hôtel du Louvre, overlooking the Place Royale. On Sunday Charles went to the English church. They walked about, through the Tuileries Gardens, along the Champs-Elysées into the Bois de Boulogne, "by which," Charles noted, one got "a fair idea of the amount of country beauty, in the way of parks, gardens, water, etc., this beautiful city manages to include. Seeing it, I wonder no more that Parisians call London 'triste.'"

On Monday they went to the Paris Universal Exhibition, and Charles admired all the art except the English examples, which he judged second-rate. In the evening he went to the theater and saw a play in which a role was played "by one of the cleverest children I ever saw . . . who could not have been more than 6 years old." On the following day they dissolved their common fund. They joined forces in the evening for a concert in the Champs-Elysées. Charles, displeased with their huge hotel, moved to the Hôtel des Deux Mondes in the rue d'Antin on Wednesday. On Thursday, again at the Exhibition, he noticed a pavilion "where Chinese music was going on," paid half a franc to enter and listen to it, "music which, once heard, one desires never to hear again." In the evening he compensated by going to the Opéra-Comique to hear *Mignon*, "with charming music and singing."

Liddon departed Paris early on the thirteenth and crossed back from Calais to Dover; Charles took the same route, but not until evening, when he left his hotel at 7 p.m., and enjoyed "a peaceful and slumbrous journey to Calais, arriving at 2 a.m." He then sailed to Dover. The crossing was smooth and he stood in the bow, "watching, through the last hour of my first foreign tour, the lights of Dover, as they slowly broadened on the horizon, as if the old land were opening its arms to receive its homeward bound children. . . ."

He traveled immediately to London, then to Croft, resuming his busy rounds. What with his many occupations, memories of the journey abroad quickly receded. Nowhere does he reflect upon it, certainly not upon his relationship with Liddon and whether their arguments and disagreements had altered the friendship. The closest we come to a remembrance is in the manuscript verse of "A Russian's Day in England," which Charles probably wrote for Lady Gwendolen Cecil in November 1874. The twenty-six lines of humorous verse draw upon the small knowledge he retained of Russians and the Russian language, but it is hardly a masterpiece.[31]

Liddon's and Charles's diaries both show the pair's interest in new and foreign adventures, in the landscape, spectacles, and mementos, and in religious duties, churches, and churchmen. The two differed enormously, however, in their attitudes. Where Liddon describes religious ceremonies, vestments, and church architecture with a fervor that reflects his spiritual and emotional commitment to the externals as representing the eternal, Charles views the same manifestations as an aesthetic rather than a spiritual experience. The same applies to much of the architecture and the visual arts. Charles took in the heady ceremonials but was more interested in the congregation—whether the people participated in the ritual, whether the devotion was genuine or mechanical. Clearly he got fed up easily with too much majesty, too much of the external display, which he thought concealed or replaced true and simple religious feeling, and he retreated from the pomp, refusing to accompany Liddon to Catholic services. Missing almost entirely from Liddon's record, but evident in Charles's, are reports of encounters with simple people—a waiter, a droshky driver, a shopkeeper. He did not meet with or talk at length with Russian church officials, he did not send home long summaries of meetings and conversations, as did Liddon. He concentrated on the culture, the language, the people, the landscape, the art, and, yes, the religion—but only as any educated traveler would do.

Disagreements obviously arose between them, and they may have had more than one falling-out. Did Charles take the trouble to pack and move to the Hôtel des Deux Mondes for the last two nights in Paris because, as he reported, the Hôtel du Louvre was too large—or was there another reason? And why did the two men cross from Calais to Dover separately within twelve hours? Something must have gone sour.

No permanent breach occurred, however. Liddon reenters Charles's diary, although not for more than a year after they had returned, when, on November 28, 1868, his name is among the guests at a dinner party Charles gave in his rooms.

The tensions that arose on the tour were inevitable, given the two personalities and their different convictions. Liddon's bent was Romeward, Charles's not. Liddon was too much like Charles's father for Charles to walk constantly by his side. Charles had probably been converted to the simpler religion in the 1850s and 1860s. He knew where he stood and what he believed in, and his beliefs did not coincide with Liddon's. The discussions on the journey brought to the surface the two men's different attitudes and must have reminded Charles of similar discussions with his father. Charles's disagreements with both men were too fundamental to resolve or reconcile.

Charles and Liddon continued meeting in Oxford and in London, and their mutual respect and affection are evident. In fact, so secure did Charles feel in the friendship that, more than once in the following years, he targeted Liddon for parody in his Oxford squibs, as he had in 1865. In 1872, for instance, in *The New Belfry of Christ Church, Oxford,* where Charles ridicules the erection at Christ Church of a wooden cube as a belfry, he asks: "Was it the Professor who designed this box, which with a lid on or not, equally offends the eye?" Charles is, as always, playing with words and sounds; as rumor had it that Liddon had designed the belfry, Charles's "lid on" was not lost on his readers.

Eighteen months later he added a burlesque of Liddon in *The Blank Cheque,* satirizing a decree authorizing the university to build new Examination Schools before anyone had determined the cost. Oxford denizens and many beyond the university walls would easily recognize "little Harry, the pet of the family." They all knew that Liddon was associated with Pusey and that he was fond of cats. Few would miss Charles's intent when they read: " 'Harry-Parry Ridy-Pidy Coachy-Poachy!' said the fond mother, as she lifted the little fellow to her knee and treated him to a jog-trot. 'Harry's very fond of Pussy, he is but he mustn't tease it, he mustn't!' "

When, in June 1870, Oxford bestowed an honorary doctorate of civil law on Liddon, Charles was proud of his friend's distinction. It was then that Liddon arranged the meeting between Charles and the newly installed chancellor of the university, Lord Salisbury, and Charles got to photograph the Chancellor and his children. Charles and Liddon were sometimes guests at Hatfield House at the same time. On the last day of 1872 Liddon noted, "Dodgson there to dinner, and very amusing."

*Charles's photograph of Lord Salisbury and sons. H. P. Liddon introduced Charles to Lord Salisbury when he came to Oxford to be installed as Chancellor of the University, and Charles did not miss the opportunity to photograph the Marquess.*

When Liddon became Canon of St. Paul's Cathedral, Charles occasionally called on him in London, but they met more often in Oxford. In May 1885 Charles lent his photographic studio to Liddon "to give a sitting to . . . an artist who is painting his picture." Their last recorded meeting appears on June 24, 1888: "Dined with Bayne to celebrate the 40th anniversary of his Matriculation," Charles writes, adding: "The other guests were Liddon, Kitchin, and Paget." Liddon also recorded the event. On September 10, 1890, Charles writes: "I see by the papers that my dear old friend, Dr. Liddon, died yesterday. It is a heavy loss, to many friends, and to the whole English Church."

The Russian journey with Liddon was a milestone for Charles. He never again left Britain, nor did he show much interest in foreign parts. He did not, for instance, record his reaction to the opening of the Suez Canal at the end of 1869 or to the Afghan or Zulu Wars. Occasionally he did cast his eye beyond England's shores, however, as when he concluded his diary for 1870 by commenting on the Franco-Prussian War: the adversaries "still unrelaxing in their struggle. . . . May Peace come with the new year." He also noted the Russo-Turkish War of 1877–78, which threatened British interests in the Suez Canal and elsewhere in the Middle East. On December 11, 1877, Charles recorded the fall of Plevna, "probably the end of the Turkish resistance. May it be the end of the war!" he added. But three days later he saw a telegram at the Oxford Union reporting diplomatic moves "thought to foreshadow war between us and Russia. *Quid Deus avertat!*" Charles's prayers were answered: the armistice between Russia and Turkey was announced six weeks later, the Anglo-Russian agreement the following May.

Charles spent most of his university vacations at Croft and later at Guildford; he entertained his sisters, his brothers, and his Aunt Lucy Lutwidge at Oxford and in London; he paid for their seaside holidays. He assisted Wilfred and Skeffington when they entered Christ Church, and saw them through their degrees, Wilfred in 1860, Skeffington in 1862. He helped the youngest, Edwin, to settle in at Rugby. He wrote to M.P.'s and other officials, soliciting posts for his brothers. On September 25, 1860, he wrote a warm, congratulatory letter to his future brother-in-law C. E. S. Collingwood, and he gave the bride away when Collingwood wed his sister Mary (April 13, 1869).

After his father died, on June 21, 1868, Charles carried out his role as head of the family diligently. He became responsible for the family's finances and for their welfare, no small responsibility when six unmarried sisters remained to a degree financially dependent upon him. For the rest of his life he was a generous benefactor, adviser, and shepherd. The years immediately after his father's death, when his younger brothers were not yet established in careers, were particularly trying. He showed a constant concern for all and was kind to a fault. Charles's niece Menella Dodgson wrote years later: "We have only lately realized how much his relations owed to his generosity during his lifetime. . . ."[32]

During the 1860s Charles followed his own religious star, testing himself, his creed, his abilities, determined to perform the duties belonging to him since his ordination in 1861. On August 17, 1862, at Malvern, he "went to the Abbey Church in the morning, and assisted at the Communion (first time)." That autumn (October 5), at Croft, he "assisted in the Communion, read the afternoon service, and took a funeral (first time) afterwards." On February 2, 1863, at F. D. Maurice's Vere Street church in London, he assisted at Communion. On the eighteenth, Ash Wednesday, at Christ Church, he "took the evening service . . . , with baptism (the first I ever performed) and a sermon."

In June 1862 his classmate and friend W. H. Ranken, Vicar of Sandford-on-Thames, asked him to preach, and he undertook to do so, spending no small amount of time preparing the sermon. His speech hesitation or stammer (even his family did not agree on how to describe his difficulty) would be an encumbrance. But he had learned to live with it in the lecture hall—why not in the pulpit? It remained for him to prepare properly and to develop a preaching style. On the eighth, the appointed Sunday, he lay awake an hour thinking about the sermon and after breakfast wrote out the headings. Later in the day he spent "about another hour" reviewing the sermon. "I found," he adds after delivering the sermon, "I had to refer to the headings constantly: it lasted, I should think, about half an hour." On August 31 he had an unsettling experience in London: "Went to the new Church [in Putney] both morning and evening, and read service in the afternoon. I got through it all with great success, till I came to read out the first verse of the hymn before the sermon, where the two words 'strife, strengthened,' coming together were too much for me, and I had to leave the verse unfinished." Home for the Christmas holidays, on December 28, 1862, he walked over to Cleasby in the evening, "as I had half promised to preach . . . [there]." He "tried it this time without any notes, and with a watch open. I found that the matter I had prepared lasted for exactly twenty-five minutes." On February 6, 1863, he resolved to begin "methodically preparing outlines for sermons."

Although he stood in for a number of other churchmen in various localities, he did not accept every invitation that came his way. On August 3, 1864, he writes to an acquaintance, Conyngham Ellis, Vicar of Cranbourne, Berkshire, refusing Sunday service; he declines the honor again on July 19, 1865: "Would I were more fit to preach to others!" he writes in his diary.

On Easter Sunday 1866, Charles assisted at 8 a.m. Communion at St. Mary's, Oxford, and preached in the afternoon: "I undertook a *short* sermon," he notes. He repeated both services in March 1867.

Then—why precisely we do not know—he gave up preaching and desisted for almost fifteen years, until June 4, 1881, when his colleague and friend T. J. Prout, Vicar of Binsey, was called to London on the death of his brother. Charles had no choice but to stand in for him. "But I was not destined to deliver" the sermon, he writes, "as Prout returned this evening [Saturday]. It is some relief to one's nerves," he adds, "as I was looking forward with terror to the ordeal." But on January 2, 1887, he was back in the pulpit at St. Mary's: "I took the headings," Charles notes, "written in my pocket, but did not refer to them."

One parishioner, Gertrude Corrie, has passed on a summary of Charles's sermon:

> In reading St. Mark's Gospel it struck him that the question put by Our Lord to the blind man was just what we all want—"What wilt thou that I should do unto thee?" Some would ask for no suffering; some thought death the greatest evil; some thought the loss of those dear to us the worst that could happen; but the real most overwhelming ill of all was sin—the blackness of sin in the world. One was tempted to infidelity in reading faithless books, and in wondering, if God be good, why this sin was permitted. He advised prayer and the reading of the Gospels. . . . To be made clean, that was what we wanted. . . . Should we be happy in Heaven if we went there with all our evil desires? If the fairy-tale wishes are always to be granted— beauty, riches, high rank—would the blind man have been happy in a fine palace, with fine meals, if still blind? Two things were necessary for our being made clean: His Will and our Will. He is always ready: we can count upon him, but we must be willing too. . . .[33]

Charles was, of course, devoted to the young and in later years felt a strong call to speak to them, to help steer them toward truth and conviction, in spite of his preference not to perform in public. He revealed his thinking in a letter to a schoolmistress, Alice J. Cooper, on May 6, 1890:

> Do you remember our talking, when last I had the pleasure of meeting you, of the possibility of my some day saying a few *serious* words to some of your elder girls? It is a thing I should both dread, and delight, to do. Physically, all such coming out of one's-self, so to speak, is a terror to me: sometimes, when I have undertaken to preach a sermon, I feel, as the time gets near, as if I really *could* not face it, and must get myself excused: and I have to say to myself "what *does* it matter what *you* feel about it? If you can say anything helpful to other immortal souls, that is the only thing that *really* signifies." . . . Just now I'm feeling rather crushed at having undertaken to preach, next Sunday, at our "College Servants' Service": but, when I've got that off my mind, I would be ready to come over, with a week's notice, if ever you could find a time, and a room, suitable, and could collect some of your elder girls

(*not* the little ones: it would be a loss, I think, of the time and the opportunity, to limit myself to what *they* would understand).

Charles did read the lessons and preach at the following Sunday's college
servants' service, but we have no account of his performance. The plan to
address Miss Cooper's girls languished and was ultimately abandoned.

If Charles had any doubts about his abilities earlier, they must have been
vanquished by the time of his twenty-eighth birthday (January 14, 1860),
when he was a strong and determined young professional with his mind
made up about most things, his personality well formed, his attitudes
shaped and framed. During the ten years that followed, his views became all
the more ingrained and emerged as expressions of his essential nature: his
responses, opinions, pronouncements came forth automatically, perhaps
even inspirationally. His genius was also evident. The forces within him that
endure most luminously and that matter to posterity add up to the flashing
wit and soaring imagination of the *Alice* books, some of the short stories,
and some of his verse. That comic genius infused many of the letters he
wrote and brought joy into the lives of a good many persons fortunate
enough to have witnessed the gymnastics of his mind at work in personal
relationships.

We saw the strain of humor in him early, as a boy of thirteen in *Useful and
Instructive Poetry*. He obviously used laughter as a release from the seriousness of life at Croft. He developed all sorts of devices, turns of mind, leaps
of language, soaring sounds. He parodied, he mimicked, he invented limericks even before Edward Lear published his; he toyed with double meanings, used foreign words and phrases for amusing effects, imitated dialects,
captured the speech and mores of tradespeople and Cockneys with divert-
ing results. He provoked laughter and relief in his associates and friends, and
with children, his favorites, he was particularly inventive. He could laugh
with them at the absurdity of the adult world in which they were compelled
to live and mature. He mastered the key to a world of frivolity that enabled
his child friends, and later a world of child readers, to banish worry, sorrow,
and fear, and, at least for a transitory minute or hour, to laugh hilariously.

"His special gift of fancy and humour," wrote H. L. Thompson, "delicate,
quaint, and quite inimitable, gave a character of its own to all that he
touched."[34] Falconer Madan recorded an incident when Charles rose in
Congregation to contribute his opinion on a proposal to raise the stipends

and the number of university professors and to curtail the personal don-to-pupil instruction within the colleges. The proposer, according to Madan, made the mistake of suggesting that the true purpose of a university was to turn out professors. " 'Quite right,' said Dodgson, 'quite right. Turn them out, turn them out!' "[35] "The truth about Lewis Carroll," wrote Viscount Simon, Oxford don and later Lord Chancellor, "is that he was always engaged in genially pulling somebody's leg and he did this very amusingly by propounding a comic mathematical problem to a non-mathematical mind. That at least was the side of him which he showed . . . at occasional dinner parties, and I think he found the Canons of Christ Church easy meat!"[36] Much of his luxuriant imagination was, in fact, devoted to making people laugh. Humor and its concomitant laughter are surely minor miracles, over-flowings of a mysterious inner force, momentary flourishes like lightning or a rainbow. They come from we know not where and last but a fleeting second. Charles was one of those rare artists who could create those flashes, and did, to divert and amuse others.

The 1860s were for Charles a time for refining his gifts, for coming to terms with his professional duties, and for establishing himself, both in the larger world of mathematics and literature, as a solid contender. His energy was enormous, his effort almost superhuman, his ambition vaulting, and his accomplishments staggeringly impressive. His willingness to take on new duties and to initiate large, lavish creative work often appears foolhardy, but, in the end, he was more controlled and accomplished than ever before. "This term has been as hard worked as any I remember," he wrote (December 12, 1867), "but I have had the comfort of feeling that the work was *all* done, and not, as last term, always in arrears"; and on the thirty-first he adds: "A year of great blessings and few trials. . . . I trust I have learned to know myself better, and have striven . . . to live nearer to God."

It is mean-spirited to attribute the *Alice* books, the early contributions in mathematics, and the photographic successes entirely to a suppression of natural drives, to a flight from his real troubled self. If the pain he suffered at coming to terms with himself and with the rejection he endured at the hands of the Liddells was the spring of some of his creative accomplishments, so be it. But whatever the origin of his creativity, posterity can hardly condemn it or him for providing us with such remarkable works of art and for softening the harsh light of day for so many young eyes.

As Charles confronted the 1870s and his fortieth birthday, he looked ahead with his characteristic humility, and on December 31, 1869, wrote: "At the close of another year, I give thanks to our Heavenly Father, who has mercifully borne with me, and spared me in life and health, yet to do something, I trust, more than I have yet done, in His service, and for the good of my fellow creatures."

*Portrait of Charles in his study at Christ Church*

# CHAPTER NINE

# The Man

*A man so various that he seem'd to be Not one,*
*but all mankind's epitome.*

JOHN DRYDEN

The telephone, the sound recorder, and even motion pictures were all invented in Charles's lifetime, and he was fascinated by them, but we have to rely entirely upon the written word and our own imaginations to see and hear him in action. Fortunately we have numerous descriptions of what he looked and sounded like in conversation, from the lecture platform, in tutorials, and from the pulpit; how he behaved in adult society, with children, to his pupils, and to his colleagues; what his likes and dislikes were, his eccentricities, and his mannerisms. Despite inherent contradictions, they help illuminate the man.

He wore no spectacles, and when he was fifty, he recorded that he weighed 10 stone 3½ (143½ pounds). He wore his hair longer than others did. He wrote mostly at a stand-up desk and could do so, by his own calculation, for "10 hours."[1] He was not fond of cut flowers. He had a tolerably good singing voice and was not shy to use it. He talked to himself: "*Talking* is a wonderful smoother-over of difficulties," he wrote in the introduction to *Symbolic Logic*. "When *I* come upon anything—in Logic, or in any other hard subject that entirely puzzles me, I find it a capital plan to talk it over, *aloud*, even when I am alone. One can explain things so *clearly* to one's self! And then, you know, one is so *patient* with one's self: one *never* gets irritated at one's own stupidity." He liked chess and spoke of it as the family occupation.

Alice recalled that he "always wore black clergyman's clothes in Oxford, but, when he took us out on the river, he used to wear white flannel trousers. He also replaced his black top-hat with a hard white straw hat on these occasions, but of course retained his black boots, because in those days white tennis shoes had not yet been heard of. He always carried himself upright, as if he had swallowed a poker."

A niece mentioned his blue or gray eyes—all the family had blue or gray eyes—and that Charles was about six feet tall.[2] "He had a pale, clean-shaven face and his thin mouth seemed almost quivering with delight at the prospect of playing with four or five little girls," another recalled. ". . . He talked delightfully, and I remember how exasperating it was to be asked whether I would like another piece of cake when I was trying so hard to hear what he was saying at the other end of the table."[3]

Still another told of coming upon him suddenly: "I caught sight of him standing at the door, waiting to be let in. . . . He held himself stiffly, one shoulder slightly higher than the other; in his almost overemphasised erectness there was an old-fashioned seriousness, an air of punctiliousness."[4]

"He was thin, and very pale," writes an Oxford lady artist. "His face presented the peculiarity of having two very different profiles; the shape of the eyes, and the corners of the mouth did not tally. He sometimes hesitated in his speech . . . and I fancied he would often deliberately use it to heighten expectancy by delaying the point of his stories." He was "the pink of propriety."[5] Another artist, Gertrude Thomson, painted this picture:

I always had a mysterious feeling, when looking at him and hearing him speak, that he was not exactly an ordinary human being of flesh and blood. Rather did he seem as some delicate, ethereal spirit, enveloped for the moment in a semblance of common humanity. . . . His head was small, and beautifully formed; the brow rather low, broad, white, and finely modelled. Dreamy grey eyes, a sensitive mouth, slightly compressed when in repose, but softening into the most beautiful smile when he spoke. He had a slight hesitancy sometimes, when speaking . . . but though Mr. Dodgson deplored it himself, it added a certain piquancy, especially if he was uttering any whimsicality.[6]

The dramatist A. W. Dubourg has recalled him as "a quiet, retiring, scholarlike person, full of interesting and pleasant conversation, oftentimes with an undercurrent of humour, and certainly with a sense of great sensitiveness with regard to the serious side of life."[7]

H. L. Thompson, a friend and colleague, wrote of him as "one of the most delightful of companions, whose keen intellect and playful fancy, united to a guilelessness and purity almost childlike in their simplicity, gave a rare and unique charm to a friendship . . . to be cherished. . . ."[8] The chemist A. S. Russell recounted: "Provided he knew you so that his shyness was not involved, provided you kept your statements and your stories on a high plane, he could be the most genial and welcome of companions, a brilliant talker, quick, witty and entirely without malice."[9] Another colleague, Frederick York Powell, remembered

> the quiet humour of his voice, the occasional laugh. . . . He was not a man that often laughed, though there was often a smile playing about his sensitive mouth. . . . All those that knew him remember . . . his kindly sympathies, his rigid rule of his own life . . . his dutiful discharge of every obligation that was in the slightest degree incumbent on him, his patience with his younger colleagues, who were sometimes a little more ignorant and impatient . . . his rare modesty, and the natural kindness which preserved him from the faintest shadow of conceit, and made him singularly courteous to every one, high or low. . . . He was an exceptionally good after-dinner speaker, but it was rarely one could get him to undertake the unthankful task, and then he would only do it when *inter amicos.* The whimsical thought, the gentle satire, the delicate allusions to the various characteristic ways of his hearers, the pleasant kindness that somehow showed through the veil of the fun, made his few post-prandial orations memorable.[10]

Another Oxford don, Lionel A. Tollemache, recorded two contrasting impressions of Charles's style of conversation. One of Charles's "intimate" friends told him that:

> Of his brilliancy there can be no manner of doubt; but it was at the same time very difficult to define or focus. . . . All he said, all his oddities and clever things, arose out of the conversation . . . of an ordinary everyday sort. . . . It was *Alice,* all kinds of queer turns given to things. You never knew where he would take you next; and all the while there seemed to be an odd logical sequence, almost impelling your assent to most unexpected conclusions. He had a great fund of stories; these again were never told independently, they were fished up from his stores by some line dropped down in ordinary talk. . . . He never told

stories against people, was never bitter or cruel, never attempted to "score off" others.

The other friend, "a man of science," told Tollemache that "Dodgson was not a brilliant talker; he was too peculiar and paradoxical; and the topics on which he loved to dwell were such as would bore many persons; while, on the other hand, when he himself was not interested, he occasionally stopped the flow of a serious discussion by the intrusion of a disconcerting epigram."[11]

T. B. Strong, Student and later Dean of Christ Church, observed Charles at close range and offered still another view:

He talked readily and naturally in connection with what was going on around him; and his power lay, as so often in his books, in suddenly revealing a new meaning in some ordinary expression, or in developing unexpected consequences from a very ordinary idea. . . . Mr. Dodgson was always ready to talk upon serious subjects; and then, though he restrained his sense of humour completely, he still presented you with unexpected and frequently perplexing points of view. If he argued, he was somewhat rigid and precise, carefully examining the terms used, relentless in pointing out the logical results of any position assumed by his opponent, and quick to devise a puzzling case when he wanted to bring objections against a rule or principle.[12]

Charles was an inveterate gadgeteer and, like the White Knight, brimming with his own inventions—except that Charles's worked. He invented his "*in statu quo*" chessboard for use when traveling,[13] and his *Memoria Technica,* as we shall see, was a great advance on the standard memory aids available for learning and remembering dates and formulae.

His inventions were legion: on July 11, 1888, he ordered a writing tablet to use in the dark, which probably led to his inventing the Nyctograph for taking notes under the covers at night. Charles explains in his diary (September 24, 1891): "An inventive day. It has long been a 'desideratum' . . . to be able to make short memoranda in the dark, without the unpleasant necessity of having to get up and strike a light. . . . Today I conceived the idea of having a series of *squares,* cut out in card, and devising an alphabet, of which each letter could be made of lines along the edges of the squares, and dots at the corners. I invented the alphabet, and made the grating of sixteen squares. It works well." He published his discovery in the *Lady* (October 29,

1891): "I do not intend to patent it," he wrote. "Anyone who chooses is welcome to make and sell the article. All I have to do, if I wake and think of something I wish to record, is to draw from under the pillow a small memorandum book, containing my Nyctograph, write a few lines, or even a few pages, without even putting the hands outside the bed-clothes, replace the book, and go to sleep again." Those who have lived in college rooms at Oxford, even in the days after electricity came to the university, will appreciate Charles's preference for remaining under the covers during winter nights. No one, it appears, took up his offer to commercialize his invention; like other inventions of his, it worked well for him, but mere mortals found the instructions too complicated.

He invented card and croquet games, an early form of what we know as Scrabble, a variety of other word games, *Doublets, Syzygies,* games of logic, *Lanrick* and other games that use a chessboard, a game of circular billiards; a rule for finding the day of the week for any date; a means for justifying right margins on a typewriter; a steering device for a velociman, a tricycle; new systems of parliamentary representation; more nearly fair elimination rules for tennis tournaments; an ingenious *Wonderland Postage-Stamp Case;* a new sort of postal money order; rules for reckoning postage; rules for a win in betting; rules for dividing a number by various divisors; a cardboard scale for Common Room, which, held next to a glass, insured the right amount of liqueur for the price paid; a substitute for "gum, for fastening envelopes . . . , mounting small things in books, etc.—viz: paper with gum on *both* sides"[14]; a device for helping a bedridden invalid to read from a book placed sideways; and at least two ciphers. On May 19, 1871, he wrote Macmillan:

> The other day I gave a little dinner-party of 8, and tried an invention of mine. . . . It is simply to draw up a plan of the table, with the names of the guests, in the order in which they are to sit, and brackets to show who is to take in whom; . . . one should be given to each guest. . . .[15]

"Now for the advantages of this plan," Charles wrote:

> (1) It saves the host the worry of going round and telling every gentleman what lady to take in.
> (2) It prevents confusion when they reach the dining-room. (The system of putting names round on the plates simply increases the confusion. . . .)

(3) It enables everybody at table to know who the other guests are—often a *very* desirable thing.

(4) By keeping the cards, one gets materials for making up other dinner-parties, by observing what people harmonise well together.

Charles tirelessly collected gadgets, toys, games, puzzles, and mechanical and technological inventions, for his own use and for the use, delight, and amusement of friends and family. From his youth onward he was an accomplished conjurer, and he added pseudomagical tricks to his repertoire: he could make paper stars, paper boats that sailed, and paper pistols that exploded; he taught children to blot their names in creased paper. He owned a machine for turning music over; six traveling inkpots; artist models of a hand, a foot, a human skull, and the skeleton of a hand and a foot; boxes of mathematical instruments and geometrical solids; a printing press; two Whiteley Exercisers, elastic appliances anchored to the wall and the floor; two pairs of dumbbells; two boxes of homoeopathic medicines; Dr. Moffatt's Ammoniaphone, which claimed to strengthen, enrich, and extend the range of the voice; a mechanical toy called "Bob the Bat" that whirred as it flew about, powered by a wound-up elastic band (once it inadvertently flew out the window, and landed on a bowl of salad a scout was carrying, causing him to drop and shatter it); a mechanical walking furry black bear; cupboards full of music boxes (he sometimes played the music backwards to amuse his friends); an American orguinette, a predecessor of the player piano; numerous Ferrometers, a friend's invention for purifying water. He collected fountain pens and pencil sharpeners; ordered five different sizes of notepaper so as to have the right size for each letter.[16]

On journeys he always took a little black bag full of games, puzzles, medications, and other items that helped break the ice with strangers and assist in an emergency; when he traveled with trunks, he wrapped each article in them separately. Discoveries and inventions fascinated him. On November 24, 1857, he described a means of cataloguing information that anticipated modern-day computers. On January 27, 1867, having heard or read that Charles Babbage had invented a new calculating machine, Charles called on the inventor "to ask whether any of his calculating machines are to be had. I find they are not. He received me most kindly," he added, "and I spent a very pleasant ¾ of an hour with him, while he showed me over his workshops, etc." On April 12 Charles bought "a calculating machine that adds up to £1,000,000." In June 1877 he acquired an "electric pen," recently invented and patented by Edison:

[It] . . . seems to me to be quite the best thing yet invented for taking a number of copies of MSS, drawings, or maps. The "pen" consists of a needle, in a holder like a pencil: the needle is worked in and out with enormous rapidity by electricity [the batteries sat in a container on his desk] and projects just far enough to go through a thin sheet of paper. The result is that every line . . . consists of a row of minute holes. . . . The paper thus prepared (. . . the "stencil") is placed in a frame with blank paper underneath, and an inked roller is passed . . . over it. . . . Copies are easily worked off at the rate of 2 a minute. . . .

On July 30, 1879, Charles recorded that he tried, "with tolerable success, the new copying 'Hektograph,' " and the device appears under its second name, the Chromograph, on August 14 of that year, when Charles did "with the Chromograph a page of a Mod[eration]s Algebra paper." On numerous occasions thereafter he entertained visitors with the duplicating device that relied upon a "master" made of special paper from which copies could be produced either by a spirit or gelatin process.

In May 1888 he acquired an early model of the "Hammond Type-Writer," set to work to improve it, and used it for letter writing and other purposes, not least of all to amuse his child visitors. On August 11, 1890, he recorded that he went to the London exhibition of " 'Edison's Phonograph' . . . a marvellous invention. As heard through the funnel, the *music* (particularly trumpet-music) was flat: the singing and speaking were better, though a little inarticulate." Two days later he returned "to hear the 'private audience' part. Listening through tubes, with the nozzle to one's ear, is far better and more articulate than with the funnel: also the music is much sweeter. It is a pity that we are not fifty years further on in the world's history, so as to get this wonderful invention in its *perfect* form. It is now in its infancy—the new wonder of the day, just as I remember Photography was about 1850."

One of his sisters wrote: "To get rid of mice in his rooms, a square live trap was used, and he had a wood and wire compartment made which fitted on to the trap whose door could then be opened for the mice to run into the compartment, a sliding door shutting them in, and the compartment could then be taken from the trap and put under water; thus all chance of the mice having an agonized struggle on the surface of the water was removed."[17]

Children saw him differently than adults. In adult society, Isa Bowman thought him "almost old-maidenishly prim."[18] But over and over again others testify that when they were children, he was as completely at ease with them as they were with him, that they found him fluent, kind, open-minded, and openhearted. He did not invariably lose his stammer in their presence, as some claim; too many of his child friends testify to the impediment and even describe its precise form. May Barber, a friend at Eastbourne, probably captured it best: "I have seen him a lot with children, and they liked him. But . . . those stammering bouts [were] rather terrifying. It wasn't exactly a stammer, because there was no noise, he just opened his mouth. But there was a wait, a very nervous wait from everybody's point of view: it was very curious. He didn't always have it, but sometimes he did. When he was in the middle of telling a story . . . he'd suddenly stop and you wondered if you'd done anything wrong. Then you looked at him and you knew that you hadn't, it was all right. You got used to it after a bit. He fought it very wonderfully. . . .[19]

T. B. Strong tells us that Charles was a "laborious worker, always disliking to break off from the pursuit of any subject which interested him; apt to forget his meals and toil on for the best part of the night, rather than stop short of the object which he had in view."[20]

He was an indefatigable record keeper. His diary, letter register, photograph register, the register of correspondence when he was Curator of Common Room are only tips of the iceberg. He kept other registers and lists, among them separate lists recording the meals he served guests and offers of hospitality that he might one day take up. "I have a book in which I write the birthdays of my little friends," he wrote (January 24, 1895). An observer remembered that "everything he did was done systematically and tidily. He was fastidious in mind and body. . . . He always appeared to have emerged from a hot bath and a band box."[21] T. B. Strong puts it differently: "He had a deep conviction of the importance of rigid processes of thought and inference. . . . It was clear that he was one man not two, and that in his mind the two elements of whimsical imagination and the love of rigid definition and inference were always present."[22]

When Charles embarked on a journey, even if it was only from Oxford to London or Guildford, he mapped out the route, distance, and time for the various legs of the trip. Then he determined how much money he would need at each stage and put the correct coins in successive pockets of his purse, ready to pay for the railway fare, his cab, his porter, and whatever newspaper, food, or drink he planned to purchase along the way. Beatrice Hatch recalled: "If you went to see Mr. Dodgson in the morning you would find him, pen in hand, hard at work on neat packets of MS. carefully arranged around him on the table, but the pen would instantly be laid aside, and the most cheerful of smiles would welcome you in for a chat as long as you liked to stay. He was always full of interest, and generally had something fresh to show: an ingenious invention of his own for filing papers, or lighting gas, or boiling a kettle!"[23] His niece Violet Dodgson wrote: "The sternest rebuke I ever received from him . . . was for leaving an open book face downwards on a chair."[24] His compulsive orderliness obviously reached into others' lives, sometimes officiously. Early on he set himself the task of bringing up to date scrapbooks of newspaper cuttings in Common Room; he supplied Common Room with blank albums and inserted loose Common Room photographs in them. He wrote in the suggestion book of the Oxford Union's library a note on how better to arrange the Union's books.[25] On January 27, 1865, he wrote to the manager of Covent Garden suggesting how to improve the arrival and departure of carriages at performances. He was troubled while seeing the play *Claudian* when a character was thrown off a bridge but his fall was not accompanied by an audible splash. He immediately wrote (May 12, 1884) to the leading man, Wilson Barrett, suggesting that "a little bit of realism . . . would be very welcome" and drawing a sketch of a "barrel half full of water," adding that "a stick ending like that in a churn, plunged into the water at the right moment, would I think produce the effect. . . ." After arriving at the Tom Taylors' before breakfast (October 3, 1863) to make their home his photographic headquarters for some days, Charles had the temerity to mention "a few little defects in [Taylor's play] *The Ticket-of-Leave Man*—two of them arithmetical ones: that Sam continues fifteen years old for nearly three years, and that May Edwards during that time appears to have saved two pounds at the rate of a shilling a week!"

Other eccentricities dominated his personality. He had his own way of making tea: Isa Bowman recalls him walking up and down his sitting room swaying the teapot to and fro for precisely ten minutes in order to achieve the desired brew.

Eating and drinking play an important role in the *Alice* books, just as they did in Victorian society. Charles was ever conscious of his child friends' needs, but he himself survived on simple food and small portions. He abjured midday meals: "Even when I *have* time," he wrote to Mrs. Mayhew (December 19, 1878), "I always decline luncheons. I have no appetite for a meal at that time, and you will perhaps sympathise with my dislike for sitting to watch others eat and drink." Planning a theater outing for three of his child friends, he wrote to the grown-up Ethel Hatch in London (October 25, 1897) inviting her to join them: "Could you give . . . the 3 girls . . . something to eat before we go? To be *very* hungry lessens one's enjoyment of a play." About to pay a visit to the headmaster of Marlborough School, he wrote (November 13, 1882): "*Please* don't make any difference, for me, in your family bill of fare. Dinner parties have too many courses for me. Even our daily High Table is much more than *I* care for."

Expecting Polly Mallalieu to come to stay at Eastbourne, Charles wrote to her mother ( July 5, 1892) detailing his

usual plan for meals when I have a child-guest. . . . Breakfast at 8-½. I have tea or coffee: Polly can have cocoa. . . . I always have meat or fish; and, when a child is with me, there is usually *jam*. . . . Luncheon about 1-½. This is *dinner* for my guest (i.e., 2 courses, meat and sweets). Polly could have ginger beer, or milk, to drink with it. . . . Tea about 5. (Cocoa for Polly.) . . . My dinner is about 7. My child-guest usually helps me with it (having, in fact, *two* dinners a day). . . . I have nothing more but milk and water and biscuits, about 10. But more could be provided, if necessary.

Charles took walks, alone and with companions. Evelyn Hatch wrote: "Walks were the special privilege of little-girl friends and he preferred to take only one at a time, considering 'three the worst possible number for a party.' During the walk he entertained his small guest with stories, riddles and jokes. . . ."[26] On July 9, 1865, at thirty-three, he recorded "a walk of twenty-one or twenty-two miles." On February 12, 1887, aged fifty-five, he took "a 25-mile walk." On March 17, 1888, he reassured a distant relative: "So long as I have the blessing of perfect health, as I have now, it is most enjoyable to take a rapid walk, in the teeth of the North or East wind. I don't mind which it is—the colder it blows, the warmer I get and the more I like it."[27] On July 29, 1897, aged sixty-five, he walked over to Hastings from Eastbourne: "altogether about twenty miles walking. I was hardly at all tired and not at all foot sore." And two days later: "Again walked over to Hastings . . . in five hours and twenty-two minutes."

"L.C. used to take me out for walks," wrote Mrs. E. L. Shute. ". . . By all the laws of right and justice, *I* should have walked with my 'good' ear to him; but no! His 'bad' ear was also the right one, and if I managed for a little to dodge round and get on the side I wanted, he always circumvented me, and it would end in my giving up the struggle, and returning home with a crick in my neck from twisting my head round to bring my hearing ear into play. . . . The walks were well worth the cricks!"[28]

Charles did not smoke and a child friend reported that he "used to say that he spent . . . [on photography] what other men spent on smoking."[29] An Oxford colleague recorded that when Thomas Gibson Bowles, editor of *Vanity Fair,* was staying with Charles at Christ Church and asked whether he might have a pipe, Charles replied, "You know that I don't allow smoking here. If I had known that you wanted to smoke, I would have ordered the Common Room Smoking Room to be got ready for you."[30] Although Charles was certainly capable of a testy remark, such rudeness was not really true to his character, and his own utterances on the subject belie the colleague's allegation. On October 14, 1890, he sent over to Common Room some cigarette samples and inquired whether the Smoking Room Committee would like to order more: "I have never tasted better!" And he wrote to the dramatist Henry Savile Clarke (November 12, 1886): "If you give me the pleasure of seeing you here, please bring the wherewithal for smoking with you. I'm not a smoker myself, but I always allow my friends to smoke in my rooms."[31]

Christopher Hussey, who occupied Charles's rooms some years later, wrote about their atmosphere in Charles's time, as reported to him by T. B. Strong, who remembered Charles's

horror of draughts. . . . The [large sitting] room is a draughty one, as it has four doors. . . . His theory was that there could be no draughts if the temperature was equalized all over the room. Accordingly he had a number of thermometers about the room, and near each one an oil stove. Periodically he made a round of the thermometers, adjusting the adjacent stove according to the reading. All cracks under doors were boarded up with coats, rugs, etc. . . . He had a very elaborate gazolier hanging from the ceiling, and elaborate instructions for lighting it pasted on the door of his room, though I gather he allowed no one to light it but himself.[32]

Seeing Charles in the pulpit as he struggled with his ideas and against his infirmities must have been memorable. "Undergraduates flocked to hear him . . . ," Michael Sadler, Christ Church Steward, wrote. "He wept when he came to the more serious parts of the sermons."[33] Claude M. Blagden, later Bishop of Peterborough, recalled that when Charles was to preach at St. Mary's, "word was passed round the University . . . and the church was

thronged, but those who expected fireworks were doomed to disappointment. What they did hear was a plain, evangelical sermon of the old-
fashioned kind. . . ."[34] Gertrude Corrie, who summarized the sermon that
Charles preached in Oxford on January 2, 1886, also recorded her impression
of him: "We liked him immensely; he has a fine face, especially profile . . . a
sweet face, seen full. He began without a text, saying how the service had altered in fifty years, and the danger of our coming for what we got—outside
accessories—for people spoke of liking and enjoying, just as if it were a musical act, or the opera. . . . We were to look on him as a fellow wanderer in
the garden—a fellow traveller hoping for light. . . ."[35]

"His sermons were picturesque in style," wrote T. B. Strong, "and strongly
emotional. . . . They came from real and sincere devotion: he delivered them
slowly and carefully, and he held his audience."[36] When Charles died, H. L.
Thompson wrote: "Some will remember his sermon at St. Mary's last Lent
Term; the erect, gray-haired figure, with the rapt look of earnest thought;
the slow, almost hesitating speech; the clear and faultless language; the intense solemnity and earnestness which compelled his audience to listen for
nearly an hour, as he spoke to them of the duty of reverence, and warned
them of the sin of talking carelessly of holy things."[37]

"He has often told me that he never wrote out his sermons," Beatrice
Hatch remembered. "He knew exactly what he wished to say, and completely forgot his audience in his anxiety to explain his point clearly. He
thought of the subject only, and the words came of themselves. Looking
straight in front of him he saw, as it were, his argument mapped out in the
form of a diagram, and he set to work to prove it point by point, under its
separate heads, and then summed up the whole."[38]

May Barber accompanied him to some of his sermons: "I think for him
to go and preach was a very plucky thing to do. . . . He liked to take somebody with him and put them in the back seat of the church, and then, walking home, you had to tell him what you remembered of the sermon."[39]

Howard Hopley, Vicar of Westham, Hastings, recalled that on the Sunday that Charles preached in his church, "our grand old church was
crowded, and, although our villagers are mostly agricultural labourers, yet
they breathlessly listened to a sermon forty minutes long, and apparently
took in every word of it. It was quite extempore, in very simple words, and
illustrated by some delightful and most touching stories of children."[40]

When Derek Hudson was working on his life of Charles, he spoke to an
old man at Guildford "who used to sit in the choir when . . . [Charles]

preached there. He told me," wrote Hudson, "that the choir-boys were rather sorry when Mr. Dodgson preached because he took such a long time about it. And he added that he was 'the most terribly thin-looking man he had ever seen. He looked as if he could have done with a good dinner.' "[41] Collingwood emphasized his uncle's "shy and sensitive nature";[42] T. B. Strong insisted that Charles's "ministry was seriously hindered by native shyness";[43] H. A. L. Fisher, Warden of New College, wrote that his "intense shyness and morbid dislike of publicity made him a figure apart";[44] and Mark Twain, meeting Charles at the MacDonalds (July 26, 1879), found him "only interesting to look at, for he was the stillest and shyest full-grown man I have ever met except 'Uncle Remus.' "[45] A good many of Charles's child friends concurred. "With grown-ups he was shy," wrote Enid Stevens, ". . . he was obviously terrified of my mamma."[46] And he himself made the point from time to time: "If people are shy with me, I generally feel so too" he wrote Mrs. Rix (June 7, 1885). Inviting a young friend to dine with three other young ladies in his rooms at Christ Church, he wrote (May 24, 1882): "Do come as soon as you can. I will begin to expect you about 6-½. Then I shall have time to get over the shyness produced by meeting so many ladies at once." "It always makes me a *little* shy to have to talk with several people (strangers) looking on and listening, and I feel obliged to keep to the most *general* topics of ordinary 'small-talk,' of which material my supply *soon* comes to an end," he explained to Mrs. Stevens (May 4, 1891) after she threw him in with a group of her lady friends. ". . . And I was made *doubly* shy by your beginning to talk about my 'books'! I am quite sure you had not the least idea how I *hate* having my books, or myself, *en évidence* in the presence of strangers."

Indulging in a double standard, as he did, did not trouble him. He disliked having uninvited visitors show up at his door but defended his right to make unannounced calls on others. Consider, too, his attitude about giving and collecting autographs. His photograph albums were his special art treasure, and when he deemed a photograph worth including, he trimmed and mounted it artistically, found for some an appropriate literary quotation or legend to help the viewer grasp his dramatic intent, and often, especially with portraits, had the sitter autograph the page the portrait appeared on. He also solicited autographs for child friends. He captured one from "*the* Kate Terry" for Lily MacDonald (May 19, 1868); he sent one of Tenniel for a friend of a friend (June 12, 1876); he got Liddon and Ruskin to sign a child friend's autograph book (November 11, 1883); and Ellen Terry obliged him by sending autographs and notes to any number of child friends (October 30, 1885). On July 14, 1893, he sent one young friend sixteen autographs.

But he staunchly objected to giving his own autograph to anyone. On May 11, 1883, he pleaded with Mrs. C. A. Heurtley, the wife of a professor of divinity, not to give away any "specimen of my handwriting" and explained: "My constant aim is to remain, *personally*, unknown to the world; consequently I have always refused applications for photographs or autographs, as my features and handwriting belong to me as a private individual—and I often beg even my own private friends, who possess one or the other, *not* to put them into albums where strangers can see them."[47]

He was relentless in adding to his own collection photographs of the famous and the attractive, but he adamantly refused to give his own photograph. He had many photographs of himself taken and gave them to cherished friends, but he refused to send any to casual acquaintances or collectors. He confesses to a friend (December 10, 1881) that "I so much *hate* the idea of strangers being able to know me by sight that I refuse to give my photo. . . ."

He set his sights even beyond the famous in the art world, the theater, and letters: he tried to snare aristocrats and, to a degree, succeeded. He was less successful with royalty. We know that he managed interviews with the Prince of Wales and succeeded in photographing Queen Victoria's youngest son and the Crown Prince of Denmark. During a visit to Hatfield House he encountered the Duke of Albany's widow and her two children and pursued them for years through their governor. He got within striking distance of the Queen at the deanery in December 1860 and recorded that Lady A. Stanley, wife of the Dean of Westminster and Resident Bedchamber Woman to the Queen, "has shown my photographs to the Queen, and is commanded to say that 'Her Majesty admires them very much.' " But the Queen chose not to keep any. He sent Princess Beatrice, the Queen's youngest daughter, a specially bound presentation copy of *Alice;* and once, when walking in Windsor Park ( July 1, 1865), he "met the Queen driving in an open carriage" and fancied that he "got a bow from her all to myself."

Charles never made it to either Buckingham Palace or Windsor Castle, but on two separate occasions at least, he wittily feigned acquaintance with the Queen in letters to child friends. Replying to Maggie Cunnynghame (April 7, 1868), who had requested a better photograph of himself, he wrote: "How *can* you ask for a better one of me than the one I sent! It is one of the best ever done! Such grace, such dignity, such benevolence, such ——— as a great secret (please don't repeat it) the Queen sent to ask for a copy of it, but . . . [I was obliged to answer:] 'Mr. Dodgson presents his compliments to Her Majesty, and regrets to say that his rule is never to give his photograph except to *young* ladies.' I am told she was annoyed about it, and said, 'I'm not so old as all that comes to.' " He also composed a fake letter from the Queen inviting him to a garden party and sent it to the three Drury sisters, but, alas, the idea, while amusing, was all air.

Although he lionized the great and the desirable, he resented any efforts to lionize him. "Perhaps your book of poetry has not brought on you all the annoyances of one who, having been unlucky enough to perpetrate two small books for children, has been bullied ever since by the herd of lion-hunters who seek to drag him out of the privacy he hoped an 'anonym' would give him," he wrote to a friend (December 10, 1881). "I have had to keep a printed form ready, and constantly use it, in answer to such people, stating that I acknowledge *no* connection with books not bearing my name," he wrote (August 17, 1892). The printed form is *The Stranger Circular,* copies of which he had printed in 1890:

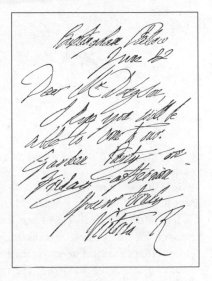

*Charles's fake letter from Queen Victoria purporting to invite him to a garden party, which he sent to the Drury sisters, whom he had met on a railway journey*

> Mr. Dodgson is so frequently addressed by strangers on the quite unauthorised assumption that he claims, or at any rate acknowledges the authorship of books not published under his name, that he has found it necessary to print this, once for all, as an answer to all such applications. He neither claims nor acknowledges any connection with any pseudonym, or with any book that is not published under his own name. Having therefore no claim to retain, or even to read the enclosed, he returns it for the convenience of the writer who has thus misaddressed it.

*Believe me, dear Madam,*
*faithfully yours,*
*C. L. Dodgson*
*[alias "Lewis Carroll"]*

*A rare instance*
*when Charles*
*signed both his*
*real name and his*
*pseudonym to a*
*letter*

But Charles's efforts to keep his two identities separate were motivated by more than his wish for privacy. He realized that if the world knew that Charles Dodgson and Lewis Carroll were one, professional pundits might shrug off his mathematical works; indeed some reviews of his serious books fell into that superficial mode when the writers linked the two names.

Other inconsistencies arose. He vented his displeasure (April 16, 1855) over an editor who had taken liberties in interpolating Euclid, insisting that no editor had the right "to *mangle* the original writer. . . ." But in a letter to his sister Mary (August 23, 1854), he advised her to improve a poem by William Cullen Bryant by altering a line before writing it into the family magazine. Even more remarkable, he repeatedly advised Ellen Terry and Henry Irving to modify passages in Shakespeare to improve both the material and their stage performance. He also put in train the idea of publishing an expurgated Shakespeare for girls, not content with available texts.

He drew caricatures of himself, one depicting what he looked like when he lectured, his hand over his mouth;[48] another showing a gross creature eating a whole plum pudding;[49] a third, after he had made friends with a real live princess at Hatfield House, showing his head held so high that he would not be able to see his correspondent were they to meet (see page 477). He composed verbal portraits of himself too. "Are you gradually making up your mind to the catastrophe of a call from me?" he wrote (March 5, 1877) to a new friend who has sent him a fan letter. "For I really think you will see me some day soon. Please picture to yourself a tallish man (about 6 feet 4 inches), very fat, with a long white beard, a bald head and a very red face—and then, when you see me you will be agreeably disappointed." Yet, when he caught Isa Bowman, to whom he sent the raised-head sketch, making a caricature of him, he flushed, snatched up her drawing, and tore it to bits.[50]

In his prime he was an agreeable social creature, attending all sorts of public events, traveling hither and thither to the homes of mere acquaintances, attending dinner parties. As time went by, however, he grew more restrictive, more particular, even irascible. One of his young friends reported that he "disliked parties, especially dinner-parties—'bandying small talk with dull people' was his description of them—and if he did not talk it was not from shyness but from boredom."[51] In early years he was happy to give tea and take it with friends; later he grew to abhor it as "that unwholesome drug" (April 29, 1880). He decided to shun dinner parties altogether, but before he did (May 30, 1882), dining at his friends the Faussetts', during "a good part of the evening, I read *The Times*, while the party played a round game of spelling words—a thing I will never join in: rational conversation and *good music*, are the only things which, to me, seem worth meeting for. . . ." But he enjoyed parties at Hatfield House and sat up until one in the morning talking to fellow guests in the smoking room.

"*No carte has yet been done of me that does real justice to my smile,*" *Charles wrote in 1868 to his child friend Maggie Cunnynghame,* "*and so I hardly like, you see, to send you one. . . . Meanwhile, I send a little thing to give you an idea of what I look like when I'm lecturing. The merest sketch, you will allow—yet still I think there's something grand in the expression of the brow and in the action of the hand.*"

He certainly shied away from parties where there was a danger of his being lionized, and as he grew older, he shunned groups of people and came to prefer individuals. "Please let me know if you are one of the ladies who are 'At Home' on a fixed day each week," he asked Mrs. Henderson (April 12, 1891), ". . . that we may *avoid* such a day!" On April 30, 1881, writing to the editor of the *St. James's*

*Charles's drawing of "a whole plum-pudding" in a letter to Edith Blakemore. "And what do you think I am going to have for my birthday treat?" Charles wrote. "A whole plum-pudding! It is to be about the size for four people to eat: and I shall eat it in my room, all by myself! The doctor says he is 'afraid I shall be ill'; but I simply say 'Nonsense!'"*

*Gazette* on "The Purity of Elections," Charles dreamed publicly of a utopia without dinner parties. On November 18, 1881, he dined with the Bonamy Prices: "An excellent host," Charles observed, "but the noise was too great for comfort. I weary more and more of dinner-parties and rejoice that people have almost ceased to invite me." He then begins to decline "all visits, parties, etc." (June 26, 1887).

Not quite all, however, for, as he wrote to the novelist Anne Isabella Thackeray (October 24, 1887), "every law has its exceptions." He continued calling on some friends and giving his special brand of dinner parties, but almost unconditionally rejected invitations. He even resisted the lure of Hatfield House, but, as he explained to Lord Salisbury (June 7, 1897), he was not cutting himself off from the Cecils: "Although I was boorish enough to decline . . . Lady Salisbury's last kind invitation to Hatfield, yet I do not consider communications with your family to have *ceased.* I still occasionally venture to appear in Arlington Street [the Cecils' London home] and I *frequently* take advantage of the always-ready hospitality which [Lady] Maud [the Cecil daughter married to the Earl of Selborne] provides, for me and any friend I happen to bring, in Mount Street. Once, not long ago, she gave luncheon, on *four* consecutive Saturdays, to me, her *old* friend, and to a new *young* friend each time!"

He was tightly bound up in Victorian values and decidedly class-conscious. Recounting to his brother Edwin an extraordinary backstage visit at the Haymarket Theatre to watch a group of child actors prepare for a performance, he wrote (March 11, 1867): "There was not much real beauty [in the little actresses], but 2 or 3 of them would have been much admired, I think, if they had been born in higher stations in life." Commenting to Miss Thomson (January 24, 1879) on some draft sketches she had sent him, he objected to "the diameter of the knee and ankle" of one of the children she had drawn. "Still," he added, "you *may* have got those dimensions from real life, but in that case I think your model must have been a country-peasant child, descended from generations of labourers: there is a marked difference between them and the upper classes—especially as to the size of the ankle." Again he wrote Miss Thomson (September 27, 1893), after the Moberly Bells (Mrs. C. F. Moberly Bell was Gertrude Chataway's older sister) agreed to allow her to use their children as models, asking her "to put them into a few pretty attitudes, and make a few hasty *sketches* of them. . . . These you could *finish*," he added, "with the help of hired models. But hired models," he insisted, "are plebeian and *heavy;* and they have thick ankles, which I do *not* agree with you in admiring. *Do* sketch these two upper-class children. One doesn't get such an opportunity every day!"

On September 29, 1881, Charles made a new child friend on the beach, one Julia Johnstone, "who proved very pleasant and quite free of shyness. . . . The mother is pleasant, but hardly looks a lady. I fancy the father is in business . . . but of course I shall not drop her acquaintance for that." Weighing the wisdom of publishing a cheap edition of *Alice,* he concluded (March 4, 1887) to Edith Nash: "It isn't a book *poor* children would much care for." And writing to a lady friend in Oxford from Eastbourne, he complained (July 27, 1890): "The children on the beach are not the right sort, *yet.* They *are* a vulgar-looking lot! I should think there's hardly any one here, yet, above the 'small shop keeper' rank."

On the day after telling an assembly of fifty or sixty girls "Bruno's Picnic" and other stories at a school where Beatrice Hatch was teaching, he wrote her (February 16, 1894): "I should like to know . . . who that sweet-looking girl was, aged 12, with a red nightcap. . . . She was speaking to you when I came up to wish you good-night. I fear I must be content with her *name* only," he added; "the social gulf between us is probably too wide for it to be wise to make *friends.* Some of my little *actress*-friends are of a *rather* lower status than myself. But, below a certain line, it is hardly wise to let a girl have a 'gentleman' friend—even one of 62!"

Insensitive in some social situations, he could also be rude, rigid, and off-putting. His niece Violet Dodgson reported that "many . . . found him difficult, exacting, and uncompromising in business matters and in college life." And, she continued, he "had undoubtedly his foibles. For instance . . . he had a disconcerting way (on becoming aware that the informal tea which he was settling down to enjoy was a real *party,* with people invited to meet him) of rising and departing with polite but abrupt excuses, leaving an embarrassed hostess and a niece murmuring scared apologies."[52] On July 25, 1891, he preached to the mother of a child friend about the syntax of her letters. After he gave a firm permission to produce a *Looking-Glass* biscuit tin and they undertook to send the tins to the hundreds of names and addresses he provided, he complained (September 7, 1892) about an advertisement pasted inside the tins: "What is an even greater annoyance to me, and a more unwarrantable liberty, they have [made] me responsible, not only for the vulgarity of a piece of bad English, but also for being the sender of 'kind regards' to my friends. There is not a single one, on the whole list I sent you, to whom I should dream of sending such a message."

He frequently wrote stinging letters of complaint: letters to the Steward of Christ Church were often officious and, alas for Charles, sometimes make him sound ridiculous. On February 7, 1881, "devoured . . . with anxiety for the fate of a paper parcel" he had sent by messenger, he suggested that Christ Church provide its messengers with waterproof capes with high collars and "for the security of our letters and parcels" a set of deep baskets with waterproof covers. On November 19, 1886, he protested that more milk than he had ordered arrived each morning at his door; on December 11 he was troubled by the outbreak of a fire in the scout's chimney: "The Scout here, and his assistant, are, I should think, stupid enough and forgetful enough to cause *any* amount of accident," he wrote. On February 13, 1887, he detected "a dangerous effluvium, caused by some defect of drainage, arising from somewhere under the Scout's room"; on March 28 he requested that the scout engage a competent assistant: "I have suffered so much, in breakage of glass and china from the clumsiness of the last assistant. . . ." On April 14 he wrote for a colleague and himself because they had agreed that

it is about time to make a formal representation to you as to the very inferior cookery now prevalent. During the last 10 days or so, we have had

(a) Beefsteak almost too tough to eat.

(b) Mashed potatoes that were a mere sop.

(c) Portugal onions quite underboiled and uneatable.

(d) . . . Baked apple-dumplings. Their idea of that dish seems to be this: "take some apples: wrap each in the thinnest possible piece of pastry: bake till nearly black, so as to produce the consistency of—say pasteboard."

(e) Cauliflowers are always sent with no part soft enough to eat except the top of the flowers. . . .

(f) Potatoes (boiled) are *never* "mealy," as cooked here.

On February 27, 1888, he worried about the arrangement of bells summoning the porter in case of need or in an emergency; on April 19 he recommended a Ferrometer for Christ Church water closets; on December 23, 1889, he objected to the messengers clearing the postbox before the appointed time, not allowing for last-minute additions; and on February 24, 1890, he insisted that the messenger did not pick up the post on time. On April 13, 1891, he wrote: "On Saturday morning, just after I had got out of bed, a ladder was reared against the bedroom window, and a man came up

*Charles's drawing of a basket for delivering the post, in a letter to the Steward of Christ Church. "Devoured as I am with anxiety for the fate of a paper parcel I sent by a messenger this morning," Charles wrote, "which I fear will arrive wet through . . . it occurs to me to suggest . . . [that you] provide for our Messengers . . . a set of deep baskets . . . with water-proof covers."*

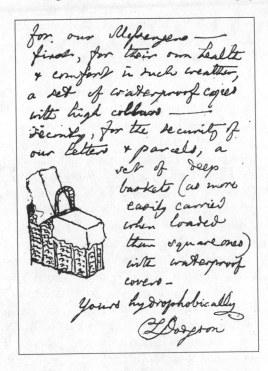

to clean it. As I object to performing my toilet with a man at the window, I sent him down again, telling him 'You are not to clean it now,' meaning, of course, that *that* window was to be left till I was dressed. [But] . . . they went away, and have not returned. So the bedroom-window, the 2 windows of the sitting-room, and the window of the pantry, are not yet cleaned. . . ."

Mind you, his fastidiousness stood Christ Church in good stead during his more than nine years as Curator of Senior Common Room. He kept efficient records, conducted business on an impersonal, professional level, established a wine committee, held wine tastings, expanded the wine cellars, and filled them with valuable vintages to slake the dons' thirst for many years to come. The acerbic tone of his letters to merchants arose from his desire to maintain proper relationships with them and to schoolmaster their behavior. His stern need for privacy provoked a third-person letter to one vintner: "Mr. Dodgson . . . understands . . . that . . . wine-merchants . . . are in the habit of calling periodically on the Curator. This practice he hopes he may, without giving offence, request may be discontinued."

His search for information about wine and determination to maintain decorum often merged. In deciding to shift some sherry to another location, Charles asked whether the move would harm the wine, and if not, how long it would take the wine to settle and be drinkable after the move. On November 25, 1888, he sought advice from a wine merchant about the most effective way to use port of different vintages. On December 24, 1889, he wrote a rather un-Christmaslike letter to Messrs. Snow and Company: "Mr. Dodgson has given directions to return to Messrs. Snow the box of Portugal fruit. . . . He would have thought it hardly necessary to point out that the Curator, whose duty it is to try to procure the *best* goods he can for Common Room, cannot possibly accept *presents* from any of the tradespeople concerned. . . . He thinks it only fair to warn Messrs. Snow that any repetition of such attentions may seriously affect their position as Wine-merchants dealt with by Common Room."

Charles's relationship with his publisher, Macmillan, has provoked a good deal of comment, almost all unfavorable to the author, declaring him compulsively fussy and obdurate, and picturing the publisher as long-suffering. But just as the myth about Charles's relationship with Tenniel vanishes before the evidence, so do these accusations. True, Charles made incessant and uncompromising demands upon the publisher. He was, particularly in the production of his books, a perfectionist who wanted his readers to have the finest possible quality he could provide. Not only did he require Macmillan to suppress the first edition of *Alice* in 1865, but in 1886 he also instructed him to dispose of an inferior edition of *The Game of Logic.* In 1889 he condemned the entire first run of ten thousand copies of *The Nursery "Alice"* because, as he wrote Macmillan (June 23, 1889), the pictures "vulgarise the whole thing"; and in 1893, when he found that a later run (the sixtieth thousand) of *Looking-Glass* had come from the presses with the illustrations not well printed, he ordered Macmillan to scuttle them as well.

In condemning Charles, however, critics overlook his role as sole provider. He, not Macmillan, paid for all production costs: he paid the illustrator, the engraver, the printer; he paid for advertising. While his books bear the Macmillan imprint, Macmillan functioned more like contractor and distributor than publisher, and in a complete reversal of what we would expect of a publisher-author arrangement today, Macmillan got a 10 percent commission on sales and transmitted the balance to Charles. Publishing a book involved a huge investment of capital for an Oxford don and, given Charles's uncompromising standards, made for an almost endless exchange of correspondence and some acerbity.

Some of Charles's least attractive behavior occurred in response to what he considered violations of religious rectitude. According to Ethel Arnold, his "sense of humour . . . failed absolutely when any allusion to the Bible, however innocuous, was involved. The patriarchs, the prophets, major and minor, were as sacrosanct in his eyes as any of the great figures of the New Testament; and a disrespectful allusion to Noah or even to Nebuchadnezzar would have shocked and displeased him quite as much as any implied belittlement of St. Paul. . . . I shall never forget the snub administered to one unfortunate acquaintance . . . who ventured to tell him . . . [a story] which, in his opinion, treated religious matters with levity."

In early May 1887 Charles heard the Bishop of Ripon, William Boyd Carpenter, deliver the Bampton Lectures at Oxford. At one point Carpenter employed the analogy "of a domestic quarrel, wherein you find the father and mother in absolute antagonism to each other upon the origin of the passionate nature of their child, and each says to the other, 'This is the fault of that terrible temper which you know belongs to *your* family.' " Charles reacted instantaneously and sent Carpenter a rebuke (May 8): "I write, as one of the large University congregation who listened this morning to the Bampton Lecture, to make one single remark—that I feel very sure that the 2 or 3 sentences in it, which were distinctly *amusing* (and of which *one* raised a general laugh) went too far to undo, in the minds of many of your hearers, and specially among the *young* men, much of the good effect of the rest of the sermon. Feeling profoundly (as who can fail to do?) what enormous powers have been given to your Lordship for influencing large bodies of men, I feel an equally profound regret that anything should occur likely to lessen their influence for good."[53]

In the mid-1880s Charles conducted a friendly transatlantic correspondence with the editors of a student newspaper called *Jabberwock* at the Boston Latin School for Girls. The editors looked upon Charles as a special friend, a sort of patron, and sent him copies of their paper, to which he contributed a three-stanza verse entitled "A Lesson in Latin." But then he received a copy of their paper that contained a limerick ascribed to a Unitarian minister:

> There was an old deacon of Lynn,
> Who confessed he was given to sin,
>   When they said, "Yes, you are,"
>   Oh, how he did swear!
> That angry old deacon of Lynn.

Again Charles reacted instantaneously and, as the girls' newspaper reported, "he sat down and with a quill of wrath stopped the *Jabberwock* once for all, saying that he never wanted to see a copy again, and that he was deeply disappointed that the young editors could allow anything in their columns which made light of so solemn a subject as the confession of sin!"[54]

He even wrote to the Duchess of Albany on July 1, 1889, about some remark one of her children made "on a scene in the life of Our Lord—a remark which . . . gave a humorous turn to the passage. . . . Is it not a cruelty (however unintentionally done)," he asked, "to tell any one an amusing story of that sort, which will be for ever linked, in his or her memory, with the Bible words, and which *may* have the effect, just when those words are most needed, for comfort in sorrow, or for strength in temptation, or for light in 'the valley of the shadow of death,' of robbing them of all their sacredness and spoiling all their beauty?"

He dealt mercilessly with the parents of a twelve-year-old actress friend, Polly Mallalieu, who visited him at Eastbourne in June 1891. When he measured the child's height, she reported that her parents insisted that she was an inch shorter than she actually was in order to secure acting engagements for her. Charles wrote accusing the parents of committing "a sin in God's sight" and of teaching the child "to think lightly of sin."

Did his role as minister enable him to sit in judgment on the actions of others and to intrude so blatantly into other people's lives? The answer is probably complex. He had a fiercely religious cast of mind, a faith worked out by his own stern rules of logic. To compromise it in any way would have been to abandon it altogether and to find himself in a spiritual desert. His devotion to the rigid laws of logic led to a rigid, uncompromising set of rules that governed his life and spilled over into the lives of others. The fixed rules were essential, too, for him to enjoy the friendship of children with a free conscience. Surely he knew that his uncompromising approach pained others, despite his effusive apologies, disclaimers, and sympathetic language. But he had to turn a blind eye to the hurt he caused: his obdurate principles had to prevail at all cost.

On more than one occasion Charles stalked out of a theater in the middle of a performance because the playwright had violated his idea of religious sanctity. He also wrote about occasions when stage performances offended his conscience. In his essay "The Stage and the Spirit of Reverence," he takes W. S. Gilbert to task for violating the principles he holds sacred: "Mr. Gilbert . . . seems to have a craze for making bishops and clergymen contemptible." He had seen *H.M.S. Pinafore,* with a considerable cast of youngsters, and, as he puts it, "as performed by *children,* one passage in it was to me sad beyond words. It occurs when the captain utters the oath 'Damn me!' and forthwith a bevy of sweet innocent-looking little girls sing, with bright, happy looks, the chorus 'He said "Damn me!" He said "Damn me!" ' I cannot find words to convey . . . the pain I felt in seeing those dear children taught to utter such words to amuse ears grown callous to their ghastly meaning."

His criticism once offended Ellen Terry:

> Mr. Dodgson . . . once brought a little girl to see me in *Faust.* He wrote and told me that she had said (where Margaret begins to un- dress): "Where is it going to stop?" and that perhaps in consideration of the fact that it could affect a mere child disagreeably, I ought to alter my business! . . . I had known dear Mr. Dodgson for years and years. He was as fond of me as he could be of any one over the age of ten, but I was *furious.* "I thought you only knew *nice* children," was all the an- swer I gave him. "It would have seemed to me awful for a *child* to see harm where harm is; how much more when she sees it where harm is not." . . . But I felt ashamed and shy whenever I played that scene.[55]

The actress's generosity enabled their friendship to survive. In fact, she, through the years, was extremely kind to Charles. At his behest, she gave elocution lessons to at least one of his child friends, procured walk-on parts for others, provided him and his child friends with choice theater seats. Charles was, of course, enchanted by the mystique of the theater and the people connected with it, but in the early years, he idolized Ellen Terry above all. For him, she personified the theater itself, and he worshiped her as his thespian goddess. His diaries contain eighty-three entries about her. He saw virtually every play she acted in and frequently went backstage to visit her.

Then, suddenly, a dramatic change occurred. All at once, no visits are recorded, no letters exchanged. The cause of the abrupt cooling off was Ellen Terry's private life. In 1868 Charles learned that she had left her hus- band, G. F. Watts, and gone to live, out of wedlock, with Edwin Godwin, an architect, by whom in time she bore two children. Charles broke with her completely and for almost twelve years shunned her. "I felt that she had [so] entirely sacrificed her position that I had no desire but to drop her acquain- tance," he wrote (April 12, 1894). Then, when Godwin abandoned Miss

Terry and their two children and she married in 1877 the actor C. C. Wardell (stage name Charles Kelly), Charles sought her out again. "It was a most generous act, I think, [for Mr. Wardell] to marry a woman with such a history," Charles wrote. In any case, she was again a true wife in Charles's eyes, and he could resume the friendship.

Gone, however, was the old adulation; she was still a tainted woman. In 1894 the nineteen-year-old Dolly Baird confided to him that she wanted to try the stage. Charles wanted to help, and he knew that Miss Terry would take an interest in Dolly if he requested it. But, in person and in a letter he sent Dolly's mother (April 12, 1894), he warned Dolly's parents about Miss Terry's past. Mrs. Baird was less censorious and allowed Charles to appeal to the actress on behalf of her daughter, and Dolly, with Ellen Terry's help, went on to become a leading West End actress.[56]

Charles's uncompromising moral stance, his harsh judgments of others, his occasional priggishness would be even more objectionable were it not leavened by sincere and abject humility and extraordinary generosity. We have seen that even as a young man, as he approached his twenty-fourth birthday, he yearned to shake off all pride and selfishness. On August 6, 1865, he preached at Croft on "*self-sacrifice*." In a letter to Ellen Terry on March 20, 1883, he thanked her for her kindness to one of his protégées: "I think you have learned a piece of philosophy which many never learn in a long life—that, while it is hopelessly difficult to secure *for oneself* even the smallest bit of happiness, and the more trouble we take the more certain we are to fail, there is nothing so easy as to secure it *for somebody else*. . . ."

He wrote to Edith Rix (July 29, 1885): "May you treat me as a perfect friend, and write anything you like to me, and ask my advice? Why, *of course* you may, my child! What else am I good for? But oh, my dear child-friend, you cannot guess how such words sound to *me!* That any one should look up to *me,* or think of asking *my* advice—well, it makes one feel humble . . . rather than proud—humble to remember, while others think so well of me, what I really *am* in myself. 'Thou, that teachest another, teaches thou not thyself?' . . . Anyhow, I like to *have* the love of my child-friends, though I know I don't deserve it."

His generosity was boundless. One child friend recalled that during a London outing she and Charles were in a pastry shop buying some cakes when Charles noticed "a small crowd of little ragamuffins . . . assembled" outside staring hungrily through the window at the cakes. He piled up seven of the cakes on one arm and took them out to the seven hungry little youngsters.[57]

He undertook heavy social burdens on behalf of his child friends. He got the artist Hubert von Herkomer to examine Ethel Hatch's work and give a professional opinion of her talent; he solicited similar advice from Joseph Noël Paton for Heartie Hunter. He composed and sent to numerous friends a circular letter recommending they attend a violin concert to be given by Angela Vanbrugh. He got Ellen Terry to provide a box for young Lottie Rix to see her in *King Lear,* and again for his cousins, the Quin girls, and yet again for Dolly Baird. He offered his Eastbourne lodgings to distant relatives and friends and paid their railway fare down to the sea.[58] He gave each of his nieces a watch when they reached an appropriate age. A veritable legion of children benefited from his untiring attentions. One of them, Edith Alice Litton, records the warm afterglow of her friendship with Charles. Her father, E. A. Litton, Fellow of Oriel College and Vice-Principal of St. Edmund Hall, Oxford, and Charles were well acquainted. Charles took the daughter fishing and brought her a kitten named Lily.

> I always attribute my love for animals to the teaching of Mr. Dodgson; his stories of animal life, his knowledge of their lives and histories, his enthusiasm about birds and butterflies, passed many a tiresome hour away. The monkeys in the Botanical Gardens were our special pets, and oh! the nuts and biscuits we used to give them! He entered into the spirit of the fun as much as ... [I] did. ... [Christ Church and Merton meadows] were remarkable then for the quantity of snails of all kinds that, on fine days and damp days, came out to take the air, and to me they were objects of great dislike and horror. Mr. Dodgson so gently and patiently showed me how wonderfully they were made, that I soon got over the fright and made quite a collection of discarded shells. ...[59]

His generosity extended beyond children. After his father's death, he was the constant mainstay of his Guildford family. He regularly allotted funds to the widow of his cousin William Wilcox. His nephew wrote that he "was always ready to do one a kindness, even though it put him to great expense and inconvenience. The income from his books and other sources, which might have been spent in a life of luxury and selfishness, he distributed lavishly where he saw it was needed, and in order to do this he always lived in the most simple way. ... In several instances, where friends in needy circumstances have written to him for loans ... he has answered them, 'I will not *lend,* but I will *give* you the £100 you ask for.' "[60]

He was charming about birthday presents. In *Looking-Glass,* the White

King and Queen give Humpty Dumpty a cravat as an *un*birthday present, of course, and Humpty Dumpty tells Alice that he prefers unbirthday presents to birthday presents because you can get 364 of them a year as opposed to only one birthday present. Charles himself insisted that he never gave birthday presents. "You see," he explained to his young actress friend Polly Mallalieu (September 7, 1892), "if once I began, *all* my little friends would expect a present *every* year, and my life would be spent in packing parcels." But he liked to give presents and treats to child friends on his own birthday. "He brought me a present one day," wrote Ruth Gamlen, ". . . a copy of *Alice's Adventures Under Ground* in facsimile. . . . 'How lovely,' I cried, 'and it's my birthday.' 'Oh dear, that won't do at all,' said Mr. Dodgson. 'I don't approve of birthdays and I never give birthday presents and so I can't give you this book.' I must have looked very disappointed. 'Never mind,' he said, 'you shall have it as an *un*-birthday present and that will make it all right,' and that is what he wrote with my name inside the book with his fountain pen. . . ."[61]

To help people searching for work or advancement, Charles printed and sent out circulars. One concerned T. J. Dymes, classical scholar and schoolmaster, and his large family. After Charles learned in 1883 that they were poverty-stricken, he sent "about 180 copies of a letter (printed) about the Dymeses." Charles wrote about Dymes as "a friend of mine . . . in great distress" who had lost his post as under-master at a boys' school and sought employment for him and other members of the family. "Mr. Dymes has settled with his landlord for a payment of £219.7*s.* . . . ," Charles wrote Frederic Harrison, another friend of Dymes (October 4, 1883). "This sum I have lent him. Also I sent him some while ago £200 (which, though nominally a loan, was really meant to be a gift until he should be able, with perfect convenience to himself, to repay it): and for this debt of £419.7*s.* . . . I am to have a Bill of Sale on his furniture, thus saving it from all risk of being seized by other creditors." Dymes must have found work and resolved his problems, and Charles later called on and dined with the Dymeses, then comfortably settled in London.

Other circular letters sought an appropriate governess for his nieces, situations for two acquaintances, a teaching post for a cousin-godson, an assistant curate to help his brother-in-law, and an appointment for his brother Wilfred.

Charles gave many copies of his books to children's hospitals. He printed *Circular to Hospitals* in 1872 and again in 1890 and *Letter and Questions to*

*Hospitals* in 1876, all offering copies of the *Alice*s and other books. He gave copies also to mechanics institutes, village reading rooms, and other worthy establishments. He turned over the profits from the facsimile of *Alice's Adventures Under Ground* to children's hospitals and convalescent homes for sick children. "You are most welcome to print for the use of the blind anything I have published," Charles wrote (January 5, 1890) to a stranger.

On January 29, 1880, he produced with his electric pen thirty copies of a testimonial to the Christ Church cook. When Charles mysteriously disappeared from his usual Christ Church haunts for two whole days, some learned that he was nursing a poor, friendless man—a minor college servant—stricken with typhoid fever in his lodgings in an obscure part of the city.[62]

Charles and Jowett had reason enough to be at loggerheads. Yet on March 1, 1883, after Jowett became Vice-Chancellor of the university, Charles called on him "at his request, to speak about the backs I wish to give to the seats in the gallery at St. Mary's." The seat backs with iron supports, costing £145, were duly installed.

Some of those who knew him sought to capture his unique charm in words. One of his young friends wrote of a visit that she, her father, and Charles paid to a friend, a Fellow at Magdalen, who was "very much interested in the study of the big drum. . . . With books before him and a much heated face, he was in full practice when we arrived. Nothing would do but that all the party must join in the concert. Father undertook the 'cello, Mr. Dodgson took a comb and paper, and, amidst much fun and laughter, the walls echoed with the finished roll, or shake, of the big drum. . . . All this went on till some other Oxford Dons (mutual friends) came in to see 'if anybody had gone suddenly cracked.' "[63]

Another youngster, Lottie Rix, whose older sister was already a friend of Charles, wrote (May 31, 1885) to her mother from her school in London after a surprise visit from Charles:

> The first thing he did after shaking hands with me and asking if I was Miss Rix, was to turn me round and look at my back. I wondered what on earth he was doing, but he said that he had been made to expect a tremendous lot of hair, and that he hadn't had the *least* idea what I was like, except that he had a vague vision of *hair*. We sat down and talked for a few minutes, and then he wanted to know if I should be allowed to come out with him, and if we were allowed "to go forth" with

friends. I said we were, so then he said, "Well then, would you go and
ask the lady principal (or dragon, or whatever you call her) if you may
come now?" I went and after a little questioning from S. Louisa got
leave.

Charles took Lottie to visit Harry Furniss's studio in St. John's Wood. On
the journey, she reported, "we talked and he sent me into fits over one thing
and another pretty well all the way. At the studio the starry-eyed youngster
saw art in the making. "The whole time I was there, I had to keep saying to
myself '*That*'s an artist who has a picture in the Academy, *that*'s Mr. Furniss
and *that*'s Lewis Carroll'!" . . . It is quite absurd how fond he is of children—at least of *girls* . . . and whenever he saw the picture of one he flew to
it." Lottie continued:

He said that he had been talked to sometimes about himself; and that
once when he was staying at Eastbourne he made friends with a little
girl on the sands, and after he had known them a little time, asked her

if she knew a little book called *Alice's Adventures in Wonderland.* She hadn't got it so he promised to give it to her. Her Mother said to him "Ah, have you heard about the author of the book? He's gone *mad!*" He said "Oh really, I had never heard it," and I think he added that he knew something about him. She stuck to it though and said "Oh yes, it was *quite* true," she could *assure* him. She had it from a friend at Lincoln who knew it for certain. . . . "He had written 3 books . . . and now he had gone mad." Two or three days afterwards he sent the little girl the book and put in it, "For So and So/From the Author." Soon afterwards he met the girl's mother, and when she saw him, she threw up her hands and said "Oh Mr. Dodgson. . . . I'll *never* say anything about anybody *to* anybody again!" To which he cheerfully replied "Oh yes Mrs.———you will."[64]

We get other glimpses of Charles in action in September 1876. Sir John Martin-Harvey, the actor-manager, gives an account of Charles's meeting with a child who would later become Martin-Harvey's wife. Little Nellie de Silva

> had watched with growing anger the way in which Bates, the man who kept the bathing-machines [at Sandown], treated the old horse that drew them up the shore from the water's edge, and suspected that the animal was insufficiently fed. She had also noticed that Bates kept his midday luncheon, carefully wrapped in a newspaper, tucked away . . . in a boat drawn up on the sands. Seeing an opportunity—she snatched the luncheon from its hiding place and fed it to the old horse. Then, armed with a stick, she deliberately smashed the glass in all the little peep-holes of the machines she could reach. This, of course, attracted the outraged holiday-folk upon the shore. The culprit was held up to popular indignation and Bates demanded full recompense for the damage done to his property. Then, from the crowd which had gathered upon the sands a meek little gentleman stepped forward, paid for the damage, and lifting the naughty little girl on to his shoulder, bore her away.[65]

The Curate of Christ Church, Eastbourne, remembered that Charles chose to attend services at his church "because the prayers were said more slowly there than anywhere else in Eastbourne; he, being deaf, liked to join in the congregational parts at a slow pace and not be left behind." Charles, he added, "rented two pews: one for himself and one for his silk hat."[66]

Along with his eccentricities went his belief that Tuesdays were his lucky days and his penchant for interleaving the number 42 and elements of it in his works and letters.

As the years passed, Charles complained more and more about an imperfect memory, an attribute he shared with the King in *Looking-Glass.* "Your bag was got back from Scotland Yard," Macmillan wrote Charles (August 26, 1876), after some forgetfulness. Langford Reed told of Charles dining with a man to whom he had recently been introduced. The following morning, while walking, the very same man stopped Charles. " 'I beg your pardon,' " Charles was reputed to have said, " 'but you have the advantage of me. I do not remember ever having seen you before.' " " 'That is very strange,' " came the reply, " 'for I was your host last night!' "[67]

A nephew recalls that Charles, having been invited to a children's party, went one afternoon to the house where he believed the party was taking place.

He had no sooner been admitted than he dropped on his hands and knees and crawled into a room where a hubbub of voices suggested the party was in progress. Both his attitude and his ululation were intended to suggest a bear, but, unfortunately for his make-believe, instead of entering his friends' house he had mistakenly selected the one next door, where a conference of serious females was taking place in connection with some reform movement or other. The spectacle of an elderly, growling clergyman entering on all-fours created an immense sensation, which was increased when the embarrassed Mr. Dodgson suddenly rose to his feet and, without attempting any explanation, fled from the house with a celerity considerably more equine than ursine.[68]

Eccentric he was, like many dons, but there was something magical about him, too, particularly with children. In the summer of 1860 he encountered two of the MacDonald children in Alexander Munro's studio, Mary and her brother Greville, who was posing for Munro's *Boy with the Dolphin,* still to be seen at the fountain in Hyde Park. "I . . . began at once to prove to the [six-year-old] boy . . . that he had better take the opportunity of having his head changed for a marble one. The effect was that in about two minutes they had entirely forgotten that I was a total stranger, and were earnestly arguing the question as if we were old acquaintances." Collingwood added that Charles "urged that a marble head would not have to be brushed and combed. At this the boy turned to his sister with an air of great relief, saying, 'Do you hear *that,* Mary? It needn't be combed!' " Charles then argued

*Charles's photograph of Bertram Rogers, his godson*

"that a marble head couldn't speak, and as I couldn't convince either that he would be all the better for that, I gave in."[69] Greville himself later remembered Charles as "very dear to us. We would climb about him as, with pen and ink, he sketched absurd or romantic or homely incidents, the while telling us their stories with no moral hints to spoil their charm. . . . Then again he would take us to . . . the Polytechnic, to see the 'dissolving views' of Christmas Fairy Tales. No pantomime or circus ever gave me the same happiness. There was a toy-shop in Regent Street where he let us choose gifts, one of which will remain my own as long as memory endures . . . an unpainted, wooden horse. I loved it as much as any girl her doll."[70]

Charles frequently insisted that he did not like boys as a breed, but he often befriended individual boys. A good many Greville MacDonalds entered his life and he was kind and avuncular to them. Bert Coote, the ten-year-old actor, "a wonderfully clever little fellow," Charles wrote of him (January 13, 1877), was another who cherished Charles's friendship. "Mr. Dodgson often came behind the scenes," Bert wrote, "and all the children in the show adored him. I well remember my sisters, Carrie and Lizzie, and I spending a day with him at Oxford and being vastly entertained by his collection of elaborate mechanical toys. The autographed copies of his books and photographs which he gave me are among my most cherished possessions." Bert also recorded that although he and his sister mimicked the mannerisms of grown-ups,

we never gave imitations of Lewis Carroll, or shared any joke in which he could not join—he was one of us, and never a grown-up pretending to be a child in order to preach at us, or otherwise instruct us. We saw nothing funny in his eccentricities, perhaps he never was eccentric among children. . . . I shall never forget the morning he took my sister and I over the Tower of London and how fascinated we were by the stories he told us about it and its famous prisoners. . . . He was a born story-teller, and if he had not been affected with a slight stutter in the presence of grown-ups would have made a wonderful actor, his sense of the theatre was extraordinary.[71]

*Wilfred Hatch as Cupid, taken by Charles. Wilfred, later in life a curate, was the brother of Charles's three friends whom he christened BEE—that is, Beatrice, Evelyn, and Ethel Hatch.*

Charles's nephew Maj. C. H. W. Dodgson reminisced about his uncle: "When I was a little boy of about six [in May 1882] he would give me pick-a-back rides, and I remember that as I hung on with my arms round his neck, his chin and cheeks were rough. You see, he shaved in cold water with a blunt razor."[72]

Charles repeatedly gave parents advice on the schools and universities where they should send their sons and offered the boys help in preparing for Oxford examinations. He took genuine interest in his nephews' careers and paid for the schooling of at least one cousin.

Gertrude Thomson contributes an anecdote that illustrates Charles's quaint charm. Having admired her Christmas cards with fairy designs, Charles wrote her and arranged to meet her at the Victoria and Albert Museum. She recalled:

> A little before twelve I was at the rendezvous, and then the humour of the situation suddenly struck me, that *I* had not the ghost of an idea what *he* was like, nor would *he* have any better chance of discovering *me!* . . . Just as the big clock . . . clanged out twelve . . . a gentleman entered, two little girls clinging to his hands, and as I caught sight of the tall, slim figure, with the clean-shaven, delicate, refined face, I said to myself, "*That's* Lewis Carroll." He stood for a moment, head erect, glancing swiftly over the room, then bending down, whispered something to one of the children; she, after a moment's pause, pointed straight at me. Dropping their hands he came forward, and with that winning smile of his that utterly banished the oppressive sense of the Oxford don, said simply, "I am Mr. Dodgson; I was to meet you, I think?" To which I as frankly smiled and said, "How did you know me so soon?" "My little friend found you. I told her I had come to meet a young lady who knew fairies, and she fixed on you at once."[73]

On September 4, 1868, at Whitby during the summer vacation, Charles encountered the Bennie family. Mrs. Bennie later described the meeting:

> At the *table d'hôte* . . . I had on one side of me a gentleman whom I did not know, but . . . a very agreeable neighbour, and we seemed to be much interested in the same books, and politics also were touched on. After dinner my sister and brother rather took me to task for talking so much to a complete stranger. I said, "But it was quite a treat to talk to him and to hear him talk. Of one thing I am quite sure, he is a genius." My brother and sister, who had not heard him speak, again laughed at me, and said, "You are far too easily pleased." . . . Next morning nurse took out our two little twin daughters in front of the sea. I went out a short time afterwards, looked for them, and found them seated with my friend at the *table d'hôte* between them, and they were listening to him, open-mouthed, and in the greatest state of enjoyment, with his knee covered with minute toys. I, seeing their great delight, motioned to him to go on; this he did for some time. A most charming story he told them about sea-urchins and Ammonites. When it was over, I said, "You must be the author of 'Alice's Adventures.' " He laughed, but looked astonished, and said, "My dear Madam, my name is Dodgson,

and 'Alice's Adventures' was written by Lewis Carroll." I replied,
"Then you must have borrowed the name, for only he could have told
a story as you have just done." After a little sparring he admitted the
fact . . . and thus I made the acquaintance of one whose friendship has
been the source of great pleasure for nearly thirty years. . . .[74]

Having heard the voices seeking to capture the man, what, in the end, are
we to make of him? Some generalities are permissible. His religious, conservative upbringing marked him deeply, and he remained, through the
years, traditional, nostalgic, although not regressive. He did not approve of
what man had made of society, nor altogether how man sought to change it.
He was forced to work with undergraduates with inadequate preparation
and lackadaisical attitudes to learning. He struggled against lowering standards of education at Oxford, but at the same time was in the vanguard in
demanding reforms aimed at governing his college more democratically. He
was forward-looking in matters mathematical, logical, scientific, mechanical, technological. But he retreated from social involvements as he grew
older, being happy, most of the time, to dwell within Tudor walls pursuing
his occupations. When he ventured forth, it was not as a wanderer or a
seeker after new adventure; he preferred to return to tried and tested haunts,
to the Royal Academy, to theatrical citadels, to the soothing seashore.
Wherever he went, he looked out for the natural child, the unsocialized
angel, who, he knew, would enable him to glimpse what he considered
heaven on earth and to recapture the innocence of his own childhood. He
devoted himself to searching out the Elysium of childhood, the purity he
himself had once known. The mystery of childhood lay at the core of his
being; it was magical for him, and he valued it beyond most things; he
sought it relentlessly and found it, and with it came a transcendent joy. Such
was the nature of the man.

# CHAPTER TEN

# *The Man's Father*

*Father's sorrow, father's joy*

ROBERT GREENE

Charles's mother was, by the few accounts we have of her, almost too good to be true: "sainted Fanny" an aunt called her; "I do not think I ever heard of anyone so highly favoured—as daughter—wife and mother—and few surely have ever passed into Glory knowing so little of earthly stain or sorrow."[1]

When, in 1827, she married her cousin, the Reverend Charles Dodgson, she was twenty-four, he twenty-seven. She gave birth to her first child, Frances Jane, in 1828, when she was twenty-five; and to her eleventh, the youngest, Edwin Heron, in 1846, at forty-three. Charles, her third child and first son, was born when she was twenty-eight. She died on January 26, 1851, aged forty-seven, the day before Charles's nineteenth birthday.

Her family was all to her, and the few letters of hers that survive and the all-too-few references to her by others show her to have been an intelligent, concerned parent—and a gentle, affectionate mother. Two letters that she wrote to her sister Lucy Lutwidge show a particular love for her eldest son and a doting mother's pride in his accomplishments. On June 25, 1847?, she wrote:

> Dearest Charlie came home [from Rugby] safely yesterday bringing with him *two* handsome prize books! one gained last Christmas . . . the other . . . just *now* gained for having been the best in Composition

(Latin and English verse and prose) in his form during the Half. He is also 2nd in Marks—53 boys in his Form—they have marks for *every*-thing they do in their daily work and at the end of their Half they are added up. . . . Dearest Charlie is *thinner* than he was but looks well and is in the *highest* spirits, *delighted* with his success at School.

Almost two years later, on March 24, 1849?, she wrote:

> *You* will I am sure be as much surprised as *we* are to hear that dear-est Charlie *really has* got the Hooping cough, after having been so proof against the complaint during the whole of his last summer holi-day, constantly nursing and playing with the little ones who had it so *decidedly*. I cannot of course *help* feeling anxious and fidgety about him, but at this very *favourable* time of year for it, I trust the complaint will be of very *short* continuance and that with care he will get through it as well as our other darlings have done. He writes [from Rugby] in excel-lent spirits and evidently feeling quite well. For this I am indeed *most thankful.* . . .

By July 5 she was able to report, once more to her sister, that "dearest Charlie's Hooping cough has quite gone."[2]

Before Charles left home to go to school, the parents went off to visit Mrs. Dodgson's father in Hull, whence the mother wrote to her eldest son:

> My Dearest Charlie,
>    I have used you rather ill in not having written to you sooner, but I know you will forgive me, as your Grandpapa has liked to have me with him so much, and I could not write and talk to him comfortably. All your notes have delighted me, my precious children, and show me that you have not quite forgotten me. I am always thinking of you, and longing to have you all round me again more than words can tell. . . . It delights me, my darling Charlie, to hear that you are get-ting on so well with your Latin, and that you make so few mistakes in your Exercises. . . .[3]

Charles valued the letter and guarded it from his young sisters by writing on it: "No one is to touch this note, for it belongs to C.L.D.," adding: "Cov-ered with slimy pitch, so that they will wet their fingers."

The mothers that enter Charles's work are usually shadowy abstractions. The old sinner of Charles's brooding poem "The Valley of the Shadow of Death" addresses his son from his deathbed:

Thy mother, boy, thou hast not known;
So soon she left me here to moan—
Left me to weep and watch, alone,
   Our one beloved child.

. . . . . . .

She passed into the perfect light
   That floods the world above. . . .

Undoubtedly Charles saw his own mother as having passed into the perfect light, and for him the force of love unites this world with the higher one.

In his poem "Solitude," written three years after his mother's death, and which may, more than any other of Charles's utterances, intimate the pain he felt at his mother's absence, we see the early formulation of the theme that idealizes the child upon the mother's breast, the breast that, in Charles's case, no longer existed. In the poem, the speaker flees from society to nature and finds solace in solitude:

Here may the silent tears I weep
   Lull the vexed spirit into rest,
As infants sob themselves to sleep
   Upon a mother's breast.

Later in the poem, he casts his mind back to the days when his mother was still alive and he young and carefree:

Ye golden hours of Life's young spring,
   Of innocence, of love and truth!
Bright, beyond all imagining,
   Thou fairy-dream of youth!

And he concludes with a wish "To be once more a little child / For one bright summer-day." The sentiment, the amalgam of childhood innocence, love, the implied mother, the fairy-dream, is Charles's mystical expression of the way of the world and the universe.

The dedicatory poem in *The Nursery "Alice"* again pictures the child-at-mother's-breast:

A Mother's breast:
Safe refuge from her childish fears,
From childish troubles, childish tears,
Mists that enshroud her dawning years!

Here again the mother is guardian.

In another dedication acrostic, this one appearing at the outset of *Sylvie and Bruno Concluded* and embodying the name of his special friend Enid Stevens (in the third letter of each line, read downward), Charles fabricated a verse that blends dreams, a sprite, a child, and a dead mother:

> Dreams, that elude the Maker's frenzied grasp—
> Hands, stark and still, on a dead Mother's breast,
> Which nevermore shall render clasp for clasp,
> Or deftly soothe a weeping Child to rest—
> In suchlike forms me listeth to portray
> My Tale, here ended. Thou delicious Fay—
> The guardian of a Sprite that lives to tease thee—
> Loving in earnest, chiding but in play
> The merry mocking Bruno! Who, that sees thee,
> Can fail to love thee, Darling, even as I?—
> My sweetest Sylvie, we must say "Good-bye!"

Sylvie, the child heroine of the *Sylvie and Bruno* books, is the fanciful, ethereal creature from beyond with angelic powers. Charles believes that life is transitory, a dream, and he evokes a dead mother and a child's stark, still hands on her lifeless breast to illustrate that death is real, eternal, a symbol of the life beyond earthly existence. Sylvie is guardian; childhood and motherhood and love are entwined in her. The living mother's breast is the natural, secure place for the living child; the dead mother's breast is a talisman: it too provides a haven, an answer to the riddle of life and death. The dead mother and the living child are both angels, proof of the real life that exists before birth and after death.

In *An Easter Greeting to Every Child Who Loves "Alice,"* Charles wallows in a bath of nostalgia as he once more invokes the mother of his childhood:

Do you know that delicious dreamy feeling when one first wakes on a summer morning. . . . And is not that a Mother's sweet voice that summons you to rise? To rise and forget, in the bright sunlight, the ugly dreams that frightened you so when all was dark—to rise and enjoy another happy day. . . .

Trying to assuage any fear of death in his child readers, Charles ends the essay with the image of an eternal mother, who, when death comes to the child reader, will with angel-hands shall undraw your curtains, and sweeter tones than ever loving Mother breathed shall wake you to a new and glorious day—and when all the sadness, and the sin, that darkened life on this little earth, shall be forgotten like the dreams of a night that is past!

In Charles's poem "Stolen Waters," he again pictures a living child and a dead mother; in "A Song of Love," a religious oratorio in *Sylvie and Bruno,* he blends rational faith with intuition, again picturing a mother cuddling and crooning her infant to rest.

For Charles, God is the force of love in the universe, and he sees both the dead mother (who has left the tainted earth and returned to the purity of heaven) and the child (who has recently come from that heaven and is still pure) as embodiments of God's love. If that love linked his own dead mother with the child, it allowed Charles to venerate the child and value above all other treasures the child's friendship. Somewhere deep within him, he may even have responded to the love of children as a manifestation of his mother's love; he may have seen children as the vessels containing a semblance of the love that he and his mother shared before she died.

Charles's memory of his mother is intertwined with his piety: the word *mother* does not appear in either *Alice* tale; in the published volumes of Charles's letters, she is mentioned only once, when, as a boy, Charles writes home to his sister Elizabeth from Rugby; and he alludes to her but twice—once, as we

*Silhouette of Charles's mother*

have seen, when his sister gave birth to Stuart, Charles's future biographer. More extraordinary, he does not mention or allude to his mother in the nine volumes of his diary that survive, covering in detail thirty-eight of his sixty-six years of life. What Charles feels is more than what we think of as earthly mother love: a pious reverence infuses his memory of her.

Charles created another close tie to his mother five years after her death, when he invented the pseudonym by which the world would know him, in linking his own first name, Charles, to his mother's family name, Lutwidge, to arrive at *Lewis Carroll.*

\* \* \*

We know much more about Charles's father than about his mother. He enters Charles's diary and letters repeatedly, and Charles depicts many fathers in his works. No question: he respected and revered his father; the man was formidable, the son faithful and dutiful. The father was gifted and justly distinguished. Having achieved a double first in classics and mathematics at Christ Church, he received a studentship, but within two years, in April 1827, he married and, by Christ Church regulations, forfeited it. He was then appointed successively to a college curacy at Daresbury in Cheshire, summoned in 1836 by his friend C. T. Longley, Bishop of Ripon, to be his Examining Chaplain,[4] and in time, with powerful voices interceding in his behalf with the Prime Minister, awarded the living at Croft in Yorkshire.

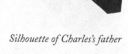

At Croft he came into his own, built a school, and revitalized the parish. He was a keen theologian, an engaging, original lecturer and preacher, and his influence reached well beyond his parish. When Charles was five, his father delivered a sermon at Ripon Cathedral that appeared in print "by decree of the Lord Bishop." More published sermons followed, and when Charles was ten, he held in his hands a huge book, his father's translation of the works of Tertullian, with a preface by E. B. Pusey, one of the leading churchmen. We cannot tell whether the elder

*Silhouette of Charles's father*

Dodgson actually chose Tertullian as his subject, or whether Pusey, general editor of the series "The Library of the Fathers," had assigned it to him. Dodgson could not have undertaken so massive a labor, however, had he felt no sympathy for Tertullian, a second-century pagan who converted to Christianity, lived an exceedingly ascetic life, and preached strict personal discipline and restraint in all things. This volume established Dodgson's reputation in the Church, and in 1852 he was made Canon of Ripon, and two years later Archdeacon of Richmond.

Charles and his brothers and sisters fell under the spell of the father's strong character and position. Wherever the Dodgson children went, to whomever they spoke in the parish, they saw their father almost idolized. He ruled their community, their whole world—how could he not have ruled the home?

The father was a brilliant and serious man—and he had a sense of humor. Collingwood wrote that "in moments of relaxation his wit and humour were the delight of his clerical friends, for he had the rare power of telling anecdotes effectively."[5] One letter illustrates his lighter side. He wrote from Ripon (January 6, 1840) to Charles, not quite eight:

My dearest Charles,

. . . You may depend upon it I will not forget your commission. As soon as I get to Leeds I shall scream out in the middle of the street, *Ironmongers, Ironmongers.* Six hundred men will rush out of their shops in a moment—fly, fly, in all directions—ring the bells, call the constables, set the Town on fire. I WILL have a file and a screw driver, and a ring, and if they are not brought directly, in forty seconds, I will leave nothing but one small cat alive in the whole town of Leeds, and I shall only leave that, because I am afraid I shall not have time to kill it. Then what a bawling and a tearing of hair there will be! Pigs and babies,[6] camels and butterflies, rolling in the gutter together—old women rushing up the chimneys and cows after them—ducks hiding themselves in coffee-cups, and fat geese trying to squeeze themselves into pencil cases. At last the Mayor of Leeds will be found in a soup plate covered up with custard, and stuck full of almonds to make him look like a sponge cake that he may escape the dreadful destruction of the Town. . . . Then comes a man hid in a teapot crying and roaring, "Oh, I have dropped my donkey. I put it up my nostril, and it has fallen out of the spout of the teapot into an old woman's thimble and she will squeeze it to death when she puts her thimble on."

At last they bring the things which I ordered, and then I spare the Town, and send off in fifty waggons, and under the protection of ten thousand soldiers, a file and a screw driver and a ring as a present to Charles Lutwidge Dodgson, from

his affectionate Papa

The letter has its charm, and wit, but it is virtually the only documented evidence of the father's capacity for fun. It is also a clear model for the violence in Charles's juvenilia and, for that matter, in the *Alice* books and later works.

Dodgson *père* was certainly ambitious for his eldest son. On February 18, 1843, he wrote from Daresbury to his brother Hassard Dodgson a long, revealing letter. "I am strongly of the opinion that a sum of money *spent* in

Education is far more profitable to a Boy who will profit by it, than the prospect of getting it at his Father's death," he wrote. "Looking at the constitution of the Chapter of Christ Church, it is certainly not impossible that I might be able some day to get for Charles a Studentship from some individual member. . . ."[7]

Only a few letters from the father to Charles survive, and they are mostly concerned with practical matters, answering Charles's queries on mathematical problems, arranging with Charles to help install Skeffington and Wilfred as Christ Church undergraduates. The father's words when Charles gained his studentship at Christ Church are all affection:

My dearest Charles,

. . . I am glad that you should have had so soon an evidence so substantial of the truth of what I have so often inculcated, that it is the "steady, painstaking, likely-to-do-good" man, who in the long run wins the race against those who now and then give a brilliant flash and, as Shakespeare says, "straight are cold again."

In a series of letters from the father to his second son, Skeffington, the father seems ever diligent and consoling. Skeffington did not meet with the ready success at Oxford that Charles and Wilfred had achieved. He worked hard but repeatedly failed examinations. The father's reaction was not recriminatory; quite the opposite. On April 26, 1861, he wrote:

I can most truly say that all my sorrow is for the vexation that this failure cannot but cause your own feelings. . . . Any failure so totally unconnected with anything in the smallest degree *discreditable* can hardly be imagined. The *fault* is exactly that of a man who cannot get into the Guards because he is 5 foot 8 instead of 5 ft. 10 in height. We can no more take out of God's hands the height of our minds than we can that of our bodies. Our duty in this world is not to make ourselves what God has not made (for this is impossible) but to do *the best* with ourselves *as we are,* and the whole experience of my life does not furnish a stronger example, if so strong a one, of the *thorough* performance of this duty than *your own.* . . . God bless you, my dear Boy, and be assured that no son ever more thoroughly satisfied a Father by his whole manner of going on than you do.

On October 31, after Skeffington endured another defeat, the father wrote another, similarly comforting letter. When, in December 1862, after struggling with Oxford examinations for six years, Skeffington succeeded in getting his degree, the father and the rest of the family were jubilant.[8]

Letters from Charles to various members of the family tell us more about the relations between father and son. He wrote three letters from school to Croft, and all went to brothers and sisters, not to a parent. Was it merely an accident that he wrote his long reports to them and not directly to his parents? Perhaps. But of Charles's earliest fourteen letters to come to light, which take him past his twenty-third birthday, one was to his nurse, one to a cousin, and twelve to brothers and sisters. Only the fifteenth was to his father. That one came from Christ Church on May 3, 1856, when Charles was twenty-four; it answers his father's query about Skeffington and Wilfred's impending matriculation at Christ Church and is brief, giving only the required information. The letter is important because it tells us that the family kept even this trifle along with the more friendly, chatty letters to Frances, Elizabeth, Skeffington, and Mary.

The Dodgsons, conscious of their family history, did not discard letters lightly. References in Charles's letters to his sisters prove that he wrote more than this one letter to his father—and the father in letters to Skeffington alludes to letters from Charles that seem not to have survived. Why did these and perhaps others not survive? Was the father less diligent about keeping the letters his children wrote him than other members of the family were about the letters they received? He was, of course, overwhelmed with work and responsibilities, so much so that perhaps the children hesitated to trouble him with letters. Writing from Rugby, Charles complains: "Papa has taken no notice of the book I had set my fancy on getting, Whiston's *Josephus,* in 2 vols., 24*s.*," and he adds: "will you please ask him what he thinks of it?" In the same letter: "I must not forget to send my hearty thanks to Papa and Mamma for their kind present." He encloses in this letter, for his father's delectation, the answer to a geometry problem worked out by his mathematics master at Rugby and adds that he would like to buy Liddell and Scott's *Greek-English Lexicon* if his father will allow it.

In another letter from Rugby to Elizabeth, he confesses to having bought a new hat, "which I suppose Papa will not object to, as my old one was getting very shabby." Six weeks after taking up residence at Christ Church, writing to his sister Mary, he asks her to remind their father of two questions that he had put earlier to him: What is he to do about a name plate for the front door of his rooms and what is he to do about acquiring a Greek history? And may he buy a copy of a standard Horace?

Charles later reported to Elizabeth that he had acquired August Böckh's *Public Economy of Athens,* "which . . . Papa had desired me to get last term." Toward Christmas of that first year at Oxford, Charles reports, again to Elizabeth, that Osborne Gordon has given him a copy of his Censor's speech "printed for private circulation," and adds, "I will bring it home with me for Papa to read. I think it beautiful Latin." Then, to Mary the following August, he writes: "Will you thank Papa for his essay on Multiplication of Lines."

Charles spent a lot of time with his father; he walked and traveled with him. They visited relatives and friends together, they talked together, but the subjects of their discussions were seldom noted. On March 23, 1855, Charles gave precedence to divinity reading for ordination over other activities: "I must consult my Father on the subject," he told his diary. On July 5 of that year, he observed his father teach, "as I was to begin trying myself soon." Diary entries touching upon his father were generally factual. He often capitalizes the word *Father,* but on one occasion, on January 20, 1865, he refers to him as "the Archdeacon." The formal designation is curious. Was conversation at the rectory full of reports of the forthcoming publication of *Alice's Adventures in Wonderland?* And had the Archdeacon's reaction been less than jubilant?

While the Dodgson children freely contributed to the family magazines and while most of the household, even Aunt Lucy, contributed, the father is noticeably absent.

Charles was a dutiful son who made every effort to please his family and particularly to stay in Papa's good graces. But one is struck by how often he took a circuitous route to communicate with his father and sent messages by way of his sisters. For some reason, Charles did not address his questions, requests, and remarks directly to the paterfamilias. Of course, there is nothing wrong with using one's sisters as deputies. Charles's restraint may simply have been out of consideration for his father's busy life.

We know that duty was one of the strongest themes in Charles's early years—duty to God, duty to parents, duty to his father's parish, duty to Christ Church, duty to his pupils, duty to his colleagues, duty even to needy strangers. But his relationship with his father went beyond duty. In one surviving letter to his father, he ends by sending "love to all" and signs himself "your affectionate son." Collingwood tells us that the father was the son's "ideal of what a Christian gentleman should be" and that when the father died, "a cloud . . . settled on . . . [Charles's] life which could never be dispelled."[9] Indeed Charles himself wrote to a child friend on June 24, 1868, three days after his father's death: "I am in great sorrow just now, as my dear dear father has been taken away from us"; and much later (March 22, 1879), to a bereaved widower, he described his father's death as "the deepest sorrow *I* have known in life."

A close reading of Charles's diaries and letters, an examination of some of his independent decisions, and a look at his literary works lead us to confront two forces in Charles's life that were working at cross-purposes: filial devotion and filial rebellion. All was not sweetness and light between father and son. To begin with, those indirect appeals, apprehensive requests, and entreaties suggest an undercurrent of fear of displeasing Papa. And there is more, for father and son disagreed on issues so basic as to drive a wedge between them, and their divergent views might even have led to an irreconcilable rift.

The father "was a man of deep piety," Collingwood tells us, "and of a somewhat reserved and grave disposition. . . . His reverence for sacred things was so great that he was never known to relate a story which included a jest upon words from the Bible."[10] This reverence for sacred subjects and the Bible obviously imbued Charles as well. Florence Becker Lennon, who, while writing her life of Charles, spoke to family members, reports: "All the stories about the elder Dodgson emphasize his charm, merely implying the iron hand in the velvet glove. The most the Misses Dodgson [Wilfred's daughters] would say about their grandfather was that he was a man of strong personality, with definite ambitions for developing his children's characters."[11]

The letters that the father wrote Charles and Skeffington were indeed affectionate, but also full of advice that he expected them to act upon. His voice was the voice of authority. When he extended Skeffington's and Wilfred's stay at Keswick with a private tutor, he wrote (March 14, 1856): "You must receive it also as a mark of confidence which I have in you both that you will not let the attractions of the Lakes and Hills prevent your attending to the *chief* purpose for which you are placed under a Private Tutor. This extra stay . . . will cost me an *additional* 100 Guineas—so make the best use of it. . . ." When the pair entered Christ Church, he wrote Skeffington (October 14, 1856): "I shall hope to hear of good Collections, and no scrapes about Chapel or the like. I will thank you to keep an exact account of all that you spend on what we call the *first outfit*. . . . I have commenced two separate books of accounts, one for you and one for Wilfred. I *particularly* beg

from the first that your account may not be mixed up with Wilfred's. . . .
Whenever you get a cheque . . . from Charles for both of you, let the money
be divided as required and let each put down his own share in his account
book *with the date*." When Skeffington was due to return to Croft to be ordained, his father wrote (November 22, 1865), "Pray do not do anything foolish, either in the way of walking, or reading, or sitting up at night, so as to
hinder you from being clear headed, brisk, and vigorous on your return
home. I shall give up a great deal of time to you between that time and the
ordination."[12]

Archdeacon Dodgson, having arranged for Charles to follow in his footsteps to Christ Church, surely hoped that he would follow him into the
Church. Was he content with his son's taking only deacon's orders* and not
proceeding to the priesthood? Can we believe that father and son did not
discuss the son's decision to halt, in a manner of speaking, in midstream?

　　Charles's choice of an academic career was by no means discreditable. His
first in mathematics must have brought approbation, and his elevation to
Student and then Lecturer more of the same. It was, nonetheless, not the
course his father favored. The letter the father wrote to his son on August
21, 1855 (see pages 54–55) was full of financial advice—and predicated on his
taking a living in ten years' time, implying that Charles would, like his father, marry and surrender his studentship.

　　They must have discussed and disagreed on various issues, the theater for
one. The father did not object to his children engaging in amateur theatricals at home or to his eldest son's entertaining the family with his marionette
theater. But High Church pronouncements would have led the father to
condemn public performances, while Charles, once at Oxford and independent, not only took to the theater hungrily but defended it publicly as a positive force for good, knowing full well that his father could not countenance
his opinion or his behavior. No indication exists that father and son discussed the issue, but they surely did.

　　Collingwood says nothing negative about the father. Derek Hudson, in
his life of Charles, endorses the accepted interpretation of the symbiotic relationship between father and son. But Hudson does suggest that the head

---

* A deacon is a member of the third order of the ministry, ranking below bishops and priests.
He is able to assist the priest in divine service and is expected to visit the sick and carry out
other charitable functions.

of the family was "authoritarian." He nonetheless attributes "a great perse-
verance and much dignity and poise" to Dodgson *père*. The father, Hudson
suggests, citing a graphologist, was "somewhat narrow in his emotional
range, 'austere, puritanical and fond of power,' unlikely to make allowances
for shortcomings or disobedience. His more human side would be likely to
show itself . . . 'with people in trouble or children whom he would protect,
provided that his authority was not challenged . . . and . . . considerable ir-
ritability [was] usually controlled behind a benign facade.' "[13]

Even leaving the graphologist's analysis aside, we still see the Archdeacon as a strong personality with perhaps authoritarian tendencies and
Charles smarting under the stern parent's yoke. A cursory look at Charles's
juvenilia makes the case clear. We see a good deal of humor in *Useful and
Instructive Poetry*, which Charles produced when he was thirteen, possibly
even the dawning imagination that produced the *Alice* books. But we see
much more. For just as the *Alice* books, with all their whimsy and fun, live
on the bedrock of Charles's personal history, so the earlier creations live on
that same foundation.

Several verses in the slim volume echo the moral maxims and the rules
of conduct that Charles and his brothers and sisters heard over and over
again in their daily rounds. Note the third verse in the collection, entitled
"Punctuality":

> Better to be before your time,
>  Then e'er to be behind;
> To ope the door while strikes the chime,
>  *That* shows a punctual mind.

The moral tag at the end appears in quotation marks, as do all the other
moral tags:

> Moral:
> "Let punctuality and care
>  Seize every flitting hour,
> So shalt thou cull a floweret fair,
>  E'en from a fading flower."

Other verses bear other moral tags: "Don't get drunk"; "Keep your wits
about you"; "Don't dream"; and even "Never stew your sister." Then there is
that brilliant piece of doggerel, "Rules and Regulations":

Learn well your grammar,
And never stammer,
Write well and neatly,
And sing most sweetly,
Be enterprising,
Love early rising,
Go walks of six miles,
Have ready quick smiles. . . .
Drink tea, not coffee;
Never eat toffy.
Eat bread with butter.
Once more, don't stutter.
Don't waste your money,
Abstain from honey.
Shut doors behind you,
(Don't slam them, mind you.)
Drink beer, not porter.
Don't enter the water,
Till to swim you are able.
Sit close to the table.
Take care of a candle.
Shut a door by the handle,
Don't push with your shoulder
Until you are older.
Lose not a button.
Refuse cold mutton,
Starve your canaries,
Believe in fairies.
If you are able,
Don't have a stable
With any mangers.
Be rude to strangers.

And the moral tag is one simple word: "Behave." Wonderfully clever and splendidly witty—and all from the pen of a young teenager. And yet, beneath the cleverness and wit resounds the voice of authority, the voice that dictates the precepts that must guide all behavior, the voice of the father.

Another early piece is engaging—and curious also. It is entitled "A quotation from Shakespeare with slight improvements" and is Charles's own rendering of the King's deathbed scene in *Henry IV, Part 2,* when the wayward Prince Hal, sitting at his dying father's bedside, picks up the crown that his father so jealously prizes and puts it on to see how majesty would sit upon him, all the time believing his father already dead. Then, the father-king stirs and accuses Hal of wishing him dead so that he can ascend the throne and fill the court with his low companions—his "weeds." It is a troubling scene, a classic version of parent misunderstanding child and attributing to him baseness and villainy where none exists, where on the contrary the child is deeply affected by what he sees as his father's sad end.

What Charles does with the scene is instructive, for, as in other pieces in this collection, he spreads a humorous veneer over the hard rock of reality. Charles starts with Shakespeare's own words at the beginning when Prince Hal, believing his father dead, soliloquizes on the subject of "majesty":

> P. Why doth the crown lie there upon his pillow
> Being so troublesome a bedfellow?
> Oh polished perturbation! golden care!
> That keepst the ports of slumber open wide
> To many a watchful night—sleep with it now!
> Yet not so sound, and half so deeply sweet,
> As he whose brow his homely biggin bound
> Snores out the watch of night.

At this point we get Charles's first interpolation. The King opens his eyes and speaks:

> K.          Harry I know not
> The meaning of the word you just have used.
> P. What word, my liege?
> K. The word I mean is "biggin."

Hal explains that a biggin is a peasant nightcap; the King thanks him for his explanation and tells him to proceed. And so it goes, Hal trying to get through his soliloquy on "majesty" and the King interrupting at every second line. They quibble over the use of another word, they squabble over the truth of one of Hal's protestations, and the King concludes that his son is "not fit to reason with."

And that is it. The humor evinced by the absurd deathbed colloquy between father and son is mildly amusing. But why did Charles choose that

"He  gave  it  to  his  father."     Ossian.

*Charles's drawing in* Mischmasch, *one of the Dodgson family magazines*

particular scene? The choice is certainly a tribute to the youngster's familiarity with Shakespeare's histories—but the scene is not one of the poet's
grand dramatic moments. The reason for the choice becomes clear only in
the context of the real father-son relationship. The conflict between the
once powerful and ambitious king on the one hand and the seemingly wayward prince on the other is close enough to Charles's heart for him to take
it for his own. He builds a superstructure of humor upon it, but only to conceal the pain beneath.

The grumbling-father theme keeps cropping up in Charles's works as he
grows older. In *The Rectory Magazine,* which materialized three years after
*Useful and Instructive Poetry,* when Charles was sixteen, we find more figures
of unshakable authority, and in a lengthy story entitled "Sidney Hamilton,"
Charles again depicts the troublesome relationship between a father and son
in a setting that resembles Croft Rectory. Here too is a clash between father
and son, the son driven out, the son reclaimed—and lest the meaning hit its
real target, the whole thing is punctured, in the end, by an amusing tag line:
"Oh, my son, whatever you do—never—never again leave your breakfast
unfinished!"

In *Mischmasch,* Charles produced a series of drawings entitled "Studies
from English Poets." The third one, captioned "He gave it to his father" shows
a Herculean youth about to bludgeon his father with an enormous club.

Years later the *Alice* books appear, stories not about an uncompliant lad but about an uncompliant lass. While the early themes recur here, Charles's targets have increased in size and number. The fictional Alice becomes his vehicle for depicting clashes between figures of arbitrary authority and long-suffering youngsters. Charles is now older, a more refined artist, better at disguising the obvious, more skilled at concealing the original models for his fictional characters, and deft at transferring his own thoughts and feelings to characters seemingly different from himself. Surely no obvious resemblance exists between the Queen of Hearts and any real person in Charles's life, but the devastating injunction that rings with horrid finality, "Off with his head," must come from somewhere.

Wonderland is, in fact, overpopulated with downright tyrants, heartless figures of authority. Besides the Queen of Hearts, we have the Caterpillar, the Hatter, the Duchess, the Red Queen, and even Humpty Dumpty—all vying for first prize. The Duchess is particularly interesting. Tenniel's model for her was a real duchess, sometimes called the ugliest woman in the world. But look at Tenniel's Duchess again: she is a man. Whether Charles urged Tenniel to make her appear masculine or not, he apparently did not complain about Tenniel's rendering. Nor must we forget the Duchess's lullaby:

> Speak roughly to your little boy,
>    And beat him when he sneezes:
> He only does it to annoy,
>    Because he knows it teases.

Why does Charles turn G. W. Langford's civilized advice—

> Speak gently to the little child!
>    Its love be sure to gain;
> Teach it in accents soft and mild,
>    It may not long remain

—into that harsh and brutal verse that the Duchess sings? And then there's the verse the Caterpillar makes Alice recite:

> "You are old, Father William," the young man said
>    "And your hair has become very white;
> And yet you incessantly stand on your head—
>    Do you think, at your age, it is right?"
>
> "In my youth," Father William replied to his son,
>    "I feared it might injure the brain;

But now that I'm perfectly sure I have none,
Why I do it again and again."

Charles parodies Southey's poem about Father William, transforms it from serious to comic, and changes Southey's characters significantly. Southey refers throughout his poem to "the young man"; in Charles's parody, the young man becomes Father William's son. In the Southey poem, Father William is a genial, soft-spoken, religious gentleman. Charles puts harsh, nonsensical words into the mouth of both Father William and the son. Finally, in Southey's poem, the young man asks straightforward questions that enable Father William to expound his gentle philosophy; in Charles's parody, the friendly dialogue turns into a hostile confrontation, the son chastising his father, the father berating the son. Moreover, in Charles's own illustration of Father William standing on his head, the old man wears a clerical collar, or something very much like one.

Much later Bruno, in the *Sylvie and Bruno* books, is a typical, mischievous, unruly lad, and when his sister, Sylvie, tries to educate him and imbue him with the proper moral values, he rebels. At one point she arranges a group of letters that spell *evil* and she asks Bruno to speak the word they spell. Insisting on reading them backwards, he says they spell *live*. Bruno does not suffer from dyslexia—and while Bruno is not at all like the youth

*Charles's own illustration of "You are old, Father William"*

Charles must have been, he has in him a young man's defiance of authority, a quality Charles apparently respected. The need for freedom of spirit and independence constantly clashes with imposed rules and regulations from without, as much for Bruno as for Charles.

Two clear character types live prominently in all of Charles's creative works, at opposite poles: on the one hand, we have the authoritarian figures, the brutish, unfeeling, father-king-queen-duchess-caterpillar type; on the other, the innocent, misunderstood, lost, abused, deprived Sidney Hamilton–Alice–Bruno type. Charles must have been deeply impressed and moved by Dickens's *Hard Times:* the Gradgrind–Cissy Jupe dichotomy lies behind much of his creative work. To ignore the pattern, to dismiss Charles's creations as mere targets of fun, is to reject the insight they offer about his motivations. They provide a gloss on his inner self.

But we have been looking only at Charles's works, not at his life. Is there anything in the diary, say, or in his letters, that suggests troubled lines of communication between father and son?

The diary reports that in June 1855 Charles, age twenty-three and already a junior don at Christ Church, left Oxford for the long vacation. Before joining the family circle at Croft, he spent a few days in London, visiting friends and going to the theater and to art galleries. On Friday, June 22, he went to see Charles Kean and Ellen Tree in Shakespeare's *Henry VIII.* It impressed him profoundly; in fact, he called it "the greatest theatrical treat I ever had or ever expect to have." He was particularly struck by the final scene of Miss Tree's performance as the dying Queen Katherine. "I never enjoyed anything so much in my life before," Charles writes, "and never felt so inclined to shed tears at anything fictitious, save perhaps at that poetical gem of Dickens, the death of Little Paul."

The allusion to Paul's death in *Dombey and Son* is significant. Charles read Dickens avidly, liked his work, and quoted him frequently. *Dombey* first appeared in monthly parts between October 1846 and April 1848, and Charles probably read it then. The tale about a father's spiritual murder of a son had a special appeal for him: for "Dombey and Son" he could easily have read "Dodgson and Son," particularly because it is a tale about an insensitive father and an exceptionally sensitive son. It is, moreover, in the early chapters, something of a *Bildungsroman* turned on its head, the story of Paul's birth and growth, his education, his trials, and then his premature death.

Paul's education is not like Charles's: Dr. Blimber's school is no Richmond or Rugby. But despite this difference, Charles might have seen many parallels between his own education and Paul's. He surely found in Dickens's pages echoes of his own early years. When Paul Dombey is installed at Dr. Blimber's cram school and Blimber asks, "Shall we make a man of him?" Paul replies: "I had rather be a child." Dickens describes Blimber's institution as a "great hothouse, in which there was a forcing apparatus incessantly at work. All the boys blew before their time. Mental green peas were produced at Christmas, and intellectual asparagus all the year round. Mathematical gooseberries . . . were common at untimely seasons. . . . Every description of Greek and Latin vegetable was got off the dryest twigs of boys, under the frostiest circumstances. Nature was of no consequence at all. No matter what a young gentleman was intended to bear, Doctor Blimber made him bear to a pattern, somehow or other."[14] Imagine Charles's reaction to that passage—and to the following:

> Such spirits as he had in the outset, Paul soon lost. . . . He kept his character to himself. He grew more thoughtful and reserved. . . . He loved to be alone; and in those short intervals when he was not occupied with his books, liked nothing so well as wandering about the house by himself, or sitting on the stairs listening to the great clock in the hall. He was intimate with all the paper-hanging in the house; saw things that no one else saw in the patterns; found out miniature tigers and lions running up the bedroom walls, and squinting faces leering in the squares and diamonds of the floor-cloth.[15]

The daily routine at Blimber's was enough to undo hardy, bullish lads, and in gentle, delicate Paul it wreaks havoc. It drains him of what little strength he has and ultimately saps his life away.

Charles's own school days were not happy ones, we know. His days at Rugby, working from seven in the morning to ten at night six days a week, were, in memory, a virtual reification of young Dombey's schedule. And we know that Charles, like Paul, yearned for solitude and privacy at school. As Charles read through Dickens's account of young Paul, he must have suffered many of Paul's agonies, and he surely resented Mr. Dombey's inept and arbitrary decisions, pronouncements, and his rigid, even brutish treatment of his son. Most keenly Charles must have felt at one with little Paul's despair, his repeated efforts to live up to his father's expectations and, finally, his humiliation at failing to fulfill them.

Charles easily couples Dombey's tragedy with Queen Katherine's in *Henry VIII*. The play summoned up his vivid memory of the novel. The Queen is a gentle creature, victimized, neglected, and rejected by a tyrant king. The three cases of Mr. Dodgson, Mr. Dombey, and King Henry are not by any means parallel. Each differs enormously from the others, just as Charles, Paul, and Queen Katherine differ. But the emotional parallels are there. The latter trio each sought to please the former, and each, in different ways, failed.[16]

Although Charles depicts a number of benevolent and innocuous males, the autocratic figures that appear in a bad light in his work send a clear message. He often paints his figures of authority as monsters, and they are, in the end, invariably vanquished or subdued. The formula enables Charles to write himself free of his father, at least for a moment, to rebel figuratively, and to assert his own authority.

The letters, like the diary, do not offer any outright clash between father and son, no outward indication of tension or disagreement between them. But it would not be in Charles's nature, nor in the nature of any Victorian of his cut of cloth, to parade any unpleasant difference with his father. However, a letter that Charles wrote to Aunt Lucy Lutwidge, who, after Mrs. Dodgson's death in 1851, became surrogate mother and housekeeper at Croft, is revealing. The letter is dated June 27, 1866—Charles was thirty-four and already the author of the first *Alice* book. He still spent summers within the family circle at Croft and at one point took rooms for a short holiday at Whitby, on the North Sea. "By the way," he wrote, "I may as well mention my Whitby plans for this year, that the family may have ample time for deliberation, and that *I* may have time to engage good rooms. . . ." He planned to go for a fortnight, and "in order to enable some of the family to go also . . . I am willing to go as far as £20, or £25 if necessary. How many go, and which, is a question I leave entirely to the sisterhood to settle among themselves: with them I include you . . . and Edwin. I need not offer to treat Skeffington, being now a gentleman of independent income." Charles wanted to book the rooms for the end of the summer, in August or September, by which time, in his own words, "I shall find the Croft air disagreeing with me."

He cannot be writing literally. Croft and Whitby are only thirty-five miles apart, and nothing is wrong with the "air" at Croft in August or September. It is far enough north not to become oppressively hot, nor is it particularly damp: it is inland and quite dry. Anyone who could survive a clammy Oxford winter, and Charles lived through many, would find Croft in the summer balmy and pleasant.

Charles means something other than climate: people perhaps or, conceivably, one person. Charles is clearly on excellent terms with his sisters and with the two brothers still in residence. He was on affectionate terms with

Aunt Lucy, to whom he confides all this. Who, then, is left? Papa, who is not mentioned in the letter and certainly was not invited to join the seaside party. Charles simply knows in advance that his father will make the air at Croft disagreeable for him and that by late August he will yearn to escape.

Let us compare father and son in a different way. Father was a strong, healthy man with a great gift for learning. He earned a double first at Oxford, became the shepherd of a flock, a theologian of high esteem with a voice in the Church General, a preacher whose sermons were worth publishing and preserving, who became an examining chaplain to a bishop, a canon, an archdeacon. He was a man who apparently never hesitated, in speech or in deed, who married young and sired eleven children.

But the son was deaf in his right ear from childhood, a stammerer, not vigorous, by many accounts unassertive, by some accounts a recluse, who took only a single first at Oxford, who became only a deacon, not a priest, who sought no parish of his own, who published mathematical works—and children's stories—not theological tomes, who did not marry, who desired the companionship of female children.

What did the father think of his eldest son? Was he altogether pleased with his character, with his career, with his overall accomplishments? What did he think of his failure to marry and to provide him with grandchildren, his refusal to follow in his footsteps in the Church? What was his opinion of the son writing and publishing *Alice's Adventures in Wonderland*? And how did he view his son's attachments to female children? He surely noticed it when the son was home, in Ripon with the Longley children and others. Charles could not mask the preference nor would he if he could have. Even if the father were the most considerate of parents, could he have concealed his disappointment?

Could the son have avoided comparing himself to his father, and did that comparison not sow the seeds of inadequacy in him? He could not match his father's strength, his father's accomplishments as a man, a husband, a father, a churchman, a community leader. Was not the stern, authoritarian nature of the older man, his self-confidence, his vigor, a source of some resentment in the younger?

And the son was, moreover, inclined to veer away from the pomp and ritual of his father's High Church and move to the simpler, less heady environment of the Broad Church, which sought to interpret the Creeds liberally and to foster faith based on inner conviction; and he rejected his father's belief that the theater is evil and championed the stage as a vehicle for uplifting entertainment and education—he must have been aware of his father's expectations and displeasure. He knew that he was offending, disappointing that paragon when he embraced the broader church, when he attended theatricals and defended them in print, when he did not take priest's orders, when he sought no curacy, when he wrote on mathematics and not on religion, when he preferred child companions to adults and wrote children's books, when he remained a bachelor and produced no heirs. Charles was aware of all this; his relationship with his father could not have been easy or agreeable; and he had to bear the scars of guilt at not living the life that Papa hoped he would.

Although father-son conflicts are ever common, what Charles had to face again and again was that he simply was not as good, as able, as brilliant as his father. First fear, then resentment, and ultimately guilt attack him. From childhood he bristled at the prohibitions and somewhere along the way realized that he must defend his beliefs and live a life congenial to his own makeup—not the life his father expected him to lead.

Let us reconsider Collingwood's statement that after his father's death, "a cloud . . . settled" on Charles's life that "could not be dispelled." Perhaps that cloud could not be dispelled because, with the death of the father, Charles could never expunge the fact that he had left the road his father chose for him, nor could he now make up for it to him. His father's death left him with the memory of his rebellion, with a permanent scar for not having provided the father, in his lifetime, with the satisfaction, the progeny, the joys that he as eldest son was meant to provide. Never, now, could he have an exculpatory dialogue with his father; never, now, could he hope to explain himself, to achieve some degree of reconciliation. With the father's death, Charles was permanently weighed down by a guilt he could never purge. Like Dr. Johnson, he was left standing in the rain in his fruitless effort to expiate his remorse.

Collingwood conceded that, in examining his uncle's serious verse, one could not avoid seeing "the shadow of some disappointment . . . over Lewis Carroll's life . . . that gave him his wonderful sympathy with all who suffered."[17] In reply to speculation that the disappointment was the result of a love affair, Collingwood adds, long after his uncle's death: "Nothing I have read in L.C.'s diaries or letters suggested . . . that he had ever had any affaires de coeur. . . . I *think* that Aunt Fanny [Charles's eldest sister] once told me that it was the family's opinion that Uncle Charles had had a disappointment in love, and that they thought . . . that the lady in question was Ellen Terry." However, "it was *Alice*," Collingwood adds, "who was undoubtedly his pet, and it was his intense love for her (though she was only a child) which pulled the trigger and released his genius. Indeed it is quite likely that Alice's marriage to Hargreaves may have seemed to him the greatest tragedy in his life."[18]

Charles may well have worshiped the actress, but love and marriage between them was entirely out of the question: when he first met her, she was already married, and as time went by, she became all the more ineligible for such a union. Collingwood's speculation about the Alice affair is more to the point. Add to the cloud that settled on Charles at his father's death Alice's rejection of him and her marriage to Hargreaves, and we see ample reason for the guilt and disappointment that belie the happy man he sometimes claimed to be and for an anguish he bore the rest of his life.

The world knows Charles as a greatly gifted human being, one who lived a life of moral virtue, sound professional and popular achievement, and a good deal of personal reward. But how did Charles himself regard his life? Did he consider himself successful? Perhaps he did when he contemplated the outward successes. But inwardly he probably saw his life as a journey on an impaired vessel, through rough and troubled seas, tossed about by harsh and hostile elements. He did his best, but he was limited. Was he himself satisfied? Did he succeed in clearing his conscience? Or was there always the nagging apprehension that his success was not the right kind of success?

He worked hard to survive, to succeed, but safe harbors repeatedly eluded him. The ultimate success for Charles would have been to be true to himself, to please his father, to be happy in wedded love. But he could not attain those goals; they were incompatible, irreconcilable, beyond his reach. Had he managed to gain his father's approbation before the Archdeacon's death, had he managed to forge a union with Alice or some other object of his desire, he would have been a far happier man than he was. But the happiness he sought remained ever out of reach, even though he tried

> To seek it with thimbles, to seek it with care;
>     To pursue it with forks and hope;
>  To threaten its life with a railway-share;
>     To charm it with smiles and soap!

Perhaps humor was the only real consolation. It offered at least momentary relief, laughter, an illusion of success. But when the humor was stripped off, success, like the Baker, softly, and with the death of Papa and then again with the loss of Alice, suddenly, but decisively, vanishes away.[19]

# CHAPTER ELEVEN

# The Man's Faith

*. . . When the fight begins within himself,*
*A man's worth something.*

ROBERT BROWNING

Charles's beliefs are not difficult to grasp because he was forthright about them in his letters and in his works. How he arrived at them and where their roots lie are more difficult to determine. Although his father inculcated his own faith in his eldest boy, and although Charles accepted virtually all his father's teachings, he slowly veered from High Church doctrine and practice.

One knows that the nineteenth century was deeply concerned with religious questions. It was an age of spiritual crises among thinking men and women. Mill, Carlyle, George Eliot, Matthew Arnold, Tennyson, Newman, Mrs. Ward, and others produced an unprecedented volume of literature depicting religious despair, doubt, and conversion. It was an age of inner debate, outer *Weltschmerz,* when diligent readers like Charles listened carefully to the sad music of Tennyson's "O"s and Matthew Arnold's "Ah"s, an age of splintered alliances, when minority allegiances, Methodists, Congregationalists, Baptists, mushroomed and grew, when the 1851 Religious Census revealed that half of England attended nonconformist chapels rather than established Anglican edifices.

A double schism occurred, moreover, in England in Charles's infancy, one between government and Church, the other within the Church itself. A monolithic society ruled by the Church was battered by opposition from nonconformists who opposed paying taxes to maintain a church whose beliefs they did not embrace and from political liberals, jubilant after their success in the Reformed Parliament of 1832. Coleridge's *On the Constitution of the Church and State* (1829) led to rethinking the relationship between tower and temple. New rules put an end to the power of archbishops and bishops, and even lesser clergy, to raid Church treasuries for their private coffers; and placed strict controls on the old abuses of pluralism, the practice of holding more than one benefice, and upon nonresidence. The requirement that the senior Dodgson live at the Residence in Ripon no less than three months of the year stemmed from these reforms.

Reformers were also disturbed by the listlessness afflicting parishioners. Comfortable, content, and cozy, the clergy, like Trollope's Dr. Vesey Stanhope, neglected the flock, which wandered aimlessly. Observing a breed of self-indulgent and self-satisfied clergy, the laity despaired. Followers remained nominally Anglican and paid both lip service and tithes to the Church, but religious fervor died.

Concerned leaders, in and out of the Church, sought ways to reinspire their followers and to revive a genuine religious feeling, while reforming both Church and clergy. Reform followed upon reform, engineered by successive parliaments, altering dioceses, creating new sees, limiting clerical incomes and funneling money to impoverished parishes.

Because neglect and abuse within the Church had been so devastating, liberal forces, critical of the rot, moved with conviction and strength. Conservatives saw the danger all too readily: if the liberals had their way, the Anglican establishment could even disappear, and some vague theism replace inherited doctrine. The only sure riposte was to strengthen the institution along traditional lines and reaffirm the divine authority of the Church and its shepherds, to refute all challenges by reviving age-old holy words and dogmas.

Oxford was a natural center of Church power. While doctrinal disputation flourished there, over glasses of port and in easy chairs, Oxford remained true, at least in externals, to tradition. Canons and deans still held sway, nowhere more than at Christ Church. Oxford and Christ Church did not waver: not until the 1870s could anyone matriculate who was not a member of the Church and who did not swear to uphold the Thirty-nine Articles.

Even here, however, little religious fire glowed. The need to rejuvenate the Church was clear to some, however, and a movement that looked back

to original religious texts and ancient reverences came from within, ultimately taking the university's name: the Oxford Movement looked backward to the beginnings of Christianity, though born paradoxically alongside
the railroad speeding full steam into the future. For Newman and other
Tractarians, studying the ancients carefully secured and strengthened doctrines laid down centuries earlier and even led some of them back to Rome.

For John Keble, John Henry Newman, and, to a lesser degree, E. B.
Pusey, Hurrell Froude, and H. P. Liddon, only one Church existed, the
Apostolic Church, with holy and divine doctrines that came down from the
Apostles. Apostolic Descent became their credo, and it appealed to many,
including Charles Dodgson senior. The Tractarian debate absorbed Oxford
and caused thinking people to examine their beliefs and take sides. The established Church reaction to the Tractarians was so fierce that Newman was
accused of heresy and had to leave Oxford altogether. Pusey fared somewhat
better. Although he too was accused of heresy and banned from preaching
within the university for two years, he survived and retained his professorship and his canon's stall at Christ Church. He became the leader of a group
who believed that the Church of England, while part of the Church of
Rome, was independent and had its own Anglican divines and its own inspired traditions.

In addition to the groups already contending at Oxford, when Charles
entered the university and during his years there, a "new current came in
from Rugby, and the influence of Dr. Arnold," according to Andrew Lang.
". . . Liberalism in history, philosophy, and religion, was the ruling power;
and people believed in Liberalism. What is, or used to be, called the Broad
Church, was the birth of some ten or fifteen years of Liberalism in religion
at Oxford. The *Essays and Reviews* were what the *Tracts* had been. . . .
Homeric battles . . . [left] the ship of the University lurching and
rolling. . . ."[1] G. M. Young added that in "the forties we are aware of a new
type issuing from the Universities and public schools, somewhat arrogant
and somewhat shy, very conscious of their standing as gentlemen but very
conscious of their duties, too, men in tweeds who smoke in the streets, disciples of Maurice, willing hearers of Carlyle, passionate for drains and co-
operative societies . . . the Arnoldians."[2]

An entry in Charles's diary (April 23, 1856) captures the explosive possibilities of the time: "Heard [Alessandro] Gavazzi[3] lecture in the town Hall
on Tractarianism: very little could be heard, as the undergraduates present
hooted and hissed a great part of the time. [William] Ince [later Canon of

Christ Church] . . . made a speech from the platform to try to obtain order, but it had almost no effect. The lecture was well delivered, but mere rhetorical nonsense in substance: he quoted (in order to refute) an argument for the Pope's infallibility, that he claims this on the grounds of being called 'Most Holy': I doubt the argument ever having been seriously put forward."

Charles actually received his baptism in doctrinal controversy well before he came to Oxford, when he witnessed denunciations of his father's own fervid creed. The dispute arose in 1847, when he was fifteen. The Reverend G. C. Gorham, Fellow of Queen's College, Cambridge, publicly questioned the validity of baptismal regeneration, a fundamental Church dogma, and the Bishop of Exeter, Henry Philpotts, refused to install him as Vicar of Brampton Speke. Gorham appealed to the judicial committee of the Privy Council and was vindicated, his argument being judged consistent with Church formularies. The case attracted considerable attention, the Church party insisting that by the judgment, the Crown had invaded sacred Church territory. The controversy dragged on, and in 1850 Charles's father published *The Controversy of Faith: Advice to Candidates for Holy Orders on the Case of Gorham v. the Bishop of Exeter,* reviewing the history of the dispute and, as Ivor Ll. Davies summarizes it, taking the view that "liberty of opinion and unity of faith are two principles in perpetual opposition and that tension must always exist between them."[4]

In early February 1852, when Charles was already set at Oxford, Dodgson senior preached at the consecration of St. Thomas's Church in Leeds a sermon that was published as *Ritual Worship,* a work that encapsulates High Church differences with Lower Church and reform movements as it describes the clash between Romanists and Dissenters.

Dodgson senior looked strictly to the past for authority and accepted only orthodox words and sacraments as holy: "The self-same argument which makes toleration a duty makes compromise a sin." He agreed with the Tractarians on the principle of Apostolic Descent, that no cleric is properly ordained without the laying on of hands.

The sermon caused something of an uproar, at least in the north of England. William Goode, then Dean of Ripon, charged the senior Dodgson with following Newman and Henry Edward Manning Romeward and with "publishing and preaching false doctrines," and branded him a heretic. But Dodgson's longtime friend Bishop Longley persuaded Goode to withdraw the charge. Dodgson nevertheless insisted on defending his position and later that year published *A Letter to the Lord Bishop of Ripon,* iterating the stout conservative position on baptism, absolution, and Holy Communion. Dodgson insists upon the real presence of Christ in the Eucharist: "I . . . hold most strongly that the language both of the Scripture and of the Church is to be regarded as purely *mysterious,* not as metaphorical." He achieved a considerable reputation in the Church of England, went on preaching and publishing his sermons, and emerged not as a Romanizer but as a formidable champion of High Church and Tory orthodoxy, defending compulsory church tithes and opposing nondenominational education.

Charles observed his father's adroit and logical explanations of his beliefs. He was, at the same time, fully aware of the schisms that had taken some Oxford churchmen Romeward; he followed the struggles in Parliament and within the university for extreme reform, even disestablishment, and saw others trying to steer a middle course, retaining the character of the English Church as distinct from Rome and relying upon its own orthodoxies rather than on popish decrees. Somewhere, somehow, he sorted out the arguments for himself. His course ultimately differed significantly from his father's, and in swerving from the parental path, he tempered not only the orthodoxies by which his father lived and breathed but also those held firmly by his Christ Church sponsor, Pusey, his dear friend Liddon, and his Bishop, Samuel Wilberforce.

Seeds of his own brand of Christianity may very well have been sown when Charles was in his teens, at Rugby, "the shrine as well as the breeding ground of liberals."[5] Archibald Campbell Tait, Charles's headmaster and housemaster, like Dr. Arnold before him, was a liberal churchman, opposed as strongly as his predecessor to shackling Christianity in rigid chains. In the early 1840s, as Fellow of Balliol College, Oxford, Tait sought to have Newman's *Tract XC* censured; he assisted in getting W. G. Ward, also Fellow of Balliol, but one who bent even more readily toward Rome than Newman, dismissed from his lectureship, and played a part, in early 1859, in having Liddon dismissed as Vice-Principal of Cuddesdon Theological College, near Oxford.

Tennyson, Charles's favorite living poet, surely helped him form his beliefs: Charles read him diligently, quoted him, echoed his verse, and forged an acquaintanceship with him and his family. Charles noted Tennyson's religious liberalism, and at some point he himself embraced the "larger hope" philosophy of *In Memoriam,* a faith ruled by "the Power in the darkness whom we guess." Tennyson rejected rational doubt and replaced it with an inner emotional certainty. Charles in his own way also dispelled doubt. He also saw the connection between Tennyson and the other liberals, most particularly Frederick Denison Maurice, seen by many as the leader of Broad Church liberalism. Tennyson and Maurice were not only close in spirit but also devoted friends. Maurice dedicated his *Theological Essays* (1853) to Tennyson and was godfather to Tennyson's elder son, Hallam. In 1854, appalled at Maurice's being ejected from his King's College, London, professorship on the charge of heterodoxy, Tennyson wrote a consoling poem, "To the Rev. F. D. Maurice," with whom he shared a belief that the idea of eternal punishment is superstition, unworthy of doctrinal sanction.

Charles recognized in Tennyson what Frederic Harrison characterized as the "exquisitely graceful re-statements of the current theology of the broad-Churchmen of the school of F. D. Maurice."[6] Maurice, Stanley, Jowett, and Baden-Powell formed a loose brotherhood and, as Owen Chadwick put it, "were all working separately and cautiously and in different modes towards restating certain Catholic doctrines," even though no one knew "quite who was in the party, or what it was supposed to represent."[7] Tennyson sang the anthem of the new religious liberalism, and Charles, joining Tennyson in acknowledging the mysterious nature of the universe, decided that he too could believe where he could not prove and refused to exclude non-Christians from salvation; like Tennyson, he found the strength of his faith within himself. He saw that Tennyson could question traditional dogma, turn from his father's beliefs, and yet remain an Anglican with a strong, positive Christian faith.

In 1859, two years after Charles met Tennyson, he encountered George MacDonald and quickly became his firm friend and admirer. Both were poets and novelists, both keenly interested in drama, and both struggling with a religious inheritance they could not fully accommodate. MacDonald—like Charles, a clergyman without an ecclesiastical appointment—descended from a stern Calvinist family in Aberdeen and probably faced a difficult struggle to make his way toward a more moderate faith. "Dodgson believed," wrote MacDonald's biographer, "as MacDonald did, that the center-point of the Christian message is that God is a God of love. . . . In the debates then raging . . . these two men . . . must have had much to talk about."[8] Charles would not open up publicly and talk to just anyone about his faith, but to such a sympathetic friend, he found it easy to do.

It was courageous of Charles even to consider deviating from High Church doctrine, and while he made no early pronouncements about his reservations, he probably asked his father to explain some points of dogma and discussed troubling points with him, as he did with Liddon well before their Russian journey. But he did not jump to any early conclusions. At Oxford he tested the water. He scrutinized many branches of the Church tree, and he certainly did not write off the Tractarians, for, through his father's inculcation, he was practically one of them.

On February 25, 1855, Charles went to hear Charles Marriott, one of Newman's disciples, preach at St. Mary's, Oxford: "He scarcely came up to my expectations," Charles wrote, "as his delivery is very monotonous, but his manner is earnest—the sermon itself I liked very much."

Charles admired John Keble (another Victorian thinker who broke away from his own father's religion), included his name in his select list of twelve of "our great poets" (July 24, 1862), and quoted him in the preface to *Sylvie and Bruno*. He went over to Keble's living at Hursley (December 18, 1857) hoping to see him, but the service hour, he learned, had been changed; on October 17, 1862, he wrote to Keble hoping to solicit a contribution to *College Rhymes;* and on May 24, 1864, he heard Keble preach at Cuddesdon: "a nervous, feeble delivery, but a beautiful sermon."

We have no record that Charles ever heard Newman preach, but on November 22, 1868, he read one of Newman's sermons. Eight years later he encountered Newman through an intermediary. The children of R. W. Church, Dean of St. Paul's and an old acquaintance of Charles, introduced Newman to *Alice* and then, evidently, sent him a copy of the *Snark*. Newman wrote to Helen (April 19, 1876), the eldest Church daughter, acknowledging the book, and Church sent Charles either the letter or a copy: "Let me thank you and your sisters without delay for the amusing specimen of imaginative nonsense which came to me from you and them this morning. . . . The little book is not all of it nonsense. . . . 'The Easter greeting to every child, etc.' is likely to touch the hearts of old men more than of those for whom it is intended." Charles and Newman met and Newman agreed "to sit for a photo. . . . But he couldn't come to me: so nothing came of it."[9]

Charles was interested in the Tractarians, perhaps even was eager to join his father's religious party. But he could not follow them all the way, given their rigidities and his own conviction that God "has created beings with *free-will,* and thus has created that which *can* then act in opposition to the Will of its creator. . . ."[10] On the other hand, Charles by no means abandoned his father's precepts in one fell swoop, and never believed that he deserted his father's party altogether: as late as July 7, 1885, he wrote to Mrs. Rix: "I myself belong to the 'High Church' school." But six months later, on January 15, 1886, he wrote to Mrs. Rix's daughter Edith: "I hope you won't be *very* much shocked at me as an ultra 'Broad' Churchman."

Obviously a gradual searching and sifting preceded these remarks. Much of what he believed coincided with Tractarian dogma, but much of it differed sharply. As he grew older, he diverged and refined his faith, still planted in his father's High Church but somewhat modified. No other single force shaped Charles's religion as did his father's teachings, but he had difficulty walking so narrow a path.

The publication of *The Origin of Species* in 1859 and the fierce debates Darwin's book generated shook to the core the faith of many thinking believers—but not Charles. We cannot be absolutely certain that Charles attended the 1860 meeting of the British Association in the University Museum in Oxford, but he probably did. He served "on the reception committee for the men of science from foreign countries and distant parts of the UK"[11] and was not likely to miss so important an event. There "Darwin's bulldog," T. H. Huxley, openly disputed with "Soapy Sam" Wilberforce, Bishop of Oxford, the thorny questions of the descent of man and the oversimplified question of man's relationship to primates, and Wilberforce asked Huxley whether he was descended from the ape on his mother's or his father's side. If Charles was not present, he certainly got an earful about it.

In any case, Charles approached Darwin and *The Origin of Species* in his usual measured way and added to his library no fewer than nineteen volumes of works by Darwin and his critics.[12] His shelves also housed no fewer than five works by Herbert Spencer, the founder of social evolutionary philosophy.

Only a single entry (December 26, 1872) in Charles's surviving diary mentions Darwin by name. Thirteen years after *The Origin of Species* appeared, Charles read Darwin's *The Expression of the Emotions in Man and Animals* (1872), illustrated by Charles's idol Rejlander, sent Darwin a print of one of his photographs, and wrote probably suggesting that if the scientist planned to publish any further work on humanity's expressions, he would be happy to supply appropriate photographs as illustrations. Darwin was happy to have the photograph Charles sent, "although," he added (December 10, 1872), "I am doubtful whether I shall ever make any actual use of it." On the fourteenth he wrote that he planned no further work on expressions, but would not forget Charles's offer should an "occasion occur."[13]

Evidently Charles was not entirely repelled by Darwin's theories, or he would not have been willing to associate his own work with them. He did not swallow Darwin's speculations whole but believed that the scientist's work deserved attention.

In chapter 5 of *Sylvie and Bruno*, he invents "Darwinism reversed" when a lady fellow-traveler suggests that the speed of railway travel has added a new compressed species to English literature, where "the Murder comes at page fifteen, and the Wedding at page forty." The narrator then suggests that when we move forward and travel by electricity, we shall have further compression, mere leaflets with the Murder and the Wedding on the same page. "A development worthy of Darwin!" the lady exclaims.

Another jocular reference to Darwin occurs in May 1872, in *The New Belfry*, section 8, "On the Feelings with Which Old Ch. Ch. Men Regard the New Belfry": "Bitterly, bitterly do all old Ch. Ch. men lament this latest lowest development of native taste. 'We see the Governing Body,' say they: 'Where is the Governing *Mind?*' And Echo (exercising a judicious 'natural selection' for which even Darwin would give her credit) answers— 'where?' "

In a letter that Charles published (October 29, 1874) in the *Pall Mall Gazette*, "Original Research," he ridiculed as ill conceived a proposal for three-year endowments for scientists engaged in original research and pointed out, tongue in cheek, that "all great things . . . come slowly to the birth. . . . Darwin for two-and-twenty years pondered the problem of the origin of species." Charles alluded again to Darwin in June 1875 in his *Fortnightly Review* essay, "Some Popular Fallacies about Vivisection." Fallacy 4 asserts: *"That man is infinitely more important than the lower animals, so that the infliction of animal suffering, however great, is justifiable if it prevent human suffering, however small."* On which Charles comments: "A strange assertion this, from the lips of people who tell us that man is twin-brother to the monkey!"

By November 1, 1874, Charles had "read the whole of [St. George] Mivart's *Genesis of Species* [1871], a most interesting and satisfactory book, showing, as it does, the insufficiency of 'Natural Selection' *alone* to account for the universe, and its perfect compatibility with the creative and guiding power of God." Charles read the book even though its author had been ostracized by the scientific community. He was more interested in ideas than reputation and was willing to look for "answers" in the work of a Roman Catholic zoologist who put forth a reasoned and informed argument admitting the validity of evolution but emphasizing the distinction between organic and inorganic matter.

Charles made a modest bow toward "Natural Selection" when he invented a chessboard game that, in 1878, he called first by that name (he later changed it to *Lanrick*), and in which, of course, the winner is the survivor of the fittest.

Perhaps his most blatant comment is a monkey-baboon that he pictures in his own drawing of the animals in the pool of tears in *Alice's Adventures Under Ground*. Some see the *Alice* books as expressing Charles's anxieties about Darwin's theories. They see in the "Pool of Tears" episode the fall into the salty primeval pool; Alice, as the only human being in the scene, outnumbered by animals, representing humanity no longer in control of nature (as if it ever is); the brutality ("speak roughly," "off with his head") as the mode of primitive existence; and the hovering danger of regression from human being back to ape, back to pig. But Charles is only having fun, making a topical joke in his drawing, knowing that the Liddell girls would appreciate the humor.

Charles's reaction to *Essays and Reviews* (1860), that rebellious volume of Broad Church challenges to established doctrine, holds no surprises either. Instead of exploding in agreement or dissent, he observed and waited. As we shall see, the essay by H. B. Wilson fueled strong doctrinal fires by rejecting eternal punishment. Charles was certainly in Wilson's camp on this one point of dogma, and yet he objected to the flagrant display of dissension: in his 1865 humorous skit on Jowett's stipend, *The New Method of Evaluation as Applied to* $\pi$, he says that the authors of *Essays and Reviews* inhabit a two-dimensional plane and lack novelty. F. D. Maurice's view was similar: the essayists should have plumbed deeper waters.[14] Charles does not, however, limit his criticism to the essayists, but points to the shortcomings of positions taken by Pusey, Liddon, Liddell, and others, all only faintly disguised by their initials. The narrowness of their approaches offends Charles; he wants a larger, more encompassing approach to religious faith. He detests theological controversy most of all because it goes contrary to Christ's teaching and his own belief that instead of contending, Christians should practice self-denial and love.

Of all the influences on Charles's faith, two men, Samuel Taylor Coleridge and Frederick Denison Maurice, were especially significant. They, in fact, helped Charles shape a faith that he could believe in wholeheartedly; in time they won his deep devotion. Metaphorically he sat at their feet. Both theological giants had themselves rebelled against their Unitarian upbringing and sought a new understanding within the boundaries of Christianity. Historians of religion often dub Coleridge the spiritual founder of the Broad Church movement and Maurice its high priest, although neither man made such claims.

*F. D. Maurice, the controversial churchman whom Charles knew and admired*

Maurice was a contemporary of Charles's father, a preacher, and a theologian. Charles knew his written work, sought Maurice out, and became acquainted with him. Coleridge died when Charles was two years old. Charles knew him only from his work, particularly a single work that Coleridge published late in life: his theological *apologia, Aids to Reflection.* First published in 1825, it was the mainspring of Charles's conversion.

Before addressing Coleridge's tome, however, let us turn to the Victorian figure who personally played a significant role in Charles's life. F. D. Maurice is not today a household name, but in his time he was enormously influential. Maurice was from the 1850s a friend of Daniel and Alexander Macmillan, the brothers who founded the publishing house; they published his books and spoke of him as "the Prophet." He was the guiding light behind *Macmillan's Magazine* and its liberal religious credo. As Alan Hertz puts it, the magazine "consistently opposed all attempts to define Anglican theology precisely and fought to keep the unorthodox and the eccentric in the Church."[15] When Daniel Macmillan's second son was born, he was named Maurice after his godfather. His son, the future prime minister and first Earl of Stockton, was, in turn, named Maurice Harold.

Maurice was born a quarter of a century before Charles. He was the son of a Unitarian minister, but, his mother and sisters being staunch Calvinists, he grew up in a home riven by religious conflict. In time Maurice went off to Cambridge, where, with John Sterling, he founded the renowned Apostles and openly fought the Utilitarian Benthamites, then the dominant philosophical party at Cambridge. Maurice never met Coleridge, but he steeped himself in the poet's works, including *Aids to Reflection*, and saw in them great meaning. Coleridge's teachings helped lead Maurice to convert from his father's Unitarian Church to the Church of England. He left Cambridge without a degree and became an undergraduate again, this time at Exeter College, Oxford. He read for holy orders and was baptized and ordained in 1834, the year Coleridge died. From that time on, and especially during the early years after Coleridge's death, when Coleridge's teachings came under severe attack, Maurice preached Coleridgean doctrine, sought to make his work accessible to everyone, and defended Coleridge as an inspired teacher and thinker.

What Maurice found in Coleridge and then preached and taught was a belief in a personal—not an abstract—God. Along with Coleridge, he believed that God revealed himself to human beings through themselves, that they were created to feel and to know God. The trouble with the age, he insisted, was that people did not speak directly to God. Religion did not consist of belief in God but was about God, even against God. "We have been dosing our people with religion when what they want is . . . the Living God. . . ."[16]

Maurice insisted that man's rationality cannot prove religious truth. One arrives at religious truth not by discussing it or by voting on doctrine; religious truth possesses its own evidence, the evidence that it satisfies an inner need. In *The Kingdom of Christ* (1838), which Charles must have read, Maurice examines the religious principles of a Quaker, a Protestant, a Unitarian, and a modern philosopher, insisting that truth does not belong to any one party but exists partly in what each sect believes, and he finds condemning the beliefs of others reprehensible. He was opposed to systems and believed that the Bible, the Creeds, and the Book of Common Prayer were the true Christian's protection against religious systems. While Maurice was not a Universalist, his was a universal faith set within a universal church that embraced all parties. The most secure and binding force is the Bible, which he regarded as the revelation of the kingdom of God. Within a huge enclave of different religious parties, each individual must find his own truth. He cannot come by it secondhand, not from church authority, from church party, from teacher, from parent—he himself must search for it and discover that divinely inspired spark in himself. Religious truth comes not through the intellect but through revelation. And yet, although one's faith is individual, Maurice sees a unifying element within all believers and seeks to make that universal element live within Christendom.

Like Coleridge, Maurice believed in free will and the need to exercise it. He broke with the Tractarians because they interpreted Christianity along restrictive lines. He criticized them for endeavoring, as he puts it, "to pull down other men's truth because it is not the same position as their own."[17] Truth, for both Coleridge and Maurice, lived only in an ethos that enabled one to search and choose.

Maurice's principal teaching is that "the *starting-point* of the Gospel . . . is the absolute Love of God; the reward of the Gospel is the knowledge of the love."[18] With Coleridge, he is concerned about the young and fears that all the philosophies, all the divided sects, factions, parties, and branches only confuse them, that sectarian argument swallows up truth. He urges them to replace argument with inner enlightenment.

Maurice possessed a magnetic personality, and his oratorical skill made him a persuasive preacher and teacher. He attracted a large following of young people to his church in London and, both in his sermons and in private conversation, preached to them that evil exists in "the inclination of every man to set up himself, to become his own law and his own centre, and so to throw all society into discord and disorder."[19]

He wrote prolifically, challenging restricted views on the nature of God, Judgment Day, the Bible, and eternal punishment. Through Christ, Maurice teaches, we are assured divine love even in death. In *Theological Essays* (1853), a copy of which Charles owned, he rejects eternal punishment, a doctrinal bulwark of the Church, and was consequently accused of heresy and expelled in 1853 from his post as Professor of Divinity at King's College, London.

Maurice did not fit into a mold. Much of his teaching, like that of his mentor Coleridge, was liberal. But he revered the past and the Sacraments; he valued history and held that studying it yielded truth. And while he could not accept orthodox readings of the Thirty-nine Articles, especially as interpreted by those he called the "Oxford Proctors," he eloquently defended the Articles themselves.

In one important detail Maurice went beyond Coleridge: he not only wrote about his beliefs but also practiced them by developing, with John Malcolm Ludlow and Charles Kingsley, the Christian Socialist Movement, by founding Queen's College, London, for educating women, and by helping to inaugurate the Working Men's College. He believed that faith without good works is useless.

Unlike Maurice, Charles had no distinct socialist inclinations. He was generous and charitable and did much for good causes, but he did not believe in the possibility of instituting social democracy. Maurice's liberal religious philosophy, however, attracted Charles. On July 20, 1862, when Charles was thirty, he went, while in London, to both morning and afternoon services at Maurice's church. "Mr. Maurice preached both times," Charles wrote. "I like his sermons very much." On February 2, 1863, he "went to Mr. Maurice's church. . . . There was communion, and as there seemed to be no one to help him, I sent him my card, and offered to help. This lucky accident led to my making his acquaintance. I went back to Lunch with him and Mrs. Maurice." Eleven days later, what Charles called a "shower of newspaper letters" appeared in the press concerning the proposed prosecution of Benjamin Jowett at Oxford for heresy for his views on atonement and for insisting that St. Paul's words must not be taken literally. Maurice wrote a letter in reply to one by Pusey. Charles believed that "there was . . . much that . . . [Maurice] had misunderstood" and wrote him a long letter on the subject. Two days later Charles "got a long earnestly written answer from Maurice," and on the following day Charles "wrote a 2nd long letter to Maurice."

This exchange over Jowett, who was forced to resubscribe to the Thirty-nine Articles, advanced Charles's friendship with Maurice. Five months later (July 19, 1863), Charles, again in London, went once more to Maurice's church to hear him preach and, on the following Sunday, attending with the George MacDonalds, met with Maurice after the service. On the next day "Mr. Maurice came to Luncheon and sat for his picture."

When, on January 24, 1864, Maurice preached in Westminster Abbey, Charles was in the congregation. In June and July of that year, Charles heard Maurice preach at least twice. Then a two-year hiatus seems to have occurred. But on June 24, 1866, he writes: "Maurice's church as usual. . . ." As usual? Well, yes, very much a standard pattern for Charles: when his activities became ordinary or cyclical, he never mentioned them. He had undoubtedly been attending Maurice's church often when in London, and going to hear Maurice preach had grown into a custom, if not a ritual. Again on April 7, 1867, Charles went "as usual to Vere Street Chapel. . . . As a great many stayed for the Communion I offered my help: even with three it took a long time. . . ." By this time Maurice's skill as preacher had spread wide and his services were well attended. The following spring Charles went "to Maurice's church in the morning. . . . The 'Benedictus' chant was . . . very beautiful." That is the last reference in the diary to Maurice. Maurice preached his last sermon at Vere Street in 1869 and died in 1872.

It is reasonable to suppose, given Charles's friendship with and admiration for Maurice, that he read much of his published work. In fact, reading Maurice may have led him to Maurice's church in the first place. His close acquaintance with Coleridge's theological philosophy and the connection between Coleridge and Maurice in all likelihood also drew him from one to the other.

We would not ordinarily associate Charles with Coleridge. True, he owned Coleridge's collected works along with individual volumes of his poems and prose. But we all own many books we rarely dip into, let alone read from cover to cover. And even among the books we read, few touch us deeply. Charles quotes here and there from "The Rime of the Ancient Mariner," but so do we all. One might fairly expect Charles to know Coleridge's major poetry because he was keen on the Romantic poets. Indeed he alludes to Coleridge as early as 1854, in his story "Wilhelm von Schmitz." He read part or all of Coleridge's *Biographia Literaria* and the treatise on church and state because the subject matter interested him. We know for a fact that he read Coleridge's *Aids to Reflection* and that it meant a great deal to him. If we look at *Aids to Reflection* along with Charles's interest in Maurice's teachings, we see where Charles came by some of his less-than-conventional beliefs and where his faith took its nourishment.

It is no secret that Charles was a prodigious reader, eclectic and thorough as in his other interests. Here too he was systematic. What is more, he often went back to books he truly valued, memorized passages, and, in a few cases, actually analyzed their contents, breaking the subject matter down into categories to allow himself easy access to the various parts. When he analyzed a book this way, it meant a great deal to him and was likely to influence his thinking. Such a book was *Aids to Reflection*. It is not exactly light reading. "What is the good of a book without pictures?" Alice asks. Well, no pictures here, but it is a book important for understanding Charles and his time.

Charles read *Aids to Reflection* "in the evening—it is one of those books that improve on a second reading: I find very little in it even obscure now" (January 14, 1855). That would appear to be his second reading of the book. Just over six months after the first entry in his diary about Coleridge's work appears, on August 5, he wrote: "Began an analysis of Coleridge's *Aids to Reflection*." Two and a half years after he first resolved to analyze the book (January 3, 1858), he wrote: "Began Coleridge's *Aids to Reflection*, for the second time"—it must actually have been at least his third—and he added: "I intend to make a sort of analysis of it this time, and also to apply the system

given opposite to page 100," where we read: "I want to organise some regular means, by which all valuable reading may be available afterwards . . .
[that is,] that I may be able in a moment to refer to any part of it. This must
be done by various 'indices' which like the absorbent ducts in the human system, shall each mechanically take up and secrete what belongs to its department. I will make a list of the subjects opposite, with the means provided or
to be provided for the prosecution of each." His list comprises seven headings: (1) Miscellaneous, (2) Etymology, (3) Theological Questions, (4)
Metaphysics, (5) Political Economy, (6) Undesigned Coincidences, (7) Subjects to be Investigated. When he began to analyze Coleridge's *Aids to Reflection,* one can assume that he broke the contents down into these
categories. The book obviously had a firm grip on him and helped to shape
his thinking and his faith.

If *Aids to Reflection* presented almost nothing obscure to Charles, he was
truly exceptional, because the work is an intricate mesh of thought and impression, woven together with tenuous and fleeting connectives. It is at once
daunting, inspiring, substantial, and ethereal. It was ahead of its time when
it appeared in 1825, and claimed no significant audience. While the Christian world was reaching for external evidence to justify faith, Coleridge au-
daciously offered inner light and conviction as the only evidence worth
seeking. Written in his last decade, it embodied the fruits of all his earlier
efforts to arrive at a spiritual understanding of life.

Like Kant and Fichte, Coleridge insists that the essential source of moral
knowledge is the intuition, not the intelligence. He writes as a teacher,
specifically addressing young men starting on their careers, offering them
advice in a series of aphorisms. It is difficult, even today, to paraphrase his
adages or educe from them a logically developed philosophy, partly because
his maxims are complex and partly because Coleridge sometimes contradicts
himself. His distinctions, between reason and understanding for instance,
and in fact among the numerous subtle forces he writes about, are not conventional. He sets at conflicting poles elements of personality that we ordinarily do not see as opposing one another because, seen together, they
illuminate one another. Essentially, he argues that

1. Man possesses Understanding and Reason, and Understanding is the
   lesser faculty of the two.
2. Understanding gives us access to everyday, common or garden hearing and seeing, enabling us to perceive impressions and to deal with

them; it concerns the practical business of daily life, the empirical side of life.

3. Reason—used in a sense altogether different from what we mean by *reason*—is mysterious, romantic, metaphysical; it gives us access to the real, universal, divine truth; it is the fountain of the moral force that guides our free will; it provides us with our instinct for what is right; it establishes a link between our humanity and the divine; it is the basis of all faith.

4. Animals and men possess Understanding, but only men possess Reason.

5. Man realizes the truth of religion through Reason, through revelation from within.

6. We possess free will, but it is supernatural, literally a free will above nature; if we acknowledge our spiritual promptings and exercise our free will, we achieve both moral and religious unity with God.

7. We need not deny our emotional promptings, but we must subject them to the power of Christian conscience and thereby imbue them with morality.

8. Faith is organic, ever growing, ever changing; the best faith is repeatedly challenged by doubts, giving us the opportunity successively and successfully to overpower temptation and doubt.

9. Conscience requires us to believe in God; morality without faith is inadequate.

10. Christianity is necessary to bolster morality, for Christianity is the crown, the apex, of all religious philosophical thinking; it is a way of life, life itself, and a living process: try it!

11. We must strive to achieve a quality of life that intimates life after death.

Coleridge challenges the view of Christianity that the nineteenth century inherited from the eighteenth, an age sworn to a mechanical epistemology, strict rules of thought, and logic at the expense of feeling and intuition. The eighteenth century was, in Coleridge's view, a time when Understanding held sway and Reason lay dormant.

The Bible, as the Word of God, is the heart of Coleridge's faith. "In the Bible there is more that *finds* me than I have experienced in all other books put together," he writes. There he finds "irresistible evidence of its having proceeded from the Holy Spirit."[20] Contesting a precept of the American

Declaration of Independence, that product of some fine eighteenth-century minds, Coleridge denies that we should pursue happiness as an end in itself. If we pursue virtue instead, he argues, happiness will come as our reward. We must not seek even the happiness that derives from doing good; we must simply strive to do good. We must seek the rainbow for itself, not for the proverbial pot of gold.[21]

*Aids to Reflection* surely gave Charles a lot to think about, and he must have found in it support for some thoughts of his own that his High Church father and associates would have considered iconoclastic. In view of Charles's odd poems about sinners and his outpourings about his own sins and sleepless hours, he must surely have listened closely to Coleridge on the subject of sin. According to Coleridge, man cannot be a moral human being without free will: he must be able to choose between good and evil to achieve a moral state. If he errs and chooses evil or, to put it bluntly, commits a sin, Coleridge insists that repentance is in the sinner's power, just like the choice between good and evil. That reassurance must have been most welcome to Charles.

Charles did not have to learn from *Aids to Reflection* about Christian dogma, the Gospel, about life after death, sin and redemption: he had all that hammered into him early. Here he found the liberal philosophy of an inner spirituality that, if not new to him, supported and helped him refine his own belief.

Much of Charles's work as well as his letters show us how his thinking ran parallel to Coleridge's and Maurice's. Take, for instance, the letter to Ellen Terry on November 13, 1890:

> And so you have found out that secret—one of the deep secrets of Life—that all, that is really *worth* the doing, is what we do for *others?* Even as the old adage tells us, "What I spent, that I lost; what I gave, that I had." Casuists have tried to twist "doing good" into another form of "doing evil," and have said "you get pleasure yourself by giving this pleasure to another: so it is merely a refined kind of selfishness, as your own pleasure is a motive for what you do." I say "it is *not* selfishness, that my own pleasure should be *a* motive so long as it is not *the* motive that would outweigh the other, if the two came into collision."

Charles clearly lives by Coleridge's dictum that happiness is not a proper goal and is instead a by-product of a virtuous life.

Charles's attitude toward the Bible, his belief in immortality, his reliance on intuition all suggest Coleridge, and it is these parallels with Coleridge's and Maurice's preaching that signal Charles's movement away from his father's orthodoxy to the less conventional.

We have seen already that in June 1855, when Charles was twenty-three, he eagerly attended theatrical offerings in London. His experience in seeing *Henry VIII* was nothing less than a deeply moving, religious experience for him. And yet he knew that in embracing the theater, he was going against his father's wishes and defying his Bishop's pronouncements that "to attend theatres or operas was an absolute disqualification for Holy Orders."[22]

Charles summarized his departure from various religious strictures in a reply (May 12, 1892) to the father of a child friend who staunchly believed that no true Christian should attend theaters:

> The main *principle,* in which I hope all Christians agree, is that we ought to abstain from *evil,* and therefore from all things which are *essentially* evil. This is one thing: it is quite a different thing to abstain from anything, merely because it is *capable* of being put to evil uses. Yet there are classes of Christians (whose *motives* I entirely respect), who advocate, on this ground only, total abstinence from
> (1) the use of wine;
> (2) the reading of novels or other works of fiction;
> (3) the attendance at theatres;
> (4) the attendance at social entertainments;
> (5) the mixing with human society in any form.
> All these things are *capable* of evil use, and are frequently so used, and even at their best, contain, as do *all* human things, *some* evil. Yet I cannot feel it to be my duty, on that account, to abstain from any one of them.
> . . . Many a Christian parent would say "I do let my daughters read novels; that is, *good* novels; and I carefully keep out of their reach the *bad* ones." And so *I* say as to the theatres, to which I often take my young friends, "I take them to *good* theatres, and *good* plays; and I carefully avoid the *bad* ones." In this, as in all things, I seek to live in the spirit of our dear Saviour's prayer for his disciples: "I pray not that thou shouldest take them out of the world, but that thou shouldest keep them from evil."

He moved out of the mainstream on other issues. Isa Bowman reports that on Sundays in Eastbourne they went twice to church. Yet he would not

force children to attend church service against their will; he opposed making Sunday for them a day of gloom and tried to make it interesting. Isa also
tells us that when the choir entered and the congregation rose, Charles remained seated.

Charles knew well that both Saint John and Saint Paul were unsure about
the destiny of sinners and that Cicero, in his *Tusculans,* wrote that contrary
to the old myths, there were no torments in the hereafter. Charles broke
with Church establishment on the concepts of hell and eternal punishment;
on both these points he stands shoulder to shoulder with both Coleridge
and Maurice. Mary Brown had confided in him her concern about the notion of hell. In his reply in June 1889, he asserts that God "will not punish
*for ever* any one who *desires* to repent, and to turn from sin. If any one says
'It is certain that the Bible teaches that when once a man is in *Hell,* no matter how much he repents, there he will stay for ever,' I reply '*if* I were certain the Bible taught that, I would give up the Bible.' . . . And if any one
urges 'then, to be consistent, you ought to grant the *possibility* that the Devil
himself might repent and be forgiven,' I reply 'and I *do* grant it!' "

He stated his position on eternal punishment again and again, in letters,
in his published work, and most elaborately in an essay he left behind in
proof at his death. There, as elsewhere, he explores logically various positions. He concludes that because God is perfectly good and eternal punishment wrong, God cannot inflict eternal punishment upon anyone repenting
of his sin. If one believes the Bible to be inspired by God, one must hold that
the word *eternal* or *everlasting* is a misconception or mistranslation and that
the Bible says only that God will inflict suffering of an unknown, not eternal, duration. "My own view," Charles wrote to his sister Elizabeth (November 25, 1894), "is that, if I were forced to believe that the God of
Christians was capable of inflicting 'eternal punishment' . . . [unjustly], I
should give up Christianity." These utterances exemplify Coleridge's and
Maurice's reliance upon internal conscience.

Charles was a moderate. He avoided religious zealots just as he distanced
himself from both aristocrats and commoners who came to Oxford to while
away their time, to shoot, to drink, to gamble, but not to work. His humanity and charity reached out to embrace a far larger world of souls than
the High Church would sanction: "Surely one ought not to wish anything
but *good* for *any* living being," he wrote to an invalid in July 1886. "I wonder
if I shall seem to you utterly heretical in confessing that I pray for God's
mercy . . . on all in rebellion against Him." And in October 1890, to the

same recipient: "More and more I am becoming content to know that Christians have *many* ways of looking at their religion, and less confident that my views must be right and all others wrong, and less anxious to bring everybody to think as I do."

He reached out to non-Christians. After seeing Ellen Terry and Henry Irving in *The Merchant of Venice,* he wrote to Terry in January 1880 praising her and Irving for their performances. But he argued with Shakespeare:

> Now I am going to be very bold, and make a suggestion. . . . I want to see that clause omitted (in the sentence on Shylock)—
>
> That, for this favour,
> He presently become a Christian.
>
> It is a sentiment that is entirely horrible and revolting to the feelings of all who believe in the Gospel of Love. Why should our ears be shocked by such words merely because they are Shakespeare's? In his day, when it was held to be a Christian's duty to force his belief on others by fire and sword—to burn man's body in order to save his soul—the words probably conveyed no shock. To all Christians now . . . the idea of forcing a man to abjure his religion, whatever that religion may be, is . . . simply horrible.

Charles insists that the textual jolt destroys the artistic merit of the scene, and he even goes so far as to rewrite the speech.

At the center of understanding Charles's own formularies is the matter of his ordination. Even after resolving in 1857 to prepare for ordination, he waited four years to take the critical step. We do not know the reason for his delays, but they certainly had nothing to do with indolence: no person worked harder toward clear goals. He had already steeped himself in Coleridgean liberalism, and while his own religious principles were strong and his faith genuine, the texture of that faith and his awareness of current doctrinal controversies surely gave him pause. He was not a man to accept dogma blindly; like many of his contemporaries, he had to ponder religious doctrine before making it his own.

But, given the regulations and governing practice of the day, given his own sensitive conscience, how could he remain a member of the cathedral college and do God's work on earth without taking holy orders? That question troubled him deeply. One wonders what discussions Charles had with his father when preparing himself for ordination. He records none, but why not? Did they not discuss, dispute, argue? Was the father so stern in his own religious convictions that the son could not challenge him? In any case, Charles had close at hand, in Oxford, Church authorities and one friend who could surely help him see his position clearly and aid in resolving any conflicts.

Liddon was perhaps easy to talk to and familiar with the problems and the arguments that Charles faced. We lack details of their discussions, but a quarter of a century later (September 1885), Charles took a long, detached look backward when writing his godson-cousin, William Wilcox, a matter-of-fact account of these early days, when he was embarking on his career:

Dr. Pusey . . . sent for me, and told me he would like to nominate me [for a studentship], but had made a rule to nominate *only* those who were going to take Holy Orders. I told him that was my intention, and he nominated me. That was a sort of "condition," no doubt: but I am quite sure, if I had told him, when the time came to be ordained, that I had changed my mind, he would not have considered it as in any way a breach of contract. . . . When I reached the age of taking Deacon's Orders, I found myself established as the Mathematical Lecturer, and with no sort of inclination to give it up and take parochial work: and I had grave doubts whether it would not be my duty *not* to take Orders. I took advice on this point (Bishop Wilberforce was one that I applied to), and came to the conclusion that, so far from educational work (even Mathematics) being unfit occupation for a clergyman, it was distinctly a *good* thing that many of our educators should be men in Holy Orders.

And a further doubt occurred. I could not feel sure that I should ever wish to take *Priest's* Orders. And I asked Dr. Liddon whether he thought I should be justified in taking Deacon's Orders as a sort of experiment, which would enable me to try how the occupation of a clergyman suited me, and *then* decide whether I would take full Orders. He said "most certainly"—and that a Deacon is in a totally different position from a Priest: and much more free to regard himself as *practically* a layman. So I took Deacon's Orders in that spirit. And now, for several reasons, I have given up all idea of taking full Orders, and regard myself (though occasionally doing small clerical acts, such as helping at the Holy Communion) as practically a layman.

Charles's memory served him well in this case. Liddon's diary reveals that he met Charles on and off during 1861. On January 22, 1861, Liddon recorded "Tea with Dodgson"; on March 21 "In afternoon a walk with Dodgson"; on May 2 "In evening dined at Christ Church. Short walk with Dodgson—called on Dr. Pusey." On August 5, 1861, when he was not quite thirty years of age, Charles took the crucial step and offered himself for examination "to be ordained Deacon." On December 7 Liddon recorded "Afternoon walked with Dodgson to Iffley and Park Crescent"; and on the eleventh that Charles came to his rooms in the evening. During these visits Charles and Liddon must have discussed Charles's ordination. On December 22 Charles was ordained Deacon and received his certificate of ordination reading that Bishop Wilberforce "did admit . . . into Holy Orders . . . Charles Lutwidge Dodgson . . . he having first in our presence freely and voluntarily subscribed to the Thirty-nine Articles of Religion, and to the three Articles contained in the 36th Canon, and he likewise having taken the oath appointed by him to be taken."[23]

Even after ordination, Charles still had doubts about his status. He sensed that he was, among the priests and Canons of Christ Church, a sort of odd man out. On October 21, 1862, ten months after ordination, he called on Liddell "to ask him if I was in any way obliged to take Priest's Orders." Charles added: "I consider mine as a Lay Studentship." The "Liberal" Dean at first opposed Charles's partial commitment: "His opinion was that by being ordained Deacon I became a Clerical Student, and so subject to the same conditions as if I had taken a Clerical Studentship, viz: that I must take Priest's Orders within four years from my time for being M.A., and that as this was clearly impossible in my case [five years having passed], I have probably already lost the Studentship, and am at least bound to take Priest's Orders as soon as possible." Charles "differed from this view," however, and the Dean "talked of laying the matter before the electors." Charles may already have become something of an embarrassment at the deanery, and the Dean might have been clinging to a technicality in the hope of disposing of the source of the embarrassment.

The following day brought a complete reversal, but we know not how or why. All we have is Charles's diary entry: "The Dean has decided on not consulting the electors, and says he shall do nothing more about it, so that I consider myself free as to being ordained Priest." Charles's refusal to go on to the priesthood may have become a point of contention between him and other college members. It seems clear that the Dean did not look favorably upon Charles's decision, and this point of disagreement might have rankled, setting the stage for later disputes.

Charles probably discussed religion with George MacDonald as well as continuing his talks with Liddon. The Liddon conversations would have been more significant, for where Charles found in MacDonald a Congregationalist, a friend in assent, in Liddon he encountered a *père manqué.* Liddon wrote in his diary (August 14, 1867): "I had a warm argument with Dodgson about Prayers for the Departed: he appealed as usual to the general practice of the actual church of England." Evidently that was not Liddon's, or Charles's father's, position. In a letter to his sister Elizabeth (November 25, 1894), Charles wrote: " 'Prayers for the dead' I need not say much about. Though I can't go so far as Dr. Liddon, who held that the English Church distinctly *enjoins* it, I can't see that she anywhere *forbids* it. And whatever the *Church* holds, I think it a good practice, quite consistent with the will of God." Prayer was important to Charles, as to Coleridge, who saw it as the intercessory between man and God, and it is affecting to think of Charles on his knees, praying not only for his own deliverance but also appealing on behalf of all of humanity. "I have not forgotten my promise to pray for you," he wrote Edith Miller (April 9, 1893). "I have done so ever since, morning and evening. There are a good many names that I specially mention: and yours has been one." On August 30, 1893, he wrote Gertrude Chataway: "I believe, and *realize* it more as life goes on, that God hears, and answers, our prayers for *others,* with a special love and approval that does not belong to prayers offered for *ourselves.* In that hope I pray for you. . . ." "I have had prayers answered—most strangely sometimes," he wrote an invalid (November 1885), "—but I think our heavenly Father's loving-kindness has been even more evident in what He has *refused* me. . . ."

Nowhere did Charles reveal the "several reasons" that worked against his ever taking full orders. Collingwood speculated about his uncle's decision to go no further, and other speculations weave their way through the accumulated literature on Lewis Carroll. Some believe that he felt encumbered by his speech impediment; that he chose not to submit to the strict rigors of the priesthood; that he was not convinced he could endure the hard labors and constant service that he saw his father perform at Daresbury and Croft; that he would have had to curtail, if not suppress entirely, his interest in both the theater and photography; that he did not wish to give up lecturing for parochial work; that he dearly valued his academic environment and the creative work it made possible; that, without so much as defining the cause, he instinctively saw himself unfit for such an undertaking. Perhaps some of these elements influenced him, but an equally weighty cause for the lesser commitment was surely that he could neither abide the elaborate pomp nor digest the rigid strictures of the main Church.

When Charles entered Oxford at eighteen, he had no difficulty subscribing to the Thirty-nine Articles. On the threshold of his thirtieth birthday, when he came to be ordained, still able to subscribe to the Articles, he nevertheless chose to stop at becoming a deacon—not because of his stammer, not because he was deaf in his right ear, not because he was disinclined to be a shepherd to a flock, nor for the other reasons already detailed, but most likely because he harbored reservations about some of the orthodox dicta. His conscience put a hold on his commitment to the narrow religious principles he had difficulty accepting. Langford Reed reports that Charles, while walking one morning with Irene and Violet Vanbrugh at Eastbourne, admitted his inability to subscribe to the Thirty-nine Articles. He did not meet the Vanbrugh girls until the 1880s, but it would seem that, if true, Charles was confiding a conclusion reached years earlier.[24]

The Thirty-nine Articles, strict in their demands, might have, in part, become a source of difficulty for Charles because of his all-encompassing view of Christianity. He might especially have had trouble subscribing, as required, to the damnatory clauses of the Athanasian Creed, condemning all nonbelievers.

"I find that as life slips away," Charles wrote in a letter in mid-1882, ". . . the life on the other side of the great river becomes more and more a reality, of which *this* is only a shadow. . . ." His view that life is but a dream grew stronger as he grew older. He believed that he was occasionally touched by a greater force than life on earth revealed, that he, from time to time, caught a glimpse of the white radiance of eternity. Some such instances relate to his inspirations for storytelling. He explains, for instance, in the preface to *Sylvie and Bruno*, how he came to write the story:

I jotted down, at odd moments, all sorts of odd ideas, and fragments of dialogue, that occurred to me—who knows how?—with a transitory suddenness that left me no choice but either to record them then and there, or to abandon them to oblivion. Sometimes one could trace to their source these random flashes of thought—as being suggested by the book one was reading, or struck out from the "flint" of one's own mind by the "steel" of a friend's chance remark—but they had also a

way of their own, of occurring, *à propos* of nothing—specimens of that
hopelessly illogical phenomenon, "an effect without cause." Such, for
example, was the last line of *The Hunting of the Snark,* which came into
my head . . . quite suddenly, during a solitary walk; and such, again,
have been passages which occurred in *dreams,* and which I cannot trace
to any antecedent cause whatever.

One may question the quality of inspiration behind the *Sylvie and Bruno*
books, but the same process must have taken place with the *Alice* books, and
the value of that inspiration is beyond dispute.

Given his belief in another world, Charles's interest in the theories of psychical exploration current at the time was natural. He was a charter member of the Society for Psychical Research, in company with Conan Doyle,
Gladstone, A. J. Balfour, Frederic Leighton, Ruskin, G. F. Watts, and many
more, and a member of the Ghost Society. Not only is his longest poem
about a ghost, but he took a particular interest in ghost stories that came his
way and in ghost pictures. "I have taken many photographs lately," Charles
notes (July 13, 1863), ". . . and 2 of the Donkins were 'ghost' pictures and
seem to have succeeded very fairly."[25] He recorded (January 12, 1856) that
Henry Wadsworth Longfellow ostensibly saw the ghost of George Washington ride on horseback past his house, once Washington's headquarters.

He was not immune to the spiritualist fever of the time. On New Year's
Day 1875, at Hatfield House, Charles talked with other guests about "spiritualism," and gradually his interest in spiritualism, thought transmission, and
all supernatural phenomena grew. Indeed, in the *Alice* books, hallucinatory
elements abound, as young people of the marijuana generation have realized.

Charles himself had unusual experiences. "At the evening service," he
noted (September 6, 1891), ". . . a curious thing happened, suggestive of
'telepathy.' Before giving out the 2nd hymn, the curate read out some notices. Meanwhile I took my hymn-book, and said to myself (I have no idea
*why*) 'it will be hymn 416,' and I turned to it. It was not one I recognised as
having ever heard: and, on looking at it, I said 'it is very prosaic: it is a very
unlikely one.' And it was really startling, the next minute, to hear the curate
announce " 'Hymn 416'!" In a letter to his friend James Langton Clarke of
December 4, 1882, he reports that he has just read a pamphlet on

"thought-reading." The evidence, which seems to have been most carefully taken, excludes the possibility that "unconscious guidance by

pressure" . . . will account for all the phenomena. All seems to point to the existence of a natural force, allied to electricity and nerve-force, by which brain can act on brain. I think we are close on the day when this shall be classed among the known natural forces, and its laws tabulated, and when the scientific sceptics, who always shut their eyes, till the last moment, to any evidence that seems to point beyond materialism, will have to accept it as a proved fact in nature.

Charles's library contained numerous volumes on occult subjects; he was aware of the literature on supernatural exploration, and he wrote about fairies. When thirteen, he revealed in a poem that he had a fairy by his side; later he called *Alice's Adventures in Wonderland* a fairy tale. When he asked an eight-year-old niece whether she believed in fairies and she replied that she did not know, he said, "Ah, that is because you have never seen one."[26] A good many fairies romp through Charles's verse and letters; one of his favorite gift books was William Allingham's *Fairies;* and when he engaged Gertrude Thomson to draw pictures for him, he asked her to draw only fairy pictures. "It may interest some of my Readers," he wrote in the preface to *Sylvie and Bruno Concluded,* "to know the *theory* on which this story is constructed. It is an attempt to show what might *possibly* happen, supposing that Fairies really existed; and that they were sometimes visible to us, and we to them; and that they were sometimes able to assume human form: and supposing, also that human beings might sometimes become conscious of what goes on in the Fairy-world—by actual transference of their immaterial essence, such as we meet with in 'Esoteric Buddhism.' "

He believed us capable of "various psychical states, with varying degrees of consciousness," and he described three: first, our ordinary state of consciousness; second, the "eerie" state, in which the person, while still in an ordinary conscious state, is aware of fairies; and third, a trancelike condition, in which, while the person is unconscious and probably asleep, "his immaterial essence" migrates to another realm and is absolutely conscious of fairies. Naturally the narrator of the tale experiences all three states.

While Charles did not join the scientists of the time who tried to relate miracles to natural science, he believed that miracles might occur, and by April 11, 1880, was making "a few investigations" in connection with a paper he was writing, "Miracles—why have they ceased?" If he wrote such a paper, however, we have not found it. Charles sent Edith Rix a copy of a sermon by F. W. Robertson on Christ's miracles, where Robertson wrote of the character of miracles as "the outward manifestation of the power of God, in order that we may believe in the power of God in things that are invisible."[27]

Charles stood on the threshold of modern exploration into psychological and supernatural phenomena. He tried to assemble evidence that would enable him to think one way or another, but his belief in the Bible and the teachings of Christ was never shaken. He embraced and practiced charity in the face of theological bickering, but kept an open mind about unexplained forces. If his speculations seem naïve, we must remind ourselves that we do not have many more certain answers to his questions than he had.

A stern critic of personal behavior and social conduct, especially in matters concerning religion, Charles might have censured himself sharply for the humor in his work. For him, however, there was no harm in fun and laughter, as long as it was kept separate from sacred subjects. While the Calvinist and Evangelical traditions of the time deplored the light and the frivolous, Charles did not subscribe to their restrictions. He would not allow humor to trespass where sanctity lived, but insisted that humor had its place in our lives. He touched upon the "relation of *laughter* to religious thought" in a letter he wrote his young lady friend Dora Abdy (December 8, 1896): "While the laughter of *joy* is in full harmony with our deeper life, the laughter of amusement should be kept apart from it. The danger is too great of thus learning to look at solemn things in a spirit of *mockery,* and to seek in them opportunities for exercising *wit.* . . . Surely there is a deep meaning in our prayer, 'Give us an heart to love and *dread* Thee.' We do not mean *terror:* but a dread that will harmonise with love; 'respect' we should call it as toward a human being, 'reverence' as towards God and all religious things."

But in his *Easter Greeting to Every Child Who Loves "Alice,"* he makes the point differently: "Surely . . . innocent laughter is as sweet in . . . [God's] ears as the grandest anthem that ever rolled." And in the preface to *Sylvie and Bruno,* he defends his decision to introduce graver thoughts along with the nonsense of the tale; he does not see them as incompatible at all. Charles recognized the natural link that exists between mathematics and humor: they are, in fact, both forms of play; and just as a joke or a witty anecdote relies upon a polished and terse delivery, so a mathematical proof does upon an elegant brevity. Unlike Dickens and Meredith, who use laughter "to ridicule in order to correct, or at least to unsettle things and ideas,"[28] Charles uses laughter as relief, like a holiday from the seriousness of life.

Because he was a mathematician-logician, his interest in fairies and miracles and his reliance on intuition suggest to some a basic contradiction in his mental framework. But he had no difficulty in reconciling these seemingly disparate elements. "Mathematical patterns are pure, timeless concepts," writes Martin Gardner, "uncontaminated by reality. Yet the outside world is so structured that these patterns in the mind apply to it with eerie accuracy. Nothing has more radically altered human history than this uncanny, to some inexplicable, interplay of pure math and the structure of whatever is 'out there.' The interplay is responsible for all science and technology."[29]

Victorian England optimistically believed that science served as the norm of truth and that, as one historian puts it, "mathematical truth was central to theology," an "exemplar of the perfect truth to which the human intellect aspired." Some even argued that "knowledge of the divine partook of the same transcendental necessity as knowledge of mathematics" and that knowledge of God had the "unquestioned status of geometrical truth."[30] Mathematics was seen as uniquely capable of providing truths about the nature of reality. This conviction rested on two beliefs: that truths about the nature of reality are conceivable and that they can be generated from axioms. Geometry is paramount in this scheme of things, because, of all the branches of mathematics, it uses axioms to arrive at truth. Charles's mathematical writings deal more with geometry than with any other branch of mathematics: *Euclid and His Modern Rivals* and *Curiosa Mathematica, Part I, A New Theory of Parallels* went far beyond his needs as a teacher, and, as Francine Abeles indicates, were truly "works of devotion."[31] In Euclid's dependence on "meaningful self-evident axioms," Charles found "the beauty and intellectual significance . . . of mathematics": he would surely have agreed with Edna St. Vincent Millay that "Euclid alone has looked on Beauty bare."[32]

As Charles wrote in one of his letters to an Agnostic (May 31, 1897), a proposition based on these axioms would force even someone "anxious *not* to believe it" to acquiesce: "He would not be able to help himself: he *must* believe it." He knew, however, that religion differed from mathematics. Indeed he understood too much about mathematics and logic to believe that either could provide *a priori* proof of God's existence. Still, while conceding that Christian belief could not compel the same universal obedience as Euclidean propositions, he thought at times about both mathematics and religion in scientific terms. Some Christian beliefs, he wrote in the same letter,

are what would be called in Science "Axioms," . . . quite incapable of being *proved*, simply because *proof* must rest on something already granted. . . . The existence of Free Will is an Axiom of this kind. Consequently, if, in any discussion . . . one accepts some Axiom . . . , and the other does not, there is not more to be said: further discussion is useless.

The other beliefs of Christianity are mostly, if not wholly, believed as a *balance of probabilities:* one who is resolved *not* to believe never finds himself *compelled* to believe: there is always room for *moral* causes to come in, such as humility, truthfulness, and, above all, the resolution to *do what is right*.

Thus, in mathematics, Charles sought reasoned proofs of logical propositions; in matters of religion, he recognized that although, as in Euclidean geometry, a believer had to accept certain axioms, he must move on from them to religious tenets that depend in part on intuition, the balance of probabilities, and moral causes.

Charles must have realized that his altered view of religion would not be welcome in the main Church, nor would his liberal notions be acceptable on the hearth at Croft, in the sitting room at Guildford, or with many of his stiff-collared colleagues in Common Room. T. B. Strong, who had ample opportunity to converse with Charles, refers to his disinclination to discuss religion: "It is difficult to speak of a side of his character in regard to which he was very reserved."[33] "I *hate* all theological controversy," Charles confessed to Mrs. Rix (July 7, 1885). "It is wearing to the temper, and is I believe (at all events when viva voce) worse than useless." Controversy is, in any case, a breeding ground for animosity, for hate, and Charles believed that love "makes the world go round."

What have we here, then, in Charles Dodgson? A renegade? A heretic? Hardly. A socialist like William Morris or Charles Kingsley? No. A militant liberal like Dr. Thomas Arnold? Certainly not. An iconoclast like Jowett? No again. A freethinker like Matthew Arnold or T. H. Huxley? Not a bit. The sum of his beliefs, like Coleridge's and Maurice's, defies labels. But like Coleridge and Maurice, he harbored a reverence for the past, a holy respect for the Bible and the teachings of Christ, an insistence on inner knowledge, a reliance on intuition and conscience—in other words, a mixture of elements that we can call both liberal and conservative. When all is said and done, he was his own man, having forged a faith intricately wrought and unique.

There emerges a man who thought carefully, deeply, and constantly about what is right and wrong, who asked all the crucial questions about life and death, good and evil, seeking answers from congenial guides, and ultimately tested and shaped his own faith and destiny. He was, in essence, a solid Christian, and he lived by Christian principles, more diligently than most of those high-minded churchmen who despised his moderation.

Charles's faith did not, then, derive entirely from domestic and school-house instruction; even though he aligned himself with his father, he rejected much of his father's teaching. Looking inward, as he so often did, must have gone against the grain of accepting traditional dicta without examining them. "God has given . . . [us] conscience (that is an intuitive sense of 'I ought,' 'I ought not'), and this . . . we ought to obey," he wrote Mary Brown (December 20, 1889). When he said that we must subject our faith to conscience, he echoed not his father, but Coleridge and Maurice, particularly Coleridge's Reason. He subscribed to a belief in the spark of divinity he found within himself, the spark that his two mentors helped him recognize.

One overpowering paradox is that no man lived more by the rules of logic or placed so much value on reasoning power than Charles Dodgson; and yet, the writings of his religious mentors, Coleridge and Maurice, are often cloudy and sometimes opaque. Even their most fervent disciples were often baffled by the vagueness and confusions that arose from their unconnected, disjointed illogicalities. But here is where Charles's own logical faculties come into play: he internally organized his mentors' utterances so that they became reasonable for him. He did not find *Aids to Reflection* difficult because of his own inner power to see through the difficulty. What is more, he was able to listen to his inner voice, to the advice Coleridge gave him in "Dejection: An Ode"—

> Ah! from the soul itself must issue forth
> A light, a glory, a fair luminous cloud
> Enveloping the Earth

—and to stand firmly by the sage's side when he read:

> I may not hope from outward forms to win
> The passion and the life, whose fountains are within.

If a human being "acts without attending to that inner voice," Charles wrote to Mary Brown (December 26, 1889), ". . . he is . . . doing wrong, *whatever* the resulting act may be. . . . Don't worry yourself with questions of *abstract* right and wrong. When you are puzzled go and tell your puzzle to your Heavenly Father . . . and pray for guidance, and then do what seems best to *you*, and it will be accepted by Him." This "inner voice," the intuition, is, as we have seen, what Blake, Coleridge, and Charles Dodgson saw as intrinsic, and what they worshiped, in the child.

When Charles wrote Mrs. Rix in 1885, he went on to say: "My dear father was a 'High Church' man . . . and I have seen little cause to modify the views I learned from him, though perhaps I regard the holding of different views as a less important matter than he did." Charles was writing seventeen years after his father's death, and his guilty burden and the aura of nostalgia might have led him to forget some facts and to gloss over others. If his father could be accused of leaning Romeward, and he was, and could contribute his most elaborate single labor, his translation of Tertullian, to the Tractarians, even if he was not an absolute Ritualist, as Charles insists he was not, he was a solid pillar of the Church, one who embraced its rigid dogma and ritual. And as Charles intimates, his father could not brook "different views." One cannot imagine the son asking the father about an inner voice, but if he did, what answer did the father give?

Writing to an unidentified recipient three years earlier, in mid-1882, Charles revealed his alliance more accurately:

I am a member of the English Church, and have taken Deacon's Orders. My dear father was what is called a "High Churchman," and I naturally adopted those views, but have always felt repelled by the yet higher development called "Ritualism." . . . But I doubt if I am fully a "High Churchman" now. I find that as life slips away (I am over fifty now) . . . the petty distinctions of the many creeds of Christendom tend to slip away as well—leaving only the great truths which all Christians believe alike. More and more, as I read of the Christian religion, as Christ preached it, I stand amazed at the forms men have given to it, and the fictitious barriers they have built up between themselves and their brethren. I believe that when you and I come to lie down for the last time, if only we can keep firm hold of the great truths Christ taught us . . . we shall have all we need to guide us through the shadows.

He bent toward the straightforward, uncomplicated, direct approach to God, and his personal approach to matters divine was so sacred that he wanted no undergrowth to obstruct his passage. While he had examined various options in earlier years and even along the way, he was not really unbiased or willing to listen to just any argument. The hard core of his belief was too sacred to be tampered with by what he believed to be heretical elements. As early as May 14, 1855, when he was still in his early twenties, he finished reading J. A. Froude's *Shadow of the Clouds* (1847), an autobiographical novel in which the hero endures, like his model in Carlyle's *Sartor Resartus,* a spiritual crisis that causes him to question the validity of his orthodox upbringing. Charles could not even then brook such outright and forthright challenges to what he considered divine precepts, and cut out "the objectionable parts of the book." Less than two years later, when he finished Kingsley's *Hypatia,* although he judged it "powerful," he found it "outrageous to taste in some parts . . . I mean especially the sneers at Christianity which he puts into the mouths of some of the heathen characters."

Charles's unwillingness to allow incursions into holy ground makes humbug of the notion that the *Alice* books are allegories or parodies of doctrinal controversies. While Charles could criticize the liturgy and even some churchmen, anyone who sees him plain knows just how inconceivable it would have been for him to parody, mock, or satirize any part of Church doctrine. It is surprising that Alexander L. Taylor, one of the more perceptive of Charles's biographers, reads "Jabberwocky" as a parody of the religious controversy raging in Charles's time: "The Tum-tum tree is certainly the Thirty-nine Articles," he writes, and he sees the Jubjub and Bandersnatch as Catholic and Protestant adversaries.[34] Charles would never have suggested anything of the sort. He placed his grave words about religion and his nonsensical verses and narratives side by side, particularly in the *Sylvie and Bruno* books, but he used them alternately and did not blend them. Sacred subjects, while discussed in pages that also bear nonsense, remain sacred subjects and he deals with them reverently.

Charles also disdained extremes, particularly extremes in religious practice, more evident in the High Church than in the Low. Ritualism was one of his bugbears, and in the preface to *Sylvie and Bruno Concluded,* he asserts that what he calls the " 'Ritual' movement" has "introduced many new dangers" into the Church service. Much in the way Church services were conducted he found repugnant. It must have distressed him that his youngest brother, Edwin, became "an extreme 'Ritualist.' "[35] On the other hand, he spent many hours writing letters to a confessed agnostic explaining in excruciating detail the basis of his own faith and trying to argue the recipient into belief.

Charles's heterodoxy led him to take more moderate positions than his father ever could or would. In one of his charges, the elder Dodgson opposed admitting Dissenters to Oxford and insisted that Oxford was "a Religious Seminary attached to the Church of England."[36] Charles, on the other hand, embraced all of humanity. In a letter he wrote to the Lowrie children in Boston, Massachusetts (August 18, 1884), he tells them what he likes to think best, about the *Alice* books:

I've had a lot printed on cheaper paper, in plain bindings, and given them to hospitals and Convalescent Homes—for poor, sick children:

and it's ever so much pleasanter to think of one child being saved some weary hours, than if all the town followed at my heels crying, "How clever he is!" . . . Some rather droll things happened about those hospitals: I sent round a printed letter, to offer the books, with a list of the Hospitals, and asking people to add to the list any I had left out. And one manager wrote that he knew of a place where there were a number of sick children, but he was afraid I wouldn't like to give them any books—and why, do you think? "Because they are Jews!" I wrote to say, of course I would give them some: why in the world shouldn't little Israelites read *Alice's Adventures* as well as other children!

On March 9, 1885, he wrote to Mrs. Rix: "Do not . . . suppose that, because I am a clergyman . . . it would make any abatement in the friendship . . . if you were to tell me you were not 'Church people.' " In the letter of July 7 of that year, he wrote her: "You may be sure that, whether Edith [Mrs. Rix's daughter] were a Roman Catholic, or Wesleyan, or Baptist, or 'Plymouth Sister,' it would be all one to me. . . . And I would escort her, with pleasure, to (the door of) *any* place of worship she liked to attend!" In *Sylvie and Bruno Concluded,* Charles made the Earl say: "How slight the barriers seem to be that part Christian from Christian, when one has to deal with the great facts of Life and the reality of Death!"

In a letter to his niece Edith Dodgson (March 8, 1891), he put the same notion into an ecumenical context: "A truth that is becoming more and more clear to me as life passes away—that God's purpose, in this wonderful complex life of ours, is mutual *inter*action, all round. *Every* life . . . bears upon, or ought to bear upon, the lives of others." Charles became more and more an *amicus humani generis* in the spirit of Coleridge's idea of unity and Maurice's Church Universal. What perhaps is most admirable about the cast of mind and faith that Charles shared with Coleridge and Maurice was a desire to embrace all of humanity, to include sinners and Dissenters, where the obdurate dicta of both the established Church and the Tractarians would have sent them into spiritual exile. He managed to steer his faith confidently through all the religious squalls of his time, and it survived them: the Evangelicals, the Tractarians, the Romanists, Darwin and evolution, *Essays and Reviews,* the Higher Criticism, Mark Pattison and the rise of the "Humanists," Charles Gore's *Lux Mundi,* Huxley's Agnosticism. An essential decency and charity prevailed in this faith that Charles carved out for himself; it served him well and did him honor.[37]

# CHAPTER TWELVE

# *Years of Harvest*

*A chacun selon sa capacité,*
*à chaque capacité selon ses oeuvres.*
MOTTO OF THE SAINT-SIMONIANS

The beginning of 1870 heralded the birth of Charles's first nephew, Stuart Dodgson Collingwood, his godson and, in time, his official biographer. Charles, now thirty-eight, was busy preparing *Through the Looking-Glass,* and in due course it appeared, at the end of 1871. That major effort behind him, he took to the press, determined again to speak his mind publicly where he saw the need for correctives. His letters and articles shot out from Oxford in many directions, appearing in some twenty different periodicals.

He also had privately printed a torrent of pamphlets, broadsides, and booklets, not only for adults and students but also for children, games and puzzles in prose and verse conceived to enlighten and train but mostly to amuse. He concocted some of his most entertaining letters, launched a small parade of whimsical pamphlets connected with his curatorship of the Senior Common Room, and assailed the press with his ruminations and explosions on subjects as diverse as lawn tennis, vivisection, parliamentary elections, and the shower bath. The years ahead would see a good many creative works as well: *The Hunting of the Snark, Rhyme? and Reason?,* the facsimile of *Alice's Adventures Under Ground, The Nursery "Alice,"* and the two *Sylvie and Bruno* books. He would also make some impressive contributions to the study of higher mathematics and logic.

The Christmas season of 1869–70 was full of activity. Charles was at Guildford, as usual, but before returning to Oxford for the new term, he traveled about a bit: to Barnack to visit his friends the Argles, where, in a game of charades one evening, with the assistance of a team of youngsters, he acted out "Carte-ill-age"; to Doncaster on January 14 to stay with another family, the Jebbs, where he inspired more charades at the Vicar's party; to Leicester on the fifteenth to visit the Bennies; then back to Guildford, and from there to London with Arthur Hughes and his family to see a pantomime.

The first German and French translations of *Alice* became realities in 1869, and Charles was arranging for the first Italian translation. Throughout the late 1860s edition after edition of *Alice* appeared, and by 1868 he had recouped all his expenses and was making a profit. He hovered over his *Alice* enterprises like a mother hen over her brood and toyed with various ideas touching the books. He asked Alexander Macmillan what the *Alice* copyright was worth in cash. Macmillan, outraged by the query, wrote (April 12, 1870): "*Alice!* What is she worth? Who knows! If you want to sell I will give you £1000. I don't think I would like to give more. But there or thereabouts is right." Charles retreated. A year later (April 5, 1871), he asked how many *Alice*s had been sold so far that year, and Macmillan replied that they had sold 1,100 copies "against about 1200 at the same time last year."

Charles wanted all later copies of *Alice* to contain a message asking each child reader to send him a photograph in care of Messrs. Macmillan. Macmillan replied to the suggestion in Carrollian terms (March 3, 1870):

> Did you ever take a Shower Bath? Or do you remember your first? To appeal to all your young admirers for their photograph! If your Shower Bath were filled a-top with bricks instead of water it would be about the fate you court! But if you will do it . . . we will help you to the self-immolation. Cartes! I should think so, indeed—cart loads of them. Think of the postmen. Open an office for relief at the North Pole and another at the Equator. Ask President Grant, the Emperor of China, the Governor General of India, the whatever you do call him of Melbourne, if they won't help you. But it's no use remonstrating with you.

Charles again drew back.

He continued ever watchful and tracked down pirates of his work both in England and the United States. He proposed (February 3, 1872) that Macmillan issue a "small and cheap" edition "without pictures" of "Selections" from *Alice* in French and German, with English running parallel to the foreign tongues to help children learn idioms. But this idea also did not bear fruit, until more than half a century later, when Japanese and other foreign-language editions adopted the idea.[1]

Although Charles oversaw the fortunes of his *Alice* books during the first two years of the decade, he was otherwise listless, almost idle, even neglecting what he himself at other times would have considered the very machinery of living. His diary entries during 1870 and 1871 are often perfunctory, not accounting at all for large stretches of time. Even though he was still involved in photography, the theater, art galleries, his reports are matter-of-fact, without a hint of white-stone markers. Not only are the diary entries truncated and infrequent, but the Charles Dodgson–Lewis Carroll publishing enterprises slowed down almost to a halt.

His Christ Church duties were now routine, and lectures no longer gave difficulty. His family was settled in Guildford, and his publishing success had assuaged his earlier financial concerns. But his lassitude could not have been the result of either his work routine or the absence of family or financial worries. It may indicate how deep a scar he bore from the break with the Liddells in 1863—long ago, but still green in emotional memory. His old feelings occasionally surged; on May 4, 1871, for instance, his thoughts flew back to the past: "On this day, Alice's birthday," he writes, "I sit down to record the events of the day. . . ." And when a music publisher wanted to copy some pictures from *Alice* for the title page of their sheet music *The Wonderland Quadrilles* and suggested that they dedicate the music to him or to some member of his family, Charles suggested (November 23) dedicating it to Alice.

His father's death also had a powerful effect upon him. True, he died eighteen months before the new decade began, but a gnawing anguish might have been eating away at Charles, guilt at having denied his father the gratification he had hoped to derive from his eldest son.

Charles made noble efforts to keep the past in perspective and to compensate for his twofold loss. He traveled about a good deal, to homes populated with children who offered him the companionship he needed. These new child friends, in fact, occasionally sparked the old creative fire, and he wrote letters and verses that stand well beside some of his best inventions.

Although Charles never was a social butterfly, he certainly moved about in society during the 1870s. On March 12, 1870, he escaped from Oxford for his first London weekend that term. He went to Moray Lodge, where he was warmly received by a party of five: "Mr. and Mrs. (Kate Terry) Lewis with their little child Katie (aged 2) and 2 charming little nieces of his, Kathleen and Alice Holdsworth (8 and 6), with whom I became great friends by the time I left next day. . . . Mr. and Mrs. [George] du Maurier called in the course of the afternoon," Charles reports. From Moray Lodge he walked to the Terrys', "where nearly all the party were at home." Then back to Oxford by ten that evening. Later that year (December 18), he wrote to Arthur Lewis: "When are you going to have the little Katie and Alice down with you again? I think I fell in love, half with one and half with the other, when I met them at your house—an unfortunate occurrence in this country, where bigamy is not regarded with favor."[2]

In arranging for a visit from the MacDonalds to Oxford in the spring of 1870, he wrote (May 12) to the eldest daughter, Lily, assuring her that the more MacDonald daughters that come the better: "Even such a little one as Mary [sixteen then] might enjoy *some* things in Oxford, you know—such as the toy-shop and the confectioner's, for instance."

The diary entries continue patchy, belying Charles's seemingly active life. "There was little worth recording during term," he wrote (June 25), "and I only paid one visit to Guildford." He singles out Commemoration as "more eventful": the installation of Lord Salisbury as Chancellor of the university, the honorary degree bestowed on Liddon, the inauguration of Keble College, and, what must have been the high point, Liddon's intervention to bring Charles and his camera into the Salisbury circle. He met and photographed all the Cecils present: "I fancy *Wonderland* had a great deal to do with my gracious reception," he wrote. On the afternoon of June 23 "Lady Salisbury and the children came again, first to my rooms, where I showed them pictures, etc., including the seven first pictures for *Through the Looking-Glass*. Then Lady Salisbury went away to make calls, leaving me the children, of whom I took two pictures, one of the two girls, the other of all four. They seem a very pleasant and good natured family, and the children are charming."

Term over, Charles set off on his accustomed rounds: Guildford, London with camera, Eastbourne, and Margate. He actually spent five weeks at Margate with three of his sisters. "I made very many pleasant acquaintances," he notes (October 20, 1870), "chiefly on account of being attracted by their children: very few turned out to be above the commercial class—the one drawback of Margate society. . . . The vacation has produced nothing in the way of work," he added; "however, the entire idleness . . . has . . . been of the greatest possible service to me."

Praising idleness is a new theme for him, a change from recriminations for not achieving his self-styled goals. Six days after returning to Christ Church in the autumn, he wrote to the Dean (October 27) "proposing (now that Sampson is to be Lecturer [in Mathematics]) that in future I shall take Pass-work [instructing students who were taking standard degrees] only, and he Class [honor-degree students], and that, as this will fairly equalise the work, the £500 shall be divided evenly between us, instead of £350 to me and £150 to the assistant-lecturer. I want some spare time very much for reading, etc., and am quite willing thus to buy it. [The Dean] . . . quite approved."

His uncharacteristic desuetude continued through the latter half of 1870. He recorded no depressions, sadness, or grief, but his old vigor was absent; he seems, rather, to float numbly through the days.

Lady Salisbury sent two invitations to Hatfield House. The first he declined because he would not be absent from a Christ Church meeting scheduled to select a new Senior Student; the second, for the New Year's festivities—"the children also wrote a joint invitation"—he accepted. He attended that election meeting on the nineteenth: "The best two [candidates] were very close . . . ," he wrote, "and a motion (proposed by me . . . ) that *two* should be elected was carried by a large majority." At December's end he noted: "No event of interest for the rest of the year." He does not reflect upon the past year, his own state of mind, or his hopes for the future.

He published a few minor items in 1870: two student aids at the University Press, *Algebraical Formulae and Rules for the Use of Candidates for Responsions* and *Arithmetical Formulae and Rules for the Use of Candidates for Responsions,* and near the end of 1870 "Puzzles from Wonderland" in *Aunt Judy's Magazine,* seven puzzles, mostly in verse, invented for the Cecil children. On November 17 he received a copy of *The Songs from "Alice's Adventures in Wonderland,"* the music composed by William Boyd of Worcester College. For Boyd's version he added two lines to "'Tis the voice of the lobster." All in all, not much for Charles Dodgson.

His humdrum existence persisted through 1871. The year began badly. He put up at the White Lion Hotel at Guildford because the Chestnuts was full of visiting relatives, and because of a bad cough, he forwent the Hatfield House New Year's party. Again he dwelled upon his "solitary leisure," finding it "very enjoyable." He tried drawing up "a collection of examples for Lectures," but did not expect to finish during vacation. Then he concludes (January 3) with one of his standard prayers, which is followed by two later "Amen"s. On the following day he finished the text of *Looking-Glass,* "begun before 1869." On the thirteenth he reflected that the sequel "has cost me, I think, more trouble than the first, and *ought* to be equal to it in every way."

Again lacunae appear in the diary, until February 14, when he reports that he had returned to Christ Church on January 17 and has been working as usual ever since. "A working life is a happy one," he writes, "but oh that mine were better and nearer to God!" Another gap occurs between February 14 and March 11, when term ends. Charles lingered on at Oxford, however, to finish his work and avoided Guildford, "because they have 'tonsilitis' [*sic*] going through the family." Another term ensued with a minimum of diary recordings. His life was routine. On June 5, 1871, he felt obliged "to record the events of today, as a specimen of my life just now": breakfast with his friend Faussett; "off (soon after 11) to borrow Julia Arnold for a photograph, brought her back (with Ethel) and did a very good negative of her in Chinese dress." Out walking after lunch, he "again fell in with the Arnolds," took them to St. John's gardens, and then returned home, "where I stayed an hour or so to play croquet with them. . . ." Then he walked with another colleague, dined with Bayne and others, had a visit from W. E. Jelf, classical scholar, who "started, and maintained a long theological talk on Rome, etc.," evidently unaware of or indifferent to Charles's displeasure with such discussions.

Having sent the completed text of *Looking-Glass* to Macmillan, his lassitude set in again. He produced one piece on college matters, *Suggestions for Committee Appointed to Consider Senior Studentships* (fifty-eight lines), which probably grew out of that earlier election meeting. No mathematical items appeared, nor any printed puzzles or games. On May 4 he began working on the Fifth Book of Euclid, but on August 16, after a holiday at Whitby, he recorded "no progress whatever." During the year, two of his verses from *Wonderland* appeared in *Aunt Judy's Magazine*, set to music by the Gatty son, Alfred.

Toward the end of the year Charles composed prologues for two plays that the Hatches planned to perform, and he wrote and printed his leaflet *To All Child-Readers of "Alice's Adventures in Wonderland,"* "a few grave words" he termed it, in which he salutes his unseen child friends with holiday greetings and hopes that they have found "that truest kind of happiness, the only kind that is really worth the having, the happiness of making others happy too!" The leaflets were tucked into copies of the 1872 *Alice* and in the new *Looking-Glass*.

The year ended, however, with the enormous satisfaction of seeing *Looking-Glass* in print and moderately well reviewed, but again he was not well:

from December 7 to 18 he was imprisoned with chills and a cough. Recovered, he joined the family circle at Guildford on the twenty-third.

The change of focus and pace in his activities during these two years is significant. His new emphasis on holidays and leisure, the modicum of published items, and his decision to reduce his lecture load (and his emolument) tell us that he was, at least temporarily, recasting the pattern of his life.

Beginning in 1872, however, the man we knew earlier reappears and indeed produces a cascade of works on diverse themes in numerous forms and for different audiences. Good news about his second *Alice* arrived early in 1872. "My birthday," he writes on January 27, when he turned forty, "was signalised by hearing . . . that . . . [Macmillan] have now sold 15,000 *Looking-Glass*es, and have orders for 500 more." Back at Christ Church for Hilary term, Charles made fresh plans. He wrote out "the Definitions, etc., of Euclid Book I on plan of improving by modern lights, but keeping as much of the original as possible" and discussed the idea with Price. "I want the University to bring out a revised Euclid," he wrote. That evening Charles and his fellow lecturer in mathematics, E. F. Sampson, "went over part of the subject of G.C.S. [Geometric Conic Sections]. Besides these two," Charles added, "I have also a MS. in progress on the summation of series, and a paper about Scholarships as at present given in Oxford." Finally, "I am writing this at 2 a.m. in the morning. . . . God grant that *I* may have grace to recover from the weakness and wilfulness of my life past!"

Euclid dominated Charles's thought and work. His adoration of the past, the hallowing of tradition, the impulse to render the past useful in his world of change, imbued his work. He understood Euclid and believed him a great original thinker. Unlike others, he did not tamper with Euclid's text, and sought to clarify it, to make it available to new generations, to make Euclid meaningful for his time.

Euclid's *Elements,* the classic work on geometry even in its own time, was not an easy crib. The story goes that when King Ptolemy I asked whether there was not an easier road to the comprehension of geometry than the *Elements* provided, Euclid replied, "There is no royal road to geometry." Euclid's *Elements,* comprising thirteen books, ruled the roost for twenty centuries, until early Victorian times, when a spate of anti-Euclidean textbooks appeared. While these did not so much defy as alter Euclid, they presented Euclidean geometry in so many forms that they confused the study of geometry altogether. Charles may have been particularly provoked when the Association for the Improvement of Geometrical Teaching moved to displace Euclid. In any case, he was challenged to stem the tide of these Euclidean contaminators by revitalizing the true Euclid. It was an enormous enterprise.

Between 1860, when Charles published both *A Syllabus of Plane Algebraical Geometry* and *Notes on the First Two Books of Euclid, Designed for Candidates for Responsions,* and 1888, when he saw *Curiosa Mathematica, Part I, A New Theory of Parallels* into print, he published at least twelve items on Euclid. *Euclid, Books I, II,* brought out privately in 1875 and then published by Macmillan in revised form in 1882, reached its eighth edition in Charles's lifetime. It is his early effort to make Euclid's first two books accessible to undergraduates and other beginners. While he retains Euclid's methods of proof and logical sequences, he added some axioms, postulates, and conventions to clarify the material.

*Euclid and His Modern Rivals* (1879), followed by a *Supplement* and a revised edition (1885), was a major effort. It did not come easily and required enormous labor: "Have been at work every day and all day," he wrote on the last day of 1876, "at my . . . *Euclid*"; then, on September 23, 1877, he was struck by the novel idea "of throwing my pamphlet . . . into an entirely different form, viz., a series of dialogues between 'Geometer' on the one hand and Euclid . . . , etc., on the other. The dramatic form will popularize it, and will make any 'chaff' much less out of place than in a regular treatise." He plunged afresh into the new plan, "working 6 or 8 hours a day" at it. On October 23 he was "writing the Euclid book day and night." He put off publication time and again because he was not entirely satisfied with his work. Finally, on February 21, 1879, he took the whole of it to the press. He received printed copies on March 27.

Charles's long and hard labors accomplished two goals: they made Euclid more accessible to Charles's contemporaries and endowed Euclid with a new, modern dignity. But the one fresh quality that Charles brought to this work came from his idea to cast the whole in a Platonic dialogue, enhanced by a trump card—his whimsy.

This four-act comedy, for that is what it is, on a subject excruciatingly difficult to most, is, if not light and airy, at least wise and witty. One may not grasp its subtleties or follow its intricate sequences, but everyone can appreciate the play, the fun. The curtain rises on a don's study. It is midnight. Minos, the Mathematics Lecturer, sits correcting a mountain of student papers, muttering to himself. Enter his colleague Rhadamanthus (probably Charles's fellow mathematical lecturer, Sampson), and they discuss how to mark the answers. Rhadamanthus leaves, and Minos falls into a deep sleep punctuated by snores. We enter his dream world, full of echoes of *Wonderland, Looking-Glass,* and "Phantasmagoria." The ghost of Euclid appears. He will provide Minos with a devil's advocate, Professor Niemand, to represent each of the challengers to Euclidean geometry. In this world of phantoms, less than something (*minus*) plus nobody (*niemand*) adds up to an odd if vigorous team of judges. They consider thirteen rivals as well as a new Syllabus of Geometry (included in "a phantasmic procession" reminiscent of the shades in *Macbeth*). Each rival's work embodies fallacies or inconsistencies, and each falls victim to the superior logic and arrangement of Euclid's *Elements.* Although some of Minos's ripostes are not altogether convincing, Euclidean geometry clearly wins the day.

The dramatic form is engaging, even enchanting. And the wit, although often dependent upon technical subtleties, leavens the loaf. The popular press took note. *Vanity Fair* (April 12, 1879) judged it "absolutely refreshing" and believed it "a book marvellous for the labour contained in it, and still more marvellous for the brightness of the humour with which the ponderous stuff of geometry is handled." The *Saturday Review* (May 10) ran a lengthy dissent: "Mr. Dodgson has brought great knowledge and acuteness to his task, but we must regret the form in which he has cast his book . . . because . . . the effect is to make the argument much harder reading than it would be otherwise." The *English Mechanic* (May 2) insisted, however, that Charles put the case for Euclid well: "On the whole . . . we regard our author as having triumphantly proved that, so far, no work has been produced which is comparable with Euclid's immortal *Elements,* as an introduction to geometry for *beginners.*" The edition sold out in six weeks, and Macmillan suggested printing another 250 copies. But Charles wanted to incorporate the good advice and criticism he had received before proceeding. Then, in July, Macmillan reported no further demand for *Euclid,* and Charles put off a second edition for six years.

"Time has justified Dodgson's scorn" of Euclid's thirteen rivals, wrote H. S. M. Coxeter in 1973, "for all save . . . [two] have been forgotten. . . . Were Dodgson still alive, he would be equally indignant about a new generation of textbook writers. . . . There is much to be said for his standpoint that the degree of rigor in Euclid's *Elements* is just right for high school: a modern axiomatic treatment . . . should be left for mature students in universities."[3]

\* \* \*

All this time Charles kept a critical eye on life in his college, his university, his society, and the world. When he uncovered ugliness or injustice, he put his pen to paper and wrote scathing attacks and proposed reasonable remedies. Often he flew straight in the face of entrenched authorities—Dean Liddell, other university administrators, those in high public office, and even Church leaders. In doing so, he was not so much conservative as humane, and while he was indeed a Conservative by conviction, he was often radical in thought and action, a man of principle, and unafraid. He functioned often as a gadfly on the rump of his college and university, and fellow dons grew to look forward to the witty, sardonic cannonades emanating from his quiet staircase in Tom Quad. They were not disappointed during the 1870s.

From the day Henry George Liddell took up the mantle of Dean of Christ Church, he set into motion a grand plan to refashion it. The deanery, where he and his family were to live, came first, and he turned it into a most comfortable dwelling where Mrs. Liddell might even accommodate the Queen and her entourage. The deanery dealt with, Liddell looked elsewhere in his Xanadu and soon was adding to, subtracting from, refining, restoring, and refashioning the towers, halls, and walls of his domain.

The first project after the deanery to demand his attention was a sacred gem, the cathedral. He made immediate changes, but it took him more than fifteen years to carry out his full-scale renovation. He turned the drawing room of an old canon's house into a double archway that afforded a new approach to the church, he removed screens and replaced stained glass, he reconstructed the eastern end, he built a new bay at the western end. The bells presented a special problem, and because the tower in which they were housed had grown too weak to support them, he removed them to a new belfry above the grand staircase leading to the dining hall. Above the splendid edifice, of which William Townesend, surveying it in 1720, said, "There never was in England a better building for fineness and curiosity as well as for strength and the goodness of the materials"[4]—the bells were encased in a simple wooden box.

Charles reacted instantaneously to the eyesore. He climbed up to the roof of the Hall with his camera, recorded the monstrosity, and then fired off a twenty-four-page pamphlet, *The New Belfry of Christ Church, Oxford,* "a Monograph by D.C.L." At six pence, it became the hottest item in Oxford and ran to five issues.

It is remarkably clever, given the speed with which Charles wrote it, and touches with mock seriousness on "the etymological significance of the new Belfry," "the impetus given to Art in England by" the belfry, the feelings with which old and resident Ch. Ch. men regard it, the logical and dramatic treatment of the belfry, and "the Moral of the new Belfry."

Charles calls the style " 'Early Debased': very early, and remarkably debased." By an almost mystical coincidence, the architect engaged to oversee the belfry's construction was named Scott, like the Dean's collaborator on the *Lexicon*, allowing Charles to accuse the Dean of wishing to embody in the belfry "a gigantic copy of the Greek Lexicon." He waxes eloquent over what he calls the "Tea-chest" and urges his readers to dare look upon it only at midnight, "For the least hint of open day/Scares the beholder quite away."

On May 29, 1873, a writer in the *Oxford Undergraduate's Journal* addressed himself to the cathedral's restoration. He quotes Charles's epithet for the belfry as a "meat-safe" and adds: "it is an ill wind that blows no one any good; and if the lovers of architectural beauty have just cause for their wrathful indignation the general public enjoy a hearty laugh over the *brochures* which Mr. Dodgson is continually publishing on these hideous monstrosities."

The belfry endured, but only until 1879, when Charles and his fellow critics had the satisfaction of seeing it replaced by a more appropriate pseudo-Tudor belfry tower.

*The New Belfry* was only the beginning. On March 19, 1873, Charles noted that "the new West entrance to the Cathedral was revealed today and almost rivals the Belfry in ugliness!" That very evening he dipped his pen in acrimony again. To add to the new offense, at least in Charles's view, was a performance scheduled in the cathedral for the following day of Bach's *St. Matthew Passion* for an audience of some twelve hundred people, timed to show off the new entrance. "I did not go," Charles wrote bluntly. "I think it a pity churches should be used so."

His new blast is entitled *The Vision of the Three T's: A Threnody*, "by the Author of 'The New Belfry.' " The "Three T's" stand for the Tea-chest (the belfry), the Trench (created by removing part of the Hall's roof parapet to show the new belfry to better advantage), and the Tunnel (the new entrance to the cathedral). A drama parodying *The Compleat Angler*, it depicts two visitors standing in Tom Quad in anguish as they regard the Dean's alterations. By the pool Mercury in the center of the quad, Piscator discourses on the "fish proper to these waters." The allegory is ingenious: Commoners are easily plucked from the waters but are seldom worth the trouble. Then he speaks of "the Nobler kinds, and chiefly of the Gold-fish, which is a species highly thought of, and much sought after in these parts not only by men, but by divers birds, as for example the King-fishers . . . ," an allusion to Mrs. Liddell's pursuit of highborn suitors for her daughters. This forty-page blast cost nine pence and went through three editions.

The *Three T's* rebukes the Liddell daughters as well. They managed the seat allocations for the celebration of Bach in the cathedral. Charles's objection to performing Bach's *Passion* in the cathedral stemmed perhaps as much from his emotional involvement as from religious or aesthetic scruples. He was fond of good music and admired music in churches, as, for instance, when he traveled with Liddon on the Continent. He could have thought himself displaced at the deanery by John Ruskin, at that time a welcome friend of the Liddells and favored with a ticket to the Bach concert.

Charles was not done with the Dean even now. In May 1873 he published a four-page appeal against further altering Tom Quad, quoting a passage from Ruskin's *Stones of Venice* complaining that many English cathedral doors "look as if they were made, not for open egress, but for the surreptitious drainage of a stagnant congregation." Charles wanted a single, broad, imposing entrance, not a puny, double-arched tunnel. In a serious, carefully reasoned address entitled *Objections, submitted to the Governing Body of Christ Church, Oxford, against certain proposed alterations in the Great Quadrangle,* he expressly opposed plans to alter the terrace that lines the four sides of the quadrangle and to replace the terrace wall with a grassy slope.

Charles kept the fires of controversy alive with more blasts. In June 1874 he published *Notes by an Oxford Chiel,* a collection of six of his pamphlets on college and university matters, one of which, *The Blank Cheque,* a stinging critique he published four months earlier, opposed a proposal to build new Examination Schools before even obtaining cost estimates. It tells the tale of a Mrs. Nivers and how she goes about selecting a school for her daughter Angela (Alice no doubt, but also an allusion to the Angel Inn, which had occupied the site where the schools were to be built). Angela's mother, Mrs. Nivers, must be Mrs. Liddell, at the heart of the u*niver*sity.

Plans for change at Christ Church progressed, and on October 21, 1874, Charles recorded a Governing Body meeting: "The Committee for lowering and narrowing the Terrace (a measure that I vainly opposed last summer) reported on their progress. They have uncovered the foundations meant by Wolsey for buttresses of cloisters, and these they are casing in stone. (It will cost about £300 and has a very ugly effect). I proposed their removal, but was not even seconded." On November 3 his letter "Architecture in Oxford" appeared in the *Pall Mall Gazette*. It discussed the proposal "to erect cloisters, and so utilise the grotesque foundations we are now enshrining in stone." Erecting cloisters would be "a piece of wanton extravagance. . . . We have [at Christ Church] a debt of more than £90,000 to pay off, and . . . such funds as we have are not our own to spend as we will, but held . . . on trust for educational purposes." A second letter of his on the subject appeared in the *Pall Mall Gazette* on the fifth, with more details.

How much influence Charles's agitation had upon the planners is not clear, but he both won and lost battles. The terrace was made narrower and lowered to reveal the range of supports originally intended for a cloister. But the grassy slope never became a reality, nor were the cloisters ever constructed.

This vendetta against the Dean's grand design crippled Charles's relationship with all the Liddells. Victorian gentlemanly and donnish decorum notwithstanding, Charles and the Dean were flesh and blood. They stood at opposite poles on many issues; their temperaments and politics differed sharply. Charles was Conservative; the Dean Liberal, a close friend of Stanley, a champion of Jowett, and a supporter of Gladstone. Charles's repeated assaults upon the Dean, although he could defend them on principle, conviction, and Ruskinian aesthetics, owed much to personal animus, a reaction to his pain at being rejected. For their part, the inhabitants of the deanery took Charles's onslaughts in silence, or so it seems, but feathers were no doubt ruffled. How could they not be, particularly by the thinly veiled jab at Mrs. Liddell in *The Vision of the Three T's.*

Through these years Charles closely watched all matters touching college and university affairs, and it did not take much to set his ink flowing. Another dozen or so papers descended his staircase for public consumption. In November 1872 he had Macmillan print, privately and secretly, a burlesque, as he put it (November 28), "on the proceedings of a very advanced school of reformers who met in London the other day, to consider the subject of the 're-distribution' of our revenues at Oxford and Cambridge, for the benefit of scientific men, who are not to teach, but only to 'investigate.' To me . . . this seems to savour a little too strongly of a very unscientific affection for the 'loaves and fishes.' " He wanted not to be identified as the author and asked Macmillan to get it printed at Cambridge and to distribute copies to both Oxford and Cambridge booksellers, Cambridge combination rooms, and Oxford common rooms. Macmillan complied and succeeded too well, because the puff remains undiscovered to this day.

In 1876 the Vice-Chancellor of the university proposed to relieve Friedrich Max Müller, Professor of Comparative Philology, Honorary Member of Christ Church, and a great friend of Liddell, of his academic duties to enable him to pursue his studies on full salary and, in his place, to appoint a deputy professor at half Max Müller's salary. Liddell delivered an eloquent speech supporting the proposal; Charles disapproved and issued a three-part argument, *Professorship of Comparative Philology*, declaring it unfair to cut in half the salary of anyone replacing the Professor on the principle that the post should dictate the salary regardless of who held it. But Charles did not carry the day: Convocation approved the measure, 94 to 35. Charles bore no animus against Max Müller personally, but the philologist neither forgot nor forgave. Years later, Max Müller praised Liddell unconditionally and wrote of his detractors: "Even in the University there were those who could not bear his towering high above them . . . not in stature only, but in character and position. Nasty things were said and written, but everybody knew from what forge those arrows came."5

Undergraduate examinations always interested Charles. On April 16, 1877, he composed "a letter to the Vice-Chancellor on the anomalies of Responsions last term—45 per cent passing in one section, and 69 in the other." He listed the sharp differences in percentage of passing students in different years and in the several sections in each sitting. "No accidental circumstance can possibly account for so large a discrepancy," he argued, "and the conclusion seems inevitable that the candidates in the first section were judged by far too high a standard, and that many failed in consequence who would have passed if they had happened to be in the other section." The *Oxford & Cambridge Undergraduate Journal* commented (May 3, 1877) that "Mr. Dodgson's recent circular demonstrates beyond all doubt the injustice perpetrated in Smalls [Responsions] last term."

Charles's *cacoëthes scribendi* does not wane. On May 15, 1877, he finished "a letter . . . on the proposal to give a degree in Natural Science which shall confer the same privileges as the M.A. degree, and sent it to the *Pall Mall Gazette*." It appeared four days later, a long, sarcastic, and amusing diatribe defending traditional values. Charles deplored the notion of doing away with the Latin and Greek requirement for newly established degrees in science. If Congregation approves the proposal, he wonders whether "the destinies of Oxford may some day be in the hands of those who have had no education other than 'scientific' " and seeks "to rouse an interest, beyond the limits of Oxford, in preserving classics as an essential feature of a University education." But Charles lost again: the new degree requirements passed, 63 to 40.

During the 1870s Charles also published briefs on subjects in the public domain, reaching beyond university concerns. One such was vivisection. His concern for animals and opposition to vivisection will not surprise readers of his children's books. An item that appeared in the *Spectator* in early February 1875 provoked him to write to the *Pall Mall Gazette* a letter entitled "Vivisection as a Sign of the Times," where he depicts vivisection as a metaphor for the malaise of the age, highlighting, in a long and convoluted argument, what he describes as social depravity. He deplores his fellow man's "enslavement of his weaker brethren . . . the degradation of woman" as well as "the torture of the animal world." And he attributes these ills to the secularization of education in schools resulting from the Education Act of 1870. Charles doubts that vivisection can aid civilization and sees it as contributing to moral decay. He fears that the future will become an "age when all forms of religious thought shall be things of the past; when chemistry and biology shall be the A B C of a State education enforced on all; when vivisection shall be practised in every college and school; and when the man of science, looking forth over a world which will then own no other sway than his, shall exult . . . that he has made of this fair green earth, if not a heaven for man, at least a hell for animals."

Charles was bucked up by "several communications," including a flattering letter from Frances Power Cobbe, the joint-secretary of the National Anti-Vivisection Society, who later quoted Charles's letter in an article she published in the *New Quarterly Magazine*. He also heard (March 4, 1875) from the Society for the Prevention of Cruelty to Animals, asking permission to reprint his letter, which he gave.

He wrote a second paper, called "Some Popular Fallacies about Vivisection," which, after the *Pall Mall Gazette* rejected it, appeared in the *Fortnightly Review* (June 1, 1875). It is an even longer sermon, formulating and classifying thirteen fallacies. The "fallacies" include the idea that man's superiority over animals gives him an innate right to inflict pain upon them in his effort to prevent human suffering; the notion that if one may legally kill animals in sport, one may surely do the same in the less selfish practice of vivisection; the question of whether vivisection, if practiced on animals, will not, in time, lead to experiments with human beings.

He makes another controversial assertion in this essay: that man's nature is not to be trusted to restrict his investigations only to scientific ends, but that he is constructed with enough of the "wild beast" in him to enable vivisectors to grow accustomed to inflicting pain without qualms, to become ensnared in the process, and ultimately to take pleasure in it. It will be a small step for these men of science to carry on their experiments on what they might consider the lower reaches of humanity—condemned criminals, incurables, lunatics, paupers—and paints a picture prophetic of George Orwell's *Nineteen Eighty-four* and Nazi concentration camps. He asks readers to think into the future to the day when such experiments on human beings will occur: "Will you represent to that grim spectre, as he gloats over you, scalpel in hand, the inalienable rights of man? He will tell you that this is merely a question of relative expediency—that, with so feeble a physique as yours, you have only to be thankful that natural selection has spared you so long."

In July 1876 he printed a thirteen-stanza poem, "Fame's Penny-Trumpet," "affectionately" dedicated "to all 'original researchers' who pant for 'endowment,' " berating scientists in search of lavish emoluments. "Blow, blow your trumpets till they crack,/Ye little men of little souls!" he shrieks at "vivisectors, log-rollers, flatterers and other mountebanks." So intemperate was the verse that the *Pall Mall Gazette, Punch,* and *World* would not print it, and he had to publish it himself, in *Rhyme? and Reason?*

Almost a decade later Charles returned to vivisection yet again, when Convocation considered (March 10, 1885) a proposed grant for the study of physiology, which Charles opposed because it did not restrict "the practice of vivisection for research." But again he lost; the proposal was carried by 412 to 244. Four days later Charles wrote another article on the subject for the *St. James's Gazette,* which appears on the nineteenth as "Vivisection Vivisected," reacting to an earlier piece in the paper which he did not believe presented "a complete view of the 'pros and cons' of this difficult question."

Having taken up the cudgels again, he tried to influence legislation. On May 9, 1875, for instance, he wrote to Lord Salisbury: "There is a terrible need for legislation—not so much in the interest of the poor tortured animals as of the demoralised and brutalised medical students." He also sent Salisbury various items, including his own *Pall Mall* letter.

Charles's voice must have counted for something when, on June 22, 1875, just after two of his pieces appeared, the Royal Commission on Vivisection, with T. H. Huxley a member, was established. It sat for the rest of the year and brought into being the Cruelty to Animals Act of 1876, which established licensing regulations for experiments on living animals. Much later C. S. Lewis took up the call for stricter controls in his essay *Vivisection* (1948): "The alarming thing is that the vivisectors have won the first round," he wrote, alluding to the Nazi experiments on human beings. "Lewis Carroll protested . . . on the very same ground which I have just used."[6]

From vivisection Charles turned to vaccination. Although Edward Jenner had invented a vaccination against smallpox in the late eighteenth century, smallpox epidemics continued to rage in England through the nineteenth century. Charles was aware and cautious: "The alarm about smallpox in the neighbourhood seems on the increase, and I went today [May 14, 1863] . . . to be vaccinated." On August 14, 1871, he decided not to visit his sister Mary, near Sunderland, because "smallpox is raging" there. And again on November 1 of that year, before returning to Oxford from a visit to his sister at Dover, he was vaccinated "on account of the smallpox at Oxford."

Although the smallpox vaccine originated in England and the first Vaccination Act passed in 1840, resistance to vaccination persisted, especially among the poorly educated, who, aware that the vaccine came from cows, feared a "beast's disease" or held with the old prejudice that any injection would introduce evil "humours" into their bodies. In 1866 the Anti-Vaccination League was formed and argued that compulsory vaccination was a denial of freedom.

In early August, seeing in the *Eastbourne Chronicle* a letter from one William Hume-Rothery defending the anti-vaccination position, Charles wrote to the paper challenging Hume-Rothery's use of statistics. An exchange of letters between Hume-Rothery and Charles followed in the *Chronicle,* until Charles, in his third letter (August 22), closed the debate asserting that he and Hume-Rothery "do not take quite the same view, either as to what is honourable in controversy, or as to what is courteous in language."

Charles the gadgeteer, the innovator, the inventor was very much in evidence during the 1870s, as well as the writer and the fighter. His rooms at Christ Church sometimes resembled a toy shop or a museum, even a laboratory or an engineer's workshop. He acquired the latest mechanical inventions, and they lined the shelves and tables of his rooms. In mid-1877 he added the newly patented "electric pen" and made it part of his arsenal.

A little earlier (May 31, 1877), Charles revised his *Memoria Technica* and judged that it "works beautifully. I made rhymes for the foundations of all the Colleges. . . ." His *Memoria Technica* is a significant improvement on Dr. Richard Grey's system, set down in 1730, for memorizing dates and events. Charles's method assigns two consonants to each number from 0 to 9, fills in vowels to make words, and sets the words in rhymed couplets that help the user to remember not just dates but almost any other body of facts. The rhymes turn the previously cumbersome method into something of a game. This is how he lets us remember the year 1492:

> Columbus sailed the world around
> Until America was FOUND.

The consonants *F N D* represent 492, the prefix 1 is always assumed.

A week after Charles bought his electric pen, he used it to punch out his *Memoria Technica* and was then able to distribute it among friends and later to use it in teaching the system. With his *Memoria Technica* refined and operational and his electric pen at hand, he devised couplets giving the specific gravities of metals and other elements.

He kept so busy, so involved, that numerous projects never reached the printer. One yearns to know what prompted him to compose an essay (July 22, 1877), "Marriage Service," bearing the epigraph "Till Death Us Do Part." It is a treatise defying the absolute position of the Church on remarriage after divorce. Charles finds circumstances where remarriage may be condoned: an oath "becomes unmeaning when one side has ceased to observe it," he wrote; in other words, "by the act of the one . . . the other is released from further obligation." The same is true when "the fulfilment of an oath becomes impossible," that is, "when one party . . . makes it impossible, by breaking the oath, for the second party to fulfil it." Remarriage in these circumstances would not, in his view, be "displeasing to God." Here again we have Charles departing from establishment dogma: "Those who object to *all* re-marriage, even after the *death* of a husband or wife, take a view that seems to me at variance with Scripture as well as with common sense," he wrote.

All through these years Charles is the Dodgson family's most ardent protector, not only in financial but in all practical matters, and a provider of entertainment. He retained his early skills of amusing audiences with sleight of hand in wig and drapery and developed and refined other techniques for public performances. He was good at charades, he sang, he told stories. Soon enough, jokes, puzzles, games, questions-and-answers, tricks with numbers and with words, and mental exercises became for him a means of everyday amusement and for his family and friends a source of fun and diversion. He also played traditional games—chess, croquet, billiards, cards—but his mind was not content with these, and he expanded, extended, and experimented with all forms and fashions, pushing traditional

MEMORIA TECHNICA.
for Numbers.

| 1 | 2 | 3 | 4 | 5 | 6 | 7 | 8 | 9 | 0 |
|---|---|---|---|---|---|---|---|---|---|
| b | d | t | f | l | s | p | h | n | z |
| c | w | j | qu | v | x | m | k | g | r |

Each digit is represented by one or other of two consonants, according to the above table: vowels are then inserted *ad libitum* to form words, the significant consonants being always at the *end* of a line: the object of this is to give the important words the best chance of being, by means of the rhyme, remembered accurately.

The consonants have been chosen for the following reasons.

(1) *b, c,* first two consonants.

(2) *d* from "*deux*"; *w* from "*two*"

(3) *t* from "*trois*"; *j* was the last consonant left unappropriated.

(4) *f* from "*four*"; *qu* from "*quatre*."

(5) *l* = 50 ; *v* = 5.

(6) *s, x,* from "*six*."

(7) *p, m,* from "*septem*."

(8) *h* from "*huit*"; *k* from ὀκτώ.

(9) *n* from "*nine*"; *g* from its shape.

(0) *z, r,* from "*zero*."

They were also assigned in accordance, as far as possible, with the rule of giving to each digit one consonant in common use, and one rare one.

Since *y* is reckoned as a vowel, many whole words, (such as "ye", "you", "eye"), may be put in to make sense, without interfering with the significant letters.

Take as an example of this system the two dates of "Israelites leave Egypt — 1495," and "Israelites enter Canaan — 1455" :—

"Shout again! We are free!"
Says the loud voice of glee.
"Nestle home like a dove,"
Says the low voice of love.

Ch. Ch.
June 27/77

---

*Charles's aid to memory,* Memoria Technica, *which he produced with his "electric" pen — an early device invented by Thomas Edison that enabled the user to create stencils from which could be produced numerous copies of a composition.*

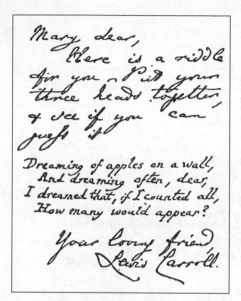

Mary dear,
        Here is a riddle
for you — Put your
three heads together,
& see if you can
guess it

Dreaming of apples on a wall,
  And dreaming often, dear,
I dreamed that, if I counted all,
  How many would appear?

        Your loving friend
          Lewis Carroll

*A riddle letter that Charles sent to Mary Watson;*
*his answer to the riddle was:*
*If ten the number dreamed of, why 'tis clear*
*That in the dream ten apples would appear.*

entertainments to their outer limits and inventing new ones. In the 1870s he created a veritable cornucopia of conundrums and mental challenges, brilliant additions to the store of magic and game playing, as effective today as they were when he devised them. He was so creative and so productive that his games and diversions fill sizable anthologies.

For Charles, his family and friends, indeed for all the Victorian middle class, domestic entertainments were the accepted form of leisure. They had no movies, radio, or television, and while they did have three-decker novels, novel-reading is a solitary activity, and closely knit families and circles of friends enjoyed communal activities. Both participant and spectator sports loomed large as leisure diversions. Cricket became a national pastime when the All-England Eleven was established in 1852; in the 1870s football became not just a school game but a game of the people; and lawn tennis was patented in 1874. Croquet was one outdoor game that everyone could play; by 1850 it became one of the most popular sports, and in 1870 the All-England Croquet Club was founded.

Charles was a croquet fan: it was one of his frequent pastimes, and he had already invented his own version, *Croquet Castles*. We have photographs of him with his family with croquet mallets on the lawn at Croft Rectory; he often played the game with the Liddells at the deanery; and, of course, he staged a memorable game of croquet in *Wonderland*.

But outdoor activities were suitable only in good weather; for the larger part of the year, Charles adapted outdoor games for indoor use and invented others suitable for drawing rooms and nurseries. "Wrote out, and sent to

Gwendolen Cecil, the rules of a mental game I invented a short time ago, which I call 'Numerical Croquet,' " Charles noted (October 24, 1872).

His motives for creating these games and puzzles went beyond the pleasure of organizing communal pastimes. Like photography, merrymaking afforded entrées into the homes and friendships that he yearned for, they helped amuse his child friends, and they eventually led to a public audience of children, the world of child game players. His success at invention must have given him deep satisfaction and compensated partly for his failure to achieve a fully rounded emotional life.

Charles is often tarred with the anti-sport brush: he is not good at sport, *ergo* he does not like it. The facts prove otherwise. For one thing, there is sport and there is sport. Hunting, shooting, and killing, as we might expect, were odious to him. He often made his case against them, particularly in the prefaces to both *Sylvie and Bruno* books. In the earlier preface, he refused to apologize for treating "with such entire want of sympathy the British passion for 'Sport.' " He admired men who hunted man-eating tigers, but not those who hunted harmless and defenseless animals. After *Sylvie and Bruno* appeared, Charles received letters protesting his harsh words against "Sport," and in the preface to *Sylvie and Bruno Concluded,* he replied: "God has given to Man an absolute right to take the *lives* of other animals, for *any* reasonable cause, such as the supply of food: but . . . He has *not* given . . . the right to inflict *pain,* unless when *necessary* . . . pain, inflicted for the purposes of *Sport,* is cruel, and therefore wrong."

Blood sports aside, his nephew assures us that Charles's "abilities did not lie much in the field of athletics," and his niece Violet Dodgson testifies that "at Rugby, Charles . . . avoided games as far as possible."[7] But at school, Charles must have had to play football, or Rugby as it came to be called, though we find no evidence that he took to the game. It must have amused him, nevertheless, to see a leader in the *Oxford & Cambridge Undergraduate Journal* (November 16, 1876), about student football headed "Slithy Toves," quote the first two lines of Charles's poem and call it "one of the most popular of modern ballads."

It is wrong to conclude, however, that Charles hated all physical sports, for he participated in some, in a few continually, and he was a spectator at others, particularly cricket and the Oxford Eights. From the earliest entries in his diary we know that he was a cricket fan, and as late as September 4, 1882, at Eastbourne, he brought together a group of young men for a cricket match. He played other games as well and even modified some for his and others' delectation. When he spent a day with the Liddells (June 26, 1857), his "photographing was . . . plentifully interspersed with swinging, backgammon, etc." On January 6, 1868, he tried "with Margaret [his sister] a new kind of backgammon, which I think of calling 'blot-backgammon.'" And over the years, he invented other versions: "Thirdie Backgammon," "Co-operative Backgammon," and "Co-operative German Backgammon," this last largely inspired by Enid Stevens. Charles recorded "Co-operative Backgammon" for posterity, in the personal columns of *The Times* (March 6, 1894).

His mathematical bent led him to construct games, puzzles, and riddles in multiple forms. He enjoyed mental challenges, and his early interest in magical tricks came into good use. He showed Isa Bowman numerous things made with his handkerchief. "If he took you up to London to see a play," Beatrice Hatch wrote, ". . . you were no sooner seated in your railway carriage than a game was produced from his bag, and all occupants of the compartment were invited to join in playing a kind of 'halma' or 'draughts' of his own invention, on the little wooden board that had been specially made at his design for railway use, with 'men' warranted not to tumble down, because they fitted into little holes in the board!"[8] Enid Stevens also recalled "lovely games. . . . And he loved ciphers: he very often wrote letters to me in cipher, and I had to solve them. What really pleased me was when I wrote him back a letter in cipher and he couldn't solve it."[9]

Pen-and-pencil games, games that he could illustrate with his own crude sketches, were among his favorites. He reveled in trick drawings. One picture story, about a man and his wife who live in a house on the shore of a lake, concludes with the legend "My dear, you are a Perfect Goose." When Charles finished telling the story and drawing the picture, he turned the picture of the bucolic lakeside setting upside down to reveal the Perfect Goose. Another, called "Mister Fox," is a tale of how a little girl named Mary outwits an evil fox. For this story Charles drew nine pictures. Another is the story of "Mr. C. & Mr. T.,"[10] accompanied by the drawing of a huge cat with a house for a head.

Riddles in verse were another specialty. As early as August 24, 1855, he was composing them, and throughout his life he fashioned a long stream of them, some

*Charles's puzzle "Mr. C. and Mr. T."*

as dedicatory acrostics, others as verses that have tricky, jokey answers in them.

Charles delighted in provoking his friends—adults and children—with challenging puzzles and problems. "Sometimes while paying an afternoon call he would borrow scraps of paper," Beatrice Hatch recalled, "and leave neat little diagrams or word puzzles to be worked out by his friends."[11] Evelyn Karney remembered when her father first brought Charles home: "In two minutes the stranger had . . . drawn a fascinating game. . . . Then he cut out a quantity of paper counters, while I watched with expectant eyes, and in five minutes our heads were close together, deep in wonderful and engrossing games."[12] Isabel Standen recalled a chance meeting in a Reading public garden. "Presently he took me on his knee and showed me various puzzles that he always carried about with him. . . . One puzzle he showed me was to draw three interlaced squares without taking the pen from the paper or going over the same line twice. . . . Another was to make figures of men and women from five dots, which he did most cleverly."[13] Dorothy Burch remembered another puzzle: "One day Mr. Dodgson cut out a circular hole the size of a sixpence in a piece of paper. 'Can you put a ha'penny through it?' he asked. [The children gathered round him] . . . could not. 'Yes, you can,' he said, 'but you have to know how.' The answer was that you doubled the circle over, and then it would stretch to allow the halfpence through." Another time Charles appeared at the Burch home early one morning, an unusual time for him to call, and asked to see her specifically. He had a problem he was putting into a book, and he wanted to see if a child of five could do it, whether a child's mind could grasp it.[14]

Lancelot Robson recalled that Charles once turned up at a children's party:

He asked us if, at our school, we did sums. A chorus answered, "Yes." . . . Then Lewis Carroll said, "I am afraid you go to a very poor school. I never do sums; I always put the answer down first and set the sum afterwards."

There was silence. . . . Then he continued. "We will do some sums." He wrote some figures on a piece of paper, and gave it to my stepmother, saying, "That will be the answer to our sum when we have set it."

Then he wrote 1,066 on another piece of paper. Choosing a little girl, he let her put down any four figures she liked under his 1,066. Then he put down four figures under hers and a small boy contributed another line. Lewis Carroll added the fifth line, so the column stood:

1,066 Lewis Carroll
3,478 Little Girl
6,521 Lewis Carroll
7,150 Little Boy
2,849 Lewis Carroll

A rather cheeky youngster was allowed to add it up, and he pronounced the answer to be 21,064. . . . My stepmother then read the figures on the paper Lewis Carroll had given her: 21,064. There were cries of "Oh!" from the children.

. . . We begged him for another trick, so he asked a little boy to write the number 12345679. He surveyed it in silence, then said, "You don't form your figures very clearly, do you? Which of these figures do you think you have made the worst?

The boy thought his 5 was poorest. Lewis Carroll suggested he should multiply the line by 45. The child laboriously worked it out and to his surprise found the result was 555555555. "Supposing I had said four, what then?" the boy queried. "In that case we would have made the answer all fours," Carroll replied. He would have told the boy to multiply by 36, another multiple of nine. But he did not attempt to explain "mystic nines" to us. . . .[15]

His catechisms were not confined to children. "At the dinner table [at Christ Church] he liked to 'quiz' his neighbours with occasional conundrums with a mathematical air," Viscount Simon recalled. On one occasion Charles set this problem:

A man wanted to go to the theatre, which would cost him 1s. 6d., but he only had 1s. So he went into a Pawnbroker's shop and offered to pledge his shilling for a loan. The Pawnbroker satisfied himself that the shilling was genuine and lent him 9d. on it. . . . The man then came out of the shop with 9d., and the Pawnbroker's ticket for 1s. Outside he met a friend to whom he offered to sell the Pawnbroker's ticket and the friend bought it from him for 9d. He now had 9d. from the Pawnbroker and another 9d. from the friend and so was able to go to the theatre.

"The question is," said Lewis Carroll, "who lost what?"[16]

Charles's diaries and letters bubble with games invented, games played, puzzles thought up, riddles put into verse. In the summer of 1890 he sent Princess Alice, the Queen's granddaughter, the Möbius ring-puzzle (which he describes in *Sylvie and Bruno Concluded*); and on August 27 he inquired of the royal comptroller of the Albany household whether Princess Alice or her brother, Prince Charles, "possess a wire-puzzle, lately published, called 'Home-Rule?' If not," he added, "I want to give it . . . [to them]." On the twenty-fourth the young Prince wrote acknowledging it: "I thank you very much for the puzzle you so kindly sent to me. I watched Mother do it up and un-do it, so that now I can do it myself." On July 27, 1870, staying with his Uncle Skeffington in London, Charles received visits from four of the Cecil children on two successive days, and he wrote some verse riddles expressly for them.

At Christmastime 1877 Charles invented for Matthew Arnold's nieces, Julia and Ethel Arnold, a word game first called *Word-Links* and later *Doublets*. "The rules are simple enough," Charles wrote. "Two words are proposed of the same length; and the Puzzle consists in linking these together by interposing other words, each of which shall differ from the next word *in one letter only. . . .* As an example, the word 'head' may be changed into 'tail' by interposing the words 'heal, teal, tell, tall.' I call the two given words 'a Doublet,' the interposed words 'links,' and the entire series 'a chain.' " *Vanity Fair* published the game in March and April 1879 and inaugurated a Doublets competition. Charles published *Word-Links* separately in 1878 and *Doublets* in 1879. He refined the game and printed subsequent editions.

In 1879 he published *A Game for Two Players*, which soon became *Lanrick*, a game that uses sixteen men (each player has eight chess pawns, draughts, or counters of one color), a chess- or draughtsboard, and nine markers the size of chess squares. As *Lanrick* it appeared in Charlotte Yonge's *Monthly Packet* in 1880 and 1881, and Charles published it separately in 1881.

Charles lost none of his sense of humor or his ability to conjure up, in a flash, a memorable conundrum, tale, or letter. In a letter he writes to Florence Terry in January 1874, he pleads with her to placate her brother Tom about a photograph that Charles promised him in 1867 but had not yet delivered. He enlists Florence's effort

to make him see that, as hasty puddings are not the best of puddings, so hasty judgements are not the best of judgements, and that he ought to be content to wait, even another 7 years, for his picture, and to sit "like patience on a monument, smiling at grief." This quotation, by the way, is altogether a misprint. Let me explain it to you. The passage originally stood "*They* sit, Like patients on *the* Monument, smiling at

*Greenwich.*" In the next edition "Greenwich" was printed short "Green" and so got gradually altered into "Grief." The allusion of course is to the celebrated Dr. Jenner, who used to send all his patients to sit on the top of the Monument (near London Bridge) to inhale fresh air, promising them that, when they were well enough, they should go to "Greenwich Fair." So of course they always looked out towards Greenwich, and sat smiling to think of the treat in store for them. A play was written on the subject of their inhaling the fresh air, and was for some time attributed to him (Shakespeare), but it is certainly not in his style. It was called *The Wandering Air,* and was lately revived at the Queen's Theatre.[17] The custom of sitting on the Monument was given up when Dr. Jenner went mad, and insisted that the air was worst up there, and that the *lower* you went the *more airy* it became. Hence he always called those little yards, below the pavement, outside kitchen windows, *"the kitchen airier,"* a name that is still in use.

All this information you are most welcome to use, the next time you are in want of something to talk about. You may say you learned it from "a distinguished etymologist," which is perfectly true, since any one who knows me by sight can easily distinguish me from all other etymologists.

The most remarkable segment of the harvest of the 1870s is Charles's literary output. Enmeshed as he was in college affairs and duties, attending to family and friends, writing letters and working at mathematics, some impulse nonetheless led him along the road that the *Alice* books took—the fanciful, the imaginative, the humorous, the literary.

*Alice* having succeeded, an *Alice* industry came into being, and Charles must have been gratified by the increasing evidence that his books were being read and influencing others. In 1872 he received a copy of music set to songs in *Looking-Glass,* matching William Boyd's earlier music to *Alice.* In 1871 and 1872 he saw a succession of songs set to his verses from *Alice* appear in *Aunt Judy's Magazine.* In March 1872 he held the first Italian *Alice* in his hands. In that same month a fellow don of Trinity College produced an "ideal" Latin translation of Charles's nonsense verse "Jabberwocky." In 1874 he got the first, albeit abridged, Dutch translation. And on November 6, 1879, he received a dramatized version of *Alice* intended to be acted for children, adapted by Kate Freiligrath-Kroeker, who then, in 1882, went on to adapt *Looking-Glass* for the same purpose.

Through the 1870s Charles played numerous airs on his dexterous pipes. He printed a variety of circular letters to hospitals, offering copies of the

*Alice* books for children's wards. "In the afternoon I wrote a large piece of MS. for *An Easter Letter* which I am again thinking of printing to insert in copies of my Easter book," Charles wrote (February 5, 1876). "I am afraid the religious allusions will be thought 'out of season' by many, but I do not like to lose the opportunity of saying a few serious words to (perhaps) 20,000 children." It was, in fact, a more substantial piece than the earlier Christmas greeting. He distributed copies to friends, put it on sale, and indeed had copies inserted in some of his new books and reprints of others. Later he had it printed inside some of the books. It also got pirated.

*An Easter Greeting to Every Child Who Loves "Alice"* is a revealing work, a disguised confessional. Here he reaches out not only to loving children but also to his own childhood, seeking to recapture, and to share with his unseen child audience, the comfort that a child feels in a mother's love. Allusions to the Bible, Blake, and Wordsworth blend in his effort to cast off the heavy weight of years and return to a pure and simple past, an unfettered, untroubled, uncorrupted, romantic faraway world he believes he once knew. The essay is, however, about the innocence that Charles had lost, and while it reaches out to the world's children, it affirms his discontent with his sullied adulthood. His guilt drives him here to justify writing lighthearted works: "If I have written anything to add to those stores of innocent and healthy amusement . . . it is surely something I may hope to look back upon without shame and sorrow . . . when *my* turn comes to walk through the valley of shadows."

Charles's most magnificent literary creation after the *Alice* books grew out of a sickroom. On July 14, 1874, he recorded: "Wrote to Fanny [his sister, at Guildford], offering to come over to take a share in nursing Charlie Wilcox." Charles Hassard Wilcox was the seventh son of the Whitburn Wilcoxes, cousins and dear friends. Charles had spent many happy days on the Wilcox hearth. The twenty-two-year-old Charlie was, moreover, Charles's godson. He was suffering from "inflammation of the lungs," a Victorian euphemism for tuberculosis, and probably came to stay with cousins in Guildford because Guildford, over 250 miles south of Whitburn, enjoys a milder climate and, with autumn and winter approaching, was thought to offer more hope of a recovery or a postponement of the inevitable. Other families sent their children similarly infected to Italy, Greece, or Spain, but the Wilcoxes probably could not afford that luxury. Perhaps Guildford's proximity to London and London doctors was another consideration.

Charles, titular head of the family, took charge of any crisis at Guildford.

Three days after he wrote to Fanny, he went there. Charlie's condition, which had deteriorated since his coming to Guildford, must have shocked Charles on his arrival on the seventeenth, and he immediately started nursing the invalid through the long nights. It was a sorrowful task; seeing the young man consumed by fever and pain weighed heavily on him.

The next morning, after only three hours' sleep, Charles left the sickroom to walk on the Surrey Downs. He needed to get away, to breathe fresh air, to see new sights. Thirteen years later he recalled, in his essay " 'Alice' on the Stage," an extraordinary occurrence that morning:

> I was walking on a hillside, alone, one bright summer day, when suddenly there came into my head one line of verse—one solitary line—"For the Snark *was* a Boojum, you see." I know not what it meant, then: I know not what it means, now; but I wrote it down: and, some time afterwards, the rest of the stanza occurred to me, that being its last line: and so by degrees, at odd moments during the next year or two, the rest of the poem pieced itself together, that being its last stanza. And since then, periodically I have received courteous letters from strangers, begging to know whether "The Hunting of the Snark" is an allegory, or contains some hidden moral, or is a political satire: and for all such questions I have but one answer, *"I don't know!"*

"For the Snark *was* a Boojum, you see" became the vehicle that impelled him forward, or, rather, backward, to create the longest, most intricate nonsense poem in the English language.

But first Charles returned to the Chestnuts and continued his nightly vigil. During those long, sad hours he pondered that light, nonsensical cluster of words. Line by line, verse by verse, he built upon that initial inspiration, probably filling page after page as he sat with the ailing figure before him. It is no accident that *The Hunting of the Snark* moves away from reality and into a mythical, unreal world; that it renounces logic and correct order, even the natural order, and violates all rational expectations. Charles saw clearly that his first inspiration was to be the last line of the long poem and that he had to build the work from back to front. And so it evolved, with parallel illogic, that the ship that takes the band of eccentric travelers on their hunt for the Snark also makes its journey backwards. Time, place, direction are irrelevant; meaning is elusive. All that matters is relief, which Charles achieves through suspense and laughter as the journey unfolds.

Charlie Wilcox's fate is detailed in his godfather's diary. At the end of July

Charles arranged for a London physician to come to Guildford to consult with the two Guildford doctors in attendance. The London man "pronounced the case . . . to be a serious one— one lung entirely diseased (phthisis), the other (at present) sound. He is to stay here 6 weeks at least before thinking of moving, and then to go to the seaside or on a voyage," Charles recorded. Charlie then appeared to enjoy a degree of recovery, and Charles felt free to go for "two or three days in the Isle of Wight." He returned to Guildford on the twenty-ninth, and then went off again in early September for a longer time.

*Henry Holiday's cover drawing for* The Hunting of the Snark

In September Charles arranged for his ward to move to the Isle of Wight. But the milder climate notwithstanding, Charlie survived for less than four more months. On November 11 Charles recorded the bleak fact: "Received the news of the death of my dear cousin and godson, Charles Wilcox, which took place . . . yesterday morning."

Charles nowhere connects Charlie Wilcox's illness and death and *The Hunting of the Snark,* but they are certainly intertwined. Why else would Charles choose for a subtitle *An Agony, in Eight Fits,* and why should the poem, intended to divert and amuse, packed as it is with hilarious episodes, jingling, jangling sounds, and absurd characters—why should this lark of a tale end tragically?

One can surmise—Charles does not tell us—that he wrote some of the poem during those cloistered nights at the Chestnuts, and perhaps as he added verse to verse, he shared them with the ailing youth. Perhaps they even worked on the verses together, and the invalid, if only for a little time now and then, got some relief from his fever and pain as he laughed and helped shape the tale. But all we really know is that twelve days after Charlie died, on November 23, 1874, Charles mentions the *Snark* for the first time in his diary, noting that John Ruskin "came by, at my request, for a talk about the pictures Holiday is doing for the 'Boojum.' "

The friendship with Henry Holiday had begun before Charles undertook his role as night nurse. "It was an agreeable surprise," Holiday wrote, "when one morning Lewis Carroll . . . came to see me and my work. We became friends on the spot." When the Holiday family first enter Charles's diary ( July 6, 1870), they were already well acquainted, Charles staying with them in Hampstead and using their home as a photography studio. Then, after Charles started writing the *Snark,* he asked Holiday if he "would design three illustrations to *The Hunting of the Snark,* in three cantos, of which he sent me the MS. It was a new kind of work and interested me. I began them at once, and sent him the first sketches, but he had in the meantime written another canto, and asked for a drawing for it; I sent this, but meantime he had written a new canto and wanted another illustration; and this went on till he pulled up the eighth canto, making with the frontispiece, nine illustrations."[18]

Charles took no steps to publish the *Snark,* even while Holiday was illustrating the verses. Not until October 23, 1875, do we read: "A sudden idea occurred, about which I wrote to Holiday and Macmillan, of publishing the 'Snark' poem this Christmas." *The Hunting of the Snark* had to be put off to Easter 1876, when Macmillan published it. The first printing was ten thousand copies, and the book was reprinted eighteen times between 1876 and 1910.

The reviews were not good. The *Standard* (April 24, 1876) condemned it: "Mr. Carroll, having made one success in the domain of 'delicious romance,' has essayed another and failed. There is neither wit nor humour in the little versified whimsicality; its 'nonsensicalities' fail either to surprise or to amuse." The *Saturday Review* (April 15) applauded the *Snark* but added that "the illustrations display that strange want of any sense of fun which distinguishes most comic draughtsmen in these days." The *Courier* missed "the delicate grace of Tenniel . . . ; by the side of . . . [the illustrations] in *Alice,* these in the *Snark* look poor and coarse. . . ." Andrew Lang, in a long notice in the *Academy* (April 8), objected to the medium of verse over prose, suggesting that if the book "is rather disappointing, it is partly the fault of the too attractive title. . . ." The *Athenaeum* (April 8) disapproved, speculating that Lewis Carroll "may . . . merely [have] been inspired by a wild desire to reduce to idiocy as many readers, and more especially reviewers, as possible. At any event, he has published what we may consider the most bewildering of modern poems. . . ." The *Spectator* (April 22) called it an outright "failure" without humour. But the reviewer judged the line "For the Snark *was* a Boojum, you see" "better than anything in *Alice*" and thought it might become a proverb. The *Graphic* (April 15) offered one of the few rave notices, praising its "singular facility of verse. . . . Everybody ought to read the book—nearly everybody *will*—and all who deserve the treat will scream with laughter." *Vanity Fair* (April 29) was severe: Carroll "goes from good to bad, and from bad to worse. . . . This book . . . deserves only to be called rubbish." *Punch* reviewed it among its Christmas books (January 6, 1877) and concluded that "the *Snark* . . . is not the Jabberwock."

*The Hunting of the Snark,* like the *Alice* books, is a tale of adventure. But unlike the *Alice* books, it is all verse, 141 rhymed four-line stanzas. It tells the story of a handful of eccentrics—a Baker, a Butcher, a Beaver, a Barrister, a Bonnet-maker, a Banker, a Boots, a Broker, a Billiard-marker—all of whom set off in an ailing ship that sometimes sails backward and is captained by a wise Bellman. The purpose of the journey is to find, lure, and capture the mythical Snark.

Although we never learn where the strange crew set out from or where they sail to, we know that they sail for many months. As they approach their destination, the Bellman gives them a pep talk and reminds them of the five unmistakable traits by which they may recognize the Snark: first, the way it tastes (meager and hollow, but crisp); second, its habit of getting up late (it frequently breakfasts at five-o'clock tea and dines on the following day); third, its slowness in taking a jest (it always looks grave at a pun); fourth, its fondness for bathing machines (which it constantly carries about); and fifth, its ambition.

We have no idea what the Snark looks like, nor apparently do the crew. Charles would not allow the drawing of the Snark that Holiday supplied to appear—he wanted to leave the beast to the reader's imagination—but the poem's refrain describes how the crew, having arrived in Snarkland, conduct their hunt:

> They sought it with thimbles, they sought it with care;
>   They pursued it with forks and hope;
> They threatened its life with a railway-share;
>   They charmed it with smiles and soap.

Snark hunting is a treacherous occupation, for our heroes encounter frightful animals along the way: the Jubjub, for instance, a dangerous bird with a high, shrill screech; and the Bandersnatch, with its savagely snapping

frumious jaws. The Bandersnatch attacks the Banker, but the rest of the
party drive it off. Finally, as evening comes on, the Baker, out ahead of the
pack, encounters the Snark from the top of a crag. He pursues it, plunging
courageously into the chasm, shouting: "It's a Snark. . . . It's a Boo—" and
then, nothing but silence.

> They hunted till darkness came on, but they found
>     Not a button, or feather, or mark,
> By which they could tell that they stood on the ground
>     Where the Baker had met with the Snark.
>
> In the midst of the word he was trying to say,
>     In the midst of his laughter and glee,
> He had softly and suddenly vanished away—
>     For the Snark *was* a Boojum, you see.

"You see" indeed! But surely no two readers agree on what they see. All
manner of meaning lurks within these quizzical stanzas, suggestive, tanta-
lizing; and like the *Alice* books, the whole is not really about meaning at all.
With the poem lending itself to individual interpretations, it is remarkable
that there is nothing at all tentative about the nonsense world that Charles
creates here, nothing hypothetical: it is as real as the traffic jam in the heart
of New York or London on a rainy Friday afternoon. Even though the journey cannot be plotted (the map the Bellman consults is, of course, blank), it
is, in spite of its tragic ending, an affirmative statement. This is where
Charles's genius lies, in seeing not only that we take the journey but also that
we get something out of it. From the start we are drawn into the thing, become members of the beamish crew, get totally involved in the bumbling adventure, share the hope of success and the disappointment, the sense of loss,
at the end.

Charles knew that most of his creative works bore currents of hidden
meaning. But he could also tease about meaning. "In answer to your question, 'What did you mean the Snark was?' " Charles wrote to May Barber
(January 12, 1897). "I meant that the Snark was a *Boojum*. I trust that . . . you
will now feel quite satisfied and happy." When a young man asked him, "Mr.
Dodgson, what is a snark?" he laughed and said: "When you find out tell
me."[19] And when someone asked him why the crew's names all begin with
a *B,* he answered: "Why not?" Just as Humpty Dumpty can make words
mean what he wants them to mean, Charles is prepared to have each reader
make whole books of his mean what each wants them to mean.

In the preface to the *Snark*, he playfully called the work "a brief but instructive poem . . . [with] a strong moral purpose." Is he pulling our leg? In a letter to some children (August 18, 1884), he tried seriously to answer their question: "As to the meaning of the *Snark?* I'm very much afraid I didn't mean anything but nonsense! Still, you know, words mean more than we mean to express when we use them: so a whole book ought to mean a great deal more than the writer meant. So, whatever good meanings are in the book, I'm very glad to accept as the meaning of the book. The best I've seen is . . . that the whole book is an allegory on the search for happiness. I think this fits beautifully in many ways."

The poem's real meaning, like the meaning in the *Alice* books, is anti-meaning. It is more about *being* than *meaning*, listening than seeing, feeling than thinking. Charles would have been surprised to be thought the creator of art for art's sake, or frivolity for frivolity's sake, but in a sense he created both: he was more interested in entertaining, in engaging the aesthetic sensibilities and the emotions, than in instructing, preaching, or devising clever meanings. He well knew that in the high noon of Victorian prudery, laughter was too often suspect, fun equated with sin, humor judged irreverent, even sacrilegious. Matthew Arnold, after all, downgraded Chaucer because he lacked "high seriousness." In too many homes, instruction and improvement were the only sanctioned activities. But in Charles's scale of values, there was room for fun and nonsense, and they did not diminish either the seriousness of life or the intensity of one's religious convictions.

Critics notwithstanding, the story produces the effect that Charles sought: it amuses young and old alike. They blanch with fear at the Jubjub's screech and hold their breath at the Baker's courage—but mostly they laugh. And this power to provoke mirth and laughter is what has won the *Snark* an ever-growing audience. Snark clubs have grown up at both Oxford and Cambridge, and the Universal Snark Club meets annually in London on Charles's birthday. The *Snark* has been set to music, adapted for the stage, and performed as a musical comedy. It was read by Alec Guinness and Alan Bennett on BBC radio and recorded on disc by Boris Karloff. The band of declared Snarkists includes W. H. Auden, Willa Cather, John Galsworthy, A. P. Herbert, Elspeth Huxley, C. S. Lewis, Cardinal Newman, and Theodore Roosevelt. Translations of it have appeared in French (the earliest by Louis Aragon), Latin, Italian, Swedish, Danish, German, Spanish, and Dutch.

Despite the press notices, the *Snark* grows in stature as the years go by. Devereux Court devoted six pages to the poem (*Cornhill Magazine,* March

1911) when a new cheap edition appeared. "The reissue of this old favourite," for Court, "is like an invitation to renew our youth." Serious critics, philosophers, psychologists, and psychoanalysts have compiled a mountain of commentaries on the poem.[20] Specialists in wit, nonsense, and comic theory have addressed themselves to this landmark poem, and their critiques sometimes illuminate, but more often obfuscate, and are often absurd.

Perhaps the most repulsive reading of the *Alice* books came from Edmund Burke, who suggested that they are about toilet training and bowel movements; similarly exceptional readings occur for the *Snark*. Some see it as an expression of Charles's sexual repression, others as an allegory of one sort or another—of Charles's search for the absolute, fame, wealth, popularity. For some, it is a burlesque of the Tichborne case, an anti-vivisection tract, an existential drama, a satire on religion-science controversies; others have argued that it was inspired by one of the Arctic expeditions, that it is an explanation of how a national economy or a board of directors works.

Meaning? Certainly the *Snark* has meaning, subterranean meaning. But Charles was not addressing his fear of death or annihilation. Underscoring everything he wrote and did and said was his conviction of a moral universe and life after death. His faith in God and a world beyond human comprehension was absolute. Beneath that staunch faith there could not lurk the worm of doubt, the belief in a void. Otherwise Charles's fierce honesty would have forced him to own up to it. It simply is not there. He was tied intellectually, emotionally, subconsciously, and consciously to a merciful God and a beneficent afterlife. The voyage in the *Snark* must in some way represent the voyage of life, just as the *Alice* books do, but the message is not one of despair. The voyage is a grand adventure, like life, and each of the crew represents some strain of society, perhaps even some personal quality in Charles himself. The Baker's vanishing is not an inevitable negation, the result of doubt, or the fate that awaits everyone. We do not know where the Baker has vanished to, and most of the party do survive. The vanishing may be metaphorically a sign of what Charles knows well: that we on earth live within the inviolable rules of nature.

Charles was always concerned with rules, natural, social, religious. The Baker is supposedly courageous for going ahead of the pack in search of the Snark, but perhaps courage alone is not enough, perhaps the Baker is intruding upon the mystery of the universe, perhaps he is presumptuous in doing so, and perhaps his derring-do is, in fact, immoral transgression rather than courage. Charles does not allow the Snark to be pictured: for him, the mystery was awesome and represented a sacred force that governs the world and that sets the boundaries between temporal and infinite. Perhaps the poem symbolically speaks, as well, about the hallowed relationship of person to person, of Charles to his child friends, about a sacredness that must never be violated. And when it is violated, annihilation results. Perhaps the Baker does not deserve so stark a fate, but he is singled out for it. He vanishes because he seeks to penetrate the unknown, to dispel its romance, to capture and domesticate its sacred mystery.

*The Hunting of the Snark* soars at least as high as the *Alice* books in its invention. It is taut and measured, like a symphony or a mass. Its musical quality is important. The critics have spent much energy analyzing its minutiae, but they fail to hear its greatness. For it is through the music of the words that Charles gets to his readers, not through the transmission of thought. The sound of the words and the accumulated sound in the lines and the verses have an effect upon us like music: the sounds filter through our minds and go directly to our hearts—our emotions soar, our laughter bubbles up. Similar sounds, contrasting sounds, contrapuntal sounds, echoes—they are all there; they coalesce, opposites clash and are reconciled, and they come together to fuse into something transcendent. Memorize the refrain, say it over and over again, and see what it does to you. The sound of *Snark* is about as far from the sound *Boojum* as we can get; the one is brief, high-pitched, and sharp, the other slow, low, and mellow. Together they encompass an extreme range of sound, a diversity and a unity of existence, the contradictions we face with life and death. That is why the Snark *was* a Boojum, you see. The Baker has vanished but the mystery survives, and the universe goes on its merry way.

Two years before Charles completed the *Snark,* he was on his way to publishing another volume of his verse, this one, unlike the earlier *Phantasmagoria,* to be illustrated. With all his other publications and activities, however, the book developed slowly. On January 7, 1878, he wrote a flattering letter to the illustrator Arthur Burdett Frost, who agreed to illustrate the book. Frost, one of the earliest American artists to achieve popularity in England, illustrated *Rhyme? and Reason?* The correspondence between poet and artist was extensive: fine points were ironed out, delays occurred, but *Rhyme? and Reason?,* with sixty-five illustrations by Frost and nine by Holiday (the book includes the *Snark*), appeared in December 1883. It sold out quickly.

Apart from Frost's illustrations, the volume contains little new material.

It is mainly a reprint of *Phantasmagoria and Other Poems*. Charles made some textual changes and added four new poems. One is "Empress of Art," a riddle in verse, which is an adulation of Ellen Terry as actress. Another, "The air is bright with hues of light," is a charade in verse inspired by Marion Terry's performance as Galatea in W. S. Gilbert's *Pygmalion and Galatea*. The other two new items are poems entitled "Echoes" and "A Game of Fives." "Echoes" is a twelve-line bit of nonsense about an eight-year-old Lady Clara Vere de Vere. The inspiration could hardly have come from Tennyson's fully realized dramatic monologue "Lady Clara Vere de Vere," but perhaps the name stuck in Charles's mind. "A Game of Fives" is a humorous account of five little girls from childhood passing through various stages of growth and maturity, until they become

> Five *passé* girls—Their age? Well, never mind
> We jog along together, like the rest of human kind:
> But the quondam "careless bachelor" begins to think he knows
> The answer to that ancient problem "how the money goes"!

The poem was probably inspired by the five sisters who lived in Guildford supported in good part by their bachelor brother.

As Charles neared the 1880s, he could look back upon a decade of enormous accomplishment. When the 1870s ended, he was forty-seven, was established professionally, and was accomplished in many disciplines, not least of all mathematics, photography, and literature. If his personal life was not all it might have been, not what he wanted it to be, he could console himself with second best, with friendships galore. He could now sit back and savor his many successes. But that, we know, was not like Charles. He was eager to get on with life, to do much more, to prove again and again to himself and to the world that he had much to offer, that he had earned his way to the green pastures, or whatever there might be, on the other side of the river. He entered the 1880s almost frantic with plans, determined to work, to add more to an already considerable array of accomplishments.

# CHAPTER THIRTEEN

# Yellowing Leaves

*The things which I have seen I now can see no more.*
WILLIAM WORDSWORTH

As Charles stepped into the 1880s, he paid no attention to the new era. He did not sit down to his diary, as was his custom earlier, look backward, and make resolutions for the year to come: the last eleven days of 1879 go entirely unrecorded.

His conscience seems not to prick him so fiercely as it used to. Only once in 1879, on April 17, did he appeal to God in his diary: "At the beginning of this new Term I ask . . . pardon for my many sins past, and grace to serve Him better during this Term and in my future life." The first year of the new decade is free of any appeal. On January 26, 1881, on the eve of his birthday, he writes: "Tomorrow I shall end my 49th year. May God help me to spend the remaining time better than the years that are now gone beyond recall!"

He was growing older and he knew it. He had memories to console him, but the sense of loss and loneliness were ever with him, and he struck despondent chords, sometimes in odd places, as in an acrostic verse he composed for Agnes Hull about this time. It echoes his earlier poem "Faces in the Fire" but adds a positive note, a determination to seek and find new harvests:

> Around my lonely hearth, to-night,
>     Ghostlike the shadows wander:
> Now here, now there, a childish sprite,

Earthborn and yet an angel bright,
Seems near me as I ponder.

. . . . . . .

New raptures still hath youth in store.
Age may but fondly cherish
Half-faded memories of yore—
Up, craven heart! repine no more!
Love stretches hands from shore to shore:
Love is, and shall not perish!

Charles's energy did not wane; he continued active, acute, productive. Toward the end of the old decade (December 12, 1879), he invented "a new way of working one word into another." The new game is called *Syzygies*.

The 1880s dawn with Charles guiding new editions of his *Easter Greeting* and *Doublets* into print, while he worked busily on various projects and made plans for others. On January 1, 1880, he penned a letter to Ellen Terry suggesting that she might want to take her children to a recital by the Weblings, a family of acting children. Charles attended the performance on the eighth at Steinway Hall, treating two sisters and a brother. Miss Terry was also present, and he "went and sat by . . . [her] through part of the time." On the fourteenth he returned to Christ Church for the new term.

His devotion to his family continued. His brothers found their way in the world and settled into careers, Wilfred as estate agent for Lord Boyne's Shropshire estates, Skeffington and Edwin in the Church. On September 4, 1880, Aunt Lucy Lutwidge died at the Chestnuts. Charles was present, and read the commendatory prayer and the thanksgiving at the burial service. He saw Wilfred married to Alice Donkin in 1871; on September 21, 1880, he tells his diary that Skeffington has just got married: "He had kept it all a secret, and I am thankful to have no responsibility." He appended a note— "see May 28, 1879"—but a later hand has cut that page from the diary.

Another event that neither enters Charles's diary nor is mentioned in his letters, although it was widely reported in the press, was Alice Liddell's marriage to Reginald Hargreaves on September 15, 1880, in Westminster Abbey. The news must have moved Charles deeply, but he took refuge in silence.

As he approached his half century, he made two major alterations to his life, one perhaps by default, the other deliberate. The first occurred in July 1880, when Charles took his last photograph; the second he accounts for in his diary on July 14, 1881: "Came to a more definite decision than I have ever

*Charles's photograph of his brother Wilfred with bicycle*

yet done that it is about time to resign the Mathematical Lectureship. My chief motive for holding on has been to provide money for others (for myself I have been for many years able to retire) but even the £300 a year I shall thus lose I may fairly hope to make by the additional time I shall have for book-writing. I think of asking the Governing Body, next term, to appoint my successor, so that I may retire at the end of the year, when I shall be close on 50 years old. . . ." The decision held, and on October 18 Charles, having written the Dean about his plans, mused: "I shall now have my whole time at my own disposal, and . . . may hope . . . to do some worthy work in writing—partly in the cause of Mathematical education, partly in the cause of innocent recreation for children, and partly, I hope (though so utterly unworthy of being allowed to take up such work) in the cause of religious thought. May God bless the new form of life that lies before me, that I may use it according to His holy will!"

On November 23 Charles heard that the Dean accepted his resignation, but rejected his suggestion that he continue to give the Euclid lectures. Restraint rules Oxford behavior, and one expects no formal acknowledgment of Charles's departure from the lectureship, either in college or Common Room. But it is odd that the exchanges with the Dean were restricted to pen and ink. However awkward the relations between Charles and the deanery, should the Dean not have spoken to him and expressed some thought if not emotion? And should the other Liddells not somehow have noticed this milestone in the life of a man who, if no longer cherished, had been so kind and generous to them? But no—nothing.

One week later Charles found "in my journal that I gave my first Euclid Lecture . . . on Monday, January 28, 1856. It consisted of twelve men, of whom nine attended. This morning I have given what is probably my *last:* the lecture is now reduced to nine, of whom all attended on Monday: this morning being a Saint's Day, the attendance was voluntary, and only two appeared. . . . I was lecturer when the *father* of . . . [one of the two] took his degree, viz., in 1858. There is a sadness in coming to the *end* of anything in life. Man's instinct clings to the Life that will never end."

While Charles was no longer Lecturer, he retained his studentship, his residence, and full voting power in Christ Church and the university. On the day he got the Dean's approval of his resignation, he recorded a list of nine books he contemplated writing, including *Euclid, Books I, II* ("a sort of chatty book" for schoolboys); a new edition of *Euclid and His Modern Rivals;* a "Collection of [Mathematical] Problems"; a book on "Series: Limits of Circle-Squaring"; "my method of finding Logarithms and Sines without tables"; a new edition of *Phantasmagoria;* a new edition of serious poems; "Games and Puzzles"; and *Sylvie and Bruno.*

*Euclid, Books I, II* is a reprint in 1882 of his privately printed 1875 version. It is not a defense of Euclid like his *Euclid and His Modern Rivals,* but an attempt to modify the original form of Euclid's *Elements,* books 1 and 2, for modern use. "This book is admirably suited to Oxford men who require to know the first two books of Euclid, and desire nothing more," the *Glasgow Herald* said (April 14, 1883). "It is charmingly neat, 'free from all accidental verbiage and repetition,' and yet Euclid. Mr. Dodgson's slight alterations of the text . . . are fully stated and explained in the introduction." The *Educational Times* (May 1) said that "Mr. Dodgson . . . has brought his considerable experience to bear upon the modelling of this exposition of Euclid's method."

Neither before nor after Charles withdrew from his lectureship did he lose sight of issues touching college and university affairs. In the spring of

1881 Christ Church undergraduate shenanigans made newspaper headlines. "The row-loving men in College are beginning to be troublesome again," Charles wrote (May 26), "and last night some 30 or 40 of them, aided by out-college men, made a great disturbance, and regularly defied the Censors. I have just been, with the other tutors, into Hall, and heard the Dean make an excellent speech to the House. Some 2 or 3 will have to go down, and 12 or 15 others will be punished in various ways." The *Observer* ran a leading article on the fracas (May 29). "Once again we . . . ask why the Cathedral House of Christchurch [*sic*] in the University of Oxford should be the perpetual occasion of University scandal," the piece began, and ended with an appeal to the University Commissioners to "do something to sever the unfortunate union which cripples a rich and noble College by tying it to the skirts of an episcopal chapter house."

Charles rose to the defense of his college in a long letter (June 5). He pointed to the many inaccuracies in the *Observer* article and quoted two particularly objectionable statements: "Christ Church is always provoking the adverse criticism of the outer world" and "The Dean . . . neglects his functions, and spends the bulk of his time in Madeira." Charles rebuts these and other accusations, pointing out that more than twenty years before, the Dean spent two successive winters away because of ill health and student uprisings had always been dealt with properly. "The essence of . . . [your] article," Charles wrote, "seems to be summed up in the following sentence: 'At Christ Church all attempts to preserve order by the usual means have hitherto proved uniformly unsuccessful, and apparently remain equally fruitless.' It is hard . . . to believe that this is seriously intended as a description of the place. . . . Permit me, as one who has lived here for thirty years and has taught for five and twenty, to say that in my experience order has been the rule, disorder the rare exception."

If Oxford wags noticed a mellowing in Charles's public utterances concerning the Dean, they must also have known that it had now been twenty years since the deanery sent Charles into exile and almost ten since he fired his cannonballs against the Dean's reforms.

A letter appeared in the *Guardian* (February 1, 1882) complaining that in "a recent Responsions examination . . . more than half the candidates were 'plucked,' " attributing the failures to a "sudden raising of the standard" and asserting that the "great majority of failures in mathematics were due to ignorance of the first two books of Euclid—in other words, to inadequate preparation, and neglect of the elementary parts of the work by teachers and [those] taught." This thrust hit right home, and Charles counterattacked with a letter that instructed the complainer on the correct way to determine the numbers and percentages: "The true answer to the question raised by your correspondent, 'How are we to account for this phenomenon?' is simply that there is no phenomenon to be accounted for." The editor added a note of rebuttal to Charles's analysis, and that provoked Charles to set to work seriously on the results of Oxford Responsions. On February 9 he published *An Analysis of Responsions-Lists from Michaelmas, 1873, to Michaelmas, 1881,* proving statistically that the average number of passes from 1873 to 1881 was 64 percent, and in 1881 63 percent, even though the variations over the years went from 54 to 82.

Through all his years as a teacher, achieving fair student examinations was one of Charles's great concerns, and he did everything he could to prepare students for the examinations. He nonetheless questioned the value of examinations and even systems of competition. More than fiction lay behind what he wrote in 1893, in chapter 12 of *Sylvie and Bruno Concluded,* where Mein Herr, a visitor, learns about how young people are brought up and taught in the narrator's country. The narrator explains:

> "In an over-crowded country like this, nothing but Competitive Examinations—"
> Mein Herr threw up his hands wildly. "What *again?*" he cried. "I thought it was dead, fifty years ago! Oh this Upas tree of Competitive Examinations! Beneath whose deadly shade all the original genius, all the exhaustive research, all the untiring life-long diligence by which our fore-fathers have so advanced human knowledge, must slowly but surely wither away, and give place to a system of Cookery, in which the human mind is a sausage, and all we ask is, how much indigestible stuff can be crammed into it!"

Having devised schemes and procedures for making the branches of mathematics more accessible to undergraduates, Charles took a tangential step to try to simplify everyday calculations for everyone. In May 1884 he contributed to the journal *Knowledge* a letter entitled "Divisibility by Seven"; and on March 8, 1887, he discovered "a Rule . . . for finding day of the week for any given day of the month" with ". . . less to remember than in any other Rule I have met with," he wrote, and published it in *Nature* at the end of the month. "I am not a rapid computer myself," he confesses in the article, "and as I find my average time for doing any such question is about 20 seconds, I have little doubt that a rapid computer would need 15." He explains his method, which, however accurate, is complex and beyond the ability of most lay readers to commit to memory. But following the instructions carefully leads to success. The rule later inspired the mathematician John Conway to base on it a system for even more rapidly calculating in one's head the day of the week for any given date.[1] A decade after Charles published the day-of-the-week rule, he published, also in *Nature*, two other discoveries, his "Brief Method of Dividing a Given Number by 9 or 11" and his "Abridged Long Division." These inventions became additional lessons Charles could teach children, individually and in groups.

At a Common Room meeting on November 30, 1882, J. Barclay Thompson, Reader in Anatomy and an abrasive colleague, "brought (by implication) charges of obstinacy and extravagance," in Charles's words, "against the [Common Room] Curator," Charles's old friend T. Vere Bayne, who had held the post for twenty-one years. "These I now attempted to rebut," Charles added. ". . . A new Curator [was] elected. I was proposed by Holland, and seconded by Harcourt, and accepted office with no light heart: there will be much trouble and thought needed to work it satisfactorily: but it will take me out of myself a little, and so may be a real good. My life was tending to become too much that of a selfish recluse."

He was keenly aware that time was slipping by. On May 24, 1882, aged fifty, having received a letter from Agnes Hull, he replied that "it is pleasant even to find one is not quite forgotten, when one is getting old, and grey, and stupid. . . ." Later that year he wrote of "life on the other side of the great river" becoming "more and more a reality . . ."; and on October 11, 1882, he described himself as "distinctly 'elderly,' if not 'old.' " The refrains on the subject of aging, accompanied by complaints of bad memory, intensify from that point onward.

Given his concern about his age, his search for more time for writing, and his resignation from his lectureship, it seems singularly odd for him to have taken on what surely was a thankless job and one that, while enormously time-consuming, could never be creative. The decision cannot be attributed to vanity; Charles was not flattered by being wanted for the task, nor would he have relished the power inherent in the post. The real reason must have been as he said, that it would take him out of himself—he was still apprehensive about idleness and indolence. He had not shaken off his penchant for self-recrimination, for wearing a hair shirt, for checking solipsistic tendencies. He was still eager to do penance for wayward thoughts and past habits. The job would certainly help keep whatever furies he feared at bay.

Immediately after his election, he was "hard at work learning my new business, and planning forms and ledgers: the accounts have not been *fully* kept by any means." He set up a battery of records and charts and kept them carefully throughout his nine-plus years in the job; they include a miscellaneous notebook with records of the wine committee's "tasting luncheons"; numerous miscellaneous lists of members, cellar books, records of expenditures, drawings he made of the wine cellars, a complaint book that he inaugurated, a letter register, and booklets containing carbon copies of his outgoing letters. His duties were so numerous, varied, and time-consuming that today we would think of them as a full-time occupation, something like those performed by the manager of a club. He had to do all the ordering (wine and liqueurs, food, coal, newspapers, magazines, stationery, and more), approve the bills, pay the servants, keep up the furniture, post notices, and see that Common Room functioned smoothly.

Through the years of his curatorship Charles deluged members of Common Room with printed notices soliciting their opinions, announcing changes in rules or procedures, and even offering for sale marmalade his brother-in-law concocted from an old recipe. His notices were customarily printed and cover a myriad of subjects. Here is one of the more bubbly sort:

---

### Christ Church Common Room.

——

## CHAMPAGNE.

——

A DESIRE having been expressed that a better *quality* of wine should be supplied as "Champagne A" (though not accompanied by any expression of willingness to pay a higher *price*), the Curator has procured samples, which Members are invited to taste, in Common Room, at 1.30, on


Sandwiches, &c. will be provided.


C. L. DODGSON,
*Curator of Common Room.*


*Nov.     , 1887.*

He paid scrupulous attention to the members' comfort, added furnishings, improved the lighting, and sought an aesthetically agreeable ambiance. He engaged William De Morgan to install a surround of colorful tiles, which exists still in the Common Room fireplace. He also extended the wine cellars and filled them with the best of economical vintages. Wine is central to all common-room life, and Charles went to great lengths to provide the cellars with proper temperature controls. Soon after he took over the curatorship, he wrote (January 25, 1883) to a London wine merchant, seeking his advice on two or three points concerning the treatment of wine:

(1) What amount of damp is desirable in a wine cellar?
(2) Is ventilation desirable?
(3) Should light be admitted?

Charles was himself fond of wine, although, as one member noted, not overwhelmed by its mystique: "He held the view that amateur wine-tasters deceived themselves when they professed to distinguish one vintage from another, and that they really were guided by the label supplied by the wine merchant. To prove this, he once secretly interchanged the labels on the bottles which the wine committee met to taste, and maintained that his colleagues had reacted exactly as he had foretold."[2]

A crisis apparently arose when Charles discovered that the cellars contained a considerable quantity of brown sherry but no port, a taste for port having reemerged among members. He sent out to a local grocer for some, leading one colleague to complain that he was running the Common Room "on the lines of a lower middle-class family." Nonetheless, for years after Charles's tenure as Curator, the port he laid down circulated after dinner in the Common Room.

In those latter Victorian days, Christ Church constituted, according to one member, "a very happy and animated society. . . . Most of us who dined found our way to Common Room afterwards, and quite a number looked in there each day for afternoon tea." (Charles, in fact, introduced afternoon tea in 1884.) "Dinner is of course in Hall, then comes the descent into the dim, religious light of the Common Room, with its panelled walls and its choice paintings of Cuyp and Frans Hals and Gainsborough, and its many engravings of Chancellors of the University and Governor-Generals and Viceroys of India, where Telling, the Common Room man—who, with his side-whiskers and choker, looked as if he had come straight out of a Dickens portrait gallery, who never seemed to sit down or take a holiday . . . —[would be] asking whether any gentleman wished to drink claret."

Charles was efficient and insisted upon proper decorum in Common Room, but he also enjoyed and encouraged good fellowship. Testimonials of life in Common Room during his curatorship confirm both. One member recalled that evenings in Common Room "were much enlivened by the presence and conversation of such men as Dr. Liddon and Mr. Dodgson."[3] Others report on Charles's natural sense of fun and whimsy, which went beyond the bounds of his children's books. "Sometimes," Blagden writes, "if the audience was small and appreciative, he would sit . . . and tell us stories in his own inimitable way. Then we realised what children must have found in him, and what supreme gifts he had to charm and hold them."

A pamphlet, *Twelve Months in a Curatorship by One Who Has Tried It*, signaled Charles's first anniversary as Curator. In it Charles begins by assuring his colleagues that his essay is not a plagiarism of "Five Years in Penal Servitude" but instead "largely autobiographical (a euphemism for 'egotistic'), slightly apologetic, cautiously retrospective, and boldly prophetic: it will be at once financial, carbonaceous, aesthetic, chalybeate, literary, and alcoholic: it will be pervaded with mystery, and spiced with hints of thrilling plots and deeds of darkness." The light touch continues as Charles addresses a number of Common Room topics. One section is entitled "Of Wine": "The consumption of Madeira (B) has been, during the past year, zero. . . . After careful calculation, I estimate that, if this rate of consumption be steadily maintained, our present stock will last us an infinite number of years." "Of Liqueurs": "The asterisks . . . indicate the degree of goodness according to the view of a certain Member of the Wine-Committee, who, in the noblest spirit of self-sacrifice, came day after day to taste the samples."

On February 27, 1884, Charles reported that colleagues "have been *most* kind about my pamphlet, and the worry I have had during the last year. I had printed a supplement announcing that I would not again serve with a Wine-Committee, but there is evidently so strong a wish to keep it and me, that I have given way, and drawn up a code of Rules I *could* work with—the last code being intolerable and absurd." On the following day the "new rules were adopted, so that I retain office."

Having his way helped. He carried on diligently and in 1886 published another report, *Three Years in a Curatorship by One Whom It Has Tried*, another witty effusion on Common Room affairs whose breezy tone reflects his success. He declares that "long and painful experience has taught me one great principle in managing business for other people, *viz.*, if you want to inspire confidence, *give plenty of statistics*. It does not matter that they should be accurate, or even intelligible, so long as there is enough of them. A curator who contents himself with simply *doing* the business of a Common Room, and who puts out no statistics, is sure to be distrusted." He turns to practical matters—ventilation, lighting, and furniture, or, in his words, "Of Airs, Glares, and Chairs"—and, after he has dealt with them, concludes: "Enough, enough! I have said my say, gentle reader! Turn the page, and revel, to your heart's content, in . . ."—and he provides a table of the present stock of wine, over twenty thousand bottles, with their prices.

Although pressured by his own writing schedule and the demands of Common Room, Charles remained throughout the 1880s enmeshed in college affairs and published a number of papers dealing entirely with tempests in teapots. These publications, however, represent only a fraction of his output. "I have a bewildering number of 'irons in the fire,' " he wrote to Alice Cooper (November 14, 1883). Having entered the sphere of public affairs earlier, he kept on commenting on issues, sending out letters to the press, writing articles, and preparing privately printed pieces designed to influence opinion and change.

Charles's interest in British politics remained keen. At this time he entered an entirely new arena, taking up the esoteric subject of social choice—that is, the study of the mathematical properties and paradoxes of voting systems. On June 28, 1872, he was in the House of Commons listening for four hours to the debate on the House of Lords' amendments to the Ballot Bill. Ten days later (with a pass from Lord Salisbury), he was in the gallery at the House of Lords to hear the debate on those amendments which the Commons had refused to accept. He was surely pleased ultimately, when the Act of 1872 created the secret ballot for the first time in England. Charles's ingrained sense of fairness drew him to seek formulae for improving voting systems, first in his own college, then in Parliament, and ultimately the world, and he published no fewer than eight separate items on the subject as well as a number of letters to the press. As early as 1873 he issued his first pamphlet, *Discussion of Procedure in Elections,* intended to alter voting methods in Christ Church elections and appointments.

The pamphlet articulates a philosophy that remained constant in all of Charles's proposals: that we can achieve more nearly perfect reflections of voters' desires not by conventional majorities, not by staging successive elections to eliminate candidates, or by other procedures in common use, but by a system of awarding marks or points, which he describes in detail, supplying charts and symbols to help advance his complex argument. He achieved some local success with this first effort: on December 18 he recorded "Election of Baynes and Paget: we partly used my method." The subject had him in its thrall. Perhaps his efforts to alter voting procedures at Christ Church grew out of the old smoldering animosity toward the Dean.

On December 29 he was "writing about Elections very constantly lately," and in June 1874 he printed *Suggestions as to the Best Method of Taking Votes Where More Than Two Issues Are To Be Voted On,* also based on a marks system and containing even more complex formulae than his earlier work. He labored intermittently on elections theory through the ensuing years, and on February 9, 1876, recorded that the "question of a system for taking votes at an election was again postponed [by the Governing Body]. Afterwards I arranged with Bayne that we should try to get information as to the rules adopted in the other Colleges." The opinion of C. W. Lawrence, Christ Church Chapter Clerk, "given today, that 'the greatest number of votes does not necessarily mean an absolute majority,' gives us the means of a final settlement of the matter, when there is a 'cyclical majority' that will yield to no other remedy." By a "cyclical majority," a term Charles coined, he means a situation where A may win a majority over B, B over C, and C over A, all at the same time. Charles was the first writer in English to recognize the existence of this phenomenon. Later that month he revised his 1874 pamphlet and published it as *A Method of Taking Votes on More Than Two Issues.* "The principle of voting makes an election more of a game of skill than a real test of the wishes of the electors," he writes here, "and as my own opinion is that it is better for elections to be decided according to the wish of the majority than of those who happen to have most skill in the game, I think it desirable that all should know the rules by which this game may be won."

For a time, voting theory could not compete with Charles's other concerns, but in 1877 he was back at it, sending out electric-pen circulars soliciting suggestions for improving his method. Then, four years later, he learned that "Mr. [Frederick] Greenwood [editor of the *St. James's Gazette*] approves my theory about General Elections (that the *results* should all be announced at once), and wants me to write on it in the *St. James's Gazette.*" "Purity of Election," appeared on May 4, taking Charles's voting concerns beyond Oxford, into the world. In this letter, he does not argue for his system of marks; he is more concerned with temporal matters as they affect a general or national election. He supports the recent innovation of the secret ballot and calls for keeping the ballots sealed and uncounted until all polling has been completed. General elections were being held over several days, and early results, made public, influence later voters, who, Charles suggests, wanted to be on the winning side. Charles sent copies "to Gladstone . . . Lord Salisbury, etc."

For the remainder of 1881 Charles was occupied with any number of other concerns. He nevertheless kept an eye on Parliament, and on March 23, 1882, another letter of his appears in the *St. James's Gazette,* this on the subject of parliamentary cloture. "May I," Charles wrote, "[make] an announcement which will shake . . . the whole scientific world? The *Perpetuum Mobile* is discovered." Charles was questioning whether the Gladstone government, after voting a resolution of cloture in the House "by a bare majority" may legitimately go on to pass legislation being debated by the same bare majority.

Charles's attention was caught, even before his cloture letter appeared, by tennis tournament rules that he deemed inherently unjust. "Did the best experiment I have made in devising a new and better rule for Lawn Tennis (or any other) tournament," he recorded (September 17, 1881). Almost a year later (July 12, 1882), his letter "Lawn Tennis Tournaments" appeared in the *St. James's Gazette.* A year and a day after that, Charles was "hard at work . . . on the Lawn Tennis Tournament Question. The most practicable form, for a *true* method," he wrote, "seems to be 32 competitors: 3 prizes only: and half-day contests, until the *invicti* are reduced to 2, when they have a whole day." He followed with another letter, "The Fallacies of Lawn Tennis Tournaments," in the *Gazette* (August 1, 1883), then with two more on the same subject (August 4 and 21) and a pamphlet, *Lawn Tennis Tournaments: The True Method of Assigning Prizes.*

His plan would settle the first prize by the end of the fourth day, the second by the middle of the fifth, and the third by the end of that day. His pamphlet contains four elements: (1) "proof that the present method of assigning prizes is, except . . . the first prize, entirely unmeaning"; (2) proof that the current method is unjust; (3) his own system for conducting tournaments, "which, while requiring less time than the present system, shall secure equitable results"; and (4) "an equitable system for scoring in matches." He proves that current practice insures the best player of the first prize, but the odds that the second-best player would take second prize are only 16/31, and a 12–1 chance that the top four players would not emerge in their rightful places.

Charles's objections were valid, but his own rules were not easy to follow or to implement. They were consequently ignored in his time. Today, however, theorists applaud his system.[4]

He had not yet finished with voting systems. On May 1, 1884, he wrote: "Spent yesterday afternoon with [R. E.] Baynes [another fellow Student], in calculations on subject of Proportionate Representation." His attention was also engaged by the controversy over suffrage. On February 29 Gladstone introduced the Government's Franchise Bill, extending the vote to rural householders. It provided for near-universal male suffrage by adding two million voters to the rolls, nearly four times the number added in 1832 and twice that in 1867, and by extending the same privileges to Scotland and Ireland, the bill unified the franchise throughout the United Kingdom. Conservatives feared the "radicalism" of the new voters and objected to giving Ireland eighty to ninety members who might all favor Home Rule. The unamended bill nevertheless passed the Commons on June 26.

Conservatives in the Lords tried to amend the bill to require the Government to join to it a complete plan for redistributing parliamentary seats, an issue that set the parties at each other's throats. Lord Salisbury championed the plan on July 7, arguing that by extending the franchise to Ireland, the Government threatened the integrity of the Empire. He also rejected as inadequate the Government's promise to introduce a plan for redistributing parliamentary seats in the next session of Parliament. The Lords amendment requiring redistribution carried and created a legislative deadlock until December.

Charles got into the thick of these proceedings early, with letters to the *St. James's Gazette* in May and June 1884. All the while he worked at honing his system, and on June 3 came up with a formula that he termed "the best I have yet devised. . . . The chief novelty in it is the giving to each candidate the power of transferring, to any other candidate, the votes given to him." On the fourth his letter appeared in the *St. James's Gazette*, and on that very day he was already working on "a new version, which I hope Mr. Greenwood will print as an *article*."

It appeared on July 5, and on the eighth Charles sent a copy to Lord Salisbury with a covering letter: "How I wish the enclosed could have appeared as *your* scheme!" he wrote. "Then it would have been attended to. That *some* such scheme is needed, and much more needed than *any* scheme for mere redistribution of electoral districts, I feel sure." On the following day Salisbury, involved in negotiating the distribution bill with the Liberals, replied, acknowledging the need for a scheme of electoral reform but stressing the difficulty of getting a hearing for "anything . . . absolutely new . . . however Conservative its object." On the tenth Charles protested to Salisbury: "*Please* don't call my scheme . . . a 'Conservative' one! ('Give a dog a bad name, etc.') . . . *All* I aim at is to secure that, *whatever* be the proportions of opinions among the Electors, the *same* shall exist among the Members. Such a scheme may at one time favour one party, at one time another: just as it happens. But really it has *no* political bias of its own."

Charles favored a general franchise, as he indicated in still another letter sent to the *St. James's Gazette* in 1884, "the first time . . . I have written a letter straight off for print, and not even corrected it," he noted (August 7) on the day that it appeared (signed "Dynamite"), merely quoted under the miscellaneous column called "Notes." He picked up and quoted a metaphor Joseph Chamberlain used: " 'I have read somewhere of a patient who was ordered a shower-bath by his physician. He had never seen one before, and when he was introduced to the startling invention he stoutly declared "I will not enter that machine without an umbrella." . . . Now Lord Salisbury insists on an umbrella. . . . He will not submit the Constitution to a bracing shower of new voters unless he can preserve it from the shock by a carefully manipulated scheme of redistribution.' "

Charles says that Chamberlain "has not got the details quite right, but the correction is easily made. The patient," he continues, "discovered that there was only one hole at the top of the shower-bath, through which the whole of the water would have fallen *en masse* upon one shoulder only; and prudently declared 'I will not enter that machine until a proper system of holes is made, so that the water may be fairly distributed.' Everyone knows," Charles concludes, "that the bracing effect of a shower-bath wholly depends on this distribution."

Charles's labors on proportionate representation and fair voting systems merge in a fifty-six-page pamphlet entitled *The Principles of Parliamentary Representation,* dated November 5, 1884. The date is significant. A second reading of the Franchise Bill was scheduled in the House on November 18, and Charles wanted to distribute his ideas as widely and early as possible. When it was published, he breathed a sigh of relief: "At last received 50 finished copies of the pamphlet. So I hope that during today and tomorrow, copies will go to all M.P.'s." The booklet distills the material from Charles's earlier letters to the *St. James's Gazette.*

The journal *Knowledge* (November 28, 1884) gave "unstinted praise to Mr. Dodgson's tract, which lays down, on mathematical principles, the numbers of voters to be assigned to each electoral district, and the number of members to be returned. He treats also of the mode of counting the votes, and goes into other practical details, which cannot fail to be of the highest value. . . . The party politician may look askance at equations as applied to . . . representation, but the wise man will read, mark, learn, and inwardly digest this little book, with the result of finding that its conclusions are at once sound and valuable."

Charles's theory of parliamentary representation assumes a two-party political system in which each side knows the number of its own supporters and controls their votes. He views an election as a two-person zero-sum game in which the votes that one party wins the other party loses, and where the outcome of the election depends both on the number of supporters each side has and on the strategy each side adopts. Assuming each side adopts an "optimal" strategy, he calculates the percentage of voters represented on the average in any given electoral system. Comparing these percentages, he can judge which system is the most representative. He concludes that the largest percentage of voters is represented where each constituency has four or five seats and where each elector has a single vote.

The system is algebraic and difficult, and Charles goes on to refine it even further. In presuming the existence of a two-party system, his proposals were appropriate enough for his time, but not for times when third parties enter the fray. Nonetheless, Charles here breaks new ground and develops highly cogent theories. His work "presents the longest connected chain of reasoning in Political Science," writes Duncan Black: "In fact the argument throughout . . . based on the 2-person zero-sum game . . . could have been put into mathematical form only after 1928 when the first exposition of the 2-person zero-sum game was given by John von Neumann."[5] In *The Principles of Parliamentary Representation*, writes Francine Abeles, "Dodgson showed a grasp of ideas on the intuitive level that were not formalized until 1928 by [E. V.] Huntington and in 1975 and 1979 by [M. L.] Balinski and [H. P.] Young."

Charles's work on voting theory remains significant today. The Marquis de Condorcet's *Essai sur l'application de l'analyse à la probabilité des décisions rendues à la pluralité des voix* (1785) made the most significant contribution to voting theory before Isaac Todhunter revived an interest in Condorcet's work in the mid-nineteenth century. But Todhunter "fails to understand" Condorcet, according to I. McLean and A. B. Urken, and others had to try to apply voting theory to current needs.[6]

Charles knew Todhunter's work and corresponded with him. On September 12, 1863, he spent "most of the morning reading Todhunter's *Theory of Equations*" and added on the twenty-first: "I have made good progress in Todhunter . . . reducing it to a formal series of enunciations." Charles included, with permission, extracts from Todhunter's essay "Elementary Geometry" in the appendix to *Euclid and His Modern Rivals* and acknowledged his help in the prologue. But Charles went beyond Todhunter. "Proportional representation was independently developed by numerous thinkers," write McLean and Urken, "but few . . . [were] capable of expressing their principles clearly and only two [succeed]—G. C. Andrae, a Danish mathematician and politician, and C. L. Dodgson—trained in axiomatic reasoning."[7] Another expert, Michael Dummett, deeply regrets "that Dodgson never completed the book that he planned to write. . . . Such were his lucidity of exposition and his mastery of the topic that it seems possible that, had he ever published it, the political history of Britain would have been significantly diffcrent."[8] Jenifer Hart finds "Dodgson's analysis of the existing system . . . acute: he saw that in some circumstances the House of Commons could consist wholly of one party, and that in other circumstances a majority, even a large majority, of the electors might not secure a majority in the House."[9]

Accustomed to subjecting all inherited practices to the strictest test of logic, Charles also challenged the entrenched British system of bookselling. Publishers customarily gave booksellers huge discounts for paying their bills promptly and booksellers gave discounts to customers for cash. Charles first wrote Macmillan about the practice at the end of 1875. He had analyzed the *Alice* accounts, come to "some startling conclusions," and drawn up tables showing that it cost 2*s*. 5½*d*. to produce a single book; his profit on that outlay was then 1*s*. 1½*d*., the publisher's 5*d*., and the bookseller's, the largest, 1*s*. 5*d*.

Macmillan's reaction was cool: he defended the bookseller, who had to keep stock and take risks. Charles was not impressed and deluged Macmillan with further analysis. "On every 1000 copies sold," he wrote (December 29), "your profit is £20.16.8, mine is £56.5.0, the bookseller's £70.16.8. This seems to me altogether unfair. . . . His profits should be the least of the three, not the *greatest*." Macmillan still defended the bookseller, producing his own figures about rents, wages, and the like. Charles, with so much else on his plate, seemed to succumb. But not entirely. In the 1880s he made a more determined assault.

Booksellers' profits were closely tied at this time to "underselling," a system of cutthroat competition that sometimes allowed discounts of as much as 25 percent off the published price for cash payments. Booksellers pressed publishers for higher discounts, often forcing them to operate on the brink of bankruptcy. In 1871 John Ruskin sought to free himself from what he saw as the pernicious practice of underselling by setting up his own publishing house; in 1882 he began fixing the sales price of his books, allowing booksellers a discount too small to permit them to undersell one another.[10] Charles also wanted his books sold at announced prices, and he insisted that Macmillan notify booksellers that for his books, the publisher in future would no longer supply "odd books," that is, twenty-one books for every twenty ordered.

Booksellers were hostile: on August 4, 1883, a letter from "A Firm of London Booksellers" appeared in the *Bookseller;* headed "Authors as Dictators," it objected strongly to

the new regime inaugurated by Mr. Lewis Carroll . . . [who] is determined to govern the retailer . . . by refusing to supply . . . [his books] to them under ten pence in the shilling, with "no odd books." . . . When an attempt is made to dictate terms to the whole of the booksellers of the United Kingdom by one individual . . . then the time has evidently come for the trade to say it will not submit to dictation of the kind from any individual, be he who he may; and rather than buy on the terms Mr. Lewis Carroll offers, the trade will do well wholly to refuse to take copies of his books, new or old, so long as he adheres to the terms he has just announced.

Charles inserted an explanation of the terms on which his books might be bought in the advertisement on the last page of *Rhyme? and Reason?* (December 1883). It reads: "N.B. In selling the above-mentioned books to the Trade, Messrs. Macmillan and Co. will abate 2*d.* in the shilling (no odd copies), and allow 5 per cent. discount for payment within six months, and 10 per cent. for cash. In selling them to the Public (for cash only) they will allow 10 per cent. discount." This marked a considerable cutback in booksellers' profits.

In the years that followed, Charles's books were sold to booksellers and the public on his terms, in the face of the continuing discount system applied to almost all other books. Underselling remained a thorn in all parties' sides, but little more than desultory discussion arose over it in the later 1880s.

Frederick Orridge Macmillan, eldest son of Daniel Macmillan and a partner in the firm, emerges as the next important actor in the discounting drama. A letter of his appeared in the *Bookseller* (March 6, 1890) entitled "A

Remedy for Underselling," proposing a net system "which would abolish discounts to the public altogether." Although his scheme met with stiff opposition, it actually led to the Net Book Agreement of 1899, eliminating the discount system altogether. Frederick Macmillan emerged the architect and hero of the Net Book Agreement, but his efforts and blueprint are related to and may be a direct result of Charles's struggle over the same issues sixteen years before. Frederick Macmillan knew about the exchanges between Charles and his uncle, Alexander Macmillan; he may even have written some of the letters the firm sent Charles on the subject. Macmillan's own writings, particularly *The Net Book Agreement 1899, and the Book War 1906–1908* (1924), show him aware of Charles's efforts. In any event, Charles deserves a prominent place among those who fought successfully for a just peace in the nineteenth-century battle of the books.

Charles's mathematical writings, his polemics on academic affairs, his calculations on voting systems and lawn tennis tournaments, and his efforts to change the economics of bookselling add up to an enormous effort. He nevertheless addressed himself to other subjects of public concern. On July 6, 1885, for instance, he read in the *Pall Mall Gazette* the first of a series of inflammatory exposés of the traffic in child virgins.

W. T. Stead had succeeded John Morley as editor of the respectable *Gazette,* bringing with him his peculiar mixture of moral zeal and flamboyant journalism. After consulting with the social reformer Josephine Butler, he undertook to expose the practice of supplying child virgins for a "fiver," not only to native roués but for export to Paris and Brussels. To document his case, he got intermediaries to supply him with one such child and to set the stage for deflowering her while she was chloroformed. Then, stopping short of the ultimate deed, he reported the sordid details in his articles entitled "Maiden Tribute to Modern Babylon" in the *Gazette.*

The first installment was enough to set Charles's teeth on edge. He wrote to Lord Salisbury (July 7, 1885) on "a matter that seems of great national importance, and to need *immediate* attention. . . . I would ask you to look at the *Pall Mall Gazette* of last night, and see if it seems to you that the publication, in a daily paper sure to be seen by thousands of boys and young men, of the most loathsome details of prostitution, is or is not conducive to public morality. If not, the *sooner* legal steps are taken, *the better.*"

We do not know whether Charles saw the succeeding three articles, which appeared on the seventh, eighth, and tenth, but he sent off a letter to the *St. James's Gazette* (which had replaced the *Pall Mall Gazette* in his favor), "Whoso Shall Offend One of These Little Ones —," and it appeared on July 22:

> The question at issue is *not* whether great evils exist — not again whether the rousing of public opinion is *a* remedy for those evils. . . . The real question is, whether this mode of rousing public opinion is, or is not, doing more harm than good. . . . And the worst of the danger is that all this is being done in the sacred name of Religion. . . . I plead for our young men and boys, whose imaginations are being excited by highly-coloured pictures of vice, and whose natural thirst for knowledge is being used for unholy purposes by the seducing whisper "read this, and your eyes shall be opened, and ye shall be as gods, knowing good *and evil!*"

He went on to plead for women, enticed to attend meetings where they listened to vile descriptions. And above all: "I plead for our pure maidens, whose souls are being saddened, if not defiled, by the nauseous literature, that is thus thrust upon them — I plead for them in the name of Him who said 'Whoso shall offend one of these little ones which believe in me, it were better for him that a millstone were hanged about his neck, and that he were drowned in the depth of the sea.'"

Charles was not alone: all London buzzed with astonishment at Stead's lurid revelations and the manner he had used to bring them to light. Meetings were held, the largest being in Hyde Park on Saturday, August 22, with two hundred thousand attending, demanding legislation to curb child prostitution. Many, like Charles, realized that Stead's vivid descriptions opened a door to professional pornography, and mounted their own protests, objecting to the sale of "indecent" publications that fed an appetite awakened by Stead's crusade. As a result of the outcry, Parliament passed the Criminal Law Amendment Bill (August 24), raising the age of consent from thirteen to sixteen, tightening controls over brothels and their owners, and making traffic for the purpose of prostitution illegal. Stead was sent to prison and historians are divided as to whether his depiction of white slavery helped or hindered civilization's progress.[11]

Charles's brief letter "Hydrophobia Curable" appeared in the *St. James's Gazette* on October 21; his position here was the same as on vaccination: because he had read in the *Gazette* that some correspondents "assert hydrophobia to be absolutely incurable," he argued that prevention was better than cure and that "an increased dog-tax, with a greater diligence in shutting up all dogs found wandering without owners, are perhaps the best available means for meeting the danger."

In the early 1880s Charles took up the cause of the inhabitants of Tristan da Cunha, a remote British island in the South Atlantic, where his brother Edwin served as missionary-priest-schoolmaster from 1881 to 1889. By 1883 Edwin was convinced that because the hundred or so inhabitants were living under such extreme privation, Britain should resettle them on the Cape or in Australia. Charles supported his brother's efforts, wrote to influential people he knew and a good many he did not know, and spent hours in the corridors of power trying to provoke action. On December 12, 1885, he sent a plea to Lord Salisbury, but Lord Salisbury could offer no immediate solution.

Edwin returned to Tristan with emergency clothing and provisions and plodded on with the dwindling population. Charles, for his part, continued his campaign in London. But their efforts were fruitless. Edwin was forced to leave the island at the end of 1889 because of his deteriorating health and returned to London with a handful of Tristanites.[12]

It is hardly surprising, given Charles's devotion to the theater, that he staunchly defended it when it was under attack or needed moral or financial support.

At the end of January 1882 the dramatist A. W. Dubourg asked him to circulate a prospectus for a plan to found a school of dramatic art. Charles complied and had the University Press print an accompanying letter. "The stage," he wrote, "as every playgoer can testify, is an engine of incalculable power for influencing society; and every effort to purify and ennoble its aims seems to me to deserve all the countenance that the great, and all the material help that the wealthy, can give it; while even those who are neither great nor wealthy may yet do their part." He wrote two letters on the subject to the *St. James's Gazette* (February 27 and March 6, 1882), appealing for support of the dramatic school, pointing out the advantages to young people of being properly trained and how much more enjoyable theatergoing would be if actors were taught to project their voices properly.

On May 15 a meeting took place at the Lyceum Theatre in aid of the project. The school, supported also by Matthew Arnold, Wilkie Collins, Henry Morley, Tennyson, and others, opened in October and was an important step toward establishing the Royal Academy of Dramatic Art.[13]

Charles pursued his dream of "Bowdlerising Bowdler" by editing an edition of Shakespeare "absolutely fit for *girls,*" as he put it (March 13, 1882) to the mother of Marion Richards. "For this I need advice, from *mothers,* as to which plays they would like to be included." He also got the headmistress of the Edgbaston High School for Girls, Alice J. Cooper, to help him in the venture, but the enterprise never bore fruit.

One dream that did come true, although it took a long time to realize it, was getting *Alice* onto the stage. On January 24, 1867, Charles saw a Christmas extravaganza, *Living Miniatures,* at the Haymarket Theatre, with a cast of twenty-seven children. It was "far beyond anything I have yet seen done by children," he noted, and wrote to Thomas Coe, the manager, and engineered an invitation to go backstage to "see how the whole thing was managed." After seeing the production a second time, he reported to his brother Edwin on his visit to the wings and, at the end of the long letter, wrote that he had presented Mr. Coe with "a copy of *my* 'juvenile entertainment,' *Alice.* I have vague hopes (although I haven't suggested the idea to him) that it may occur to him to turn it into a pantomime. I fancy it would work well in that form." But Coe did not take the hint. Charles tried other means of getting *Alice* onto the West End stage, but with no success.

In April 1876 he permitted the London Polytechnic Institute to stage an amateur version of *Alice* and went to see it. "The 'Alice' was a rather pretty child about 10," he noted (April 18), ". . . who acted simply and gracefully," but he objected to an "interpolated song for the [Cheshire] Cat."

Charles was now convinced that *Alice* had theatrical possibilities, and in March 1877 he tried to engage Arthur Sullivan to write some songs for a musical production. Sullivan was enamored of the idea and suggested a collaboration, Charles to write the libretto, he the music. But Charles demurred, not wishing to commit either himself or his prize object before seeing what Sullivan could do with a song or two. Furthermore, he found Sullivan's proposed fees exorbitant, and when he finally ordered only one song, the proposal died, and posterity is left to wonder what a collaboration between Lewis Carroll and Arthur Sullivan might have produced.

Ten years passed, and Charles was still looking for an appropriate way of mounting *Alice* in the West End. Then, on August 28, 1886, he heard from Henry Savile Clarke, playwright, drama critic, and newspaper editor, requesting permission to make an operetta of the *Alice* books. "There is one, and only one, condition which I should regard as absolutely *essential* before allowing my name to appear as 'sanctioning' any dramatic version . . . ," Charles replied on the thirtieth, asking for a "written guarantee that, neither

*Phoebe Carlo, the first Alice on the professional stage, with Dorothy d'Alcourt as the Dormouse. The West End production of the Alice dream play opened for Christmas 1886 and was both a theatrical and a critical success. The play was revived at least twice in Charles's lifetime.*

in the libretto nor in any of the stage business, shall any coarseness, or anything suggestive of coarseness, be admitted." Charles believed that most pantomimes were spoiled for children and people of good taste by indecencies. He also set two more conditions: that the production have no harlequinade tacked onto it and that only one of the *Alice* books be the subject of the operetta—"I do not believe that *any* genuine child enjoys mixtures." He also wanted the songs and parodies that were based on old nursery rhymes to be sung to the old, not new, airs. And he asked Clarke not to give any publicity to his real name and to let him know what plays, etc., Clarke was the author of. "I am very ignorant of names of dramatic authors."[14]

The succeeding months produced a flood of letters to and from Clarke, and from time to time the two met to discuss details. Charles was full of suggestions, and Clarke always listened attentively, commented respectfully, and did what he thought best. He engaged Walter Slaughter, a young, little-known composer he had worked with earlier to supply the music.

For the role of Alice, Charles proposed his twelve-year-old friend Phoebe Carlo, with whom he had become acquainted after hearing her sing in *Whittington and His Cat* (by Joseph A. Cave) and later in *The Silver King* (by H. A. Jones). Clarke acceded.

Another suggestion from Charles went down less well. He wanted a

three-act structure and, despite his aversion to "mixtures," suggested sand-
wiching *The Hunting of the Snark* between the two acts of *Alice* in order to
give Phoebe a rest between her two lengthy acts. Clarke knew better and ve-
toed that idea as well as Charles's plan to create Phoebe's costume himself
and to arrange acting lessons for her. The discussions went on in good spirit,
however: "I will now execute the beautiful strategic movement known as
'giving way all along the line,' " Charles wrote Clarke (November 2), "and
withdraw my suggestions 'en masse,' the 'dress' question included. Amateurs
have no business to put in their oar: it only spoils things." Clarke asked
Charles to supply some extra lines of verse, and Charles complied. Charles
got his wish about omitting a harlequinade, but the operetta is based on both
*Alice* books.

*Alice in Wonderland*, "A Musical Dream Play, in Two Acts, for Children
and Others," opened at a two-thirty matinee on Thursday, December 23,
1886, at the Prince of Wales Theatre. The play text was on sale in the foyer,
arranged and published by Clarke, for those who wanted more than the conventional playbill. But Charles was absent. On that day, the beginning of his
Christmas vacation, he traveled from Oxford to Guildford and did not stop
in London.

Clarke sensibly stayed close to the published stories. He dressed the characters as Tenniel pictured them, and although he did not appropriate the
text verbatim, he used crucial lines and exchanges to remind the audience of
the original.

Charles did see the production, a week after it opened, taking a cousin of
his and a twelve-year-old child friend. "The first Act ('Wonderland') goes
well," he wrote, "specially the Mad Tea Party. . . . Phoebe Carlo is a splendid 'Alice.' Her song and dance, with the Cheshire Cat . . . was a gem. The
second Act went flat. The two Queens . . . were *very* bad (as they were also
in the first Act as Queen and Cook): and the 'Walrus, etc.,' had no definite
finale. But, as a whole, the play seems a success." He saw the production on
other occasions, with more young friends.

On Friday, December 24, the day after the play opened, at least ten papers noticed it. "*Alice in Wonderland* must become a highly popular production," wrote *The Times*. "It is exceedingly pretty, and every scene is crammed
with innocent jokes and witty sayings that cannot fail to amuse." The *Daily
News* proclaimed that "a more sweet and wholesome combination of
drollery and fancy, of humour and frolic, of picturesque beauty and brilliant
pageantry—in brief, a more refined and charming entertainment—has not

been seen upon our stage for many a day." The *Daily Telegraph* wrote that "surprise and delight are certain" for those who venture to see it. "They will see pretty stage pictures . . . hear a lot of delightful music . . . rejoice in effective dances . . . and laugh till their sides ache. . . . Laugh! Yesterday afternoon big children and little children did nothing but laugh." Similar praise came from all of the other critics.

*Alice in Wonderland* ran for fifty performances and closed on February 26, 1887. It then went on a successful tour of Britain's major provincial cities.

On February 18, 1887, Charles noted that Clement Scott, editor of the *Theatre*, was "willing to receive a paper on *Alice in Wonderland*" as the first in a series of papers about the stage. It appeared as " 'Alice' on the Stage" in April 1887. Charles fancied that some readers might be "interested in sharing" his "special knowledge" of what he meant the *Alice* stories to be. He recalls the river picnics with the "three little maidens," how he told the original Alice tale, and then, "to please a child I loved (I don't remember any other motive), I printed the manuscript, and illustrated it with my own crude designs . . . that rebelled against every law of Anatomy or Art." He reports that "every . . . idea and nearly every word of the dialogue . . . *came of itself.* Sometimes an idea comes at night, when I have had to get up and strike a light to note it down—sometimes when out on a lonely winter walk, when I have had to stop, and with half-frozen fingers jot down a few words which should keep the new-born idea from perishing. . . . I cannot set invention going like a clock, by any voluntary winding up. . . . *Alice* and *Looking-Glass* are made up almost wholly of bits and scraps, single ideas which came of themselves. Poor they may have been; but at least they were the best I had to offer."

Charles bristled when new regulations interfered with what he considered the theater's positive social value. "Mr. J[ohn] Coleman [actor and theatrical entrepreneur], who is bringing out a book on 'Stage Children' and the new law passed by the Commons [the Prevention of Cruelty to Children Bill] forbidding those under age ten to appear, had asked me for my letter about 'Brighton Pier,' " Charles noted (August 4, 1889). "I sent it, and a new one, which he has printed in today's *Sunday Times*, of which he has sent a copy to every member of the Lords!"

The "Brighton Pier" letter, "Children in Theatres," appeared in the *St. James's Gazette* (July 19, 1887), defends the practice of allowing children under ten to act professionally, and gives an account of Charles's five-hour outing on Brighton Pier with three child actresses from the cast of his *Alice,*

0438

"happy and healthy little girls" who benefited much from their careers. The *Sunday Times* letter, "Stage Children," argues also that children should be allowed to act and proposes regulations governing their employment. "But I do not believe," he writes, "that the law can absolutely prohibit children under ten from acting in theatres without doing a cruel wrong to many a poor struggling family, to whom the child's stage salary is a Godsend, and making many poor children miserable by debarring them from a healthy and innocent occupation which they dearly love." Other voices joined with Charles's and the bill was changed to allow children to work on the stage under careful supervision.

Charles saw no clash between his involvement with the theater and his religion, despite voices in the Church condemning the theater as a source of dubious pleasure and even of evil and vice. His major defense was "The Stage and the Spirit of Reverence" in the July 1888 *Theatre.* He suggests that good deeds transcend any particular religious affiliation. Good includes "all that is brave, and manly, and true in human nature. . . ." And "a man may honour these qualities, even though he own to no *religious* beliefs whatever." This kind of good, that transcends religion, Charles calls "reverence." He then claims that in " 'reverence' such as this . . . the standard reached on the Stage is fully as high as in the literature of Fiction, and distinctly higher than what often passes without protest in Society."

He notes that when evil is portrayed on the stage, the audience's natural moral instinct prompts them to manifest their indignation by uttering a low, fierce hiss. "The reader can no doubt recall many occasions when the Pit and Gallery have shown equally keen sympathy with self-denial, generosity, or any of the qualities that ennoble human nature."

He widens the definition of *reverence* to include "the belief in *some* good and unseen being . . . to whom we feel ourselves responsible," insisting that we must deal with all religious subjects . . . with care, respect, and reverence. He condemns the " 'irreverence' with which . . . [religious] topics are sometimes handled, both on and off the Stage." He deplores anecdotes based on phrases from the Bible, the worst abuses being "the utterances of *reverend* jesters." He has heard from the lips of clergymen anecdotes whose "horrid blasphemy outdid anything that would be even *possible* on the Stage."

Then he asks: To what extent "can the Stage use of oaths, or phrases introducing the name of the Deity, be justified?" His answer is: Not when these oaths and phrases are "lightly and jestingly uttered." "Used gravely, and for a worthy purpose," they are admissible. "But we must never take the name of the Lord in vain or allow it to be used in *badinage.*" The act of prayer and places of worship are generally treated with reverence on the Stage, although he would not shield "ministers of religion," from ridicule "*when they deserve it.*"

He concludes by proposing that much in the Bible is especially suitable for stage drama, particularly the parables and most particularly "The Prodigal Son," especially where the "wretched outcast" returns and the old father rushes forth to clasp him to his breast: "Might not some eyes, even among the roughs in the Gallery, be 'wet with most delicious tears,' and some hearts be filled with new and noble thoughts, and a spirit of 'reverence' be aroused." The long essay is an extraordinary mixture of conservative rigidity and humane liberality.

On October 25, 1887, Charles went to talk to Clarke "about his proposed revival of *Alice.*" They conferred again the following year. On July 4, 1888, Charles wrote Clarke suggesting that the next Alice should be a little actress who had a minor role in the original production, Isa Bowman, whom Charles had befriended and who was becoming one of his chief child friends. Clarke agreed. In the following months Charles sent Clarke a spate of suggestions for improving the dream play, and the play, incorporating some, but not all, of Charles's changes, opened at the Globe Theatre on December 26, 1888. The musical director, Edward German, later recalled that "the principals, chorus and orchestra seemed like a large family—so happy was everyone"; and Irene (Vanbrugh) Barnes, making her London debut as the Knave of Hearts and the White Queen, remembered that Charles made himself "so entertaining to the children during rehearsal . . . that more than once he was politely requested to leave the theatre by the worried stage manager."[15] Again the notices were rapturous and Charles, who saw the production on January 3, 7, and 15, was pleased.

Clarke's dream play was revived time and again, during Charles's lifetime and after, and other adaptations followed, by Nancy Price, Clemence Dane, Eva Le Gallienne, Florida Freibus, and more. Charles's *Alice* traveled beyond the stage; it has been made into films, notably the Paramount and Walt Disney versions, and has been adapted for television a number of times, once by Jonathan Miller; and the whole Charles-Alice story is the subject of Dennis Potter's film *Dreamchild.* Ballets too have spawned, notably one by Glen Tetley with David del Tredici's music, and even operas.

Nigel Playfair recalled that when he produced *Alice* in Worcester College Gardens in 1894, Charles "took no outward interest in the performance, but . . . came to the rehearsals, secretly . . . to a secure hiding place behind a rhododendron bush."[16] Max Beerbohm, reviewing a 1900 rendition, judged its "ingenuity . . . delightful. . . . None of . . . [the incidents] has lost its savour, and all of them grow out of and into one another in the right kind of reasonable-unreasonable sequence. The result is a perfect little pantomime. Every adult must revel in it."[17]

Charles embarked on another *Alice* venture during these years. He had thought for some time of publishing an *Alice* for the very young and wrote Macmillan on the subject in early 1881. But he was too busy to do much about it. On March 29, 1885, at fifty-three, even he was impressed with the number of irons he had in the fire: "Never before have I had so many literary projects on hand at once," he noted. "For curiosity I will here make a list of them," and he listed fifteen, *The Nursery "Alice"* appearing ninth. He added that "20 pictures are now being coloured by Mr. Tenniel" for the nursery volume. But Tenniel had other occupations, and three years passed with no action on the project. Finally, with Tenniel's colored pictures before him and with some spare time on his hands during the Christmas holiday, Charles "began [on December 28, 1888] text of 'Nursery Alice' "; he sent off the last bit of the manuscript on February 20, 1889. But when he first saw the printed drawings, he was appalled, wrote Macmillan (June 23) that they were "far too bright and gaudy," canceled the entire edition of ten thousand copies, and had another ten thousand printed. By Easter 1890 the book finally appeared and Charles went to town (March 25) to inscribe a hundred copies for friends and family.

*The Nursery "Alice"* is a larger, thinner volume than its parent, contains fifty-six pages of text, about one-quarter of the full *Alice*, a cover in color by Gertrude Thomson, and those twenty colored Tenniel illustrations. Charles omitted most of the verse, appended at the end *An Easter Greeting to Every Child Who Loves "Alice"* and *Christmas Greeting (From a Fairy to a Child)*, and wrote a preface:

I have reason to believe that "Alice's Adventures in Wonderland" has been read by some hundreds of English Children, aged from Five to Fifteen: also by Children, aged from Fifteen to Twenty-five: yet again by Children aged from Twenty-five to Thirty-five. . . . And my ambition *now* is (is it a vain one?) to be read by Children aged from Nought to Five. To be read? Nay, not so! Say rather to be thumbed, to be cooed over, to be dogs'-eared, to be rumpled, to be kissed, by the illiterate, ungrammatical, dimpled Darlings, that fill your Nursery with merry up-roar, and your inmost heart of hearts with a restful gladness!

Such, for instance, as a child I once knew, who—having been care-fully instructed that *one* of any earthly thing was enough for any little girl; and that to ask for *two* buns, *two* oranges, *two* of anything, would certainly bring upon her the awful charge of being "greedy"—was found one morning sitting up in bed, solemnly regarding her *two* little naked feet, and murmuring to herself, softly and penitently, "deedy!"

Charles did more than merely condense his story; he tried to explain the story and teach the child about the characters. The text is really addressed to the mothers acting as Charles's surrogates in bringing the book, the text, and the pictures to the child's awareness. He took great pains with the tale, leaving much out and adding new material. The pictures are the primary focus. For example, on page 11, we find the famous picture of Alice and the Mouse in the pool of tears. Here is how Charles deals with the episode:

Now look at the picture, and you'll soon guess what happened next. It looks just like the sea, doesn't it? But it *really* is the Pool of Tears—all made of *Alice's* tears, you know!

And Alice has tumbled into the Pool: and the Mouse has tumbled in: and there they are, swimming about together.

Doesn't Alice look pretty, as she swims across the picture? You can just see her blue stockings, far away under the water.

But why is the Mouse swimming away from Alice in such a hurry? Well, the reason is, that Alice began talking about cats and dogs: and a Mouse always *hates* talking about cats and dogs!

Suppose you were swimming about, in a Pool of your own Tears: and suppose somebody began talking to *you* about lesson-books and bottles of medicine, wouldn't *you* swim as hard as you could go?

Here we have Charles the teacher at work, and we also have Charles try-ing to get into the child's mind, getting close to what he lovingly thinks of as "child nature." First he makes the tiny tot concentrate on the picture, then he prods the child's curiosity by asking questions that a youngster can an-swer by examining the picture. He makes sure that the child can recognize colors, and he tries to help the child develop habits of close observation. He cleverly suggests certain truths about human and animal nature, and he opens up a realm of fun and nonsense that the child can share with the adult reading the story.

*Vanity Fair* (May 31, 1890) judged it "a very charming nursery book"; the *Athenaeum* (June 14) lumped it with nine other children's books, but *The Nursery "Alice"* leads the pack and gets almost half the space given to the ten. The writer has only praise for it: he calls it "very brilliant and entertaining."

Charles went on writing occasional verse and papers through the 1880s, the subjects varying from public censure to public aid. He also penned other memorable compositions that did not reach the printed page in his life-time — for example, a letter (February 14, 1880) ostensibly written by Mabel to Emily, two dolls owned by his young friend Beatrice Hatch. Charles en-dowed it with all the misspellings and orthographic oddities one might ex-pect from a very young letter writer. He wrote a draft in purple ink, and then, improving it, put it onto a stencil with his electric pen. The result is delightful.

When, in November 1880, his friend C. H. O. Daniel, founder of the Daniel Press, asked Charles to contribute a verse for a volume celebrating the first birthday of Daniel's daughter Rachel, Charles demurred, but even-tually succumbed and wrote a twenty-eight-line bauble for *The Garland of Rachel,* now a rarity (only thirty-six copies were printed), joining a luminous company of versifiers including Austin Dobson, Andrew Lang, J. A. Symonds, Robert Bridges, Edmund Gosse, and W. E. Henley.

In early 1881 he printed a four-page pamphlet, *On Catching Cold.* It merely quotes extracts from two medical authorities, and he sent Ellen Terry a copy on January 11, having produced it for "the benefit of my cold-catching friends."

On September 22, 1884, Charles paid a visit to an old child friend, Edith Denman, now married to W. H. Draper, Vicar of Alfreton, a few miles north of Derby, and Draper persuaded Charles to address a small gathering of his parishioners. Although Charles normally spoke from memory with the help of a few jottings, this time he wrote out the entire piece, which he apparently had before him while he spoke. Draper later recalled Charles's "nervous, highly-strung manner as he stood before the little room full of simple people, few of whom had any idea of the world-wide reputation of that shy, slight figure before them." When the sermon was over, Draper tells us, "he handed the manuscript to me, saying: 'do what you like with it.'" This is another instance, like so many others, where Charles's manuscripts, letters, and inscribed books later enriched the recipient. Draper not only shepherded the piece into print, in a number of editions, but sold the man-uscript to an antiquarian dealer.

The essay, published posthumously, is *Feeding the Mind*, and in it Charles suggests that feeding the mind is as important as feeding the body. We suffer dire physical consequences if we neglect to feed the body, Charles begins, while the results of failing to feed the mind are less apparent. It might be better if we also saw tangible results when we neglected to feed the mind,

> if you could take it, say, to the doctor and have its pulse felt. "Why, what have you been doing with this mind lately? How have you fed it? It looks pale, and the pulse is *very* slow." "Well, doctor, it has not had much regular food lately: I gave it a lot of sugar-plums yesterday." "Sugar-plums? What kind?" "Well, they were a parcel of conundrums, Sir." "Ah, I thought so. Now, just mind this: if you go playing tricks like that, you'll spoil all its teeth, and get laid up with mental indigestion. You must have nothing but the plainest reading for the next few days. Take care, now! no novels on any account!"

It is possible, Charles asserts, to tell a healthy from an unhealthy mental appetite. Give a person "a short, well-written, but not too exciting treatise on some popular subject. . . . If it is read with eager interest and perfect attention, and *if the reader can answer questions on the subject afterwards,* the mind is in first-rate working order: if it be politely laid down again, or perhaps lounged over for a few minutes, and then, 'I can't read this stupid book!' . . . you may be equally sure that there is something wrong in the mental digestion."

Early in 1888 Charles engaged in a correspondence with the editors of the school magazine of the Latin School for Girls in Boston. He wrote them (February 6) in the third person permitting them "with much pleasure" to name their magazine *Jabberwock*. He toyed with a possible history for the word and suggested that the Anglo-Saxon word *wocer,* or *wocor,* signifies "offspring" or "fruit." Taking *jabber* in its ordinary sense of "excited and voluble discussion," this would give the meaning of "the result of much excited discussion." "Whether this phrase will have any application to the projected periodical, it will be for the future history of American literature to determine." To the editors' delight, Charles sent them an original twenty-one-line poem to publish, entitled "Lesson in Latin":

> Our Latin books, in motley row,
> > Invite us to our task—
> Gay Horace, stately Cicero;

Yet there's one verb, when once we know,
  No higher skill we ask:
This ranks all other lore above—
We've learned "'*Amare*' means '*to love*'!"

So hour by hour, from flower to flower,
  We sip the sweets of Life:
Till, all too soon, the clouds arise,
And flaming cheeks and flashing eyes
  Proclaim the dawn of strife:
With half a smile and half a sigh,
*"Amare! Bitter One!"* we cry.

Last night we owned, with looks forlorn,
  "Too well the scholar knows
There is no rose without a thorn"—
But peace is made! We sing, this morn,
  "No thorn without a rose!"
Our Latin lesson is complete:
We've learned that Love is Bitter-Sweet!

It is an odd verse to send across the Atlantic for admiring schoolgirls to contemplate. But it follows the pattern of Charles insinuating the story of his life into his work. However light some of it seems, a serious confession is there as well.

Later in the year Charles composed *Isa's Visit to Oxford*, a sixteen-page diary to commemorate the fourteen-year-old actress's visit as his guest (July 11 to 16, 1888). According to this diary, Isa and the A.A.M. (Aged, Aged Man) have breakfast at Christ Church "and then Isa learned how to print with the 'Type-Writer,' and printed several beautiful volumes of poetry, all of her own invention." On Saturday "Isa had a Music Lesson, and learned to play an American Orguinette. It is not a *very* difficult instrument to play, as you have only to turn a handle round and round: so she did it nicely." She and the A.A.M. put one sheet of music in the wrong end first, listened to a tune backwards, "and soon found themselves in the day before yesterday. So they dared not go on, for fear of making Isa so young she would not be able to talk."

Isa's ten-year-old sister, Maggie, came to Oxford the following June 10 to 12 to act in *Bootle's Baby*, and Charles took charge of her. He composed a diary for her, too, in verse. Charles happened to introduce Maggie to the Bishop of Oxford, William Stubbs, who asked her what she thought of Oxford. " 'I think,' said the little actress with quite a professional aplomb 'it's the best place in the provinces!' " In the poem, Charles expanded the encounter with the Bishop:

> They met a Bishop on the way . . .
>   A Bishop large as life,
> With loving smile that seems to say
>   "Will Maggie be my wife?"
>
> Maggie thought *not*, because, you see,
>   She was so *very* young,
> And he was old as old could be . . .
>   So Maggie held her tongue. . . .

The May-September marriage theme suggests that again Charles was writing from the heart.

He continued inventing games, puzzles, and riddles. He taught the Hulls (August 13, 1880) "my new game . . . where one player names 3 or 4 letters in a word, and the other guesses the word. The game acquired the name "Mischmasch," after the early family magazine. Its "essence," Charles wrote in the introduction when he published it (June 1881) in the *Monthly Packet*, "consists of one Player proposing a 'nucleus' (i. e. a word known in ordinary society, and not a proper name), containing it. Thus 'magpie,' 'lemon,' 'himself,' are lawful words containing nuclei 'gp,' 'emo,' 'imse.' "

Charles continued to compose what he called "charades," verses of considerable length embodying puzzles. Sometimes the puzzle consisted of a double acrostic and contained a series of riddles which, when solved, displayed the name of the recipient or some other solution.

He used every device and technique he knew to turn mathematical calculation into a game. He undertook to create a series of "Knots" for the *Monthly Packet* and offered to publish the answers along with the names of respondents who untied the knots. "Romantic Problems" is the early title of what later became in book form *A Tangled Tale*, with illustrations by A. B. Frost, containing ten knots, each built around at least one mathematical problem. All ten and follow-up answers appeared in the *Packet* between April 1880 and March 1885, and the book in 1885. Charles set the first knot,

446 LEWIS CARROLL

"Excelsior," a tale of two medieval knights, thus: "Two travellers spend from 3 o'clock till 9 in walking along a level road, up a hill, and home again: their pace on the level being 4 miles an hour, up hill 3, and down hill 6. Find distance walked: also (within half an hour) time of reaching top of hill." He published the winners' names and printed one solution submitted in "tuneful verse."

The critical reception of *A Tangled Tale* ranged from lukewarm to antagonistic. The *Pall Mall Gazette* (January 4, 1886) noticed the "higgledy piggledy mixture of sense and nonsense that at once compels a reading," but concluded: "We decidedly prefer the simple nonsense of *Alice in Wonderland*. Mathematics will be mathematics," no matter how well one coats it with sugar, and the writer conjectured that "children's stories, alas! will soon not be children's stories at all in this improving age."

Charles next devised a method for teaching perhaps a less-than-hungry public to reason logically and become aware of the rules of formal logic. In time this project became his major occupation and made an important contribution to posterity. He started modestly, with *The Game of Logic*. Charles was trying to make deductive logic easy and entertaining by casting syllogisms amusingly instead of dryly and adding spice to explanatory material. The game, Charles wrote in the preface, "requires one Player, *at least*. . . . At the same time, though one Player is enough, a good deal more amusement may be got by two working at it together, and correcting each other's mistakes." The syllogism is at the heart of Charles's game. "I don't guarantee the Premises to be *facts*," he cautions. ". . . It isn't of the slightest consequence to us, as *Logicians*, whether our Premises are true or false: all *we* have to make out is whether they *lead logically to the Conclusion*, so that, if *they* were true, *it* would be true also."

When Charles received the first copies of *The Game of Logic* (December 5, 1886), he was so dissatisfied with the printing, he decided that it was fit only for the American market, and had the book reprinted. *The Game of Logic* served him as a textbook for teaching classes of girls and mistresses in Oxford, Eastbourne, and elsewhere and for private instruction of his child friends. With Charles as teacher, the *Game* sometimes succeeded. After all, his syllogisms serve up a variety of cakes, uncanny dragons, canny Scotchmen, brave Englishmen, rich Jews, Gentile Patagonians, selfish lobsters, lots of *x*'s and *y*'s, of course, and plenty of diagrams. It works well for those whom nature has endowed with a facile mathematical talent—it was one of Max Ernst's favorite books—but hardly for most of the children for whom it was intended, as the novelist and critic Marghanita Laski discovered when she tried it out on her own children.[18] Most children find the instructions and explanations indigestible. Perhaps the notice in *Punch* (March 19, 1887) was most perceptive: "What does he mean by it? . . . It may yet have its use, however, as pages of it, or fifty lines at a time, might be set as a punishment to naughty boys and girls to write out or learn. . . . Lewis Carroll has been 'chopping logic,' and has given young'uns some uncommonly dry chips."

Charles's dedication in *The Game of Logic* to the eleven-year-old niece of the *Snark*'s illustrator, Climène Mary Holiday (her name is revealed in the second letter in each line, read downward), is an acrostic verse that serves more than the occasion, for it too shows him sadly and painfully becoming reconciled to the loss of childhood and child friendships:

> I charm in vain: for never again,
> All keenly as my glance I bend,
>> Will Memory, goddess coy,
>> Embody for my joy
> Departed days, nor let me gaze
>> On thee, my Fairy Friend!
>
> Yet could thy face, in mystic grace,
> A moment smile on me, 'twould send
>> Far-darting rays of light
>> From Heaven athwart the night,
> By which to read in very deed
>> Thy spirit, sweetest Friend!
>
> So may the stream of Life's long dream
> Flow gently onward to its end,
>> With many a floweret gay,
>> A-down its willowy way:
> May no sigh vex, no care perplex,
>> My loving little Friend!

Memory is not a coy mistress, but a goddess, and she seems to be failing Charles by preventing him from recapturing the joys of his youth. He faces the reality that his claim to child friendship is vanishing. He has no choice, now that he is aging, but to accept the inexorable passage of time and the changes it brings.

\* \* \*

The two *Sylvie and Bruno* books constitute Charles's most ambitious literary enterprise—they are also his most disastrous. The roots of this wayward tree reach back twenty years to June 24, 1867, when Charles was struck with an idea for a story, "Bruno's Revenge," for *Aunt Judy's Magazine.* Charles told the tale again and again to child friends and strangers, individually, in small groups, and in large assemblies. The success of the tale suggested that he do more of the same, and he did, adding segment after segment over the years. He reported its genesis in the preface to *Sylvie and Bruno:* "I found myself at last in the possession of a huge unwieldy mass of literature . . . which only needed stringing together, upon the thread of a consecutive story, to constitute the book I hoped to write. Only! The task, at first, seemed absolutely hopeless, and gave me a far clearer idea, than I ever had before, of the meaning of the word 'chaos': and I think it must have been ten years, or more, before I had succeeded in classifying these odds-and-ends sufficiently to see what sort of a story they indicated: for the story had to grow out of the incidents."

Ruskin had hoped that Charles's next book "would not be a mere unconnected *dream,* but would contain a *plot.*" Charles assured Ruskin (January 8, 1890), through Ruskin's cousin, Joan Severn, that the book contained "no *dreams,* this time: what look like dreams are meant for *trances*—after the fashion of Esoteric Buddhists—in which the spirit of the entranced person passes away into an actual Fairyland." To satisfy Ruskin further, Charles supplied not just one plot but two. He also created three separate worlds and dealt at length with impalpabilities, with fathomless time and space.

The episodes of one of the plots occur in the real world; those of the second in Outland, an imaginary spiritual kingdom with medieval trappings; the third in Elfdom, the most rarified of the three planes of existence and available only to the few.

The narrator—Charles disguised as an old London lawyer, bald and bespectacled—acts both as commentator and as a character within the drama. He is also able to induce trances or hallucinations allowing him to move to Outland and back freely.

The structure is complex, and it is difficult to keep the three different spheres in mind. Readers in search of the diversion and entertainment they expect from Lewis Carroll, particularly his young admirers, are all at sea here. Had Charles taken a few steps backward, evoking the principles that rule his earlier work and remembering what he knew about a child's mind and heart, he would have seen that he had lost touch with those he most ardently wished to address. By the time he set himself the task of assembling the stray episodes, he was blinded by an overpowering interest in supernatural forces and set on a course that required him to reconcile extraordinary psychic soundings with a Christian universe. The result, while chronicling Charles's own development, is both fuzzy and perplexing.

*Sylvie and Bruno* appeared for Christmas 1889. It contained precisely four hundred pages, a thirteen-page preface, a table of contents, forty-six illustrations by Furniss, and a five-page index. A glance through the index alone would put a novel-reader off instantly, replete as it is with technical, scientific, and conceptual entries like "Artistic effect dependent on indistinctness(!)"; "Barometer, sideways motion of"; "Brain, inverted position of"; " 'Convenient' and 'Inconvenient,' different meanings"; "Darwinism reversed"; and "Electricity, influence of, on Literature." This is not the meat of narrative prose, and even though they are subjects that engaged Charles and many of his contemporaries, in a novel they make for heavy weather. Charles once knew precisely how to involve a reader in a problem, how to steer a young mind slowly and carefully through a puzzle or a game and bring that mind to victory. But by the late 1880s something had gone awry.

The illustrations for *Sylvie and Bruno* grew out of a prickly saga. On March 1, 1885, Charles wrote to Harry Furniss, in Charles's words "a very clever artist in *Punch*," to ask "if he is open to proposals to draw pictures for me." On March 9 he heard "from Furniss, naming terms, etc.: and wrote accepting them, and proposing to send him a poem to begin on." Furniss would illustrate both *Sylvie and Bruno* books, with forty-six drawings for each, but the road that Charles and Furniss traveled was a rocky one, and both men endured much unpleasantness along the way. The partnership began amicably enough, but gradually passed through misunderstandings, disagreements, and even near-collisions. Charles was intent upon getting illustrations as close as possible to the pictures he imagined. He sketched many himself in his barrage of letters to Furniss to help him achieve what he wanted. Furniss was agreeable up to a point, then chafed and bridled.

Tenniel could not accommodate Charles's wish to have him draw a wasp; Furniss had trouble over a spider: "My idea is that there is no necessity for being so entomologically accurate as you aspire to be," Charles wrote Furniss (August 25, 1886), "and that a creature, mostly human, but *suggestive* of a spidery nature, would be quite accurate enough." On November 29, 1886: "*Please* don't give Sylvie high heels! they are an abomination to me." By 1889 matters had gone from bad to worse. On August 26 Charles wrote: "It is a severe disappointment to me to find that, on account of a single square-inch of picture, as to which we disagree, you decline to carry out your engagement. Well, I have far too much horror of the 'Law,' to *insist* on your promise being carried out: moreover I am not quite so foolish as to believe that Art-work, extorted by legal process, would be worth anything at all. So I release you from all your engagements." Furniss had evidently threatened Charles with publishing an account of the author's unreasonable demands, and Charles welcomed the challenge. "*You* shall have your say first: and my paper will come out . . . as an answer to yours. I not only fully authorise you to print the '5 pages' of my letter [alas missing], which you say would win you 'the sympathy of all the Artists,' but I call upon you to do so. . . . Like you, I shall await with confidence the verdict of 'all the Artists' . . . as to whether the figure of Sylvie is, or is not, in the correct proportions of an ordinary child of 11 or 12."

The articles by artist and author never materialized, and the two came to a fresh understanding. Furniss wrote offering to redraw the pictures Charles objected to, and Charles took (August 30) "in good part" all Furniss said, and rejoiced "that we are still friends. . . . Your words, 'I in no way decline to carry out my engagement to illustrate the book,' are truly welcome."

But the reconciliation did not deter Charles from pursuing perfection in the pictures for volume 2. On September 8 he wrote Furniss: "You *do* give me a lot of extra trouble by ignoring the text so much! Several passages I have re-written, in order to make the text agree with the picture. . . ." Then he wrote (October 21, 1893): "I must really *beg* you to make *both* dresses more opaque. If you look through a magnifying-glass, you will see that the 'hind-quarters' still show very plainly through."

Not all the letters between the two men were acerbic. Painstakingly particular as Charles was, he invariably behaved well. Time and again he was gracious to Furniss, complimenting him on the pictures, apologizing for his entreaties, and, in a crunch, giving way entirely to the artist's view. "I am *most* grateful for all the thought and trouble you expend on my book," he wrote (August 25, 1886). "It is really *most* kind of you, to be so ready to accept other ideas for the pictures than what you had already devised," Charles wrote (November 29, 1886). When Furniss's work on *Sylvie and Bruno* was finished, Charles wrote (November 1, 1889) to congratulate him.[19]

Well after the *Sylvie and Bruno* books were launched, however, another unpleasantness arose between the two. In the spring of 1896 an advertisement appeared in the *Oxford Review* announcing Furniss's entertainment

*Charles's sketch and Harry Furniss's finished drawing for "the Tottles" in* Sylvie and Bruno Concluded. *Charles wrote a sarcastic verse to describe the relationship of husband and wife. In part it runs:*

> *See now this couple settled down*
> *In quiet lodgings, out of town:*
> *Submissively the tearful wife*
> *Accepts a plain and humble life.*

"NEVER!" yelled Tottles And he meant it.

31/8/87

*America in a Hurry.* Charles bought four tickets. But well before Furniss arrived in Oxford, Charles fired off a blistering letter to him, telling him that an hour after buying the tickets, he noticed in the program "A Sermon in Spasms" and, in the quotations from notices printed in the program, a description of that item as "clever imitations" of sermons by the preacher Thomas de Witt Talmage. Charles "immediately went and returned the tickets," fearing a public "insult to Christianity, and . . . profaning of holy things." Furniss did not forget the insult, and in one of his memoirs wrote: "The Rev. C. L. Dodgson . . . in some respects was a typical Oxford Don— once a schoolmaster always a schoolmaster. He lectured his friends as he had lectured his youths, and treated grown-up men of the world as if they were children. In . . . [*America in a Hurry*] I gave a wordless imitation of that eccentric American, Talmage . . . carefully pointing out to my audience that I imitated his gestures and voice—not Talmage in the character of a preacher, but as a showman. . . . I always had a number of clergymen in my audience, and those who had heard me found nothing whatever objectionable, nor could they detect in what I did anything touching upon sacred things."[20]

Furniss was so bruised by his exchanges with Charles that after Charles's death, when he started publishing the volumes of his reminiscences, he claimed his pound of flesh. Again and again he recounts, exaggerates, and invents unpleasant incidents, scurrilous accounts of the way Charles dealt with him, sent him manuscripts in strips and in code, making him promise never to let anyone see his work, not even his family. The reports are largely figments of Furniss's heated need for vengeance, even though he was very well paid for his labors. Furniss was an extravagant popularist, a flamboyant showman, unscrupulous in dealing with cartoon subjects, whom even Tenniel could not swallow whole.

If the *Sylvie and Bruno* books are not captivating adventure tales for the young or easy romantic novels for the mature reader, they are much else and not to be undervalued. They present a store of issues that gripped most thinking Victorians, not least of all the science-versus-faith dilemma that Charles Lyell, Robert Chambers, and Darwin posed. And they deal with a myriad of other topical concerns, offering us a mirror of the Victorian mind in flux and in contention with itself.

Again autobiographical elements enter. The dedicatory nine-line acrostic verse built on Isa Bowman's name, which one expects to be light and airy, turns philosophical and glum:

Is all our Life, then, but a dream
Seen faintly in the golden gleam
Athwart Time's dark resistless stream?

Bowed to the earth with bitter woe,
Or laughing at some raree-show,
We flutter idly to and fro.

Man's little Day in haste we spend,
And, from its merry noontide, send
No glance to meet the silent end.

Charles used *Sylvie and Bruno* to set out some philosophical notions. An old earl concedes that probably some forms of science transcend human life: "Mathematics, for instance. . . . One can't imagine *any* form of Life, or *any* race of intelligent beings, where Mathematical truth would lose its meaning." Charles puts his ideas of life after death in the mouth of the hero of the novel, Arthur Forester:

"I have imagined a little child, playing with toys on his nursery-floor, and yet able to *reason,* and to look on, thirty years ahead. Might he not say to himself 'By that time I shall have had enough of bricks and ninepins. How weary Life will be!' Yet, if we look forward through those thirty years, we find him a great statesman, full of interest and joys such as no baby-language could in the faintest degree describe. Now, may not our life, a million years hence, have the same relation, to our life now, that the man's life has to the child's? And, just as one might try, all in vain, to express to that child, in the language of bricks and ninepins, the meaning of 'politics,' so perhaps all those descriptions of Heaven, with its music, and its feasts, and its streets of gold, may be only attempts to describe, in *our* words, things for which we *really* have no words at all."

Within that argument rests Charles's view of life, death, and the universe. He may be rationalizing, but he believes it heart and soul.

Both Lady Muriel, the grown-up equivalent of Sylvie, and Sylvie herself are probably fictional incarnations of Alice. Charles found an early Furniss sketch of Lady Muriel unsatisfactory because he could not possibly fall in love with the lady in that sketch. Nor did Furniss draw Arthur Forester, Charles's vision of himself at an eligible age, satisfactorily: he looks forty and not right for a man in love with the young Muriel. Charles wanted him to be "about twenty-five, powerful in frame and poetical in face," capable of being a passionate lover.

The story's narrator suffers from a heart ailment, and the purpose of his journey is to consult his friend Arthur, a physician, about his condition. Before the journey ends, however, the narrator and Muriel meet by coincidence and talk. In time Arthur confides in his older friend (the young Charles confiding his emotional state to the older Charles), that he "*cannot* read her feelings towards me. If there is love, she is hiding it! No, I must wait, I must wait!" Time passes, and the narrator presses Arthur: "Well, old friend, you have told me nothing of . . . nor when the happy day is to be?" Arthur replies that it is not to be soon: "I dare not speak till I am sure that my love is returned." "Don't wait too long!" the narrator urges. "Faint heart never won fair lady! . . . You are running a risk that perhaps you have not thought of. Some other man—" Arthur can only say that "if she loves another better than me, so be it! I will not spoil her happiness. The secret shall die with me. But she is my first—and my *only* love!" The narrator suggests that, while that is a beautiful sentiment, Arthur's approach is not practical. "I dare not ask the question whether there is another!" Arthur replies. "It would break my heart to know it!"

Did Charles draw these words and feelings from memory? Do these two voices echo the debate of the early 1860s on the path through Tom Quad to the deanery? Do the villains of the tale, Sibimet and Tabikat, caricature the Liddell parents? Mrs. Liddell had a reputation for being "catty," and Tabikat is ruthlessly ambitious, like Mrs. Liddell in life: because she is the wife of the Warden, she asks: "And I am Vice-Wardeness?"

The denouement of the love triangle is Charles's private fantasy of what he wanted to have happen between him and Alice. Eric, the two-dimensional sub-hero, who earlier claims Muriel's loyalty, releases her from their engagement, enabling the real hero to win his heart's desire: Arthur wins Muriel, and in his fantasy Charles wins Alice.

When Charles embarked on these books, he wanted to write a different sort of book from the *Alice*s. He struck out on "another new path," in the hope of supplying, "for the children whom I love, some thoughts that may suit those hours of innocent merriment which are the very life of Childhood: and also, in the hope of suggesting, to them and to others, some thoughts that may prove . . . not wholly out of harmony with the graver cadences of Life." But he knew, in his heart, that *Sylvie and Bruno* was not entirely suitable for children: "I'm giving it to *mothers*," he confessed to a cousin (November 30, 1889), "not to *daughters*: as it is a book intended for *all* ages—not for children only, as *Alice* was."

Charles had lost the sense of appropriateness, proportion, and aesthetic balance that he possessed earlier. He retreated inward where he should have traveled outward, and the *Sylvie and Bruno* books are overburdened by seriousness, calculated messages, ponderous cogitations, and fulminations that reflect the map of Charles's aging mind and broken heart. They are at one and the same time his *apologia pro vita mea* and his *consolatio philosophiae*.

Unlike the *Alice* books and the *Snark*, these volumes are not works of genius, despite some inventive moments of intellectual pyrotechnics, wit, verse, and nonsense. The poetry, liberally supplied, is both good and bad, the nonsense verse tending to be the best. As a novel it is trite; as a work of philosophical speculation, hazardous. But as a treatise on art, science, technology, religion, society, and other subjects, it is an encrusted mirror of nineteenth-century life and thought. For us, it illustrates the state of Charles Dodgson's mind, with its logical conviction that life is purposeful, that God and eternity are real.

The *Alice* books are brilliant tales of growing up, magical reconstructions of childhood confronting adulthood, and the search for identity in the social fabric. *The Hunting of the Snark* is a journey in search of universal verities, a search for proof that the journey of life has meaning and that death, while mysterious, is the engine of a greater, inscrutable force. The *Sylvie and Bruno* books show us the possibilities of the world outside what we know of reality and argue in favor of an eternity for all. For the narrator, for Charles, the story is about perceiving occasional beams of light that filter through the many-colored dome and allow him to sense eternity. The books are not great works of inspiration; they are self-indulgent, self-justifying, even self-congratulatory autobiography, but as such the most personal, most revealing of Charles's works.

*Sylvie and Bruno* earned the notices it deserved. The *Academy* (December 21, 1889) asked outright: "What are we to say about this new book by 'Lewis Carroll'?" It insisted that no critic who had read *Alice* wanted to speak ill of its author. "But ah, the pity of it! . . . We can assure . . . [the reader] that he will become weary and puzzled long before he reaches the end." The *Literary Churchman* (January 10, 1890) found that it fell short of the *Alice* books, although it also found much in it attractive and thought Sylvie and Bruno "delightful little creatures." The *Spectator* (January 18), in a long notice, said bluntly that Charles had "failed in his attempt to produce a third work which can be put on a level" with the *Alice* books; but the *Athenaeum* (January 4), in another long notice, all jam and no vinegar, thought it "full of amusing things," the characters "delightful," and Carroll a "gay and witty writer."

The 1880s were for Charles years of great accomplishment, intense activity, many rewards, and a time of significant invention but less creation. As he passed through his fifties, his inspirations diminished, the green leaves turned yellow, and while he still labored remarkably well and produced an avalanche of works of integral interest in numerous disciplines and arenas, the earlier free-flowing sap of his imagination had dried to a trickle. The delicate rivulets that reached from the child's mind and heart to his and taught him, or so he thought, the essence of existence, had atrophied, and all was now calculation, intelligence, and rationality. Sadly, he did not fully recognize the change and did not entirely come to terms with it.

# CHAPTER FOURTEEN

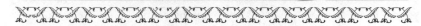
# And No Birds Sing

*Still nursing the unconquerable hope,*
*Still clutching the inviolable shade.*

MATTHEW ARNOLD

Writing to an old family friend on December 19, 1889, Charles offered a line "in answer to the anxiety you so kindly express about my presumed 'delicacy of health.' It consists at present of the malady called 'being fifty-seven.' I've never known serious illness," he continued; "that bout of ague, in which you so kindly nursed me, is one of the worst I have had. . . . But years go quick at 57, and one cannot count on 10 or 20 more of active life, with *quite* the gay confidence of a man of 27!"

The intertwining themes of aging, the passage of time, and the state of Charles's health, which had sounded in the 1880s, ring stronger throughout the 1890s, as do complaints about a defective memory. His nephew writes that he "had a wonderfully good memory, except for faces and dates,"[1] but by the time he was fifty-three, he confessed (March 1, 1885) in a letter to Alice: "I am getting to feel what an old man's failing memory is, as to recent events and new friends. . . . For instance, I made friends, only a few weeks ago, with a very nice little maid of about 12, and had a walk with her—and now I can't recall either of her names." On April 4, 1893, he asked a friend: "Please tell me . . . what your husband is, as regards the Royal Family, and what as regards the late and present governments, and what he is doing in Ireland. Excuse my bothering you so. You told me all these things: but old people forget so!"

He was anxious about time's winged chariot, eager to complete his numerous writing projects: On April 10, 1890, he wrote to a friend: "As life shortens in, and the evening shadows loom in sight, one gets to grudge *any* time given to mere pleasure, which might entail . . . leaving work half-finished that one is *longing* to do before the end comes. There are several books I *greatly* desire to get finished, for children," he adds. "I am glad to find my working-powers are as good as they ever were. Even with the mathematical book (a 3rd edition) which I am now getting through the Press [*Curiosa Mathematica, Part I*] I think nothing of working 6 hours at a stretch. . . . There is one text that often occurs to me—'The night cometh, when no man can work.' " In January 1892 he wrote another friend: "God's Presence [is] . . . more clearly felt, from the amount of sickness and death one hears of. . . . I hope I am *ready* to go, if God pleases to call me, but I should *like* a few more years of work first!"

Charles compiled several lists of books he still intended to write. One such list, included in the preface to *Sylvie and Bruno,* is incomplete but significant: a Child's Bible, with chosen passages suitable for the very young; another selection from the Bible of passages worth committing to memory; an anthology of prose and verse from books other than the Bible also worth memorizing; and his expurgated version of Shakespeare for girls. With so many projects on hand, including the sequel to *Sylvie and Bruno* and other works, he felt pressed as never before. "If only I could manage without annoyance to my family," he wrote a cousin (June 25, 1891), "to get imprisoned for 10 years, 'without hard labour,' and with the use of books and writing materials, it would be simply delightful!"

His job as Curator of Senior Common Room had grown onerous and now interfered with his private labors. He sought to rid himself of it, but he had to put all the records perfectly right and find a successor. Finally, on March 4, 1892, he recorded: "A memorable day . . . having heard that [T. B.] Strong was willing to be elected, and Common Room willing to elect him, I most gladly resigned. The sense of relief, at being free from the burdensome office . . . is very delightful."

He suffered no serious health problems, but minor illnesses plagued him, especially that ubiquitous Victorian malady, ague. "Since the afternoon of the 24th," he noted (October 31, 1890), "I have kept [to] my rooms, suffering from a combination of ague, cystitis, and lumbago." At other times he reported boils, eczema, synovitis, migraines (during which he saw "moving fortifications"), influenza, pleurisy, "liver trouble," diarrhea, laryngitis, bronchitis, erythema, attacks of fever, vesical catarrh, rheumatism, neuralgia, insomnia, and toothaches. He remained physically hardy, took long walks, rode his velociman (a tricycle that proved more tiring than walking), did other exercises, ate little, and followed a rigorous regime. But despite his highly strung temperament, he remained vigorous.

On February 6, 1891, while working on *Sylvie and Bruno Concluded,* he experienced what might have been an epileptic attack. He had had one previous incident like it, described in his diary (January 20, 1886): "On the morning of the New Year (I think it was) I had an attack ('epileptiform' Dr. Morshead called it) which left me with a sort of headache and not feeling my usual self for a week or 10 days. . . . It seems to have been but a mild attack: and I don't think it's in the family. . . ." (Charles's memory deceived him, for on June 23 and 28, 1881, he recorded his brother Skeffington's epileptic attacks.)

Charles provided details of his 1891 episode: "I must have fainted just at the end of morning chapel, as I found myself, an hour afterwards, lying on the floor of the stalls; and had probably struck my nose against the hassock, as it had been bleeding considerably. It is the first time I fainted away. . . . I had some headache afterwards, but felt very little worse. It is of course possible it may have been epilepsy and not fainting, but Dr. Brooks thinks the latter." Six days later he added: "Nearly well again though still not free from headache. Dr. B. now thinks it was an epileptic attack, passing off into sleep."

These health problems inconvenienced him, but more serious were his struggles against depression. Gloom closed in on him from without and from within: on March 17, 1888, he confided in the invalid Loui Taylor that every day of his life was "as full of business as it will hold—which is a thing not to complain of but to be thankful for: *occupation* is a real blessing, if only that it keeps one from thinking about one's self and one's own troubles."[2]

In January 1892 the annual censors' dinner was canceled out of respect for the memory of the Duke of Clarence (eldest son of the Prince of Wales), who died on January 14; and a fortnight later Charles noted that term "is put off till February 5, as Oxford is so full of influenza . . . [and] not thought safe to let the undergraduates return. I, however, stay on here: three of the four sisters at Guildford are in bed with influenza. My knee is not well yet, and I live a hermit, as I have done for two months." By the thirtieth he is "allowed to walk about a little in my room, each day." Three days earlier he had turned sixty. "Alas, what ill spent years they have been! Father, forgive me, and help me to spend the remnant of my days as in Thy sight!" Without a succession of child visitors he was lonely. Writing to Mrs. Stevens (June 1, 1892), he begged her to intercede with a local mother of three daughters "in order that I may try if I can add, to my *very* small list of child-friends here (which contained, till Saturday, *one* name only!)."

But his despondency was temporary. Two years later his spirits seem brighter: "To say I am quite well 'goes without saying,'" he wrote Mary Brown (August 21, 1894). "In fact my life is so strangely free from all trials and troubles, that I cannot doubt my own happiness is one of the 'talents' entrusted to me to 'occupy' with, till the Master shall return, by doing something to make other lives happy." He informed his sister Louisa (September 28, 1896) that his health had been "splendid" for the last year and a half and that his "working powers" were "fully as great as, if not greater than, what I have ever had." A year later still (September 1, 1897), his "health is something to be *most* thankful for. I work at the Whitely Exerciser . . . and feel myself distinctly stronger and better for it."

Concerned about how best to use his time, he grew increasingly reluctant to make social commitments. He categorically rejected dinner invitations tendered from the deanery. On May 31, 1890, the Duchess of Albany arrived there on a visit, and the Liddells gave a dinner in her honor. Charles was invited (the Duchess "had wished to meet me"), but he declined.

Occasionally he played the role of the withdrawn private person. "*Solitude* is very much to my taste," he wrote to Caroline Erskine (April 12, 1890). "Nature evidently meant me for a Hermit." On August 19 he wrote to Edith Lucy: "For 5 weeks now, I have hardly had a *word* of conversation with anybody but Mrs. Dyer [his Eastbourne landlady]! . . . It has been a positive relief. My thoughts have gone out in *writing*, not in talk." On August 28 of that summer, he wrote to Maud Standen: "I came down here on July 5, and have been here ever since (nearly 8 weeks) all alone, and scarcely ever interchanging 'sweet words of human speech' with *any* one," and he added: ". . . You will perhaps pity me! But your pity would be thrown away. I am so busy, and as happy, as the day is long: in fact it isn't nearly long *enough*, for me to do all I want to do in it."

But despite his own characterization, he was not by nature a recluse or hermit. People, the outer world, and its events were essential to his happiness. He continued to go to the theater and concerts and enjoyed spectacles. He encouraged friends and acquaintances to call and welcomed overnight guests both at Oxford and at Eastbourne. He did not turn permanently inward, and soon enough he was whirling about again in society.

He was now thinner, and his rodlike appearance made him look taller. He could still be seen every afternoon he was in Oxford "in his tall silk hat and flowing clerical black striding out to take the air."[3] Ethel Hatch, one of Charles's child friends in Oxford, recalled him as "tall and thin, with thick, dark hair turning iron-grey, clear-cut features, and light-blue eyes which seemed to take in everything as he looked about him; and his thin lips were generally twisted into a humorous smile. He was dressed in the usual clerical dress of that day, a black frock-coat and white cravat, and a top-hat rather at the back of his head. . . ."[4] Isa Bowman, the actress who became one of his closest child friends late in Charles's life, remembered him as

a man of medium height. . . . [His] hair was a silver-grey, rather longer than it was the fashion to wear, and his eyes were a deep blue. He was clean shaven, and, as he walked, always seemed a little unsteady in his gait. . . . He was a little eccentric in his clothes. In the coldest weather he would never wear an overcoat, and he had a curious habit of always wearing, in all seasons of the year, a pair of grey cotton gloves.

But for the whiteness of his hair it was difficult to tell his age from his face, for there were no wrinkles on it. He had a curiously womanish face, and, in direct contradiction to his real character, there seemed to be little strength in it. . . . He was as firm and self-contained as a man may be, but there was little to show it in his face.

Yet you could easily discern it in the way in which he met and talked with friends. When he shook hands with you—he had firm white hands, rather large—his grip was strong and steadfast . . . the pressure of his [hand on yours] was full of strength, and you felt here indeed was a man to admire and to love. The expression in his eyes was also very kind and charming.[5]

Charles cultivated the companionship of mature women more than before. On July 27, 1890, he encouraged his artist friend Mrs. Chad to come to stay with him at Eastbourne. He wrote to Mrs. G. J. Burch (May 20, 1893), the mother of two girl friends, reporting an expedition he had made with a child friend, to London, then on to Guildford: "Now, I *may* be able . . . to make a similar expedition with *you*, if you can come. . . . Could Irene & Co. spare you from Saturday morning till Monday evening?" In fact, Mrs. Burch joined him for the outing on June 28 and 29. They first went to town, spent the morning looking at paintings, then lunched with Lady Maud Wolmer, and went off to see Henry Irving and Ellen Terry in W. G. Wills's *Charles I* at the

Lyceum. Afterward they traveled to Guildford, spent the night there, and returned to Oxford the next day. Within the week he wrote Mrs. Burch again: "May I fetch you, some day this week, at (say) 3-½, for a stroll, tea, dinner, and as much evening as you feel equal to? I don't *think* we should bore each other to any unendurable extent!" A number of other London outings follow without children. To Mrs. Stevens he suggested (March 3, 1896) that instead of having her daughter to dine, "her *mother* ought to be the next to come. . . . Won't you name the day, when I may have the pleasure of coming for you at 6.15?" Writing to Mrs. Poole (November 16, 1896) to thank her for the "loan of Dorothy," he added: "Now I wonder whether *you*, encouraged by the circumstance that your daughter has returned alive, will brave the ogre's den, and come and dine with me?" And she did, on December 1.

What did these women make of such attentions? Both Mrs. Chad and Mrs. Stevens were widows, but Mrs. Burch's husband was very much alive, Professor of Physics at University College, Reading, as was Mrs. Poole's, Lecturer at Jesus College. But all obviously felt free to accept Charles's invitations without compromising either themselves or him.

He continued seeking child friends as well, even if, by his own confession, he now preferred them a bit older: "My views about children are changing," he wrote Macmillan (December 18, 1877), "and I *now* put the nicest age at about 17!" "Twenty and thirty years ago," he wrote (March 8, 1894) to the mother of a quartet of new friends, " 'ten' was about my ideal age for such friends: now 'twenty' or 'twenty-five' is nearer the mark. Some of my dearest child-friends are 30 and more: and I think an old man of 62 has the right to regard them as being 'child-friends' still."

In the spring of 1887 and again in 1894 he taught logic classes at the Oxford High School for Girls, and his classrooms provided green fields for finding new friends. He asked Mrs. Poole if he might have her daughter Dorothy, aged thirteen, to dine with him at Christ Church and succeeded. His pursuit of child friends, his dependence upon their companionship, his need to fill the void that repeated rejections and inevitable coolings created as the girls grew up, continued unabated. They were the major source of calm for an unquiet heart.

He had great success with the Bowman children, whose friendship he made in his mid-fifties and which he cultivated with great success. Charles actually did much to put that family on the stage and insure their success. As we know, he first encountered Isa, the eldest, aged twelve, in 1886, at a rehearsal of the first production of Clarke's *Alice*, in which she had a small

Dreams, that elude the Waker's frenzied grasp—
Hands, stark and still, on a dead Mother's breast,
Which nevermore shall render clasp for clasp,
Or deftly soothe a weeping Child to rest—
In suchlike forms me listeth to portray
My Tale, here ended. Thou delicious Fay—
The guardian of a Sprite that lives to tease thee—
Loving in earnest, chiding but in play
The merry mocking Bruno! Who, that sees thee,
Can fail to love thee, Darling, even as I?—
My sweetest Sylvie, we must say 'Good-bye!'

*An acrostic verse dedication to Enid Stevens (using the third letter of each line to spell her name) in* Sylvie and Bruno Concluded

part. She made a singular impression, but not until September 27, 1887, did he ask for and receive permission to take Isa on a day's outing in London. He had her sit for a professional photographer, and when he brought her back home, to Stratford, east London, he met her whole family, parents and four other children, three girls and a boy.

On the following Saturday, with Mrs. Bowman's leave, Isa came for a week's visit with Charles at the seaside. On Friday, October 7, the day before she was due to return home, Charles declared her visit "a success. . . . On Tuesday we went to [a] . . . swimming entertainment; on Wednesday to [a] concert and fireworks at Devonshire Park; and yesterday we walked to Beachy Head and back—about six miles. . . . We have had daily Bible-reading together, and I have taught her three propositions of Euclid!"

With Charles's help, all the Bowman children went on the stage, the daughters to full-time professional careers. Isa became one of Charles's all-time favorites. She visited him again, at Eastbourne and Oxford, he saw her in London, he observed her on the stage, he wrote some of the most enchanting whimsicalities ever to "My own darling Isa."

Although this friendship was intense and gratifying, other friendships developed in the autumn of his life. When he brought home Winifred Stevens, one of the girls in his logic class at the Oxford High School, after taking her for a walk and tea (February 27, 1891), he "met, for the first time her beautiful [eight-year-old] sister Enid, who seems a sweet child." On the following day he wrote Mrs. Stevens: "I have lost a considerable fraction (say .25) of my heart to your little daughter: and I *hope* you will allow me further opportunities of trying whether or no we can become real *friends*. She would be about my only child-friend—in Oxford."

His friendship with Enid developed slowly but well. He "borrowed" her regularly, took her on walks, printed calling cards for her, entertained her and Mrs. Stevens and her alone, to tea in his rooms, and had Gertrude Thomson paint a portrait of her, which he hung over his Christ Church mantel. On his sixty-second birthday he took Enid to a London matinee of Arthur Wing Pinero's *Sweet Lavender*.[6] He dedicated *Sylvie and Bruno Concluded* to her with an acrostic verse. "We were the very greatest friends," she wrote later. "I don't think anybody else ever had so much of him as I had. . . . I was the last child-friend." Elsewhere she recalled: "When I was twelve I had scarlet fever, and for six long weeks I was shut away from all society. In all that time not a day passed without a letter from 'my old gentleman' (as the family always called him)."[7]

When Charles found that some fellow lodgers at Eastbourne possessed a young daughter, he struck up an acquaintance. Gladys Baly later reminisced:

> I was six years old . . . when a letter arrived addressed to me. It . . . was typewritten, at a time when few people used typewriters. . . . It was an invitation to tea from the gentleman staying in the rooms above ours. . . . Next day, I was dressed in my best and sent upstairs to my party. I was shy, and he teased me about my funny little mannerisms, but all in the kindest way. I was a tiny bit afraid of the tall, thin gentleman, with a halo of grayish hair round a not too handsome face, yet I recollect him best as someone who really understood my feelings when grown-ups told me that I could not, or must not, do certain things. . . . Happy engrossing hours were those I spent with Mr. Dodgson, when he showed me tricks and puzzles and . . . how to make a paper pistol that would go off with a bang.[8]

Because he believed that his age absolved him from any Grundyish suspicions, Charles grew more determined to have child guests to stay at Eastbourne. And thus it was: with the wave of his magic wand, he summoned child friends to stay. Charles met Marie Van der Gucht, "a quite charming child aged 11" at the Frederick Holidays' (July 24, 1885), and five days later invited her to come as his guest to Eastbourne. She "at once said 'yes,' and her mother consented: but afterwards she lost courage." But she came the following year and stayed from September 1 to 6. On August 29, 1885, Mrs. Rix and her daughter Edith came to Eastbourne as his guests for over a week. On September 7 Mrs. Rix departed, "leaving Edith (*mirabile dictu!*) in my care till tomorrow. After the decision of Mr. and Mrs. Rix, only a week ago, that such a thing could not be thought of because of 'Mrs. Grundy,' it is rather droll to have that position entirely abandoned! It will make an excellent precedent for having other visitors," Charles writes, "of any age up to 19."

From August 17 to 23, 1887, he had as guest the first of the Barnes sisters, Irene, aged fifteen. Within a fortnight, on September 5, he went to London to fetch Edith Lucy, also aged fifteen, but that visit was a disaster. "Edith was in such tribulation," Charles wrote the following day, ". . . that I took her back to town by the 12:00 train, her visit having lasted exactly 17 hours! I don't know which of us was best pleased, when we parted at Victoria—she to be back with her mother, or I to part with her!" Charles consoled himself, however, with a visit from another Barnes sister, Edith, aged nineteen, from September 10 to 15. On the day after Edith departed, he had more consolation in having Edith Lucy's older sister, Katie, aged seventeen, to visit, from the sixteenth to the twenty-second. On October 1 he journeyed to London to fetch Isa Bowman, then thirteen, for a full week. Isa returned the following summer, 1888, and remained five weeks, "a very happy time for both of us." After she left, life felt "rather lonely without Isa." The following summer, Isa arrived on July 17, and three days later Charles produced, as a surprise, her sister Nellie. "My children," as Charles styled them, remained with him for almost six weeks.

Other visitors enlivened his summers, and he reported (September 6, 1891) on a memorable one to Lorina Liddell, now Mrs. Skene, "professing to be my own publisher of any scandal likely to be laid to my charge!" He explained: "Mr. Toole's company was (on tour) at Eastbourne . . . and his 'leading lady' was staying with me! Please don't be more shocked than is absolutely necessary. She is Miss Irene Vanbrugh on Stage. . . . A very nice girl, and her elocution is simply *lovely*." Isa arrived at the end of September for her fifth visit and remained a month. On January 13, 1892, approaching his sixtieth birthday, he wrote to Mrs. George MacDonald: "In my old age

I have begun to set 'Mrs. Grundy' entirely at defiance, and to have girl-friends to brighten, one at a time, my lonely life by the sea: of all ages from 10 to 24. Friends ask, in astonishment, 'did you ever hear of any *other* elderly clergyman having young-lady guests in this way?' and I am obliged to confess I never *did:* but really I don't see why they shouldn't. It is, I think, one of the *great* advantages of being an old man, that one can do many pleasant things, which are, quite properly, forbidden to a younger man." More child guests filled the visitors' roster, and on August 23, 1892, Charles's niece Violet Dodgson, aged fourteen, came for eleven days.

> I came to know . . . [Uncle Charles] better when . . . I was honoured but slightly alarmed by an invitation to spend ten days with him in his rooms at Eastbourne—ten days so crowded with good things that I had no time to feel lost or homesick. . . . We did "lessons" in the morning—Bible-reading, a few sums, a little symbolic logic, some poetry-reading—all of an unexpectedly spicy quality which raised them above ordinary "lessons." They included an exciting attack on the first few propositions of Euclid, hitherto only a name to me. I shall never forget my bewilderment when paper, pencil, rule, and compasses were laid before me with the smiling request that I should, unaided, draw an equilateral triangle on the line *A–B* ruled for me. I had learned no geometry. It got done, but I need scarcely say *not* "unaided"! He made it quite fascinating, as also the symbolic logic. The rest of the day went on a variety of amusements, expeditions to here, there, and everywhere, concerts, theatres (five plays in ten days), talks which removed my bed-time almost into the small hours and sent me home finally a somewhat washed-out little person. I probably bored him: he liked children to talk and we were rather dumb. But he never let me see it and was the most thoughtful, courteous, and unwearying of hosts. Moreover, he made one feel that one was of interest to him as an individual—a novel experience to a child picked out of the middle of a large family. He invited opinions and discussed them with respect and understanding. His face lighted up with appreciation of my feeble little jokes or my admiration of something he was showing or explaining. He was always a cheerful, keen, and sympathetic companion, and I had not a dull moment.[9]

Charles's diaries chronicle similar visits every year at Eastbourne until his last stay there in 1897. That year a new guest, Dolly Rivington, aged four-

*Charles's drawing of Edith Blakemore on the beach at Eastbourne, where he spent the summer of 1877. Charles wrote on August 2: "This evening, on the pier, I have made friends with quite the brightest child, and nearly the prettiest, I have yet seen here." He and Edith soon became great friends.*

teen, came for eleven days (August 13 to 24), and Charles took her to Winchelsea to visit Ellen Terry: "She sent a carriage to meet us.... In the afternoon ... we were out in the garden, and Miss Terry and Dolly were swinging, side by side, in hammocks." Later that week Terry was in Eastbourne and Charles called on her and tried unsuccessfully to lure her over for tea. These were his last visits with his favorite actress.

"Much of the brightness of my life, and it has been a wonderfully happy one," Charles wrote (March 8, 1894) to Mrs. J. C. Egerton, the mother of a logic pupil at the Oxford High School, "has come from the friendship of girl-friends." Writing to a new young friend (November 15, 1897), he looked back at having known "some 200 or 300 children." He clung to the memories of them as he did to the few former child friends who had matured and remained "faithful," but was always aware that the connections were tenuous and might snap any moment. As he wrote Edith Blakemore (February 1, 1891): "When we have reached the exact moment when you are beginning to give me up finally, as a hopeless correspondent and a useless friend ... [I shall] write you just *one* more letter, so as to wind up the works of friendship (please observe this quite new original simile—treating friendship as a clock! You see it needs the joining of *two hands:* and though things are sometimes at *sixes and sevens,* yet they always *come round* at last) and set it going again." Wit and whimsy helped him escape any possible embarrassment.

He acquired the Drury sisters on a railway journey in 1869, and they remained on good terms as the girls grew. In 1882 Minnie, the eldest, married and soon was raising her own family. Charles kept in touch and asked (November 3, 1895) whether Minnie "would be disposed to give me a bed, and to lend me a daughter as companion to take to . . . [a] play." On November 8 he arrived in time for lunch and took the daughter, Audrey, to her first play, *The Professor's Love Story* by J. M. Barrie. Audrey and her mother were largely responsible, in 1898, for establishing by subscription a new children's bed to be known as the "Alice in Wonderland Cot" at Great Ormond Street Hospital.

Occasionally he encountered parental censure. "Heard again from Mrs. Richards," Charles noted (October 6, 1893), ". . . about her wish that Marion should not dine with me again, or even walk with me." A year later (August 14, 1894): "Dear May Miller was engaged to dine with me, but Mrs. Miller wrote to say there was so much 'ill-natured gossip' afloat, she would rather I did not invite either girl without the other. No doubt it is Mrs. Richards's doing: she means well, but it is a pity she should interfere with other people thus."

A wary schoolmistress interfered with another friendship. On September 28, 1894, Charles, traveling from London to Eastbourne, "made friends with a nice girl of about 15 (surname 'Newby') who was on her way to a school in Eastbourne. I gave her my card and promised her a wire-puzzle." The following day he sent the youngster (not knowing her first name, he addressed her as "My dear + + + + +") a ring-puzzle and asked whether she would "try to propitiate your mistress for me, and get her permission for me to call on her—in the wild hope that she will let our friendship continue? If she can find a time when she and her girls have a spare half-hour (or, better, hour), I shall be happy to teach them one or two things which I have taught . . . to the girls at the Oxford High School. . . . I have many a young friend of your age," Charles boasted, "and *hope* to be allowed to add *you* to the list." On October 5 Charles noted: "Heard from Miss Wilkie, the mistress . . . to tell me that Miss N. is a Ward in Chancery, and may not make any acquaintances unless with the approval of her guardians. (She also returns the puzzle. I wonder if Miss N. has my letter!)." According to Evelyn Hatch, Mary "told her [railway] adventure to her school-mistress and gave her the letter which she received a few days later. But the proposed classes never took place, and the offer of friendship was rejected, as the mistress seems to have regarded the old gentleman with some suspicion and discouraged Mary from sending him a reply. Years later, on the death of the school-mistress, the letter was found among her possessions and returned to Mary Newby."[10]

Charles knew well that ultimate disappointment awaited him with most of these child friendships, but was nevertheless saddened when the inevitable occurred. He often took pen in hand to send best wishes to a child friend upon her engagement or wedding. On September 17, 1891, he wrote Maud Standen sending "sincere wishes for the happiness of yourself and your future husband," and added: "My child-friends are all marrying off, now, terribly quick! But, for a solitary broken-hearted hopeless old bachelor, it is certainly soothing to find that some of them, even when engaged, continue to write as 'yours affectionately'! but for that, you will easily perceive that my solitude would be simply *desperate!*"

He began to decline invitations to attend the weddings of his once-little friends. "A few years ago I went, in the course of about three months," he wrote to Kathleen Eschwege (January 20, 1892), "to the weddings of three of my old child-friends. But weddings are not very exhilarating scenes for a miserable old bachelor; and I think you'll have to excuse me from attending *yours.*" When Kate Terry Lewis invited him to her wedding (to Frank Gielgud), he wrote her (July 4, 1893), ironically on the anniversary of the famous river journey: "You surely do not *expect* a 'lone, lorn creature' like me—a wretched old bachelor—to cloud the happy day by his sombre presence?" And he signed himself "With an old man's love, I am, Affectionately yours. . . ." Weddings were taboo, and when Lady Muriel married in *Sylvie and Bruno Concluded,* Charles describes the event as "more like a funeral than a wedding." (Admittedly, in the book the groom is about to go off to a plague-ridden town.) He did, however, wish his marrying friends well: on June 7, 1890, he wrote Helen Feilden, "God bless you and your chosen husband, and help you to love each other with a love second only to your love for Him who Himself is 'Love.' "

On March 31, 1890, he confided to Edith Blakemore, who never married and remained a friend: "Usually the child becomes so entirely a different being as she grows into a woman, that our friendship has to change too: and *that* it usually does by sliding down, from a loving intimacy, into an acquaintance that merely consists of a smile and a bow when we meet! . . . That is partly why I have written you all this long letter—that you continue to honour me with an affection that is a *sort* of love, and that we haven't yet got to the "smile and bow" stage! I hope we may continue equally good friends during the years—few or many—that I have still before me."

But Charles was not too old to savor new adventures; he reveled in them and wrote about one to Edith Rix on the day before 1890 dawned:

> Can you easily believe that I have been standing on a stage, curtain up, foot-lights dazzling me and turning all beyond them into black darkness (I never knew before what it was like, for actors to look over footlights into a dark abyss), and telling a fairy-tale . . . with an audience of nearly 300? The head-mistress of a large High School at Birmingham had invited me to witness a performance by the girls—scenes from *Julius Caesar* in German, and then Mrs. Freiligrath-Kroeker's dramatic version of *Alice:* and I had rashly offered to tell the little ones a story after it was over. I expected to have an audience of 40 or 50, mostly children, and had no idea there would be such a host of elder girls and parents. However, when I saw what I had to face, I thought I would go through with it, for the sake of the younger children: I tried to ignore the presence of the others. . . . I gave them "Bruno's Picnic." . . . The children, who acted in *Alice,* came on . . . at my suggestion, and sat on the floor, and, with the table of the "Mad Tea Party" to lean against, and the little Alice herself standing by me . . . it wasn't *quite* such a formidable ordeal as it would have been to stand alone on an empty stage.

Writing (September 13, 1893) from Eastbourne to Enid Stevens, then eleven, he recounted two more adventures:

> I was taking a walk the other day, and I came on a boy and girl about 12 and 10 years old; and . . . they were carefully examining her finger. So I said "is anything the matter?" And they told me she had just been stung by a wasp. So I told them to put some hartshorn to it, as soon as they got home, and that would take away all the pain. And I gave them a tiny lesson in chemistry, and explained that, if you mix an acid and an alkali, they fizz up, and the acid loses its acidity: and the wasp's poison is an *acid,* and hartshorn is an *alkali.* When I got home, I thought "Now I won't be so badly provided, next time I come across a stung little girl" . . . so I bought myself a little bottle of strong ammonia (which is better than hartshorn): and I put it in my pocket when I go [for] a walk. And now, if it happens again, I can make the little girl happy in a minute. But *no* little girl has ever got stung since, that *I* have met with. Isn't it a sad sad pity?

Now here's *another* adventure for you. I have a very dear girl-friend here (about twenty-five, so she's a *little* older than you): and the other day I took her in the steamer to Brighton. It's about 2-½ hours' voyage: and it was deliciously rough: and we pitched up and down all the way. And every now and then a wave struck the bow, and a lot of it splashed over the deck. At first there was in the bow a young man . . . and my friend (May Miller) and me. Soon the young man got so wet, that *he* fled. May bore 2 or 3 more shower-baths, and then she said *she* was getting drenched. So we went back to the middle of the steamer: and all the passengers, up on the "bridge" and the upper deck, clapped their hands, in honour of the brave young lady. However, *I* was so wet by this time that I had got reckless: so I went back to the bow, and climbed up to the very point, and sat there, riding up and down *grandly* over the waves, and every now and then getting a wave all over me. . . . When we got to Brighton, I was wet to the skin, and May nearly as bad. We *had* meant to go and have tea with my sister, who lives in Brighton: but we decided it wouldn't be wise to risk a chill, by going into a house *at all*. It wanted about an hour to the time of the train back to Eastbourne: and we spent it walking up and down in the sun and wind, and trying to get dry. . . . When we got to my lodgings . . . I told . . . [May] she had far better dine with me [than go home], and I was sure Mrs. Dyer could lend her enough clothes to dine in, and would dry her own things while we dined. So she . . . came to dinner dressed up in clothes lent her by the maid! (Mrs. Dyer's things would have been too large.) And she *did* look so pretty in the maid's Sunday-gown!

In these latter years Charles's life was punctuated by his frequent talks before child audiences, sometimes numbering in the hundreds, not only entertaining them with tales and games but dwelling more on serious messages, mini-sermons. "It is a great privilege to be allowed to talk to them on the *realities* of life," Charles wrote (July 22, 1894). One of his sermons to a children's service at St. Leonards-on-Sea appeared in the *St. Mary Magdalen Church Magazine* (November 1897). He took a simple approach, plunging at the outset into the first of three tales; and after telling the stories, he added a message:

And now, dear children, I want you to promise me that you will each one try, every day, to do some loving act of kindness for others. Perhaps

you have never really tried before; will you begin to-day—the beginning
of a new week? Last week is gone for ever; this week will be quite different. As you rub out the sums on your slate that have not come right,
and begin all over again, so leave behind the disobedience, or selfishness,
or ill-temper of last week, and begin quite fresh to try your very best,
every day, to do what you can towards fulfilling God's law of love.

Charles's adventures continued. In the summer of 1894, at Eastbourne, he
paid particular notice to a young actress named Florence Ada White appearing in a play entitled *Our Eldorado* at the Seaside Theatre, and he left a
copy of *Alice* at the theater for her on the following day with a note inviting
her to call on him. "She arrived at 5," Charles noted, "and stayed till 7. She
is fourteen, and seems a very nice child." That evening he saw the play a second time and afterward went round to see "Florrie" and her father and
walked them home. More meetings with Florrie followed. With permission
from the person who was both the author of the play and the male lead,
F. A. Scudamore (Michael Redgrave's grandfather), Charles stood "in the
wings through the whole piece (the only stranger there), which was a new
and most interesting experience. . . . Florrie was with me a good deal of the
time, and it added much to the interest of watching her on the stage to have
just had her with me. Her make-up, even when seen quite close, did not
spoil her at all. It was a pretty sight, once, when the curtain was down, to see
her on the stage, dancing (to the music of the orchestra) a gavotte." Then
Charles again walked home with the actress and her father, and on the following day brought her back to his rooms to dine while he lunched, and kept
her till about four.

He recorded another royal occasion at Oxford on May 12, 1897. "As the
Prince of Wales comes this afternoon to open the Town Hall, I went round
to the Deanery [since 1892 occupied by Francis Paget], etc., to invite them
to come through my rooms up on the roof, to see the procession arrive. A
party of about twenty were on my roof in the afternoon, including . . . most,
if not all, of the children in Christ Church." Charles dined with the celebrities in Hall that evening. "The Dean had the Prince on his right, and Lord
Salisbury on his left. My place was almost *vis-à-vis* with the Prince." Then
Charles fetched two of his young friends "to see the illuminations. About
11 we . . . had tea in my rooms, and saw from the roof the illuminated
Quad, and the return of the Prince from the Mayor's 'reception' at the Town
Hall."

Charles got very much into the swim of Jubilee Week celebrations in June

1897. Edith Rix came to Oxford as his guest. After she arrived, he had his three nieces over to tea with her and in the evening gave a dinner party in her honor. More tea and dinner parties followed; together they called on various friends; and on June 20, a Sunday, Edith being Catholic, Charles accompanied her to St. Aloysius's. "There was much beauty in the service," he wrote. Parties dominated Jubilee Day itself, the twenty-second, and in the evening Charles took Edith, Enid Stevens, and Margaret Mayhew to see the Oxford illuminations, which "were splendid." Parties continued until Edith left on the twenty fourth. Charles found reasons still, from time to time, for assigning a white stone to a particular day.

Charles continued giving logic lectures here and there, especially to schoolgirls and their mistresses. Having lectured on his "Game of Logic" at the Oxford High School in May and June 1887, he now lectured there on formal logic. On June 7, 1886, he began logic lectures at Lady Margaret Hall and went on with them into 1887. On May 7, 1894, he began lecturing to thirteen girls at St. Hugh's Hall, Oxford. On October 12 he began a week's course at Mrs. Barber's girls' boarding school at Eastbourne. Years later the pupils of that school helped to endow the "Lewis Carroll Cot" at the Throat and Ear Hospital, Brighton.[11]

He did not give these lectures because he missed the contact with undergraduates. Actually he no longer felt *en rapport* with undergraduate education and made no effort to take on any male pupils. He simply and unabashedly wanted to teach young girls and their mistresses.

He gave some of his logic pupils personal tuition in his rooms. The Rowell sisters, for instance, accepted his invitation for instruction during the Easter vacation, 1894. Many years later Ethel Rowell recalled:

When Mr. Dodgson stood at the desk in the sixth-form room and prepared to address the class I thought he looked very tall and seemed very serious and rather formidable . . . and, with the ready docility of a schoolgirl of the nineties, I soon settled down to the subject in hand and forgot the lecturer in his own fascinating "Game of Logic." . . . There was a very ingenious diagram marked in squares, and there were red and gray counters, and by placing counters on appropriate squares we were able to try conclusions with such facts as:

> All cats understand French;
> Some chickens are cats

or

All selfish men are unpopular;
All obliging men are popular.

Mr. Dodgson came to school several times and gave us further elaborations of his most ingenious method, and as he proceeded I think the facts became more fanciful and the fancies more fantastic. . . . I went to and from Mr. Dodgson's rooms . . . and as the subject opened out I found great delight in this my first real experience of the patterned intricacies of abstract thought. . . . Mr. Dodgson compelled me to that independence of thought I had never before tried to exercise. . . . Gradually under his stimulating tuition I felt myself able in some measure to judge for myself, to select, and if need be, to reject. . . . In Mr. Dodgson's presence I felt proud and humble, [and enjoyed the] grace conferred thus upon an ignorant schoolgirl by the magnanimity of a proud and very humble and very great and good man. . . . He was so patient of all one's limitations, so understanding, so infinitely kind.[12]

Irene Vanbrugh was less rapturous. She remembered that when she visited him, his "great delight was to teach me his Game of Logic. . . . This made the evening rather long, when the band was playing outside on the parade and the moon shining on the sea."[13] Evelyn Hatch recalled the amazement she and her classmates at St. Hugh's experienced when they realized that during Charles's lessons, his pupils "were actually expected to *laugh!*" She found that

though such propositions as:

Some new Cakes are nice
No new Cakes are nice
All new Cakes are nice

and

All teetotalers like sugar
No nightingale drinks wine

sounded rather like extracts from a child's reading-book . . . considerable intelligence, as well as much skill and attention were required to learn the game and work out a conclusion on the diagram. How patiently he bore with our stupidity![14]

Besides giving logic lessons and appearing before school assemblies, Charles now accepted more invitations to preach. On April 5, 1885, at Guild ford for Easter, he discerned a shortage of hands at the service at St. Mary's and "unwillingly . . . helped Mr. Beloe with the mid-day Communion. . . . But I do not intend to do so again," he wrote, "as I much dislike the observances with which he concluded the service (for example, washing the cup, and his fingers in it, and then drinking the water!) which savour too much of Romanism." He then called on the Reverend Mr. Beloe and had "a long chat, about the ritual observed here, etc., etc., etc." By January 4, 1891, however, Mr. Beloe had departed St. Mary's, and Charles returned to the pulpit there.

On January 26, 1890, Charles preached at the college servants' service, and, recalling that last time (the previous Sunday) "I was over the half-hour," he put his watch before him, and "by omitting a portion, ended it in about 20 minutes." Altogether he preached four times to the servants that year. He went on preaching, at Oxford, Guildford, Taunton, Worcester, and Eastbourne and vicinity.

Charles had left photography far behind by now, but he continued sketching for pleasure. Arranging a meeting with Gertrude Thomson, he planned (September 6, 1890) "to allow myself an hour or two at your studio before we go off to the play. And I would come even earlier, so as to have a couple of hours, *if* you could get a child-model that . . . *you* might copy, and that I might *try* to copy. I tried Maud Howard, the other day, at the studio of my friend Mrs. Chad. . . . She has a beautiful figure, I think. And she seems nice and modest: but she is turned 14, and *I* like drawing a *child*, best. However, if you wish to get a model for Wednesday, and *cannot* find a child, Maud would be well worth having for an hour. . . . But *don't* get a grown-up model, any time you are expecting *me*."

While Gertrude Chataway stayed with him at Eastbourne in September 1893, she put him in touch with her eldest sister, Ethel, the wife of C. F. Moberly Bell, assistant manager of *The Times,* and their children, particularly Hilda, Enid, Iris, and Cynthia. Mrs. Bell was most agreeable about permitting Miss Thomson to come and sketch and photograph her daughters nude. When Charles visited the Bells (September 26, 1893), he found them "a delightful family." They are "*charming*," he wrote Miss Thomson, "not quite *beautiful,* in face, I admit; still, I would *much* like to have the *figures* of the youngest (Cynthia), and perhaps (if she doesn't mind) the ten year old (Iris), among the fairies" that Miss Thomson was drawing for Charles's projected book.

He asked Miss Thomson to photograph them as well. "Yes, I know of Iris' scar," he wrote (October 2, 1893). "But *still* I want that photo, while it is possible to get it: in 2 or 3 years it will be impossible. The scar does not matter: the photo is only for *me*, not for exhibition." On the fourteenth Charles and Miss Thomson both arrived in the morning at the Bells': "She made, and I *tried* to make sketches of Iris and Cynthia, who were very willing and very patient models, with lovely figures, and yet more lovely innocence. It purifies one even to see such purity." Four days later, however, he wrote Miss Thomson: "So far as any picture done for *me* is concerned, neither Iris nor Cynthia is ever to be drawn again, at their house, in anything but *full-dress*. The *risk*, for that poor little boy, is too great to be run again." The youngest Bell son, Clive, aged eight, must have stumbled into the room during the previous session.

On November 20, 1897, Charles celebrated "a delightful day," sketching with Miss Thomson. Three days earlier he had written her: "Could you have a *camera*, as well as the model on Saturday? Drawing takes *time*, of which we shall have little to spare. But the lens, with which you did the Bells, is a terribly *small* one: some of the photos are very much out of proportion. Could you *hire* one, for the day, with a better lens? Charge *me* with the costs involved." Miss Thomson got the camera, but it must have given them some difficulty because Charles asked her (November 21) to get fuller instructions for operating it the next time she hired it.

Letter writing remained important to Charles, but in the 1890s some of it became onerous. On April 25, 1890, he acknowledged to Isabel Standen that her name had been "ever so long, on a list of unanswered correspondents: but I'm generally 70 or 80 names in arrears: and sometimes *one* letter will take me an afternoon." Laid up with a troublesome knee joint, he wrote to Gertrude Chataway (January 1, 1892): "I am taking advantage of all this abundant leisure and silence, to make a desperate effort to work off my arrears of unanswered letters. I began by making out a list of the people who are waiting (some of them from 5 to 10 years) for letters. There are more than 60 of them." Writing to a Sheffield clergyman on January 11 of that year, he said: "Your kind, sympathising and most encouraging letter about *Sylvie and Bruno* has deserved a better treatment from me than to have been thus kept waiting more than 2 years for an answer."

He continued to be an accomplished letter writer; his inventive impulses did not fail him and he produced some remarkable epistles. Of course, these fanciful creations were to his young female friends, who still sparked the flame, and some of the best went to his special friend Isa Bowman.

Part of Charles's routine when he had a child friend "on loan" was to take her to the theater and to art galleries, and to beg meals for her from adult friends in London. He especially enjoyed introducing his child friends to "lions," and while his overture to the Duchess of Albany (May 11, 1889) proposing to bring "some sweet children" did not bear fruit, he frequently succeeded with Lady Wolmer, and on May 11 took Isa to lunch with the Wolmers and their daughter Mabel, nicknamed "Wang." Three weeks later Charles was staying at Hatfield House, about which he must have told Isa, and he wrote her on Hatfield House letter paper.

June 8, 1889

My darling Isa,

. . . This is Lord Salisbury's house. . . . It *is* such a nice house to stay in! they let one do just as one likes—it isn't "Now you must do some geography! now it's time for your sums! the sort of life *some* little girls have to lead when they are so foolish as to visit friends— but one can just please one's own dear self. There are some sweet little children staying in the house. . . .

Then there is the Duchess of Albany here, with two such sweet little children. She is the widow of Prince Leopold (the Queen's youngest son), so her children are a Prince and Princess: the girl is "Alice," but I don't know the boy's Christian name: they call him "Albany," because he is the Duke of Albany. Now that I have made friends with a real live little Princess, I don't intend ever to *speak* to any more children that haven't titles. In fact, I'm so proud, and I hold my chin so high, that I shouldn't even *see* you if we met! No, darling, you mustn't believe *that*. If I made friends with a *dozen* Princesses, I would love you better than all of them together, even [if] I had them all rolled up into a sort of child-roly-poly. . . .

Your ever loving Uncle,
C.L.D.
X X X X X X X

Charles first met Sydney Bowles, aged eleven, a month after he sent her the letter below. She was the elder daughter of Thomas Gibson Bowles, with whom Charles was corresponding at the time about his new word game *Syzygies,* soon to appear in Bowles's *The Lady.* Charles visited the Bowles family on June 11–12: "Sydney is a *very* sweet-looking child," he noted. (Incidentally, the novelist Nancy Mitford was Sydney Bowles's eldest child.) The letter is reproduced here in its actual size:

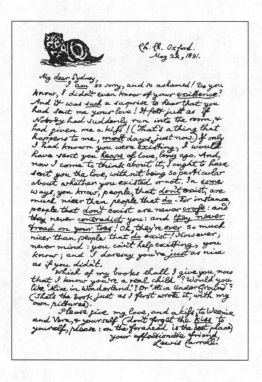

Charles must have mustered time and ingenuity for his looking-glass letters. One went to Edith Ball, a child model who sat for Miss Thomson's fairy drawings. Charles was sending a copy of *The Nursery "Alice"* to Edith's younger sister, Maud, who also sat for Miss Thomson.

From age fifty-five, a fierce, unbridled determination dominated Charles's life. He had turned into the last lap and set himself a rigid goal: to complete his serious work. If, in taking this road, he was escaping the despair of old,

*Nov. 6, 1893,*

My dear Edith,

I was very much pleased to get your nice little letter: and I hope you won't mind waiting a little while longer for the real one. Some day I will send you the other book I told about, called "Through the Looking-Glass" that you had not read, the first time you ever saw

should get them mixed in your mind. Which W. you like best, do you think, a horse that drowns you in a cab, or a lady that blows your picture, or a dentist, or a street-newsman, or a Matron. that draws you into her arms, to give you a kiss? but rather oxen would you put the other in? Do you find looking Glass writing easy to read? I remain your loving, Lewis Carroll.

*Charles's looking-glass letter to Edith Ball, whom he engaged to pose for Miss Thomson's drawings for his book* Three Sunsets and Other Poems.

his unsuccessful attempts to lead a more fulfilling personal life and his disappointments in love, he never acknowledged it. For him, those projected books were to be his further contribution to the march of humane thought and faith, the oblation to mark his little while on earth, his offering to other troubled souls to help them avoid despair and to believe that their lives were not in vain.

He worked obdurately, frantically. Responding to an invitation from his friends the MacDonalds, then living in Italy, he wrote (January 13, 1892): "It would be a very pleasant thing to do: but I can see no prospect at all of my ever going outside England again. Life is wearing away fast . . . and more and more I grudge the hours that *must* be given to so many other things, when *I* would like to work, 24 hours a day, at the books that I have on hand, nearly done, or half done, or only begun." On August 17, 1892, he wrote the novelist Mrs. A. S. Walford: "I feel that the number of working hours, now left, is very finite indeed: and I would like to give all that is left, of time and brain-power, to *work*." So intent was he upon this course that he once even denied himself the pleasure of watching the Oxford boat races with his friend Enid Stevens. On May 21, 1897, he wrote her: "My darling . . . What is it you want? If it is, to go *with* you to see the Eights, I fear I must beg off. I can give you a small fraction of my love (say .0001 of a very hard heart), or I can give you a written request, which would secure the admission, to our [Christ Church] Barge . . . but I can't give you time!"

The result of this driving force was considerable. Charles now wrote "useful" books, books that aid in developing intelligence, that help clarify and simplify moral and religious questions. With few exceptions, the works were larger, thicker, heavier, and weightier in content.

As he withdrew from college and university affairs during the 1890s, he produced only a few items touching upon academia. On December 4, 1890, he read in the *St. James's Gazette* an account of an astonishing masquerade at Queen's College, when some rowdy undergraduates dressed in clerical garb marched through the college, imitating and mocking religious ceremonies, including Communion, forcing fellow students to participate. This behavior was too much for Charles, and he wrote a long letter to the *Gazette* (December 6) deploring the incident but, returning to an old refrain, castigating his fellow dons and clergy for telling inappropriate anecdotes. In his nearly forty years at Oxford, he had heard, "at a moderate computation, some twenty thousand anecdotes, many of them jests on sacred things, some even taking the name of God in vain." He hoped that the recent Oxford scandal would do some good by opening eyes to the general practice of making holy things ludicrous.

Charles's letter provoked a reply from "An Essex Vicar," suggesting that Charles, as Lewis Carroll, had parodied a verse in the Book of Proverbs by his use of "'Tis the voice of the sluggard." The charge is interesting, but Charles did not address it. He was appalled at having his anonymity invaded this way and wrote to the editor begging him never again to violate his privacy by connecting his real name with his nom de plume.[15] And he never wrote again for the *St. James's Gazette*.

He marked his resignation after more than nine years as Curator of Common Room with a circular and a pamphlet, *Curiosissima Curatoria,* a fifty-six-page "parting gift" to his colleagues from "Rude Donatus" (late summer 1892). It is an amiable if dull anthology of Christ Church Common Room resolutions and other miscellanea culled from college archives enlivened by a wry quip here and there. He thoughtfully wrote to the Common Room's

Upper Servant (March 4, 1892) to express "the regret I feel in thus ending our relations . . . and my thanks for the thoughtful attention with which you have always carried out my wishes."

More than ever before, he kept several projects going at the same time. While working on the sequel to *Sylvie and Bruno,* he labored at his scheme to produce texts on three levels of formal logic and mulled over a book on current religious problems. Elements of this latter project had already entered into *Sylvie and Bruno* and into a good many of his letters (to a sister, to a nephew, to some child friend, and to an agnostic with whom he corresponded). He never finished the book, but he left behind a set of six galley proofs dealing with eternal punishment. The printer dated them October 28, 1897, but their genesis and composition occurred earlier. In fact, on June 20, 1895, Charles sent the printer the manuscript of "Eternal Punishment," part of a book to be entitled "Solvent Principles." According to what he wrote Macmillan on May 14, 1895, it would "attempt to treat some of the religious difficulties of the day from a logical point of view."

Charles's nephew-biographer, who received at least one of his uncle's letters on eternal punishment, reported that Charles's heart was set on writing his book on religion because "he felt that, as a clergyman, to associate his name with such a work would be more fitting than that he should be known as a writer of humorous and scientific books."[16] Charles himself never said so. What really spurred him on was his desire to be useful to others.

Although by the time he first came to Oxford, the tumult and the shouting that attended the rise of the Oxford Movement had subsided, religious controversy was still stage center. The nature of the afterlife, if it existed, was one of the disputed points of dogma and belief, and Charles's idol F. D. Maurice stood at the heart of the controversy, a major challenger of the established view on eternal punishment. Charles's own view runs parallel to what Maurice preached. Both men believed that all souls would achieve salvation and remission from eternal punishment.

Charles rubbed intellectual and spiritual shoulders with other radical theologians, including Frederick William Robertson, who echoed Coleridge's doctrine of internal spiritual inspiration. Charles owned Robertson's *Sermons,* read them, and sent an extract on miracles from his copy to Edith Rix (June 7, 1885) when he was mobilizing his thoughts for his book on religious questions. He used Robertson again, when, in 1889, in the preface to *Sylvie and Bruno,* he quoted him on the perils of nocturnal hauntings, evil desires, unholy images, and how to dispel them. He also turned to Robertson in his essay entitled "The Stage and the Spirit of Reverence"; when arguing that a person need not own to any *"religious* beliefs whatever" to possess reverence, he quotes Robertson's account of the reverence among members of a tribe of Eastern robber-hillsmen.

Charles wrote to Robert William Dale, a Congregationalist minister in Birmingham and the author of numerous works of theology with a liberal Mauricean flavor. "I am reading your delightful book *The Living Christ and the Four Gospels* [1890] with the greatest interest and profit," Charles wrote him (March 3, 1892).

Charles believed *Essays and Reviews* an unfortunate enterprise and probably agreed with Pusey's judgment that the authors were "Seven against Christ." He must, however, have read at least one essay with interest and sympathy. Henry Bristow Wilson, lately Professor of Anglo-Saxon at Oxford, later tried by the Court of Arches and found guilty of heresy, wrote on eternal punishment in "The National Church," pleading for a more moderate look at the facts and advocating a broader understanding and less restrictive orthodoxy. He urges that sinners are not necessarily doomed eternally and suggests that "all, both small and great, shall find a refuge in the bosom of the Universal Parent."[17]

*Eternal Hope* (1878) is another book that Charles probably knew well. Based on a series of sermons, delivered in Westminster Abbey by Frederic William Farrar, Canon of Westminster, later Dean of Canterbury, and the author of *Eric, or Little by Little, Eternal Hope* also challenged the conventional doctrine of eternal hell, arguing that it was the result of a misinterpretation of the original text. Farrar was significant enough to Charles for him to note (April 19, 1885) that "Farrar is too ill to give the 'Bampton' [Lectures]. . . ." Presumably Charles planned to attend.

Charles's letters are sprinkled with his thoughts about eternal punishment; he wrote of it in *Sylvie and Bruno Concluded,* and he preached on the subject from the pulpit. One Oxford graduate recalled "a sermon in St. Mary's . . . towards the end of his life in which he quaintly and characteristically disproved everlasting punishment on the logical principle of 'excluded middle.' Either God is just or unjust; there is no third alternative. Everlasting punishment cannot be just in any accepted meaning of the term; therefore a just God cannot impose it."[18] Charles used this logical approach in his manuscript on eternal punishment, which his nephew published in *The Lewis Carroll Picture Book* (1899). His argument is intricate and deals with a sequence of propositions that he examines individually. Like Farrar, he concludes that "the word, rendered in English as 'eternal' or 'everlasting,' has been mistranslated, and that the Bible does not really assert more than that God will inflict suffering, of unknown duration but *not* necessarily eternal, punishment for sin."

Charles wrote the essay in the first person, seeking answers to these heaven-and-hell questions by applying formal logic to them. Some critics believe him something of a sophist here. But long ago he had heard the truth, from within, from the intuition that Coleridge helped him recognize. He wanted to offer spiritual comfort and a road to salvation to other sinners, and he appealed to their reasoning powers, but when he personally fashioned a proleptic future for himself, he relied on his inner voice. It told him to reject church dogma, even as, in listening to Coleridge, Maurice, and Farrar, he rejected the voices closest to him and his own development, the voices of his father, of his sponsor Pusey, and of his good friend Liddon.

Charles's attention in these declining years was not frequently caught by events abroad. The perennial Irish questions interested him, but he apparently took no notice of the war between China and Japan over Korea that broke out in 1894, nor did he mention the dispute between Britain and the United States over the boundary between Venezuela and British Guiana of 1895 that so concerned Parliament. The Armenian Massacre and the Greco-Turkish War of 1895 also passed without comment, as did events leading up to the Boer War in South Africa. Even at home, he made no nod to the founding of the socialist Fabian Society or to the unrest and agitation of the 1890s that led to the founding of the Labour Party.

He did keep a close watch on his pet projects. The cause of working people continued to interest him, and in mid-August 1890 he sent one of the few public letters of his later years, "Eight Hours Movement," to the *Standard*. It dealt with issues unskilled workers raised during the London Dock Strike of 1889 and appealed for justice:

> Supposing that employers of labour, when threatened with a "strike" in case they should decline to reduce the number of hours in a working day, were to reply, "In future we will pay you so much per hour, and you can make up days as you please," it does appear to me—being, as I confess,

an ignorant outsider—that the dispute would die out for want of a *raison d'être,* and that these disastrous strikes, inflicting such heavy loss on employers and employed alike, would become things of the past.

Charles wrote again to Lord Salisbury, who began his third ministry in June 1895. Having read that a fire had badly damaged the Criterion Restaurant, Piccadilly, Charles warned (August 30) him about the dangers of fire in London, suggesting that the Government set up lookout stations at the highest points to detect fires as soon as possible. Replying, Lord Salisbury promised to take up his suggestion with an official of the Fire Brigade.

Four days later Charles dispatched another letter advocating that "Members of the Government of either House be allowed to appear in the other, to answer questions, and join in discussion"; and that the House of Lords "might do more of the work that now falls on, and almost crushes, the House of Commons." Charles here anticipated in part Lord Bryce's suggested reforms in 1918.[19] Replying (September 6), Lord Salisbury found "much to be said for" Charles's suggestions. "The practical answer to both," he wrote, ". . . is that they would be inconsistent with the *amour propre* of the House of Commons. This is in practice a more than adequate reason why they should not be adopted, but I know no other." On the seventeenth Charles wrote again, asking the Prime Minister to consider his brother Edwin for a clerical post. But Crown livings were not in the Prime Minister's gift, and Edwin departed again for foreign shores: from 1896 to 1899 he was Vicar of Jamestown, St. Helena, in the South Atlantic.

Home Rule was a burning issue during the last quarter of the nineteenth century, and Charles took a keen interest in it, even as he did in other Irish questions. When, in early 1873, for instance, Parliament turned down Gladstone's proposal to create a university for Irish Roman Catholics, and Gladstone resigned as Prime Minister, Charles exulted over the event in his diary (March 11 and 25). When, in early 1881, Charles Stewart Parnell resorted to obstructive measures in Parliament in the hope of achieving Home Rule, Charles reports (February 3) the "Grand historical scene in the House of Commons—37 Irish Obstructives turned out of the House, and a new Act passed, under which the Speaker is made a sort of Dictator for the purpose of passing an Irish Coercion Bill."

Parnell was not chastened; he continued his disruptive tactics, and Gladstone, back in office, invoked the provisions of the Coercion Bill. On October 14 Charles "heard the welcome news of the arrest of Mr. Parnell." On the following May 7 he recorded the news "of the murder in Dublin of . . . the new Secretary for Ireland, and of . . . [the] Under-Secretary." Four years later, on June 7, 1886, Charles jubilantly notes a "memorable" night: "at 1-½ a.m. . . . the great division took place on the second reading of Gladstone's Home Rule Bill, which was thrown out. . . . I trust the nation will never again be so near to a gigantic catastrophe." Charles's position remained firm. On May 7, 1890, he heard Joseph Chamberlain speak against Home Rule at a Liberal Unionist meeting at Oxford and thought him "clever and interesting." Later that year (November 29), he noted: "History is moving briskly just now! First, Parnell's disgrace as co-respondent in a divorce suit. Then Gladstone's letter, calling on him to resign the leadership of the 'Home Rule' party. And this morning Parnell's Manifesto to the Irish people, disclosing Gladstone's negotiations with him, and the sham 'Home Rule' Bill he proposed to bring in when next in power, offering Parnell the Irish Secretaryship as a sop!"

Years later, on June 7, 1897, he turned his mind to the Emerald Isle again when he wrote Lord Salisbury expressing dismay that the Queen had never graced Ireland: "If, once in every few years . . . she had paid a visit to Ireland it would have made an *incalculable* difference in the history of Great Britain. Those two miserable Home-Rule Bills would never . . . have been ever heard of." He urged the Prime Minister to persuade the Queen to visit or even to establish a royal residence there. The Duke of York (later George V) visited Ireland in August 1897, only two months after Charles wrote, but no known connection exists between Charles's letter and the visit. The Queen herself visited Ireland in 1900, but it is unlikely that Charles's letter influenced that visit either.

Degrees for women at Oxford became a real issue in 1896, and Charles got involved. In March Congregation was to vote on whether Oxford should grant women degrees. Twelve years earlier (April 29, 1884), the university admitted women to some examinations by a large majority vote, but Charles voted "*non-placet.*" In the crucial vote on March 18, 1896, the vote went against the women, 215 to 140, and Charles probably voted with the majority. His vote did not mean that he opposed higher education for women. Four days after the vote, he composed a four-page pamphlet, *Resident Women-Students,* arguing that to admit women would overwhelm the present resources and cause chaos, diminishing the quality of education. Rather than suffer these debilities, he urged Oxford, Cambridge, and Dublin to "join in a petition to the Crown to grant a charter for a Women's University.

Such a University would very soon attract to itself the greater portion of young Women-Students. It takes no great time to build Colleges; and we might confidently expect to see 'New Oxford,' in the course of 20 or even of 10 years, rivaling Oxford, not only in numbers, but in attainments." Women's halls and colleges already existed at Oxford, but not until 1920 did the university grant degrees to women.

Games, puzzles, charades, anagrams, riddles, acrostics, rebuses, palindromes, rhyming letter games, alphabet games, poetic parodies, concrete poetry, tongue twisters—all were part of Charles's bag of tricks and virtually all for the delectation, diversion, and development of young minds. He could usually get even the less than eager young friends to try word puzzles, and his patience was immense. In one case, when he sent the "Mischmasch" nucleus *eon* to Elisabeth Bury and asked her to find words in which it appears, she confessed she was baffled. Charles replied (March 8, 1896), pretending to be grateful that "in an age of so much greediness and over-eating, that there is at least *one* young lady in Oxford, who not only never *takes* luncheon, but has never even *heard* of such a meal." In the same letter, Charles sent her some *Doublets* and showed her how to turn CAT into DOG by drawing a vertical list of words:

CAT
COT
DOT
DOG

"Invented a new way of working one word *into* another," Charles announces in his diary on December 12, 1879. This is *Syzygies,* a more complicated game built upon the *Doublets* principle. In this early diary entry, he sets out his first three specimens:

Send MAN on ICE.           MAN
                    per m a n ent
                         enti c e
                              ICE
RELY on ACRE.              ACRE
                    sa c r e d
                      c r edentials
                         enti r e l y
                              RELY

Prove PRISM to
be ODIOUS.

PRISM
p r i s matic
dramatic
melo drama
melo d i o u s
ODIOUS

In 1891 *Syzygies* appeared in the *Lady* as a competition, and Charles had it separately printed; in 1893 he republished it along with a revised *Lanrick*.

In 1890 he invented *Circular Billiards* and published three versions of the rules. It is a weird game, requiring a round table (Charles apparently had one built) covered in baize but without pockets or spots, and three billiard balls. The point of the game is to make the cue ball hit the other two balls *seriatim*.

"Invented what I think is a *new* kind of riddle," Charles recorded (June 30, 1892). "A Russian had three sons. The first, named Rab, became a lawyer; the second, Ymra, became a soldier. The third became a sailor: what was his name?" The names read backwards spell out their professions; as the third was in the navy, his name must be Yvan.

"The idea occurred to me," Charles noted (February 4, 1894), "that it might be a pleasant variation of Backgammon to throw *three* dice, and choose any two of the *three* numbers: the average *quality* of the throws would be much raised. I reckon the chance of '6,6' would be about two and a half what it now is. It would also furnish a means, similar to giving points at billiards, for equalising players: the weaker might use three dice, the other using two. I think of calling it 'Thirdie Backgammon.'" It evolved into "Co-operative Backgammon," and on March 6 Charles published a notice in the agony column of *The Times,* giving the rules for the game.

He invented alphabet and number-guessing games. During January 1895 he was both creating and improving on two such games. The first, a primitive version of Scrabble, he described in a letter to Winifred (Stevens) Hawke on New Year's Day 1895:

If ever you want a *light* mental recreation, try the "30 letter" puzzle. I tried it for the first time, the other day, with one of my sisters: and I think it is very interesting. I have taught it to Enid, I think: but we have improved it. Here is our rule.

"Take 4 or 5 complete alphabets. Put the vowels into one bag, the consonants into another. Shake up. Draw 9 vowels and 21 consonants. With these you will make 6 real words (excluding proper names) so as to use up *all* the letters. If *two* people want to do it, then after drawing a set of 30, pick out a set of duplicates for the other player. Sit where you cannot see one another's work, and make it a *race*. It seems to take from 5 to 10 minutes. It makes a shorter, but very good, puzzle, to draw 6 vowels and 14 consonants, and make 4 words; and yet a shorter one to draw 3 vowels and 7 consonants and make 2 words."

The second, "Number-Guessing," he dated February 6, 1896. It has to be seen to be believed (see opposite).

Charles's second part of *Curiosa Mathematica* appeared in 1893 with the subtitle *Pillow-Problems Thought Out During Sleepless Nights*. Following his interesting introduction are seventy-two problems in algebra, geometry, and trigonometry, with which Charles had distracted himself from troublesome thoughts during the night and now was sharing with others. One overpowering difficulty was that his readers were not all as interested or talented as he was in dealing with the subject matter or in following the sinewy lines of his solutions. Still, when the book appeared, the *Spectator* (August 10, 1893) gave it a lavish notice, with minor reservations: "The formula is . . . attractive," the reviewer wrote, suggesting that if one cannot cope with Charles's problems, one can apply the formula in other ways, by designing, during sleepless hours, "a perfect gentleman's residence with pineries and hothouses" or by devising "a new scheme for hanging the pictures in the National Gallery" or by inventing plans for "reorganising the Army and Navy." The *Athenaeum* (October 21) found the introduction to the volume more engrossing than its mathematical problems and went on to make the obvious point that tackling the problems might very well have the opposite of the desired effect by keeping one awake.

*Pillow-Problems* remained in print and demanded attention. Eugene Seneta, for instance, devoted a long article to the "probabilistic contents of the 72 problems" and concluded that the work reflects the nature, standing and understanding of probability within the wider English mathematical community of the time."[20]

Charles was not one to worry about negative notices of his books, in particular those that greeted *Sylvie and Bruno*, but as he worked away at the sequel, he bethought himself about the puzzlement expressed in many quarters over the book, and on January 10, 1890, a letter of his appeared in the *St. James's Gazette:*

<u>Number - guessing</u>                    6/2/96

A. "Think of a number."

B. [thinks of 23]

A. "Multiply by 3. Is the result odd or even?"

B. [obtains 69] "It is odd."

A. "Add 5, or 9, whichever you like."

B. [adds 9, & obtains 78]

A. "Divide by 2, & add 1."

B. [obtains 40]

A. "Multiply by 3. Is the result odd or even?"

B. [obtains 120] "It is even".

A. "Subtract 2, or 6, whichever you like."

B. [subtracts 6, & obtains 114]

A. "Divide by 2, & add 29, or 38, or 47, which-
-ever you like."

B. [adds 38, & obtains 95]

A. "Add 19 to the original number, & tack on
     any figure you like".

B. [tacks on 5, & obtains 425]

A. "Add the previous result."

B. [obtains 520]

A. "Divide by 7, neglecting remainder"

B. [obtains 74]

A. "Again divide by 7. How often does it go?"

B. "Ten times".

A. "The number you thought of was 23".


[This is an improvement on the
puzzle containing the direction "Multiply
by 3. Is the result odd or even?" & after-
-wards "Divide by 2." Four times, in the
course of it, B has the choice of certain
numbers, & need not say which he uses!
I don't think this phenomenon occurs
in any other such puzzle.]

"Lewis Carroll." autograph C L Dodgson

*Charles's "Number-Guessing" game*

You will, I believe, be doing a kindness to many readers of this book, who have found difficulties unforeseen by me, in the sudden change of scene, and the introduction into real life of what they suppose to be "dream-children," if you will allow me to explain that the book is written on the theory of the actual existence of fairies, and of their being able to assume human form. The "I" of the story goes through three different stages of being (1) real life, (2) the "eerie" stage in which he can see fairies, (3) trance, in which while his body remains apparently asleep, his spirit is free to pass into fairyland and witness what is going on there at that moment. There are no "dreams" in the book: the many imitations that have appeared of my two "dream-stories" have effectually barred me from any further attempt to write fiction of that kind.

But not even this explanation helped the story come alive.

After years of hard labor, Charles declared *Sylvie and Bruno Concluded* ready. He encountered the usual difficulties with his illustrator and printer, and the book missed the Christmas sale of 1893 by appearing on December 29. The dedication is, as we have seen, to Enid Stevens and is again a sad farewell, a verse that begins with "Dreams" and ends with " 'Good-bye!' "

By now Charles's books automatically claimed immediate attention in the press; this latest one earned occasional respect but nowhere any of the once customary acclaim. The *Athenaeum* (January 27, 1894) asked: "Where is the wit; where the 'flashes of merriment'? The story—if story 'it can be called which shape has none'—has, however, been constructed on a theory. . . . There are many good things in the book, of course, but it is much too long." The *Spectator* (March 24) exclaimed: "What a loss the world had when Lewis Carroll took to writing sense!" and continued mercilessly: "His sense is but indifferent." If he had lost the ability to write nonsense, no one would blame him. "But Lewis Carroll shows us that the power of saying wise and witty things without sense is still his, and that the filling of half his two last books with the trivialities of reason and convention was deliberate. That being so, we have a good ground for a grievance. . . . Let us hope that Mr. Lewis Carroll's next book will be all fancy and nonsense. . . ." The critic accused Charles of committing "a sin which ought to lie heavy on his conscience, and make him repent that he was ever unwise enough to stoop to real people." The *Publishers' Circular* (January 13) admitted that "it has delighted us, though in a fairy story we could dispense with discussions on ethics, on charity, on 'fate, free-will, foreknowledge absolute,' and similar topics. . . . [It] is perhaps a trifle too deep and satirical for childish understandings; yet the didactic and ironical parts are so mixed up with bits of pure fun that when we would protest we find ourselves unexpectedly in a burst of laughter." Sales of the book disappointed Charles, and copies of the first edition were available into the twentieth century.

If Charles was at all saddened to realize that the audience he had acquired through his humorous works of fancy was less interested in his graver words, he could find consolation in the flourishing *Alice* industry. *Alice* and *Looking-Glass* themselves gained in popularity, and Charles reported to Alice Hargreaves (December 8, 1891) that "your adventures have had a marvellous success. I have now sold well over 100,000 copies." In late 1887 and early 1888 he had both books reset and reissued at modest prices, in separate volumes and in one combined volume, as the People's Editions. When, toward Christmas 1893, he received copies of a new batch of *Looking-Glass*es, the sixtieth thousand, with the illustrations badly printed, he again had the entire run canceled and inserted an announcement in *The Times* requesting buyers of the books to return them to Messrs. Macmillan in exchange for copies with better printing.

Translations proliferated, the *Alice* characters inspired all manner of art and commercial enterprises, imitations and parodies burgeoned, sequels appeared, and poems that Charles never wrote were attributed to him. Charles continued to generate new ideas connected with the *Alice* books. On October 29, 1888, he "invented a 'stamp-case,' which I got [his sister] Louisa to make for me. I hope to get it published." Macmillan refused to distribute the case, but Emberlin and Son of Oxford published it, and it went on sale with a miniature pamphlet entitled *Eight or Nine Wise Words about Letter-Writing,* both tucked neatly inside an envelope.

Charles designed the stamp case himself. Drawings of Alice appear on the case and the cover, and the case produces two neat tricks. When one pulls it out from the cover, the cover picture of Alice holding the Duchess's baby is replaced by one of her holding the pig; likewise, on the back the entire Cheshire Cat is replaced by the residual grin. The case, when unfolded, contains slots for various denominations of postage stamps. On September 15, 1889, Charles, at Eastbourne, sent a prepublication copy of the stamp case to Mary Jackson, a chum of Isa Bowman, and he enclosed in one of the stamp slots a letter the size of a postage stamp.[21]

*Eight or Nine Wise Words about Letter-Writing,* while enormously entertaining, grew out of some actual disappointments, like the one described in a letter (April 27, 1892) to Nellie Thorne, niece of the actress Sarah Thorne:

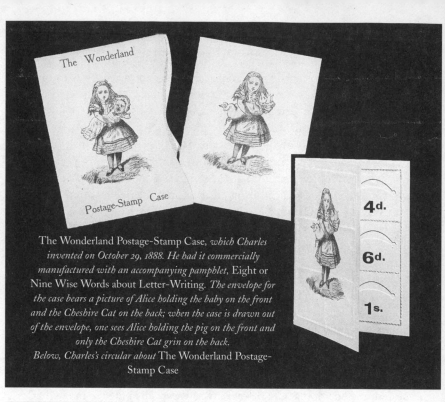

The Wonderland Postage-Stamp Case, *which Charles invented on October 29, 1888. He had it commercially manufactured with an accompanying pamphlet,* Eight or Nine Wise Words about Letter-Writing. *The envelope for the case bears a picture of Alice holding the baby on the front and the Cheshire Cat on the back; when the case is drawn out of the envelope, one sees Alice holding the pig on the front and only the Cheshire Cat grin on the back. Below, Charles's circular about* The Wonderland Postage-Stamp Case

Oh dear, oh dear, what vague creatures girls are! Here is Norah writing to me (who have undertaken to meet her in London) that she will arrive at "Euston" on "Friday": but she names no *hour:* evidently she expects me to stand on the cheerless platform for 24 hours at a stretch. And, while I am still simmering in wrath at *this,* I get a letter from Nellie, telling me she is "going to play" in "a first piece" at the Vaudeville, but naming no *date,* and not giving the *name of the piece,* and adding "I hope if you come to Town while I am acting that you will come and see me": evidently *she* expects me to attend that theatre every night for the next few months, till she appears!

Now I'll give you a heap of good advice. When you ask a friend to come and see you act, state (in round numbers) the *year* in which you expect to appear, and give (within 15 letters) the initials of the *piece.* Also, if his name happens to be "Dodgson," don't omit the "g" in writing to him. Also, if he happens to live at an Oxford College, don't call it "Christ College" ("Christ College" is at *Cambridge*). . . . Also, when you've directed your letter to him, don't suddenly lose your temper, and hurl it to the ground, and trample on it with muddy boots! That has evidently been the fate of your last letter to me: and I've laid the envelope aside, as a memorandum of the sort of child *Nellie* is!

The essay itself is practical, sensible, and tongue-in-cheek. Some of the cardinal rules it sets down are: Read through the letter you are answering before you begin writing the answer; address and stamp the envelope in advance; put your return address and the date on the top of the letter; write legibly; don't fill more than a page and a half with apologies for not having written sooner; if your correspondent has made a severe remark, ignore it or answer it with something less severe; and so on.

The *Postage-Stamp Case* along with *Eight or Nine Wise Words* sold for one shilling and was still available in stationers' shops for that price well into the twentieth century. Today, however, when one comes up for sale, it can easily fetch one hundred pounds.

When a poet friend inquired of Charles on behalf of her brother whether Messrs. Barringer, Wallis and Manners, Tin Plate Decorators and Manufacturers of Decorated Enamelled Tin Boxes, might undertake to manufacture a *Looking-Glass* biscuit tin, Charles asked (April 14, 1891) "for more information . . . as I do not the least know what 'a children's tin' *is.*" The tin manufacturers sent Charles samples, Charles was pleased with their artistic merit, gave permission (April 21, 1891) "for the *Alice* pictures to be similarly treated," and further agreed (February 14, 1892) to the tins bearing the legend "by permission of Lewis Carroll" or "of the author." On March 30 he wrote to say that a sample box "seems charming," and on April 1 that the "*Alice* tin is indeed a great success." Despite his contretemps with the manufacturer, fifty thousand tins decorated with characters from *Looking-Glass* in color were produced, and Charles sent three hundred to his family, to the Albany children, and to many other friends. The tins are among the rarest Carrollian collector's items today. An inscribed tin he sent to Alice survives in the Pierpont Morgan Library.

The House of Macmillan remained Charles's publisher to the end. The relationship, begun in 1863, lasted thirty-five years, and was a credit to both author and publisher, who together made publishing, book production, and bookselling history. Charles was never easy to please, and his insistence upon perfection could have driven any but the most patient publisher to break with him. But he was also considerate and generous as well as gifted, and Alexander Macmillan must have valued those qualities in him, just as Charles valued the firm's patience and reliability.

On April 28, 1871, Charles, having detected a misunderstanding in his correspondence with Macmillan, wrote: "I began dealing with your house with full confidence in it in every way—and that confidence is undiminished." After Alexander Macmillan retired and Frederick Macmillan took over, the firm grew larger and efficiency and personal attention declined. Charles was not one to overlook cursory treatment, and his letters to the firm and his diaries reflect his irritation: "I fear the Firm is going down, and I may have to find another publisher," he noted (December 13, 1889). But he did not leave Macmillan. In important matters he got his way, and as late as March 20, 1896, he was able to write Frederick Macmillan: "Thanks for your letter, and especially for what you say about not accepting any share of the profits, should any such accrue, of a French Edition of *Symbolic Logic*. It is by no means the first time that I have had to notice, with gratitude, the handsome way in which my Publishers deal with me." Charles's most lavish tribute to Macmillan, however, came in a snippet of a quote in Collingwood from *The Profits of Authorship*, an essay which has gone lost:

> The publisher contributes about as much as the bookseller in time and bodily labour, but in mental toil and trouble a great deal more. I speak, with some personal knowledge of the matter, having myself, for some twenty years, inflicted on that most patient and painstaking firm,

Messrs. Macmillan and Co., about as much wear and worry as ever publishers have lived through. The day when they undertake a book for me is a *dies nefustus* for them. From that day till the book is out—an interval of some two or three years on an average—there is no pause in "the pelting of the pitiless storm" of directions and questions on every conceivable detail. To say that every question gets a courteous and thoughtful reply—that they are still outside a lunatic asylum—and that they still regard me with some degree of charity—is to speak volumes in praise of their good temper and of their health, bodily and mental.[22]

Charles's most exacting efforts of the 1890s went into his three-layered work on symbolic logic, beginning with elementary and reaching ethereal, theoretical heights. He did not, however, work systematically from simple to complex but shifted from one to the other, conducting something of a logical three-ring circus.

Only in recent years have we become aware of the extent to which Charles pushed out the intellectual boundaries of thinking about logic while simplifying the subject and seeking to make it all easier to comprehend. He was in constant exchange with other pundits tilling similar furrows and published his findings in learned papers and journals, questioning others' assertions and asking daunting logic questions. Eventually he produced "one of the most brilliantly eccentric logic textbooks ever written."[23]

His first volume, *Symbolic Logic; Part I, Elementary* appeared in February 1896. He addressed schoolteachers in a separately printed prospectus:

> Any one, who has to superintend the education of young people (say between 12 and 20 years of age), must have realised the importance of supplying them with healthy mental recreations, to occupy times when both brain and muscles have done their fair share of work for the day.
>
> . . . I claim, for Symbolic Logic, a very high place among recreations that have the nature of games or puzzles; and I believe that any one, who will really *try* to understand it, will find it more interesting and more absorbing than most of the games or puzzles yet invented.
>
> . . . Symbolic Logic has one *unique* feature, as compared with games and puzzles, which entitles it, I hold, to rank above them all. . . . The accomplished Logician has not only enjoyed himself, all the time he was working . . . but he finds himself . . . the holder of an "Open Sesame!" to an inexhaustible treasure-house of varied interest. He may apply his

skill to any and every subject of human thought: in every one of them it will help him to get *clear* ideas, to make *orderly* arrangement of his knowledge, and, more important than all, to detect and unravel the *fallacies* he will meet with in every subject he may interest himself in.

People harbor three false ideas about the study of logic, Charles claims: that it is too hard for average intellects, that it is dry and uninteresting, and that it is useless. He rebuts all three and concludes with a modest claim: "This is, I believe, the very first attempt (with the exception of my own little book, *The Game of Logic* . . .) that has been made to *popularise* this fascinating subject. . . . But if it should prove, as I hope it may, to be of *real* service to the young, and to be taken up, in High Schools and in private families, as a valuable addition to their stock of healthful mental recreations, such a result would more than repay ten times the labour that I have expended on it."

In his effort to make the rigors of logic easier, he uses diagrams, but his most significant contribution is his inventive wit, for he couched his examples in humor and sought to help his readers learn without a mighty struggle.

He begins with syllogisms, by setting his reader to solve problems or puzzles with three propositions; gradually he works them up to more difficult problems with as many as ten premises. In all cases, one has to proceed logically to find the solution. If one follows Charles's cardinal rule of never moving beyond a point until one has mastered it, one may progress slowly and comprehend the more difficult exercises.

Charles's propositions feature an enormous and amusing cast of players: Achilles and the Tortoise, small girls and a sympathetic friend, a crocodile and a liar, a logician fond of pork chops, and a gambler—and we meet three barbers, five liars, and other odd characters.

*Symbolic Logic, Part I* earned favorable notices. The *Athenaeum* (October 17, 1896) gave it more than a full page, describing it as "well arranged" and praising it because "its expositions are lucid . . . and not a few witty and amusing. . . ." It is "an interesting and useful little work." The *Educational Times* (July 1) judged it "a *tour de force* of originality, throwing light on its subject from fresh angles."

Charles's contribution to the grand historical sweep of formal logic is not significant in this first volume: he intended merely to introduce his readers to the discipline of thinking logically, not to make a major contribution. By devising a more flexible box diagram to supplant earlier circle diagrams for illustrating relationships, he did improve a traditional crutch. It is his drama and humor that raise his exercises above the ordinary and claim a significant niche for him. His genius lay in dressing logic in a literary garment and giving a splash of color to it.

His work should not be underestimated. The logic that underpins his *Alice* books, the *Snark,* and other creative products, as well as Charles's distinct method and style, influenced logicians of the twentieth century, who in turn broke new ground and often used Charles's work as a point of departure. Philip E. B. Jourdain added an appendix of leading passages from the *Alice* books to *The Philosophy of Mr. B\*rtr\*nd R\*ss\*ll* (1918); and R. B. Braithwaite, writing in 1932, reported that "in Cambridge it is now *de rigueur* for economists as well as logicians to pretend to derive their inspiration from Lewis Carroll."[24] Serious mathematicians and stolid philosophers to this day smile wryly when they refer to Charles's Barber-Shop Paradox or his Moonlight Sonata and Guinea Pig problem. Many have tried to imitate him and inject drama and humor into their own work, but usually with lumbering and ponderous results.

The succeeding two volumes of *Symbolic Logic* were meant to be "Advanced" and "Transcendental," and Charles worked away at them. He had much of both volumes worked out in manuscript and almost all of volume 2 set in type when he died. The family, although well-meaning and concerned about his work, were compelled to clear his Christ Church rooms quickly, had to make hasty decisions, burning many seemingly less important papers. Without a doubt parts of the two advanced logic books went up in flames during those unhappy days.

By a marvelous accident of history, however, much of the second volume, though scattered here and there, survived, as have bits and pieces of the third. The late W. W. Bartley III set out, in 1959, to find what he could of Charles's remaining logical work and found enough to keep him on the trail for eighteen years. Early on he found some of Charles's neglected logic papers *in situ* in Christ Church Library. He approached Charles's publisher, but found nothing there. He inquired of Charles's printers, but they had suffered badly in the London Blitz and also had nothing. In time Bartley wrote asking whether I had ever encountered any of Charles's logic, and I reported that in the mid-1960s, when I was searching for Charles's letters, John Sparrow, then Warden of All Souls, sent me a group of Charles's letters on logic written to another Oxford logician, John Cook Wilson, Fellow of Oriel and Wykeham Professor of Logic. Accompanying the letters was a set of proofs of a large portion of Charles's second logic book. Bartley came to examine the papers and, as he put it, "had the exhilarating experience, in Cohen's apartment in Greenwich Village, of reading for the first time three of the books (that is, chapters) . . ." of Charles's second book on symbolic logic. In 1977 Bartley published this material and everything else he found of Charles's logic, making possible, for the first time, a valid assessment of Charles's contribution.

Although not all logicians agree with Bartley, he makes high claims for Charles's work in *Symbolic Logic, Part II,* asserting that he reached "beyond the practice of his Cambridge contemporaries," the avant-garde logicians of the time. He points out that in solving logical problems Charles employed "truth tables." Even here, Charles's ingenuity continued to breathe free, as did his paradoxical wit, his dramatic power, and his ability to create humorous examples.[25] Bartley also shows that after working with truth tables as early as 1894, Charles proceeded, between 1894 and 1896, to develop a "Method of Trees" to determine "the validity of what were . . . highly complicated arguments." As Charles's truth tables anticipate work to be done in the 1920s, so his method of trees anticipates "Semantic Tableaux," which did not appear until 1955.[26]

The Cook Wilson connection was crucial, and not just because it allowed Charles's work to survive. British logicians were mostly concentrated at Cambridge during Charles's life, while he worked in virtual isolation at Oxford, where logic was not in fashion. His only logic colleague was Cook Wilson, who publicly criticized his work on symbolic logic in what appears now as a prolegomenon to his later outbursts against Bertrand Russell and Alfred North Whitehead's remarkable *Principia Mathematica* (1910). Charles, eager to convince Wilson and to have his reaction, sent him a set of proofs of his work on part 2. A correspondence ensued, and when Cook Wilson died, the proofs passed to A. S. L. Farquharson, editor of Wilson's papers, who turned them over to Sparrow.

Charles and Wilson had clashed in print earlier. On February 21, 1891, Charles wrote to the mathematical editor of the *Educational Times* offering to review E. T. Dixon's *The Foundation of Geometry.* "The book is on the 'direction' theory," Charles recorded, "and involves, I believe, the same logical fallacy as lies at the root of Wilson's treatise." Wilson, Dixon, and Charles were all inquiring into the origins of axiomatic truths, or first principles, and Charles believed that the other two incorrectly accepted as axioms propositions that Euclid had proved.

Charles and Wilson met for the first time in the 1880s. Charles noted (February 27, 1885) that Wilson "called about his MS. on Parallels, which he had sent me to read. He has *tried* to prove Euclid's last axiom, but of course in vain." On April 25 Wilson "came about 9, and staid till nearly 1 a.m. discussing parallels: he has made some curious discoveries—but Euclid's axiom remains unproved." On November 23, 1886, Wilson dined with Charles, "and we talked afterwards till nearly midnight about his series of Theorems for proving Euc. Ax. 12. He uses infinite *lines,* but not as infinite *magnitudes,*" Charles noted. On May 30, 1891, "Wilson came in to talk about 'Direction,' and I found that all I have done about 'grills' has been worked by him, and some I have done wrong! I shall omit that chapter." On January 21, 1893, Charles was "still unsuccessfully trying to convince . . . Wilson . . . that he has committed a fallacy!"

Relations became strained, evidently, and on February 5 Charles "heard from . . . Wilson, who has long declined to read a paper (which I sent January 12, and which seems to me to *prove* the fallacy of a view of his about Hypotheticals). He now offers to read it, if *I* will study a proof he sent, that another Prob. of mine had contradictory data. I have accepted his offer, and studied, and answered, his paper. So I now look forward hopefully to the result of his reading mine." But we find no record of a reply from Wilson. A year later (February 1, 1894), Charles was jubilant: "I got from . . . Wilson what I have been long trying for, an *accepted* transcript of the fallacious argument over which we have had an (apparently) endless fight. I think the end is near, *now.*" And on March 31 Charles reported: "Have just got printed, as a leaflet, *A Disputed Point in Logic*—the point . . . Wilson and I have been arguing so long. This paper is *wholly* in his own words, and puts the point very clearly. I think of submitting it to all my logical friends."

As was his fashion, Charles set up the argument as a dialogue between "Nemo" (Wilson) and "Outis" (Charles), again choosing names that mean "Nobody." But before doing more with the dispute, Charles rewrote the problem and put it into an entirely different dramatic format, about three alphabetical men: Allen, Brown, and Carr. Charles had it printed in May and pursued the matter further; instead of sending copies only to logic friends, he sent another version of it to *Mind,* the quarterly review of psychology and philosophy, and it appeared in July. Here the problem emerges through a dialogue between "Uncle Joe" (Wilson) and "Uncle Jim" (Charles), still about Allen, Brown, and Carr. Before he was done with the problem, which became known as the "Barber-Shop Paradox," Charles wrote eight different versions of it.

Its appearance in *Mind* elicited various solutions from some of the most highly respected logical thinkers of the day. John Venn, whose earlier work on symbolic logic Charles was trying to improve, published a solution in his own book entitled *Symbolic Logic* in 1894; Alfred Sidgwick published two papers on the subject, also in *Mind* in 1894 and 1895; W. E. Johnson did likewise, in the same numbers of *Mind* as Sidgwick.

Charles did not give up: the problem of hypotheticals haunted him. When replies to the letter he sent to his logic friends arrived, he collated them, evaluated them, and awarded them points. "I am in correspondence with about a dozen logicians," he wrote to the logician James Welton.[27]

"I am giving all my time to Logic," he wrote (December 11, 1894), "and have at least got a workable theory of Hypotheticals." On December 21 he recorded: "My night's thinking over the very puzzling subject of Hypotheticals seems to have evolved a new idea—that there are 2 kinds, (1) where the Protasis is *in*dependent of the Hypothetical, (2) where it is dependent on it." Although he kept working on the problem, not until after his death did the importance of his work gain recognition.

Bertrand Russell discusses Charles's Paradox in *The Principles of Mathematics* (1903). Even Wilson, shortly after Charles's death, paid tribute to Charles in a lecture he gave, and in 1905 he published an article in *Mind* finally accepting Charles's solution.[28] In 1950 Charles's Paradox was again at the center of two essays in *Mind,* by the logicians Irving Copi and Arthur W. Burks, and it continues to provoke discussion in connection with material implication and modal logic.

Charles published "What the Tortoise Said to Achilles," another part of book 2 of his opus, in *Mind,* arguing that universal hypotheses or natural laws must be included in the premises of explanatory arguments to avoid the logical absurdity of infinite regress. This section too is cast as a drama and leans heavily upon the ancient myth of the race between the Greek hero and the lowly animal, where the handicap in favor of the Tortoise suggests that Achilles can never win the race even if the participants raced into infinity. In Charles's tale, the race is less important than the conversation between Achilles and the Tortoise, with its puns and playful references to the *Alice* books. The exchange is in fact a complex logical fusillade, but the final image and exchange are choice. Achilles ends up sitting on the Tortoise's back, "writing in his note-book." The Tortoise speaks:

"Have you got that last step written down? Unless I've lost count, that makes a thousand and one. There are several millions more to come. And *would* you mind, as a personal favour—considering what a lot of instruction this colloquy of ours will provide for the Logicians of the Nineteenth Century—*would* you mind adopting a pun that my cousin the Mock-Turtle will then make, and allowing yourself to be re-named Taught-Us?"

"As you please!" replied the weary warrior, in the hollow tones of despair, as he buried his face in his hands. "Provided that *you*, for *your* part, will adopt a pun the Mock-Turtle never made, and allow yourself to be re-named A Kill-Ease!"

A three-page manuscript in Christ Church Library entitled "An Inconceivable Conversation between S. and D. on Indivisibility of Time and Space" shows that Charles was working on the problem as early as November 1874.[29]

"What the Tortoise Said to Achilles" has become a standard item of discussion among logicians and philosophers. William A. Wisdom, writing in 1974, lists half a dozen of the most important responses to Charles,[30] and Bartley augments them and explains some.[31] Jourdain cites Charles's two papers in *Mind* as exceptional, particularly "What Achilles Said to the Tortoise," which is, for logicians, "a beautiful insight into the need to distinguish theory from meta-theory in logic. . . ."[32] R. B. Braithwaite asserts that Charles "was ploughing deeper than he knew. His mind was permeated by an admirable logic which he was unable to bring to full consciousness and explicit criticism. It is this that makes his . . . casual puzzles so profound."[33]

These casual puzzles underlie all Charles's creative work and are essential for grasping his cast of mind, but the final assessment has yet to be made, even if only of the fractured shards. Bartley and Braithwaite offer lavish evaluations; others, not least of all P. T. Geach, while conceding that "the great attraction" of Charles's work "is the collection of ingenious and amusing concrete examples and puzzles," believes Bartley's claims "absurdly exaggerated."[34] Nevertheless, as time passes, Charles's work earns plaudits. In 1979 D. R. Hofstadter tried, for instance, to rekindle a pedagogic interest in Carroll's logic. "It is a great pity for the teaching of logic (and some other subjects)," wrote Ivor Grattan-Guinness in 1991, "that while . . . works by Carroll are still easily available and are even partly translated into several languages, their potential use has not yet been recognized."[35]

To the end Wilson remained Charles's dueling partner. Eleven months before he died, Charles wrote in his diary: "Made a splendid Logic Problem, about 'great-grandsons' (modelled on one by De Morgan). My method of solution is quite new, and I greatly doubt if *any* one will solve the Problem. I have sent it to . . . Wilson."

Between November 1879 and February 1, 1899, when a piece of his appeared posthumously, Charles contributed eleven items to the *Educational Times* on various mathematical and logic problems, almost all of them reprinted, some expanded, in *Mathematical Questions and Solutions from "The Educational Times."* From 1888 onward he printed a series of nine "Papers on Logic," rare items now, that set specific problems in forms of propositions, all dressed in his usual humorous drapery, some meant for his young female logic students. In 1892 he printed a *Challenge to Logicians* with propositions, in June 1894 *A Theorem in Logic,* a mathematical problem in hypotheticals with an algebraical example. In the following year he produced *Logical Nomenclature, Desiderata,* a list of eight cases where logical positions were in need of a distinctive name. He continued to work with numbers, devising what appear to the layman as mysterious and magical formulae, some of which found their way into print. His "Abridged Long Division," for example, appeared in *Nature* (January 20, 1898), six days after his death.

"For the first (and probably only) time in my life," Charles tells his diary (May 21, 1896), "I have passed for 'Press,' *two* books in one day! One being Georgie [Wilcox] Allen's *The Lost Plum-Cake* and the other the second edition of *Symbolic Logic.*" He actually got Macmillan to publish his cousin Mrs. Allen's children's book, and he wrote an introduction, one of his last literary compositions. The story is "A Tale for Tiny Boys"—not girls—but Charles pitched in wholeheartedly nonetheless.

His introduction praises both his cousin's special gift for writing books for very young children and Miss Thomson's clever cover design. Then he addresses mothers on the behavior of their children in church. He knows that although children's attention can be caught by hymn singing, by the lessons and prayers, sermons are usually far beyond their grasp.

> It goes to one's heart to see, as I so often do, little darlings of five or six years old, forced to sit still through a weary half-hour, with nothing to do, and not one word of sermon that they can understand. Most heartily can I sympathize with the little charity-girl, who is said to have written to some friend, "I thinks, when I grows up, I'll never

go to church no more. I thinks I'se getting sermons enough to last me all my life!" But need it be so? Would it be so *very* irreverent to let your child have a story-book to read during the sermon. . . . For my part, I should love to see the experiment tried. I am quite sure it would be a success.

He concludes that Mrs. Allen's book would be an ideal "Sunday-treat" for children to read during sermon-time.

We may marvel at his success, but we are also likely to be saddened by the need that drove him so relentlessly, weakening his constitution, aging him before his time. Perhaps the force that motivated him, that lay behind the feverish activity, behind the austere, oppressive determination, was the need to produce works of serious intent as acts of obeisance, of repentance. In any case, the well of imagination was now running dry, and if it did produce a trickle, that moiety was channeled into the examples or the dramatic dialogues within the serious works, not into fairy tales. The end was near, the battle nearly done.

*One of the late photographs of Charles*

# CHAPTER FIFTEEN

# Gentle into That Good Night

*I have lived long enough, having seen one thing,*
*that death hath an end.*

A. C. SWINBURNE

The cherished image of the real Alice never ceased to live in Charles's memory or to elicit a pang of loss. Through his later years Charles's consolation was to summon up those golden days of yore and let them flash upon his inward eye. Memory carried with it the ache of hope unfulfilled, but it also brought back the days of happy frolic. Since the mid-1860s Charles's relationship with the various Liddells was at best sporadic, but whenever their paths crossed, they all embraced propriety; they were formal, distant, cold—but civil.

Alice's biographer writes about the "cloud" that hung over Alice's horizon. "The rift between Dodgson and their parents was a calamity to all the little girls," Anne Clark writes, "but especially to Alice. She was a most affectionate, tender-hearted child and deeply attached to him. . . . [She] often saw him from afar as he crossed Tom Quad or strode about the High Street and St. Aldate's with that stiff and curiously jerky gait. It pained her not to be able to go to him as before, to bask in his affection and enjoy his inimitable nonsense. There was now a void in her life which could never be filled in the same way again."[1]

After Mrs. Liddell brought the fully grown Ina and Alice to be photographed in Charles's studio on June 25, 1870, few meetings ensued. Those

*Charles's last photograph of Lorina Liddell*

sittings survive and show two rather glum young ladies, dressed formally, their hair properly pinned up, both sitting wooden before Charles's lens. Gone the glee, the old impetuosity.

Throughout the 1870s a deliberate distancing was manifest, and after a few casual encounters, a four-year silence followed. Charles must have been invited to Alice's wedding in Westminster Abbey on September 15, 1880, but we have no evidence that he noted it anywhere. At the time he was at Eastbourne.

On December 19, 1881, Charles attended a Governing Body meeting at Christ Church, when a discussion took place on whether or not to give the college servants Christmas presents. Charles and some colleagues feared setting a precedent that might become "a tax on our successors," and Charles cast the deciding negative vote, observing: "If I had not gone . . . they would have been 7 to 5, and the Dean would most likely have given his 2 votes and casting vote, thus carrying it for this time, and making a precedent difficult to set aside for the future." On the following June 15 (and on June 19, 1884) Charles again opposed the Dean on the issue of appointing R. W. Macan, a controversial churchman, to a vacant studentship.

Toward Christmas 1883 Charles wrote Alice, addressing her as "Dear Mrs. Hargreaves," and sent her a copy of *Rhyme? and Reason?* The letter is warm with reminiscence: "Perhaps the shortest day in the year is not *quite* the most appropriate time for recalling the long dreamy summer afternoons of ancient times: but anyhow if this book gives you half as much pleasure to receive as it does me to send, it will be a success indeed." He signed himself "Sincerely yours" and inscribed the book to "Mrs. Hargreaves, with sincere regards and many pleasant memories of bygone hours in Wonderland, from the Author."

Refurbishments, repairs, and alterations went on in various quarters during these years, and on July 11, 1884, Charles admired a "beautiful view of the Cathedral interior, which, now that the organ is down, can be had from just outside the west door." He feared the Dean would put the organ back, and with Liddon suggested that it be placed at the west end, where indeed it is now.

On March 1, 1885, Charles, forgetting that he had written to Alice just over a year earlier, wrote again: "I fancy this will come to you almost like a voice from the dead, after so many years of silence—and yet, those years have made no difference, that I can perceive, in *my* clearness of memory of the days when we *did* correspond." He goes on to ask whether she would permit him to publish a facsimile of the original *Alice* tale, and if so, whether she would be kind enough to lend him the booklet he had written out for her. "There can be no doubt that I should incur the charge of gross egoism in

*Charles's last photograph of Alice Liddell. He took these rather sullen portraits on June 25, 1870, years after the laughter and the glee had fled from his friendship with the sisters.*

publishing it," he adds. "But I don't care for that in the least: knowing that I have no such motive: only I think, considering the extraordinary popularity the books have had (we have sold more than 120,000 of the two) there must be many who would like to see the original form." She consented; he acknowledged her kindness in a letter on March 7, and on the twenty-first received the manuscript booklet. He wrote five more times in the next twenty months, reporting progress and working out details about the preface and the use of the profits, which he suggested should go to a children's hospital. The book appeared as *Alice's Adventures Under Ground* in 1886, and Charles was magnanimous in sending a copy to Mrs. Liddell inscribed "To Her, whose children's smiles fed the narrator's fancy and were his rich reward."

Along the way, on June 18, Charles attended another Governing Body meeting at which the "Macan question" was finally shelved by appointing a different man Lecturer. On February 6, 1886, the two M.P.'s for Oxford came to Common Room with the Dean, and Charles went over to meet them; and at another Governing Body meeting, on May 26, 1886, Charles and the Dean were, *mirabile dictu,* at one on a single issue: E. F. Sampson moved that Common Room should pay rent for its drawing room. Charles reminded his colleagues that Christ Church had given the dons the room, rent free, in 1878, and consequently it was not a matter that the Governing Body could deal with. "The Dean thought so too," Charles added, "so the matter was deferred."

On October 25, 1887, returning from a hasty visit to London where he had gone to talk to Henry Savile Clarke and Harry Furniss about his projects, Charles had as railway companions Rhoda and Violet Liddell, the two youngest daughters. He noted the occasion in the diary but made no comment. A year later (November 1, 1888), Lorina's husband, W. B. Skene, Christ Church Treasurer, brought "as his guest, Mr. Hargreaves (the husband of 'Alice')," Charles recorded, "who was a stranger to me, though we had met, years ago, as pupil and lecturer. It was not easy to link in one's mind," he adds, "the new face with the olden memory—the stranger with the once-so-intimately known and loved 'Alice,' whom I shall always remember best as an entirely fascinating little 7-year-old maiden."

After he declined to dine with the Liddells and the Duchess of Albany in May 1890, he did go "in the evening, about a quarter to ten, and had a little chat with the Duchess . . . and Mrs., Rhoda, and Violet Liddell, etc." On June 9 Charles, traveling from Guildford back to Oxford, encountered Mrs. Liddell at the Guildford station. She "had come over to look at houses (to take for the summer)," Charles writes. "I had given her the names of the house-agents there. She had a list with her of houses to be enquired about: and went off, at my suggestion, to call at the Chestnuts and get information." On October 17 of that year, returning to Oxford from Eastbourne, he heard "the important news that the Dean means to resign at Christmas."

On November 12 he wrote to Mrs. Liddell, again refusing an invitation to meet the Duchess of Albany at the deanery. He explained at some length his habit of declining *all* invitations and included a paragraph on the Dean's impending retirement, which he calls a

very *great* loss, to the University, the College, the City, and to myself. . . . And, to *me,* life in Christ Church will be a totally different thing when the faces, familiar to me for 36 years, are seen no more among us. It seems but yesterday when the Dean, and you, first arrived: yet I was hardly more than a boy, then; and many of the pleasantest memories of those early years—that foolish time that seemed as if it would last for ever—are bound up with the names of yourself and your children: and now I am an old man, already beginning to feel a little weary of life—at any rate weary of its *pleasures,* and only caring to go on, on the chance of doing a little more *work.*[2]

Four days later Charles had a "remarkable day. The Duchess of Albany was at the Deanery with her children, and sent the children to my room soon after 10. The little Alice is improved, I think, not being so unruly as she was two years ago: they are charming children. I taught them to fold paper pistols, and to blot their names in creased paper, and showed them the machine which, by rapid spinning, turns the edging of a cup, etc., into a filmy solid: and promised to send Alice a copy of *The Fairies* [by William Allingham]. . . . I mark this day with a white stone."

On the following day, the seventeenth, Charles went "across to the Deanery for a minute, just before the Duchess left, to see her." On the nineteenth he wrote Mrs. Liddell another long letter: "I feel that I am largely indebted to *you* (for, if the Royal party had not been staying with *you,* they would assuredly never have come near *me!*) for the unique honour I have enjoyed—enough to make me conceited for the rest of my life. There are, possibly, other commoners who have been honoured by *single* visits from Princesses: but I doubt if any others have ever had *two* visits, in one day from the same Princess!" But, by his own confession, he thirsted for more:

> The honour I now covet is that a certain pair of young ladies should come some day and take tea with me. I have a store of ancient memories of visits from your elder daughters but I do not think that Miss Rhoda and Miss Violet Liddell have ever even been inside my rooms: and I should like to add to my store *one* fresh memory at least, of having had a visit from them. . . . If the reply be favourable, will they kindly choose a day . . . when they have *plenty* of spare time on their hands? I do *not* enjoy brief hurried visits from my young lady friends. A couple of hours would certainly not tire *me* of *them,* however much it might tire *them* of *me!*

Six days later, on the twenty-fifth, the girls did pay a visit: "Rhoda and Violet Liddell came to tea (first time of entering my rooms!). They insisted on waiting on me, as I was laid up with a 'synovitic' knee: and we had a very pleasant 2 hours."

On December 3 he had a "yet more wonderful experience. Mrs. Liddell and Mrs. Skene came to tea, and proved very pleasant guests." Within the week, on the ninth, Charles, learning that "Mrs. Hargreaves, the original 'Alice,' is now at the Deanery . . . invited her also over to tea. She could not do this, but very kindly came over, with Rhoda, for a short time in the afternoon." Charles gave Alice one of his *Postage-Stamp Cases*, inscribed to "Mrs. Hargreaves, from the Inventor." And that is the last mention of Alice by name in the diary.

On January 7, 1892, Charles wrote to Alice to ask whether he might send her some umbrella handles carved in ivory representing characters from the *Alice* books which a friend of his had sent him. On the first of March he went to Christ Church Library, "to aid in presentation, to Mrs. Liddell," of a portrait of her husband that Hubert von Herkomer had been commissioned to paint: "New Dean presented it, in a graceful speech, to which she made a very feeling reply." Charles's name does not appear, however, in an album of well-wishing signatories presented to the Dean.

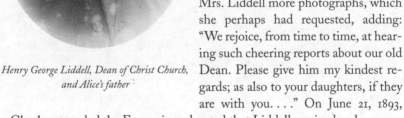

On February 2, 1893, Charles sent Mrs. Liddell more photographs, which she perhaps had requested, adding: "We rejoice, from time to time, at hearing such cheering reports about our old Dean. Please give him my kindest regards; as also to your daughters, if they are with you. . . ." On June 21, 1893,

*Henry George Liddell, Dean of Christ Church, and Alice's father*

Charles attended the Encaenia and noted that Liddell received an honorary doctorate of civil law.

Thus ends the tale of Charles's friendship with the Liddell family. The Liddells lived on, the Dean and his wife in retirement at Ascot, Alice with her family at Cuffnells, near Lyndhurst in Hampshire, but their paths and Charles's do not cross again. Charles lived on a few more years, becoming more and more withdrawn, "having now settled down into the hermit-life of old age," as he put it to Lord Salisbury (June 7, 1897), declining an invitation to Hatfield.

The Liddells' impact on Christ Church, the university, and on the town of

Oxford was formidable. "He did more than any one of his time to bring the University and the City into harmonious relations," wrote his biographer.[3] From 1870 to 1874 he was Vice-Chancellor, and in 1881, when A. P. Stanley died, he was offered, but refused, the deanery of Westminster. He remained strikingly handsome into old age, a classic figure, almost a colossus.

The *Lexicon* alone gave him a genuine claim to scholarly distinction. But he also produced, in the year that he became Dean, a two-volume *History of Ancient Rome,* and he spent the rest of his life adding, altering, revising, and condensing both his *Lexicon* and *History.* The *Lexicon* was really the first of its kind, used by students and scholars, and it was a reflection on the Liddell posture, grandeur, and aloof bearing that provoked dons and undergraduates alike to compose and circulate amusing anecdotes and jingles about the man and his work. One such runs:

> Two men wrote a Lexicon, Liddell and Scott;
> One half was clever, one half was not.
> Give me the answer, boys, quick, to the riddle,
> Which was by Scott, and which was by Liddell?

Variations on the theme were current, for example:

> Part of it's good, and part of it's rot:
> The part that is good was written by Scott:
> By Liddell was written the part that is not.

Political bias and even jealousy do not entirely explain the repeated imputations by Liddell's contemporaries. Even his own disciple-biographer painted him as "unsympathetic in demeanour."[4] To undergraduates he "perhaps for many years presented a somewhat stern aspect." He "was not ready with compliments, and he was not given to many words when commenting on work and conduct."[5] The painter William Blake Richmond recalled that one had to choose one's words carefully in the Dean's presence: "Those . . . rash enough not to do so, brought a cartload of bricks down on them without delay."[6] Margaret L. Woods found his "manner . . . always haughty."[7] "Among some of the Oxford undergraduates the Dean was not always popular," wrote a commentator on "Politics and Persons" in the *St. James's Gazette,* who quotes a member of Christ Church reminiscing "a few years ago":

I wondered at his unpopularity, for no one could be more courteous or more scrupulously just and impartial. . . . He was quite capable of making a caustic remark in the peculiar Oxford manner. On one occasion he was taking stock of the intellectual attainments of an undergraduate who vaunted himself to be somebody. "What Sophocles do you know?" inquired the Dean. "Oh, I know all Sophocles," was the ready answer. "Really," was the Dean's reply. "How I wish I could say the same!" The youth then proceeded to translate, and gave an extraordinary rendering to one of the phrases. "Where did you get that from?" asked the Dean. "Oh, Liddell and Scott" was the answer. "Then," said the Dean with much gravity, "I am sure it must have been Dr. Scott, and not I."

Other observers were harsher. A niece of Alice told me point-blank that the Dean was "a pompous bore" and Mrs. Liddell "a prude." "From a theological viewpoint Liddell proved an even damper squib than Jowett," writes the historian W. R. Ward; and the Regius Professor of Modern History at Oxford, E. A. Freeman, himself a staunch liberal, asserts that it proved "the hollowness of Oxford liberalism that they cannot see through such a humbug" as Liddell, who was "a rogue as well as a 'blockhead and blunderer.' "[8] On a lighter note, when the Oxford Union launched a campaign for funds to restore its premises, Robert Cecil, third son of the Prime Minister and an undergraduate at University College, appealed to his father, Lord Salisbury, for a contribution. The father complied but confided that he sent the money only after "very complicated negotiations" and that it came as "a ransom by which your mother has escaped the obligation of dancing with the Dean of Christ Church."[9]

When the January 30, 1875, number of *Vanity Fair* appeared with a caricature of Liddell in its "Men-of-the-Day" series, the author of the biographical blurb was aware, as the artist "Ape" clearly was when he painted Liddell with turned-up nose, that the Dean appeared somewhat too self-satisfied: "Dr. Liddell is a great man in the University of Oxford. . . . He has so comprehended the relative importance of men and things as to believe most thoroughly in the necessity for maintaining the British Aristocracy as a superior and privileged race. . . . Dignified in appearance and with much superficial sternness of demeanour, he . . . is . . . fine-looking, and thoroughly domesticated."

Domesticated indeed, for he seems to have bowed his lofty head only to his lady. And she, by marrying this nephew of a baron and first cousin of an earl, raised her station considerably and quickly saw her mission in life as leading her family into higher social prominence. In this enterprise she had more than her husband's birthright and credentials to aid her, for she was herself a beauty, a forceful woman, an engaging raconteur and disputant, and, if on occasion fiery and sharp in opinion and criticism, all the same a magnetic personality. When, in 1859, the royals sent the Prince of Wales to Oxford for his university education, their having known Liddell since his Westminster days, when he was domestic chaplain to Prince Albert, no doubt influenced them. Mrs. Liddell must have taken great satisfaction in the visits from the Queen herself, from seeing princes and princesses strung like exotic pearls around her dinner table.

Mrs. Liddell's hunger for aristocrats had no bounds. She was an insatiable collector of the "right" people and, whether she knew them or not, ardently sought and amassed their autographs. One short letter from Thackeray to the Dean was a special prize all her life and she mentioned it in her will.[10] And yet she destroyed all the letters that Charles wrote to her children—"he must have written . . . [them] hundreds . . . ," Alice's son Caryl wrote[11]—evidence enough of her disdain. She would not let her daughters retain reminders of what she saw as Charles's overzealous attentions, which she judged excessive, intrusive, improper, perhaps impure. Did she not value those letters for their commercial worth alone, for Charles was clearly a rising literary star? Apparently not. When the Dean died and she commissioned his friend H. L. Thompson to write his life, she saw to it that neither Charles nor the *Alice* books were mentioned, not once. Her distaste for Charles, in spite of all outward appearance, was deep, firm, and permanent. Sadly, the letters that the young Alice wrote to Charles do not survive either, having probably met a similar fate as his to her at the hands of Charles's heirs.

Mrs. Liddell governed the deanery with an iron hand. Charles's unkind parody of her as Tabikat, the domineering wife of the evil sub-warden in *Sylvie and Bruno,* underscored her reputation of being "catty" and pushy. Some of the jingles that went the rounds suggest the same. One written in my copy of Thompson's life of the Dean, published in 1899, bears an inscription that places the origin of the quatrain at the time the Liddells ruled the roost; it reads "Christ Church 1867":

An Oxford Epigram

I am the Dean and this is Mrs. Liddell,
She plays the first, and I the second fiddle.
She is the Broad; I am the High:
And we are the University.

Proper though Mrs. Liddell was, she stood on no ceremony in her relentless search for highborn suitors for her daughters. On October 15, 1884, the young Robert Cecil wrote home to his mother: "Mrs. Liddell has had the impudence to ask me to dinner. I don't know the old hag and don't want to and so have refused rather shortly."[12]

In 1872, when the Queen decided that her youngest son, Prince Leopold, should follow his elder brother to Christ Church, the decision must have given Mrs. Liddell considerable satisfaction, even though the Prince was not robust and suffered from hemophilia. The Dean and Mrs. Liddell took particular interest in the young royal, inviting him to the deanery on all suitable occasions. Those visits became "more and more frequent," Anne Clark writes, "for was not the Dean his mentor; was not the Deanery at Christ Church the hub around which the social life of Oxford revolved? And was not the Dean's wife sympathetic and understanding; and were not her daughters charming, gifted and very beautiful?"[13] The Prince even attended Lorina's wedding to W. B. Skene on February 7, 1874.

Marriage was in the air, and in that season when the eldest Liddell daughter wed Skene, Fellow of All Souls and a wealthy landowner—not a bad catch—Mrs. Liddell hoped for an even better match for her second daughter, Alice. The carefully kept secret was that Prince Leopold had fallen in love with Alice and she with him. When the Prince completed his undergraduate studies and was in Oxford to attend Commemoration, everywhere "he went, Alice was with him, always accompanied by her mother and sisters." At Encaenia, when "the Vice-Chancellor presented the Prince with his diploma, the crowd cheered and sang 'For he's a jolly good fellow.' It was a proud and emotional moment, especially for Alice as she watched the young man who had come to mean so much to her."[14]

Nothing, alas, came of the romance. The Queen's priorities were quite different from Mrs. Liddell's. She insisted that her sons marry royalty and undoubtedly quashed Leopold's affair with Alice. The Prince, like so many British royals, looked to Germany, married Princess Helen Frederica Augusta, daughter of H.S.H. George Victor, Prince of Waldeck-Pyrmont.

Charles's path crossed the Prince's during the Prince's undergraduate days. When Robinson Duckworth was tutor to the Prince, Charles noted (November 12, 1867) that he sent Duckworth a collection of autograph letters for his royal pupil, obviously another autograph collector. Even while the Prince was courting Alice, Charles wrote (May 24, 1875) to the Prince's tutor, then R. H. Collins, to ask if the Prince would sit for a photograph.

Collins replied "that the Prince will sit" and asked Charles to lunch. Charles paid his "first (possibly my only) visit to Wykeham House [May 25]: We were six at luncheon. . . . I found myself treated as senior guest, and had to sit next to the young host, who was particularly unassuming and genial in manner: I do not wonder at his being so universal a favourite. . . . I showed the Prince a few photographs I had taken with me, and after arranging for a sitting on Wednesday next, took my leave." On June 2, "the Prince came alone about 11-½. . . . He staid till nearly 1, and I took 2 photographs of him, but neither was quite free from moving. He looked over a number of photographs, and chose some for me to give him." At least one of Charles's takes of the Prince was good enough for Charles to keep as part of his own collection.

*Charles's photograph of Prince Leopold, Queen Victoria's youngest son, who courted Alice*

Five years after the Prince died, Charles encountered the Prince's widow, the Duchess of Albany, and her two children for the first time, at Hatfield House, found them pleasant, and cultivated a friendship, particularly with the children, Prince Charles and Princess Alice. Certainly he saw the irony of his becoming friendly with the surviving children of the Prince who wooed, if he did not wed, Alice Liddell.

When the Prince and Alice appeared to be more than friends, Charles launched his most virulent attacks upon the Dean and, indeed, upon Mrs. Liddell's "king-fisher" activities. His unbridled vitriol may well have had something to do with the rejection and the pain he suffered as he stood by, an observer where he might have been a participant.

But Charles was not the only observer-critic of the drama being played out at the deanery. In the same year that he published *The Vision of the Three T's*, which was devastating enough, an anonymous lampoon even more humiliating descended upon the university community. *Cakeless*, a verse drama dressed in Greek names and togas, satirizes the Liddell parents' jockeying for suitable suitors for their three daughters. It wields a blade even sharper than Charles's and must have cut deeper into the Dean and Mrs. Liddell's composure. Lorina was already wed to Skene in real life, but in the piece

Skene is not good enough, despite his extensive landholdings. Much better is required for the other three, and possible suitors are named: Yerbua (Aubrey Harcourt, the Earl of Sheffield's grandson and the son of E. W. Harcourt, of Nuneham Park, M.P. for Oxford; the young Harcourt had been once engaged to Alice's sister Edith, who died the previous year) and Rivulus (Lord Brooke, at that time an undergraduate at Christ Church, who would later become fifth Earl of Warwick). Psyche, the youngest daughter, announces that she has "trapped a Pr*nce, the youngest of his race," named Regius, evidently meant to be Prince Leopold, the author not having observed carefully enough whom the Prince was courting.

A triple wedding takes place in the second act. At the outset, among the wedding party, settled in the church, is Kraftsohn (Dodgson) "biting his nails." He interrupts the ceremony: "I do protest against this match, so let me speak." Apollo (the Dean), "irate," gives orders: "Strip, strip him, scouts! this is the knave we seek."

> Kraftsohn: By circles, segments, and by radii,
> Than yield to these I'd liefer far to die.

The scouts descend upon him and he must flee to the cloisters. Romanus, one of the Dean's entourage, directs the scout phalanx:

> Take him through trench and tunnel to the chest,
> Nor ever leave the cursed fiend at rest.
> Leave him in Wonderland with some hard-hitting foe,
> And through the looking-glass let him survey the blow;
> Confine him in the belfry, not in Peck,
> And make him sign at pleasure your blank cheque.

The scouts obey and lock Kraftsohn in the belfry. Apollo is so pleased to get rid of him that he forgives his wife (Diana) when the wedding cake does not arrive:

> Bother the cake! yonder within the chest
> My foeman Kraftsohn bites his nails at rest.

Act 3 moves to the belfry, where Kraftsohn is imprisoned, still biting his nails in rage:

> My fate is sealed; my race is run,
> My pilgrimage is wellnigh done.

Farewell to pamphlets and to angles round!
I seek a shore where Euclid is not found.[15]

*Cakeless* stuck in the Dean's throat. He suppressed it and had its author, later identified as John Howe Jenkins, sent down.

But what about Alice Liddell; what happened to her? If she bore any affection for Charles, she was first forced to repress it. Then her strong attachment to Prince Leopold went nowhere. She clearly suffered more than her share of emotional battering. The death of her sister Edith having occurred in the same season as the demise of her affair with the Prince, she must have been miserable during much of 1876. But, according to Clark, "she sought to forget the sorrows . . . in a whirl of gaiety."[16] Holidays away from Oxford were the prescription. One evening in 1878, during a visit to Scotland, Clark reports, "Alice and Rhoda astonished the company with conjuring tricks, a relic no doubt of the days when Charles Dodgson had taught Alice to practice sleight of hand."

But earlier, even while Prince Leopold paid court to Alice, she was already the idol of another Christ Church undergraduate, ironically a pupil of Charles's, Reginald Gervis Hargreaves, the only son of a wealthy mill owner and property magnate from Lancashire. Reginald was a dashing, stylishly dressed young man who cultivated leisure and enjoyed cricket, riding, shooting, clubbing, sailing, and golf. Sent to Eton and then to Christ Church, he trudged his way through both. "He hated Latin and Greek," Clark tells us, "and did not even care for French."[17]

The Hargreaves family began as farmers in the north and later branched out into textiles. Reginald's father succeeded in turning the family's calico printing firm to excellent account, and Reginald, the only son, would inherit a vast estate in the north and another, Cuffnells, which his father bought in the New Forest.

Young Hargreaves fell in love with Alice, danced with her at university balls, took his bachelor's degree in 1878, and proposed marriage in July 1880, when Alice had turned twenty-eight. They were married in Westminster Abbey eight weeks later. The classic Victorian list of wedding presents is recorded, but the name of Charles L. Dodgson is missing. Curious that, and it speaks of Mrs. Liddell's censorious blue pencil, because together with Vere Bayne, Charles gave the couple an R. P. Spiero watercolor of Tom Quad. Clark tells us that Alice treasured the picture "until her dying day."[18]

Cuffnells, the Hampshire house, shut up since Reginald's mother's death in 1872, was reopened, aired, and made suitable for the newlyweds, and here they lived out their lives. Fifteen months after the marriage, their first son, Alan Kynaston, was born. Fifteen months later another son, Leopold Reginald, was born, and the Prince agreed to be godfather. Seven weeks later, when the Prince's first child was born, he named her Alice. Later she became one of Charles's child friends. Finally, four years after Leopold Reginald, a third son arrived and was named Caryl Liddell.

Alice, well trained by her mother in practical matters and manners, made an agreeable chatelaine of the large and beautiful house with its many servants. She and "Regi" sought out society's cream for their soirées, balls, and shooting parties and gave the appearance of a happy, thriving couple with three healthy, growing sons. "And yet curiously," writes Clark, "everyone who knew her commented on an air of sadness . . . never far from the surface. However much she laughed and sang, however much she indulged that insatiable curiosity, the sadness was somehow always there." True, she grieved for her sister Edith, but deeper, even more personal emotions were locked within.

Reginald Hargreaves's estates encountered the fate of so many Victorian country fortunes: the income became inadequate to maintain them. In the early 1890s he began to sell off the northern estate, first the crumbling house and park, then, after the turn of the century, the outlying farms. The proceeds enabled him and Alice to carry on at Cuffnells as before. They continued to live in self-indulgent comfort, lacked for nothing, and were always lavish to their sons. Then a twofold disaster struck: both Alan and Leopold were killed in action during the Great War.

The parents and the younger son carried on as before. Reginald died at Cuffnells on February 14, 1926, aged seventy-three. Caryl inherited Cuffnells, but not enough money to insure a lucrative future either for him or the estate. Well established in a social set in London, he spent most of his time in town. Alice remained at Cuffnells and grew lonely in the huge house, with Caryl making only occasional short visits. Alice did not always approve of Caryl's London life: "There were often raised voices and banged doors," Clark reports. "But they showered affection on each other for all that. He was her life now."[19]

Caryl's lifestyle and the upkeep of Cuffnells created a financial crisis. This time Alice came to the rescue. She had locked away in her study all those magnificent first editions, lovingly inscribed, and the other gifts that Charles had showered upon her so long before—and she had also the unique green leather notebook containing the first manuscript rendering of the Alice story. She decided to sell. Lewis Carroll was now a worldwide household name, his manuscripts and inscribed first editions treasures sought by rich collectors everywhere. No scruple held her back. A Sotheby auction on April 3, 1928, brought Alice £15,400, an enormous sum at that time. According to Alice's niece, she wished to leave Caryl enough money to pay the death duties on Cuffnells. But he was not good with money; he invested it unwisely and lost the lot.

The manuscript booklet, at least, had a dignified future. Initially it was bought by Dr. A. S. W. Rosenbach, who, after exhibiting it in the Philadelphia Free Library, sold it to Eldridge Johnson, president of the Victor Talking Machine Company. Johnson died in 1944, and when the manuscript came up for auction again, in 1946, at the Parke-Bernet Galleries in New York, Rosenbach again bought it, this time for $50,000. The bibliophile Lessing Rosenwald then hatched a plan that would honor everyone concerned: it should go back to its country of origin and become the property of the British nation. Rosenbach could not resist, nor could other benefactors, and on November 6, 1948, Luther Evans, Librarian of Congress, sailed on the *Queen Elizabeth* with the booklet in his charge. For part of the voyage he kept the precious object under his pillow, checking frequently to assure himself that it was still there. On November 12 he appeared with it at the British Museum, where, in a modest ceremony, he presented the treasure to the British nation "as an expression of thanks to a noble people who held Hitler at bay for a long period single-handed." The Archbishop of Canterbury formally accepted the gift and called it "an unsullied and innocent act in a distracted and sinful world—a pure act of generosity." The booklet went on immediate display in the British Museum and has been there under glass ever since.[20]

After Alice sold the manuscript, she lived on at Cuffnells, taking some interest in local affairs. Life had few pleasures, however, for the solitary woman sitting for hours beneath Richmond's painting of the three young Liddell sisters.[21] Gone the dinner parties, the flow of dignitaries, the shooting parties; gone Reginald, gone her two soldier sons, and, though still alive, gone Caryl too. For, against Alice's clear opposition, Caryl, now in his early forties, in June 1929 wed a war widow. The seventy-seven-year-old Alice not only objected to the marriage but thought a widow who remarried immoral. The couple did not dislodge her from Cuffnells; they lived in London, leaving Alice lonelier than ever, a once bright creature made dull by dullness.

Times Wide World Photo.
Mrs. R. L. Hargreaves Arriving
Yesterday From England.

*Alice Hargreaves on a visit to New York to*
*commemorate the hundredth anniversary of*
*Charles's birth. Columbia University*
*awarded her an honorary degree on the*
*occasion.*

But in 1932, the hundredth anniversary of
Charles's birth, Alice was suddenly transformed. The world, by now enthralled by
the *Alice* books, hailed Lewis Carroll as the
greatest children's writer ever. His books
had been translated into dozens of languages, and people from all nations were
ready to celebrate the writer's wit and
wisdom. Columbia University, led by its
dynamic president, Nicholas Murray
"Miraculous" Butler, invited Alice to participate in an elaborate sequence of celebratory
events, enticing her from her country life in
Hampshire to the bright lights and sky-
scrapers of Manhattan. She succumbed,
and the university arranged for her to have
both her sister Rhoda and her son Caryl
come as traveling companions.

News of the eighty-year-old immortal's
arrival in New York was splashed across the
country's newspapers. She was met and
whisked off, by police escort, to a suite in
the Waldorf-Astoria, taken on sightseeing
tours, received by society, and paid homage
by the American reading public. Her visit
inspired a special edition of *Alice,* copies of
which she inscribed, and in a formal ceremony she received an honorary doctorate of
letters from Columbia. She appeared in a
Paramount newsreel and addressed the
American people on the radio, reading from
the letters she had received from Charles in
later years. "America and New York City are
such exciting places that they take me back
to Wonderland," she confided.[22] She and
Caryl were paid to record her reminiscences
of Carrollian days in a long article in the
*New York Times.* Alice blossomed, re-

*Alice Hargreaves as an old woman*

sponded graciously during interviews, and warmly conjured up the past. All this because of her friendship, so long ago, with the rejected Mr. Dodgson.

On her return to England, she participated in the London celebrations of Charles's hundredth birthday. And when the corks stopped popping and the excitement died down, she had yet another busy life before her, because all manner of letters and requests now descended upon her. She was asked to unveil a White Rabbit memorial at Llandudno, where the Liddells once had a summer home, and when she declined, David Lloyd George, the former prime minister, stepped in instead. In time she confessed to Caryl that she was "tired of being Alice in Wonderland. Does it sound ungrateful? It *is*— only I do get tired!"[23] She still felt isolated, however, and rented another house, The Breaches, at Westerham, a mile from her younger sister Rhoda, where she found some solace in family visits. On November 16, 1934, at age eighty-two, she died peacefully. Cuffnells became a hotel, luring guests to stay at the home of the famous Alice. During the Second World War it was used to billet soldiers, but after the war, decayed, it was demolished.

But is that all? Is nothing more to be said about this woman and the way she dealt with the memory of her friendship with Charles, the gifts he gave her, the way she accepted the plaudits and money that came her way because of that friendship?

We have seen that the Liddells valued breeding and social position. Perhaps because Alice saw a veritable parade of aristocratic and royal visitors at the deanery, the Cuffnells Hargreaves aspired to duplicate those connections. Clark tells us that the Hargreaves sons "were never allowed to forget their social class. There was no hob-nobbing with the people in the village. Regi was daring enough to introduce a professional cricketer into the New Forest cricket team," Clark continues, "but this man was not permitted to socialise with the rest of the team because of his inferior status. Artisans were not allowed to use the gentlemen's changing-rooms, much less join them for refreshments and conversation after the game. Good works and charitable acts were one thing, but Alice was acutely class-conscious."[24]

"Cuffnells was a focal point for high society," Clark writes. Lords and ladies came and returned invitations, among them the Duchess of Albany and her daughter Princess Alice; Mr. and Mrs. Gladstone; J. E. Millais; Lord Leighton; and a good many other world figures. Perhaps not surprisingly, the Cuffnells servants called Alice "Lady" Hargreaves.

Alice and her husband chose not to stoop to consort with the surviving Dodgson family, whom they saw as beneath them. The Dodgson family got a cold shoulder even when they wrote with a legitimate inquiry about some historical fact. Alice was not obliged to concern herself with them, of course, but one can only imagine the reaction of Charles's sisters living modestly at the Chestnuts in Guildford when they read about the sale of the *Alice* manuscript.

In the early days, Charles rejoiced in the young Alice's ebullience, but he also knew that beneath her charming and beautiful exterior lurked an unpleasant petulance. Indeed, in chapter 9 of *Looking-Glass,* the Red Queen speaks of Alice's "nasty, vicious temper." The same was apparently true of "Lady" Hargreaves. One of her servants, who customarily arrived at Cuffnells at five-thirty every morning, was supposed to open some shutters. One winter morning the pain of chilblains in her hands prevented her from doing it. Instead she cleaned a fire grate, thinking she would ask one of the other servants to open the shutters later. Suddenly, "she was startled by an icy voice from the doorway. . . . 'I thought I told you to open the shutters before you begin the grate. You know I want it done first thing. Why have you disobeyed me?' " The servant explained, "Alice was a strict disciplinarian, and she had no intention of allowing any of the servants to imagine that she could be disobeyed." She sent another servant into the village to fetch some ointment for the housemaid's hands, but she deducted the cost from her wages—an entire week's pay.[25]

The tale of the chilblained hands is symptomatic. The son of another housemaid at Cuffnells writes in a private letter: "It was whilst dusting that . . . [my mother] broke a vase one day. On telling Mrs. H. of the catastrophe, my mother was, according to her oft-repeated story, thanked for being honest, rebuked for being clumsy and advised [that] all breakages [would] be made good from her wages." Alice, we read, "had been brought up to deal with servants, and knew well the value of letting them know that she was continually on the watch and might turn up at any time to see what was going on, even in the servants' quarters."[26]

One thinks back to the days when Charles and Alice were frequent companions, when he lavished so much attention on her and she responded with wit and charm to his provocative teasing. Did she then feel any emotional attachment to him; did she respond to his love with similar, if younger, even childish affection? She must have felt something, for her preference for him over other companions was real. If so, why did she so steadfastly refuse to speak about Charles up until the celebrations of 1932, when she was drawn into a web of publicity? And if not, why did she give her third son the curious name Caryl? When asked why she chose the name, she said she saw it in a novel just before the child was born. Is that all? Perhaps she did see the name in print, and perhaps, while the name is spelled differently, the sound of it summoned up loving memories, memories that came to mind every time she heard or spoke the name of her youngest son. Perhaps.

Over the last twenty years of his life Charles contemplated bringing out a volume of what he considered his "serious poems." On resigning his lectureship, the list of possible future books contains "Serious Poems." The project remained on a back burner for years. He completed it, however, just before he died, and it appeared posthumously, a slender volume entitled *Three Sunsets and Other Poems.* It contains all but two of the poems in the second "serious" part of *Phantasmagoria and Other Poems,* five new poems, and twelve "fairy fancies" by Gertrude Thomson. These pictures are antiseptic nudes that have nothing to do with the poems, simply pleasant artworks conforming to Charles's taste.

Among the five new items, two come from the *Sylvie and Bruno* books: "A Song of Love"; "Far Away," a romantic piece about a lass who overcomes

*Gertrude Thomson's "fairy fancies" in* Three Sunsets and Other Poems, *Charles's last book, published posthumously*

doubts about her sailor-boy suitor when he brings her a precious pearl; the poem he wrote for the girls' school newspaper in Boston; and two acrostic verses written for the Albany children.

The poems from *Phantasmagoria,* almost all of them composed in the 1850s, are those star-crossed utterances of youth, tales of unrequited love, unfulfilled hopes, rejection, and dismay. The dominant note throughout is the morbid strain that shrouded Charles's life as he grew to manhood. Although these verses were moth-eaten garments of the long ago, they meant a great deal to him, and he offered them up for another showing. They are self-indulgent regressions to an emotional past and, while negligible as poetry, they tell us what was in his heart.

Most of these soul-searing pieces, written either before or in the early days of Charles's involvement with the Liddells and his friendship with Alice, are not products of his estrangement from the Liddells; rather, they are tokens of his early self. They chart the growing awareness of his emotional preferences, his perception that he is different from other men and that the difference bears within it the seeds of tragedy. True, when he wrote them, he was a young man in his twenties, with the usual *Weltschmerz* of romantic youth, influenced by Byron and Tennyson. But when, so many years later, he set himself to refurbish and republish these effusions, he was young no longer. Why, then, did he unearth and resuscitate them? Did he believe them works of literature? Perhaps. But his decision means more than that, for he did not revive his humorous poems, those for which he was and is hailed. The serious poems were dearer to him, they captured the underlying theme of his life. They made his emotional life come full circle, were proof of how accurately he had predicted his voyage on earth, and provided an Aristotelian unity.

What did he make of the prophecies enshrined in them? How could he not see miraculously etched there his failures with Alice Liddell and, later, with other child friends? What a painful exercise to indulge in. But, then, he never shirked from duty, however painful, and in reviving these "serious poems," in writing the *Sylvie and Bruno* books, in preparing his essay on eternal punishment, in pouring years into his books on mathematics and logic, he did as duty bade. He was holding up mirrors of a soulful struggle that might perhaps show something to others and help those who shared his brand of rejection and dejection to see that they were not alone, not necessarily abandoned by God and the universe. He issued them as one of the last gestures of his life, confessing to himself and to the world that here was the heart of Charles Dodgson writ plain: those youthful, romantic lines are not fiction; they are fact.

Charles's death, unlike his life, was unremarkable. Victorians dramatized death more than we do and readied themselves for it from a much earlier age. Dickens, Trollope, and certainly Charles often meditated on their mortality. On September 28, 1896, when Charles was well along toward his sixty-fifth birthday, he wrote to a sister: "It is getting increasingly difficult, now, to remember *which* of one's friends remain alive, and *which* have gone. . . . Also, such news comes less and less of a shock: and more and more one realises that it is an experience each of *us* has to face, before long. The fact is getting *less* dreamlike to me, now: and I sometimes think what a grand thing it will be to be able to say to oneself 'Death is *over*, now: there is not *that* experience to be faced, again!' " Still, he remained fit through 1897. In September he boasted to the same sister that he made his eighteen-mile walk from Eastbourne to Hastings often, twice in one week and hardly felt tired.

On December 23 he traveled from Oxford to Guildford to join the family for the Christmas holiday. Shortly after the New Year they all learned that their sister Mary's husband, C. S. Collingwood, had died suddenly. Charles himself was then down with a bad chest cold and fever. Today the condition would cause no alarm and would respond to antibiotics. But at the close of the nineteenth century, bronchial infections were much more serious. Actually Charles suffered a good amount of bronchial trouble through his later years, owing in part, no doubt, to the miasmal river climate of Oxford, but we should now consider another possible irritant. In the latter part of the Victorian era, advocates of change replaced coal fires with cleaner, more efficient asbestos gas fires. On December 5, 1884, Charles had one installed in his upper bedroom at Christ Church and by March 19, 1887, could boast four, in "both sitting-rooms, turret room, and upper bedroom . . . and no coals at all." On December 31, 1889, he installed one in his room at Guildford, and on December 9, 1890, wrote his Eastbourne landlady asking her to install an asbestos fire in his bedroom there, pointing out the "*great* convenience of . . . being able to keep it burning all night without having to attend to it." Breathing in friable asbestos particles may have damaged his lungs and made them more vulnerable to infections. His condition worsened and he faded. On January 14, 1898, thirteen days before his sixty-sixth birthday, he was dead.

He left instructions that his funeral be "simple and inexpensive, avoiding all things which are merely done for show, and retaining, only what is, in the judgement of those who arrange my Funeral, requisite for its decent and reverent performance." He also requested that "there be no expensive monument. I should prefer a small plain head-stone."[27] His wishes were honored. The new dean of Christ Church, Francis Paget, and the Rector, C. F. Grant, conducted a simple funeral service at St. Mary's in Guildford, where Charles had preached in earlier days. Members of his family, colleagues from Oxford, and a good many friends attended. But Alice Hargreaves was absent, and no Liddells appeared. Four days after Charles died, his friend and nemesis Henry George Liddell passed peacefully from the world. On January 23, Dean Paget preached a sermon in Christ Church Cathedral honoring the memory of both men.[28] The irony of the conjunction could not have been lost on many in the congregation.

Charles's artist friend Gertrude Thomson was on hand at Charles's funeral and later remembered

a grey January day, calm, and without sound, full of the peace of God which passeth all understanding.

A steep, stony, country road, with hedges close on either side, fast quickening with the breath of the premature spring. Between the withered leaves of the dead summer a pure white daisy here and there shone out like a little star.

*Charles's grave in Guildford Cemetery*

A few mourners slowly climbed the hill in silence, while borne before them on a simple hand-bier was the coffin, half hid in flowers.

Under an old yew, round whose gnarled trunk the green ivy twined, in the pure white chalk earth his body was laid to rest, while the slow bell tolled the passing—

> Of the sweetest soul
> That ever looked with human eye.

Ten days before his death, Charles sent off, as usual, a half-yearly gift to Fanny Wilcox, the widow of his cousin, whom he had helped to support since her husband's death twenty-two years earlier. On the following day, when he heard of his brother-in-law's death, he sent his sister Mary fifty pounds "on account," in case she should need some "ready money."

His will is only fifteen lines long, dividing all his worth equally among his surviving brothers and sisters and appointing his brothers Wilfred and Edwin executors. T. Vere Bayne and A. Vernon Harcourt appear as witnesses.

Institutions traditionally lack hearts, and Christ Church was no exception. After Charles's death, his family was forced to clear out his rooms quickly, and while Charles's relatives were sorting out his papers, a constant pillar of smoke rose from the chimney over his rooms as bundle after bundle of his papers, letters, and manuscripts went up in flames. But Charles's fireplace was an inadequate incinerator, and in a letter to an unidentified recipient who was managing the disposal of Charles's effects, Charles's brother Wilfred wrote: "I thought at the finish that it would be a great deal of trouble bringing the sacks of papers all the way down here, and, as you stated that you could have them burnt in the manner we wish at Oxford, I should be glad if you would do so."[29]

The family retained some of his possessions and papers for themselves, and many which they chose not to keep came up for auction in Oxford on May 10 and 11 that spring. Charles's collection of gadgets, his games and puzzles, his huge library, his furniture, the portraits of friends and his artist friends' paintings and sketches, his own artwork, photographs, photograph albums, photograph equipment, his Nyctograph, and much, much more— all were knocked down to the highest bidder and scattered to the four winds. The sale brought in a total of slightly over seven hundred pounds, less than 5 percent of the amount that Alice garnered from the sale of her Lewis Carroll treasures. Charles's colleague Frederick York Powell was moved to write a poem about the event:

> At a Certain Auction . . .
>
> POOR playthings of the man that's gone,
> Surely we would not have them thrown,
> Like wreckage on a barren strand,
> The prey of every greedy hand.
>
> Fast ride the Dead! Perhaps 'tis well!
> He shall not know, what none would tell,
> That gambling salesmen bargain'd o'er
> The books he read, the clothes he wore,
>
> The desk he stood at day by day
> In patient toil or earnest play,
> The pictures that he loved to see,
> Faint echoes of his Fantasy.

He shall not know. And yet, and yet,
One would not quite so soon forget
The dead man's whims, or let Gain riot
Among the toys he loved in quiet:

Better by far the Northman's pyre,
That burnt in one sky-soaring fire
The man with all he held most dear.
'He that hath ears, now let him hear.'[30]

Charles's death was more than a national event. Obituaries appeared in papers all over the world, funeral wreaths arrived from many admirers, the family was inundated by letters of condolence. "In many a home and many a schoolroom," wrote *The Times*, "there will be genuine sorrow to-day when it is announced that the author of *Alice in Wonderland* and *Through the Looking-Glass* has passed away."

The world quickly acknowledged that Charles was no ordinary mortal. True, he lived up to stern Victorian standards, embraced strict, correct, old-fashioned, inhibiting mores and manners, was rigidly uncompromising, could be irascible, imperious, testy, hasty in reprimand, curt and cutting in conversation. But he was much more than the typical Oxford don. To say that he was remarkably gifted is banal. He was more than gifted, and he possessed more than a unique imagination—he was magical. Ethel Arnold remembers when she first met him:

It was a typical Oxford afternoon in late autumn—damp, foggy, cheerless; the grey towers of the distant Colleges across the "Parks" . . . looked greyer than usual in the dim autumnal light. A number of little girls, bursting with youthful spirits, and all agog for mischief, danced along one of the paths, a staid governess bringing up the rear. Presently one of their number spied a tall black clerical figure in the distance, swinging along towards the little group with a characteristic briskness, almost jerkiness, of step. —"Here comes Mr. Dodgson," she cried. "Let's make a barrier across the path so that he can't pass." No sooner said than done—the children joined hands and formed a line across the path; the clerical figure, appreciating the situation, advanced at the double and charged the line with his umbrella. The line broke in confusion, and the next moment four of the little band were clinging to such portions of the black-coated figure as they could seize upon. Two little people, however, hung back, being seized with shyness and a sudden

consciousness of their audacity, a sudden awe of this tall, dignified gentleman in black broadcloth and white tie. But in a moment he had
shaken off the clinging, laughing children, and before the two little
strangers had time to realize what had happened, they found themselves
trotting along either side of him, a hand of each firmly clasped in the
strong, kind hands of Lewis Carroll, and chattering away as if they had
known him all their lives. Thus began a lifelong friendship between
Lewis Carroll and the younger of these two little girls, myself. . . .

His genius with words, his creative nonsense, his hilarious dramatis personae, his amusing episodes, his tickling absurdities, his way of appealing to
ear, eye, head, and heart—they are all elements of his magic. Perhaps he
himself needed to flee the harsh realities of his solitude, but he equally
needed to share all his gifts with others; if his creative work helped him alleviate his own frustration, it also brought sacks full of amusement and entertainment to friends and strangers alike.

He sought to live a respectable life and succeeded. His stern rules of
thought and behavior insured rectitude even with his child friends. He convinced himself that his interest in these dryads was purely social, aesthetic,
and spiritual, and if we see a hidden sexual force as well, we know, too, that
he effectively suppressed it. He could not, in all likelihood, prevent suggestive thoughts and images from invading his bedroom at night or altogether
extirpate the consequent guilt that haunted him. But he fled those nocturnal hobgoblins to a daylight filled with innocence, where he imposed iron
control on thought and action and never compromised his moral conscience
and religious faith.

In a way he was himself ever childlike, but only in that he appreciated, for
much longer than most of us can, the child's mind and heart and knew how
to make them easy and happy. He was not at all emotionally retarded, but
rather a person with a passionate orchestra playing within his breast. Either
because of genetic inheritance or because of the way he was reared and grew,
or a combination of the two, his sexual energies sought unconventional outlets. But our analytical techniques are not good enough to provide conclusive medical, scientific, or psychological explanations for differing sexual
appetites. Even without complete scientific insights, however, society has
come to be more and more understanding about sexual variance and to ponder the possibility that there is, in this complex universe, a place for diverse
sexualities.

The forces that shaped Charles's sexual orientation are still mysterious. If we read the hillock of psychoanalytical tomes that have tried to get at the essence of this man's psyche, we come away with numbing contradictions. Charles never saw any of the works of Freud or other early writers on psychoanalysis, he could not have read any medical or psychological works that might suggest that his feelings had a legitimate place in the world. It cannot have been easy for him growing up at Daresbury and Croft or during his schooling or at Herculean Oxford, first as undergraduate, then as don, to confront inner promptings that he recognized as different, extrasocietal, awkward, embarrassing, punitive, completely at odds with what he observed in other boys and men, opposed to what he had been taught to believe to be right in the eyes of those he loved and in the dicta of his faith.

Living with that inner self must have caused many sleepless hours, to be sure; it must have made him pause at personal encounters; it must have required him to fashion a very special external persona; it must have brought him untold anguish. But carefully, gradually, deliberately, he found a way through his immense difficulty, he learned how to deal with his feelings as a man. He made the most of his strengths, learned to avert or subdue his weaknesses. The great paradox of the life of this paragon, this prodigy of wit and laughter, is that he carried in his breast a heavy, brooding, somber, sullen burden.

It is a burden of incompleteness, another paradox for so publicly successful, so accomplished a life. The fact of his unfulfilled state confronted him daily, and was humbling, humiliating, and obdurate. He felt that he did not succeed in his father's eyes; he never married to continue the line that his father hoped for. He knew, too, that his father could never approve of his slide away from High Church dogma and discipline. His filial failure was matched with his inability to fit into an approved social mold. His desires and open preference for the companionship, the love, of little ones destroyed any chance that he might have had of taking his place on an equal footing with other men and women. Instead he became the odd man out, an eccentric, the subject of whispers and wagging tongues.

All his successive friendships with his young friends were doomed. We cannot be sure that Charles ever seriously proposed marriage to any of them, but he was inclined to do so, and if he ever did, he failed. The rejections and the rebuffs were as evident as they were inevitable. He was, in the end, a man with a broken heart, one who loved but was never really loved in return. He clung to memories of the past, but his consolations were tinged with pain.

The two poems that frame *Looking-Glass* reveal the sadness that closed in
when the Liddells rejected him, but the ache found its expression time and
time again, wrapped in sentimentality, as, for example, when he wrote his
essay " 'Alice' on the Stage" in the spring of 1887:

> Stand forth, then, from the shadowy past, "Alice," the child of my
> dreams. Full many a year has slipped away, since that "golden after-
> noon" that gave thee birth, but I can call it up almost as clearly as if it
> were yesterday . . . the three eager faces, hungry for news of fairy-land,
> and who would not be said "nay" to: from whose lips "Tell us a story,
> please," had all the stern immutability of Fate!

He revealed his deep disappointment again in 1889, in, of all places, the
preface to *The Nursery "Alice,"* where he refers to the "weariness of the
solemn mockery, and the gaudy glitter, and the hopeless misery, of Life" and
alludes to "Children of a 'certain age,' whose tale of years must be left untold, and buried in respectful silence." It is an odd comment in an odd place
that Charles wrote from an aching heart.

A deep sadness permeates these musings and the occasions when a child
friend grew up, deserted him, and went off to lead her own life. One such
incident occurred on May 28, 1895, when Isa Bowman, playing at Oxford as
leading lady in a musical comedy, came to see him and told him that she was
engaged to be married. For a moment, she recalled, he was upset and, in irritation, snatched some roses from her belt and flung them out the window,
exclaiming, "You know I can't stand flowers."[31] Charles evidently took hold
of himself and on the following day entertained Isa and her fiancé. But as
far as we can tell, he never heard from Isa again. "I don't even know whether
the report is true," he wrote (November 19, 1896) to Isa's friend Mary Jackson, "that she is married." One of the first reminiscences of Charles to be
published after his death is Isa's, for which she was presumably well paid,
and those charming letters that Charles wrote her found their way, soon
enough, into the marketplace.

Charles's impairments and disillusionments forced him to become precise, exacting, and sometimes testy with people who swam into his orbit.
His public life, however, more than made up for his shortcomings. He found
satisfaction most of all in preaching to young and old and in writing serious
works that eased his pain of rejection and solitude and that he hoped would
help others contend with their difficulties.

All his life he struggled against the limits of his nature; all his life he sought to correct, to improve upon, what he was and what he did, to free himself of his guilt, his sins, his lonely isolation. He achieved a degree of peace through his feverish activity on behalf of others, for his conscience did not prick him toward the end as it had done in his prime. But with child friends, although they came and went, he never truly succeeded.

Perhaps his failure to correct his speech impediment was the overarching symbol of his entire life. He learned to live with his stammer; he knew what it permitted him to do, what not, where it would snare him and destroy the effects he sought to achieve, and how to avoid the traps. A letter he wrote nine days before he died in response to a request that he help in church at Guildford shows how carefully he had thought out his position:

> My note to your wife was written too briefly and hastily to explain my position with regard to giving help in church. The hesitation, from which I have suffered all my life, is always worse in *reading* (when I can *see* difficult words before they come) than in speaking. It is now many years since I ventured on reading in public—except now and then reading a lesson in College Chapel. Even that I find such a strain on the nerves that I seldom attempt it. As to reading the *prayers*, there is a much stronger objection than merely my own feelings: every difficulty is an interruption to the devotions of the congregation, by taking off their thoughts from what ought to be the *only* subject in their minds. I am sorry that I cannot undertake what you ask.

Deprived of full, flowing speech, Charles accommodated the difficulty that characterized his entire life, a life hampered by inescapable limitations, blotted by imperfections and lacking emotional fulfillment.

There is, nonetheless, something noble, selfless, and generous in what Charles Dodgson fashioned of himself and in the way he reined in his impulses and set them to serve his family, his young friends, his society, his God—and himself. In the end, one wants not only to say "Well done!" but also to congratulate him for so successfully transforming a life that might easily have teetered on the brink and fallen into the abyss into one that was useful, dignified, and creative. For he, and he alone, shaped that precarious youth of unusual talent and scrupulous character into a man who made many valuable and distinguished contributions to his world and to posterity—who made himself, in short, into a man worth writing about.

# Appendix

In spite of his stammer, Charles, as an undergraduate and junior don, succeeded as an orator when called upon to be one. As mentioned in Chapter 2, his compositions were chosen three times as the best weekly theme required of Christ Church men on a moral subject beneath a Latin tag, and he consequently read out those essays in Hall on Saturday afternoons to the assembled body. Neither these essays nor the two that follow them below have, to the best of my knowledge, ever been published.[1]

The earliest is followed by the subscription in Charles's hand: "Read out in Hall, November 22, 1851." The quotation is attributed to Publilius Syrus and translates as "A beautiful face is a silent recommendation." Charles was nineteen years old when he wrote it.

### Formosa facies muta commendatio est

Many, if not most, of the objects of nature are endued with a certain principle, inseparable from them, and as it were a part of their being, which affects the eye, and through the eye the mind, with a sensation of pleasure; which makes us dwell long on, and be unwilling to lose sight of, the object of our delight, and this principle we call Beauty. It has been affirmed also, and with great show of reason, that this peculiar pleasure, and the faculty of enjoying it, is confined to the human species, as if it were too exalted a delight to be wasted on the inferior orders of living creatures.

Such is the Beauty in scenery, in trees, lakes, and mountains, in the vastness of the Ocean, in the splendour of Sunrise, and in the rich glow of Sunset, in the broad daylight, and in the majesty of Night, in animals, and last, highest, and grandest of all, in the divine form and features of Man.

Now whether this faculty, which the mind doubtless possesses, of perceiving and enjoying these beauties of Nature, be conferred on it from above, or be a part of our gross and corporeal nature, we have no means of knowing: certain it is, however, that the pleasures thence derived are among the highest, the most ennobling, and the most enduring which our nature is capable of receiving.

Nor is it to the eye alone that this power is given of gratifying the soul within, the ear also bears it's [*sic*] part: and there is a Beauty in *sound* allied, if not closely analogous, to that which belongs to form and colour; and tho' we might vainly endeavour to assign to either a superiority over the other, yet it surely were no fanciful theory which would confine to these the power of satisfying the cravings of our higher and spiritual nature, and leave to the others the task of gratifying the animal and earthly passions.

Closely connected with this perception of Beauty in natural objects follows the sensation of love and admiration for the object in whom this Beauty is perceived, and hence it is that an outward Beauty in the form and features of others exercises an imperceptible influence over us, even when we know nothing of the character and real nature of the person.

How unjust in effect this principle is, may be easily seen from the consideration that the possession of Beauty is as much beyond the will and control of the individual admired, as the faculty of enjoying it is independent of and unattainable by the powers of the mind, it being in fact a gift born with us rather than an acquisition which self-education can bring us in after years.

The manuscript of this second undergraduate theme bears the subscription: "Read out in Hall. May 22, 1852." Unlike the earlier manuscript, this one bears a good quantity of cross-outs. The Latin tag is from Ovid's *Tristia* and translates as: "Nothing aids which may not also injure us." Charles was twenty when he wrote it.

### *Nil prodest quod non laedere possit idem*

Alike within us and without us, alike in the gifts of Nature, in the faculties of our own minds, and in the various events and changes of life, there is nothing that is not alloyed with some mixture of evil, nothing that the wayward genius of man has not at some time or other wrested to his own hurt. The fault lies not in the things themselves which are thus abused, but in the abuser: it was of his own free choice

# Appendix

that he sought out the evil in them, and not the good: his unhappiness is of his own earning, and he has himself to blame for what he has done. The evils we ourselves experience, and the misery we see around us, all show how much more ready the nature of man is to derive harm and sorrow from what lies in his way rather than good.

Hence we may learn how vain it is to expect that we shall find unmixed happiness in any conceivable condition of life, or to believe that others ever have done so, or ever will: how vain to envy the rich and the powerful their outward show of happiness, or to imagine that they feel no more and no other than what we see. How different would be our language if we could look into their hearts, and see the stings of Care which those very rich have planted there, and the load of anxiety crushing down and stifling all the buoyancy of spirit, and all the capability for enjoyment which may once have been theirs. The very name of "miser" is suggestive of that unhappiness which universal experience teaches us is the constant result of an excessive love for riches.

And yet none would say that riches may not be made of the very greatest benefit to ourselves and to others: none will deny that the power of doing good which they confer on us is one of the highest and purest sources of enjoyment we can possess. Virtue alone, as Aristotle has shown us, forms an exception to the rule: as from it's [sic] very nature it must ever do, for it is only by being carried to excess that any of those faculties of the mind, which we call Virtues can become a means of injury, and in this very act of abuse they cease to be Virtues.

We may not then, in judging of any faculty, consider only the good it is capable of doing, but also the evil to which it is liable, remembering that, however mighty it may be as an instrument of good, abuse will make it as mighty an instrument of ill.

A third essay of this genre is undated, but the handwriting puts it closest to the earliest of these youthful efforts. The Latin tag is from Tacitus's *Annals* and translates as: "To despise fame is to despise merit."

### Contempta fama contemni virtutes

That a due regard for our reputation, and for the opinion our fellow creatures around us have of us, is a great check upon many vices, and a powerful encouragement to the cultivation of many of the most manly and ennobling virtues, there can be little doubt. And yet we may run into extremes in both directions, either in paying too much respect to the opinion of men, or in utterly disregarding it. For in the former case we shall be constituting our fellow men, who are probably as ignorant and as erring as ourselves, almost divine arbiters of right and wrong, while in the latter we shall be treating them as though, like brute beasts, they were unable to distinguish at all between them.

The love of fame is at the same time one of the most noble and one of the most powerful motives which can inspire the human breast: for while the love of money, or power, or pleasure frequently debase the mind,[2] and sink their votary into the most mean and grovelling vices, the pursuit of fame is of itself a safe guard against such temptations, and though it does not and can not raise the moral standard to perfection, yet it never can suffer it to fall below a certain level, as long as civilised men retain a regard and respect for virtue, and a contempt, if not a hatred, of vice.

This it is which rouses and supports the spirit of the conqueror under difficulties and dangers of every kind, which urges him to the most arduous enterprises, and encourages him in the most desperate circumstances, while he feels that the eyes of the world are upon him, and that his achievements, his talents, and his courage, will be recorded on the page of history, and emulated by posterity.

This it is which upholds the student through the long days and nights of incessant toil, which enables him to persevere in obscurity, in poverty, and in distress, content to bear all so that his name may be known hereafter as a mighty philosopher, as a discoverer of the hidden things of science, or as one who has benefitted mankind by the results of his labours.

This too, it must be confessed, it is which drives men to deeds of reckless folly and excess, if not to worse crimes, which arms the traitor against his sovereign's life, and makes the murderer exult in his fate, nay, which causes men to commit suicide itself, to obtain a hideous notoriety, and to be talked about, no matter how, by the world.

Though the lovers of fame are occasionally found to be guilty of crimes like these, yet in general they will be found among the noblest and best of mankind, while those who affect an utter disregard and contempt for it, can hardly be otherwise than sordid and vicious.

While still an undergraduate, in the spring of 1854, Charles delivered a "declamation" in Hall. It was something more than the result of the weekly theme competition, written as it is entirely in Latin and Greek and taking a passage from Aristotle's *Ethics* as its subject. We can only infer that because he had distinguished himself in classical studies, he had been asked to write and deliver this declamation at some regularly scheduled college event. The essay bears no title but is subscribed at the close: "Declamation read in Hall, May 3, 1854." Charles was twenty then and in the following December would sit for his final examinations for his bachelor's degree; he would obtain a second-class in classics.

Aristotle begins the Nicomachean Ethics by writing, "Every art and method aims at some good" [*Nic. Eth.* 1094a2]. In these words, he sets out two notable principles of his doctrines: first, he was less diligent in seeking truth than in determining what was good; next, he believed that some truth inhered in every man's opinions, and that therefore, it was possible, by carefully scrutinizing the ancients' doctrines, to find truth.

But our author scarcely deserved being called a philosopher. For philosophy has a double nature: first, it seeks after pure and simple truth, scrutinizes the secrets of nature, and establishes theories and axioms; secondly, it rules life's ways and loves virtue and justice. Everyone agrees that the name of philosophy rightly belongs to the first and should be denied to the second.

But if Aristotle tried harder to rule and enforce everything than he did to seek truth, he ought to be called *philopraktos* [one who loves action] rather than *philosophos* [one who loves wisdom]. Indeed this fact is entirely clear just from reading these words: "Furthermore, a young man, being disposed to follow his passions, listens vainly and without profit, for the end he seeks is not knowledge but action" [*Nic. Eth.* 1095a4].

Nevertheless, philosophy is not entirely separated from living a good life. For one should seek wisdom if it makes men blessed, if it teaches them to govern themselves with moderation. And so Aristotle sought such wisdom, and if certain errors are to be found in his search, he did not err without good cause. Three factors must be noted which greatly stood in his way in making this search and led his mind into error. First, he wanted concord and unity in all things so much, that he erected a lofty structure upon feeble foundations. Next, because he spent his life amid war and warlike people, he thought that the largest part of virtue consisted in waging war, and he held that those things most fitted for war were the most deserving of praise. Third, the ancients either gave no thought to life after death or they doubted, rather than believed in it.

Our author's reasoning followed naturally from these factors. He did not at all believe that fixed doctrines could be derived from *a priori* principles. Indeed, he felt that everything we do in life arises from pleasure and must be judged solely by the outcome. The result is that, since Aristotle related everything to pleasure, he would hardly agree to what today we call the "final" cause. Moreover, he felt that life ended with death, or rather, was extinguished by it. How therefore could Aristotle and today's believers in a "final" cause agree in this regard? What cause is adequate to bring a soldier into battle unless death, if not actively sought, is despised and scorned?

Philosophy deserted Aristotle as he investigated this matter. However, he by no means gave up the attempt, since he was not one who could believe that truth did not exist at all. He conceded an immortal nature to men, but he speaks of it cautiously and doubtfully: "a most fearful thing is death." If he dared to affirm anything on this subject, he seems to be trying to comprehend shadows, as it were. And so, in this obscurity, or rather falsity of all things, if we contemplate that faith with which he constantly sought truth, we cannot admire him too much. The true and the good are permanent—which indeed he announced clearly when he wrote: "virtue is steadfast."

An early entry in the first volume of Charles's surviving diary occurs on March 3, 1855: "Spent most of the morning over a Latin Theme to be read out in Hall . . . ," but the manuscript of this theme has not surfaced, nor does any further mention of it enter the diary. By this time Charles was a graduate and a Student teaching mathematics.

It was the custom in the nineteenth century to celebrate a Christ Church dignitary of the past at the Gaudies. On May 6, 1856, Charles wrote in his diary: "The Dean sent for me to tell me he wishes me to read out the 'Life' at the Gaudy this time. He chose 'Richard Hakluyt,' author of a book of travels." Charles fulfilled his assignment, wrote the essay and read it out in Hall on June 31 "and afterwards dined at the high table." The essay survives in Christ Church Library, has never been published, but is hardly more than a potboiler, reveals little about Charles, and perhaps should continue to lie dormant.

One other unpublished manuscript has come to light and deserves our attention. It is of a different sort altogether, really a rough draft of an essay or a talk or a sermon, written hastily with numerous cross-outs, in pencil, and in a handwriting that puts it much later than the earlier themes and declamation. When it came up for sale at Sotheby's in 1932, it was part of various lots of Charles Dodgson material owned by his sister Louisa, who died in 1930. It is untitled, but it deals with the subject of "Pleasure."

There is this difference between those who pursue pleasure as their ultimate object, and those who direct their chief endeavours to the acquirement of virtue, knowing that it alone is capable of conferring the purest, the most exalted, the most enduring happiness, namely that the former party seek to gain their end in any way which appears most likely to forward their hopes, without regard to the natures of the means they employ, which are often evil as well as good, the evil in many cases appearing more attractive than the good, while the latter, guiding themselves by the criterion of virtue, abstain from anything which they see to be evil, choosing only those things which reason and conscience tell them to be consistent with right and equity.

If pleasure were the object to which our chief aims and hopes ought to be directed, we should err, not only from the uncertainty of our guide, since few agree in their notions as to what pleasure really consists in, but also from our ignorance as to what means are most proper to be employed to attain that end. For there are many things which to one who has not made trial of them would appear to be conducive to happiness, and there are many states of life, which appear happy to those who are otherwise situated, and who set in comparison the privations and hardships they feel in their own condition with the pleasures and advantages they perceive in the other.

Thus the poor man may with some appearance of reason envy his richer neighbour, and wish that he could enjoy the same luxuries, and the same exemption from labour, and it is experience alone that can teach him how great anxieties riches often bring with them, and how the pleasures of luxury soon cease to please, when they become the business of life, instead of its relaxation. And the rich man may well envy the poor the keen relish with which he enjoys the little pleasure which falls in his way, and would sometimes gladly exchange his luxurious couch and table loaded with dainties for the labourer's hard pallet and simple fare, to which labour and hunger bring a zest it is not in the power of riches to supply.

But as to the actual nature of pleasure, and what it may be that really gives it, how few there are who have any other idea of it than as that which gratifies the senses. The wise however, who propose to themselves virtue as the mark they are chiefly to aim at, perceive that true pleasure consists in it's [*sic*] attainment, and in the consciousness of inward purity. So that although they do not take it at all as a motive for action, yet they do more surely and more constantly obtain it and more thoroughly enjoy it, than do those who blindly aim at pleasure, believing it to be good in itself and think that way the best, which appears to lead straight to their object.

There is this difference then, etc. [and the essay breaks off].

# Abbreviated Titles

| | |
|---|---|
| *Alice* | Lewis Carroll, *Alice's Adventures in Wonderland* |
| Alice Liddell | "The Lewis Carroll that Alice Recalls," *New York Times*, May 1, 1932; and, somewhat altered, "Alice's Recollections of Carrollian Days, as Told to her Son," *Cornhill Magazine*, July 1932 |
| Bartley | W. W. Bartley III, ed., *Lewis Carroll's Symbolic Logic, Part I and Part II* (1977) |
| Beatrice Hatch I | Beatrice Hatch, "In Memoriam: Charles Lutwidge Dodgson (Lewis Carroll)," *Guardian*, January 19, 1898 |
| Beatrice Hatch II | Beatrice Hatch, "Lewis Carroll," *Strand Magazine*, April 1898 |
| Bill and Mason | E. G. W. Bill and J. F. A. Mason, *Christ Church and Reform* (1970) |
| Blagden | Claude M. Blagden, *Well Remembered* (1953) |
| Collingwood | Stuart Dodgson Collingwood, *The Life and Letters of Lewis Carroll* (1898) |
| *Diaries* | *The Diaries of Lewis Carroll*, 2 vols., ed. Roger Lancelyn Green (1953) |
| Ethel Arnold | Ethel M. Arnold, "Reminiscences of Lewis Carroll," *Atlantic Monthly*, June 1929; and *Windsor Magazine*, December 1929 |
| Ethel Rowell | E. M. Rowell, "To Me He Was Mr. Dodgson," *Harper's Magazine*, February 1943 |
| Evelyn Hatch | Evelyn M. Hatch, ed., *A Selection from the Letters of Lewis Carroll to His Child Friends* (1933) |
| Hudson | Derek Hudson, *Lewis Carroll* (1954; new ed., 1976). All references are to the first edition. |
| Isa Bowman | Isa Bowman, *The Story of Lewis Carroll* (1899), reprinted as *Lewis Carroll As I Knew Him* (1972) |

*Jabberwocky*            *Jabberwocky* (The Journal of the Lewis Carroll
                         Society)
Johnston                 John Octavius Johnston, *Life and Letters of Henry
                         Parry Liddon* (1904)
*Letters*                *The Letters of Lewis Carroll,* 2 vols., ed. Morton N.
                         Cohen, with the assistance of Roger Lancelyn Green
                         (1979)
*Looking-Glass*          Lewis Carroll, *Through the Looking-Glass and What
                         Alice Found There*
*Picture Book*           *The Lewis Carroll Picture Book,* ed. Stuart Dodgson
                         Collingwood (1899)
*Real Alice*             Anne Clark, *The Real Alice* (1981)
Reed                     Langford Reed, *The Life of Lewis Carroll* (1932)
*Snark*                  Lewis Carroll, *The Hunting of the Snark*
Violet Dodgson           Violet Dodgson, "Lewis Carroll—as I Knew Him,"
                         *London Calling,* June 28, 1951

# Notes

## 1. Beginnings

1. It appeared on January 31.
2. Collingwood, p. 11.
3. Ibid., pp. 11–12.
4. Anne Clark, *Lewis Carroll: A Biography* (1979), p. 14.
5. Collingwood, p. 11.
6. Ibid., p. 8.
7. Christ Church Treasury Papers, MS. Estate 19, 160, January 23, 1832.
8. Collingwood, p. 8.
9. *Diaries*, p. 29.
10. January 13, 1870.
11. Collingwood, p. 14.
12. Ibid., pp. 12–13.
13. In a letter to her sister Lucy Lutwidge (Dodgson Family Papers).
14. *Diaries*, p. 6.
15. Edward Baines, *History, Directory & Gazetteer, of the County of York . . .* (1823), vol. 1, p. 431.
16. In 1846 the Reverend Mr. Dodgson published *A Short Account of the First Establishment of the Croft National School*, which describes the school and playgrounds, payments required from the children's families (two pence per week for one child in a family, three pence for two children from a family, and so forth). The list of contributions for the building of the school shows that Mr. Dodgson himself gave more than half of the total amount collected.
17. *Northern Echo*, January 5, 1932, as quoted in *Diaries*, p. 9.
18. *Diaries*, p. 9.
19. Collingwood, pp. 19–20; Hudson, pp. 34–35.
20. Stuart Dodgson Collingwood, "Before *Alice:* The Boyhood of Lewis Carroll," *Strand Magazine*, December 1898.
21. Collingwood, pp. 24–25.
22. "At the Intersection of Mathematics and Humor: Lewis Carroll's *Alice*s and Symbolical Algebra," *Victorian Studies*, Autumn 1984, p. 160.
23. Collingwood, p. 23.
24. Frederick H. Forshall, *Westminster School Past and Present* (1884), p. 113; John Field, *The King's Nurseries: The Story of Westminster School* (1987), pp. 62–66.
25. J. B. Hope Simpson, *Rugby Since Arnold* (1967), esp. pp. 10–22.
26. W. H. D. Rouse, *A History of Rugby School* (1898), pp. 343–44. I have also used David Newsome, *Godliness and Good Learning* (1961), esp. pp. 64–65; Eugene L. Williamson, Jr.,

*The Liberalism of Thomas Arnold* (1964), esp. pp. 223–27; and John Chandos, *Boys Together: English Public Schools, 1800–1864* (1984), pp. 80–81.

27. Rouse, p. 257.

28. George Melly, *School Experiences of a Fag at a Private and Public School* (1854), pp. 106–107.

29. Simpson, pp. 32–34.

30. Collingwood, p. 29.

31. Dodgson Family Papers.

32. A. G. Butler, *The Three Friends: A Story of Rugby in the Forties* (1900), p. 24.

33. Collingwood, p. 30.

34. Hudson, p. 48.

35. Collingwood, p. 85.

36. In addition to the works already cited in this section, I have drawn upon the following: Philip Dodgson Jaques, "Lewis Carroll and the Dodgson Lineage," *Mr. Dodgson: Nine Lewis Carroll Studies* (1973); *History, Gazetteer, and Directory of Cheshire* (1860); Edna De Prez, "Lewis Carroll—His Birthplace and Childhood," *Jabberwocky*, July 1991; W. White, *Yorkshire Directory* (1840); Brenda Dane Matheson, *Lewis Carroll Around the North* (n.d.); Arthur Penrhyn Stanley, *The Life and Correspondence of Thomas Arnold, D. D.*, 2 vols., 9th ed. (1868); Godfrey, A. Solly, ed., *Rugby School Register* (1933); J. R. de S. Honey, *Tom Brown's Universe* (1977); Michael McCrum, *Thomas Arnold, Headmaster: A Reassessment* (1989).

## 2.   *Cap and Gown*

1. Dodgson Family Papers; Collingwood, p. 55.

2. [C. W. Collins], "Oxford in Fact and Fiction," *Blackwood's Magazine*, December 1895.

3. "The Scholar-Gypsy."

4. *Praeterita* (reprint, 1989), pp. 182–83.

5. *Tom Brown at Oxford*, chap. 3.

6. W. E. Sherwood, *Oxford Yesterday: Memoirs of Oxford Seventy Years Ago* (1927), p. 27.

7. Meriol Trevor, *The Arnolds* (1973), p. 114.

8. *Early Victorian England, 1830–1865* (1934), vol. 2, p. 493.

9. (Reprint, 1869), pp. 3, 16, 29, 74–75.

10. [Frederick] Oakeley, "Personal Recollections of Oxford," *Time* 2 (1880): 681.

11. [C. W. Collins].

12. [Unsigned], "Reminiscences of My Time at Oxford," *Temple Bar*, November 1890.

13. [W. C. Collins]; Stephen Page and J. M. C. Crum, *Francis Paget* (1912), pp. 130–32.

14. Charles LLoyd, the oldest son of the late Bishop of Oxford, was Student and Tutor at Christ Church; George Marshall was Student and Censor.

15. [W. C. Collins].

16. G. M. Young, "The Schoolman in Downing Street," *Daylight and Champaign* (1937), p. 60.

17. As reported in Henry L. Thompson, *Christ Church* (1900), p. 150.

18. [Unsigned], "Reminiscences. . . ."

19. Edward Wakeling, "Lewis Carroll's Rooms at Christ Church, Oxford," *Jabberwocky*, Summer 1983.

20. [G. J. Cowley-Brown], "Personal Recollections of the Author of 'Alice in Wonderland,'" *Scottish Guardian*, January 28, 1898.

21. *Tom Brown at Oxford*, chap. 1.

22. *Praeterita,* p. 184.

23. Dodgson Family Papers.

24. Christ Church Archives.

25. Collingwood, pp. 53–55.

26. *Letters,* p. 1133.

27. Collingwood, p. 57.

28. See Appendix for the full text.

29. *Symbolic Logic, Part I* (1896), p. 180.

30. Collingwood, p. 57; [Thomas Fowler], "Our Lewis Carroll Memorial," *St. James's Gazette,* March 11, 1898.

31. Collingwood, p. 57.

32. Blagden, p. 121.

33. Frederic Harrison, *Autobiographic Memoirs* (1911), vol. 1, p. 108.

34. Collingwood, p. 61.

35. Ibid., pp. 64–65.

36. In addition to the works already cited in this section, I have drawn upon the following: E. G. W. Bill, *Education at Christ Church, Oxford, 1660–1800* (1989); J. P. C. Roach, "Victorian Universities and the National Intelligentsia," *Victorian Studies,* December 1959; Charles W. Boase, *Oxford* (1887); H. C. Michen, *Oxford* (1905); Hugh de Selincourt, *Oxford from Within* (1910); Keith Briant, *Oxford Limited* (1937); Stephen Paget, ed., *Henry Scott Holland* (1921); W. G. Hiscock, *A Christ Church Miscellany* (1946); Christopher Hobhouse, *Oxford* (1939); C. B. Dawson, *The Mirror of Oxford* (1912); G. W. Kitchin, *Ruskin in Oxford and Other Studies* (1904); James Morris, *Oxford* (1965); Jan Morris, ed., *The Oxford Book of Oxford* (1978).

## 3. *The Don, The Dean, and His Daughter*

1. Henry L. Thompson, *Christ Church* (1900), pp. 215, 217; Bill and Mason, pp. 132–41.

2. *Oxford* (new ed., 1909), pp. 246–47.

3. Goldwin Smith, *Reminiscences,* ed. Arnold Haultain (1910), p. 103.

4. *Praeterita,* pp. 190–91.

5. Henry L. Thompson, *Henry George Liddell* (1899), p. 196.

6. A. M. W. Stirling, *The Richmond Papers* (1926), pp. 190–91.

7. Gordon N. Ray, ed., *The Letters and Private Papers of William Makepeace Thackeray* (1945), vol. 2, pp. 641–42.

8. The letter comes from Ripon and is dated February 6, 1856. See Anne Clark Amor, ed., *Letters to Skeffington Dodgson from His Father* (1990), p. 12.

9. In marking exceptional days or events with "a white stone," Charles appropriates Catullus's "*Lapide candidiore diem notare,*" of which he may have been reminded when reading *Tom Brown's Schooldays,* where Tom, in chapter 4, after an enjoyable day's journey and a splendid meal at the Peacock Inn, marks the day with a white stone.

10. Charles invented two ciphers in 1858, the first (Key-Vowel) on February 23, the second (Matrix) on February 26. According to Francine Abeles, the Matrix cipher is probably the first cipher constructed on mathematical principles. See Francine F. Abeles, *The Mathematical Pamphlets of Charles Lutwidge Dodgson and Related Pieces* (1994), pp. 328–30, 339–40.

11. "Syllabus, etc., etc. (done) [*A Syllabus of Plane Algebraical Geometry,* published in 1860]; Notes on Euclid (done) [*Notes on the First Two Books of Euclid,* also published in 1860]; Ditto on Algebra (done—will be out this week, I hope) [*Notes on the First Part of Algebra,* indeed

published that year]; Cycle of Examples, Pure Mathematics (about ⅓ done) [*General List of (Mathematical) Subjects, and Cycle for Working Examples*, to appear in 1863]; Collection of formulae (½ done) [probably *The Formulae of Plane Trigonometry*, published that year]; Collection of Symbols (begun) [either for *The Formulae of Plane Trigonometry* or for *Symbols and Abbreviations for Euclid*, the latter to appear in 1866]; Algebraical Geometry in 4 vols. (about ¼ of Vol. I done) [possibly an early version of *The Fifth Book of Euclid Treated Algebraically*, to appear in 1868]." Some claim that *The Fifth Book of Euclid Treated Algebraically* by "A College Tutor" (1858) is Charles's first published book. But it is inconceivable that he would omit his first book from this list.

12. Collingwood, p. 91.

13. Catherine Sinclair, *Holiday House*, in Robert Lee Wolff, ed., *Masterworks of Children's Literature*, Part 1, Vol. 5, 1837–1900, "The Victorian Age," p. 7.

14. Roger Lancelyn Green, "The Golden Age of Children's Books," in Sheila Egoff et al., eds., *Only Connect* (1969), p. 3.

15. Roger Lancelyn Green, *Tellers of Tales* (1953), p. 17.

16. Dodgson Family Papers.

17. The passage is from a letter from T. B. Strong dated March 13, 1895, quoted in Sidney Herbert Williams and Falconer Madan, *A Handbook of the Literature of Rev. C. L. Dodgson* (1931), p. 212.

18. "Mr. Dodgson: Lewis Carroll at Oxford," *The Times*, January 27, 1932.

19. A. S. Russell, "Lewis Carroll, Tutor and Logician," *Listener*, January 13, 1932.

20. *The Times*, December 19, 1931.

21. Ibid., December 22, 1931.

22. Ibid., January 30, 1932.

23. Isa Bowman, p. 6.

24. Violet Dodgson.

25. Alice Liddell.

26. Ibid.

27. Meteorological records report rain and argue against the accuracy of the "golden afternoon" the participants recalled.

28. " 'Alice' on the Stage," *Theatre*, April 1887.

29. Collingwood, p. 96.

30. Alice Liddell.

31. *Picture Book*, pp. 358–60.

32. Mavis Batey, *The Adventures of Alice* (1991), to which I am indebted for, as she so aptly subtitles this book, "the story behind the stories that Lewis Carroll told."

33. Alice Liddell.

34. "Oxford in the 'Seventies,' " *Fortnightly Review* 150 (1941): 276–82.

35. Hatfield House MSS. 3M/D XIII/101.

36. Charles confesses this to her, as Mrs. Hargreaves, in a letter dated March 1, 1885.

37. Deborah Gorham, "The 'Maiden Tribute of Modern Babylon' Re-examined: Child Prostitution and the Idea of Childhood in Late-Victorian England," *Victorian Studies*, Spring 1978.

38. Mrs. E. M. Ward, *Memories of Ninety Years* (n.d.), pp. 32–33.

39. David Williams, *Genesis and Exodus: A Portrait of the Benson Family* (1979), pp. 10–19.

40. *Real Alice*, p. 21.

41. Dodgson Family Papers.

42. Caryl Hargreaves, "The Lewis Carroll that Alice Recalls," *New York Times Magazine*, May 1, 1932.

43. *Victoria through the Looking-Glass* (1945).

44. Edward Wakeling, "Two Letters from Lorina to Alice," *Jabberwocky*, Autumn 1992.

## 4.  *The Child*

1. Charles Dodgson, *A Short Account of the First Establishment of the Croft National School* (1845), as quoted in Anne Clark, *Lewis Carroll* (1979), p. 35.

2. *The Letters of William Blake*, ed. A. Geoffrey Keynes (1980), p. 9.

3. *The Poetical Works of William Blake*, edited with a prefatory memoir by William Michael Rossetti (1875), p. lxx. Although Rossetti's edition of Blake's poetry did not appear until Charles was in middle age, I use it because it is probably close to whichever edition Charles himself used.

4. *Poor Monkey: The Child in Literature* (1957), p. 15.

5. For instance in a letter to his sister Mary, September 19, 1871.

6. Charles quotes from Milton's "Il Penseroso" and from the Bible (Malachi 4:2).

7. A. Charles Babenroth, *English Childhood* (1922), p. 299.

8. W. M. Rossetti, p. xci.

9. See *Picture Book*, p. 343.

10. Jeffrey Stern, ed., *Lewis Carroll's Library* (1981), p. 25.

11. Book 2, chapter 9.

12. In addition to the works already cited here, I am indebted to Arthur A. Adrian, *Dickens and the Parent-Child Relationship* (1984).

## 5.  *The* Alice *Books*

1. Alice Liddell.

2. *George MacDonald and His Wife* (1924), p. 342; and *Reminiscences of a Specialist* (1932), pp. 15–17.

3. *Confessions of a Caricaturist* (1901), vol. 2, pp. 103–104.

4. The letter is in the Huntington Library, San Marino, California.

5. The letter is in the Berg Collection, New York Public Library. Miss Rossetti's children's book *Speaking Likenesses* (1874) owes a debt to *Alice*, as the author confesses in a letter to her painter brother: *The Family Letters of Christina Georgina Rossetti*, ed. W. M. Rossetti (1908), p. 44.

6. The letter, dated February 2, 1866, is in the Houghton Library, Harvard University. A year later, on February 7, 1867, Rossetti wrote again on the subject (MS., New York Public Library): "I am very glad to see what a decided and continuous success *Alice in Wonderland* is. Nothing could be better deserved."

7. The letter, undated, is in the Houghton Library, Harvard University. Kingsley also wrote to Macmillan about the book: "What a charming book you have published for Dodgson. He was staying with us the other day, and has sent us a copy" (S. M. Ellis, *Henry Kingsley* [1931], p. 138). Kingsley's children's story, *The Boy in Grey*, published five years later, shows the influence of *Alice;* and in *Valentin: A French Boy's Story of Sedan* (1872), Kingsley makes Valentin comment upon "The Walrus and the Carpenter" as a satire on the Franco-Prussian War.

8. Other notices are reprinted in *Jabberwocky* (Winter 1979/80, Spring 1980, Summer 1980, and Autumn 1980).

9. Collingwood, p. 139.

10. Ibid., pp. 142–43.

11. Selwyn H. Goodacre, "Lewis Carroll's 1887 Corrections to *Alice*," *Library*, June 1973.

12. *What Books to Lend and What to Give* (1887), p. 76.

13. Preface to the facsimile edition of *Alice's Adventures Under Ground.*

14. Mavis Batey, *The Adventures of Alice* (1991), provides the most extensive account of the Oxford models for the people, places, and events in the *Alice* books.

15. Ethel Rowell.

## 6.    *The Pursuit of Innocents*

1. *Illustrated Times,* January 28.

2. Una Taylor, *Guests and Memories* (1924), p. 312.

3. Charles spells it Frederi*k*a.

4. See *Letters,* p. 33.

5. [Unsigned], "Lewis Carroll Interrupts a Story," *Children's Newspaper,* February 7, 1931.

6. Alice Liddell.

7. "Lewis Carroll as I Remember Him," *Queen,* July 20, 1932.

8. They are in the Philip H. and A. S. W. Rosenbach Museum in Philadelphia and have been reproduced in Morton N. Cohen, ed., *Lewis Carroll, Photographer of Children: Four Nude Studies* (1979).

9. Private letter.

10. Hudson, pp. 322–26.

11. See *Letters,* pp. 385, 441, 460, 466.

12. Isa Bowman, p. 60.

13. "Lewis Carroll Interrupts a Story," *Children's Newspaper,* February 7, 1931.

14. "Oxford in the 'Seventies,'" *Fortnightly Review* 150 (1941): 276–82.

15. *Index to the Story of My Days* (1957), p. 32.

16. Kenneth Rose, *The Later Cecils* (1975), p. 31.

17. *Diaries,* p. xxvi.

18. Isa Bowman, pp. 2–3.

19. Beatrice Hatch I.

20. Harry R. Mileham, "Lewis Carroll," *The Times,* January 2, 1932.

21. *Without Knowing Mr. Walkley* (1938), p. 176.

22. Mrs. E. H. B. Skimming, "More Recollections of Lewis Carroll," *Listener,* February 6, 1958.

23. Letter to *The Times,* April 2, 1928.

24. Isa Bowman, pp. 72, 77, 131.

25. Morton N. Cohen, ed., *Lewis Carroll and the Kitchins* (1980), p. 43.

26. Isa Bowman, p. 3.

27. Morton N. Cohen, ed., *Lewis Carroll, Photographer of Children: Four Nude Studies* (1979), p. 31.

28. "Lewis Carroll," in *The Moment and Other Essays* (1948); reprinted in Robert Phillips, ed., *Aspects of Alice* (1974), pp. 78–80.

29. Reed, p. 95.

30. See *Letters,* pp. 395–96.

31. Letter to *The Times,* January 3, 1932.

## 7. *The Fire Within*

1. W[illiam] H[enry] H[ewett], in an article that appeared in the *Eastbourne Gazette* in 1898 and is reprinted as "The Late 'Lewis Carroll,' " *Jabberwocky*, Winter 1973.

2. In extracting Charles's repeated appeals to heaven and his resolutions to correct his faults, I have quoted from or alluded to his diary entries for: May 10 and November 12, 1856; February 2 and September 1, 1857; May 9 and 17, June 12 and 20, July 10, 14, and 22, August 27, October 17, November 6 and 26, December 6 and 18, 1862; January 22, February 5 and 6, March 9, 29, and 31, April 1, May 19, June 12 and 23, July 3 and 9, August 21 and 22, September 21, October 19, 26, and 30, December 16, 28, and 30, 1863; June 28, 1864; June 5, July 1 and 10, 1866.

3. The last recorded take is on June 23, 1863, when Charles, in photographing the Deanery, had Ina and Alice sit in the window of the royal chamber.

4. Collingwood, pp. 146–49.

5. See, for instance, Peter Gay, *The Bourgeois Experience*, vol. 2 (1986); Michael Mason, *The Making of Victorian Sexuality* (1994); and *The Making of Victorian Sexual Attitudes* (1994).

6. Joy Melville, *Ellen and Edy* (1987), p. 28.

7. Modern examinations of Victorian sexual attitudes are legion. I have used Walter E. Houghton, *The Victorian Frame of Mind* (1957); Don Richard Cox, ed., *Sexuality and Victorian Literature* (1984); Philippe Ariès and André Béjin, *Western Sexuality*, trans. Anthony Forster (1985); Roy Porter and Lesley Hall, *The Facts of Life: The Creation of Sexual Knowledge in Britain, 1650–1950* (1995).

8. Collingwood, pp. 385–86.

9. Private conversation with Brigadier Cecil Keith, Agnes Hull's son.

10. See A. A. Brill, *Basic Principles of Psychoanalysis* (1985), chapter 11.

11. See *Letters*, February 28, 1889.


## 8. *Years of Triumph*

1. Letter to Frances Hardman, May 24, 1882.

2. Edward Wakeling, "Lewis Carroll's Rooms at Christ Church, Oxford," *Jabberwocky*, Summer 1983.

3. Beatrice Hatch I.

4. Beatrice Hatch II.

5. See, for instance, Isa Bowman, pp. 20–23; and Ruth Gamlen in Hudson, pp. 314–18.

6. The letter is in the Dodgson Family Papers.

7. *Letters of Dante Gabriel Rossetti*, ed. Oswald Doughty and John Robert Wahl (1965), vol. 2, p. 495.

8. Charles's long letter to Tom Taylor in which he sketches the plot by act and scene survives: see *Letters*, pp. 84–85.

9. Although Charles's ciphers are not truly new inventions (Blaise de Vigenère used the double-alphabet substitution method for coding messages in the sixteenth century and Giovanni Sesti is thought to have devised the polyalphabetic substitution cipher that anticipates *The Telegraph-Cipher* in the seventeenth century), Charles believed that he did invent them because he thought them up independently. See Edward Wakeling, ed., *The Cipher Alice* (1990), p. 8; Francine Abeles and Stanley H. Lipson, "Some Victorian Periodic Polyalphabetic Ciphers," *Cryptologia*, April 1990.

10. *Diaries,* p. 263.

11. Chapter 3 deals with these works in some detail.

12. A facsimile of the text appears as plate 4 in Bill and Mason.

13. Bill and Mason, p. 113.

14. *Christ Church, Oxford* (1911), p. 42.

15. Bill and Mason, pp. 110–11.

16. Ibid., p. 128.

17. E. T. B. Twistleton, chief commissioner of the poor laws in Ireland, as quoted in ibid., p. 159.

18. In this section on Oxford reform I have drawn upon the following works: Henry L. Thompson, *Christ Church* (1900); G. M. Young, "Portrait of an Age," in *Early Victorian England, 1830–1865* (1934), vol. 2, pp. 493–95; A. J. Engel, *From Clergyman to Don: The Rise of the Academic Profession in Nineteenth-Century Oxford* (1983); W. R. Ward, *Victorian Oxford* (1965).

19. See *Diaries,* p. 277; *The Lewis Carroll Handbook,* rev. ed., ed. Denis Crutch (1979), p. 49.

20. No. 84, 1866.

21. See A. Adrian Albert in "Determinants," *Encyclopaedia Britannica* (1967), vol. 7, p. 313.

22. See, for instance, Thomas Muir, *The Theory of Determinants in the Order of Development* (1920), vol. 3, pp. 24–27.

23. See, for instance, David P. Robbins and Howard Rumsey, Jr., "Determinants and Alternating Sign Matrices," *Advances in Mathematics,* November 1986.

24. Private letter.

25. "Determinants and Linear Systems: Charles L. Dodgson's View," *British Journal for the History of Science* 19 (1986): 331–35.

26. "Lewis Carroll's 'Pillow Problems': On the 1993 Centenary," *Statistical Science* 8 (1993): 180–86.

27. Francine Abeles, as above and in *The Mathematical Pamphlets of . . . Dodgson . . .* (1994), pp. 170–81; Martin Gardner, *The Annotated Alice* (1936), pp. 181–82; Edward Wakeling, private letter.

28. Private letter.

29. Liddon's unpublished diary is in Liddon House, South Audley Street, London. The segment of the journey with Charles is published in *The Russian Journal—II: A Record Kept by Henry Parry Liddon of a Tour Taken with C. L. Dodgson in the Summer of 1867,* ed. Morton N. Cohen (1979).

30. The diary that Charles kept of the journey, covering July 12 to September 14, 1867, is separate from the other surviving volumes and is in the Parrish Collection, Princeton University Library. It has been published in at least three separate editions: *Tour in 1867 by C. L. Dodgson . . .* (1928); *The Russian Journal and Other Selections from the works of Lewis Carroll,* ed. John Francis McDermott (1935; reprint, with a new preface, 1937).

31. The text appears in *Russian Journal—II,* pp. 51–52.

32. Quoted in her obituary, *Wantage Herald,* November 7, 1963.

33. Quoted in *Diaries,* p. 446.

34. "The Late Rev. C. L. Dodgson," *Oxford Magazine,* January 26, 1898.

35. *Oxford Outside the Guide-Books* (1925), p. 164.

36. Hudson, pp. 312–14.

## 9.  *The Man*

1. See *Letters,* February 12, 1887.

2. Irene Dodgson Jaques, private conversation at Little Croft, Canford Cliffs, Dorset, December 9, 1978.

3. Ruth Waterhouse, in Hudson, pp. 314–18.

4. Ethel Rowell.

5. E. L. Shute, "Lewis Carroll as Artist," *Cornhill Magazine*, November 1932.

6. "Lewis Carroll: A Sketch by an Artist-Friend," *Gentlewoman*, January 29 and February 5, 1898.

7. *Picture Book*, pp. 161–63.

8. "Lewis Carroll: Obituary," *Oxford Magazine*, January 26, 1898.

9. "Lewis Carroll, Tutor and Logician," *Listener*, January 13, 1932.

10. Quoted in Oliver Elton, *Frederick York Powell* (1906), vol. 2, pp. 361–67.

11. "Reminiscences of 'Lewis Carroll,'" *Literature*, February 5, 1898.

12. "Lewis Carroll," *Cornhill Magazine*, March 1898.

13. See *Diaries*, December 24, 1866.

14. Ibid., June 18, 1896.

15. Although the names Charles sends Macmillan in this diagram are fictitious, the diagram that appears in his diary for May 15, 1871, shows his guests to be three of his sisters, his brother Wilfred, Friedrich Max Müller and his wife, and Dr. Franz Kielhorn, the Sanskrit authority.

16. For the most extensive list of Charles's possessions, see the *Catalogue of the Furniture, Personal Effects and Library of the Late "Lewis Carroll" . . . Which will be Sold by Auction at the Holywell Music Room, Oxford, On Tuesday, May 10th, and the following days* (1898), reproduced in Jeffrey Stern, ed., *Lewis Carroll's Library* (1981).

17. *Picture Book*, p. 358.

18. Isa Bowman, p. 12.

19. H. T. Stretton, "More Recollections of Lewis Carroll—II," *Listener*, February 6, 1958.

20. "Lewis Carroll," *Cornhill Magazine*, March 1898.

21. A. S. Russell.

22. "Mr. Dodgson: Lewis Carroll at Oxford," *The Times*, January 27, 1932.

23. Beatrice Hatch II.

24. *Diaries*, pp. xxii–xxiv.

25. *Diaries*, April 30, 1857.

26. Evelyn Hatch, p. 4.

27. Jon A. Lindseth Collection, Cleveland, Ohio.

28. "Lewis Carroll as Artist," *Cornhill Magazine*, November 1932.

29. Isabel Standen, "Lewis Carroll as I Remember Him," *Queen*, July 20, 1932.

30. Blagden, pp. 113–16.

31. Fales Library, New York University.

32. Florence Becker Lennon, *The Life of Lewis Carroll* (1962), pp. 194–95.

33. *Michael Ernest Sadler . . . A Memoir by his Son* (1949), pp. 90–91, 95.

34. Blagden, pp. 115–16.

35. Quoted in *Diaries*, p. 445.

36. "Mr. Dodgson: Lewis Carroll at Oxford," *The Times*, January 27, 1932.

37. *Oxford Magazine*, January 26, 1898.

38. Beatrice Hatch I.

39. H. T. Stretton, "More Recollections of Lewis Carroll—II," *Listener*, February 6, 1958.

40. Collingwood, pp. 327–29.

41. "In Search of Lewis Carroll," *Everybody's Weekly*, February 19, 1955. See also Mark Goodacre, "The Preaching of Lewis Carroll," *Jabberwocky*, Summer 1993.

42. "Lewis Carroll: An Interview with his Biographer," *Westminster Budget*, December 9, 1898.

43. "Lewis Carroll," *Cornhill Magazine*, March 1898.

44. *Unfinished Autobiography* (1940), p. 54.

45. In 1895 Twain told an Australian reporter that he had always regarded Carroll as "a true and subtle humorist"; in October 1908 he referred to "the immortal Alice" in a letter; and in his "No. 44, the Mysterious Stranger" (1902–1908), Twain wrote of one of his characters: "She smiled quite Cheshirely (my dream-brother's word . . .)." *Diaries,* p. 382, quoting Twain's *Autobiography* (1906), vol. 2, p. 232; and Alan Gribben, *Mark Twain's Library* (1980), vol. 1, p. 198.

46. Enid Shawyer, in a letter to the *Observer,* February 14, 1954.

47. *Letters,* p. 446, n. 1.

48. Ibid., p. 743.

49. Ibid., p. 452.

50. Isa Bowman, p. 19. Joseph Brabant, in the privately published monograph *Sacred Topics and Lewis Carroll's Double Standard* (1987), points out that Charles was capable of parodying verse of religious flavor and of making comic allusions occasionally to biblical subjects. Charles would have been shocked to think that he did either.

51. Ethel Hatch, "Lewis Carroll Remembered," *Listener,* August 4, 1966.

52. *Diaries,* pp. xxii–xxiv.

53. W. Boyd Carpenter, *The Permanent Elements of Religion* (1889), pp. 177–78.

54. *Letters,* pp. 695, 705–706.

55. Edith Craig and Christopher St. John, eds., *Ellen Terry's Memoirs* (1933), pp. 141–43.

56. Laurence Irving, *The Successors* (1967), esp. p. 77.

57. Collingwood, p. 388.

58. For instance, *Letters,* pp. 960, 1030.

59. Edith Alice Maitland, "Childish Memories of Lewis Carroll by One of his Alices," *Quiver,* 1899, pp. 407–15.

60. Collingwood, pp. 324–25.

61. Ruth Waterhouse, in Hudson, pp. 314–18.

62. Reed, p. 109.

63. Maitland, pp. 407–15.

64. *Letters,* pp. 578–80.

65. *Autobiography* (1933), pp. 128–29.

66. Stanley Godman, "Lewis Carroll at the Seaside," *The Times,* July 27, 1957.

67. Reed, p. 64.

68. Ibid., pp. 64–65.

69. Collingwood, pp. 83–85.

70. *Reminiscences of a Specialist* (1932), pp. 15–16.

71. Reed, p. 63, 95.

72. "Memories of Lewis Carroll—III," *By the Tum Tum Tree* (published by the Lewis Carroll Society), January 1981.

73. "Lewis Carroll," *Gentlewoman,* January 29 and February 5, 1898.

74. Collingwood, pp. 99–101.

## 10. *The Man's Father*

1. *Diaries,* p. 29.

2. These letters are among the Dodgson Family Papers.

3. Collingwood, pp. 13–14, n.d.

4. His duties were to serve on a panel examining candidates for holy orders.

5. Collingwood, p. 8.

6. Surely "pigs and babies" find their way into *Alice.*

7. *Diaries,* p. 8.

8. For these and the other surviving letters from the father to Skeffington, see *Letters of Skeffington Dodgson from His Father,* ed. Anne Clark Amor (1990).

9. Collingwood, p. 131.

10. Ibid., p. 8.

11. Florence Becker Lennon, *The Life of Lewis Carroll* (1962), p. 44.

12. *Letters to Skeffington Dodgson from His Father,* ed. Anne Clark Amor (1990), pp. 13, 15, 26.

13. Hudson, p. 25.

14. Chapter 11.

15. Chapter 12.

16. In chapter 22 of *Dombey,* Mr. Toots writes an acrostic on "Florence." Could it have spurred Charles on to write his own acrostics? None of his recorded acrostics appears to predate the Dickens reference.

17. Collingwood, p. 355.

18. Hudson, p. 191.

19. For some material in this chapter, I am indebted to an unpublished paper by Jessica Gerard of the University of Wisconsin (Milwaukee) entitled "Parent-Child Relationships in the Nineteenth-Century Country House," presented at the Midwest Victorian Studies Association, April 26–27, 1985.

## 11. *The Man's Faith*

1. *Oxford* (1909 ed.), pp. 242–44.

2. *Early Victorian England, 1830–1865* (1951), vol. 2, p. 474.

3. Italian orator of the Risorgimento who fled to England in 1849 after being declared a heretic for criticizing the government of the papal states and preaching for a united Italy. He was, when Charles heard him, associated with the Italian Protestants in London.

4. Ivor Ll. Davies, "Archdeacon Dodgson," *Jabberwocky,* Spring 1976, which I have used throughout this section on Charles's father.

5. W. R. Ward, *Victorian Oxford* (1965), p. 130.

6. *Tennyson, Ruskin, Mill and Other Literary Estimates* (1900), p. 10.

7. *The Victorian Church,* part 1 (1971), pp. 544–45.

8. William Raeper, *George MacDonald* (1987), p. 174.

9. *Diaries,* pp. 250–51; Mary C. Church, ed., *Life and Letters of Dean Church* (1895), esp. pp. 189–90; Wilfred Ward, *Life of John Henry Cardinal Newman* (1912), vol. 2, pp. 318–19.

10. *Letters,* p. 951.

11. Mavis Batey, *The Adventures of Alice* (1991), p. 35.

12. W. John Smith, "Dodgson's Scientific Interests with Reference to the Books in His Library," *Jabberwocky,* Winter 1984/85.

13. The earlier letter from Darwin is in the Houghton Library, Harvard University, the later one among the Dodgson Family Papers.

14. Frederick Maurice, ed., *The Life of Frederick Denison Maurice* (1884), vol. 2, p. 384.

15. "The Broad Church Militant and Newman's Humiliation of Charles Kingsley," *Victorian Periodicals Review,* Winter 1986.

16. Frederick Maurice, ed., *The Life of Frederick Denison Maurice* (1884), vol. 1, p. 369.

17. Ibid., p. 205.

18. Ibid., vol. 2, pp. 16–17.

19. *Theological Essays* (1871 ed.), p. 45.

20. *Confessions of an Inquiring Spirit* (1956 ed.), p. 43.

21. I have used the 1983 edited reprint (Chelsea House) of the 1884 edition of *Aids to Reflection* (George Bell and Sons). John Beer's magisterial edition (1994) was published after I completed my typescript.

22. Collingwood, p. 74.

23. The certificate is in the Muniments Room of the Castle Arch Museum, Guildford.

24. Reed, p. 103.

25. What Charles's "ghost" pictures looked like is not certain. They may have been double exposures like the one he took of the Barry children and called "The Dream." See *Letters,* facing p. 220.

26. *Diaries,* p. xxi.

27. "Christ's Way of Dealing With Sin," a sermon delivered on November 9, 1851, in *Sermons on Christian Doctrine* (n.d.), pp. 108–18. I have also used Selwyn Goodacre, "Lewis Carroll and Hypnogogic Phenomena," *World Medicine,* August 28, 1974; Lucille Iremonger, *The Ghosts of Versailles* (1957), esp. p. 146.

28. Donald J. Gray, "The Uses of Victorian Laughter," *Victorian Studies,* December 1966.

29. "Count Up," *New York Review of Books,* December 3, 1987.

30. Joan L. Richards, *Mathematical Visions: The Pursuit of Geometry in Victorian England* (1988), p. 104.

31. Private letter, November 7, 1989.

32. Helena M. Pycior, "At the Intersection of Mathematics and Humor . . . ," *Victorian Studies,* Autumn 1984; and Millay, Sonnet 45, *The Harp-Weaver* (1922).

33. "Lewis Carroll," *Cornhill Magazine,* March 1898.

34. *The White Knight* (1952), p. 80.

35. See his letter to Gertrude Chataway, December 2, 1890.

36. *A Charge Delivered to the Clergy . . . of Richmond* (1855), p. 33.

37. In addition to those already cited, in this chapter I have drawn on the following works: Charles Richard Sanders, *Coleridge and the Broad Church Movement* (1942); Arthur Michael Ramsey, *F. D. Maurice and the Conflicts of Modern Theology* (1951); E. L. Woodward, *The Age of Reform, 1815–1870* (1954 ed.); Alex R. Vidler, *F. D. Maurice and Company* (1966); Olive J. Brose, *Frederick Denison Maurice* (1971); Frank Mauldin McClain, *Maurice: Man and Moralist* (1972); Basil Willey, *Samuel Taylor Coleridge* (1972); Elizabeth Longford, *Piety in Queen Victoria's Reign* (1973); David Forrester, *Young Doctor Pusey* (1989); John R. Reed, *Victorian Will* (1989); Lance St. John Butler, *Victorian Doubt* (1990); Richard J. Helmstadter and Bernard Lightman, eds., *Victorian Faith in Crisis* (1990); Michael Wheeler, *Death and the Future of Life in Victorian Literature and Theology* (1991).

## 12. *Years of Harvest*

1. Warren Weaver, *Alice in Many Tongues* (1964), p. 46.

2. D & D Galleries (Somerville, New Jersey), Catalog 10 (1993), Lot 1 (Letters).

3. Introduction to the Dover edition of *Euclid and His Modern Rivals* (1973), pp. v–viii.

4. W. G. Hiscock, *A Christ Church Miscellany* (1946), p. v.

5. *The Life and Letters of the Right Honourable Friedrich Max Müller,* edited by his wife (1902), vol. 2, pp. 7, 450–53; "Dean Liddell as I Knew Him," in *Last Essays* (n.d.), as quoted in Alexander L. Taylor, *The White Knight* (1952), pp. 164–65.

6. C. S. Lewis, *Vivisection* (1948), p. 10.

7. Collingwood, p. 26; and Violet Dodgson.

8. Beatrice Hatch II.

9. E. G. Shawyer, "More Recollections of Lewis Carroll—III," *Listener,* February 6, 1958.

10. It is reproduced in *Diaries,* pp. 572–73; another version appears in John Fisher, *Further Magic of Lewis Carroll* (n.d.), pp. [9–10].

11. Beatrice Hatch II.

12. In a letter to *John O'London's Weekly,* April 9, 1932.

13. "Lewis Carroll as I Remember Him," *Queen,* July 20, 1932.

14. From an interview in Miss Burch's home near Farnham, Surrey, in August 1974 and first published in *Letters,* pp. 955–56.

15. "Give my Love to the Children," *Reader's Digest,* February 1953. Although Charles never published his "Number-Guessing" game, a manuscript of an "improved" version survives in the Fales Library, New York University.

16. Hudson, pp. 312–14.

17. Charles Reade's drama based on the Tichborne Case (the famous Victorian legal battle over whether or not an impostor had impersonated the eldest son of the dead Sir James Tichborne), *The Wandering Heir,* was playing at the Queen's Theatre.

18. *Reminiscences of My Life* (1914), pp. 165, 244–46.

19. Evelyn Karney, in a letter to *John O'London's Weekly,* April 9, 1932.

20. See Martin Gardner, *The Annotated Snark* (1962), for a range of these speculations.

## 13. *Yellowing Leaves*

1. "Tomorrow is the Day after Doomsday," *Eureka,* October 1973.

2. This and the quotations in the next two paragraphs are from Blagden, pp. 114–16.

3. Arthur Hassall, *Christ Church, Oxford* (1911), p. 136.

4. I. McLean and A. B. Urken, eds., *Classics of Social Choice,* 1995. I have also used G. C. Heathcote, *Lawn Tennis* (1890).

5. "Evaluating Lewis Carroll's Theory of Parliamentary Representation," *Jabberwocky,* Summer 1970.

6. Francine Abeles, "C. L. Dodgson and Apportionment for Proportional Representation," *Ghānita Bhāritī* 3 (1981): 71–82. In this section I have also consulted: Duncan Black, "The Central Argument in Lewis Carroll's 'The Principles of Parliamentary Representation,'" *Papers on Non-Market Decision Making* [later *Public Choice*], Fall 1967; Duncan Black, "Lewis Carroll and the Cambridge Mathematical School of P. R.; Arthur Cohen and Edith Denman," *Public Choice,* Spring 1970; Duncan Black, "Lewis Carroll and the Theory of Games," *American Economic Review,* May 1969; Duncan Black, *The Theory of Committees and Elections* (1958); Francine Abeles, "Ranking by Inversion: A Note on C. L. Dodgson," *Historia Mathematica* 6 (1979): 310–17; Jeremy Corlett Mitchell, "Electoral Strategy under Open Voting: Evidence from England, 1832–1880," *Public Choice,* Winter 1976; McLean and Urken, Introduction; and Iain McLean, Alistair McMillan, and Burt L. Monroe, "Duncan Black and Lewis Carroll," *Journal of Theoretical Politics,* April 1995.

7. Introduction.

8. *Voting Procedures* (1984), p. 5.

9. *Proportional Representation* (1992), p. 110.

10. E. T. Cook, *The Life of John Ruskin* (1912), chap. 18, esp. vol. 2, pp. 330–31.

11. I have used Raymond L. Schultz, *Crusader in Babylon* (1972); and Deborah Gorham, "The 'Maiden Tribute of Modern Babylon' Re-examined: Child Prostitution and the Idea of Childhood in Late-Victorian England," *Victorian Studies,* Spring 1978.

12. In this section I have used H. Martyn Rogers, "Life on the World's Loneliest Island: Tristan da Cunha, South Atlantic," *Landmark* 5 (1923): 587; and Allan B. Crawford, *I Went to Tristan* (1941), pp. 63–64.

13. Allardyce Nicoll, *A History of English Drama, 1660–1900* (1967), vol. 5, pp. 62–66; Hamilton Aidé, "A Dramatic School," *Theatre,* February 1882; "A Dramatic School of Art," *Truth,* June 1, 1882.

14. Clarke's earlier dramatizations were considerable. In 1873 he collaborated with the playwright L. Du Terreaux on the comedy *Love Wins;* then with A. Watson on *Pendarvon;* then again with Du Terreaux on *A Fight for Life.* Then he himself wrote farces and burlesques, including *That Beautiful Biceps, A Tale of a Telephone,* an adaptation of "Rip Van Winkle," and comic operas. A few of Charles's letters to Clarke appear in *Letters.* Quotations from letters that do not appear in that section are in the Fales Library of New York University.

15. Reed, p. 73.

16. *Hammersmith Hoy: A Book of Minor Revelations* (1930), pp. 88–89.

17. *Around Theatres* (1953), pp. 109–12.

18. See Hudson, pp. 279–80; Jeffrey Stern, "The Game of Logic," *Jabberwocky,* Winter 1980/81; and Edward Wakeling, "The Game of 'Logic: 1887,'" *Jabberwocky,* Winter 1981/82.

19. A few of Charles's letters to Furniss are published in *Letters.* Quotations here from those that do not appear in that selection are in the Pierpont Morgan Library, New York.

20. *The Confessions of a Caricaturist* (1901), vol. 2, pp. 179–80.

## 14.   *And No Birds Sing*

1. Collingwood, p. 267.

2. Jon A. Lindseth Collection, Cleveland, Ohio.

3. H. A. L. Fisher, *Unfinished Autobiography* (1940), p. 54.

4. "Recollections of Lewis Carroll—III," *Listener,* January 30, 1958.

5. Isa Bowman, pp. 9–12.

6. See *Letters,* January 26, and *Diaries,* January 27, 1894.

7. *Diaries,* pp. xxiv–xxvi; "Lewis Carroll," letter to the editor, *Observer,* February 14, 1954; "Recollections of Lewis Carroll—III," *Listener,* January 30, 1958.

8. "G.B.H.," "Recollections of Lewis Carroll," *Christian Science Monitor,* February 23, 1932; "Alice in Wonderland," *The Times,* April 2, 1928.

9. *Diaries,* pp. xxii–xxiv.

10. Evelyn Hatch, p. 235.

11. Stanley Godman, "Lewis Carroll at the Seaside," *The Times,* July 27, 1957.

12. Ethel Rowell.

13. *To Tell My Story* (1948), pp. 18–20.

14. Evelyn Hatch, pp. 1–13.

15. Desmond Chapman-Huston, *The Lost Historian: A Memoir of Sidney Low* (1936), pp. 74–76.

16. *Picture Book,* p. 344.

17. *Essays and Reviews* (1860), pp. 205–206.

18. Guy Kendall, *Charles Kingsley and His Ideas* (n.d.), p. 129.

19. Bernard Crick, *The Reform of Parliament* (1964), pp. 195–96.

20. "Lewis Carroll's 'Pillow-Problems': On the 1992 Centenary," *Statistical Science* 8 (1993): 180–86.

21. The letter is in the Pierpont Morgan Library, New York.

22. Collingwood, pp. 227–28.

23. Bartley, p. 3.

24. "Lewis Carroll as Logician," *Mathematical Gazette* 16 (1932): 174–78.

25. Bartley, esp. p. 31.

26. Ibid., pp. 31–32.

27. Ibid., p. 448.

28. Ibid., pp. 447–49; John Cook Wilson, *Statement and Inference* (1926), esp. vol. 1, pp. xli–xliii; vol. 2, pp. 635, 638, 639; also W. W. Bartley III, "Lewis Carroll's Lost Book on Logic," *Scientific American,* July 1972; W. W. Bartley III, "Lewis Carroll as Logician," *Times Literary Supplement,* June 15, 1973.

29. The "S." could be Charles's mathematical colleague E. F. Sampson.

30. "Lewis Carroll's Infinite Regress," *Mind* 83 (1974): 571–73.

31. Bartley, pp. 466–70.

32. *The Philosophy of Mr. B\*rtr\*nd R\*ss\*ll* (1918), p. xxxix.

33. "Lewis Carroll as Logician," p. 300.

34. Geach's review of Bartley's work appears in *Philosophy,* January 1978.

35. *Gödel, Escher, Bach: An Eternal Golden Braid; A Metaphoric Fugue on Mind and Machines in the Spirit of Lewis Carroll* (1979), as quoted in Ivor Grattan-Guinness, ed., *Philip E. B. Jourdain: Selected Essays on the History of Set Theory and Logics (1906–1918)* (1991), p. xxxix.

## 15.   *Gentle into That Good Night*

1. *Real Alice,* p. 88.

2. On December 19 Charles wrote directly to the Dean, expressing his "personal sense of our loss in your departure from among us, and my most cordial wishes for the health and happiness of yourself and your family."

3. H[enry] L[ewis] T[hompson], "Henry George Liddell, D.D.," *Oxford Magazine,* February 2, 1898.

4. H. L. Thompson, in *The Dictionary of National Biography* (compact ed., 1975), p. 2439.

5. H. L. Thompson, in the obituary in the *Oxford Magazine,* February 2, 1898.

6. A. M. W. Stirling, *The Richmond Papers* (1926), p. 192.

7. "Oxford in the 'Seventies,' " *Fortnightly Review* 150 (1941): 276–82.

8. *Victorian Oxford* (1965), pp. 132, 236.

9. Salisbury Papers, Doc. 1, p. 58.

10. *Real Alice,* pp. 106–107.

11. "The Lewis Carroll That Alice Recalls," *New York Times Magazine,* May 1, 1932.

12. Papers of the third Marquess of Salisbury, Box 1-H, Hatfield House.

13. *Real Alice,* p. 144.

14. Ibid., p. 160.

15. Derek Hudson first called attention to *Cakeless,* in his 1954 biography of Charles; Anne Clark republished it in *The Real Alice* (Appendix 2, pp. 256–62).

16. *Real Alice,* p. 170.

17. Ibid., p. 177.

18. Ibid., p. 182.
19. Ibid., p. 232.
20. Edwin Wolf II with John F. Fleming, *Rosenbach: A Biography* (1960), pp. 538–39; and Luther H. Evans, "The Alice Manuscript," preface to *Alice's Adventures Under Ground* (1964); and personal conversation with Luther Evans. The manuscript traveled to the Pierpont Morgan Library, New York, in 1982, for the sesquicentennial celebration of Charles's birth.
21. *Real Alice,* p. 241.
22. *New York Times,* May 1, 1932.
23. The letter is in Christ Church Library.
24. *Real Alice,* p. 211.
25. Ibid., p. 237.
26. Ibid., pp. 236–37.
27. Dodgson Family Papers.
28. *The Virtue of Simplicity, A Sermon Preached . . . on . . . January 23, 1898,* privately printed.
29. The letter is in the Dodgson Family Collection at the Castle Arch Museum Muniments Room, Guildford.
30. Quoted in Oliver Elton, *Frederick York Powell* (1906), vol. 2, p. 393.
31. *Diaries,* p. 518.

## Appendix

1. The manuscripts of the first three undergraduate themes are in the Pierpont Morgan Library, New York. The manuscripts of the Latin-Greek declamation and the essay on "Pleasure" are in the Fales Library, New York University.
2. Charles wrote the word *soul* above the word *mind.*

# Index

*Italicized* page numbers refer to illustrations.

ILLUSTRATION CREDITS

Grateful acknowledgment is made to the following people and organizations for providing artwork included in this volume:

Anne Clark Amor: page 65 (bottom left and right)

Mavis Batey: page 87

The Governing Body of Christ Church, Oxford: pages 28, 31, and 61

Gernsheim Collection, Harry Ransom Humanities Research Center, University of Texas at Austin: pages 154–156 (all)

Philip Dodgson Jaques: page 232

The Pierpont Morgan Library, New York: pages 506 (AAH 651) and 507 (AAH 661)

The New York Public Library, Henry W. and Albert A. Berg Collection, Astor, Lenox and Tilden Foundations: page 489

The New York Public Library, General Research Division, Astor, Lenox and Tilden Foundations: page 97

Morris L. Parrish Collection of Victorian Novelists, Department of Rare Books and Special Collections, Princeton University Libraries: pages 2, 64 (bottom), and 95

The Rosenbach Museum and Library, Philadelphia: pages 166 (bottom) and 167 (all)

All other photographs are from the collection of the author. Copyright material by Charles L. Dodgson has been reproduced by permission of A. P. Watt Ltd. on behalf of The Trustees of the Charles L. Dodgson Estate.

## A NOTE ABOUT
## THE LEWIS CARROLL SOCIETY

The Lewis Carroll Society of North America is a nonprofit organization devoted to the study of the life, work, times, and influence of Charles Lutwidge Dodgson. The hundreds of current members include leading authorities on Carroll, collectors, students, and general enthusiasts. The Society meets twice a year at the site of an important Carroll collection and features well-known speakers and exhibitions. It maintains an active publication program and publishes a newsletter. Further information is available from the Secretary, Genevieve B. Smith, 1655 34th Street, Washington, D.C. 20007.